A Practical Guide to Immigration Law relating to Students

A Practical Guide to Immigration Law relating to Students

Elena Tsirlina
Solicitor, Blokh Solicitors

Bloomsbury Professional

Bloomsbury Professional Ltd, Maxwelton House, 41–43 Boltro Road, Haywards Heath, West Sussex, RH16 1BJ

Bloomsbury Professional is an imprint of Bloomsbury Publishing plc

A CIP Catalogue record for this book is available from the British Library.

ISBN 978 1 84766 571 3

Typeset by Phoenix Photosetting, Chatham, Kent
Printed in Great Britain by Hobbs the Printers, Totton, Hampshire

Foreword

Study has always been one reason for coming to the United Kingdom for a temporary purpose, and s 1(4) of the Immigration Act 1971 requires the Secretary of State to make rules of practice as to the entry and stay of persons coming for study. However the contents of the rules and associated requirements have varied widely in the intervening 40 years and continue to do so. Indeed such is the pace of change in immigration law today, that any book on voluntary immigration schemes such as the points based system is a potentially perilous enterprise if changes after the publication date distort the guidance that was formally accurate. The same is true of jurisprudence. In the summer of 2010 the Court of Appeal gave its judgment on the legality of reliance on Policy Guidance detached from the Immigration Rules in the case of *Pankina* [2010] EWCA Civ 719 [2010] 3 WLR 1526. The Upper Tribunal IAC followed shortly after with a number of decisions deciding which student applications that failed to apply the letter of the guidance could still be upheld on appeal, but those decisions in turn were replaced by new rules incorporating those elements of the previous scheme that the executive considered important.

The admission of non-nationals for study engages a number of different issues of policy: for universities the ability to attract non resident students who can pay the higher overseas charges; for the private sector the ability to teach English and provide related course for profit; for business the ability to attract and retain skilled professionals whose educational achievement can give stimulus to the economy; for the European Union to ensure that there is a free movement of citizens for Treaty purposes; for the government of the day concern to ensure that numbers are not excessive and the purpose for entry is bona fide study at a reputable institution; and for the judiciary to ensure that the practice approved by Parliament is followed and applicants are treated fairly and where appropriate in accordance with any applicable human rights.

All of the above makes a work such as this an ambitious challenge, to which the author has risen with experience, insight and exposition of the law and practice. I hope that this is a work that will prove its worth to users of the system and take its place in the library of immigration literature.

The Hon Mr Justice Blake
President, Upper Tribunal
Immigration and Asylum Chamber

Preface

The ephemeral nature of the immigration scheme relating to international students and their sponsors has dictated the pace at which this tome has been written and subsequently revised to fall into step with the unremitting onslaught of changes in the Immigration Rules, policy guidance and other extraneous documents. Since the introduction of Tier 4 of the Points Based System the body of immigration law has become both complex and ambiguous requiring understanding of the underlying political and social issues driving the system forward. Justifiably, the main purpose of the book is to present the relevant law and procedure in a straightforward way made ready for practical application. The book takes the reader on a journey from first coming to the United Kingdom to obtaining British citizenship.

Chapter 1 offers a broad introduction interspersed with commentary on the new system's historical viewpoint laying down the marker for future changes in law and policy to be phased in over the coming year. Chapter 2 goes on to analyse the legal underpinning of the sponsorship and licensing scheme concluding that it poses a constitutional conundrum for judges and parliamentarians. Chapter 3 deals with students and related categories who wish to undertake study or other forms of activity in the United Kingdom on a temporary or long-term basis while Chapter 6 goes on to deal with categories for academic staff, parents of children at school and sponsored researchers. Chapter 4 is devoted solely to sponsors of international students wishing to attain or renew their sponsor licence or Highly Trusted Sponsor status dealing in detail with various deadlines and checkpoints. Chapter 5 acquaints the reader with a range of legal remedies coupled with information about the multifarious role of legal representatives. Chapter 7 addresses the subject of international students staying on in the United Kingdom after finishing their studies or related activities, an objective made almost impossible by the recent and forthcoming changes. Concluding the book, Chapter 8 offers a keyhole perspective of public perception of the new system.

The book is dedicated to my mother, friends and colleagues who have given their support throughout. I would like to express my immense gratitude to Laurie Fransman QC and Duran Seddon, both of Garden Court Chambers, for inspiring me to write this book and for taking the time to read through and edit some of the earlier drafts – it has been an arduous task. A special thank you goes to The Hon Mr Justice Blake. I would also like to offer my thanks to Kiran Goss, Jane Bradford and the tenacious marketing team at Bloomsbury Professional – if it were not for them you would not be reading this book.

Elena Tsirlina
London
October 2011

To my late father

Contents

Table of Legislation

References to the European Convention on Human Rights are tabled under Schedule 1 to the Human Rights Act 1998

Statutes

Statutory Instruments

EC Legislation

Immigration Rules

Table of Cases

Chapter 1

Paving the way to new Immigration Policies for International Students

'Deconstruction is not a dismantling of the structure of a text, but a demonstration that it has already dismantled itself. Its apparently solid ground is no rock, but thin air.'

J. Hillis Miller, 'Stevens' Rock and Criticism Cure' (1976)

Brief historical outlook

1.01 On 18 June 1999 the Prime Minister launched the first phase of the Prime Minister's Initiative ('PMI') for International Education to increase the number of international students studying in the United Kingdom and promote British education abroad by encouraging partnership between universities and colleges in the United Kingdom and abroad. The Government aimed to increase by 75,000 the number of overseas students in higher and further education by 2005. This target was exceeded ahead of schedule 'with an extra 93,000 in HE[1] and 23,300[2] in FE'.[3]

1.02 Following consultation with UKCOSA,[4] the Home Office introduced the 'student batch scheme' on 1 August 2000 whereby universities could submit applications for visa renewals (leave to remain extension applications) on behalf of their students. The scheme was launched to streamline the application process. However, there was a downside to the scheme. A senior welfare officer at

1 UK higher education.

2 UK further education.

3 'Prime Minister Launches Strategy to Make UK Leader in International Education', www.dfes.gov.uk, 18 April 2006. A copy is available at http://www.egovmonitor.com/node/5644.

4 United Kingdom Council for Overseas Student Affairs: Council for International Education, incorporated on 8 August 2002, now known as United Kingdom Council for International Student Affairs.

Leicester University said: 'Home Office documentation is confusing and difficult to understand, and the person checking the application requires knowledge of, and training in, immigration issues.'[5] A similar sentiment was expressed in the UKCOSA survey report *Broadening Our Horizons* published in November 2004[6] which said that the batch scheme 'requires institutions to take on a significant extra administrative burden in handling and checking students' applications, taking up staff time…'. In its May 2007 survey *Benchmarking the Provision of Services for International Students in Higher Education Institutions*[7] UKCOSA reported that the student batch scheme was available to all students at 69% of educational institutions and available to students with complex applications at only 3% of educational institutions. At the same time 95% of educational institutions provided immigration advice to students.

1.03 A series of terror attacks was launched on the USA on 11 September 2001. In the aftermath it emerged that one of the terrorists was a foreign student who got a visa to study English at a language school which he never attended. Two other terrorists were awaiting approval of their student visas to attend a flight school in Florida. This is not unlike the events surrounding the 1993 World Trade Centre bombing in which one of the terrorists had entered the USA on a student visa, dropped out of school but stayed in the country. George J Borjas, a professor at Harvard University, pointed out that the foreign student programme run by the US Immigration and Naturalization Service ('INS') was in need of radical surgery as it was riddled with corruption and fraud. At the time, in order to obtain a student visa, a foreign student had to be admitted to an INS-approved educational institution, be enrolled there on a full-time basis and have sufficient funds for maintenance. The institution would then send the student a Certificate of Eligibility for Non-immigrant Student (F1) Status – For Academic and Language Students (Form I-20) which he would present at a consular post abroad. Ordinarily, a prospective student would be admitted to several schools and therefore issued with a number of I-20s.

1.04 The system was criticised for lack of monitoring and reporting of non-enrolment. The US Government responded by proposing to develop a computerised system to track the students and making schools record any changes in their status. This was done as far back as 1996. However, the system, called the Student Exchange Visa Information System ('SEVIS'), authorised by the US Congress, was not fully implemented before 11 September 2001, due to lack of funding and objections from the education community.

5 'International Pressure', Guardian Unlimited, 30 November 2004, http://education.guardian.co.uk/students/overseasstudents/story/0,,1362095,00.html.

6 'Broadening Our Horizons', UKCOSA, November 2004, http://www.ukcisa.org.uk/files/pdf/BOHsummary.pdf.

7 'Benchmarking the Provision of Services for International Students in High Education Institutions', UKCOSA, May 2007, http://www.ukcosa.org.uk/files/pdf/pmi/benchmarking_report.pdf.

1.05 The system was met with scepticism by Professor Borjas, who wrote extensively on the subject. He said: 'this approach will probably not be very effective, since the INS lacks the resources to take any action if, for example, the University of Southern California reports that ten of its foreign students dropped out in the past semester.'[8] In September 2002, Professor Borjas highlighted another problem; that of accreditation. He said that 'there are only 4,000 colleges and 6,000 state-accredited vocational schools in the United States, but around 73,000 institutions have the authority to accept foreign students.'[9]

1.06 SEVIS implements section 641 of the Illegal Immigration Reform and Immigrant Responsibility Act 1996. The renewed interest in SEVIS was reinforced by two laws passed by Congress – the Patriot Act of 2001 (which amended section 641) and the Enhanced Border Security and the Visa Entry Reform Act of 2002 under which SEVIS was set to become operational by January 2003. The purpose of SEVIS is 'to track and monitor schools and programs, students, exchange visitors and their dependents throughout the duration of approved participation within the US education system'.[10] The system provided necessary information accessible by stakeholders such as the Department of State, US Customs and Border Protection, US Citizenship and Immigration Services and U.S. Immigration and Customs Enforcement. It required schools to report a student's failure to enrol and/or attend school. Schools were allowed a transition period in order to register their students on SEVIS until 1 August 2003. It was reported that 5,937 schools had met the deadline while almost 600 schools were yet to file their applications for certification. The system has been updated at least six times since 2003 and is functioning today.

1.07 Back in Britain it appeared, at least for a while, that all Government departments involved in implementing the PMI combined their efforts to make it work. By July 2003 the Home Office faced a backlash over the introduction of additional charges on foreign students seeking to extend their stay in the United Kingdom. The Home Office announced, without consultation, that it would charge £155 for postal and £250 for same-day service extension applications. The new charges seemed excessive compared to the £36 visa fee. It was suggested in The Times in August 2003 that 'the Home Office move clashed with the Prime Minister's drive to encourage overseas students to come to Britain.'[11] With that in mind, there was a noticeable policy shift from internationalism to isolationism towards the end of 2003.

8 'Rethinking Foreign Students: A question of the national interest', National Review, 17 June 2002, http://www.nationalreview.com/issue/borjas061702.asp. Also available at http://www.hks.harvard.edu/fs/gborjas/Papers/NR061702.htm.

9 'The Student Program is Deeply Flawed', the Boston Globe (reprinted), 15 September 2002, http://www.ksg.harvard.edu/news/opeds/2002/borjas_student_program_bg_091502.htm (no longer available).

10 Student and Exchange Visitor Program, http://www.ice.gov/sevis/index.htm.

11 '£155 visa exploitation of overseas students', Times Online, 5 August 2003, http://www.timesonline.co.uk/tol/news/uk/article857417.ece.

1.08 *Paving the way to new Immigration Policies for International Students*

1.08 In a speech to Chatham House in November 2003 the Home Secretary[12] stated that the Home Office was developing an accreditation scheme for students. On 22 April 2004 the Home Secretary announced a new programme of measures to seek prevention of abuse of immigration routes to study in the United Kingdom including an accreditation and monitoring scheme for genuine colleges, and a requirement to notify the Home Office when students do not attend courses. This move informed much of the Labour immigration policy in the run-up to the 2005 general election.

1.09 The Home Secretary went on to state that 'the majority of foreign students are genuine and bring substantial economic benefits to the UK. A report from the British Council this week showed that students from overseas currently contribute £3 billion a year to our economy and predicts that this figure will be boosted by a further £13 billion by 2020. It is important that we protect this business and that these students continue to see further and higher education in our country as world-class'.[13] Thus the Government began its drive to stamp out 'visa scams' and 'bogus' colleges. On 27 April 2004 the Prime Minister instigated a comprehensive review of managed migration routes. One of the issues revealed by the review was that out of around 1200 unaccredited colleges checked by the Home Office nearly a third 'were found not to be providing education services'.[14]

1.10 At the same time as tackling abuse of the student route, the Government introduced a package of measures to make the United Kingdom more attractive to genuine international students by presenting them with routes leading to work and long term residence. From 18 September 2002 degree students became eligible to switch into employment categories. This was preceded by a policy brought in by the Secretary of State on 17 October 2001 by way of a concession outside the Immigration Rules, diminishing the importance of the 'intention to leave' requirement for degree students. On 25 October 2004 the Government introduced the Science and Engineering Graduate Scheme ('SEGS') to encourage science, mathematics and engineering graduates to pursue job opportunities in the United Kingdom. A similar scheme, the Fresh Talent: Working in Scotland scheme was launched on 22 June 2005. This was followed by the widening of eligibility criteria allowing international graduates who obtained undergraduate or postgraduate degrees, certificates or diplomas in any subject in the United Kingdom to participate in the International Graduates Scheme from 1 May 2007.

12 The Secretary of State for the Home Department is referred to interchangeably either as the Home Secretary or as the Secretary of State throughout this chapter.

13 'New Measures to Tackle Student and Marriage Immigration Abuse', 22 April 2004, www.bia.homeoffice.gov.uk (archived).

14 'Selective Admission: Making Migration Work for Britain', July 2005, www.bia.homeoffice.gov.uk (archived).

1.11 On 18 June 2004 the Education and Skills Secretary announced the establishment of a new register of education providers ('the Register') to address abuse in the education sector. Publicly funded institutions or those already accredited through existing UK accreditation bodies were to be automatically added to the Register. It was envisaged that from May until July 2004 all publicly funded accredited providers would be added onto the Register. A registration scheme for unaccredited private education institutions was to be developed.[15]

1.12 In August 2004 the Observer investigated a 'degrees-for-sale' scandal which revealed that 'university staff are being put under increasing pressure to pass foreign students studying for masters' degrees because the income is keeping many universities afloat.'[16] In the meantime, students and universities were becoming disconcerted over visa processing fees – this was echoed in the UKCOSA survey report of November 2004 compiled by Beatrice Merrick.

1.13 On 24 January 2005, Des Browne, the then Minister of State, signed off on a report which proposed to assess the regulatory impact of accreditation of private English language colleges.[17] The purpose of the proposal was to 'tackle the problems caused by illegitimate and poorly-run educational establishments which offer poor quality teaching and/or facilitate entry to the UK of individuals who are not genuine students'. It was accepted that 'around 300,000 students come to the UK each year to study English in the private sector. They spend around £1.2 billion, forge links with the UK which are helpful to trade, business and diplomacy and many go on to higher and further education in the UK. It is therefore crucial for the UK English language sector to maintain a good reputation overseas for providing a quality product…'. According to the report, accreditation of English language colleges is part of the measures designed to tackle abuse of the student migration route, as approximately 16% of colleges were found not to be genuine. Figures differed between UK Trade and Investment/British Council and English UK findings as to the number of non-accredited colleges. At the time it was not thought cost-effective to introduce a statutory accreditation scheme. Instead, it was recommended to build on the existing voluntary and self-financing accreditation schemes by encouraging colleges to seek accreditation from the British Council or other recognised providers and amending the Immigration Rules to refuse entry other than to students attending such colleges.

15 'New Register of Education Providers – Clarke', 18 June 2004, www.dfes.gov.uk (archived).

16 '"Degrees for sale" at UK universities', Observer, 1 August 2004, http://observer.guardian.co.uk/print/0,3858,4983540-102285,00.html.

17 'Regulatory Impact Assessment – Accreditation of Private English Language colleges', 24 January 2005, http://www.ind.homeoffice.gov.uk/6353/6356/17715/closedconsultationsprivatee1.pdf (archived).

Tightening of immigration control on foreign students

1.14 In February 2005 the five-year strategy for asylum and immigration was unveiled before Parliament, announcing that the Government was working towards a points-based system ('PBS'). It was envisaged that the scheme would have four tiers introducing a number of obligations 'on the various parties who benefit' under the scheme; primarily migrants and their sponsors. In the case of Tier 4 relating to students, sponsors were to share responsibility in ensuring that students complied with the requirements of their leave and report when they failed to attend studies. The detail of the obligations was to be worked up in consultation.[18]

1.15 On 7 February 2005 the Minister for Citizenship and Immigration announced that the Government was setting up a joint taskforce ('Joint Education Taskforce') with representatives from the education sector and other stakeholders to act as an advisory body to the Home Office on immigration policy affecting international students (eg visa charges), playing a key role in implementing measures announced in the five-year strategy.

1.16 In a speech during the 2005 General Election, the Prime Minister summed up the Government's success in the fight against 'bogus' colleges as follows: 'There has also been systematic action against addresses purporting to be education establishments for overseas students: more than 1,200 suspect colleges have been investigated, of which more than 300 have been closed as a result.'[19] At the same time concerns were raised by university officials when the Home Office gave universities only two weeks to respond to its proposals to increase visa fees from £36 to £85.

1.17 On 19 July 2005 the Government launched a consultation exercise concerning the framework of a single points-based scheme and the proposals for a new five-tier system.[20] The new system was to be operable, robust, objective, flexible, cost effective, transparent, usable and compatible with EU and international law.

1.18 The Joint Education Taskforce was to test in consultation two operational options requiring educational institutions to monitor and report international students who do not enrol and attend their courses. Option 1 (non-enrolment) was to focus on students who were issued with visas but did not enrol at the particular

18 'Controlling our Borders: Making Migration Work for Britain – Five Year Strategy for Asylum and Immigration', February 2005, www.bia.homeoffice.gov.uk (archived).

19 'Tony Blair's speech on immigration in full', Times Online, 22 April 2005, http://www.timesonline.co.uk/tol/news/politics/election2005/article384285.ece.

20 'Selective Admission: Making Migration Work for Britain', July 2005, www.bia.homeoffice.gov.uk (archived).

institution for which the visa was issued. The data gathered in the pilot was to inform the ideas behind the concept of a certificate of sponsorship and bonds being used for high risk applicants. Option 2 (discontinuation of study) was to test the impact of mandatory reporting of non-attendance on education institutions and the Home Office's resources to respond effectively. The Taskforce launched the Joint Notifications Project which began on 1 September 2005 and ran until 17 February 2006 involving consultation with 38 volunteer educational institutions.

1.19 In August 2005 further concerns were raised by Universities UK over ministers hampering efforts to recruit overseas students. A spokesperson for Universities UK said: 'In the UK, universities and colleges are doing all they can to demonstrate the UK is a high quality destination, but with the end of the Prime Minister's initiative and the considerable upheaval in the immigration system – including punitive increases in fees for visas and visa extensions as well as the proposed abolition of the right of appeal on student visas – we believe the Government is hampering rather than helping our international competitiveness.'[21]

1.20 Tony McNulty, then the Home Office Minister, announced on 12 July 2005 that Phase 2 of new entry clearance requirements (as part of the UK Residence Permit Scheme) for all foreign nationals (all non-visa, non-EEA nationals) coming to the United Kingdom for more than six months would be introduced as of 13 November 2005.[22] There was to be a grace period of two months from 13 November 2005 during which those arriving without the necessary entry clearance would not be refused if they otherwise qualified under the Immigration Rules. It was originally envisaged that the arrangements were to be introduced in stages over a two year period with Phase 1 coming online on 13 November 2003 and involving 10 nationalities: USA, Canada, South Africa, Singapore, Malaysia, South Korea, Hong Kong (but not BN(O)s), Japan, Australia and New Zealand.

1.21 At the House of Lords on 21 November 2005 the Parliamentary Under Secretary of State for the Department for Education and Skills, Lord Adonis reported that 'we have a very impressive record over the past five years of increasing the number of overseas students. The numbers were up by 57 per cent in the three years between 2001 and 2004, and the latest figures for undergraduate applications for this year show a further increase of nearly 1 per cent for 2005–06. However, we are in no way complacent, which is why the discussions are ongoing on the second phase of the Prime Minister's initiative, so that we can give substantial further encouragement to the recruitment of international students.'[23]

21 'Ministers 'hampering' overseas student recruitment', Guardian Unlimited, 2 August 2005, http://education.guardian.co.uk/students/overseasstudents/story/0,,1541084,00.html.

22 'Phase 2 of New Entry Clearance Requirements', 14 July 2005, http://www.aoc.co.uk/aoc/Members/int/immigration_visas (no longer available).

23 Lords Hansard, the House of Lords, November 2005, http://www.publications.parliament.uk/pa/ld199900/ldhansrd/pdvn/lds05/text/51121-01.htm21 (moved to another part of the Hansard website).

1.22 *Paving the way to new Immigration Policies for International Students*

1.22 In November 2005 Dr Neil Kemp was commissioned to produce a report for the Joint Education Taskforce on the impact of changing national visa regulations on the choice of destination country by international students. The report went on to compare visa regimes in other countries such as the USA, Canada and Australia and provide statistical data in respect of flow of international students to the United Kingdom.[24]

1.23 In his speech at the Association of Independent Higher Education Providers Conference on 14 December 2005, Lord Triesman (the Parliamentary Under-Secretary of State, Foreign and Commonwealth Office then responsible, among others, for UKvisas, migration policy, the British Council, etc) remarked 'I have seen myself some of the off-the-shelf packages of forged papers that potential abusers of the immigration control can buy in the markets of Lagos, Mumbai, Kingston, etc to gain entry as students. I have heard the lies that some applicants will tell during interviews to get visas. And I know of the increasing sophistication of those who have the sole intention of subverting the visa system. This Government is obliged to, and is determined to, meet these new challenges... That is why we launched the Joint Education Taskforce in May to develop a real partnership with the education sector.'[25]

1.24 On 18 April 2006 the second phase of the PMI for International Education was launched.[26] This was a five-year strategy 'to attract an additional 100,000 overseas students to study in the UK and encourage partnerships between universities and colleges in the UK and overseas'.[27] Total funding for the promotion of British education abroad in 2006-7 and 2007-8 was set at £27 million (allocated for United Kingdom/Africa, United Kingdom/Russia, United Kingdom/China and other partnership initiatives and the United Kingdom/India Education and Research Initiative). The specific targets for 2011 were: (a) to attract an additional 70,000 overseas students to HE and an additional 30,000 overseas students to FE in the United Kingdom; (b) to improve student satisfaction ratings; (c) to increase the number of international partnerships; and (d) to double the number of countries sending in excess of 10,000 students per year to the United Kingdom.[28] Priority markets for diversification and consolidation were identified as Australia,

24 'The Impact of Changing National Visa Regulations on the Choice of Destination Country by International Students', November 2005, www.keele.ac.uk/research/lpj/ESRC_Sustainability/Seminar2/HO_Report_NKemp.doc (no longer available).

25 'Speech by Lord Triesman at the Association of Independent Higher Education Providers Conference, Dorchester Hotel, London', 14 December 2005, http://www.ind.homeoffice.gov.uk/6353/18383/18679/speechbylordtriesman2.pdf (archived).

26 The second phase of the Prime Minister's Initiative coincided with the expansion in the Science and Engineering Graduate Scheme from March 2006 allowing all Masters and PhD students rather than those just from selected courses to benefit from it (see **Chapter 7**).

27 'Prime Minister Launches Strategy to Make UK Leader in International Education', 18 April 2006, www.dfes.gov.uk. The material was downloaded by the author and subsequently published on www.dcsf.gov.uk. Also available at http://www.egovmonitor.com/node/5644/print.

28 'PMI2 Overview', British Council, http://www.britishcouncil.org/eumd-pmi2-overview.htm.

Bangladesh, Brazil, Canada, China, Ghana, the Gulf States (including Saudi Arabia and UAE), Hong Kong, India, Indonesia, Japan, Korea, Malaysia, Mexico, Nigeria, Pakistan, Russia, Singapore, Sri Lanka, Taiwan, Thailand, Turkey, USA and Vietnam.

1.25 On 26 January 2007 it was announced that the new Border and Immigration Agency, would be equipped with a wide range of new powers to 'deter, detect and deport those breaking the rules and ensure that those foreign nationals legally in the UK play their part in upholding the rules'[29] under the UK Borders Bill which was published on that day.

1.26 From 30 October to 22 December 2006 the Government ran a public consultation on a new charging regime for immigration and nationality fees. The consultation attracted 340 responses from stakeholders, businesses and individuals. Further consultation was carried out with the three Taskforces: Joint Education Taskforce, Employers' Taskforce and the Arts and Entertainment Taskforce. It resulted in *A response to the Consultation on a New Charging Regime for Immigration and Nationality Fees*[30] being published in March 2007 and revised fees being announced in April 2007. In some categories the fees almost doubled.

1.27 Assuming the responsibilities of the Immigration and Nationality Directorate ('IND'), part of the Home Office, for managing immigration control in the United Kingdom; the Border and Immigration Agency, a new 'arms length' executive agency, was created on 1 April 2007 and went live on 2 April 2007 with Lin Homer as its Chief Executive operating in shadow status for the first year before being granted full agency status. It published its Business Plan and framework agreement in April 2007.[31] In the Business Plan the Border and Immigration Agency announced that it would be launching 'the register of authorised employers and educational institutions, where these organisations will need to demonstrate compliance to our immigration laws, will also act as a deterrent, and thus reduce illegal working'. It also summarised its achievements in the education sector in the past year during which it 'targeted UK educational institutions that act fraudulently to bring overseas nationals to the UK, or who act outside the rules, removing 45 colleges from the approved DfES list, and shutting down bogus colleges with action against around 20 individuals being taken further'.

1.28 In the Statement of Changes in Immigration Rules laid before Parliament by the Secretary of State on 3 April 2007 (Cm 7074), the Home Office introduced 11 policy changes, some of which (such as the revised bona fide criteria becoming

29 'New powers boost Immigration Officers' power to protect UK borders', Directgov, 20 January 2007, http://webarchive.nationalarchives.gov.uk/+/www.direct.gov.uk/en/Nl1/newsroom/DG_066141.

30 'A Response to the Consultation on a New Charging Regime for Immigration and Nationality Fees', March 2007, http://www.ind.homeoffice.gov.uk/6353/6356/17715/closedconsultationscharging2.pdf (archived).

31 'Border and Immigration Agency's Business Plan for Transition Year April 2007 – March 2008', April 2007, http://www.ind.homeoffice.gov.uk/6353/aboutus/businessplan0708.pdf (archived).

part of the Immigration Rules and external degree level students required to be registered with the UK degree awarding body) took effect from 19 April 2007 with the remainder taking effect on 1 September 2007. These changes were to provide a springboard for the imminent wide-ranging reshuffle in the immigration structure.

Emergence of Tier 4

1.29 On 18 April 2007 Liam Byrne, the then Immigration Minister, unveiled the timetable for launching PBS with Tier 1 coming online at the beginning of 2008 (in fact, it was launched on 29 February 2008), Tier 2 and Tier 5 being introduced in the third quarter of 2008 and Tier 4 following them in the spring of 2009.

1.30 In June 2007, the Home Office, with the Foreign and Commonwealth Office, published a joint report[32] setting out their international objectives, one of which was 'to help Britain gain a greater share in the … education market'.

1.31 On 24 July 2007, the Border and Immigration Agency revealed the first glimpses of Tier 4 of the PBS as it announced, elaborating further on the statements made in the Command Paper,[33] that accreditation with one of the three designated bodies would be a mandatory requirement under the new system. It would demonstrate that an accredited institution is 'a genuine education provider with sound teaching practices, recruitment procedures and progress monitoring of its students'. The requirement will only apply to private institutions (outside of the system of public reviews carried out by Ofsted and others) and will require a full institutional review.[34] Also in July 2007, the Border and Immigration Agency published its regulatory impact assessment report comparing benefits and drawbacks of mandatory accreditation.[35]

1.32 Commenting on the new Immigration Rules, Bill Rammell, the then Minister for Lifelong Learning, Further and Higher Education, said 'The government welcomes the many genuine international students who come to study in the UK each year. But a minority of less reputable colleges in this country work with people overseas helping them to get round the immigration rules and enter the UK to

32 'Managing Global Migration: A strategy to build stronger international alliances to manage migration', June 2007, http://www.ind.homeoffice.gov.uk/6353/aboutus/internationalstrategy (archived).

33 Cm 7641, March 2006: A Points-Based System: Making Migration Work for Britain, 7 March 2006, Home Office, http://www.homeoffice.gov.uk/documents/command-points-based-migration?view=Binary (archived).

34 'Points Based System: The Accreditation of T4 (Students) Sponsors', 24 July 2007, http://www.bia.homeoffice.gov.uk/aboutus/newsarchive/accreditationoft4sponsors (archived).

35 'Accreditation of Private Educational Institutions Involved in Recruiting International Students Under the Points Based System: Tier 4, Regulatory Impact Assessment', July 2007, http://www.bia.homeoffice.gov.uk/6353/aboutus/BIA_Accreditation_RIA.pdf (archived).

work illegally. That is why new rules for colleges who teach overseas students have been announced. Unaccredited institutions should seek accreditation as soon as possible.'[36] This policy direction was certainly different from the recommendations made on 24 January 2005, which favoured a more voluntary approach to accreditation. The proposals for mandatory quality assurance were developed in consultation with the Joint Education Taskforce.

1.33 On 1 September 2007, further changes to the Immigration Rules were introduced. They were to broaden the scope and definition of student provisions making three categories available to allow students to enter and/or remain in the United Kingdom and would lead to consequential changes being made to the visitor provisions (paragraph 41 of the Immigration Rules) preventing a visitor studying at any institution in the United Kingdom effective from 1 September 2007. The three student categories were: (a) student visitor category (pursuant to paragraphs 56K–56L of the Immigration Rules; (b) child visitor category; and (c) student category (pursuant to paragraph 57 of the Immigration Rules). Student visitor category was brand new while the other two categories were amended to reflect the changes.

1.34 Prior to 31 March 2009 education institutions were expected to volunteer information about students who do not enrol, fail to attend their course of study or discontinue their studies altogether. The numbers of absentee foreign students are staggering and yet there are no robust reporting mechanisms in place to ensure their cases are properly dealt with by the Home Office officials.

1.35 In an article entitled 'Mystery of the missing overseas students'[37] The Times carried out a study concerning international students who fail to enrol on courses, which shows that 'the student visa system is being abused' and 'used as a short cut for people wishing to obtain visas to enter Britain for other reasons'.

1.36 The new Immigration Rules sought to address this growing concern by introducing a limited form of mandatory reporting requiring all education institutions to maintain satisfactory records of enrolment and attendance of students and supply them to the Home Office on request within 28 days from the date of request. Failure to provide the relevant information to the Home Office would result in a number of measures being taken against the non-compliant institution which might ultimately lead to its removal from the Register (then DfES Register). Reporting would become a mandatory requirement for education institutions under the PBS after 22 February 2010.

36 'College Immigration Fronts to be Targeted', The Guardian, 24 July 2007, http://education.guardian.co.uk/further/story/0,,2133550,00.html?gusrc=rss&feed=8.

37 'Mystery of the missing overseas students', The Times, 14 July 2007, http://www.timesonline.co.uk/tol/life_and_style/education/article2073157.ece.

1.37 *Paving the way to new Immigration Policies for International Students*

1.37 In Command Paper Cm 7197 *Control of Immigration: Statistics – United Kingdom 2006*[38] presented by the Secretary of State in August 2007, it states that '309,000 non-EEA students were admitted to the United Kingdom in 2006, an increase of 9 per cent on the previous year'. In the UKvisas Annual Report 2006/2007 published on 8 August 2007, it further asserted that UKvisas received 313,000 applications from international students who annually contribute around £5 billion to the UK economy.[39]

1.38 Reading these statistics in light of the PMI made some people have reservations about the transitional changes laying foundations for the PBS. According to the consultation paper published in June 2007, *Simplifying Immigration Law: an Initial Consultation,*[40] which is at the heart of the Simplification Project seeking to consolidate and rationalise the legal framework of the immigration system, Tier 4 would be launched in the spring of 2009.

1.39 Under the PBS, institutions bringing foreign students to the United Kingdom would be designated as sponsors who would need to demonstrate that they are a bona fide education institution and accredited by a recognised body. Accreditation is ultimately an 'independent qualitative check on an institution in which the institution has demonstrated it is a genuine education provider rather than operating to facilitate the entry of bogus students to the UK'.[41]

1.40 Before they could qualify as sponsors and be registered on the register of sponsors ('Register of Sponsors'), private institutions were required to be accredited by such bodies as Accreditation UK, the British Accreditation Council and the Accreditation Service for International Colleges. Only those on the Register of Sponsors would be able to issue certificates of sponsorship which would act as an assurance from the sponsor 'that the student intends and is able to follow the relevant course of study' (Command Paper Cm 6741, March 2006, paragraph 127). Any leave given to a student would be tied to the sponsoring institution. According to the March 2006 Command Paper, Tier 4 would be separated into three categories of study: general student, school and study through work.

1.41 Education institutions would bear greater responsibility for checking the students' credentials, monitor their enrolment and attendance and comply with the Home Office's reporting procedures. On 1 November 2007 a press release was published to announce that one of the requirements under the PBS would be for

38 'Control of Immigration Statistics', 21 August 2007, http://www.official-documents.gov.uk/document/cm71/7197/7197.pdf (archived).

39 'Annual Report 2006/2007', http://www.ukvisas.gov.uk. The material was downloaded by the author and subsequently removed from the website. It was placed in the Libraries of both Houses of Parliament by Mr Liam Byrne, former Minister of State, Home Department.

40 'Simplifying Immigration Law', June 2007, http://www.bia.homeoffice.gov.uk/6353/6356/17715/immigrationlawconsultation (archived).

41 'Points Based System: The Accreditation of T4 (Students) Sponsors', 24 July 2007, http://www.bia.homeoffice.gov.uk/aboutus/newsarchive/accreditationoft4sponsors (archived).

foreign migrants coming to the United Kingdom, at least in respect of Tier 1 for now, to have an acceptable level of English. A list of tests which met the Border and Immigration Agency's requirements was published. The press release sought to encourage organisations facilitating English language tests to get on the List of Approved English Language Tests by registering with the Points Based System Operational Policy Team by 30 November 2007.[42]

Introduction of ATAS and launch of PBS

1.42 On 13 November 2007 the Border and Immigration Agency announced that from 30 November 2007 the Academic Technology Approval Scheme ('ATAS')[43] would become a mandatory requirement within the Immigration Rules for students intending to enter or remain in the United Kingdom for more than six months to undertake postgraduate studies or research in certain subjects.

1.43 This was a belated follow-up to an August 2007 announcement made by the Foreign and Commonwealth Office that ATAS would be introduced on 1 November 2007 and that as of 3 September 2007 students would be able to apply for an ATAS certificate online on the Foreign and Commonwealth Office website.

1.44 ATAS, according to the Foreign and Commonwealth Office, was established to prevent the dissemination of sensitive knowledge and skills leading to the proliferation of weapons of mass destruction ('WMD'). Non-EU/EEA nationals wishing to take postgraduate courses of study or undertake postgraduate research in the United Kingdom in the disciplines ranging from medicine, sciences and engineering to technologies would be required to obtain an ATAS certificate prior to applying for a visa, entry clearance or extension of stay in the United Kingdom. Students were required to: (a) hold a valid ATAS Clearance Certificate; and (b) hold a valid student entry clearance. The responsibility to acquire a certificate was on the student. UK, EU/EEA nationals and those applying to take undergraduate courses of study were exempt from this requirement.

1.45 The forerunner of a similar scheme was the USA. Given its Cold War history and the series of terrorist attacks in 1993 (and then in 2001) on American soil and driven by national security concerns of sensitive scientific and technical research findings, in 1994 the US Congress directed the US Department of State to develop a 'Technology Alert List' of categories of subjects that students from countries classified as 'state sponsors of terrorism' (Libya, Iran, Iraq, North Korea, Cuba,

42 'Points Based System, Procedure for Inclusion on the List of Approved English Language Tests', November 2007, http://www.ind.homeoffice.gov.uk/6353/11406/49552/pbs_procedureforinclusion.pdf (archived).

43 'Changes to Student Rules – academic technology approval scheme (ATAS)', 13 November 2007, http://www.bia.homeoffice.gov.uk/aboutus/newsarchive/atas (archived).

Sudan and Syria) should not be admitted to study. Sixteen sensitive categories were identified and added to the list. On 29 October 2001 Presidential Homeland Security Directive, Combating Terrorism Through Immigration Policies[44] stated that 'the Government shall implement measures to end the abuse of student visas and prohibit certain international students from receiving education and training in sensitive areas, including areas of study with direct application to the development and use of weapons of mass destruction. The Government shall also prohibit the education and training of foreign nationals who would use such training to harm the United States or its Allies'.

1.46 On 7 May 2002, the White House unveiled a proposal to create a panel that would screen foreign graduate students, post-doctoral fellows, and scientists enrolling on courses 'uniquely available' in the USA. The new panel, the Interagency Panel on Advanced Science Security ('IPASS') would evaluate candidates, reviewing as many as 2,000 applications, to ensure that the courses of study do not give them information or skills that could be used against the USA in a terrorist attack.[45]

1.47 In the meantime in the UK it was announced, on 14 November 2007, that immigration, customs and visa agencies would be consolidated under the new United Kingdom Border Agency ('UK Border Agency') which would see the integration of the HMRC, the Border and Immigration Agency and UKVisas.[46]

1.48 A new provision was inserted into paragraph 57 of the Immigration Rules to read as follows:

> '(v) he holds a valid Academic Technology Approval Scheme (ATAS) clearance certificate from the Counter-Proliferation Department of the Foreign and Commonwealth Office which relates to the course, or area of research, he intends to undertake and the institution at which he wishes to undertake it; if he intends to undertake either,
>
> (i) postgraduate studies leading to a Doctorate or Masters degree by research in one of the disciplines listed in paragraph 1 of Appendix 6 to these Rules; or
>
> (ii) postgraduate studies leading to a taught Masters degree in one of the disciplines listed in paragraph 2 of Appendix 6 to these Rules; or

44 'Presidential Homeland Security Directive, Combating Terrorism Through Immigration Policies', 29 October 2001, http://www.whitehouse.gov/news/releases/2001/10/20011030-2.html (also now available at http://www.dhs.gov/xabout/laws/gc_1214333907791.shtm).

45 'Visa Panel Will Focus On Science', The Washington Post, 8 May 2002, http://www.washingtonpost.com/ac2/wp-dyn/A49877-2002May7?language=printer (moved to archive at http://www.washingtonpost.com/ac2/wp-dyn?pagename=article&node=&contentId=A49877-2002May7&notFound=true).

46 'Border controls boosted by new technology and unified structure', 14 November 2007, http://www.bia.homeoffice.gov.uk/aboutus/newsarchive/bordercontrolsboosted (archived).

(iii) a period of study or research, as described in paragraph 57(ii)(b), in one of the disciplines listed in paragraph 1 or 2 of Appendix 6 to these Rules, that forms part of an overseas postgraduate qualification'

1.49 During a Joint Education Taskforce meeting on 13 November 2007 'members raised the issue on deportation of international students in respect to overstayers attempting to regularise their stay. Action by Border and Immigration Agency is generally to enforce the rules is increasing.'[47]

1.50 International students were back in the news when on 7 January 2008 a Home Office memo leaked to the press was published by the Daily Mail. The memo was written by Mr Jonathan Lindley, Director of Enforcement at the Border and Immigration Agency, on 17 December 2007 and described a recent rule change 'which was meant to crack down on student overstayers, making them automatically liable for refusal if they sought a visa extension'. The memo stated that:

> 'a proportion of these refusals have led to removal, some of which have been enforced. One such case came to Lin Homer's attention last week, resulting in the removal being cancelled and some critical comments from Lin. I am surprised that any have come sufficiently high within enforcement teams' priorities to merit such quick removal action. Please instruct your enforcement teams not to proceed with enforcing any student refusal cases unless they are deemed, at least inspector level, to be a priority due to Harm.'[48]

The case that prompted Lin Homer's intervention involved a student who entered the wrong credit card details on an application submitted in time.[49] On 29 February 2008 Tier 1 of the PBS was launched.

1.51 On 6 March 2008 it was announced that the national identity scheme would be introduced for foreign nationals in 2008 and British citizens in 2009. The scheme would begin in November 2008 and start with categories that are considered to be most at risk of abuse, such as students seeking leave to enter or remain in the United Kingdom. This had raised some legitimate concerns among education institutions and associations.

1.52 The Home Secretary announced on 3 April 2008 the unification of border, immigration, customs and visa checks under the umbrella of the new UK Border

47 Page 3, Minutes of the Joint Education Taskforce, 13 November 2007, http://www.webarchive.nationalarchives.gov.uk/20080806122547/http://www.ukba.homeoffice.gov.uk/sitecontent/documents/aboutus/workingwithus/stakeholders/jet/minutes/13november2007/jet_minutes131107.pdf?view=Binary (archived).

48 According to the Daily Mail 'Harm' is 'a reference to the Home Office system of gauging how harmful it is for an illegal immigrant to remain in the country'.

49 'Bogus Students Can't be Deported', Daily Mail, 7 January 2008 (hard copy).

Agency, an executive agency chaired by its Chief Executive, Lin Homer, and headed up by Chief Constable Roger Baker of Essex Police and Customs Commissioner Mike Eland.

1.53 The UK Border Agency announced its plan *Roll-out of new rules for foreign students* on 30 October 2008 and published a four stage plan for the implementation of Tier 4 of the PBS. The plan was subsequently updated on 13 August 2009. Phase 1 (sponsor registration) of the implementation plan commenced on 28 July 2008 requiring sponsors to apply to join the Register of Sponsors by 2 February 2009. Phase 2 (policy implementation) commenced on 31 March 2009 opening Tier 4 to prospective students to apply under the new provisions. 31 March 2009 marked the launch of Tier 4 for international students and the unveiling of the new Immigration Rules and policy guidance.[50] Phase 3 (trial and implementation of the sponsorship management system) began on 5 October 2009 and phase 4 (full sponsorship management system) – whereby sponsors could assign Certificates of Acceptance for Studies ('CAS') to prospective students and now had a mandatory duty to report on students that they were sponsoring to the UK Border Agency – began on 22 February 2010.

1.54 On 12 November 2009 the Prime Minister launched a review of the Tier 4 route, the outcome of which resulted in significant changes being introduced on 3 March 2010.[51] On 6 April 2010 the Immigration Rules were amended to introduce the Highly Trusted Sponsor Scheme and impose a number of restrictions on the level at which courses can be taught, work and work placement arrangements. With the change in Government in May 2010 came changes in immigration policy.

1.55 On 22 July 2010 the UK Border Agency announced that secure English language tests for students would be implemented from 12 August 2010. Judgments in *Secretary of State for the Home Department v Pankina*[52] on 23 June 2010 and *EnglishUK Ltd, R (on the application of) v Secretary of State for the Home Department*[53] on 9 July 2010 had a significant impact on the Immigration Rules, especially those related to international students, resulting in key amendments to the Rules on 23 July and 12 August 2010.

1.56 On 2 August 2010 the Minister of State for Borders and Immigration, Damian Green, announced an urgent review of the entire student visa system. In the ensuing months the Government made further statements on 6 September, 5

50 The new rules introducing Tier 4 were inserted by the Statement of Changes in Immigration Rules (HC 314) laid before Parliament on 9 March 2009 and in force from 31 March 2009. The new policy guidance was also introduced at this time supplementing the requirements set out in the Immigration Rules. Since its inception the policy guidance has undergone a number of changes and was used to introduce various concessions and transitional arrangements affecting international students.

51 By way of amendments to the policy guidance rather than the Rules.

52 [2010] EWCA Civ 719.

53 [2010] EWHC 1726 (Admin).

November and 23 November 2010 indicating its intention to reform the student system as a consequence of which a consultation was launched on 7 December 2010 to run for eight weeks until 31 January 2011. During this period, a new temporary concession was introduced to the student visitor route for English language students on 10 January 2011.

1.57 On 22 March 2011 the Secretary of State announced the changes affecting international students and their sponsors. The first wave of changes were introduced by way of the Statement of Changes in Immigration Rules (HC 908) published on 31 March 2011 and came into force on 21 April 2011. Other key changes were rolled out on 4 July 2011 and 5 September 2011, accompanied by interim announcements of changes on 13 June 2011, 18 July 2011 and 28 July 2011. The rest of the changes will be phased in over time until the end of 2012. From its commencement Tier 4 has had a tumultuous history courting controversy and publicity in equal measures.[54] With that in mind, the purpose of this book is to assist Tier 4 students and their sponsors in steering their way through the often uncertain provisions governing various aspects of the PBS relating to international students.

54 The history of Tier 4 of the PBS is further discussed in **Chapters 2–8** of the book.

Chapter 2

Sponsorship and Licensing

Formation of regulation and policy

Benefit and abuse of managed migration: in figures and public perception

Government initiative to boost recruitment of international students

2.01 In the past decade, the Government set out to balance the scales of proportionality between two competing forces: benefits gained by the United Kingdom from genuine student migration and harm caused by rogue misuse of the student route to the detriment of immigration control. From the Prime Minister's Initiatives launched in 1999 and 2006 to the introduction of Tier 4 of the Points Based System ('PBS') in 2009 the Government brought in often contradictory in purpose measures to increase the rewards and suppress the damage. In responding to public concern about the potential threat to national security from bogus students and their enablers the Government has ultimately put itself at odds with its earlier intention to step up recruitment of international students.

2.02 As noted in **Chapter 1,** on 18 June 1999 the Government announced the launch of the Prime Minister's Initiative ('PMI') in the form of a five year strategy aimed at increasing the number of international students by forging lasting relations between the United Kingdom and overseas to bring long-term political, cultural and economic benefits to the country. The Department for Education and Skills ('DfES'), as it was known then, was assigned with the task of leading PMI through: (a) a worldwide PR and communications strategy managed by the British Council including global launch of the Education UK brand; (b) increasing the country's marketing, counselling and information capacity; (c) initiation of new initiatives overseas to drive the campaign forward; and (d) *'improving access to, and attractiveness of, the UK as a study destination through a new package of measures and removing barriers preventing students from choosing the UK as a study* *destination*'[1] (added emphasis). The initiative involved stakeholders from various Government departments and devolved administrations, and was managed by a Project Working Group chaired by DfES and a High Level Steering Committee.

2.03 A study published by the British Council in April 2004, *Vision 2020*,[2] stated that:

> 'After a period of relative decline in terms of global market share for the UK during the 1990s, action was taken. This involved a more integrated approach by government, education institutions and the British Council (under the aegis of the Prime Minister's Initiative – PMI), and has led to a significant increase in numbers of international students in the UK in 2002–03'.

According to the Home Office figures there were significant increases in numbers of non-EU/EEA students in 2000–2002. In 2000, 313,000 students were admitted to the United Kingdom, an increase of 40,200 on 1999.[3] By 2002 the number of international students admitted to the United Kingdom rose to 369,000, an increase of 9% on 2001 with over 90% of students coming from Asia (161,000), the Americas (101,000) and Europe (76,000) and nearly 50% from the USA (69,2000), China (42,700, a 58% increase), Japan (32,500), Poland (18,400) and Russia (15,100).[4] At the same time the National Audit Office confirmed that entry clearance was granted to 128,000 visa national students in 2002.[5] However, contrary to the British Council report the figures show a decrease to 319,000 (down by 14% on 2002) in 2003[6] and 294,000 in 2004.[7] According to a report of the Home Affairs Committee on immigration control, the United Kingdom overtook the USA in becoming the most popular destination for Chinese students in 2004.[8]

1 Education UK: Positioning for Success, British Council, consultation document, 2003, http://www.britishcouncil.org/education_uk_-_positioning_for_success_-_consultation_document.pdf

2 *Vision 2020: Forecasting international student mobility, a UK perspective*, British Council, 2004, http://www.britishcouncil.org/eumd_-_vision_2020.pdf

3 Control of Immigration Statistics, United Kingdom, 2000, Home Office, November 2001, Cm 5315, http://www.archive.official-documents.co.uk/document/cm53/5315-i/5315_i.pdf

4 *Control of Immigration Statistics, United Kingdom, 2002*, Home Office, 27 November 2003, Cm 6053, http://www.archive2.official-documents.co.uk/document/cm60/6053/6053.pdf

5 *Visa Entry to the United Kingdom, the Entry Clearance Operation*, National Audit Office, Report by the Comptroller and Auditor General, 17 June 2004, HC 367, http://www.nao.org.uk/publications/0304/visa_entry_to_the_uk.aspx

6 *Control of Immigration Statistics, United Kingdom, 2003*, Home Office, October 2004, Cm 6353, http://www.archive2.official-documents.co.uk/document/cm63/6363/6363.pdf

7 *Control of Immigration Statistics, United Kingdom, 2004*, Home Office, 22 November 2005, Cm 6690, http://www.official-documents.gov.uk/document/cm66/6690/6690.pdf

8 *Immigration Control*, Fifth Report of Session 2005–2006, Home Affairs Committee, House of Commons, HC 775–i, 23 July 2006, http://www.publications.parliament.uk/pa/cm200506/cmselect/cmhaff/775/775i.pdf

2.04 The five-year objectives of the PMI were two-fold:

> 'For the UK to become the first choice for quality among international students at the higher education level, attracting an additional 50,000 students by 2004/05, worth £500 million per annum in new export earnings
>
> For the UK to become the world's leading nation for international students in further education attracting an additional 25,000 students by 2004/05, worth £200 million per annum in export earnings.'[9]

Despite the demonstrable decrease in numbers of students granted admission to the United Kingdom in 2003 and 2004, PMI was hailed a success given that it exceeded its target of 75,000 by 43,000 international students[10] by the time it came to an end in 2005. It was calculated that the estimated value to the UK economy of international students in public sector institutions in 2001/02 was £3.84 billion[11] with a potential rise to £5.84 billion by 2010 excluding programmes taught overseas. It bears noting that statistical data provided by organisations such as the Higher Education Statistics Authority, the Organisation for Economic Co-operation and Development and the Office of National Statistics differ in methodology and results. Moreover, in a study entitled *The Global Value of Education and Training Exports to the UK Economy*,[12] Dr Neil Kemp of the British Council (see para **1.22**) pointed out that 'the scope of the industry has not been defined systematically nor its full value to the UK regularly calculated.' Building on previous studies by Susan Bullivant[13] and Elizabeth Rylance-Watson[14] the study aimed at developing 'a methodology for annual calculation of exports of education and training services from the UK' to be used as a yardstick by Government departments to produce year on year comparisons. By studying in turn each aspect of the education industry: Higher Education, Further Education, English Language Teaching, Examination and Professional Bodies, Independent Primary and Secondary Education, Private Sector Training and other industries such as publishing, educational equipment and broadcasting, Professor Johnes used the data from 2001–2002 to apply his methodology to and concluded that the value of exports amounted to £10.3 billion.

9 Education UK: Positioning for Success, British Council, consultation document, 2003, http://www.britishcouncil.org/education_uk_-_positioning_for_success_-_consultation_document.pdf

10 Making It Happen. The Prime Minister's Initiative for International Education, British Council, update, 13 April 2010, http://www.britishcouncil.org/making_it_happen_-_the_prime_ministers_initiative_for_international_education.pdf

11 Education UK: Positioning for Success, British Council, consultation document, 2003, http://www.britishcouncil.org/education_uk_-_positioning_for_success_-_consultation_document.pdf

12 British Council and the UK Trade and Investment, April 2004, http://gianlucasalvatori.nova100.ilsole24ore.com/files/global-value-of-education-and-training-exports-to-the-uk-economy.pdf

13 *The value of education and training exports to the UK economy*, Bullivant Associates, October 1998, Department for Education and Employment, research report RR83.

14 *UK Exports of Training Expertise*, Elizabeth Rylance-Watson and Associates, 1999, report, Department for Education and Employment.

2.05 Global value of student migration was further tested by the British Council in its follow-up study, *Global Value: The Value of UK education and training exports: an update*[15] using methodology previously established by Professor Johnes but also incorporating new elements and providing regional breakdown of export figures. Conservative calculations showed that the estimated total value of exports for 2002–2003 was £7.7 billion and £8.6 billion for 2003–2004 (not including private sector training, consultancy and goods and services).[16] There have been no further updates of this study.

2.06 To improve on the medium term accomplishments of PMI, a consultation document, *Education UK: Positioning for Success* published by the British Council in 2003 put forward a new, more ambitious strategy; taking the initiative forward having identified the need for a new approach to marketing, building the United Kingdom's capacity to accommodate international students and nurturing relationships with them to form a potential market for 'life-long learning' by striving for a higher degree of integration, partnership and communication stretching far beyond the realms of the domestic education industry and the Government. The strategy blueprint outlined in the consultation document was a stepping stone towards the development of the five-year Prime Minister's Initiative for International Education ('PMI2') which was launched on 18 April 2006. The main aims of PMI2 were to promote the benefits of a UK education to international students through marketing and communications and to ensure that they have a positive experience in their studies (including immigration)[17] and its targets for 2011 were to:

- attract an additional 70,000 international students to UK Higher Education, and an additional 30,000 international students to UK Further Education;
- achieve demonstrable improvements to student satisfaction ratings in the UK;[18]
- achieve significant growth in the number of partnerships between the UK and other countries;

15 Dr Pamela Lenton, British Council, September 2007, http://www.britishcouncil.org/global_value_-_the_value_of_uk_education_and_training_exports_-_an_update.pdf. Liam Byrne referred to it in his foreword to the Students Under the Points Based System (Tier 4) – Statement of Intent, see below for content analysis.

16 The purpose of the methodology created by Professor Johnes in 2004 was to provide a model for year on year comparisons and to block a gap in annual data analysis calculating total value of international students to the UK economy. Unless evidence to the contrary exists, there is little to suggest that any such comparisons were produced until 2007. Moreover, the later study indicated that a direct comparison of figures between the two studies proved to be impracticable given the differences in data collection methods, changes in sampling and surveys, among others.

17 The British Council has been a stakeholder in the Joint Education Taskforce since 2006 working closely with the UK Border Agency, Government departments and education industry to share research, resources and best practice guidance feeding into new immigration policy. In its briefing note, A smoother journey, the British Council stipulates that its role is to offer guidance to students, agents and global education community to make visa arrangements user-friendly and ensure that international students have a positive experience in the UK (http://www.britishcouncil.org/british_council_role_in_visas_and_immigration.pdf).

18 See **Chapter 8**.

- double the number of countries sending more than 10,000 students per annum to the UK.[19]

2.07 In the years following the introduction of the second part of the decade long initiative, Home Office statistics showed a steady rise in numbers of student arrivals. In 2006, 309,000 non-EU/EEA students were admitted to the United Kingdom (an upsurge from 284,000 in 2005).[20] It was estimated that 358,000 non-EEA students were granted entry to the United Kingdom in 2007,[21] marking a 4% increase on the previous year, and in 2008[22] the estimated figure rose to 371,000 (including 144,000 student visitors). In its milestone report, *Making it Happen: The Prime Minister's Initiative for International Education*, published on 13 April 2010,[23] the British Council advanced an upbeat view of PMI2's adaptability in line with a myriad of changes in the global education landscape including the introduction of the PBS for international students. The report noted that the total direct value of education and training exports was over £12.5 billion and the value of international students was £8.5 billion (comprising Higher Education (transnational, tuition and spending), Further Education (tuition and spending), English Language Teaching (tuition and other) and Independent Primary and Secondary Education).

2.08 More recent figures and impact analysis can be gleaned from the following selection of reports:

- 'International higher education in facts and figures', International Unit, Universities UK, Summer 2010;[24]
- 'The Migrant Journey', Home Office, Lorrah Achato, Mike Eaton and Chris Jones, September 2010;[25]
- 'Overseas Students in the Immigration System, Types of Institution and Levels of Study', UK Border Agency, December 2010;[26]
- 'Pathway to prosperity: making student immigration work for universities and the economy', CentreForum, Thomas Brooks with Chris Nicholson, February 2011;[27]

19 PMI2 Overview, British Council, http://www.britishcouncil.org/eumd-pmi2-overview.htm.
20 Control of Immigration Statistics, United Kingdom, 2006, Home Office, 21 August 2007, Cm 7197, http://www.official-documents.gov.uk/document/cm71/7197/7197.pdf.
21 Home Office Statistical Bulletin, 2007, Home Office, August 2008, 10/08, http://rds.homeoffice.gov.uk/rds/pdfs08/hosb1008.pdf.
22 Control of Immigration: Quarterly Statistical Summary, United Kingdom, October – December 2009, Home Office, http://rds.homeoffice.gov.uk/rds/pdfs10/immiq409.pdf.
23 http://www.britishcouncil.org/making_it_happen_-_the_prime_ministers_initiative_for_international_education.pdf.
24 http://www.universitiesuk.ac.uk/Publications/Documents/InternationalHigherEducationInFactsAndFiguresSummer2010.pdf.
25 http://rds.homeoffice.gov.uk/rds/pdfs10/horr43c.pdf.
26 http://www.ukba.homeoffice.gov.uk/sitecontent/documents/aboutus/reports/pbs-tier-4/overseas-students-report.pdf?view=Binary.
27 http://www.centreforum.org/assets/pubs/pathways-to-success.pdf.

- 'The Student Immigration System: a consultation, Response from the Bell Educational Trust', Bell Educational Trust, 11 February 2011;[28]
- 'Universities UK response to the student immigration system – a consultation', Universities UK, 11 February 2011;[29]
- 'The UKBA's Proposed Restrictions on Tier 4 visas: implications for University recruitment of overseas students', Higher Education Policy Institute, Edward Acton, 18 February 2011;[30]
- 'Student Migration in the UK', Institute for Public Policy Research, Sarah Mulley and Alice Sachrajda, 22 February 2011;[31]
- 'Points Based System Tier 4 Attendance at Privately Funded Colleges', UK Border Agency, March 2011;[32]
- 'Student immigration reforms and their anticipated economic impacts', All-Party Parliamentary Group on Migration, 2 March 2011;[33]
- 'The Migrant Journey, the Second Report', Home Office, Lorrah Achato, Mike Eaton and Chris Jones, 16 August 2011.[34]

On 13 June 2011 in its impact assessment report the UK Border Agency ('UKBA') estimated that the impact of the forthcoming student reforms could cost the economy around £3.6 billion.[35] On 26 July 2011 in its follow-up report on student visas the Home Affairs Committee referred to a Monitoring Brief produced by the UK Statistics Authority on 11 July 2011 in which it confirmed that 'the currently available statistics on immigration and emigration fall some distance short of painting the comprehensive statistical picture that Parliament would want to be available to inform the public policy debate. This is true at the national level but even more pronounced at the local level where there is often little relevant data.'

28 http://www.bell-worldwide.com/media-centre/downloads/The%20Student%20Immigration%20System%20Consultation%20-%20Response%20from%20Bell%20Educational%20Trust%20January%202011.pdf.
29 http://www.universitiesuk.ac.uk/Publications/Documents/UUKresponseToTheStudentImmigrationSystem.pdf.
30 http://www.hepi.ac.uk/files/The%20UKBAs%20Proposed%20Restrictions%20on%20Tier%204%20visas%20-%20implications%20for%20University%20recruitment%20of%20overseas%20students.pdf.
31 http://www.ippr.org.uk/members/download.asp?f=%2Fecomm%2Ffiles%2Fstudent+migration+Feb2011%2Epdf.
32 http://www.ukba.homeoffice.gov.uk/sitecontent/documents/aboutus/reports/privately-funded-colleges/report.pdf?view=Binary.
33 http://www.appgmigration.org.uk/sites/default/files/APPG_migration-international%20students-briefing_paper.pdf.
34 http://www.homeoffice.gov.uk/publications/science-research-statistics/research-statistics/immigration-asylum-research/horr57/horr57-report?view=Binary (archived).
35 *"Reform of the Points Based Student (PBS) Immigration System"*, UK Border Agency, 13 June 2011, http://www.ukba.homeoffice.gov.uk/sitecontent/documents/policyandlaw/ia/reform-students-pbs/ia-students-.pdf?view=Binary.

It goes on to say that 'there is no statistical solution to this without the systematic recording, and matching, and keeping of full records, of people entering and leaving the UK.'[36]

Bogus colleges[37]

2.09 The magnetic pull of the United Kingdom as a top destination for quality education is undeniable as has been the impact of international students on its economy. The less well-intentioned have aspired to share in the good fortune and to capitalise on the influx of demand. A growing industry of 'visa factories' or 'visa shops' operating on the periphery of public attention began to catch the eye of the media as reports uncovering fake degrees increased in their number and frequency towards the end of the first round of the PMI. The role of the media in exposing the underbelly of education black market should not be underestimated. Being diametrically opposed to the aims and targets of the PMI, the phenomenon of bogus colleges requires forensic examination as one of the antecedents driving the education sector into the arms of stricter immigration regulation. The phenomenon is in no way unique to the United Kingdom, as countries like Canada, the USA and Australia are among those who have fallen prey to it, and nor are the measures introduced to tackle the problem throughout the years.

2.10 The terms 'bogus college' and 'bogus student' are not defined in the Immigration Rules although they are frequently used by the Government in policy documentation. In its Eleventh Report of Session 2008–09, *Bogus colleges*, the House of Commons Home Affairs Committee, the term 'bogus college' was defined as 'an illegitimate educational establishment set up primarily to enable non-European Economic Area (EEA) nationals to come to the UK on fraudulent student visas.'[38]

2.11 In March 2003 and January 2004, BBC News reported that several websites[39] offering fake British degrees[40] were closed down following a joint operation by trading standards officers in the United Kingdom and the USA while others continued to thrive in cyberspace despite efforts to shut them down.[41] While fake

36 *"Immigration Statistics"*, Monitoring Brief, M&A Note 5/2011, UK Statistics Authority, 11 July 2011, http://www.statisticsauthority.gov.uk/assessment/monitoring/monitoring-briefs/index.html.

37 See below at **2.90** for references to a selection of media articles.

38 'Bogus colleges', House of Commons Home Affairs Committee, HC 595, 21 July 2009, http://www.publications.parliament.uk/pa/cm200809/cmselect/cmhaff/595/595.pdf.

39 'Bogus degree sites shut down', BBC News, 7 March 2003, http://news.bbc.co.uk/1/hi/education/2829237.stm. The article named 'The University of Palmers Green', 'The University of Wexford' and 'Harrington University' among others.

40 It is an offence to supply unrecognised degrees liable on summary conviction to a fine under the Education Reform Act 1988, s 214.

41 'Fake universities thrive on the web', BBC News, 5 January 2004, http://news.bbc.co.uk/1/hi/education/3369567.stm. The article named 'Shepperton University', 'University of Dorchester' and 'GM University' as being web-based bogus universities.

universities prospered on the web, anecdotal evidence showed that there were at least 700 unregistered English language schools damaging the sector's reputation and undermining immigration control. The Secretary of State[42] 'alarmed by evidence showing that some colleges are prepared to authorise visas in return for cash'[43] was urged to get tough on unregulated colleges to deal with the lacuna.

2.12 Colleges were largely set up as private limited liability companies without any criminal checks being carried out on their staff and their activities unimpeded by regulatory bodies and voluntary accreditation. Private colleges were exposed as the weak spot in the industry, open for opportunists to engage in immigration fraud by facilitating a backdoor entry and then an extended stay in the United Kingdom for non-EU/EEA migrants, who did not wish to engage in genuine study, by providing them with forged documentation including offer letters, attendance and progress reports, and diplomas necessary to satisfy immigration officials. Calls for a clampdown gained momentum as investigative journalists posing as mystery shoppers brought to light activities of Evendine College,[44] Empire College,[45] Bedford School,[46] Anfell College and Scott's College[47] to name but a few, and the Metropolitan Police engaged in raids on suspected perpetrators of visa immigration scams under an initiative called 'Operation Maxim' to tackle organised immigration crime in London.[48]

2.13 The matter came to a boiling point when on 7 March 2004 Steve Moxon,[49] a caseworker in the managed migration section at the Immigration and Nationality Directorate ('IND'), Home Office, made public in The Sunday Times an unofficial and unpublished policy concerning waiver of checks on immigrants from Eastern Europe to reduce the backlog of cases. The policy was entitled 'Flexibility guidance: ECAA guidance for Entry Clearance cases post August 1st' issued in September 2003 as explained by Beverley Hughes, the Minister for Citizenship and Immigration who

42 David Blunkett, at the time. Secretary of State or Home Secretary are used interchangeably throughout.

43 'Language schools are 'visa factories', Times Online, 20 April 2003, http://www.timesonline.co.uk/tol/news/uk/article861610.ece.

44 'Visa scam language school is closed', Evening Standard, 23 June 2003, http://www.thisislondon.co.uk/news/article-5440144-visa-scam-language-school-is-closed.do.

45 'Exposed: the language schools that give visas to bogus students', Telegraph, 18 April 2004, http://www.telegraph.co.uk/news/uknews/4192155/Exposed-the-language-schools-that-give-visas-to-bogus-students.html.

46 'Language school visa scam', BBC Home, 14 March 2005, http://www.bbc.co.uk/insideout/extra/series2/bogus-language-school.shtml.

47 'Getting a visa without the graft', Guardian, 27 September 2005, http://www.guardian.co.uk/society/2005/sep/27/immigrationandpublicservices.internationalstudents.

48 'Raids smash student visa racket', BBC, 16 June 2004, http://news.bbc.co.uk/1/hi/england/london/3810981.stm and "Dawn raid crackdown on student visa scam", Times Online, 17 June 2004, http://www.timesonline.co.uk/tol/life_and_style/education/student/news/article446460.ece.

49 Author of *The Great Immigration Scandal*, (2nd edn, Imprint Academic, 2006). Chapter 11 of the book deals with bogus colleges.

was called to answer before the House of Commons on 8 March 2004.[50] Amidst an investigation by Ken Sutton, a senior civil servant, into Mr Moxon's claims and calls from the Shadow Home Secretary, David Davis, for the Minister to accept personal responsibility, The Times went on to publish leaked memos and emails which also revealed lack of willingness within the Home Office to commit resources to tackle the growing problem of bogus colleges and students. One of the emails published on 14 March 2004 is attributed to Mark Jones, a civil servant, and is dated 26 November 2003:

> 'Unfortunately the common factor I have found in all of my investigation (into) bogus colleges is that although ministers recognise that student abuse is on the increase, there is little commitment from anyone to investigating potentially bogus colleges/students unless a particular case or college has hit the headlines. The message from the (immigration service) at quite high level is that this kind of thing is currently low on their list of priorities.'[51]

2.14 While the inquiry report published on 25 March 2004 did not place blame squarely at the feet of the ministers, other countervailing circumstances that gave a misleading impression forced Ms Hughes to resign.[52] Swift action was called for within the IND and the Home Department not only to mitigate the damage caused by the public dressing down but also to deal with the failures and recommendations highlighted in the Sutton report.

2.15 On 22 April 2004, the Guardian reported that 'the Home Secretary, David Blunkett, has promised a package of measures to deal with the politically sensitive issue of "bogus students"' and noted that 'although the Home Office has issued guidance on what it regards as bona fide institutions, and has circulated lists of colleges accredited by the British Accreditation Council ('BAC') and English language organisations approved by the British Council, there is no *definitive list*'[53] (added emphasis). On 22 April 2004 the Secretary of State formally stated in a series of public announcements that:

> 'We are going to tighten up dramatically on the students coming in, the colleges which take those students, private adult colleges – many of them providing language courses... They are very important for our economy...but also a

50 Hansard, House of Commons, 8 March 2004, http://www.publications.parliament.uk/pa/cm200304/cmhansrd/vo040308/debtext/40308-05.htm.

51 'Minister misled Commons on immigration', The Times, 14 March 2004, reprinted at http://www.amren.com/news/news04/03/16/ukscandal.html. Also printed on page 142, Chapter 11, "The Great Immigration Scandal", Imprint Academic, Second Edition, 2006.

52 Columns 1753–1754, Personal Statement, Hansard, House of Commons, 1 April 2004, http://www.publications.parliament.uk/pa/cm200304/cmhansrd/vo040401/debtext/40401-05.htm#40401-05_head0.

53 Added emphasis. 'The real thing?', Guardian, 20 April 2004, http://education.guardian.co.uk/students/overseasstudents/story/0,12743,1195277,00.html.

> growing scam. Secondly, making sure that those students who do come actually turn up on their courses and don't disappear into the economy…'[54]

And further that:

> 'This is the right approach - ensuring the UK secures the benefits of immigration to the country while acting to tackle abuse of the system.'[55]

2.16 The Secretary of State also confirmed that the Government would be accrediting colleges to reduce the '"several thousand" bogus students that enter the system each year'[56] and would be putting in extra resources to check that those colleges actually existed. This package of measures was part of a top to bottom review of the entire immigration system. In a collaborative move the Education and Skills Secretary[57] announced on 18 June 2004 the creation of a new register of education providers aimed at tackling immigration abuse by preventing bogus institutions from bringing illegal migrants into the country. It appeared from the DfES press release that the only criterion for getting on the register was for education providers to produce evidence of legitimate business. The Education and Skills Secretary said:

> 'We know bogus providers are in the minority which is why we are working to make the scheme as straightforward and un-bureaucratic as possible for those genuine providers, who will easily be able to provide evidence of their work.'[58]

2.17 The register would be maintained free of charge under the auspices of DfES[59] but made available to the Home Office to guide them in their decisions in respect of granting leave to enter the United Kingdom to migrants wishing to study. The proposal was for publicly funded accredited education providers to be automatically included on the register (the Register of Education and Training Providers) from May to July 2004.[60] In the timeframe from May to the end of 2004, DfES set out to promote the register to private providers by urging them to be accredited and then be automatically entered on the register. The press release went on to say that:

54 Blunkett proposes immigration "blitz", ePolitix, 22 April 2004, http://www.epolitix.com/latestnews/article-detail/newsarticle/blunkett-proposes-immigration-blitz/ and 'Blunkett "blitz" on fake language schools', Guardian, 22 April 2004, http://www.guardian.co.uk/politics/2004/apr/22/immigrationpolicy.immigration.

55 'New measures tackle student and marriage immigration abuse', Number 10 website, 22 April 2004, http://webarchive.nationalarchives.gov.uk/+/http://www.number10.gov.uk/Page5692.

56 'Blunkett proposes immigration "blitz"', ePolitix, 22 April 2004, http://www.epolitix.com/latestnews/article-detail/newsarticle/blunkett-proposes-immigration-blitz/.

57 Charles Clarke, at the time.

58 'New register of education providers – Clarke', DfES, 18 June 2004, http://www.dcsf.gov.uk/pns/DisplayPN.cgi?pn_id=2004_0120.

59 'Register to deter student visa abuse', Times Online, 19 June 2004, http://www.timesonline.co.uk/tol/life_and_style/education/student/news/article448145.ece.

60 Similar to the onset of the Highly Trusted Sponsor Scheme in April 2010.

'The Register will be as un-bureaucratic as possible:

- Those education providers who receive public funding or are accredited through existing UK accreditation bodies have already undergone robust assurance measures and will automatically be added to the Register.
- A straight forward registration scheme is being developed for those private providers who are not accredited and more details of this will be made available in the coming months.'

2.18 There was no mention as to how quality assurance would factor into the register's remit. On 21 June 2004 the Committee of Public Accounts, House of Commons, demanded to know when the 'stable door' on sham colleges would be shut to stop them undermining the good name of genuine educational establishments. When probed by the Committee about attendance at 'Mickey Mouse' colleges, Bill Jeffrey, Director General of the Immigration and Nationality Department said that the Government was determined to put an end to them:

> 'This is an area that we have got into in the last month or so much more than in the past, and, as the Home Secretary announced a few weeks ago, first of all, there will be a registration scheme, and the Secretary of State for Education announced that the other day, but in the meantime we have been visiting colleges. We have already been to 300 or 400 of the ones that we thought gave most grounds for doubt, and there are a number of them we have already identified as being essentially bogus and applications in relation to them, whether made abroad or in this country, will be refused.'[61]

2.19 In respect of attendance, he expanded on what the Home Secretary and the Education and Skills Secretary said in their April and June 2004 announcements by confirming that there were ongoing discussions between the Home Office and the education industry about a possibility of there being an obligation on the education providers to inform the Home Office about students' attendance. This issue was further examined by the House of Commons, Committee of Public Accounts report published on 1 March 2005 which confirmed that 'the Home Office is addressing the problem of bogus colleges by compiling a register of genuine colleges and institutions for us in the United Kingdom and overseas' and 'consulting with the education sector and others about placing an obligation on institutions to report students who do not regularly attend their stated courses'.[62]

2.20 In a follow-up article The Times said that the initial findings presented to the Committee of Public Accounts on 21 June 2004 'follow a secret operation started

61 Response to Question 74, Minutes of Evidence, 'Visa Entry to the UK: the Entry Clearance Operation', Committee of Public Accounts, House of Commons, HC 737-i, 21 June 2004, http://www.publications.parliament.uk/pa/cm200304/cmselect/cmpubacc/uc737-i/uc73702.htm.

62 Foreign and Commonwealth Office: Visa entry to the United Kingdom: the entry clearance operation, House of Commons Committee of Public Accounts, Seventh Report of Session 2004–05, 1 March 2005, HC 312, http://www.publications.parliament.uk/pa/cm200405/cmselect/cmpubacc/312/312.pdf.

six weeks ago as part of the Government's drive against sham marriages and bogus colleges offering student visas to migrants'[63] and that the information would not be made publicly available but instead be given to a new intelligence unit dealing with these issues. This lack of transparency was picked up on by Baroness Anelay of St Johns during the debate on Asylum and Immigration (Treatment of Claimants, etc) Bill in the House of Lords on 28 June 2004.[64] During the debate Lord Avebury expressed his scepticism about the limited effect of raids on purported bogus colleges conducted on 16 June 2004 by the police (the operation was codenamed 'Taming' as part of 'Operation Maxim', see above) being confined to London and Essex.

2.21 The intelligence unit referred to by The Times must have been the new Managed Migration Intelligence Unit founded in May 2004 within the IND to tackle abuse of the student route. It worked alongside the Student Task Force set up by the Government following the review in April 2004 made up of members from the IND and DfES to carry out visits to education providers to establish their *bona fides* by checking that they comply with the following criteria:

- 'Maintain satisfactory records of enrolment and attendance of students;
- Provide courses which involve a minimum of 15 hours organised daytime study per week;
- Ensure a suitably qualified tutor is present during the hours of study to offer teaching and instruction to the students;
- Offer courses leading to qualifications recognised by the appropriate accreditation bodies;
- Employ suitably qualified staff to provide teaching, guidance and support to the students;
- Provide adequate accommodation, facilities, staffing levels and equipment to support the numbers of students enrolled at the institution;
- Comply with the latest IND guidance on notification of absent students.'[65]

2.22 The new Register of Education and Training Providers ('the Register') was ultimately incorporated into the Immigration Rules by the Statement of Changes in Immigration Rules (HC 164) laid before Parliament on 20 December 2004[66] introducing the following change into student requirements with effect from 1 January 2005:

63 'Hundred bogus colleges found', Times Online, 22 June 2004, http://www.timesonline.co.uk/tol/news/uk/article448497.ece.

64 Column 77, The Parliamentary Debates (Hansard), Fifth Series, Volume DCLXII Ninth Volume of Session 2003–2004 House of Lords, 28 June 2004, http://www.publications.parliament.uk/pa/ld200304/ldhansrd/vo040628/text/40628-22.htm.

65 Paragraph 251 in reference to the Home Office Immigration Directorate's Instructions, Chapter 3, Paragraph 3.5.3, Immigration Control, Fifth Report of Session 2005–2006, Home Affairs Committee, House of Commons, HC 775–i, 23 July 2006, http://www.publications.parliament.uk/pa/cm200506/cmselect/cmhaff/775/775i.pdf.

66 http://www.ukba.homeoffice.gov.uk/sitecontent/documents/policyandlaw/statementsofchanges/2004/hc164.pdf?view=Binary.

'For paragraph 57(i) substitute:

"(i) has been accepted for a course of study which is to be provided by an organisation which is included on the Department for Education and Skills' Register of Education and Training Providers, and is at either;
  (a) a publicly funded institution of further or higher education; or
  (b) a bona fide private education institution which maintains satisfactory records of enrolment and attendance; or
  (c) an independent fee paying school outside the maintained sector; and".'

2.23 The Statement of Changes in the Immigration Rules (Cm 7074) laid before Parliament on 3 April 2007 and issued to replace HC 418, introduced two new requirements for education providers with effect from 19 April 2007:[67] to maintain satisfactory records of enrolment and attendance of students and supply them to the Border and Immigration Agency ('BIA') on request, and for private education institutions to be *bona fide*. Paragraph 57 (i) was amended as follows:

'(i) has been accepted for a course of study which is to be provided by an organisation which is included on the Department for Education and Skills' Register of Education and Training Providers, and is at either;
  (a) a publicly funded institution of further or higher education which maintains satisfactory records of enrolment and attendance of students and supplies these to the Border and Immigration Agency when requested; or
  (b) a *bona fide* private education institution; or
  (c) an independent fee paying school outside the maintained sector which maintains satisfactory records of enrolment and attendance of students and supplies these to the Border and Immigration Agency when requested; and'.

2.24 The term *bona fide* was previously defined by a set of criteria laid out in the Immigration Directorate's Instructions but had now been incorporated into paragraph 6 of the Immigration Rules (Interpretation Section). The justification was provided in the Explanatory Memorandum which stated that the reason for this was to make the criteria more robust and to underline the importance of compliance with the requirements to the private educational establishments wishing to apply for inclusion on and to remain on the DfES' Register. The definition stipulated that:

'a *bona fide* private education institution' is a private education institution which:

(a) maintains satisfactory records of enrolment and attendance of students, and supplies these to the Border and Immigration Agency when requested;

67 http://www.bia.homeoffice.gov.uk/sitecontent/documents/policyandlaw/statementsofchanges/2007/cm7074.pdf?view=Binary.

(b) provides courses which involve a minimum of 15 hours organised daytime study per week;
(c) ensures a suitably qualified tutor is present during the hours of study to offer teaching and instruction to the students;
(d) offers courses leading to qualifications recognised by the appropriate accreditation bodies;
(e) employs suitably qualified staff to provide teaching, guidance and support to the students;
(f) provides adequate accommodation, facilities, staffing levels and equipment to support the numbers of students enrolled at the institution; and
(g) if it offers tuition support to external students at degree level, ensures that such students are registered with the UK degree awarding body.'

2.25 On 28 June 2007 DfES was divided into two ministries, the Department for Children, Schools and Families ('DCSF') and the Department for Innovation, Universities and Skills ('DIUS' which took over DfES's responsibilities) and consequently, references to DfES were removed from the Immigration Rules by the Statement of Changes (HC 40) enacted on 13 November 2007 taking effect as of 30 November 2007.[68] The Register was renamed from the DfES' Register of Education and Training Providers to the Register of Education and Training Providers. By way of clarification, Immigration Directorate's Instructions (Chapter 3 Section 3 (Nov/07))[69] were amended to say that:

> 'Caseworkers should note that the definition of a *bona fide* private education institution in paragraph 6 of the rules should ***not*** be used to refuse an application for leave to remain as a student where adverse information about an institution comes to light during the consideration of an application. As long as the institution appears on the Register of Education and Training Providers, the applicant should not be refused leave on the basis that he is not attending a *bona fide* private education institution.'

In the same policy guidance compliance officers appointed to inspect private education institutions were given basic instructions under each heading of the criteria as to how to determine whether a private college met the definition of a *bona fide* private education institution.

2.26 In January 2008 the Register came under scrutiny following reports that out of approximately 2,000 private colleges included on the Register, 256 had been inspected since 2005 with 124 being removed from the list.[70] This gave rise to legitimate concerns that more bogus colleges remained on the Register and its

68 http://www.bia.homeoffice.gov.uk/sitecontent/documents/policyandlaw/statementsofchanges/2007/hc40.pdf?view=Binary.
69 Accessed and saved 28 February 2008.
70 'Bogus college check catches 124', BBC, 8 January 2008, http://news.bbc.co.uk/l./hi/education/7177033.stm.

purpose as a gatekeeper was undermined. The concerns were further heightened by a memo dated 17 December 2007 leaked to the Daily Mail from the BIA in which the Director for Enforcement instructed student case working teams not to pass any further student refusal cases to the enforcement teams despite them being liable for removal under the Immigration Rules.[71] To address the concerns, the Government was preparing to unveil later in 2008 a new register fully under control of the UK Border Agency ('UKBA') within a framework of tighter, more centralised regulation over the education sector.[72]

2.27 The phenomenon of bogus colleges was independently examined by the House of Commons Home Affairs Committee in Summer 2009 following widespread media reports, and in particular, the investigation conducted by The Times, in relation to a number of Pakistani nationals apprehended by the police in April 2009 in 'Operation Pathway'. The Home Affairs Committee made the following suggestions in its report regarding bogus colleges on 21 July 2009:

> 'Conclusions and recommendations
>
> 1. Insufficient quality assurance procedures on the part of the Department for Innovations, Universities and Skills for private educational establishments on the Register of Education Providers, which facilitated the issuing of student visas between 2005 and 2009, allowed bogus colleges to bring foreign nationals into the UK on fraudulent student visas. We are pleased that the UK Border Agency has recognised the deficiencies of this system and introduced more rigorous regulation of educational establishments sponsoring student visas under the Points Based System. However, we remain cautious about the UK Border Agency's ability to deal with this issue and will continue to monitor sponsorship arrangements once Tier 4 of the Points Based System has been fully implemented. (Paragraph 8)
> 2. It is difficult to ascertain a precise figure for the number of bogus colleges in existence. One method of forming an estimate is to look at the discrepancy between educational establishments listed on the previous Register of Education Providers, which provided the only means of obtaining a student visa until March 2009, and those listed on the register of sponsors under the points based immigration system, which has replaced the Register of Education Providers and requires more stringent checks of educational establishments' credentials. There are around 2,200 colleges which were on the Register of Education Providers but are not on the register of sponsors. Whilst failure to transfer from the Register of Providers to the register of sponsors does not automatically mean a college is "bogus", we suspect that a significant proportion of these colleges are not legitimate. (Paragraph 13)

71 See **1.50**.
72 See **Chapter 4** for information about the Register of Sponsors under Tier 4 of the PBS.

3. Colleges not on the register of sponsors will no longer be able to facilitate student visas; however we are concerned about the number of illegal immigrants who may already have entered the UK on fraudulent student visas, the numbers of which could be in the tens of thousands. Firm enforcement action must be taken against any individual whose student visa has expired to ensure that they leave the country, as well as against those who have set up bogus colleges to perpetrate visa fraud. We have received no evidence that the Home Office has made adequate preparations to deal with this issue. (Paragraph 14)
4. We found no substantial evidence to corroborate the alleged link between bogus colleges and terrorist activity. The Pakistani nationals who entered the country on fraudulently-obtained student visas and who were arrested in Operation Pathway in April 2009 were subsequently released without charge. As far as we are aware, foreign students involved in previous terrorist plots have entered the UK on genuine student visas. Our evidence suggested that most individuals entering the UK on fraudulently-obtained student visas do so in order to work illegally. (Paragraph 16)
5. New arrangements for issuing student visas under the points based immigration system do appear to provide a more effective means of countering bogus colleges because of the requirement for independent accreditation coupled with the UK Border Agency's inspection regime. However, we are deeply concerned to hear that advance notice of inspection visits has been given in up to 85% of cases. This is unacceptable and does not give us any confidence in the rigour of the inspection regime in combating bogus colleges. The UK Border Agency should ensure that sufficient resources are provided to allow for rigorous and, critically, unannounced inspections. Any change in college ownership should require the college to be reaccredited. (Paragraph 22)
6. In addition, we note concerns amongst the education sector about the credentials of one of the accrediting bodies, the Accreditation Service for International Colleges. We understand the UK Border Agency is currently conducting a review of accrediting organisations, but the allegations are very worrying, and we suggest that they look closely at these allegations and request they make the results of the review available to us as a matter of urgency. (Paragraph 23)
7. We are extremely disappointed that the Government has ignored repeated warnings from the education sector about the problem of bogus colleges. While the new sponsorship system under the points based immigration system should help to prevent bogus colleges, we consider that a more complete means of prevention requires the compulsory regulation of private further education colleges and English language schools by the state. We therefore strongly recommend that the Government uses the Companies Act 2006 to restrict use of the term "college" in future to properly accredited institutions and instigates an inspection regime to enforce this. Alongside measures to tighten the UK's immigration controls, this would protect EEA, as well as non-EEA, students from receiving sub-

standard education at unregulated private colleges, which is highly damaging to the UK's international reputation for education and therefore the UK economy. (Paragraph 27)

8. We recommend that the Department for Business, Enterprise and Skills devises a system to make better use of intelligence provided by college networks, such as the Association of Colleges, to close down bogus colleges. We intend to revisit this issue once Tier 4 of the Points Based System has been fully implemented. (Paragraph 29)
9. Foreign nationals who apply to study in the UK in good faith but find themselves to be the victim of a scam on arrival also provide a valuable source of information about bogus colleges. However, these individuals may fear that reporting such establishments to the authorities would result in the closure of the establishments and lead to the students' status becoming that of illegal immigrants. As they have entered the UK illegally, however unwittingly, such individuals should not be allowed to remain; but to encourage greater reporting, those who do come forward with information should not be precluded from making successful immigration applications in future. (Paragraph 30)'[73]

The roots of sponsorship and licensing as applicable to Tier 4 and their phased implementation

2.28 At a managed migration event on 27 April 2004, Digby Jones, Director of the Confederation of British Industry,[74] delivered a welcome address at the London School of Business asserting that it was 'a time for political courage, swift, transparent, easily understood implementation of tough but fair rules' and encouraging the Government to show that the words 'managed' and 'controlled' had real meaning.[75] The key speaker, the Prime Minister, went on to outline principal facets of a new immigration strategy that was being put in place 'globally, nationally and locally':

> 'We will neither be Fortress Britain, nor will we be an open house. Where necessary, we will tighten the immigration system. Where there are abuses we will deal with them, so that public support for the controlled migration that benefits Britain is maintained.'[76]

73 Bogus colleges, House of Commons Home Affairs Committee, HC 595, 21 July 2009, http://www.publications.parliament.uk/pa/cm200809/cmselect/cmhaff/595/595.pdf.

74 Confederation of British Industry.

75 Speech by Digby Jones at Managing Migration Event at the London Business School, Tuesday 27 April 2004, http://www.cbi.org.uk/.

76 'PM speech on migration to the CBI', 27 April 2004, http://www.number10.gov.uk/Pag5708.

2.29 *Sponsorship and Licensing*

This 'top to bottom review'[77] was a sophisticated risk assessment exercise and the rhetoric of recognising benefits and tackling abuses exposed an uneasy equilibrium underlying the Government's proposed scheme becoming its pervasive maxim and major source of criticism for years to come.[78]

2.29 The Government presented to Parliament the blueprint of the five-year strategy for asylum and immigration, *Controlling Our Borders: Making Migration Work for Britain, Five Year Strategy for Asylum and Immigration*[79] on 7 February 2005 setting out key and large-scale areas of review and pitting the existing immigration architecture as a leviathan of complexity and confusion against the more streamlined system adopting a 'simple, straightforward and robust'[80] approach to immigration. In the preamble to the document the Prime Minister emphasised that 'the challenge for the Government is to maintain public confidence in the system by agreeing immigration where it is in the country's interests and preventing it where it is not.'[81]

2.30 In answer to the challenge the Government put forward a new single points-based system (invariably referred to as the Points Based System or 'PBS' throughout) uniting all work and study routes into four tiers:

- Tier 1, highly skilled individual
- Tier 2, skilled worker, with a job offer
- Tier 3, temporary low skilled worker schemes
- Tier 4, specialist and temporary workers, trainees and students.[82]

2.31 Points would be awarded in line with qualifying criteria and migrants, save for Tier 1, would need a *sponsor* to be admitted to the country. 'The scheme will introduce a number of obligations on the various parties who benefit',[83] the document went on to say. Moreover and most strikingly, sponsors such as

77 Paragraph 4.8, Page 13, Selective Admission: Making Migration Work for Britain, 19 July 2005, http://www.webarchive.nationalarchives.gov.uk/20100413151441/http://homeoffice.gov.uk/documents/cons-selective-admission-1907052835.pdf?view=Binary (archived).

78 In sentiment, this was a resolute departure from the Government's White Papers Fairer, Faster and Firmer – A Modern Approach to Immigration and Asylum published in July 1998 and Secure Borders, Safe Haven: Integration with Diversity in Modern Britain, Home Office, Cm 5387, published in February 2002. (http://www.archive2.official-documents.co.uk/document/cm53/5387/cm5387.pdf)

79 'Controlling our Borders: Making Migration Work for Britain,' Five Year Strategy for Asylum and Immigration', Home Office, Cm 6472, 7 February 2005, http://webarchive.nationalarchives.gov.uk/20080806122547/http://www.ukba.homeoffice.gov.uk/sitecontent/documents/aboutus/reports/fiveyearstrategy/asylumandimmigration?view=Binary (archived).

80 Home Office, Cm 6472, 7 February 2005, page 9.

81 Home Office, Cm 6472, 7 February 2005, page 5.

82 Home Office, Cm 6472, 7 February 2005, p 37.

83 Home Office, Cm 6472, 7 February 2005, p 16.

employers or educational institutions were invited to *share responsibility* of ensuring that migrants complied with the conditions of their immigration status:

> 'Sponsors will *share the responsibility of ensuring that migrants comply with the requirements attached to their leave.* They will be expected to including *[sic]* report if the migrant has left employment or is failing to attend studies.'[84] (added emphasis)

The concept of sponsorship, although not novel in the immigration context, had previously been by and large confined to, financial support associated with maintenance and accommodation undertakings for partners, children and family members given by a sponsor to gain entry to the United Kingdom.[85] In relation to students it was mostly associated with Government and international scholarship agency or private sponsorship. The emerging concept of sponsorship in the PBS went through several stages of development, constantly in a state of flux, moving and expanding its goalposts throughout.

2.32 At this point, the scope of sponsor participation, extended from individuals to private and public entities, in the managed migration process was yet to be specified. The subject was revisited in the Government consultation paper *Selective Admission: Making Migration Work for Britain* which was published on 19 July 2005[86] and dedicated solely to the PBS. The paper was more descriptive about the terms of sponsor engagement:

> 'In order to keep the system robust against abuse, a key principle is that all those who benefit from migration (not just the Government, but also employers, educational institutions and the migrants themselves) must play a part in helping to ensure that the system is not abused.'

2.33 This was the policy intent and the driving force behind the reform. The aim behind the radical redesign, as the Government pitched it, was to make it simpler and easier for the public to understand the basis and reasons for admission of migrants, for employers to access skills and experience and education providers to recruit foreign students, and for decision-makers to administer the system which had to adhere to tests of operability, robustness, objectivity, flexibility, cost effectiveness, transparency, usability and compatibility with international law.[87] The

84 Home Office, Cm 6472, 7 February 2005, p 16.

85 Ian A Macdonald QC and Frances Webber *Macdonald's Immigration Law & Practice* (6th edn, LexisNexis Butterworths, 2005), paragraphs 11.53–11.58 and Gina Clayton *Textbook on Immigration and Asylum Law* (3rd edn, Oxford University Press, 2008), paragraph 9.3.1.

86 The consultation process was to be managed in line with the Government's six consultation criteria including allowance for a minimum of 12 weeks for written consultation, clarity of proposals and timescale, accessibility, feedback, monitoring of effectiveness and ensuring that the consultation follows better regulation practice. The consultation exercise ran from 19 July until 7 November 2005.

87 These eight tests intended to set discretion and subjectivity outside the scope of consideration in favour of greater certainty making conformity to uniform criteria a qualifying requirement.

remodelled landscape of the PBS involved five tiers defining routes for settlement and temporary migration:

'Tier 1: Highly skilled individuals to contribute to growth and productivity.
Tier 2: Skilled workers with a job offer; and workers to meet specific overseas requirements.
Tier 3: Limited numbers of workers to fill low skill shortages.
Tier 4: Students: increasing exports and improving the education sector for the UK.
Tier 5: Other temporary categories: visiting workers, selected development schemes and youth mobility/cultural exchange.'[88]

The Government suggested that with the exception of Tier 1 each migrant coming to the United Kingdom through the remaining tiered routes would need a sponsor. In turn a sponsor 'could help make the system work by' assessing prospective migrants and confirming that they meet the criteria, providing evidence justifying the need for migrants in a specified category, and letting the Home Office know when a migrant leaves work or ceases studying. The Government would remain responsible for managing migration. At this developmental stage, the Government was appealing for greater involvement and support from sponsors, rather than imposing a strict burden of obligations. These initial proposals were beginning to sketch out the boundaries of shared responsibility between the Government and sponsors. To define them further, the public were asked to say whether they thought sponsors should bear a responsibility 'to contribute to the maintenance of control' (question 26) and what they should be expected to do to carry out that responsibility (question 27).[89]

2.34 Under Tier 4, sponsorship translated into the relationship between educational establishments and students being bound by a certificate of sponsorship ('CoS') which would need to be valid for the duration of students' studies. That way a CoS would serve to 'link the issuing of entry clearance or leave to remain to a specific course at a specific sponsoring institution'.[90] In relation to this the public were asked whether educational institutions should be required to 'help maintain integrity of the immigration control in order to be able to issue certificates of sponsorship'.[91] It was not proposed, at this juncture, that sponsors and migrants would be connected in the same way, by a CoS, under any other Tier.

88 Paragraph 6.2, Page 17, *Selective Admission: Making Migration Work for Britain, 19 July 2005, http://*webarchive.nationalarchives.gov.uk/20100413151441/http://homeoffice.gov.uk/documents/cons-selective-admission-1907052835.pdf?view=Binary (archived).

89 Page 27, *Selective Admission: Making Migration Work for Britain*, 19 July 2005.webarchive.nationalarchives.gov.uk/20100413151441/http://homeoffice.gov.uk/documents/cons-selective-admission-1907052835.pdf?view=Binary (archived).

90 Paragraph 6.23, Page 24.webarchive.nationalarchives.gov.uk/20100413151441/http://homeoffice.gov.uk/documents/cons-selective-admission-1907052835.pdf?view=Binary (archived).

91 Page 24, *Selective Admission: Making Migration Work for Britain*, 19 July 2005, Question 21.

2.35 In its response to the *Selective Admission: Making Migration Work for Britain* consultation, the Immigration Law Practitioners' Association ('ILPA') pointed out that while it was acceptable to leave it to the educational establishments to assess a student's ability to follow a particular course of study, 'any attempt to pass on the burden of enforcing immigration control to root out a few bad apples would incur disproportionate costs for educational establishments at a time when the UK has stated its intention to attract greater numbers of overseas students'.[92] Furthermore, ILPA stressed that putting 'the citizen or the corporation in the role of police officer is wholly inappropriate to this complex area of law'.[93]

Universities UK relayed the concerns of its 126 members in relation to sponsorship by saying that while higher education institutions consider the academic suitability of their prospective students 'it is the responsibility of the immigration authorities to assess other aspects'.[94]

2.36 Home Secretary, Charles Clarke,[95] introduced the centrepiece of the wide-ranging five-year strategy[96] for asylum and immigration, the Points-Based System on 7 March 2006, at the unveiling of the Government's Command Paper.[97] Clarke stressed that:

> 'foreign workers or students will also in future need a UK sponsor to vouch for them, ensuring that businesses and colleges *take responsibility* for making sure foreign workers and students comply with visa rules.'[98] (added emphasis)

2.37 The Command Paper set out the Government's proposals and the scope of the PBS following the preceding consultation, introducing for the first time the requirement for *all* migrants applying for leave in Tiers 2–5 to have a CoS[99] acting as an assurance from a sponsor confirming a migrant's ability and intention to do

92 Answer to Question 21, ILPA. November 2005, http://www.ilpa.org.uk/.
93 Answer to Question 26, ILPA. November 2005, http://www.ilpa.org.uk/.
94 Page 5, *Selective Admission: Making Migration Work for Britain* – Universities UK response, Universities UK, http://www.universitiesuk.ac.uk/PolicyAndResearch/PolicyAreas/Documents/International%20and%20European/Submission%20to%20the%20Home%20Office%20consultation%20on%20selective%20admission.pdf.
95 Charles Clarke was Secretary of State for the Home Department from 15 December 2004 to 5 May 2006. His Labour predecessors were Jack Straw (2 May 1997–8 June 2001) and David Blunkett (8 June 2001–15 December 2004). He was succeeded in office by John Reid (5 May 2006–27 June 2007).
96 Starting from 1928, five-year plans were a marked feature of socialist economic growth and development programmes in the Soviet Union, China, India, Pakistan, Vietnam, South Korea, Romania and other countries. Such method of economic planning came to a halt in the 1990s.
97 *A Points-Based System: Making Migration Work for Britain*, 7 March 2006, Cm 6741, Home Office, http://www.homeoffice.gov.uk/documents/command-points-based-migration?view=Binary.
98 *A Points-Based system: making migration work for Britain*, 11 March 2006, UK Border Agency, http://www.bia.homeoffice.gov.uk/sitecontent/newsarticles/2006/pointsbasedsystem.
99 There were suggestions from the education sector to change the word 'sponsorship' in the 'Certificate of Sponsorship' as it implied financial support.

a specific job or course of study, and, more importantly, likelihood of a migrant's compliance with the conditions of their leave.[100] For Tier 4 migrants their leave would be tied to the sponsoring institution and not the course, as suggested in the consultation paper[101] and only those sponsors who are on the list of approved sponsors would be able to issue CoS.[102] Tier 4 would be subdivided into three categories with different conditions attached to each: (a) general student; (b) school; and (c) study through work.[103] Sponsors listed as approved would be rated either A or B according to their past history:

> 'Sponsors *who conform with all their responsibilities* and whose migrants are found regularly to comply with their immigration conditions, can expect to be rated A. Sponsors who have a less good track record or could do more to improve their procedures, will be rated B.'[104] (added emphasis)

2.38 Going forward the Command Paper advanced a five Tier framework, similar to that set out in the consultation paper:

> 'Tier 1: Highly skilled individuals to contribute to growth and productivity
> Tier 2: Skilled workers with a job offer to fill gaps in UK labour force
> Tier 3: Limited numbers of low skilled workers needed to fill specific temporary labour shortages
> Tier 4: Students
> Tier 5: Youth mobility and temporary workers: people allowed to work in the UK for a limited period of time to satisfy primarily non-economic objectives'[105]

2.39 PBS would be designed for non-EU/EEA migrants wishing to come to or remain in the United Kingdom to work, train or study but unlike the existing system consisting of more than 80 immigration routes[106] it would be 'simpler and less bureaucratic'.[107] Entry clearance under the PBS would be mandatory for migrants regardless of Tier. Outlining the benefits of the sponsorship relationship, the Command Paper highlighted the fact that sponsors 'will have a formal role'[108] which

100 This was intended to replace the subjective tests under the existing Immigration Rules which required a judgment being made by decision-makers who may not be qualified as to the suitability of a particular course for a migrant.
101 Paragraph 126, Page 31, Cm 6741.
102 Education providers would need to demonstrate that they are *bona fide* and accredited by a recognised body (Paragraphs 62 and 128, Cm 6741).
103 Paragraph 132, Page 32, Cm 6741.
104 Paragraph 66, Page 20, Cm 6741.
105 Page 2, A Points-Based System: Making Migration Work for Britain, 7 March 2006, Cm 6741, Home Office, http://www.homeoffice.gov.uk/documents/command-points-based-migration?view=Binary.
106 It was proposed that routes such as visitors, ancestry, marriage and family reunion would be left outside the scope of the new system.
107 Paragraph 18, Page 10, Cm 6741.
108 Paragraph 11, Page 8, Cm 6741.

would be instrumental to the process unlike the existing system which was not 'clear about the responsibilities of those who seek to bring migrants to the UK'.[109]

2.40 According to the results of the consultation, the vast 'majority of respondents (82%) thought that employers, educational institutions and other sponsors should have a responsibility to contribute to the maintenance of the control'.[110] In the education sector 81% of respondents gave a positive answer to question 21 (see **2.34**)[111] whilst others voiced their concerns about the ultimate responsibility for policing the system remaining with the Government. During a meeting of the Joint Education Taskforce[112] on 7 March 2006, the Association of Independent Higher Education Providers ('AIHEP') pointed out that while the dichotomy was stated, 'there were no solutions given'.[113]

2.41 At this stage, the extent of responsibilities was not, at first glance, onerous. Sponsors were expected to check migrants' credentials and co-operate with the Home Office's monitoring. Education providers had additional responsibilities in having to report non-enrolment or discontinuation of studies by a student.[114] Reporting is the obligation that the Government has been consulting on since April 2004. In the blueprint for reforming the IND, *Fair, effective, transparent and trusted: rebuilding confidence in our immigration system,*[115] the Government outlined the delivery plan for the PBS and restated the policy intent for sponsors to take *greater responsibility* for ensuring the compliance of migrants that they bring to the United Kingdom.[116]

2.42 The conceptual importance of sponsorship as the keystone of the new PBS was further reiterated in *Securing the UK Border: Our vision and strategy for the future* published in March 2007[117] and *Simplifying immigration law: an initial consultation*

109 Paragraph 20, Page 10, Cm 6741.

110 Paragraph 56, Page 19, Cm 6741.

111 Paragraph 130, Page 32 and Page 59 in Section 1, Summary report for the Education sector on the basis of 119 received responses, Cm 6741.

112 See **Chapter 1** for information about the inception of the Joint Education Taskforce.

113 Minutes, Joint Education Taskforce, 7 March 2006, http://www.ukba.homeoffice.gov.uk/sitecontent/documents/aboutus/workingwithus/stakeholders/jet/minutes/7march2006/jet_minutes070306.pdf?view=Binary.

114 Paragraph 63, Page 20 and Paragraph 129, Page 32, Cm 6741.

115 Home Office, July 2006, http://www.homeoffice.gov.uk/documents/ind-review-250706/ind-review-eng?view=Binary.

116 Paragraph 2.14, *Fair, effective, transparent and trusted: rebuilding confidence in our immigration system,* July 2006, Home Office, http://webarchive.nationalarchives.gov.uk/20080806122547/http://www.ukba.homeoffice.gov.uk/sitecontent/documents/aboutus/consultations/closedconsultations/inspectorateconsultation/ (archived).

117 Paragraph 3.13, *Secure the UK Border: Our vision and strategy for the future*, Home Office, March 2007, http://webarchive.nationalarchives.gov.uk/20080110000624/http://www.ukba.homeoffice.gov.uk/sitecontent/documents/managingourborders/securingtheukborder/securingtheukborder.pdf?view=Binary (archived).

published in June 2007.[118] The Secretary of State began moulding the Immigration Rules so as to prepare future sponsors to comply with their proposed duties. The Explanatory Memorandum to the Statement of Changes in the Immigration Rules (Cm 7074)[119] stated that:

> 'At present the Home Office encourages education institutions to report voluntarily in respect of those students who do not enrol on or fail to attend for their chosen course of study.[120] Under the points based system for managed migration this reporting will become mandatory as part of a sponsor's responsibilities. There is a need to familiarise education institutions with this process and begin to include those institutions who have not previously volunteered this information.'

2.43 In the Statement of Intent, *Sponsorship under the Points Based System*, published in November 2007[121] the Government provided a more elaborate overview of sponsorship by integrating a further significant change into its overall architecture. The Statement defined two fundamental principles of sponsorship:

'a. Those who benefit most directly from migration (that is, the employers, educational institutions or other bodies who are bringing in migrants) should play their part in ensuring that the system is not abused, e.g. by alerting us if their migrants do not turn up for their job or course, or if they disappear; and

b. The Border and Immigration Agency needs to be sure that those applying to come to the UK to do a job, or to study, are eligible to do so and that a reputable employer or college genuinely wishes to take them on.'[122]

With this in mind, sponsorship plays two main roles in the PBS framework:

'a. It provides evidence that the migrant has a genuine job or course to go to in the UK;

b. It acts as a pledge from the sponsor that it will accept the responsibilities of sponsorship in respect of the migrant…'[123]

118 Paragraph 2.4. *Simplifying immigration law: an initial consultation*, Border and Immigration Agency, June 2007, http://collections.europarchive.org/tna/20080205132101/http://www.ind.homeoffice.gov.uk/sitecontent/documents/aboutus/consultations/closedconsultations/simplification1stconsultation/consultationdocument.pdf?view=Binary (archived). The Government announced the Simplification Project on 6 June 2007.

119 3 April 2007, http://www.bia.homeoffice.gov.uk/sitecontent/documents/policyandlaw/statementsofchanges/2007/cm7074.pdf?view=Binary.

120 Reporting was voluntary and could be submitted to the Home Office through a dedicated e-mail address icc7@ind.homeoffice.gsi.gov.uk.

121 *Sponsorship under the Points Based System, Statement of Intent*, Border and Immigration Agency, November 2007, http://webarchive.nationalarchives.gov.uk/20080110000624/http://www.ukba.homeoffice.gov.uk/sitecontent/documents/managingourborders/pbsdocs/statementofintent/sponsorshippbs.pdf?view=Binary (archived)

122 Paragraph 5, Page 6, Ibid.

123 Paragraph 21, Page 9, Ibid.

2.44 In the introduction to the paper Liam Byrne, then Minister of State for Borders and Immigration,[124] said that those who wish to act as sponsors would need a *licence* to do so. To become a sponsor an organisation would need to apply to be licensed by the BIA. A prospective sponsor would be required to supply evidence and be investigated with reference to its background to ensure that 'licences are only granted to bona fide organisations which are likely to comply with their conditions'.[125] The Statement went on to describe the circumstances in which a licence application 'will', 'will normally' and 'may' be refused,[126] and circumstances in which the prospective sponsor would be granted a licence but be 'awarded' or 'may be awarded' a B-rating.[127] If successful, a licensed sponsor would be able to apply for CoS to assign to migrants. Allocating CoS to migrants did not ensure that their entry clearance applications would succeed as the BIA reserved the right to make the final decision regarding admission of migrants to the United Kingdom. A CoS for students was renamed into a 'confirmation of acceptance of studies' to avoid any confusion with financial obligations. A licence would be issued for four years conditional upon compliance with numerous duties.

2.45 The Statement outlined duties that all licensed sponsors would be asked to fulfil: generic and specific to each Tier. The generic duties included record keeping, reporting, complying with the law and co-operating with the BIA. The specific duty for Tier 4 sponsors was to ensure that confirmations of acceptance of studies were issued only if the sponsor was satisfied as to the intention and ability of a migrant to follow the course of study. If a sponsor failed to comply with any of its duties, the penalty would be being downgraded to a B rating or having its licence withdrawn. Paragraphs 108 to 115 of the Statement describe the circumstances in which a sponsor 'will', 'will normally' and 'may' have its licence withdrawn and paragraphs 116 to 118 describe the circumstances in which an A-rated sponsor 'will be' or 'may be' downgraded to a B rating and a B-rated sponsor 'will' or 'may' lose its licence. The Statement went on to describe in some detail enforcement action to be against non-compliant sponsors.

2.46 The Statement, being an accountability document, was the precursor to the introduction of the licensing sponsorship system in the first quarter of 2008. BIA stated that it would issue 'the formal rules that will govern the licence regime

124 In office from 22 May 2006 to 3 October 2008.

125 Paragraph 27, Page 10, *Sponsorship under the Points Based System, Statement of Intent*, Border and Immigration Agency, November 2007, http://webarchive.nationalarchives.gov.uk/20080110000624/http://www.ukba.homeoffice.gov.uk/sitecontent/documents/managingourborders/pbsdocs/statementofintent/sponsorshippbs.pdf?view=Binary (archived).

126 Grounds of mandatory and discretionary refusal.

127 Paragraphs 35-38, *Sponsorship under the Points Based System, Statement of Intent*, Border and Immigration Agency, November 2007, http://webarchive.nationalarchives.gov.uk/20080110000624/http://www.ukba.homeoffice.gov.uk/sitecontent/documents/managingourborders/pbsdocs/statementofintent/sponsorshippbs.pdf?view=Binary (archived).

in advance of its introduction, and revise them periodically thereafter'[128] (see immediately below). The Government introduced a licensing system to enable those wishing to employ foreign workers from outside the EU/EEA to apply for a Tier 2 sponsor licence from 29 February 2008.[129] The provisions were contained in *Sponsorship under the Points Based System: Licensing Guidance.* Prospective sponsors under other Tiers would need to wait before making their licence applications. The Government introduced a threefold overriding principle for considering licence applications: the applicant must be: (a) a bona fide organisation operating lawfully in the United Kingdom; (b) trustworthy; and (c) capable of carrying out its duties as a sponsor.[130] The licensing guidance introduced the requirement for sponsors to appoint key members of staff to deal with the sponsorship management system ('SMS'). At paragraph 100 of the Licensing Guidance it was stated that the duties applicable to other categories 'will be added to these Rules when it becomes possible to apply for a licence in those categories'.

2.47 Education providers became eligible to apply for a Tier 4 licence and join the new Register of Sponsors from 28 July 2008. Unlike its predecessor, the register was to be run entirely by the UKBA and would no longer be within the sphere of the DIUS. In July 2008 the Government published *Students Under the Points Based System – (Tier 4) Statement of Intent.*[131] The firmly worded document put its message across quite clearly: the licence regime was the answer to reducing risk of abuse by allowing in only genuine students and cracking down on bogus colleges. It was a compromise, if not a solution, to keep the uneasy equilibrium on an even keel. To the public this arranged marriage between the Home Office and education providers was presented as panacea for withstanding the onslaught of abuse to the immigration system.

2.48 The Statement of Intent disclosed that the licensing process would replace the Register of Education and Training Providers run by the DIUS. In order to get a licence all education providers would need to show that they were inspected, audited or hold valid accreditation by one of approved accreditation bodies. Tier 4 would be split into two categories: Child Student and General Student. A confirmation of acceptance of studies, as it was denoted in the November 2007 Statement of Intent, was transformed into a 'confirmation of acceptance for

128 Paragraph 15, Page 8, *Sponsorship under the Points Based System, Statement of Intent*, Border and Immigration Agency, November 2007, http://webarchive.nationalarchives.gov.uk/20080110000624/http://www.ukba.homeoffice.gov.uk/sitecontent/documents/managingourborders/pbsdocs/statementofintent/sponsorshippbs.pdf?view=Binary (archived).

129 Sponsorship under the Points Based System: Licensing Guidance, Border and Immigration Agency, February 2008, available on http://www.aoc.co.uk/.

130 Paragraph 29, Page 10, *Sponsorship under the Points Based System: Licensing Guidance*, Border and Immigration Agency, February 2008, available on http://www.aoc.co.uk/

131 *Students Under the Points Based System – (Tier 4), Statement of Intent*, UK Border Agency, July 2008, http://webarchive.nationalarchives.gov.uk/20100303145844/http://www.ukba.homeoffice.gov.uk/sitecontent/documents/managingourborders/pbsdocs/statementofintent/studentsunderthepointsbased.pdf?view=Binary (archived).

studies' ('CAS') (as it currently stands). The Statement explained the two roles of sponsorship in the application process for the education sector:

> 'It provides an assurance that the education provider is confident that the student is capable of doing the particular course of study; and
>
> It involves a pledge from the sponsoring education provider that it will accept responsibility for the student whilst he is in the UK. Would-be students will not even be able to apply for a visa without a CAS'.[132]

2.49 The new system promised to 'dramatically simplify'[133] the immigration system while at the same time expanding on the number and description of stringent duties, checks, course type and level restrictions, and penalties for non-compliance with the requirements. The Statement also stipulated that education providers would not have a formal right of appeal against a decision by the UKBA to refuse a sponsor licence application or revoke an existing sponsor licence.[134] The Government's strict new plans were supported by Bill Rammell, Higher Education Minister, on 30 July 2008. He said:

> 'I will not tolerate the minority of individuals who seek to damage the quality of our education system through bogus colleges. This is why we have introduced tighter checks to the current Register of Education and Training Providers. The new system will toughen this process further and give extra protection from the damage bogus colleges can cause'.[135]

As indicated in the Statement of Intent, the Government published *'Students under the Points Based System – (Tier 4),* Implementation Plan on 30 October 2008. The plan was to deliver Tier 4 in four phases.

132 Paragraph 7, Page 6, *Students Under the Points Based System – (Tier 4), Statement of Intent*, UK Border Agency, July 2008, http://webarchive.nationalarchives.gov.uk/20100303145844/http://www ukba.homeoffice.gov.uk/sitecontent/documents/managingourborders/pbsdocs/statementofintent/studentsunderthepointsbased.pdf?view=Binary (archived).

133 Paragraph 26, page 10, *Students Under the Points Based System – (Tier 4), Statement of Intent*, UK Border Agency, July 2008, http://webarchive.nationalarchives.gov.uk/20100303145844/http://www.ukba.homeoffice.gov.uk/sitecontent/documents/managingourborders/pbsdocs/statementofintent/studentsunderthepointsbased.pdf?view=Binary (archived).

134 Paragraphs 75–76, Pages 16–17, *Students Under the Points Based System – (Tier 4), Statement of Intent*, UK Border Agency, July 2008, http://webarchive.nationalarchives.gov.uk/20100303145844/http://www.ukba.homeoffice.gov.uk/sitecontent/documents/managingourborders/pbsdocs/statementofintent/studentsunderthepointsbased.pdf?view=Binary (archived).

135 Strict new rules for foreign students, UK Border Agency, 30 July 2008, http://www.bia.homeoffice.gov.uk/sitecontent/newsarticles/2008/strictnewrules. This statement was later repeated almost word for word by the Minister of State for Higher Education, David Lammy on 30 October 2008 http://www.bia.homeoffice.gov.uk/sitecontent/newsarticles/rolloutofnewrulesforforeign. On 12 May 2010 the UK Border Agency announced that following the election on 6 May 2010 all news items including information about Government strategy published before April 2010 were removed from the website and placed in the UK government web archive at: http://webarchive.nationalarchives.gov.uk/20100503160445/http://www.ukba.homeoffice.gov.uk/.

2.50 According to the document, Phase 1 (Sponsor Registration) would commence from 28 July 2008 and prospective sponsors were urged to apply to be included on the Register of Sponsors by no later than 2 February 2009. Phase 2 (Policy Implementation) would commence from the end of March 2009 when Tier 4 would open to students allowing them to apply to come to the United Kingdom. Phase 3 (Trial and Implementation of the Sponsorship Management System) would commence from Autumn 2009 by rolling out IT system trials. Before the IT system was fully introduced, it was suggested that sponsors should issue potential students with a letter and that duties such as reporting would only become mandatory once the IT system was trialled. Phase 4 (Full Sponsorship Management System) would commence from February 2010 enabling sponsors to use SMS to issue CAS to prospective students. The plan was updated on 13 August 2009,[136] mostly in relation to Phase 3 (Trial and Implementation of the Sponsorship Management System for In-Country Migrant Applications). The amended plan also defined the letter to be issued to potential students by sponsors before the introduction of SMS as a 'visa letter' for the purposes of Phase 2.

2.51 A definition of a 'sponsor licence' was finally provided in the Statement of Changes in Immigration Rules (HC 1113) laid before Parliament on 4 November 2008 (see **2.63**). Further, in the section dealing with sponsorship under Tier 4 of the Explanatory Memorandum to the Statement of Changes in Immigration Rules (HC 314) laid on 9 March 2009 the Government stated that 'provisions about how an education provider becomes a licensed sponsor and how a licensed sponsor issues a prospective migrant with a visa letter are *not contained* in the immigration rules, rather in guidance published by the United Kingdom Border Agency'[137] (added emphasis). Additionally, 'in order to obtain a licence, a sponsor must satisfy the United Kingdom Border Agency that it is bona fide, honest and capable of complying with its duties.'[138]

2.52 In a news release of 22 December 2008 published on the UKBA website on 5 January 2009, the UKBA reinforced the message for colleges and universities to take greater responsibility for the international students they bring to the United Kingdom as this would weed out bogus colleges.[139] On 5 January 2009 the UKBA announced that more than 520 universities and colleges had applied to join

136 *Students under the Points Based System – (Tier 4), Implementation Plan*, UK Border Agency, August 2009, http://webarchive.nationalarchives.gov.uk/20100303145844/http://www.ukba.homeoffice.gov.uk/sitecontent/documents/managingourborders/pbsdocs/statementofintent/pbstier4implementationplan.pdf?view=Binary (archived).

137 *Students under the Points Based System – (Tier 4), Implementation Plan*, UK Border Agency, August 2009, http://webarchive.nationalarchives.gov.uk/20100303145844/http://www.ukba.homeoffice.gov.uk/sitecontent/documents/managingourborders/pbsdocs/statementofintent/pbstier4implementationplan.pdf?view=Binary (archived).

138 Paragraph 7.6. Ibid.

139 http://www.bia.homeoffice.gov.uk/sitecontent/newsarticles/foreignstudents.

the new sponsor register.[140] By way of a warning universities and colleges were reminded on 27 January 2009 to apply for a licence by 2 February 2009.[141] By then more than 800 universities, colleges and schools were reported to have signed up.

2.53 Phase 2 of the delivery plan was rolled out on 31 March 2009. In March 2009 the UKBA published *Guidance for Sponsor Applications – Tier 2, Tier 4 and Tier 5 of the Points Based System.*[142] The guidance underwent a series of transformations throughout the following months with Tier 4 sponsor provisions eventually being separated into a discrete document. 'A strict new system to crack down on bogus colleges and fraudulent applications from foreign students has so far screened out almost a quarter of applications from independent schools, colleges and universities', it was announced on 31 March 2009. More than 2,100 education providers applied to be on the Register of Sponsors with some 460 institutions not being accepted.[143] It was estimated that up to 2,000 bogus colleges would be forced to close due to the introduction of the new changes.[144] On 12 May 2009 the BBC reported that:

> 'The approved list of colleges for sponsoring UK student visas has shrunk by more than 13,000, following a crackdown against bogus colleges. There had been about 15,000 public and private educational institutions on the government's register. But the new list, vetted by the UK Border Agency, now only has 1,500 institutions registered...But the sharp fall in numbers will raise questions as to whether the previous official list included bogus institutions.'[145]

2.54 On 1 August 2009 the House of Commons, Home Affairs Committee published a 135-page report entitled *Managing Migration: The Points Based System.*[146] On 5 June 2008 the Home Affairs Committee announced its intention to launch a new inquiry by way of written submissions of no more than 2,500 words and oral evidence to take the Government to task over its implementation of the PBS including its effect on education and the proposed sponsorship arrangements.[147]

140 Universities and colleges sign up to new system for foreign students, UK Border Agency, 5 January 2009 (news release of 22 December 2008), http://www.bia.homeoffice.gov.uk/sitecontent/newsarticles/foreignstudents.

141 http://www.bia.homeoffice.gov.uk/sitecontent/newsarticles/signuptotier4.

142 Dated "010309", saved on 7 August 2009.

143 Tough new rules target bogus colleges and education cheats, UK Border Agency, 31 March 2009, http://www.bia.homeoffice.gov.uk/sitecontent/newsarticles/toughnewrulestargetbogus (archived).

144 '"Bogus" colleges lose visa rights', BBC, 31 March 2009, http://news.bbc.co.uk/l/hi/uk_politics/7973887.stm.

145 '13,500 fewer colleges for visas', BBC, 12 May 2009, http://news.bbc.co.uk/l/hi/education/8046341.stm.

146 Managing Migration: The Points Based System, Thirteenth Report of Session 2008–09, House of Commons, Home Affairs Committee, 1 August 2009, HC217–I, http://www.parliament.the-stationery-office.co.uk/pa/cm200809/cmselect/cmhaff/217/217i.pdf (archived).

147 Home Affairs Committee Press Release, Session 2007–08/43, 5 June 2008, http://www.parliament.uk/business/committees/committees-archive/home-affairs-committee/hacpn080605no43/ (archived).

2.55 *Sponsorship and Licensing*

Section 7 of the report dealing with sponsorship[148] stated that 'a key feature of the new system is the transfer of responsibility for enforcement of immigration control from the UKBA to employers'.

2.55 Strikingly, the Home Affairs Committee made no substantive comment on the fact of 'transfer of responsibility' and recommendations made by it in respect of sponsorship were primarily concerned with logistics management: quality of service provided by the UKBA in exchange for sponsors taking on greater responsibilities, processing times, testing of IT systems and gradual roll-out of the Tier 4 category to quell concerns from the education sector. In the Government reply to this report[149] the Secretary of State when responding to the recommendations made by the Committee with regard to sponsorship steered clear of any policy comments concerning the transfer of responsibility. Instead, paragraphs 18–23 of the reply deal exclusively with administrative and operational matters surrounding implementation of sponsorship arrangements and the UKBA relations with stakeholders.

2.56 On 17 September 2009 the UKBA announced that Phase 3 of the Tier 4 roll-out was set to go live on 5 October 2009 and that the voluntary trial period of SMS would run until February 2010 when use of the system would become mandatory. During this period, sponsors would be allowed to issue CAS, visa letters or a combination of both but only to would be Tier 4 migrants applying in-country.[150] Those sponsors who obtained their Tier 4 licence prior to 5 October 2009 had to perform a transition exercise to convert their allocation of CoS into CAS to enable them to use SMS. On 14 October 2009 sponsors were invited to participate in a Tier 4 sponsor survey running until 29 January 2010 to convey concerns regarding Phase 3.[151] The Statement of Changes in Immigration Rules (HC 120) hailed the introduction of Phase 4 on 22 February 2010 (and marked departure of visa letters) requiring Tier 4 migrants to have electronic CAS to enable them to score points.[152] On 22 February 2010 the duty to report on students who had been assigned a CAS became mandatory.[153]

148 Page 45, section 7, Managing Migration: The Points Based System Thirteenth Report of Session 2008–09, House of Commons, Home Affairs Committee, 1 August 2009, HC217–I, http://www.parliament.the-stationery-office.co.uk/pa/cm200809/cmselect/cmhaff/217/217i.pdf (archived).

149 Managing Migration: The Points Based System, The Government Reply to The Thirteenth Report from the Home Affairs Committee Session 2008–09 HC217, December 2009, Cm 7767, http://www.official-documents.gov.uk/document/cm77/7767/7767.pdf (archived).

150 Phase 3 launch date announced for Tier 4 of the points-based system, UK Border Agency, 17 September 2009. http://www.bia.homeoffice.gov.uk/sitecontent/newsarticles/2009/september/go-live-date-announced-tier4 (archived).

151 Take part in our survey of Tier 4 sponsors, UK Border Agency, 14 October 2009, http://www.bia.homeoffice.gov.uk/sitecontent/newsfragments/tier4-sponsor-survey (archived).

152 Statement of Changes in Immigration Rules HC120, 10 December 2009, http://www.bia.homeoffice.gov.uk/sitecontent/documents/policyandlaw/statementsofchanges/2009/hc120?view=Binary (archived).

153 See **Chapter 3** for further information.

The legal basis of the sponsorship and licensing scheme

2.57 This section does not seek to enter into a comprehensive discourse about the complexities of constitutional and administrative law and how they relate to the subject matter at hand. Such a discussion is outside the scope of this book. Instead, the purpose of this section is to raise questions concerning the legal foundation of the sponsorship and licensing scheme. The answer to these questions lies with the courts and, in part, with Parliament. Two of the most immediate and principal questions that need to be answered are: (a) what empowers the Secretary of State to establish and administer the sponsorship and licensing scheme; and (b) is the UKBA the appropriate licensing authority to regulate sponsors. Questions concerning the standing of policy guidance in the absence of statutory underpinning, licensing as a form regulation and delegation of executive powers to private actors are subordinate to these.

Absence of enabling legislation

2.58 Taken as a discrete segment of the PBS, the sponsorship and licensing scheme hinges on executive policy. There is no discernible enabling primary legislation which underpins the scheme giving the Government powers to run it. In its response dated 3 August 2010 to the author's request made under the Freedom of Information Act 2000 the Secretary of State gave the following answer to the author's question concerning specific statutory provisions which give grounding to the sponsorship scheme and, in particular, to the Sponsor Guidance:[154]

> 'Section 3(2) of the Immigration Act 1971 requires that the Secretary of State for the Home Department (SSHD) lay down rules as to the practice to be followed in the administration of the Act regulating the entry into and stay in the UK of persons required by the Act to have leave to enter. By virtue of s. 1(4) of the Act those rules are to include provision for admitting those who seek to enter the UK for the purposes of study. The Secretary of State has exercised her power to make such rules in section 6A of the Immigration Rules. Further rules relating to sponsorship are set out in Appendix A Immigration Rules. These provisions establish the requirement that an individual must have a sponsor in order to obtain Entry Clearance or Leave to Remain in the UK as a student.
>
> "*Sponsor*" and other concepts associated with sponsorship under the PBS are defined in paragraph 6 Immigration Rules.

154 Sponsor Guidance includes Tiers 2 and 5 of the Points Based System – Sponsor Guidance (current version 04/11, valid from 6 April 2011), and Tier 4 of the Points Based System – Policy Guidance (current version 09/11, valid from 5 September 2011 and referred to hereafter as 'the Sponsor Guidance') together with Appendices A to E.

2.59 *Sponsorship and Licensing*

The Points Based System Sponsor Guidance is regulatory guidance which is incorporated by the Immigration Rules. Paragraph 245AA(c) Immigration Rules states that "*Where Part 6A or Appendices A to C or E of these Rules refers to the United Kingdom Border Agency Guidance, this means guidance published by the United Kingdom Border Agency for use by Sponsors or migrants to ensure compliance with these rules. If the Sponsor or applicant does not satisfy the requirements set out in the guidance and referred to in the Rules, the applicant will not meet the related requirement in these Rules.*" As such, the guidance is a statement of practice to be followed in regulating entry into and stay in the UK of those who are subject to immigration control.'

2.59 Read side by side in full, sections 1(4) and 3(2) of the Immigration Act 1971 state:

'1(4) *The rules laid down by the Secretary of State as to the practice to be followed in the administration of this Act for regulating the entry into and stay in the United Kingdom of persons not having the right of abode shall include provision for admitting* (in such cases and subject to such restrictions as may be provided by the rules, and subject or not to conditions as to length of stay or otherwise) persons coming for the purpose of taking employment, or for purposes of study, or as visitors, or as dependants of persons lawfully in or entering the United Kingdom.' [added emphasis]

'3(2) *The Secretary of State shall from time to time (and as soon as may be) lay before Parliament statements of the rules, or of any changes in the rules, laid down by him as to the practice to be followed in the administration of this Act for regulating the entry into and stay in the United Kingdom of persons required by this Act to have leave to enter, including any rules as to the period for which leave is to be given and the conditions to be attached in different circumstances*; and section 1(4) above shall not be taken to require uniform provision to be made by the rules as regards admission of persons for a purpose or in a capacity specified in section 1(4) (and in particular, for this as well as other purposes of this Act, account may be taken of citizenship or nationality).

If a statement laid before either House of Parliament under this subsection is disapproved by a resolution of that House passed within the period of forty days beginning with the date of laying (and exclusive of any period during which Parliament is dissolved or prorogued or during which both Houses are adjourned for more than four days), then the Secretary of State shall as soon as may be make such changes or further changes in the rules as appear to him to be required in the circumstances, so that the statement of those changes be laid before Parliament at latest by the end of the period of forty days beginning with the date of the resolution (but exclusive as aforesaid).' (added emphasis)

2.60 In light of the next paragraph it is pertinent to cite the Immigration Act 1971, s 4(1):

'4(1) The power under this Act to give or refuse leave to enter the United Kingdom shall be exercised by immigration officers, and the power to give leave to remain in the United Kingdom, or to vary any leave under section 3(3)(a) (whether as regards duration or conditions), shall be exercised by the Secretary of State; and, unless otherwise allowed by or under this Act, those powers shall be exercised by notice in writing given to the person affected, except that the powers under section 3(3)(a) may be exercised generally in respect of any class of persons by order made by statutory instrument.'

2.61 In other words, the Secretary of State, by making rules of practice in accordance with the Immigration Act 1971, ss 1(4) and 3(2), regulates the entry into and stay in the United Kingdom of persons who are subject to immigration control. Depending on whether the person is applying for leave to enter or remain, the Secretary of State or immigration officers make decisions about whether to grant leave in a particular instance.[155] There is no juristic authority to suggest that the Act extends to decision making about who is entitled to come within the groups of those who benefit most directly from migration, namely, about who is entitled to be a sponsor. It would be wrong as a matter of statutory construction to decide otherwise and the pronouncement of the courts is instrumental to this issue.[156] If that proposition is right then regulation of employers and education providers by the Secretary of State is outside the scope of the Act. If that is the case, then it follows that the Sponsor Guidance cannot be 'a statement of practice to be followed in regulating entry into and stay in the UK of those who are subject to immigration control.' In a sense, the use of the Sponsor Guidance as a mechanism for regulating admission of non-EU/EEA nationals to the United Kingdom by proxy is inimitable in immigration law.

2.62 In the response to the request made under the Freedom of Information Act 2000, the Secretary of State appears to be ascribing the characteristics of the Immigration Rules contained in the Immigration Act 1971, ss 1(4) and 3(2) to the Sponsor Guidance by equating the latter to 'a statement of practice to be followed in regulating entry into and stay in the UK'. If that is the case, then arguably that concedes that the Sponsor Guidance is tantamount to the Immigration Rules. However, to be valid Immigration Rules must be subject to a negative resolution

155 Decisions regarding 'entry clearance' (defined in the 1971 Act, s 33(1)) are devolved to Entry Clearance Officers, although the constitutional status of such officers has never been defined with clarity.

156 In *New London College Ltd, R (on the application of) v Secretary of State for the Home Department* [2011] EWHC 865 (Admin) (7 April 2011) Williams J stated at paragraph 23 of the judgment that 'there is no immigration rule which identifies or defines the circumstances in which a sponsor licence will or may be granted, suspended or withdrawn. The practice of the Defendant in relation to the grant, suspension or withdrawal of such a licence is set out in guidance issued by UKBA.' Contrary to *Pankina*, Williams J went on to say that he did not consider that 'this guidance constitutes a material or substantive change in the immigration policy which is contained within the rules themselves. In my judgment it constitutes no more than an explanation of how the powers conferred by relevant rules will be exercised in practice.'

parliamentary procedure under the Immigration Act 1971,s 3(2). This must be explored further in light of the recent judicial decisions defining the role of extraneous materials.

2.63 It is true that definitions of 'sponsor' and 'sponsor licence' were inserted into paragraph 6 of the Immigration Rules on 27 November 2008,[157] the date that marked the commencement of the sponsorship scheme (for Tiers 2 and 5), and they are as follows:

> 'Under Part 6A of these Rules, "Sponsor"[158] means the person or Government that the Certificate of Sponsorship Checking Service records as being the Sponsor for a migrant.
>
> Under Part 6A of these Rules, a reference to a "sponsor licence" means a licence granted by the Secretary of State to a person who, by virtue of such a grant, is licensed as a Sponsor under Tiers 2, 4 or 5 of the Points Based System.'

2.64 Definitions of 'A-rated sponsor', 'Highly Trusted Sponsor' and 'B-rated sponsor' were inserted later:

> 'Under Part 6A of these Rules, an "A-rated Sponsor" is a Sponsor which is recorded as being "A-rated on the register of licensed Sponsors maintained by the United Kingdom Border Agency.[159]
>
> Under Part 6A and Appendix A of these Rules, a "B-rated Sponsor" is a sponsor which is recorded as being "B-Rated" on the register of licensed sponsors maintained by the United Kingdom Border Agency.[160]
>
> Under Part 6A of these Rules, "Highly Trusted Sponsor" means a sponsor which is recorded as being "Highly Trusted" on the register of licensed sponsors maintained by the United Kingdom Border Agency.'[161]

2.65 As stated in paragraph 7.5 of the Explanatory Memorandum to the Statement of Changes in Immigration Rules (HC 314) laid before Parliament on 9 March 2009:

> 'Provisions about how an education provider becomes a licensed sponsor and how a licensed sponsor issues a prospective migrant with a visa letter are not contained in the immigration rules, rather in guidance published by the United Kingdom Border Agency.'

157 Inserted by the Statement of Changes in Immigration Rules (HC 1113).

158 Official financial sponsor, rather than a PBS sponsor.

159 Inserted by the Statement of Changes in Immigration Rules (HC 1113) laid before Parliament on 4 November 2008 and in force from 27 November 2008.

160 Inserted by the Statement of Changes in Immigration Rules (HC 908) laid before Parliament on 31 March 2011 and in force from 21 April 2011.

161 Inserted by the Statement of Changes in Immigration Rules (HC 439) laid before Parliament on 18 March 2010 and in force from 6 April 2010.

2.66 Paragraph 245AA(c) was inserted into the Immigration Rules by the Statement of Changes (HC 439) with effect from 6 April 2010. Between 27 November 2008 and 6 April 2010 there was no express reference to the Sponsor Guidance in the Immigration Rules. Paragraph 245AA(a)–(b) which was inserted into the Immigration Rules on 30 June 2008[162] obliges applicants to provide documentary evidence specified in policy guidance to meet the evidential requirements in Part 6A or Appendices A to C, or E to the Immigration Rules. The Asylum and Immigration Tribunal accepted in cases such as *PO (Points based scheme: maintenance: loans) Nigeria* [2009] UKAIT 00047[163] that policy guidance was incorporated into the Immigration Rules by virtue of paragraph 245AA of the Immigration Rules although this was before the insertion of paragraph 245AA(c) into the Rules on 6 April 2010 (which specifically name checks 'sponsor guidance'). Paragraph 245AA was renumbered as paragraph 245A by the Statement of Changes (HC 863) laid before Parliament on 16 March 2011.

2.67 There are notable judicial authorities that strive to classify the atypical status and role held by the Immigration Rules as something other than delegated legislation (*R v Home Secretary ex p Hosenball* [1977] 1 WLR 766; *Pearson v IAT* [1978] Imm AR 212; *Bapio Action Ltd & Anor, R (on the application of) v Secretary of State for the Home Department & Anor* [2007] EWCA Civ 1139; *Odelola v Secretary of State for the Home Department* [2008] EWCA Civ 308). The decision in *Secretary of State for the Home Department v Pankina* [2010] EWCA Civ 719 refers to the relationship between the Immigration Rules and the Immigration Act 1971 as being constitutionally unique. The intrepid claim that the Sponsor Guidance is without foundation requires further examination and this has a bearing on the Immigration Rules. The Secretary of State has stated that the Sponsor Guidance is regulatory guidance incorporated into the Immigration Rules by way of paragraph 245AA(c). Is it necessary for policy guidance to have a statutory basis or, indeed, be incorporated into the Immigration Rules to be persuasive?

2.68 Constitutional theorists Colin Turpin and Adam Tomkins argue that while some forms of guidance stem from statutes which empower ministers to give guidance 'a great deal of ministerial guidance has no statutory basis and is without any legislative element. It may nevertheless be effective in influencing the conduct of those to whom it is directed, especially when it is based on clear constitutional understandings or if the means of compulsion are available in reserve.'[164] This mostly applies to guidance given to public bodies. They hasten to add that it is common for guidance that has a statutory basis to be 'subject to parliamentary

162 Inserted by the Statement of Changes in Immigration Rules (HC 607).

163 Heard on 28 August 2009.

164 Colin Turpin and Adam Tomkins *British Government and the Constitution* (6th edn, Cambridge University Press, 2007), p 481.

procedures similar to those applied to delegated legislation'[165] and be laid before Parliament for approval by both Houses before being issued. There are limits, Turpin and Tomkins assert, to what can be lawfully achieved by guidance as 'the government cannot override a discretionary power which a public body has under statute by giving it guidance, and the public body cannot abdicate its discretion by treating the guidance as binding on it.'[166]

2.69 In the present case, the Sponsor Guidance does not appear to have a statutory footing. In sharp contrast from earlier manifestations of Home Office policy such as IDIs[167] and DSPs,[168] it seeks to impose legal duties and sanctions on employers and education providers, the majority of whom are private, rather than public bodies. It has never been brought under parliamentary scrutiny. Material changes in the Sponsor Guidance are effected independently from the Immigration Rules and are not expressly reflected in them (although it must be noted that more recently some provisions contained in the Sponsor Guidance, especially those related to validity of CAS, have been creeping into the Immigration Rules). Certainty is a chief concern. At paragraph 33 of *Secretary of State for the Home Department v Pankina* [2010] EWCA Civ 719 (23 June 2010)[169] Sedley LJ stressed that:

> '... the statutory recognition of rules which are to have the character and, on appeal, the force of law requires such rules to be certain. That does not shut out extraneous forms of evidence of compliance, so long as these are themselves specified, but it does in my judgment shut out criteria affecting individuals' status and entitlements which...(a) have not themselves been tendered for parliamentary scrutiny, and (c) even if ascertainable at that point of time, may be changed without fresh scrutiny. As to (b), while the fact that the criterion absorbed into the rules comes from a policy document makes nonsense of the notion of policy, this is not critical: the vice would be the same if the reference

165 Colin Turpin and Adam Tomkins *British Government and the Constitution* (6th edn, Cambridge University Press, 2007), p 481.

166 Colin Turpin and Adam Tomkins *British Government and the Constitution* (6th edn, Cambridge University Press, 2007), p 482.

167 Immigration Directorates' Instructions.

168 Diplomatic Service Protocols.

169 A number of Upper Tribunal judgments followed the principles established in *Pankina.* To name but a few: *FA and AA (PBS effect of Pankina) Nigeria* [2010] UKUT 304 (IAC) (25 August 2010); *CDS (PBS "available" Article 8) Brazil* [2010] UKUT 305 (IAC) (25 August 2010); *HM and others (PBS – legitimate expectation – paragraph 245ZX(l);) Malawi* [2010] 446 UKUT (IAC) (8 December 2010); *MM and SA (Pankina:near miss) Pakistan* [2010] UKUT 481 (IAC) (26 January 2011); *Adubiri-Guimah and others (Post-study work – Listed institution) Ghana* [2011] UKUT 123 (IAC) (28 March 2011); *Aleem (Pankina-Uplift for overseas earnings) Ski Lanka* [2011] UKUT 120 (IAC) (28 March 2011); *Molla (established presence - date of application) Bangladesh* [2011] UKUT 161 (IAC) (03 May 2011).

in the rules were to a categorical criterion in some external but impermanent or undetermined source.'[170]

2.70 An earlier significant criticism made by Sedley LJ of the use of guidance by the Secretary of State can be found in paragraphs 50–55 of *Bapio Action Ltd & Anor, R (on the application of) v Secretary of State for the Home Department & Anor* [2007] EWCA Civ 1139. In that case guidance which 'directly and intentionally' affected 'immigration law and practice by imposing on the possibility of employment in the public sector a restriction beyond those contained in the Rules' and 'the exercise by NHS trusts of the private law power to enter into contracts' was declared unlawful. The final ruling was made on 30 April 2008 by the House of Lords upholding the Court of Appeal's decision (*Bapio Action Ltd & Anor, R (on the application of) v Secretary of State for the Home Department & Anor* [2008] UKHL 27).

Licensing

2.71 Under the PBS the Secretary of State regulates employers and education providers through licensing although this form of licensing differs from those described below. Licensing is a form of regulation which can create a barrier to entry. Anne Davies defines licensing as 'a form of social regulation in which the Government only permits firms or individuals to engage in a particular kind of activity if they have a licence'[171] and as long as 'minimum standards are met by all those who participate in the market.'[172] The PBS licensing scheme constitutes a regulatory measure to control the activities of recruiters of non-EU/EEA nationals in the United Kingdom – the sponsors.

2.72 In the words of Davies 'in general, the regulator publishes a set of criteria for the grant of a licence... Some licensing schemes may require review and renewal of the licence on a regular basis. In other cases, the licence continues unless and until there is evidence to indicate that it should be withdrawn... In licensing situations, a market exists for the services or products in question, and the government regulates that market by controlling who can participate.'[173]

170 Following the introduction of CAS and its replacement of visa letters on 22 February 2010 the Secretary of State added to Appendix A to the Immigration Rules, requirements on validity of CAS which affect, at least partially, Tier 4 sponsors. These substantive requirements related to CAS were extended further on 21 April 2011 and now regulate, among others, the Tier 4 interim limit, level of courses a Tier 4 migrant may be undertaking, how a sponsor's rating affects the level or institution at which a Tier 4 migrant may be studying, English language competence, examination re-sits, pre-sessional courses, work placements, etc. Perhaps, this is a move by the Secretary of State to make the sponsorship and licensing scheme resistant to a *Pankina* type challenge. However, the other issues raised in this section remain unanswered.

171 A.C.L Davies *The Public Law of Government Contracts* (Oxford University Press, 2008), p 10.

172 A.C.L Davies *The Public Law of Government Contracts* (Oxford University Press, 2008), p 12.

173 A.C.L Davies *The Public Law of Government Contracts* (Oxford University Press, 2008), p 12.

2.73 In the present context, a stark example of such regulation was the introduction of the interim cap on migration, and in particular, paragraph 63A of Appendix A (related to Tier 2 (General) migrants) inserted by the Statement of Change in Immigration Rules (HC96) on 19 July 2010:

> 'The Secretary of State shall be entitled to limit the number of Certificates of Sponsorship available to be assigned to Sponsors in any one period, and to limit the number of Certificates of Sponsorship assigned to any specific Sponsor in any one period. These limits will be specified in the Points Based System guidance.'

2.74 From 19 July 2010 the regime and criteria for issuing CoS changed so that sponsors would have their requests for additional certificates approved only in exceptional circumstances provided they could demonstrate 'a pressing need to issue further certificates of sponsorship'.[174] The initial interim cap was declared invalid by the Divisional Court on 17 December 2010 (*Joint Council for the Welfare of Immigrants, R (on the application of) v Secretary of State for the Home Department* [2010] EWHC 3524 (Admin)). With effect from 21 December 2010 the Secretary of State promulgated new Immigration Rules (HC 698) to specify in the Immigration Rules the quantum of the immigration cap and to reintroduce the interim cap which would run until 5 April 2011. The Secretary of State issued a Statement of Intent on 16 February 2011 affirming its intention to introduce from 6 April 2011 a limit of 20,700 applying to CoS for those seeking entry to the United Kingdom as a Tier 2 (General) migrant.[175] The limit was introduced on 6 April 2011, as intended, pursuant to the Statement of Changes in Immigration Rules (HC 863).

2.75 According to Anthony Ogus, licences 'are issued before the regulated activity has taken place, the ostensible purpose being to *prevent* the occurrence of what is regarded as socially undesirable; the potential quality of performance of *all* those engaged in the activity has to be assessed to ascertain whether it achieves the required standards; typically the conditions for the licence involve only *minimum* and *uniform* standards; and the sanction – prohibition of the occupation or activity – is particularly severe.'[176]

For example, licensable activities or occupations include but are not limited to betting offices,[177] gaming,[178] creation of embryos,[179] sale by retail of alcohol, supply of alcohol by or on behalf of a club, provision of regulated entertainment and late

174 Immigration limit for Tier 2 (General) of the points-based system, UK Border Agency, 28 June 2010, http://www.ukba.homeoffice.gov.uk/sitecontent/newsfragments/28-intro-limit-for-t2-pbs.

175 Tier 2 of the Points Based System, Statement of Intent, Transitional Measures and Indefinite Leave to Remain, UK Border Agency, 16 February 2011, http://www.ukba.homeoffice.gov.uk/sitecontent/documents/aboutus/reports/soi-tier2/tier2-soi-transitional-measures?view=Binary

176 Anthony I. Ogus *Regulation: Legal Form and Economic Theory*, (Hart Publishing, 2004), p 214.

177 Betting, Gaming and Lotteries Act 1963.

178 Gaming Act 1968.

179 Human Fertilisation and Embryology Act 1990.

night refreshment,[180] zoos,[181] agricultural work, gathering shellfish, processing or packaging of shellfish or any produce derived from agricultural work or shellfish.[182] These and other licensable activities or occupations are regulated by statute. Licensing functions which include the criteria for issuing and revoking licences are generally carried out by a licensing authority. A licensing authority is either appointed or established by statute, eg the Gangmasters Licensing Authority, the Human Fertilisation and Embryology Authority, the Gaming Board for Great Britain, the Horserace Totalisator Board and so on. Decisions made by licensing authorities may be challenged by way of an appeal and appeal provisions are made by statute.

2.76 For want of an enabling statute, the Sponsor Guidance contains the substantive requirements prescribed for licensed sponsors. The sponsorship and licensing scheme is administered by the UKBA. In their book *Understanding Regulation: Theory, Strategy, and Practice*, Robert Baldwin and Martin Cave noted that:

> 'Regulatory agencies are bodies that act on behalf of central government but are not central Departments of State. One of their strengths, as institutions, is an ability to combine governmental functions…[183]
>
> …
>
> There was a growing perception by policy-makers and legislators during this century that certain industries and activities required a special and continuing form of control…It was, in addition, felt necessary to mix functions such as adjudication, policy-making, and enforcement which could not be combined in a tribunal or court and could not be carried out by a government department, at least where adjudication was involved, because departments would be seen to be lacking independence, or worse, politically biased…[184]
>
> …
>
> Typically, a parent statute would empower the Secretary of State to establish an agency as a legal corporation and to appoint the Chair and member of the governing board. The agency would act independently of the ministerial department, with its own staff, but the minister would have overall powers of key appointment and direction. To summarize, agencies as regulatory institutions hold the advantage over ministerial departments in so far as they offer a greater degree of continuity of policy, they combine a wider range of

180 Licensing Act 2003.

181 Zoo Licensing Act 1981.

182 Gangmasters (Licensing) Act 2004.

183 Robert Baldwin and Martin Cave *Understanding Regulation: Theory, Strategy, and Practice* (Oxford University Press, 1999), p 69.

184 Robert Baldwin and Martin Cave *Understanding Regulation: Theory, Strategy, and Practice* (Oxford University Press, 1999), p 70.

functions successfully, they may adjudicate free from political taint, and can develop high levels of special expertise.'[185]

Licensing authority

2.77 UKBA is one of three agencies within the Home Office that came into existence on 1 April 2008. On 14 November 2007 the Prime Minister announced in a statement to Parliament the creation of a new agency, details of which were published in a Cabinet Office report on the same day.[186] With reference to that statement the Secretary of State confirmed the establishment of the UKBA on 3 April 2008:

> 'The new UK Border Agency is today established as a shadow agency of the Home Office. The agency's purpose and objectives are set out in its first business plan which I am laying in the House today. That purpose is clear: it is to secure our border and control migration for the benefit of our country; protecting our borders and national interests; preventing border tax fraud, smuggling and immigration crime; and implementing decisions quickly and fairly.
>
> The UK Border Agency will unite the work of the Border and Immigration Agency, Customs detection work at the border from Her Majesty's Revenue and Customs (HMRC) and UK Visas from the Foreign and Commonwealth Office (FCO), to create an organisation with a budget of over £2 billion, 25,000 staff, and operating in local communities, at our borders, and across 135 countries worldwide. The agency will deploy unprecedented power in pursuit of its goals.'[187]

2.78 Aside from laying down a business plan, the Home Office signed a memorandum of understanding with the Foreign and Commonwealth Office to bolster the move of UKVisas to the UKBA. This memorandum is contained in the Library of the House of Commons.[188] The Home Office also entered into a partnership agreement with the Commissioners of HM Revenue & Customs. UKBA assumed full executive agency status on 1 April 2009. On the same day it published a framework agreement[189] and a business plan setting out the agency's objectives for the three years ahead, from April 2009 to March 2012.

185 Robert Baldwin and Martin Cave *Understanding Regulation: Theory, Strategy, and Practice* (Oxford University Press, 1999), p 70.

186 House of Commons Hansard Debates, Volume 467, Column 669, 14 November 2007, http://www.publications.parliament.uk/pa/cm200708/cmhansrd/cm071114/debindx/71114-x.htm.

187 House of Commons Hansard Debates, Volume 474, Column 75WS, 3 April 2008, http://www.publications.parliament.uk/pa/cm200708/cmhansrd/cm080403/wmstext/80403m0002.htm#08040372000307.

188 House of Commons Hansard Debates, Volume 474, Column 77WS, 3 April 2008, http://www.publications.parliament.uk/pa/cm200708/cmhansrd/cm080403/wmstext/80403m0003.htm

189 Revised in December 2009.

2.79 The history of executive agencies is rooted in the Government's programme of civil service reform launched in 1988. In addressing the House of Commons on 18 February 1988 the Prime Minister introduced a report, *Improving Management in Government: The New Steps,* which called for 'more room and flexibility for the exercise of personal responsibility.' As the Prime Minister explained to the House of Commons, the Government accepted four recommendations made by the report:

> 'The report recommends, first, that to the greatest extent practicable the executive functions of Government, as distinct from policy advice, should be carried out by units clearly designated within Departments, referred to in the report as "agencies". Responsibility for the day-to-day operations of each agency should be delegated to a chief executive. He would be responsible for management within a framework of policy objectives and resources set by the responsible Minister, in consultation with the Treasury.
>
> It recommends secondly, that the Government should commit themselves to a progressive programme for attaining this objective; thirdly, that staff should be properly trained and prepared for management of the delivery of services whether within or outside central Government; and, fourthly, that a "project manager" at a senior level should ensure that the programme of change takes place.'[190]

2.80 Commenting on the functions of executive agencies, Turpin and Tomkins observed that:

> 'The policies, budgets and tasks of the executive agencies are settled by the responsible minister. For each agency a 'framework document' is drawn up (and published) which specifies, amongst other matters, the functions, aims and objectives of the organisation, its Chief Executive's financial freedoms and responsibilities and its relationship with the minister and departmental officials...
>
> The executive agencies are intended to have a large measure of autonomy in *operational* matters, while *policy* remains the responsibility of the minister and the 'core' department. This distinction has proved problematic. Policy and operations impact on each other and are not easily separated.'[191]

2.81 The Home Office (or the Home Department) was founded on 27 March 1782 following the move of domestic operations from the Southern Department. Its current sprawling structure includes three agencies, the UKBA, the Identity and Passport Service, the Criminal Records Bureau and a number of independent executive and advisory non-departmental public bodies. UKBA is divided into five broad operational areas or groups each of which is headed by a director and

190 House of Commons Hansard Debates, Volume 127, column 1149, 18 February 1988, http://www.margaretthatcher.org/document/107173.

191 Colin Turpin and Adam Tomkins *British Government and the Constitution* (6th edn, Cambridge University Press, 2007), p 410.

supported by corporate service directorates: borders, international, immigration, intelligence, criminality and detention. UK operations are split into six regions, each led by a regional director (Midlands and East, Wales and South West, North East, Yorkshire and the Humber, North West, London and South East, Scotland and Northern Ireland). UKBA board has 18 members presided over by Lin Homer, Chief Executive[192] (who has been with the Home Office since August 2005). Lin Homer was selected to be the new Permanent Secretary for the Department of Transport on 2 December 2010[193] leaving Deputy Chief Executive of the agency, Jonathan Sedgwick, as acting Chief Executive. On 15 July 2011 the Home Office announced Rob Whiteman to be the new Chief Executive.

2.82 The UKBA is undoubtedly a regulatory body controlling the sponsorship scheme as it issues and revokes licences. Conversely, there is no primary legislation appointing it to be a licensing authority for the purposes of the sponsorship scheme. The particular section within the UKBA entrusted with processing licence applications is the Sponsor Licensing Unit[194] (any mention of which has been taken out of the Sponsor Guidance) which is split into teams responsible for a wider range of functions pertaining to sponsorship and licensing.[195] The standards that must be satisfied by prospective sponsors before obtaining a licence are set out in executive policy as are the criteria for suspension, withdrawal (or revocation, as it became known after 21 April 2011) of licences and reduction of CoS/CAS. Sponsors are expressly deprived of a right of appeal but are given an opportunity to make representations or fresh applications. It may be arguable that in fact based cases in respect of suspension or withdrawal (revocation) of sponsor licences it may be necessary to have a right of appeal. As a licensing authority the UKBA lacks transparency and consistency in its decision-making processes and there are concerns of bias. One way of challenging an act of the Secretary of State is through judicial review proceedings in which points made under the Human Rights Act 1998 can be argued. As the only available remedy, judicial review is generally prohibitive for most sponsors.

2.83 In line with the Human Rights Act 1998, s 6(1), 'it is unlawful for a public authority to act in a way which is incompatible with a Convention right'. 'In relation to any act (or proposed act) of a public authority which the court finds is (or would be) unlawful, it may grant such relief or remedy, or make such order, within its powers as it considers just and appropriate', states the Human Rights Act 1998, s 8(1).

192 Our organisation, UK Border Agency, http://www.ukba.homeoffice.gov.uk/aboutus/organisation/.

193 House of Commons Hansard Written Answers, column 43W, 10 January 2011, http://www.publications.parliament.uk/pa/cm201011/cmhansrd/cm110110/text/110110w0002.htm#1101105001344

194 There are various teams related to the Sponsor Licensing Unit dealing with specific managerial facets such as the Student Systems and Control Team, Customer Service Team, Suspension and Revocation Team and others.

195 References to the Sponsor Licensing Unit have been taken out of the Sponsor Guidance as from 21 April 2011.

Improper delegation

2.84 Lastly, the sponsorship scheme, as discussed at length in the previous section, is based on two fundamental principles one of which is that 'those who benefit most directly from migration (the employers, education providers or other bodies that bring in migrants) help to prevent the system being abused.'[196] The language used by the Government in encouraging 'those who benefit most directly from migration' to share responsibility has changed over time since the publication of *Controlling Our Borders: Making Migration Work for Britain, Five Year Strategy for Asylum and Immigration*, but the meaning has remained the same. Paragraph 34 of the Sponsor Guidance advises sponsors to assign CAS only to students who, to the best of the sponsor's knowledge and belief, will meet the requirements for a valid CAS and will be able to make a successful application for leave (in previous versions of the Sponsor Guidance this requirement was much more onerous for sponsors who were asked to make a judgement call as to whether students would comply with the conditions of their leave). In her request under the Freedom of Information Act 2000 the author asked what gives the Secretary of State power to share responsibility for immigration control with sponsors and received the following response:

> 'The power to set down rules and statements of practice to be followed in the administration of the 1971 Act is set out in Section 3(2) of the Act, as outlined in the previous answer. Sponsorship allows employers and education providers to make decisions about migrants from outside the UK who wish to work or study with them, in line with ordinary practice in recruitment of employees or students. However, the final decision on whether or not to grant entry clearance or leave to remain is firmly the responsibility of the SSHD. A decision by a Sponsor to accept an individual as an employee or student is not determinative of an application for Entry Clearance or Leave to Remain.'

2.85 Does the Secretary of State have power to delegate any part of her responsibility for regulating the admission of aliens to the UK to private actors. The Government exercises statutory and prerogative powers.[197] Turpin and Tomkins state that 'the government possesses a considerable number of executive powers – powers which do not extend to alteration of the law but may affect the rights or obligations of those with respect to whom they are exercised... Most executive powers of government derive from statute and are vested in the "Secretary of State", a designated minister, or (less often) in government departments. When power is conferred upon a departmental minister it does not necessarily follow that he or she must personally decide whether to exercise the power. In practice

196 Paragraph 18, the Sponsor Guidance.

197 Prerogative powers have recently been under review (one of them is the prerogative power to issue, refuse, impound and revoke passports), see Review of the Executive Royal Prerogative Powers: Final Report, Ministry of Justice, 15 October 2009, http://www.justice.gov.uk/publications/docs/royal-prerogative.pdf.

the decision may be taken by a subordinate minister or, very frequently, by officials on the minister's behalf.'[198] Ministers must espouse the principles of individual and collective responsibility. The concept of individual ministerial responsibility makes ministers responsible to Parliament for their executive actions and for everything done by their department.

2.86 Turpin and Tomkins assert that 'a public body on which power is conferred by statute may not divest itself of the power by delegating it to some other body, unless such delegation is expressly or impliedly authorised by the statute' (*H Lavender & Son Ltd v Minister of Housing and Local Government* [1970] 1 WLR 1231).[199] Davies helpfully clarifies that 'public law contains two core principles about delegation. The first is the maxim *delegates non potest delegare*, which requires that discretions should be exercised by those to whom they have been entrusted and not delegated to anyone else. The second is the *Carltona* doctrine, which provides that discretions entrusted to a minister may be exercised by civil servants within the department.'[200]

2.87 These two principles are qualified by the existence of enduring common law powers such as contractual powers exercised by ministers under the Deregulation and Contracting Out Act 1994[201] that enable the Government to delegate ministerial functions to private contractors. According to Catherine Donnelly 'in England, the constitutional structure seems generally unsupportive of constitutional controls on governmental delegators and, as such, it seems that there are few constitutional limits on the ability of either the legislative or executive delegator to delegate power to private parties.'[202]

2.88 Donnelly also argues that 'the management of governmental programmes is increasingly delegated to private actors.'[203] For example, the Immigration and Asylum Act 1999, s 149 allows the Secretary of State to enter into contracts for the provision or running of removal centres[204] with private contractors and thus certain immigration removal centres are run by private actors, eg Campsfield House and Harmondsworth are run by the GEO, Brook House, Dungavel, Oakington and Tinsley House are run by the G4S Group, Colnbrook and Yarl's Wood are run by the Serco Group.

198 See *Carltona Ltd v Commissioners of Works* [1943] 2 All ER 560 (CA).

199 Colin Turpin and Adam Tomkins *British Government and the Constitution* (6th edn, Cambridge University Press, 2007), p 666.

200 A.C.L. Davies *Accountability, A Public Law Analysis of Government by Contract* (Oxford University Press, 2001), p 117.

201 See ss 69 and 70 concerning functions of Ministers and office holders.

202 Catherine M Donnelly *Delegation of Governmental Power to Private Parties, A Comparative Perspective* (Oxford University Press, 2007), pp 160, 161.

203 Catherine M Donnelly *Delegation of Governmental Power to Private Parties, A Comparative Perspective* (Oxford University Press, 2007), p 64.

204 The Nationality, Immigration and Asylum Act 2002, s 66 changed the name of 'detention centre' to 'removal centre'.

2.89 There is no evidence to suggest that the Secretary of State has delegated her responsibility to sponsors in a way envisaged by the Deregulation and Contracting Out Act 1994 or otherwise by contract and there is no express statutory power to so delegate. Nonetheless, employers and education providers are in a position of quasi-immigration officials who control non-EU/EEA migrants through compliance with their own sponsorship duties. One of the arguments that the Secretary of State has put forward in public statements against allegations of improper delegation is that she makes the final decision on admission to the United Kingdom. It may stem from this that the Secretary of State has reserved the right to go behind any assessments made by sponsors in respect of individual applicants. The sponsors' decision to issue CoS/CAS to employees or students at least in part determines the outcome of an application for entry clearance or leave to remain (as without a valid CoS/CAS the application would be refused outright). As a condition of keeping their licence, sponsors must assume joint responsibility for something that is solely in the Secretary of State's province. It is then for the courts to resolve whether such form of delegation is unlawful and whether the Secretary of State has acted *ultra vires*. On the other hand, it may be for Parliament to take action.

Annex

A selection of media articles on bogus colleges and bogus students

2.90

7 March 2003, Bogus degree sites shut down, BBC News http://news.bbc.co.uk/1/hi/education/2829237.stm

20 April 2003, Language schools are 'visa factories', Times Online http://www.timesonline.co.uk/tol/news/uk/article861610.ece

23 June 2003, Visa scam language school is closed, Evening Standard http://www.thisislondon.co.uk/news/article-5440144-visa-scam-language-school-is-closed.do

5 January 2004, Fake universities thrive on the web, BBC News http://news.bbc.co.uk/1/hi/education/3369567.stm

8 February 2004, Visa crackdown will hit language colleges, Times Online http://www.timesonline.co.uk/tol/news/world/ireland/article1014452.ece

14 March 2004, Minister misled Commons on immigration, Times Onlihttp://www.timesonline.co.uk/tol/news/uk/article1045856.ece

18 April 2004, Exposed: the language schools that give visas to bogus students, Telegraph

http://www.telegraph.co.uk/news/uknews/4192155/Exposed-the-language-schools-that-give-visas-to-bogus-students.html

20 April 2004, The real thing? Guardian
http://education.guardian.co.uk/students/overseasstudents/story/0,12743,1195277,00.html

16 June 2004, Raids smash student visa racket, BBC
http://news.bbc.co.uk/1/hi/england/london/3810981.stm

17 June 2004, Dawn raid crackdown on student visa scam, Times Online
http://www.timesonline.co.uk/tol/life_and_style/education/student/news/article446460.ece

19 June 2004, Register to deter student visa abuse, Times Online
http://www.timesonline.co.uk/tol/life_and_style/education/student/news/article448145.ece

22 June 2004, 100 fake colleges in visa scam, Guardian
http://www.guardian.co.uk/politics/2004/jun/22/immigrationandpublicservices.overseasstudents

12 October 2004, Paper tiger, Guardian
http://www.guardian.co.uk/education/2004/oct/12/internationalstudents.highereducation

14 March 2005, Language school visa scam, BBC Home
http://www.bbc.co.uk/insideout/extra/series2/bogus-language-school.shtml

24 June 2005, Colleges hit by bogus claims, TES Connect
http://www.tes.co.uk/article.aspx?storycode=2111821

27 September 2005, Getting a visa without the graft, Guardian
http://www.guardian.co.uk/society/2005/sep/27/immigrationandpublicservices.internationalstudents

25 July 2007, End to bogus colleges, Herald Scotland
http://www.heraldscotland.com/end-to-bogus-colleges-1.843039

8 January 2008, Bogus college check catches 124, BBC
http://news.bbc.co.uk/l/hi/education/7177033.stm

9 January 2008, Half of private language colleges struck off in crackdown on illegal immigrants, Mail Online
http://www.dailymail.co.uk/news/article-506884/Half-private-language-colleges-struck-crackdown-illegal-immigrants.html

3 November 2008, Bogus college sold on to a new owner, Herald Scotland
http://www.heraldscotland.com/bogus-college-sold-on-to-a-new-owner-1.893750

31 March 2009, 'Bogus' colleges lose visa rights, BBC
http://news.bbc.co.uk/1/hi/uk_politics/7973887.stm

15 April 2009, Determined terrorists could subvert security checks over student visas, Times Online
http://www.timesonline.co.uk/tol/news/uk/crime/article6094379.ece

27 April 2009, Bogus colleges: Closing the loophole, The Journal
http://www.journal-online.co.uk/article/5714-bogus-colleges-closing-the-loophole

12 May 2009, 13,500 fewer colleges for visas, BBC
http://news.bbc.co.uk/1/hi/education/8046341.stm

13 May 2009, Fewer colleges for foreign students following visa crackdown, Telegraph
http://www.telegraph.co.uk/education/educationnews/5314502/Fewer-colleges-for-foreign-students-following-visa-crackdown.html

21 May 2009, Pakistani gang 'pocketed millions' in bogus college scam, Guardian
http://www.guardian.co.uk/education/2009/may/21/bogus-college-scam

21 May 2009, Sham colleges open doors to Pakistani terror suspects, Times Online
http://www.timesonline.co.uk/tol/news/uk/crime/article6330301.ece

22 May 2009, 'Approved' college sells diplomas to help foreign students stay in UK, Times Online
http://www.timesonline.co.uk/tol/news/uk/crime/article6338235.ece

23 May 2009, Investigation of colleges by The Times prompts parliamentary inquiry, Times Online
http://www.timesonline.co.uk/tol/news/uk/crime/article6346204.ece

28 May 2009, Terror suspects' college found to be bogus, Times Higher Education
http://www.timeshighereducation.co.uk/story.asp?storyCode=406719&sectioncode=26

2 June 2009, Would-be terrorists don't choose bogus colleges, says minister, Guardian
http://www.guardian.co.uk/education/2009/jun/02/terrorists-avoid-bogus-colleges

19 June 2009, Register planned to bust bogus colleges, TES Connect
http://www.tes.co.uk/article.aspx?storycode=6015760

29 June 2009, Man given job of closing bogus colleges was sacked by university, Times Online
http://www.timesonline.co.uk/tol/life_and_style/education/article6597341.ece

21 July 2009, Bogus colleges 'not being tackled', The Independent
http://www.independent.co.uk/news/education/education-news/bogus-colleges-not-being-tackled-1754410.html

21 July 2009, Bogus college action 'inadequate', Educational News Digest (BBC)
http://www.edplace.co.uk/educational_news_digest?id=6163

21 July 2009, Bogus colleges: MPs criticise ministers' failure to stop illegal immigrants
http://www.guardian.co.uk/education/2009/jul/21/bogus-colleges-visas-illegal-immigrants

4 December 2009, Colleges may face ban on taking foreign students in visa crackdown, Times Online
http://www.timesonline.co.uk/tol/life_and_style/education/article6943566.ece

21 December 2009, King's College of Management gets new licence after fake places scandal, Times Online
http://www.timesonline.co.uk/tol/news/uk/article6964565.ece

29 December 2009, Suspect colleges discovered twice a month, Telegraph
http://www.telegraph.co.uk/news/newstopics/politics/lawandorder/6907115/Suspect-colleges-discovered-twice-a-month.html

30 December 2009, Bomber linked to London extremists but radicalised in Yemen, officials say, Guardian
http://www.guardian.co.uk/world/2009/dec/30/detroit-plane-bomber-yemen-radicalisation

9 January 2010, Conservatives to crack down on UK visas for foreign students, Guardian
http://www.guardian.co.uk/politics/2010/jan/09/tories-plan-visas-foreign-students

11 January 2010, Immigration system not stopping bogus students, warns leaked memo, Telegraph
http://www.telegraph.co.uk/news/uknews/immigration/6952401/Immigration-system-not-stopping-bogus-students-warns-leaked-memo.html

13 January 2010, Thousands of students from suspended bogus colleges in UK, Telegraph
http://www.telegraph.co.uk/news/newstopics/politics/lawandorder/6974143/

Thousands-of-students-from-suspected-bogus-colleges-in-UK.html

19 January 2010, English language schools fear new visa rules, Guardian
http://www.guardian.co.uk/education/2010/jan/19/foreign-student-visas

25 January 2010, 140 colleges suspended over immigration, The Independent
http://www.independent.co.uk/news/education/education-news/140-colleges-suspended-over-immigration-1878648.html

4 February 2010, Blacklisted UK colleges take Border Agency to court, The Register
http://www.theregister.co.uk/2010/02/04/ukba_student_visa/

8 February 2010, Foreign student visas to be slashed, Alan Johnson announces, Telegraph
http://www.telegraph.co.uk/education/educationnews/7181882/Foreign-student-visas-to-be-slashed-Alan-Johnson-announces.html

13 March 2010, UK's bogus colleges leave Indians in lurch, Deccan Chronicle
http://www.deccanchronicle.com/international/uk%E2%80%99s-bogus-colleges-leave-indians-lurch-566

16 March 2010, English language schools plan legal challenge on tightening of visa rules, Guardian
http://www.guardian.co.uk/education/2010/mar/16/english-language-schools-students-visas

18 March 2010, UK schools brand visa rules 'unlawful', The Guardian Weekly
http://www.guardianweekly.co.uk/?page=editorial&id=1500&catID=18

17 April 2010, Huge rise in foreign students 'undermines Labour's immigration policy', Telegraph
http://www.telegraph.co.uk/news/uknews/7601393/Huge-rise-in-foreign-students-undermines-Labours-immigration-policy.html

Chapter 3

Manual for International Students

How to apply for your initial grant of leave or extend your stay in the United Kingdom for the purpose of studies

Introduction

3.01 On 31 March 2009 the Government introduced Tier 4, a Points Based System ('PBS') route for international students requiring them to be 'sponsored' by education providers duly licensed for the purpose by the UK Border Agency ('UKBA'). Tier 4 is divided into two categories, Tier 4 (General) and Tier 4 (Child), which account for the vast majority of student applications. The main part of this Chapter deals with them. The purpose of this Chapter is to equip the reader with the rudimentary tools for unravelling Tier 4 provisions. While the general content of Tier 4 will undoubtedly change following ongoing reviews of this route, the core essentials should not. There remain some other student categories that are not dependent on the student being sponsored that are also dealt with in this Chapter. Those categories have been either created or affected also by recent developments, beginning particularly from April 2007. This Chapter deals with non-EU/EEA migrants, EEA free movement rights and studies as part of it are beyond the scope of this book.

3.02 On 3 April 2007 the Secretary of State introduced 11 policy changes, some of which were due to take effect from 19 April 2007. The rest were introduced from 1 September 2007[1] including the launch of the new student visitor category, amendments to the child visitor category to allow children to undertake a course of study and consequential amendments to the visitor category prohibiting visitors

1 Inserted by the Statement of Changes in Immigration Rules (Cm 7074).

from undertaking a course of study and imposition of mandatory entry clearance requirements on students. The student visitor category was introduced within the visitor rules to provide for short-term students wishing to study in the United Kingdom on courses lasting six months or less.

3.03 The child visitor category which was introduced on 12 February 2006[2] catered to short-term students under the age of 18 years. To ensure that existing child protection measures were being applied, an additional requirement was imported into this category to allow a child to study at a private institution which was registered on the DfES' Register of Education and Training Providers. The child provisions underwent further changes on 30 November 2007.[3] From 27 November 2008 student visitor and child visitor categories were included in a distinct new grouping of special visitors.[4] The student and child visitor rules were last amended on 1 January 2010.[5] A new temporary concession was introduced to the student visitor route for English language students on 10 January 2011.[6]

3.04 Entry clearance became a mandatory requirement for students and prospective students. This was to ensure that students' applications were systematically considered by an Entry Clearance Officer (rather than an Immigration Officer at a port of entry) in order to reduce instances of abuse.

3.05 As noted in **Chapter 1**, on 13 November 2007 the Border and Immigration Agency ('BIA') announced the launch of the Academic Technology Approval Scheme ('ATAS'). Having a valid ATAS Clearance Certificate became a mandatory requirement from 30 November 2007 for students applying for leave to enter or remain for a period of six months or more to undertake courses at postgraduate level or research in certain subjects. The ATAS Scheme is operated by the Foreign and Commonwealth Office. ATAS remains a requirement under PBS.

3.06 On 31 March 2009 the Immigration Rules were amended to include paragraphs 245ZT–245ZY related to Tier 4 (General) students and paragraphs 245ZZ–245ZZD related to Tier 4 (Child) students. As of 7 December 2010, the student route has been under review which has determined the changes in the Immigration Rules and attendant policy from 21 April 2011[7] and from 4 July 2011. The latest amendments to the Immigration Rules were introduced by way of the Statement of Changes in Immigration Rules (HC 908) laid before Parliament on 31

2 Inserted by the Statement of Changes in Immigration Rules (HC 819).
3 Inserted by the Statement of Changes in Immigration Rules (HC 40).
4 Inserted by the Statement of Changes in Immigration Rules (HC 1113).
5 Inserted by the Statement of Changes in Immigration Rules (HC 120).
6 *Written ministerial statement on English language students*, Home Office, 13 December 2010, www.ukba.homeoffice.gov.uk/sitecontent/documents/news/wms-students-english.pdf.
7 *The Student Immigration System, a Consultation,* UK Border Agency, December 2010, www.ukba.homeoffice.gov.uk/sitecontent/documents/policyandlaw/consultations/students/student-consultation.pdf?view=Binary. The consultation ran for eight weeks until 31 January 2011.

March 2011 and effective from 21 April 2011 and another Statement of Changes in Immigration Rules (HC 1148) which followed in its stead on 13 June 2011 and came into force on 4 July 2011 marking two of the four phases of changes envisaged by the statement of intent published on 31 March 2011. The Government's intention was to create a more selective system to work in conjunction with the existing PBS relating to students and their sponsors. Changes effective from 21 April 2011, 4 July 2011 and further proposed changes to the student route are dealt with in this Chapter.

3.07 Immigration Rules relating to students (paragraphs 57–62), student nurses (paragraphs 63–69), students re-sitting an examination (paragraphs 69A–69F), students writing up a thesis (paragraphs 69G-69L), postgraduate doctors and dentists (paragraphs 70–75), sabbatical officers (87A–87F) were deleted on 31 March 2009 and moved to Appendix F to the Immigration Rules. Overseas qualified nurses/midwives seeking leave to remain in the United Kingdom, remain in the main part of the student Rules, at paragraph 69M onwards enabling those already here in that capacity to extend their leave. Concessions outside the Immigration Rules related to sandwich students, Bar students, music students, pupillage scheme, Wellbeck College students, Association of American Study Abroad Programmes and Pestalozzi Children's Village Trust were also deleted. Information about these concessions can be found in Chapter 3, Section 3, IDI, June 2009.[8]

Changes and transitional measures

3.08 For the second time implementation of PBS policy relating to international students and their sponsors is being phased in over time as it allows the industry to adjust to changes.[9] From 2 August 2010 onwards the Government has repeatedly signalled its intention to transform the existing student route in line with its five-year policy programme.[10] The purpose of the reform was to make PBS, an objective system by design, more selective.[11] Following an obligatory but short consultation that drew responses from more than 30,000 corporate and individual respondents, the Secretary of State announced the changes to be made to the student visa system on 22 March 2011.[12] This was followed by a

8 See at www.ukba.homeoffice.gov.uk/sitecontent/documents/policyandlaw/IDIs/idischapter3/section3/section3.pdf?view=Binary.

9 See **Chapters 2 and 8** for more detail on the implementation of Tier 4 from 31 March 2009 onwards.

10 Tier 4 has been in perpetual flux as it underwent another major review announced by the previous Government on 12 November 2009.

11 Fundamentally, returning immigration law to its pre-PBS days.

12 Column 855 et al, Daily Hansard, House of Commons, Volume 525, www.publications.parliament.uk/pa/cm201011/cmhansrd/cm110322/debtext/110322-0001.htm#11032282000003.

written announcement on the UKBA website[13] and publication of a summary of the main changes.[14]

3.09 On 31 March 2011 the Government published its statement of intent heralding the changes to unfold over the next 18 months.[15] The statement of intent was accompanied by the Statement of Changes in Immigration Rules (HC 908) and other documents. This occasion marked the second anniversary of Tier 4. This new policy was essentially a product of compromise within the Government. The Statement of Changes in Immigration Rules (HC 908) was criticised by the House of Lords' Merits of Statutory Instruments Committee in its Thirty Ninth Report and 'drawn to the special attention of the House on the grounds that it gives rise to issues of public policy likely to be of interest to the House and may imperfectly achieve its policy objectives' for a debate on 16 May 2011.[16]

3.10 The first wave of changes that were introduced on 31 March 2011 commenced on 21 April 2011. These changes have been incorporated into the fabric of this chapter. Although strongly criticised the actual impact of these changes is yet to be determined.[17] The second set of changes was introduced on 13 June 2011 with the publication of the Statement of Changes in Immigration Rules (HC 1148). These changes came into force on 4 July 2011. Other key changes will be rolled out until the end of 2012. No fundamental changes have been made to the Tier 4 (Child) route as part of this review (other than those relating to the maintenance requirements and differentiation arrangements).[18] Changes relating to sponsors and transitional arrangements relating to them are set out in Chapter 4. Some of the more recent changes relating to sponsors, such as the change in ratings from 5 September 2011, will have a direct impact on students whose sponsors are rated anything other than HTS.

13 *Government outlines overhaul of student visas,* UK Border Agency, 22 March 2011, www.ukba.homeoffice.gov.uk/sitecontent/newsarticles/2011/march/54-student-visas.

14 *Summary of the new student policy,* UK Border Agency, 22 March 2011, www.ukba.homeoffice.gov.uk/sitecontent/documents/news/summary-student-policy.pdf.

15 *Student Visas, Statement of Intent and Transitional Measures,* UK Border Agency, March 2011, www.ukba.homeoffice.gov.uk/sitecontent/documents/news/sop4.pdf.

16 www.publications.parliament.uk/pa/ld201012/ldselect/ldmerit/137/13703.htm.

17 On 13 June 2011, the UKBA published its impact assessment of the proposed changes, *Reform of the Points Based Student (PBS) Immigration System,* UK Border Agency, 13 June 2011, www.ukba.homeoffice.gov.uk/sitecontent/documents/policyandlaw/ia/reform-students-pbs/ia-students-.pdf?view=Binary. The impact assessment was published '12 weeks after the changes to the policy were announced.' (see *Student Visas: Follow-up,* Home Affairs Committee, House of Commons, Eleventh Report of Session 2010–12, HC 1445, 26 July 2011, para 6 www.publications.parliament.uk/pa/cm201012/cmselect/cmhaff/1445/1445.pdf).

18 63% of respondents (overall number of respondents: 28,335) to the Tier 4 consultation agreed that no changes should be made in light of the low risk of abuse amongst users. *Consultation on the student immigration system: 7th December 2010 to 31st January 2011. Consultation questionnaire results,* UK Border Agency, March 2011, p 6 www.ukba.homeoffice.gov.uk/sitecontent/documents/policyandlaw/consultations/students/student-consultation-results.pdf?view=Binary.

Changes from April 2012

3.11 There will be two further changes made to the Tier 4 (General) route in Spring 2012:

- **Work placements**[19] – while the minimum study to work ratio will be maintained at 50:50 for students sponsored by higher education institutions undertaking courses at degree level or above, students not sponsored by higher education institutions will only be able to undertake courses which include work placements where the minimum study to work ratio is kept at 66:33.
- *Overall limit on time spent studying*[20] – Tier 4 (General) students will be able to spend a maximum of five years studying at degree level (NQF Levels 6 and 7/QCF Levels 6 and 7/SCQF Levels 9 to 11) in addition to the total of three years they are able to study at below degree level courses now (NQF Level 6/QCF Level 6/SCQF Level 9). The overall limit will be eight years save for some exceptions. Time spent studying pursuant to Tier 4 (Child) leave will not count towards these limits. PhD students will not be subject to the time limit. However, if they have been in the United Kingdom as students or Tier 4 (General) students for eight or more years on completion of their PhD, they will not be able to extend their leave under Tier 4 (General). Students who have been in the United Kingdom as students or Tier 4 (General) students from April 2012 will be able to finish their studies but not apply for an extension of stay under Tier 4 (General) once their leave expires.

Making an application

Entry clearance applications

3.12 Entry clearance applications should be submitted in the country of the applicant's residence and/or nationality by appointment or on an *ad hoc* basis at a diplomatic post abroad, normally through a UK Visa Application Centre ('VAC') operated by a commercial partner such as VFS Global or Worldbridge. The role of

19 53% of respondents (overall number of respondents: 26,020) to the Tier 4 consultation disagreed that the current ratio of study to work should be increased from 50:50 to 66:33. *Consultation on the student immigration system: 7th December 2010 to 31st January 2011. Consultation questionnaire results*, UK Border Agency, March 2011, p 9 www.ukba.homeoffice.gov.uk/sitecontent/documents/policyandlaw/consultations/students/student-consultation-results.pdf?view=Binary.

20 92% of respondents (overall number of respondents: 26,912) to the Tier 4 consultation disagreed that students seeking to study a new course should return home and apply overseas. Instead, the Government has proposed to implement an overall limit on time that international students can spend studying in the United Kingdom. *Consultation on the student immigration system: 7th December 2010 to 31st January 2011. Consultation questionnaire results*, UK Border Agency, March 2011, p 8 www.ukba.homeoffice.gov.uk/sitecontent/documents/policyandlaw/consultations/students/student-consultation-results.pdf?view=Binary.

VAC staff is to interface with applicants, accept their applications and, depending on local arrangements, facilitate their biometric data collection. They are not in a position to offer immigration advice and should not do so. Select VAC facilities offer additional services for an extra fee such as:

- SMS visa application tracking services;
- VIP services which includes a separate lounge, personalised service and refreshments;
- Submission of applications without passports;
- Courier returns services;
- Photocopy and printing services;
- Fax services;
- Premium services providing expedited decision times for specific application types.

3.13 It is easy to get waylaid trying to find access to the right information. Overseas posts can be found through the central hub of the Foreign and Commonwealth Office ('FCO') website.[21] Diplomatic web pages then lead to official VAC websites by going through 'Visiting the UK' and 'Visas' web pages. The VAC websites, which have become more uniform in style and content, can also be accessed through the unified UKBA website as of 4 September 2011. Application forms must be submitted electronically through the visa4UK website[22] operated by the FCO. Once submitted, they should be printed out, signed and submitted together with a photograph and supporting documents to the relevant British post abroad (UKBA acting through British Embassy, Consulate or High Commission) through a VAC or directly. Posts in some countries are not yet equipped to accept electronic forms and in such cases applicants should download and use VAF forms from the UKBA website.[23] Prospective applicants or applicants awaiting a decision can check the guide to processing times on the UKBA website.

3.14 Current visa application fees from 6 April 2011 are as follows:

Visa types covered in this chapter	Cost
Student visitor up to six months	£76.00
Student visitor – English language course only up to 11 months	£140.00
Prospective student up to six months	£76.00

21 See at www.fco.gov.uk/en/travel-and-living-abroad/find-an-embassy/.

22 Direct links from the International Group (formerly known as UKvisas), UKBA, FCO and other related websites networked by the commercial partners should lead to the visa4UK website.

23 See at www.ukvisas.gov.uk/en/.

Visa types covered in this chapter	**Cost**
Child visitor up to six months, single or multiple	£76.00
Child visitor up to two years Child visitor up to five years	£265.00 £486.00
Child visitor up to 10 years Tier 4 (General) Tier 4 (Child) Tier 5 (Youth Mobility Scheme)	£702.00 £255.00 £255.00 £190.00
Chevening Scholarship or Fellowship	free
British Marshall Scholarship	free
Fulbright Scholarship	free
Commonwealth Scholarships and Fellowships Plan	free
Clinical attachments, dental observations and PLAB test	£265.00

3.15

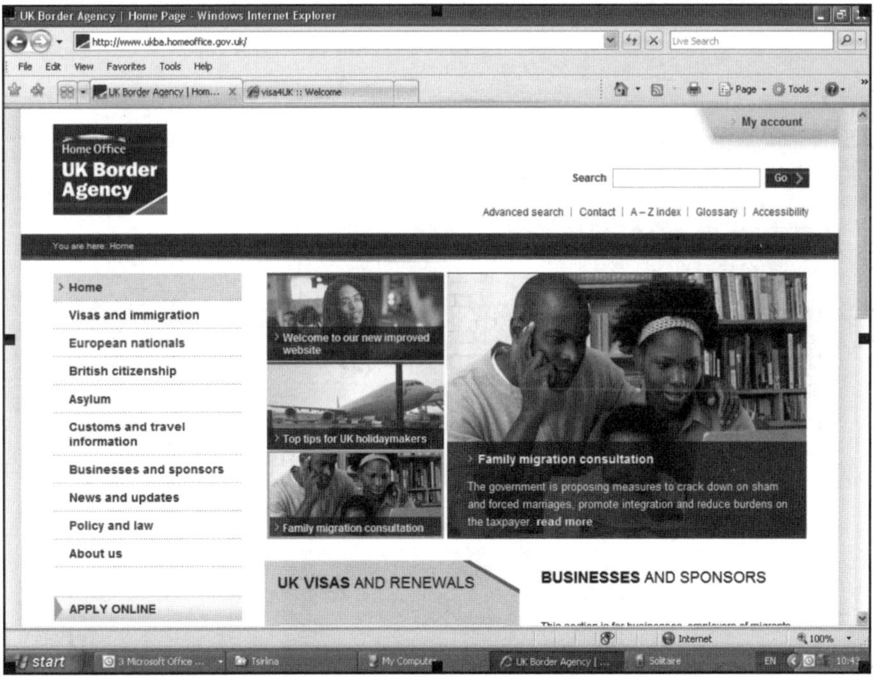

3.16

visa4UK :: Welcome - Windows Internet Explorer
http://www.visa4uk.fco.gov.uk/
Home Office
UK Border Agency
Visa4UK
the official British Government website for
online visa applications
You are here: Visa4UK Home
Visa4UK Home
Apply for a Visa
Existing Applications Login here >>
Frequently Asked Questions
Enquiries & Feedback
Welcome to Visa4UK
Welcome to the Visa4UK website. Here you can apply for a UK visa and book your appointment to submit your visa application over a secure internet connection.
If you are not yet sure whether you need a visa to visit the UK, please check the 'Do I Need a UK Visa' questionnaire on the UK Border Agency Visa Services web site.
Please note that you cannot use this website to apply for a visa to visit other countries other than the UK and UK Overseas Territories.
You can get contact details of your nearest UK visa issuing office from the UK Border Agency website.
If you wish to apply for a UK visa as a highly skilled migrant, please ensure you are aware of the latest points based system rules.
To begin a new UK visa application now, click the button below. For any other option use the navigation menu on the left of this page.
Apply for a UK visa now >
Help and support
See our Supported Countries page to check whether you can apply online from your current location.
WorldPay
We accept
VISA

3.17

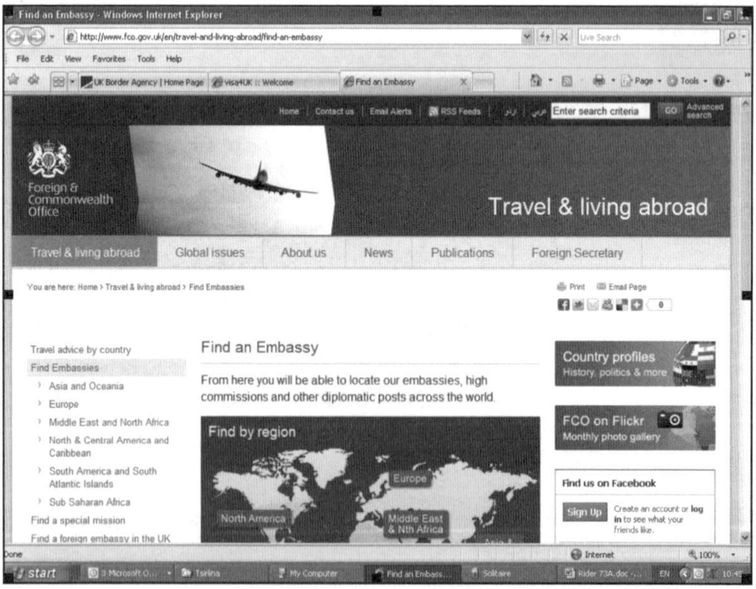
Find an Embassy - Windows Internet Explorer
http://www.fco.gov.uk/en/travel-and-living-abroad/find-an-embassy
Home
Contact us
Email Alerts
RSS Feeds
Enter search criteria
Foreign & Commonwealth Office
Travel & living abroad
Travel & living abroad
Global issues
About us
News
Publications
Foreign Secretary
You are here: Home › Travel & living abroad › Find Embassies
Print
Email Page
Travel advice by country
Find Embassies
Asia and Oceania
Europe
Middle East and North Africa
North & Central America and Caribbean
South America and South Atlantic Islands
Sub Saharan Africa
Find a special mission
Find a foreign embassy in the UK
Find an Embassy
From here you will be able to locate our embassies, high commissions and other diplomatic posts across the world.
Find by region
Europe
North America
Middle East & Nth Africa
Country profiles
History, politics & more
FCO on Flickr
Monthly photo gallery
Find us on Facebook
Sign Up
Create an account or log in to see what your friends like.

Extension applications

3.18 Some categories covered in this chapter, such as Tier 5 (Youth Mobility Scheme), do not allow migrants to make in-country extension or switching applications. Therefore, please refer to each individual category within this chapter for guidance on extension applications. The UKBA recently introduced an interactive application service which allows for most in-country non-PBS and PBS applications to be made online. The 'Apply Online' option is available at http://apply.ukba.homeoffice.gov.uk/iapply.portal.

Biometric information

3.19 Enrolling biometric information is part and parcel of the application process. It became a legal requirement on 4 July 2006. This is true of all entry clearance applications and some leave to remain applications made in the United Kingdom. Biometric information consists of an applicant's digital photograph and fingerprints and the procedure of enrolling this data should take 5–10 minutes excluding waiting time. Non-EU/EEA applicants applying for entry clearance in the special visitor, business visitor, Tier 4 and Tier 5 categories must provide their biometrics. When making their application for leave to remain in the United Kingdom, Tier 4 applicants are required to apply for a Biometric Residence Permit ('BRP') formerly known as an Identity Card for Foreign Nationals ('ICFN').

3.20 A process by which an applicant's biometrics may be obtained and recorded is set out in section 6(2) of the Immigration (Provision of Physical Data) Regulations 2006, SI 2006/1743 ('the Regulations') and is described as 'a process by which the individual who makes the application:

(a) attends a British Diplomatic mission or British Consular post where a record of his fingerprints or a photograph of his face is taken;
(b) attends a Diplomatic mission or Consular post of another State where a record of his fingerprints or a photograph of his face is taken by an official of that State on behalf of the authorised person; or
(c) attends other premises nominated by an authorised person where a record of his fingerprints or a photograph of his face is taken by a person on his behalf of an authorised person.'

3.21 Applicants who provided their biometrics during the application process may have their fingerprints checked when entering the United Kingdom. Biometric information must be destroyed 'by the Secretary of State at the end of 10 years beginning with the date on which the original record or photograph was provided' (reg 8 of the Regulations). The Secretary of State must take all reasonably practicable steps to ensure that biometric information held in electronic form which is set to be destroyed is destroyed or erased, or that access to it is blocked (reg 10(1) of the Regulations).

3.22 In accordance with reg 4 of the Regulations children under the age of 16 must have their biometrics taken in the presence of a person aged 18 or over who is the child's parent or guardian, or a person who for the time being takes responsibility for the child. This applies to applications made inside and outside the United Kingdom. Children under the age of five are exempt from having to submit their biometric data and so are people who are not subject to immigration control.

3.23 Depending on the country, applicants applying for entry clearance are required to provide their biometrics at the same time or prior to submitting their applications for consideration at a British diplomatic post. Unless applicants are making their entry clearance applications in the USA, New Zealand or Bermuda, they are required to attend a designated Visa Application Centre. Applicants in the USA will need to attend an Application Support Center operated by the Department of Homeland Security, applicants in New Zealand will need to attend the New Zealand Department of Labour Offices in Auckland, Christchurch or Wellington and applicants in Bermuda will need to make an appointment to attend the Department of Immigration in Bermuda. If successful, applicants will have their entry clearance vignette endorsed in their national passport.

3.24 Tier 4 students applying inside the United Kingdom to extend their leave must apply for a BRP as part of their extension application. Their immigration status will not be endorsed in their national passport. Adult and child students already in the United Kingdom wishing to extend their stay must make their combined applications for leave to remain and a BRP using up to date specified application forms. At the moment these forms are:

- Application for a Grant of Leave and Biometric Immigration Document under Tier 4 (General) Student – Main Applicant (Tier 4 (G) (to be used by adult applicants); or
- Application for a Grant of Leave and Biometric Immigration Document under Tier 4 (Child) Student – Main Applicant (Tier 4 (C) (to be used by child applicants)

Biometric enrolment applies to applications made by post or in person using the premium service. Applicants whose Tier 4 applications are approved will receive a BRP by post within seven working days of the date of approval of application.

3.25 In its brochure, which is now out of date, entitled Identity Cards for Foreign Nationals, Biometric Enrolment Process,[24] the UKBA provides a step-by-step overview of postal and premium application processes as follows:

24 This brochure can be downloaded at www.ukba.homeoffice.gov.uk/sitecontent/documents/visitingtheuk/identity_cards_for_foreign_1 (this brochure has been archived). A new brochure relating to Biometric Residence Permits can be found at www.ukba.homeoffice.gov.uk/sitecontent/documents/residency/brp-application-process.pdf.

Postal Applications	*Premium Applications*
Application and fee posted by applicant ∇	Applicant makes PEO appointment ∇
Application received and fee processed ∇	Applicant arrives at PEO reception (having passed through security) ∇
Application data entry into case system ∇	Application checked by reception (correct form and documents including photos) & ticket issued ∇
Application validated (correct application form and documents including photos) ∇	Applicant pays application fee ∇
Applicant identified as requiring biometrics ∇	Application data entry into case system ∇
Biometric notification letter sent to applicant ∇	Biometrics enrolled & results checked ∇
Appointment made by applicant ∇	Application considered ∇
Applicant arrives at biometric enrolment centre reception (having passed through security) ∇	Decision made (whether to grant or refuse) ∇
Appointment checked and ticket issued ∇	Applicant leaves PEO ∇
Biometrics enrolled and results checked ∇	Identity Card issued by secure delivery to address provided (successful applicants)
Applicant leaves biometric enrolment centre ∇	
Passport and documents returned to applicant with decision ∇	
Identity Card issued by secure delivery to address provided (successful applicants)	

3.26 Biometrics can be enrolled at Public Enquiry Offices or Biometric Enrolment Centres by booking an appointment on the phone or online. If an applicant is making a premium application wishing to get a same-day decision, he or she must book an appointment to apply in person at one of the seven Public Enquiry Offices throughout the United Kingdom. At the Public Enquiry Office in Croydon, for example, biometrics are enrolled in the afternoon a day before a decision is made in respect of an application. Applicants who have made their application by post will need to book their appointment to enrol their biometric information at a Biometric Enrolment Centre or a Public Enquiry Office once they are in receipt of a letter from the UKBA. There is an additional option for applicants who have made their application by post and who live within certain postcodes to enrol their biometrics at select Post Offices. Applicants are not required to make an appointment as this is a walk-in service available to sole applicants aged 16 or over.

Public Enquiry Offices and Biometric Enrolment Centres	**Post Office Biometric Enrolment**
Croydon Public Enquiry Office Address: Lunar House, 40 Wellesley Road, Croydon CR9 2BY Tel: 0870 606 7766	**Post Office – Aberdeen (Union Street)** Address: 489 Union Street, Aberdeen, AB11 6AZ
Solihull Public Enquiry Office Address: Dominion Court, 41 Station Road, Solihull, Birmingham B91 3RT Tel: 0870 606 7766	
Sheffield Public Enquiry Office Address: Vulcan House, Riverside Entrance, 6 Millsands, Sheffield S3 8NU Tel: 0870 606 7766	**Post Office – Beeston** Address: 6a Chilwell Road, Beeston, Nottingham NG9 1AA
Liverpool Public Enquiry Office Address: The Capital Building, 6 Union Street, Liverpool, L3 9AF Tel: 0870 606 7766	**Post Office – Cambridge** Address: 57–58 St Andrew Street, Cambridge CB2 3QB
Glasgow Public Enquiry Office Address: Festival Court, 200 Brand Street, Govan, Glasgow G51 1DH Tel: 0870 606 7766	**Post Office – Durham** Address: 33 Silver Street, Durham DH1 3RE
Belfast Public Enquiry Office Address: UK Border Agency Public Office, 1 Drumkeen Complex, Upper Galwally, Belfast, BT8 6TB Tel: 0870 606 7766	**Post Office – Kingstanding** Address: 25 Kingstanding Centre, Birmingham B44 9HH

Public Enquiry Offices and Biometric Enrolment Centres	**Post Office Biometric Enrolment**
Cardiff Public Enquiry Office Address: General Buildings, Ground Floor, 31–33 Newport Road, Cardiff, Wales CF24 0AB Tel: 0870 606 7766	**Post Office – London (Canning Town)** Address: 22 Barking Road, London E16 1HF **Post Office – London (High Holborn)** Address: 181 High Holborn, London WC1V 7RL **Post Office – London (Battersea)** Address: 202 Lavender Hill, London SW11 1AB
London Biometric Enrolment Centre Address: Identity and Passport Service, Hannibal House, Elephant and Castle, London SE1 6TE	**Post Office – London (Camden High Street)** Address: 112–114 Camden High Street, London NW1 0RR
Birmingham Biometric Enrolment Centre Address: Identity and Passport Service, 6th Floor, Kensington House, Suffolk Street, Queensway, Birmingham B1 1LN	**Post Office – London (Earl's Court)** Address: 185 Earl's Court Road, London SW5 9RB **Post Office – London (Golders Green)** Address: 879 Finchley Road, London NW11 8RT
Derby Biometric Enrolment Centre Address: 2nd Floor, Stuart House, Green Lane, DE1 1RS	**Post Office – London (Old Street)** Address: 205 Old Street, London EC1V 9QN **Post Office – London (Poplar)** Address: 22 Market Square, London E14 6AB
Brighton Biometric Enrolment Centre Address: 1st Floor (North Suite), 42 Frederick Place, Brighton BN1 4EA	**Post Office – Middleton** Address: 53 Manchester New Road, Middleton, Manchester M24 1SQ
	Post Office – Oxford Address: 102–104 St Aldates, Oxford OX1 1ZZ

Public Enquiry Offices and Biometric Enrolment Centres	**Post Office Biometric Enrolment**
	Post Office – Romsey Address: 15–25 Church Street, Romsey, Hampshire SO51 8WA
	Post Office – South Shields Address: Kepple Street, South Shields, Tyne and Wear NE33 1AA

Tier 4 Migrants

Introduction

3.27 The Tier 4 route is divided into two categories, Tier 4 (General) and Tier 4 (Child), which are regulated by paragraphs 245ZT–245ZZD, Part 6A of the Immigration Rules. The point scoring requirements and specific evidence related to them are contained in paragraphs 113–120[25] (relating to Tier 4 (General)) and paragraphs 121–126 (relating to Tier 4 (Child)) of Appendix A, paragraphs 10–14 (relating to Tier 4 (General)) and paragraphs 15–22 (relating to Tier 4 (Child)) of Appendix C to the Immigration Rules which form part of the substantive provisions. These provisions are amplified by the Tier 4 of the Points Based System – Policy Guidance ('Tier 4 Policy Guidance'),[26] a separate document to which references are made in Part 6A and the Appendices. Further information is contained in the Tier 4 of the Points Based System – Policy Guidance ('Sponsor Guidance'),[27] Provisions relating to sponsors are set out in detail in Chapter 4. although passing references to sponsors are made throughout this Chapter. Information about those in the residual student category (prior to 31 March 2009) can be found in Chapter 3, IDI.[28]

3.28 Tier 4 is a complex construct whose components include multiple variables which have been layered on over time since its inception. The system has been subject to continued reforms and amendments stretching its flexibility to the limit. Although it is not immediately apparent, Tier 4 provisions accommodate students, postgraduate doctors and dentists, sabbatical officers, students writing up, re-sitting examinations or retaking modules of study which prior to 31 March

25 In fact, the relevant part of the Appendix relating to CAS assigned to Tier 4 (General) migrants runs to paragraph 120B.

26 Version 07/11, 4 July 2011.

27 Version 09/11, 5 September 2011.

28 Chapter 3, IDIs, UK Border Agency, http://www.ukba.homeoffice.gov.uk/sitecontent/documents/policyandlaw/IDIs/idischapter3/.

2009 accounted for separate sub-categories within the Immigration Rules relating to students.

3.29 The chapter below goes on to examine in detail the requirements and conditions of stay of Tier 4 (General) and Tier 4 (Child) students as they are set out in the Immigration Rules, Appendices and policy guidance. There are some provisions that overlap between Tier 4 (General) and Tier 4 (Child) categories, especially where 16 or 17 year old students are concerned. References to the Tier 4 Policy Guidance and other extraneous materials are selective and do not seek to reproduce the policy documents in full.

3.30 The Immigration Rules underwent key changes on 23 July and 12 August 2010 pursuant to the Statement of Changes in Immigration Rules (HC 382) following judgments in *Secretary of State for the Home Department v Pankina* [2010] EWCA Civ 719 on 23 June 2010 and *English UK Ltd, R (on the application of) v Secretary of State for the Home Department* [2010] EWHC 1726 (Admin) on 9 July 2010. Further changes came as a result of the consultation that ran from 7 December 2010 to 31 January 2011. The first wave of these changes was introduced on 21 April 2011 and the second on 4 July 2011 forming part of this Chapter. Further changes relating to students and sponsors will be phased in from April 2012 to the end of 2012.

3.31 In order to apply for entry clearance or leave to remain in the Tier 4 (General) and Tier 4 (Child) categories, applicants must have a Tier 4 sponsor licence issued by the UKBA to recruit non-EU/EEA students. Tier 4 sponsors holding a Tier 4 sponsor licence were rated as either A or B, or have HTS Status prior to 5 September 2011.[29] As of 5 September 2011 there can only be two ratings: A and HTS status. An A rating is transitional and given for 12 months only with a view to applying for HTS status on completion of the transitional period. Various transitional arrangements have been put into place for residually rated A and B rated sponsors. Sponsors are expected to meet various deadlines in order to obtain HTS status by April 2012 at the latest. Tier 4 sponsors are listed in the Register of Sponsors which is available on the UKBA website at www.ukba.homeoffice.gov.uk/sitecontent/documents/employersandsponsors/pointsbasedsystem/registerofsponsorseducation. Their rating will determine the range of courses, levels at which the courses can be taught and work placements they can offer to international students. For more information about Tier 4 sponsors, please refer to **Chapter 4**.

3.32 In relation to Tier 4 (General) students, paragraphs 245ZV(b) and 245ZX(c) of the Immigration Rules require migrants to satisfy provisions under paragraphs 113–120 of Appendix A (Attributes) to the Immigration Rules. Paragraphs 245ZV(c) and 245ZX(d) require migrants to comply with the requirements under paragraphs 10–14 of Appendix C (Maintenance). Likewise, in relation to Tier 4 (Child) students, paragraphs 245ZZA(b) and 245ZZC(c) of the Immigration Rules

29 Prior to 21 April 2011, rating was denoted as A (Trusted) or B (Sponsor).

require migrants to satisfy provisions under paragraphs 121–126 of Appendix A (Attributes) to the Immigration Rules. In turn, paragraphs 245ZZA(c) and 245ZZC(d) of the Immigration Rules compel migrants to meet the requirements set out in paragraphs 15–22 of Appendix C (Maintenance).[30] The provisions contained in these paragraphs are qualified by the contents of paragraph 1A of Appendix C to the Immigration Rules.

3.33 Paragraphs 245ZT–245ZZD of the Immigration Rules and related attributes and maintenance provisions were inserted into the Immigration Rules by the Statement of Changes (HC 314) on 31 March 2009. In the short time since their introduction the student provisions have since undergone innumerable changes, with the policy guidance changing independently of the Immigration Rules. Tier 4 provisions are far from homogeneous and are a far cry from the student provisions in place prior to 31 March 2009. In a sense Tier 4 is like a patchwork quilt and deconstructing its design means pulling various strands together to see the whole picture. On 30 September 2009 the UKBA published a Questions and Answers summary for Tier 4 students, which barely begins to scratch the surface when it comes to explaining what the system is all about and how to navigate your way around it.[31]

3.34 PBS is a policy driven scheme and the student route is no exception. At a glance, Tier 4 policy guidance appears to be edifying and instructive to applicants. On closer examination, it contains supplementary requirements which qualify the Immigration Rules in such a way as to be restrictive. Tier 4 Policy Guidance effective from 4 July 2011 is voluminous and stands at 73 pages consisting of the main body, an addendum, five annexes and one appendix revealing a complex web of extraneous requirements and transitional arrangements superimposed on the Immigration Rules.[32] Moreover, policy guidance has been used by the Secretary of State as a mechanism for implementing swift changes to Tier 4 requirements and sidestepping parliamentary scrutiny, a practice that has been successfully challenged in *Pankina*[33] and *EnglishUK*[34] but not altogether curbed.

3.35 It is erroneous to think of Tier 4 Policy Guidance as being wholly absorbed into the Immigration Rules by virtue of paragraph 245A of the Rules. References to the guidance as well as documents specified therein are scattered throughout the Tier 4 provisions in Part 6A and Appendices A and C to the Immigration Rules. Given that the policy guidance is in continuous development and its contents are subject

30 Prior to the amendments introduced by the Statement of Changes in Immigration Rules (HC 908) there were errors contained in paragraphs 245ZV(c), 245ZX(d), 245ZZA(c) and 245ZZC(d) of the Immigration Rules in respect to the relevant paragraphs in Appendix C to the Immigration Rules.

31 www.ukba.homeoffice.gov.uk/sitecontent/documents/studying/t4-qanda-students.pdf.

32 Its predecessor was Tier 4 Policy Guidance, version 04/11, 21 April 2011, 68 pages.

33 Secretary of State for the Home Department v Pankina [2010] EWCA Civ 719 (23 June 2010).

34 English UK Ltd, R (on the application of) v Secretary of State for the Home Department [2010] EWHC 1726 (Admin) (9 July 2010).

to change without notice, it is not surprising that references to the policy guidance in the Immigration Rules are made in the vaguest and most general of terms, inevitably leading to more uncertainty. What emerges from the overwhelming menagerie of provisions is that there are two core requirements, having a valid Confirmation of Acceptance for Studies ('CAS') and required maintenance (funds), that form the backbone of Tier 4 and all the other conditions predicating validity of an application revolve around them.

Tier 4 (General) migrants

3.36 Tier 4 (General) migrants must refer to the following provisions before making their entry clearance application:

- Paragraph 245A of the Immigration Rules;
- Paragraphs 245ZU–245ZW of the Immigration Rules;
- Paragraphs 113–120 of Appendix A (Attributes) to the Immigration Rules;
- Paragraphs 1A and 10–14 of Appendix C (Maintenance) to the Immigration Rules;
- Paragraphs 320–324 of the Immigration Rules together with Chapter 9, IDI (general grounds of refusal, see modernised guidance);
- Paragraphs 325–326 of the Immigration Rules together with Chapter 10, IDI (police registration, see modernised guidance);
- Tier 4 of the Points Based System – Policy Guidance ('Tier 4 Policy Guidance');
- Photo guidance
- Study (STY) guidance for use by entry clearance staff (currently being updated);
- Entry Clearance Guidance, STY5, List of main sponsored programmes for overseas students (scholarship and award programmes).

3.37 Applications for entry clearance as a Tier 4 (General) student must be made either online or on paper using a VAF9 PBS Personal Details form. In addition, applicants must complete a hard copy of a self-assessment point scoring Appendix 8 and submit it together with the VAF9.

3.38 Tier 4 (General) migrants should be mindful of the following provisions before making their application for leave to remain in the United Kingdom:

- Paragraphs 34–34J of the Immigration Rules (provisions related to forms, procedures and formalities associated with making immigration applications);
- Paragraph 245A of the Immigration Rules;
- Paragraphs 245ZX––245ZY of the Immigration Rules;

- Paragraphs 113–120 of Appendix A to the Immigration Rules;
- Paragraphs 1A and 10–14 of Appendix C to the Immigration Rules;
- Tier 4 of the Points Based System – Policy Guidance ('Tier 4 Policy Guidance');
- Photo Guidance;
- Paragraphs 320–324 of the Immigration Rules together with Chapter 9, IDI (general grounds of refusal, see modernised guidance);
- Paragraphs 325–326 of the Immigration Rules together with Chapter 10, IDI (police registration, see modernised guidance);
- Chapter 3, IDI (for information only by those who hold leave granted prior to 31 March 2009)
- Borders, Citizenship and Immigration Act 2009, s 50;
- Entry Clearance Guidance, STY5, List of main sponsored programmes for overseas students (scholarship and award programmes).

3.39 Applications for leave to remain in the United Kingdom as a Tier 4 (General) student must be made using a specified form, Application for a Grant of Leave and Biometric Immigration Document under Tier 4 (General) Student – Main Applicant (Tier 4 (G)). The form is denoted by a version number which reflects the month and year of issue. The form also specifies the 'valid from' date.

3.40 Pursuant to paragraph 34 of the Immigration Rules[35] a form is considered specified if it is posted on the UKBA website, marked for the purpose, comes into force on the date specified on the form or related announcement. Therefore, in accordance with paragraph 34A of the Immigration Rules applications must comply with the following requirements:

'(i) the application or claim must be made using the specified form,
(ii) any specified fee in connection with the application or claim must be paid in accordance with the method specified in the application form, separate payment form and/or related guidance notes, as applicable,
(iii) any section of the form which is designated as mandatory in the application form and/or related guidance notes must be completed as specified,
(iv) if the application form and/or related guidance notes require the applicant to provide biographical information, such information must be provided as specified,
(v) an appointment for the purposes stated in subparagraph (iv) must be made and must take place by the dates specified in any subsequent notification by the Secretary of State following receipt of the application, or as agreed by the Secretary of State,

35 See also *US and MV (PBS applicants from same family) Malaysia* [2010] UKUT 167 (IAC) (2 June 2010).

(vi) where the application or claim is made by post or courier, or submitted in person:
  (a) the application or claim must be accompanied by the photographs and documents specified as mandatory in the application form and/or related guidance notes,
  (ab) those photographs must be in the same format specified as mandatory in the application form and/or related guidance notes, and
  (b) the form must be signed by the applicant, and where applicable, the applicant's spouse, civil partner, same-sex partner or unmarried partner, save that where the applicant is under the age of eighteen, the form may be signed by the parent or legal guardian of the applicant on his behalf,

(vii) where the application or claim is made online:
  (a) the photographs and documents specified as mandatory must be submitted in the manner directed in the application form and/or related online guidance notes and by such date as is specified in the acknowledgement of the online application,
  (ab) those photographs must be in the same format specified as mandatory in the application form and/or related guidance notes, and
  (b) the confirmation box (which states that the information contained in the application form is true and complete) must be completed by the applicant or, if the form is completed by an immigration adviser on the applicant's behalf, by the immigration adviser on specific instructions from the applicant that the information given is true and complete, and

(viii) the application or claim must be delivered in accordance with paragraph 34B.'

3.41 It is most likely that the reference to applications to be made online at paragraph 34A(vii) of the Immigration Rules relates to applications for a sponsorship licence (paragraph 34B(iii)). Reading through the rest of the relevant requirements, paragraphs 34E–34F make provisions for those wishing to vary their leave to remain in the United Kingdom. Paragraph 34G provides the parameters for determining the date on which an application is made:

'(i) where the application form is sent by post, the date of posting,
(ii) where the application form is submitted in person, the date on which it is accepted by a public enquiry office of the United Kingdom Border Agency of the Home Office,
(iii) where the application form is sent by courier, the date on which it is delivered to the United Kingdom Border Agency of the Home Office, or
(iv) where the application form is submitted online, the date on which it is so submitted.'

3.42 And finally, paragraph 34J of the Immigration Rules warns that if a person whose application for leave to remain is under consideration, requests for his/her passport to be returned for the purpose of travel outside the CTA,[36] the application, provided it has not yet been determined, shall be treated as withdrawn as soon as the passport is returned.

3.43 In addition to paragraph 34, paragraph 245A(a) of the Immigration Rules (which applies to both in and out of country applications) stipulates that references to specified documents made in Part 6A or Appendices A to C or E of the Immigration Rules relate to the documents specified in the PBS policy guidance and unless these are provided, the requirements to which they are attached will not be met. Paragraph 245A(a) must be read together with paragraph 245A(b)–(c):

'(a) Where Part 6A or Appendices A to C, or E of these Rules state that specified documents must be provided, that means documents specified by the Secretary of State in the Points Based System Policy Guidance as being specified documents for the route under which the applicant is applying. If the specified documents are not provided, the applicant will not meet the requirement for which the specified documents are required as evidence.

(b) If the Entry Clearance Officer or Secretary of State has reasonable cause to doubt the genuineness of any document submitted by an applicant which is, or which purports to be, a specified document under Part 6A or Appendices A to C, or E of these Rules and having taken reasonable steps to verify the document, is unable to verify that it is genuine, the document will be discounted for the purposes of this application.

(c) Where Part 6A or Appendices A to C, or E of these Rules refer to the United Kingdom Border Agency guidance, this means guidance published by the United Kingdom Border Agency for use by Sponsors or migrants to ensure compliance with these Rules. If the Sponsor or applicant does not satisfy the requirements set out in guidance and referred to in these Rules, the applicant will not meet the related requirement in these Rules.'

Requirements for entry clearance and leave to remain

Entry clearance

3.44 Non-EU/EEA migrants wishing to come to the United Kingdom as Tier 4 (General) students must apply for entry clearance in that capacity at a British diplomatic post abroad regardless of whether they are visa or non-visa nationals. It is a mandatory requirement. Migrants without valid entry clearance will be refused entry to the United Kingdom under this route (paragraph 245ZU of the Immigration Rules). Requirements for entry clearance and leave to remain are contained in paragraphs 245ZV and 245ZX of the Immigration Rules with reference

36 Common Travel Area.

to Appendices A and C to the Immigration Rules. These substantive requirements are heavily amplified by Tier 4 Policy Guidance.

3.45 Under the Immigration Rules in force prior to 31 March 2009, 'progress' and 'attendance' were key determinants behind applications for extension of leave. In the run up to the PBS, sponsors were made responsible for monitoring students' attendance and it became compulsory to report non-attendance from 22 February 2010. From 4 July 2011 Tier 4 sponsors are called upon to vouch for their sponsored students' academic progression, where appropriate.

3.46 Save for the switching requirements in paragraph 245ZX(b) which are dealt with in **Chapter 7**, the requirement for a migrant applying for leave to remain not to be an illegal entrant in paragraph 245ZX(a) and few other subtle differences, the requirements for leave to remain are uniformly similar to the entry clearance requirements.

General grounds of refusal

3.47 Under paragraphs 245ZV(a) and 245ZX(a) of the Immigration Rules applicants must not fall for refusal under the general grounds of refusal. These grounds are contained in paragraphs 320 to 324 of the Immigration Rules and are dealt with separately below in this chapter.

Point Scoring Requirements

3.48 There are two core point scoring requirements. Applicants must score:

- a minimum of 30 points under paragraphs 113 to 120 of Appendix A (paragraphs 245ZV(b) and 245ZX(c)), and
- a minimum of 10 points under paragraphs 10 to 14 of Appendix C (paragraphs 245ZV(c) and 245ZX(d)).

3.51 Appendix A deals with attributes. The only attribute a Tier 4 (General) student is required to have is a valid CAS. In order to claim points for a CAS, there is a range of additional requirements set out in Appendix A that need to be satisfied in order for the CAS to be considered valid. Appendix C relates to maintenance (funds), namely the amount of money students must have and the length of time for which they (or their financial sponsors) must have held it.

Confirmation of Acceptance for Studies

3.49 Following a period of trialling and transitional adjustments to the Sponsor Management System ('SMS') from 5 October 2009, introduction of CAS on 22 February 2010 marked the end of visa letters. The earlier versions of the Tier 4 Policy

Guidance featured a table containing broad mandatory requirements prescribed for visa letters. The inconsistency of interpretation of these requirements by sponsors often led to visa letters being invalidated and applications for entry clearance or leave to remain being refused. The switch to SMS and bulk data transfer was meant to instil uniformity and standardisation with regard to information management and issuing of CAS, leading to fewer errors. Unlike a visa letter, a CAS is not a paper based document. It is as the Tier 4 Policy Guidance defines it at paragraph 26 'a virtual document similar to a database record' which is tantamount to 'an official and unconditional offer of a place on a course of study' (paragraph 20).

3.50 In paragraph 6 of the Immigration Rules (dealing with interpretation) the definition of a CAS is broader and non-specific:

> 'Under Part 6A and Appendix A of these Rules, "Confirmation of Acceptance for Studies" means a unique reference number electronically issued by a sponsor via the Sponsor Management System to an applicant for entry clearance, leave to enter or remain as a Tier 4 Migrant in accordance with these Rules.'[37]

3.51 A CAS reference number is linked to the Confirmation of Acceptance for Studies Checking Service which is defined at paragraph 6 of the Immigration Rules as:

> 'a computerised interface with the Points Based System computer database which allows a United Kingdom Border Agency caseworker or entry clearance officer assessing a migrant's application for entry clearance, leave to enter or remain as a Tier 4 migrant under these Rules to access and review details of the migrant's Confirmation of Acceptance for Studies, including details of the migrant's Sponsor, together with details of the course of study and other details associated with the circumstances in which the Confirmation of Acceptance for Studies was issued.'

Paragraph 33 of the Tier 4 Policy Guidance states that having a valid CAS does not guarantee that an application will succeed.

Appendix A (Attributes)

3.52 Paragraphs 113 to 120 of Appendix A to the Immigration Rules deal with attributes that student applicants must possess in order to score 30 points. Applicants must score the points shown in Table 16:[38]

37 Prior to the Statement of Changes in Immigration Rules (HC 908), the definition was 'Under Part 6A of these Rules, "Confirmation of Acceptance for Studies" means an authorisation issued by a Sponsor to an applicant for entry clearance, leave to enter or remain as a Tier 4 Migrant in accordance with these Rules.'

38 The wording in tables listed in this Chapter is reproduced verbatim from the Immigration Rules.

Criterion	**Points awarded**
Confirmation of Acceptance for Studies	30

The notes accompanying Table 16 at paragraphs 115A–120B of Appendix A qualify the validity of CAS. All of the requirements that characterise a CAS in these paragraphs must be met for it to be valid.

VALIDITY OF CAS

3.53 Paragraph 115A of Appendix A states that, in order to obtain points for a CAS, the applicant must provide a valid CAS reference number. It is the licensed sponsor's responsibility to provide the applicant with that number (paragraph 27 of the Tier 4 Policy Guidance). Newly added paragraphs 115B–115I of Appendix A deal with an interim limit applicable to CAS allocation relating to certain existing sponsors from 21 April 2011 to 5 April 2012. The interim limit is dealt with in detail in **Chapter 4**. These new requirements are also mentioned in paragraphs 22–25 of the Tier 4 Policy Guidance. For completeness, the provisions relating to the interim limit are quoted below:

'115B. The Secretary of State shall be entitled to limit the number of Confirmations of Acceptance for Studies allocated to any specific Sponsor in any one period.

115C. The limit on the number of Confirmations of Acceptance for Studies allocated to specific Sponsors shall be known as the Tier 4 Interim Limit.

115D. The Tier 4 Interim Limit will apply from 21 April 2011 to 5 April 2012 (inclusive) (the "Tier 4 Interim Limit Period").

115E. The Tier 4 Interim Limit will be applied to any Tier 4 Sponsor that does not satisfy both of the following criteria throughout the Tier 4 Interim Limit Period:

(i) has Highly Trusted Sponsor status; and
(ii) is subject to and holds a valid and satisfactory full institutional inspection, review or audit by one of the following bodies:
  (a) the Bridge Schools Inspectorate; or
  (b) the Education and Training Inspectorate; or
  (c) Estyn; or
  (d) Her Majesty's Inspectorate of Education; or
  (e) the Independent Schools Inspectorate; or
  (f) Ofsted; or
  (g) the Quality Assurance Agency for Higher Education; or
  (h) The Schools Inspection Service;
  or is not:
(iii) an independent school;
(iv) the Foundation Programme Office;

(v) the Yorkshire and Humber Strategic Health Authority; or

(vi) a Tier 4 Sponsor that applied for a Tier 4 Sponsor licence on or after 21 April 2011 and meets the requirements of (ii) (but not (i)) above.

(vii) an overseas higher education institution which has Highly Trusted Sponsor Status.[39]

115F. A Tier 4 Sponsor who does not satisfy the requirements of paragraph 115E and is therefore subject to the Tier 4 Interim Limit is known as a Limited Sponsor.

115G. All Confirmations of Acceptance for Studies allocated by the Secretary of State to Limited Sponsors prior to 21 April 2011 and which have not been assigned to an applicant for entry clearance, leave to enter or leave to remain under Tier 4 prior to 21 April 2011 are withdrawn and the only Confirmations of Acceptance for Studies allocated to a Limited Sponsor are the Confirmations of Acceptance for Studies allocated in acccordance [sic] with paragraph 115H below.

115H. The Tier 4 Interim Limit will be calculated as follows:

(i) A Limited Sponsor who has that status as at 21 April 2011 will be allocated:

(a) where the Limited Sponsor had a Tier 4 Sponsor Licence for the entirety of the period 1 March 2010 to 28 February 2011, a number of Confirmations of Acceptance for Studies equal to the number assigned by that Limited Sponsor to Tier 4 Migrants which were used for an application which resulted in a grant of entry clearance, leave to enter or leave to remain, where both the assignment and grant of leave were between 1 March 2010 and 28 February 2011;

(b) where the Limited Sponsor had a Tier 4 Sponsor Licence for only part of the period 1 March 2010 to 28 February 2011, a number of Confirmations of Acceptance for Studies equal to:

(i) the number of Confirmations of Acceptance for Studies assigned by the Limited Sponsor to Tier 4 Migrants which were used for an application which resulted in a grant of entry clearance, leave to enter or leave to remain, where both the assignment and grant of leave were between 1 March 2010 and 28 February 2011;

(ii) multiplied by the appropriate factor to increase the figure in (i) until it is equal to the number of Confirmations of Acceptance for Studies that would have been assigned and granted in a period of 12 months;

(c) where the Limited Sponsor did not have a Tier 4 Sponsor licence during the period 1 March 2010 to 28 February

39 Incorporated by virtue of the Statement of Changes in Immigration Rules (HC 1148).

2011, a number of Confirmations of Acceptance for Studies equal to:

(i) the annual allocation the Limited Sponsor received when it was granted its Tier 4 Sponsor licence;

(ii) less 26% which is the average percentage of Confirmations of Acceptance for Studies assigned by Limited Sponsors which did not result in a grant of entry clearance, leave to enter or leave to remain, where both the assignment and refusal of leave were between 1 March 2010 and 28 February 2011;

(d) where the calculation in paragraphs (a) to (c) above results in 0 or a negative number, the Limited Sponsor will be allocated 0 Confirmations of Acceptance for Studies under the Tier 4 Interim Limit.

(ii) A Limited Sponsor who acquires that status after 21 April 2011 will be allocated a number of Confirmations of Acceptance for Studies:

(a) equal to the result of the calculation appropriate for the Limited Sponsor's circumstances as set out in 115H(i) above; and

(b) subject to a reduction equal to the number of Confirmations of Acceptance for Studies assigned by the Limited Sponsor to Tier 4 Migrants since 21 April 2011 which were used for an application which resulted in a grant of entry clearance, leave to enter or leave to remain since 21 April 2011.

115I. A Limited Sponsor will, on provision to the UK Border Agency of evidence that it meets the criteria set out in paragraph 115E above, be exempt from the Tier 4 Interim Limit from the date the UK Border Agency provides written confirmation that it is so exempt.'

Paragraph 116 of Appendix A states that a CAS will only be considered valid if:

'(a) it was issued no more than 6 months before the application is made,

(b) the application for entry clearance or leave to remain is made no more than 3 months before the start date of the course of study as stated on the Confirmation of Acceptance for Studies,

(c) the Sponsor has not withdrawn the offer since the Confirmation of Acceptance for Studies was issued,

(d) it was issued by an institution with a Tier 4 (General) Student Sponsor Licence,

(da) where the application for entry clearance or leave to remain is for the applicant to commence a new course of study, not for completion of a course already commenced by way of re-sitting examinations or repeating a module of a course, the Sponsor must hold an A-rated or Highly Trusted Sponsor Licence,[40]

40 Incorporated by virtue of the Statement of Changes in Immigration Rules (HC 908).

(e) the institution must still hold such a licence at the time the application for entry clearance or leave to remain is determined

(ea) the migrant must not previously have applied for entry clearance, leave to enter or leave to remain using the same Confirmation of Acceptance for Studies reference number where that application was either approved or refused (not rejected as an invalid application or withdrawn),[41]

(f) it contains such information as is specified as mandatory in guidance published by the United Kingdom Border Agency, and

(g) if it was not issued for a course of studies, it was issued for a full-time, salaried, elected executive position as a student union sabbatical officer to an applicant who is part-way through their studies or who is being sponsored to fill the position in the academic year immediately after their graduation.'

3.54 This means that a CAS will only be valid:

- for a period of six months (also see paragraph 31 of the Tier 4 Policy Guidance);
- if the application for entry clearance or leave to remain is made no earlier than three months before the start date of the course of study (also see paragraphs 29 and 90 of the Tier 4 Policy Guidance);
- if the offer to undertake a course of study with the sponsor has not been withdrawn;
- if it was assigned by a licensed sponsor whose licence is effective at the time the application for entry clearance or leave to remain is determined;
- if it contains the information specified as mandatory in the UKBA guidance (see also paragraph 26 of the Tier 4 policy guidance);
- if it was not issued for a course of studies, then it was assigned to an applicant for the purpose of embarking on a full-time, salaried, elected executive position of a student union sabbatical officer (paragraphs 58 and 73–79 of the Tier 4 Policy Guidance);
- if assigned by a licensed sponsor who is A-rated or holds HTS status where the application is made to commence a new course of study (consequently, B-rated sponsors cannot issue CAS to new students; this is further qualified by changes in the sponsor ratings from 5 September 2011);
- only once (paragraph 32 of the Tier 4 Policy Guidance).

NB: paragraph 26 of the Tier 4 Policy Guidance states that 'the information that the sponsor will include in a Confirmation of Acceptance for Studies can be found on our website: www.ukba.homeoffice.gov.uk/sitecontent/documents/employersandsponsors/pointsbasedsystem/sponsor-prep-phase-4.'

41 Incorporated by virtue of the Statement of Changes in Immigration Rules (HC 908).

This webpage is out of date. There is no definitive guidance on the mandatory information to be included in a CAS. There are piecemeal indications throughout both the sponsor and the student policy guidance. The SMS User Guide for Tier 4 sponsors proves to be more helpful in terms of identifying the mandatory fields to be completed in a CAS. The Guide can be found at: www.ukba.homeoffice.gov.uk/sitecontent/documents/employersandsponsors/sms-user-manual-t4/.[42] It is questionable whether the Guide comes within the meaning of paragraph 245A(c) of the Immigration Rules.

VALIDITY OF A CAS REFERENCE NUMBER

3.55 Paragraph 26 of the Tier 4 Policy Guidance states that each CAS is a unique reference number. Paragraph 117 of Appendix A to the Immigration Rules qualifies the validity of a CAS reference number in the following way:

> '(a) the number supplied links to a Confirmation of Acceptance for Studies Checking Service entry that names the applicant as the migrant and confirms that the Sponsor is sponsoring him in the Tier 4 category indicated by the migrant in his application for leave to remain (that is, as a Tier 4 (General) Student or a Tier 4 (Child) Student), and
>
> (b) that reference number must not have been withdrawn or cancelled by the Sponsor or by the United Kingdom Border Agency since it was assigned.'[43]

3.56 This effectively means that the CAS reference number specified by an applicant on the application form must match a related entry on the Confirmation of Acceptance for Studies Checking Service and must not have been withdrawn or cancelled by the licensed sponsor or the UKBA since being issued. Paragraph 34 of the Tier 4 Policy Guidance states that a CAS can be withdrawn or cancelled by the sponsor or the UKBA at any time. As stated above it is the sponsor's responsibility to provide the CAS reference number to the applicant (paragraph 27 of the Tier 4 Policy Guidance) and the information contained in the CAS which is relevant to the student's application (paragraph 28 of the Tier 4 Policy Guidance).

ENGLISH LANGUAGE ABILITY AND ABILITY TO FOLLOW COURSES[44]

3.57 Paragraph 118 of Appendix A to the Immigration Rules states that no points will be awarded for a CAS unless the following requirements are satisfied:

> '(a) the applicant supplies, as evidence of previous qualifications, specified documents that the applicant used to obtain the offer of a place on a

42 Last updated on 12 February 2010. From 1 October 2011 the UKBA introduced new SMS features.

43 Paragraph 117(b) of Appendix A to the Immigration Rules was deleted and substituted by virtue of the Statement of Changes in Immigration Rules (HC 908). Wording of paragraph 117(b) prior to substitution: 'that reference number must not have been cancelled by the Sponsor or by the United Kingdom Border Agency since it was assigned.'

44 See OR (Student: ability to follow course) Bangladesh [2011] UKUT 166 (IAC) (5 November 2011).

course from the Sponsor unless the applicant is sponsored by a Highly Trusted Sponsor, is a national of one of the countries listed in Appendix H, and is applying for entry clearance in his country of nationality or leave to remain in the UK. The UK Border Agency reserves the right to request the specified documents from these applicants. The application will be refused if the specified documents are not provided in accordance with the request made;[45] and

(b) for Confirmation of Acceptance for Studies assigned on or before 20 April 2011, one of the requirements in (i) to (vii) is met:[46]

(i) the Confirmation of Acceptance for Studies was assigned before 3 March 2010,[47] or

(ii) the course is degree level study; or

(iii) the course is a foundation degree course; or

(iv) the course is a pre-sessional course before a degree-level course; or

(v) the applicant is a Government Sponsored student and the course is an English language course; or

(vi) the applicant is a national of one of the following countries:
Antigua and Barbuda
Australia
The Bahamas
Barbados
Belize
Canada
Dominica
Grenada
Guyana
Jamaica
New Zealand
St Kitts and Nevis
St Lucia
St Vincent and the Grenadines
Trinidad and Tobago
United States of America, and provides the specified documents, or

(vii) the Confirmation of Acceptance for Studies Checking Service entry confirms that the applicant has a knowledge of English equivalent to level B1 of the Council of Europe's Common European Framework for Language Learning or above and:

45 From the words 'unless the applicant' to the end of the paragraph inserted by virtue of the Statement of Changes in Immigration Rules (HC 1148).

46 Paragraph 118(b) of Appendix A to the Immigration Rules was deleted and substituted by virtue of the Statement of Changes in Immigration Rules (HC 908). Wording of paragraph 118(b) prior to substitution: 'one of the requirements in (i) to (viii) below is met.' The reference to paragraph 118(b)(viii) was a drafting error as the paragraph only ran to 118(b)(vii).

47 Due to passage of time this paragraph is of limited relevance given that a CAS assigned before 3 March 2010 is already invalidated by virtue of paragraph 116(a) of Appendix A (i.e. that it was issued more than six months before the application).

(1) if the Confirmation of Acceptance for Studies was assigned before 12 August 2010, the applicant provides documents to support the Sponsor's assessment of his knowledge of English, or

(2) if the course of study stated on the Confirmation of Acceptance for Studies is an English language course, the applicant provides documents to support the Sponsor's assessment of his knowledge of English, or

(3) the applicant provides an original English language test certificate from an English language test provider approved by the Secretary of State for these purposes, which is within its validity date, and clearly shows:

i. the applicant's name,

ii. that the applicant has achieved or exceeded level B1 of the Council of Europe's Common European Framework for Language Learning in all four components (reading, writing, speaking and listening), unless exempted from sitting a component on the basis of the applicant's disability, and

iii. the date of the award, or

(4) the applicant has successfully completed a course as a Tier 4 (Child) student (or under the student rules that were in force before 31 March 2009, where the student was granted permission [sic] stay whilst he was under 18 years old) which:

i. was at least six months in length, and

ii. ended within two years of the date the sponsor assigned the Confirmation of Acceptance for Studies.

(c) For Confirmation of Acceptance for Studies assigned on or after 21 April 2011, one of the requirements in (i) to (iii) is met:[48]

(i) the course is degree level study and the Confirmation of Acceptance for Studies has been assigned by a Sponsor which is a Recognised Body or a body in receipt of funding as a higher education institution from the Department for Employment and Learning in Northern Ireland, the Higher Education Funding Council for England, the Higher Education Funding Council for Wales, or the Scottish Funding Council, and:

(1) the applicant is a national of one of the following countries: Antigua and Barbuda; Australia; The Bahamas; Barbados; Belize; Canada; Dominica; Grenada; Guyana; Jamaica; New Zealand; St Kitts and Nevis; St Lucia; St Vincent and the Grenadines; Trinidad and Tobago; United States of America, and provides the specified documents; or

48 Paragraph 118(c) et al of Appendix A to the Immigration Rules was inserted by virtue of the Statement of Changes in Immigration Rules (HC 908).

(2) has obtained an academic qualification (not a professional or vocational qualification), which is deemed by UK NARIC to meet or exceed the recognised standard of a Bachelor's or Master's degree or a PhD in the UK, from an educational establishment in one of the following countries: Antigua and Barbuda; Australia; The Bahamas; Barbados; Belize; Canada; Dominica; Grenada; Guyana; Jamaica; New Zealand; St Kitts and Nevis; St Lucia; St Vincent and the Grenadines; Trinidad and Tobago; the UK; the USA, and provides the specified documents; or

(3) the applicant has successfully completed a course as a Tier 4 (Child) Student (or under the student rules that were in force before 31 March 2009, where the student was granted permission [sic] stay whilst he was under 18 years old) which:
   i. was at least six months in length, and
   ii. ended within two years of the date the sponsor assigned the Confirmation of Acceptance for Studies; or

(4) the Confirmation of Acceptance for Studies Checking Service entry confirms that the applicant has a knowledge of English equivalent to level B2 of the Council of Europe's Common European Framework for Language Learning in all four components (reading, writing, speaking and listening), or above.

Or

(ii) the course is degree level study and the Confirmation of Acceptance for Studies has been assigned by a Sponsor which is not a Recognised Body or is not a body in receipt of funding as a higher education institution from the Department for Employment and Learning in Northern Ireland, the Higher Education Funding Council for England, the Higher Education Funding Council for Wales, or the Scottish Funding Council, and:

(1) the applicant is a national of one of the following countries: Antigua and Barbuda; Australia; The Bahamas; Barbados; Belize; Canada; Dominica; Grenada; Guyana; Jamaica; New Zealand; St Kitts and Nevis; St Lucia; St Vincent and the Grenadines; Trinidad and Tobago; United States of America, and provides the specified documents; or

(2) has obtained an academic qualification (not a professional or vocational qualification), which is deemed by UK NARIC to meet or exceed the recognised standard of a Bachelor's or Master's degree or a PhD in the UK, from an educational establishment in one of the following countries: Antigua and Barbuda; Australia; The Bahamas; Barbados; Belize; Canada; Dominica; Grenada; Guyana; Jamaica; New Zealand; St Kitts and Nevis; St Lucia; St Vincent and the Grenadines; Trinidad and Tobago; the UK; the USA, and provides the specified documents; or

(3) the applicant has successfully completed a course as a Tier 4 (Child) Student (or under the student rules that were in force before 31 March 2009, where the student was granted permission [sic] stay whilst he was under 18 years old) which:
   i. was at least six months in length, and
   ii. ended within two years of the date the sponsor assigned the Confirmation of Acceptance for Studies; or

(4) the applicant provides an original English language test certificate from an English language test provider approved by the Secretary of State for these purposes, which is within its validity date, and clearly shows:
   i. the applicant's name,
   ii. that the applicant has achieved or exceeded level B2 of the Council of Europe's Common European Framework for Language Learning in all four components (reading, writing, speaking and listening), unless exempted from sitting a component on the basis of the applicant's disability, and
   iii. the date of the award.

Or

(iii) the course is for below degree level study and:

(1) the applicant is a national of one of the following countries: Antigua and Barbuda; Australia; The Bahamas; Barbados; Belize; Canada; Dominica; Grenada; Guyana; Jamaica; New Zealand; St Kitts and Nevis; St Lucia; St Vincent and the Grenadines; Trinidad and Tobago; United States of America, and provides the specified documents; or

(2) has obtained an academic qualification (not a professional or vocational qualification), which is deemed by UK NARIC to meet or exceed the recognised standard of a Bachelor's or Master's degree or a PhD in the UK, from an educational establishment in one of the following countries: Antigua and Barbuda; Australia; The Bahamas; Barbados; Belize; Canada; Dominica; Grenada; Guyana; Jamaica; New Zealand; St Kitts and Nevis; St Lucia; St Vincent and the Grenadines; Trinidad and Tobago; the UK; the USA, and provides the specified documents; or

(3) the applicant has successfully completed a course as a Tier 4 (Child) Student (or under the student rules that were in force before 31 March 2009, where the student was granted permission [sic] stay whilst he was under 18 years old) which:
   i. was at least six months in length, and
   ii. ended within two years of the date the sponsor assigned the Confirmation of Acceptance for Studies; or

(4) the applicant provides an original English language test certificate from an English language test provider approved

by the Secretary of State for these purposes, which is within its validity date, and clearly shows:

i. the applicant's name,

ii. that the applicant has achieved or exceeded level B1 of the Council of Europe's Common European Framework for Language Learning in all four components (reading, writing, speaking and listening), unless exempted from sitting a component on the basis of the applicant's disability, and

iii. the date of the award.'

3.58 The UKBA has made different documentary requirements[49] for those Tier 4 students it considers to be 'low risk'.[50] In accordance with paragraph 12 of the Tier 4 Policy Guidance Tier 4 students will qualify under the differentiation arrangements if they are:

- sponsored by a sponsor which has HTS status; and
- applying for entry clearance in the country of their nationality or for leave to remain in the UK;[51] and
- nationals of the following countries listed in Appendix H to the Immigration Rules:[52]

'— Argentina

— Australia

— British National Overseas

— Brunei

— Canada

— Chile

49 These requirements are arguably discriminatory. The Minister for Immigration argues that the policy complies with the Equality Act 2010 (Student Visas: Follow-up, Home Affairs Committee, House of Commons, Eleventh Report of Session 2010–12, HC 1445, 26 July 2011, p 11 www.publications.parliament.uk/pa/cm201012/cmselect/cmhaff/1445/1445.pdf).

50 50% of respondents (overall number of respondents: 25,571) to the Tier 4 consultation agreed that differential requirements should be implemented for high and low risk students and 51% of respondents (overall number of respondents: 25,520) agreed that the UKBA should concentrate on the abuse of evidence as the starting point. Consultation on the student immigration system: 7th December 2010 to 31st January 2011. Consultation questionnaire results, UK Border Agency, March 2011, p 10 www.ukba.homeoffice.gov.uk/sitecontent/documents/policyandlaw/consultations/students/student-consultation-results.pdf?view=Binary.

51 Appendix H to the Immigration Rules adds that 'where an applicant is a dual national, and only one of their nationalities is listed above, he will be able to apply using the different documentary requirements that apply to these nationals, provided he is applying either for entry clearance in his country of nationality listed above or for leave to remain in the UK'.

52 Appendix H was inserted by virtue of the Statement of Changes in Immigration Rules (HC 1148).

— Croatia
— Hong Kong
— Japan
— New Zealand
— Singapore
— South Korea
— Taiwan (those who hold a passport issued by Taiwan that includes the number of the identification card issued by the competent authority in Taiwan)
— Trinidad and Tobago
— United States of America'

This list will be reviewed on an annual basis. Under the different documentary requirements, Tier 4 students will normally be required to provide less evidence as indicated in the Tier 4 Policy Guidance. The UKBA reserves the right to request the full set of documents and refuse those applications where such are not provided within a specified time.

As stated in paragraph 92 of the Tier 4 Policy Guidance, the level of English language ability and how it is to be assessed depends on:

- when CAS was assigned;
- the type of course to be undertaken;
- the type of institution at which the student will be undertaking the course.

3.59 For CAS assigned on or before 20 April 2011 this means that unless a CAS was assigned before 3 March 2010 or a student is studying at NQF Level 6 (degree level study), undertaking a foundation degree or a pre-sessional course, is Government sponsored and undertaking an English language course or is from a majority English-speaking country, and his or her CAS was assigned on or after 12 August 2010, his or her Tier 4 sponsor has to assess their English language competence and ensure that it is at a minimum level B1 on the Common European Framework of Reference for Languages by showing either that the student:

- has passed a secure English language test with an approved test provider for Tier 4 and has achieved or exceeded level B1 in reading, writing, speaking and listening unless exempt due to disability, or
- has successfully completed a course as a Tier 4 (Child) student or under the student rules in force prior to 31 March 2009 where the student was granted leave while he was under the age of 18, and the course was at least six months in duration and ended within two years of the date on which CAS was assigned (see paragraphs 94–104 of the Tier 4 Policy Guidance).

3.60 For CAS assigned on or after 21 April 2011 this means that:

- If a Tier 4 (General) migrant (unless designated to be a gifted student) is to undertake a course of study at NQF Level 6/QCF Level 6/SCQF Level 9 (degree level study) at a higher education institution (or a body in receipt of funding as a higher education institution), his/her sponsor must assess the student's English language proficiency to be at CEFR level B2 by ensuring that he/she:
  - — is from a majority English speaking country; or
  - — has completed an academic qualification equivalent to a UK Bachelor's, Master's or PhD degree which was taught in a majority English speaking country; or
  - — has successfully completed a course as a Tier 4 (Child) student or under the student rules in force prior to 31 March 2009 where the student was granted leave while he was under the age of 18, and the course was at least six months in duration and ended within two years of the date on which CAS was assigned; or
  - — is proficient at CEFR level B2 in each of the four components (reading, writing, speaking and listening) as assessed using the sponsor's own method of assessing the student's English language ability and this is confirmed accordingly on the CAS.
- If a Tier 4 (General) migrant is to undertake a course of study at NQF Level 6/QCF Level 6/SCQF Level 9 (degree level study) at a non-higher education institution (or a body not in receipt of funding as a higher education institution), his/her sponsor must assess the student's English language proficiency to be at CEFR level B2 by ensuring that he/she:
  - — is from a majority English speaking country; or
  - — has completed an academic qualification equivalent to a UK Bachelor's, Master's or PhD degree which was taught in a majority English speaking country; or
  - — has passed an English language test from the list of approved tests for Tier 4 which is still valid at the time of application and has achieved at least CEFR level B2 in each of the four components (reading, writing, speaking and listening) unless exempt due to disability; or
  - — has successfully completed a course as a Tier 4 (Child) student or under the student rules in force prior to 31 March 2009 where the student was granted leave while he was under the age of 18, and the course was at least six months in duration and ended within two years of the date on which CAS was assigned.
- If a Tier 4 (General) migrant is to undertake a course of study at NQF Levels 3, 4 or 5/QCF Levels 3, 4 or 5/SCQF Levels 6, 7 or 8 (below degree level study), his/

her sponsor must assess the student's English language proficiency to be at CEFR level B1 by ensuring that he/she:

— is from a majority English speaking country; or

— has completed an academic qualification equivalent to a UK Bachelor's, Master's or PhD degree which was taught in a majority English speaking country; or

— has passed an English language test from the list of approved tests for Tier 4 which is still valid at the time of application and has achieved at least CEFR level B1 in each of the four components (reading, writing, speaking and listening) unless exempt due to disability; or

— has successfully completed a course as a Tier 4 (Child) student or under the student rules in force prior to 31 March 2009 where the student was granted leave while he was under the age of 18, and the course was at least six months in duration and ended within two years of the date on which CAS was assigned (see paragraphs 105–117 of the Tier 4 Policy Guidance).

Evidence about either must be included in the CAS if this is how a student's English language ability was assessed by their Tier 4 sponsor (paragraphs 91–117 of the Tier 4 Policy Guidance, also see paragraphs 320–334 of the Sponsor Guidance).[53]

3.61 As a result of the Tier 4 review launched by the Prime Minister on 12 November 2009, the Secretary of State raised the minimum level of English language courses that Tier 4 (General) students could undertake (with the exception of Government sponsored students or those undertaking pre-sessional English language courses) from level A2 to level B2 of the Common European Framework of Reference for Languages on 3 March 2010[54]. Under the new provisions from this date students applying to study English language had to demonstrate an existing knowledge of English language at level B1 or above in order to show that they could study with the aim of raising their proficiency to level B2. The changes were implemented by way of updating the Tier 4 policy guidance, rather than amending the Rules and, as a result, were subsequently disputed as part of the EnglishUK[55] judicial review challenge.

3.62 The requirements in paragraph 118 were initially introduced by the Statement of Changes in Immigration Rules (HC 382) in force from 12 August

53 See Annex (Table B) of the Sponsor Guidance for information about transitional arrangements in respect of assessing Tier 4 (General) students' English language ability.

54 Changes to Tier 4 student visa applications from 3 March 2010, UK Border Agency, 3 March 2010, http://webarchive.nationalarchives.gov.uk/20100303141249/http://www.bia.homeoffice.gov.uk/sitecontent/newsarticles/2010/255022/tier4-visa-applications.

55 English UK Ltd, R (on the application of) v Secretary of State for the Home Department [2010] EWHC 1726 (Admin) (9 July 2010).

2010 as a consequence of the judgment in EnglishUK.[56] On 22 July 2010 it was announced by the UKBA that secure English language tests for Tier 4 (General) students would be implemented from 12 August 2010. In a Ministerial Statement of the same date, the Minister of State for Immigration stated that:

> 'I am also making a further change to the Tier 4 (General) category today to make it a requirement for some students studying below degree level to provide evidence of having passed a UK Border Agency-approved secure English language test at a minimum of B1 level on the Common European Framework of Reference for languages. This change builds on the previous position where the sponsors of such students were required to make their own assessment of the English language level of the student. The use of an independent test is an advance on this as it should help ensure that sponsors are not duped by students offering false or fake documents to prove their English language ability.'[57]

3.63 The approved English language tests for Tier 4 were listed in a table on the UKBA website[58] and are as follows:

- Test of English as a Foreign Language – Internet based test (TOEFL IBT);
- International English Language Testing System (IELTS) – General Training or Academic Module;
- International Legal English Certificate (ILEC);
- International Certificate in Financial English (ICFE);
- Certificate of Proficiency in English (CPE);
- Certificate in Advanced English (CAE);
- Business English Certificate (BEC) Vantage, Higher or Preliminary First Certificate in English (FCE);
- Preliminary English Test;
- ESOL Skills for Life (levels Entry 3 and above);
- Pearson Test of English Academic (PTE Academic).

3.64 On 6 April 2011 the UKBA published a new list of approved English language test providers for applications made under Tiers 1, 2 and 4 of the PBS and spouse and partner applications. On 8 July 2011 the UKBA updated this list to include:

56 English UK Ltd, R (on the application of) v Secretary of State for the Home Department [2010] EWHC 1726 (Admin) (9 July 2010).

57 Written ministerial statement on changes to the immigration points based system, UK Border Agency, 22 July 2010, www.ukba.homeoffice.gov.uk/sitecontent/documents/news/wms-on-the-changes-to-pbs.pdf.

58 List of English Language Tests that have been assessed as meeting the Agency's requirements for Tier 4, www.ukba.homeoffice.gov.uk/sitecontent/applicationforms/pbs/approvedenglishtestst4.pdf. Not valid from July 2011.

- ‘new acceptable test certificates for business language testing service (BULATS);
- clarification that we accept the test of English as a foreign language (TOEFL) ibt test (internet based test); and
- new test scores for tests conducted by Pearson’.[59]

The new updated list of approved English language tests can be found at www.ukba.homeoffice.gov.uk/sitecontent/applicationforms/new-approved-english-tests.pdf. This new list is broken down by awarding body, level, minimum grade required, test certificate validity and documents which are required with the application.

3.65 Documentary requirements for students undertaking PTE Academic were amended on 21 April 2011 by virtue of Appendix A to the Tier 4 Policy Guidance (see the section on documents below).

3.66 Further additions were made to paragraph 118 of Appendix A to the Immigration Rules, namely, the substitution of paragraph 118(b) and insertion of paragraph 118(c) of Appendix A by virtue of the Statement of Changes in Immigration Rules (HC 908) laid before Parliament on 31 March 2011 and in force from 21 April 2011 and the insertion in paragraph 118(a) of Appendix A by virtue of the Statement of Changes in Immigration Rules (HC 1148) laid before Parliament on 13 June 2011 and in force from 4 July 2011. These changes came about as a result of the latest review of the student route.

3.67 The requirements set out in paragraph 118 of Appendix A are evidential. The documents which need to be provided in support of an application to satisfy these requirements will be dealt with in the evidence section below. The requirements are twofold as they ask an applicant to provide documents used as evidence to prove their:

- ability to follow the course of study in respect of which CAS has been assigned, and
- English language ability.

3.68 English language ability is dealt with in detail at paragraphs 91–117 of the Tier 4 Policy Guidance. Paragraphs 97–98 give guidance to students undertaking English language courses with CAS assigned before 21 April 2011. Paragraphs 99–104 give guidance to students undertaking non-English language courses with CAS assigned before 21 April 2011. Paragraphs 107–109 deal with students undertaking degree level courses at higher education and non-higher education

59 Changes to the new list of English language test and providers, UK Border Agency, 8 July 2011, www.ukba.homeoffice.gov.uk/sitecontent/newsarticles/2011/july/13-list-of-english-language. The PTE scores were reduced across the board in all four components from A1 to C2.

institutions whose CAS were issued on or after 21 April 2011 whereas paragraph 110 deals with students whose courses of study fall below degree level and whose CAS were issued on or after 21 April 2011.

INTERVIEW WITH UKBA OFFICIALS

3.69 Paragraph 245ZV(ca) of the Immigration Rules[60] provides that:

> 'Where an applicant has been issued with a Confirmation of acceptance for studies on or after 21 April 2011, the applicant must, if required to do so on examination or interview, be able to demonstrate without the assistance of an interpreter English language proficiency of a standard to be expected from an individual who has reached the standard specified in a Confirmation of acceptance for studies assigned in accordance with appendix a paragraph 118(c) (for the avoidance of doubt, the applicant will not be subject to a test at the standard set out in Appendix a, paragraph 118(c)).'

3.70 Paragraph 93 of the Tier 4 Policy Guidance gives a wide interpretation to this rule. From 21 April 2011 if a Tier 4 (General) migrant is required to undergo an interview either as part of their entry clearance application or on arrival to the UK and they 'cannot show at that interview that his/her English language ability is at the standard required by the Immigration Rules and set out in this guidance, his/her entry clearance application may be refused or he/she may [sic] refused permission to enter the UK.' This applies to applicants who have been issued with CAS on or after 21 April 2011. There is no indication that this provision applies to Tier 4 (General) migrants who have made their applications in-country although it is reasonable to assume that they may also be caught out by this provision on re-entering the United Kingdom. In addition, paragraph 324 of the Sponsor Guidance states that if Tier 4 (General) students who are assigned a CAS on or after 21 April 2011 are asked to attend an interview and 'cannot hold a simple conversation without an interpreter' their application or their permission to enter the United Kingdom will be refused.

ENGLISH LANGUAGE REQUIREMENTS FOR GIFTED STUDENTS AT UNIVERSITIES

3.71 In exceptional cases where sponsors want to offer a place on a course of study at a higher education institution to a gifted student who does not meet the requisite B2 English language requirement, they may waive the requirement only 'if English language proficiency is not integral to that particular course of study and a pre-sessional course would be inappropriate' (paragraph 335 of the Sponsor Guidance). This must be approved by the Academic Registrar or equivalent. The

60 Incorporated into the Immigration Rules by virtue of the Statement of Changes in Immigration Rules (HC 908).

course to be undertaken by a gifted student must be at NQF Level 6/QCF Level 6/ SCQF Level 9 and above (paragraph 108 of the Tier 4 Policy Guidance).

3.72 When filling in the CAS, the sponsor must confirm the following in the 'Evidence provided' field (paragraph 337 of the Sponsor Guidance and paragraph 117 of the Tier 4 Policy Guidance):

- that the student is treated as gifted; and
- the reason for doing so; and
- the name of the sponsor's Academic Registrar or equivalent together with telephone number and email address.

3.73 In addition, the sponsor must provide the student with an original letter which must be signed by the Academic Registrar or equivalent (paragraph 338 of the Sponsor Guidance and paragraph 117 and 112 of the Tier 4 Policy Guidance). The letter must confirm:

- the sponsor name; and
- the sponsor licence number; and
- the student's name; and
- the student's course including the level of study; and
- that the Academic Registrar or equivalent considers the student to be gifted and the reason for it.

3.74 Students applying for entry clearance must have this letter with them on entry to the United Kingdom (paragraph 339 of the Sponsor Guidance and paragraph 117 of the Tier 4 Policy Guidance). In turn, the sponsor must notify the UKBA by email of each gifted student it has assigned CAS to. The sponsor must send the email to T4GiftedStudents@UKBA.gsi.gov.uk citing: (a) the CAS reference number in the subject of the email; and (b) providing its contact details and sponsor licence number in the body of the email (paragraph 340 of the Sponsor Guidance).

RE-SITTING EXAMINATIONS OR REPEATING MODULES

3.75 Paragraph 119 of Appendix A to the Immigration Rules states that:

> 'If the applicant is re-sitting examinations or repeating a module of a course, the applicant must not previously have re-sat the same examination or repeated the same module more than once, unless the Sponsor is a Highly Trusted Sponsor. If this requirement is not met then no points will be awarded for the Confirmation of Acceptance for Studies, unless the Sponsor is a Highly Trusted Sponsor.'

3.76 Paragraph 119 of Appendix A was substituted by the Statement of Changes in Immigration Rules (HC 439) on 6 April 2010. There is no information concerning these provisions in the Tier 4 Policy Guidance (apart from paragraph 63 of the Tier 4 Policy Guidance relating to paragraph 120B of Appendix A to the Immigration Rules, see below). In this instance, students must refer to the Sponsor Guidance where at paragraph 419 it is explained that students can re-sit examinations or repeat any part of their course up to two times in exceptional circumstances. This relates to students who are sponsored by A rated sponsors or sponsors who are B rated subject to an action plan under the Sponsor Guidance in place before 5 September 2011 (paragraph 420 of the Sponsor Guidance). Highly Trusted Sponsors (those with HTS status) are the exception to this rule and are permitted to allow further re-sits or repeats of study in exceptional circumstances. See **Chapter 4** for further information on how HTS status affects a sponsor's ability to offer courses to students.

ACCEPTABLE COURSE LEVELS, COURSE TYPES AND WORK PLACEMENTS

3.77 Paragraph 120 of Appendix A deals with courses in respect of which CAS was assigned on or before 20 April 2011 and states that:

> 'Points will only be awarded for a Confirmation for Studies assigned on or before 20 April 2011[61] (even if all the above requirements are met) if the course in respect of which it is issued meets each of the following requirements:
>
> (a) The course must meet the following minimum academic requirements:
>
> i. for applicants applying to study in England, Wales or Northern Ireland, the course must be at National Qualifications Framework (NQF) Level 3 or above if the Sponsor is:
>
> (aa) a Highly Trusted Sponsor; or (bb) an A rated Sponsor and the Confirmation of Acceptance for Studies was assigned on or before 30 April 2010; or
>
> (cc) an A rated Sponsor with application for Highly Trusted Sponsor status pending determination by the UK Border Agency and the Confirmation of Acceptance for Studies was assigned between 1 May 2010 and 30 June 2010; or
>
> (dd) a B rated Sponsor and the Confirmation of Acceptance for Studies was assigned on or before 5 April 2010; or
>
> ii. for applicants applying to study in England, Wales or Northern Ireland, the course must be at National Qualifications Framework (NQF) Level 4 or above if the requirements at 120(a)(i)(aa) to (dd) are not met; or
>
> iii. for applicants applying to study in Scotland, the course must be accredited at Level 6 or above in the Scottish Credit and Qualifications

61 The words 'assigned on or before 20 April 2011' were inserted by virtue of the Statement of Changes in Immigration Rules (HC 908).

Framework (SCQF) by the Scottish Qualifications Authority if the Sponsor is:

(aa) a Highly Trusted Sponsor; or

(bb) an A rated Sponsor and the Confirmation of Acceptance for Studies was assigned on or before 30 April 2010; or

(cc) an A rated Sponsor with an application for Highly Trusted Sponsor status pending determination by the UK Border Agency and the Confirmation of Acceptance for Studies assigned on or before 20 April 2011[62] was assigned between 1 May 2010 and 30 June 2010; or

(dd) a B rated Sponsor and the Confirmation of Acceptance for Studies was assigned on or before 5 April 2010; or

iv. for applicants applying to study in Scotland, the course must be accredited at Level 7 or above in the Scottish Credit and Qualifications Framework (SCQF) by the Scottish Qualifications Authority if the requirements at 120(a)(iii)(aa) to (dd) are not met; or

v. the course must be a short-term Study Abroad Programme in the United Kingdom as part of the applicant's qualification at an overseas higher education institution, and that qualification must be confirmed as the same as a United Kingdom degree level by the National Recognition Information Centre for the United Kingdom (UK NARI C [sic]); or

vi. the course must be an English language course at level B2 or above of the Common European Framework of Reference for Languages; or

vii. the course may be an English language course at any level, where the applicant is a Government Sponsored student or the course is a pre-sessional course before a degree course; or

viii. the course may be an English language course at level A2 or above on the Common European Framework of Reference for Languages where the Confirmation of Acceptance for Studies was assigned before 23 July 2010; or

ix. the course must be a recognised Foundation Programme for postgraduate doctors or dentists.

(b) The course must, except in the case of a pre-sessional course, lead to an approved qualification as defined in sponsor guidance published by the United Kingdom Border Agency.

(c) Other than when the applicant is actually on a work placement, all study that forms part of the course must take place on the premises of the sponsoring educational institution.

(d) The course must meet one of the following requirements:

62 The words 'assigned on or before 20 April 2011' were inserted by virtue of the Statement of Changes in Immigration Rules (HC 908).

i. be a full time course of degree level study that leads to an approved qualification as defined in UKBA guidance;

ii. be an overseas course of degree level study that is recognised as being equivalent to a UK Higher Education course and is being provided by an overseas Higher Education Institution,

iii. be a full time course of study involving a minimum of 15 hours per week organised daytime study and, except in the case of a pre-sessional course, lead to an approved qualification, below bachelor degree level as defined in paragraph 120(a).

(e) If the course contains a course-related work placement, any period that the applicant will be spending on that placement must not exceed half of the total length of the course spent in the United Kingdom except where it is a United Kingdom statutory requirement that the placement should exceed half the total length of the course. Where the student is following a course of study below degree level study (excluding a foundation degree course), the course can only be offered if the Sponsor is:

(aa) a Highly Trusted Sponsor, or

(bb) an A rated Sponsor and the Confirmation of Acceptance for Studies was assigned on or before 30 April 2010; or

(cc) an A rated Sponsor with an application for Highly Trusted Sponsor status pending determination by the UK Border Agency and the Confirmation of Acceptance for Studies was assigned between 1 Amy 2010 and 30 June 2010; or

(dd) a B rated Sponsor and the Confirmation of Acceptance for Studies was assigned on or before 5 April 2010.'

3.78 Paragraphs 120(a), 120(d)(iii) and 120(e) were last substituted and/or supplemented by the Statement of Changes in Immigration Rules (HC 382) on 23 July 2010. These paragraphs appear as they were on 23 July 2010 as they have not been changed save for the substitutions/supplements made to paragraphs 120 and 120(cc) by the Statement of Changes in Immigration Rules (HC 908) on 21 April 2011.

3.79 The relevant parts of the Rules were first amended on 6 April 2010[63] following the Tier 4 review (initiated by the Government on 12 November 2009) to stipulate that only sponsors holding a Highly Trusted Sponsor licence could offer restricted courses, namely, courses at NQF Level 3 or equivalent and courses below degree level (save for foundation degrees) including a work placement. Transitional arrangements were put in place for Tier 4 sponsors.[64]

63 Statement of Changes in Immigration Rules (HC 439).

64 Tier 4 changes for education providers and migrant students, UK Border Agency, 7 April 2010, www.ukba.homeoffice.gov.uk/sitecontent/newsarticles/2010/april/03-t4-changes.

3.80 Publicly funded institutions automatically deemed to hold a Highly Trusted Sponsor licence on 6 April 2010 had to make their applications to upgrade their licence type by 30 June 2010 to retain the status. All other A-rated sponsors who did not qualify for automatic inclusion and wanted to apply for a Highly Trusted Sponsor licence had to do so by 30 April 2010 to be able to offer restricted courses to migrant students. See **Chapter 4** for further information about the Highly Trusted Sponsor Scheme.

3.81 Paragraph 120A of Appendix A which was inserted into the Immigration Rules by the Statement of Changes in Immigration Rules (HC 908) deals with courses in respect of which CAS was assigned on or after 21 April 2011 and states that:

> 'Points will only be awarded for a Confirmation of Acceptance for Studies assigned on or after 21 April 2011 (even if all the requirements in paragraphs 116 to 119 above are met) if the course in respect of which it is issued meets each of the following requirements:
>
> (a) The course must meet the following minimum academic requirements:
>
> i. for applicants applying to study in England, Wales or Northern Ireland, the course must be at National Qualifications Framework (NQF) / Qualifications and Credit Framework (QCF) Level 3 or above if the Sponsor is a Highly Trusted Sponsor; or
>
> ii. for applicants applying to study in England, Wales or Northern Ireland, the course must be at National Qualifications Framework (NQF) / Qualifications and Credit Framework (QCF) Level 4 or above if the Sponsor is an A-Rated Sponsor or a B-Rated Sponsor; or
>
> iii. for applicants applying to study in Scotland, the course must be accredited at Level 6 or above in the Scottish Credit and Qualifications Framework (SCQF) by the Scottish Qualifications Authority and the Sponsor must be a Highly Trusted Sponsor; or
>
> iv. for applicants applying to study in Scotland, the course must be accredited at Level 7 or above in the Scottish Credit and Qualifications Framework (SCQF) by the Scottish Qualifications Authority if the Sponsor is an A-Rated Sponsor or B-Rated Sponsor; or
>
> v. the course must be a short-term Study Abroad Programme in the United Kingdom as part of the applicant's qualification at an overseas higher education institution, and that qualification must be confirmed as the same as a United Kingdom degree level by the National Recognition Information Centre for the United Kingdom (UK NARIC); or
>
> vi. the course must be an English language course at level B2 or above of the Common European Framework of Reference for Languages; or
>
> vii. the course must be a recognised Foundation Programme for postgraduate doctors or dentists;

(b) The Confirmation of Acceptance for Studies must be for a single course of study except where the Confirmation of Acceptance for Studies is:
   (i) issued by a Sponsor which is a Recognised Body or a body in receipt of funding as a higher education institution from the Department for Employment and Learning in Northern Ireland, the Higher Education Funding Council for England, the Higher Education Funding Council for Wales, or the Scottish Funding Council to cover both a pre-sessional course of no longer than three months' duration and a course of degree level study at that Sponsor; and
   (ii) the applicant has an unconditional offer to a place on a course of degree level study at that Sponsor; and
   (iii) the course of degree level study commences no later than one month after the end date of the pre-sessional course.

(c) The course must, except in the case of a pre-sessional course, lead to an approved qualification as defined in the Tier 4 (Sponsor) guidance published by the UK Border Agency on the UK Border Agency website.

(ca) A course leading to an approved qualification must be offered by a Sponsor that, if approval at a specified level is required from a relevant awarding organisation, has that approval at the specified level, as set ouf in the UK Border Agency sponsor guidance published on the UK Border Agency website.[65]

65 Inserted by virtue of the Statement of Changes in Immigration Rules (HC 1148). Paragraph 227 of the Sponsor Guidance states that 'an approved qualification for our purposes is one which is:

- validated by Royal Charter; or
- awarded by a recognised body on the recognised bodies list operated by BIS (formerly DIUS) (see link – http://www.bis.gov.uk/policies/higher-education/recognised-uk-degrees/recognised-bodies); or
- recognised by one or more recognised bodies via a formal articulation agreement with the awarding body; or
- in England, Wales and Northern Ireland on the Register of Regulated Qualifications (see link – http://register.ofqual.gov.uk/) at Qualifications and Credit Framework (QCF) or National Qualifications Framework (NQF) Level 3 or above;
- in Scotland, accredited at Level 6 or above in the Scottish Credit and Qualifications Framework (SCQF) by the Scottish Qualifications Authority; or
- an overseas qualification, on which UK NARIC is able to advise on its validity, with a level equivalent to level 3 or above on the National Qualifications Framework.
- Covered by a formal legal agreement between a UK recognised body and another education provider or awarding body, which must be signed off by an authorised signatory for institutional agreements within the recognised body. The agreement must confirm the recognised body's own independent assessment of the level of the institution's or awarding body's programme in relation to the National Qualifications Framework (or its equivalents), and also state that any student who successfully completes the education provider's or awarding body's named course can be admitted onto a specific or a range of degree-level courses offered by the recognised body.'

Paragraph 228 of the Sponsor Guidance goes on to say that distance learning courses do not lead to an approval qualification.

(d) Other than when the applicant is on a course-related work placement or a pre-sessional course, all study that forms part of the course must take place on the premises of the sponsoring educational institution or an institution which is a partner institution of the migrant's Sponsor.

(e) The course must meet one of the following requirements:

i. be a full time course of degree level study that leads to an approved qualification as defined in UKBA guidance;

ii. be an overseas course of degree level study that is recognised as being equivalent to a UK Higher Education course and is being provided by an overseas Higher Education Institution; or

iii. be a full time course of study involving a minimum of 15 hours per week organised daytime study and, except in the case of a pre-sessional course, lead to an approved qualification, below bachelor degree level as defined in the Tier 4 (Sponsor) guidance published by the UK Border Agency on the UK Border Agency website.

(f) If the course contains a course-related work placement, any period that the applicant will be spending on that placement must not exceed half of the total length of the course spent in the United Kingdom except where it is a United Kingdom statutory requirement that the placement should exceed half the total length of the course. Where the student is following a course of study below degree level study including a course-related work placement, the course can only be offered if the Sponsor is a Highly Trusted Sponsor.'

3.82 Paragraph 58 of the Tier 4 Policy Guidance provides the breakdown of the type of study Tier 4 (General) students can do:

'• a full-time course of study that leads to a qualification at Level 6 or above of the revised National Qualification Framework (NQF) or its equivalents; or

• an overseas course of degree level study that is recognised as being equivalent to a UK Higher Education course and is being provided by an overseas Higher Education Institution; or

• a full time course involving a minimum of 15 hours per week organised daytime study (daytime study is 8am – 6pm, Monday to Friday) and (except in the case of a pre-sessional course) leading to a qualification below degree level but which must be at a minimum of NQF Level 3 or its equivalents.[66]

Or undertaking:

• a recognised Foundation Programme as a postgraduate doctor or dentist in the UK;

• work as a student union sabbatical officer.'

66 See also paragraph 226 of the Sponsor Guidance.

Paragraphs 59–60 of the Tier 4 Policy Guidance describe the acceptable levels of courses that Tier 4 (General) students can undertake with CAS assigned on or before 21 April 2011 in line with paragraph 120 of Appendix A to the Immigration Rules. Students with CAS assigned on or after 21 April 2011 are dealt with in paragraphs 61–62 of the Tier 4 Policy Guidance (also partially covered in paragraphs 304–307 of the Sponsor Guidance) in line with paragraph 120A of Appendix A to the Immigration Rules. English language courses are covered in paragraphs 64–66, higher education courses at overseas institutions are covered in paragraphs 67–68 and foundation programme courses for postgraduate doctors and dentists are dealt with in paragraphs 69–72 of the Tier 4 Policy Guidance (also dealt with in paragraphs 317–319 of the Sponsor Guidance). The types of work placements a student can do are explained in paragraphs 305–309 of the Tier 4 Policy Guidance (and partially in paragraphs 364–370 of the Sponsor Guidance) and will be dealt with below in the section dealing with work provisions.

ACADEMIC PROGRESSION

3.83 Paragraph 120B of Appendix A which was inserted into the Immigration Rules by the Statement of Changes in Immigration Rules (HC 1148) deals with a new requirement applicable to CAS assigned on or after 1 July 2011[67] (although the rule came into force on 4 July 2011) and states that:

> 'Points will only be awarded for a valid Confirmation of Acceptance for Studies assigned on or after 1 July 2011 (even if all the requirements in paragraphs 116 to 120A above are met) if the Sponsor has confirmed that the course for which the Confirmation of Acceptance for Studies has been assigned represents academic progress from previous study undertaken during the last period of leave as a Tier 4 (General) Student or as a Student, except where:
> (i) the applicant is re-sitting examinations or repeating modules in accordance with paragraph 119 above, or
> (ii) the applicant is making a first application to move to a new institution to complete a course commenced elsewhere.'

This requirement is dealt with in more detail in paragraphs 371–377 of the Sponsor Guidance and is touched upon in **Chapter 4**.

67 At paragraph 371 of the Sponsor Guidance it states that 'since 4 July 2011, if you assign a CAS to a student to take another course in the UK after they finish one, it must be academic progression from the previous course'. In accordance with the Immigration Rules the provision applies to CAS assigned from 1 July 2011 onwards.

Additional requirements related to CAS not compliant with the ***Pankina*** *principle prior to 21 April 2011*

3.84 Paragraph 32 of the Tier 4 Policy Guidance imposes a requirement which restricts the validity of a CAS to the effect that it 'cannot be used more than once'. The paragraph goes on to say that 'if a student's Tier 4 application is refused, and he/she wishes to make another application, he/she will need to get a new Confirmation of Acceptance for Studies form his/her sponsor.' Prior to 21 April 2011 this provision was not reflected in the Immigration Rules and was applied by immigration officials even if the reason for refusal was unrelated to CAS. This provision has now been added to the Immigration Rules by virtue of paragraph 116(ea) of Appendix A to the Immigration Rules to bring it in line with the *Pankina* principle and make it resistant to challenge. This provision undoubtedly puts a strain on a sponsor's allocation of already restricted CAS numbers. If a sponsor was to refuse to issue more than one CAS to a student, it would make any further attempt by that student to succeed in an application for entry clearance or leave to remain impossible.

MAINTENANCE (FUNDS)

3.85 The maintenance requirements came under scrutiny in the *Pankina* case and as a result of its outcome, the Rules were amended on 23 July 2010 to insert paragraph 1A into Appendix C to the Immigration Rules. Applicants required by the Immigration Rules to score points under Appendix C to the Immigration Rules, must adhere to the requirements contained in Paragraph 1A:

'(a) The applicant must have the funds specified in the relevant part of Appendix C at the date of the application;

…

(c) If the applicant is applying as a Tier 4 Migrant, the applicant must have had the funds referred to in (a) above for a consecutive 28-day period of time;

(ca) If the applicant is applying for entry clearance or leave to remain as a Tier 4 Migrant, he must confirm that the funds referred to in (a) above are:

- (i) available in the manner specified in paragraph 13 below for his use in studying and living in the UK; and
- (ii) that the funds will remain available in the manner specified in paragraph 13 below unless used to pay for course fees and living costs;

(d) If the funds were obtained when the applicant was in the UK, the funds must have been obtained while the applicant had valid leave and was not acting in breach of any conditions attached to that leave;

(e) The applicant must provide the specified documents;

(f) Where the funds are in one or more foreign currencies, the applicant must have the specified level of funds when converted to pound sterling (£) using the spot exchange rate which appears on www.oanda.com* for the date of the application;

(g) Where the applicant is applying as a Tier 1 Migrant, a Tier 2 Migrant or a Tier 5 Migrant, the funds must have been under his own control on the date of the application and for the period specified in (b) above; and

(h) Where the application is made at the same time as applications by the partner or child of the applicant (such that the applicant is a Relevant Points Based System Migrant for the purposes of paragraph 319AA), each applicant must have the total requisite funds specified in the relevant parts of appendices C and E. If each applicant does not individually meet the requirements of appendices C and / or E, as appropriate, all the applications (the application by the Relevant Points Based System Migrant and applications as the partner or child of that relevant Points Based system Migrant) will be refused;

(i) The end date of the 90-day and 28-day periods referred to in (b) and (c) above will be taken as the date of the closing balance on the most recent of the specified documents, and must be no earlier than 31 days before the date of application'.[68]

The UKBA revised its evidential requirements of maintenance by adding a declaration to the application form asking the applicant to confirm availability of funds to cover course fees and living costs. Where concerns arise, checks will be carried out to verify that funds continue to be available.

APPENDIX C (MAINTENANCE (FUNDS))

3.86 Pursuant to paragraphs 10–11 of Appendix C to the Immigration Rules Tier 4 (General) students must score 10 points for funds in accordance with the criteria contained in the table below. Availability of funds must be evidenced by submitting documents specified in the Tier 4 Policy Guidance subject to the differentiation arrangements.

68 Paragraph 1A of Appendix C to the Immigration Rules was amended by the Statement of Changes in Immigration Rules (HC 908). It was last amended by the Statement of Changes in Immigration Rules (HC 1148) in force from 4 July 2011. The new requirements were added and/or substituted in paragraphs 1A(c), 1A(ca)(i)–(ii) and 1A(h)(i).

Criterion	**Points awarded**
If studying in inner London: Where the applicant does not have an established presence studying in the United Kingdom, the applicant must have funds amounting to the full course fees for the first academic year of the course, or for the entire course if it is less than a year long, plus £800 for each month of the course up to a maximum of nine months. Where the applicant has an established presence studying in the United Kingdom, the applicant must have funds amounting to the course fees required either for the remaining academic year if the applicant is applying part-way through, or for the next academic year if the applicant will continue or commence a new course at the start of the next academic year, or for the entire course if it is less than a year long, plus £800 for each month of the course up to a maximum of two months. **If studying in outer London and elsewhere in the United Kingdom** Where the applicant does not have an established presence studying in the United Kingdom, the applicant must have funds amounting to the full course fees for the first academic year of the course, or for the entire course if it is less than a year long, plus £600 for each month of the course up to a maximum of nine months. Where the applicant has an established presence studying in the United Kingdom, the applicant must have funds amounting to the course fees required either for the remaining academic year if the applicant is applying part-way through, or for the next academic year if the applicant will continue or commence a new course at the start of the next academic year, or for the entire course if it is less than a year long, plus £600 for each month of the course up to a maximum of two months.	10

3.87 Notes accompanying the table in paragraphs 12–14 of Appendix C to the Immigration Rules are of an explanatory nature. These have been largely substituted and/or supplemented by the Statement of Changes in Immigration Rules (HC

908) and the Statement of Changes in Immigration Rules (HC 1148). Paragraph 12 states that to be considered to be studying in inner London an institution or its branch must be 'situated in an inner[69] London Borough specified in United Kingdom Border Agency guidance.' If studies are to take place at more than one site, then in order to be considered to be studying in inner London a CAS must specify that 'the applicant will be spending the majority of time studying at a site or sites situated in inner London'. Paragraph 12A deals with the calculation of the length of the applicant's course if it includes a part of a month (prior to 21 April 2011 this was dealt with only in the Tier 4 Policy Guidance). Availability of funds is dealt with in paragraph 13.

Paragraph 13 incorporates the additional requirements that were previously imputed by the Tier 4 Policy Guidance into the Rules:

> 'Funds will be available to the applicant only where the specified documents show or, where permitted by these Rules, the applicant confirms that the funds are held or provided by:
> (i) the applicant (whether as a sole or joint account holder); and/or
> (ii) the applicant's parent(s) or legal guardian(s), and the parent(s) or legal guardian(s) have provided written consent that their funds may be used by the applicant in order to study in the UK; and/or
> (iii) an official financial sponsor which must be Her Majesty's Government, the applicant's home government, the British Council or any international organisation, international company, University or Independent school.'[70]

New paragraph 13A states that:

> 'No points will be awarded where the specified documents show that the funds are held in a financial institution with which the UK Border Agency is unable to make satisfactory verification checks. A list of financial institutions which do not satisfactorily verify financial statements is published on the UK Border Agency website.'

Reference should be made to paragraph 259 of the Tier 4 Policy Guidance. The list of financial institutions can be found at www.ukba.homeoffice.gov.uk/sitecontent/documents/studying/financial-institutions.pdf.[71]

69 The words 'inner London' were inserted into paragraph 12 of Appendix C by the Statement of Changes in Immigration Rules (HC 908).
70 From the word 'or' to 'that' added by the Statement of Changes in Immigration Rules (HC 1148).
71 Not available online at the time of publication.

3.88 The circumstances in which an applicant, be it a Tier 4 migrant, student or a postgraduate doctor or dentist will be considered to have an established presence[72] studying in the United Kingdom are defined in paragraph 14 as follows:

'(i) has finished a single course that was at least six months long within the applicant's last period of entry clearance, leave to enter or leave to remain, or

(ii) is applying for continued study on a single course where the applicant has completed at least six months of that course.'[73]

3.89 Paragraphs 35–41 of the Tier 4 Policy Guidance provide the breakdown of maintenance requirements:

- The two factors that determine the amount of money an applicant needs to have available in each individual case are the length of the course of study and the place of study (paragraph 35);
- The two components of the maintenance requirement are course fees for the first period of study (if commencing a new course) or the next period of study (if continuing a course) and living costs for up to a maximum of nine months (paragraph 36);
- The amount of course fees will be indicated by the Tier 4 sponsor on a CAS (paragraph 37);
- For those embarking on a new course the Tier 4 sponsor must indicate the course fees for the first year or the entire course, if its duration is less than a year (paragraph 38);
- For those continuing a course and applying for an extension of leave the Tier 4 sponsor must indicate the balance of course fees that remains to be paid (if the student is part way through the academic year) or the course fees payable for the next academic year (if the student is to continue the course at the start of the academic year) (paragraph 39);

72 See *DN (student; course 'completed'; 'established presence') Kenya* [2010] UKUT 443 (IAC) (15 November 2010) in which Upper Tribunal held that for the course to be 'completed' it does not have to be 'successfully completed' and the concept of 'established presence' requires the student's presence, not success achieved as a student. In *Molla (established presence - date of application) Bangladesh* [2011] UKUT 161 (IAC) (03 May 2011) the Upper Tribunal held that for the purpose of determining 'established presence', the date of application is the relevant date for calculating whether a Tier 4 (General) student has completed a course of study within specified periods of time.

73 This paragraph was supplemented by the Statement of Changes in Immigration Rules (HC 908). The wording of this paragraph prior to the changes in force from 21 April 2011 is as follows: 'if the applicant has completed a course that was a least six months long within their last period of leave as a Tier 4 migrant, student or as a Postgraduate Doctor or Dentist, and this course finished within the last four months, or the applicant is applying for continued study on a course where the applicant has completed at least six months of that course and has been studying within the last four months.'

- For those undertaking a Study Abroad Programme the Tier 4 sponsor must indicate the course fees for the first year or the entire course, if its duration is less than a year, or alternatively, indicate that no fees are due (paragraph 40);
- There is no fixed amount of living costs that an applicant must show as this will depend on the personal circumstances of each applicant (paragraph 41).

3.90 Paragraphs 141–173 of the Tier 4 Policy Guidance categorise what constitutes sufficient funds to satisfy the point scoring requirements. These provisions deal separately with course fees, living costs, place of study, established presence, the amount of maintenance (funds) to be shown, money that can be used for the purposes of applying.

COURSE FEES (PARAGRAPHS 141–147)

3.91 When issuing a CAS the Tier 4 sponsor must:

- indicate the cost of course fees, or
- confirm that there are no fees to pay.

If a student has already paid all or part of the course fees prior to making the application for entry clearance or leave to remain, this amount can be deducted from the total amount that the student must show as being available to him/her when making the application.

3.92 A student embarking on a new course or a student in the United Kingdom as part of a Study Abroad Programme who is required to pay course fees must show sufficient funds to cover course fees:

- for the first year, or
- for the entire course (if its duration is less than a year).

3.93 A student continuing a course and applying for extension of leave to continue the studies must show sufficient funds to cover course fees:

- to the end of the current academic year, or
- for the next academic year (if the course is set to continue from the start of the next academic year).

LIVING COSTS (PARAGRAPHS 148–173, ANNEX 5 TO THE TIER 4 POLICY GUIDANCE)

3.94 The amount of living costs depends on:

- the location of the site of study (which determines the monthly amount), and
- established presence (which determines whether an applicant can show this amount for a reduced number of months).

3.95 A student spending more than 50% of their study time in inner London must show £800 per month for living costs. A student spending more than 50% of their study time in outer London or elsewhere in the United Kingdom must show £600 per month for living costs. If a student has already paid all or part of accommodation fees before making the application for entry clearance or leave to remain, this amount can be deducted from the total amount that the student must show as being available to him/her for living costs when making the application. This provision does not apply to privately arranged accommodation.

3.96 Inner London encompasses the following boroughs:

- Camden
- City of London
- Hackney
- Hammersmith and Fulham
- Haringey
- Islington
- Kensington and Chelsea
- Lambeth
- Lewisham
- Newham
- Southwark
- Tower Hamlets
- Wandsworth
- Westminster

3.97 A student who does not have an established presence studying in the United Kingdom must show sufficient funds for living costs for each month of the course up to a maximum of nine months. For such a student the overall amount of funds is made up of the course fees plus:

- £800 for living costs for each month of their course up to a maximum of nine months, if studying in inner London, or
- £600 for living costs for each month of their course up to a maximum of nine months, if studying in outer London or elsewhere in the United Kingdom.

3.98 A student with an established presence studying in the United Kingdom must show sufficient funds for living costs for each month of the course up to a maximum of two months. For such a student the overall amount of funds is made up of the course fees plus:

- £800 for living costs for each month of their course up to a maximum of two months, if studying in inner London, or
- £600 for living costs for each month of their course up to a maximum of two months, if studying in outer London or elsewhere in the United Kingdom.

3.99 A student can claim points for the reduced levels of living costs regardless of whether they are applying for entry clearance or leave to remain.[74] If the length of the course exceeds an even number of months, then it will be rounded up to the next month (this is pervasive throughout the Tier 4 Policy Guidance and has now been incorporated into the Immigration Rules at paragraph 12A of Appendix C).

3.100 In line with paragraph 155 of the Tier 4 Policy Guidance students including postgraduate doctors or dentists and sabbatical officers will be considered to have an established presence if they have current leave as Tier 4 migrants, students, postgraduate doctors or dentists and on the date of the application he/she:

'• has finished a single course that was at least six months long within the applicant's last period of entry clearance, leave to enter or leave to remain, or
• is applying for a continued study on a single course where the applicant has completed at least six months of that course.'

3.101 The second limb of the definition of 'established presence' that endured up until 21 April 2011 has been done away with. The second limb of the definition required:

'• his/her last grant of leave ended no more than four months before his/her Tier 4 application was made; or
• he/she is currently following a course of study.'[75]

This requirement is no longer in place.

3.102 The emphasis on pursuing a single course means that applicants cannot combine two or more courses to make up the period of six months of study. Annex 5 contains a table of maintenance (funds) students with or without an established presence of studying in the United Kingdom will need to demonstrate to claim 10 points.

74 See Chapter 5 in relation to caselaw on 'established presence' such as *DN (student; course 'completed'; established presence') Kenya* [2010] UKUT 443 and *Molla (established presence – date of application) Bangladesh* [2011] UKUT 161.

75 Prior to 21 April 2011, paragraph 127 of the Tier 4 Policy Guidance, version 07/10, 23 July 2010.

3.103 Students can use money held in an account owned by their parents or legal guardians provided that the relationship between them is established and the consent is given for use of the money (paragraph 162 of the Tier 4 Policy Guidance). This implicitly excludes sponsorship by any other family members, friends or relatives. This is a restrictive substantive requirement which did not, prior to 21 April 2011, form part of the Immigration Rules and is now reflected in paragraph 13(ii) of Appendix C to the Immigration Rules.[76]

3.104 Students can also rely on official financial sponsorship to cover all or part of their maintenance (funds) (paragraph 171 of the Tier 4 Policy Guidance and paragraph 13(iii) of Appendix C to the Immigration Rules). The Interpretation Section also contains a general definition of an official financial sponsor for the purposes of Part 6A of the Rules as 'the person or Government that the Certificate of Sponsorship Checking Service or Confirmation of Acceptance for Studies Checking Service records as being the Sponsor for a migrant'. Students can also use a personal loan as evidence of available funds (see the documents section below) (a loan held in the name of a parent(s) or a legal guardian cannot be used as evidence of money held by the Tier 4 (General) student[77]). As maintenance (funds) is an evidential requirement, please see the documents section below.

3.105 On 22 July 2010 the UKBA announced that due to a change in the US legislation, UK institutions participating in the William D Ford Federal Direct Loan Programme administered by the US Department of Education would be authorised to offer Federal Direct Loans to students coming from the USA to study in the United Kingdom from 1 July 2010. Tier 4 sponsors participating in the programme must use a template letter when authorising loans to prospective students from the USA.[78]

76 Following challenges in *CDS (PBS 'available' Article 8) Brazil* [2010] UKUT 305 (IAC) (25 August 2010) and *FA and AA (PBS effect of Pankina) Nigeria* [2010] UKUT 304 (IAC) (25 August 2010). Upper Tribunal held in CDS that funds are considered to be 'available' to an applicant if they belong to a third party willing to arrange for the funds to be used in support of that person's application. Furthermore, in FA and AA it was established that funds held in a bank account belonging to the applicant's husband are considered to be available to the applicant. Both judgments followed the principles found in *Pankina.* Reference can also be made to the judgement in *AM and SS (PBS Tier 1 joint accounts) Pakistan* [2010] UKUT 169 (IAC) (2 June 2010) which pre-dates Pankina but determines that a joint account bearing the applicant's name satisfies evidential requirements. Given that the relevant wording has now been imported from the policy guidance into the Immigration Rules in force from 21 April 2011, these judgements are of restricted consequence.

77 See also *PO (Points based scheme: maintenance: loans) Nigeria* [2009] UKAIT 00047 (25 November 2009).

78 Changes to Tier 4 of the points-based system, UK Border Agency, 22 July 2010, http://webarchive.nationalarchives.gov.uk/20100823120706/http://www.ukba.homeoffice.gov.uk/sitecontent/newsarticles/2010/july/45-changes-to-t4.

ATAS

3.106 Diverting back to the remainder of the requirements under the Immigration Rules, paragraphs 245ZV(d) and 245ZX(e) relate to the Academic Technology Approval Scheme. These paragraphs stipulate that if the applicant wishes to undertake:

'(i) postgraduate studies leading to a Doctorate or Masters degree by research in one of the disciplines listed in paragraph 1 of Appendix 6 to these Rules, or

(ii) postgraduate studies leading to a taught Masters degree in one of the disciplines listed in paragraph 2 of Appendix 6 to these Rules, or

(iii) a period of study or research in excess of 6 months in one of the disciplines listed in paragraphs 1 or 2 of Appendix 6 of these Rules at a publicly funded institution of higher education where this forms part of an overseas postgraduate qualification

the applicant must hold a valid Academic Technology Approval Scheme clearance certificate from the Counter-Proliferation Department of the Foreign and Commonwealth Office which relates to the course, or area of research, that the applicant will be taking and at the institution at which the applicant wishes to undertake it and must provide the specified documents to show that these requirements have been met.'

3.107 Appendix 6 of the Immigration Rules contains a list of disciplines for which an ATAS clearance certificate is required under Tier 4. The Scheme is operated by the Foreign and Commonwealth Office. In accordance with paragraph 127 of the Tier 4 Policy Guidance, Tier 4 (General) students who are applying for a course starting before 1 January 2012 must obtain an ATAS clearance certificate if they intend to undertake the following courses:

'• postgraduate studies leading to a Doctorate or Masters degree by research in one of the subjected listed in paragraph 1 of Appendix 6 of the Immigration Rules; or

• postgraduate studies leading to a taught Masters degree in one of the subjects listed in paragraph 2 of Appendix 6 of the Immigration Rules; or

• study or research in the UK of longer than six months which is part of an overseas postgraduate level course, in any subject listed in Appendix 6 of the Immigration Rules.'

Paragraph 128 of the Tier 4 Policy Guidance makes ATAS provisions for students applying on or before 1 October 2011 for the following courses:

'• undergraduate or postgraduate studies leading to a Doctorate or Masters degree by research in one of the disciplines listed in paragraph 1 of Appendix 6 of the Immigration Rules, or

- undergraduate or postgraduate studies leading to a taught Masters degree or other postgraduate qualification in one of the disciplines listed in paragraph 2 of Appendix 6 of the Immigration Rules, or
- a period of study or research in excess of 6 months in one of the disciplines listed in paragraphs 1 or 2 of Appendix 6 of the Immigration Rules at an institution of higher education where this forms part of an overseas postgraduate qualification.'

Statement of Changes in Immigration Rules (HC 1148) will introduce paragraph 245ZV(da) into the Immigration Rules from 1 October 2011 dealing with the new provisions set out in paragraph 127 of the Tier 4 Policy Guidance.[79]

In accordance with paragraph 129 of the Tier 4 Policy Guidance, applications for an ATAS clearance certificate must be made online on the Foreign and Commonwealth Office website at www.fco.gov.uk/atas. The website explains that ATAS 'is used to help stop the spread of knowledge and skills that could be used in the proliferation of weapons of mass destruction (WMD) and their means of delivery.' An application for an ATAS clearance certificate can be made up to 12 months in advance of the start of the course of study. The Foreign and Commonwealth Office aims to process applications within 20 working days but may take longer during busy periods.

3.108 Before making the application, applicants are required by the Foreign and Commonwealth Office to have the following information to hand:

> 'your official letter from your Higher Education Institution is the most important document you will need to refer to is from your Higher Education Institution and this should Include your programme of study and its JACS code
>
> if you are doing a Masters course which involves research, then a research proposal is required
>
> if you are doing a Masters course which does not involve research and is taught, then the official letter will also need details of the optional modules you anticipate taking
>
> full details of any previous and current employment
>
> full details of published papers
>
> previous ATAS applications
>
> full names and contact details of 2 referees (first name(s) and family name). You must have known both of your referees for at least three years. At least one of these must be an academic from your country of origin.
>
> how you will be funding your studies.'[80]

79 See also paragraph 7.5–7.7 of the Explanatory Memorandum to the Statement of Changes in Immigration Rules laid on 13 June 2011 (HC 1148).

80 Apply Online, Foreign and Commonwealth Office, www.fco.gov.uk/en/about-us/what-we-do/services-we-deliver/atas/apply-online/.

3.109 In accordance with paragraphs 130–1131 of the Tier 4 Policy Guidance an ATAS clearance certificate remains valid for as long as the Tier 4 sponsor, course details including length of the course do not change. Students changing the course, study modules, area of research or moving to another institution will need to apply for a fresh ATAS clearance certificate. Students whose leave was issued on or after 30 November 2007 applying for further leave to write up a thesis will need a new ATAS clearance certificate. Students whose previous leave was issued prior to 30 November 2007 applying for further leave to write up a thesis will not need ATAS clearance. According to paragraph 6 of the Immigration Rules, 'under Part 6A of these Rules, "Student Writing-Up a Thesis" means a migrant who is granted leave under paragraphs 69G to 69L of these Rules.'[81] As this is an evidential requirement, please refer to the section below dealing with documents.

Postgraduate doctors and dentists

3.110 Under the Immigration Rules in force before 31 March 2009 the provisions dealing with postgraduate doctors or dentists could be found in paragraphs 70–75M. Now they are part of the Tier 4 (General) provisions in Part 6A of the Immigration Rules for entry clearance and leave to remain under paragraphs 245ZV(e) and 245ZX(f) of the Immigration Rules. Pursuant to paragraph 6 of the Immigration Rules 'under part 6A of these Rules, "Postgraduate Doctor or Dentist" means a migrant who is granted leave under paragraphs 70 to 75 of these Rules.' Pursuant to paragraphs 245ZV(e) and 245ZX(f) of the Immigration Rules applicants wishing to be a postgraduate doctor or dentist on a recognised Foundation Programme must meet the following requirements:[82]

'(i) the applicant must have successfully completed a recognised UK degree in medicine or dentistry from:
   (1) an institution with a Tier 4 General Sponsor Licence,
   (2) a UK publicly funded institution of further or higher education or
   (3) a UK bona fide private education institution which maintains satisfactory records of enrolment and attendance,

(ii) the applicant must have previously been granted leave:
   (1) as a Tier 4 (General) Student, or as a Student, for the final academic year of the studies referred to in paragraph (i) above, and
   (2) as a Tier 4 (General) Student, or as a Student, for at least one other academic year (aside from the final year) of the studies referred to in paragraph (i) above,

81 Paragraphs 69G to 69L of the Immigration Rules were deleted by the Statement of Changes in Immigration Rules (HC 314) on 31 March 2009. Now these provisions are part of the Tier 4 (General) provisions.

82 See paragraph 317 of the Sponsor Guidance relating to continued sponsorship of postgraduate students for the purposes of writing-up.

(iii) if the applicant has previously been granted leave as a Postgraduate Doctor or Dentist, the applicant must not be seeking entry clearance or leave to enter or remain to a date beyond 3 years from the date on which he was first granted leave to enter or remain in that category, and

(iv) if the applicant has previously been granted leave as a Tier 4 (General) Student to undertake a course as a postgraduate doctor or dentist, the applicant must not be seeking entry clearance or leave to enter or remain to a date beyond 3 years from the date on which the applicant was first granted leave to undertake such a course.'

3.111 Paragraphs 69–72 of the Tier 4 Policy Guidance deal with postgraduate doctors or dentists wishing to undertake a recognised Foundation Programme. The explanation provided in the guidance does not go beyond the remit of the Immigration Rules. Postgraduate doctors or dentists who were granted leave prior to 31 March 2009 should refer to Chapter 3 Section 6, IDI. To satisfy evidential requirements, please refer to the documents section below.

3.112 The Immigration Rules dealing with postgraduate doctors and dentists continue to reflect the policy aim of the Government to restrict access to UK foundation programmes and work as trainee doctor/dentist to those who have graduated from higher education institutions in the United Kingdom. The full history and background to how this category has been treated is set out in the House of Lords decision in *BAPIO* (*Bapio Action Ltd & Anor, R (on the application of) v Secretary of State for the Home Department & Anor* [2008] UKHL 27).

Official financial sponsorship

3.113 Paragraphs 245ZV(f) and 245ZX(g) of the Immigration Rules deal with additional requirements to be satisfied by officially sponsored students:

> 'if the applicant is currently being sponsored by a Government or international scholarship agency, or within the last 12 months has come to an end of such a period of sponsorship, the applicant must provide the unconditional written consent of the sponsoring Government or agency to the application and must provide the specified documents to show that this requirement has been met.'

3.114 An explanation of restrictions placed on students with official financial sponsorship is contained in paragraphs 44–47 of the Tier 4 Policy Guidance. Such a restriction is a PBS-wide phenomenon and is not limited to Tier 4. An official financial sponsor is defined in paragraph 44 as 'Her Majesty's Government, the student's home Government, the British Council or any international organisation, international company, university or UK independent school.' As of 21 April 2011 this definition is also reflected in paragraph 13(iii) of Appendix C to the Immigration Rules.

3.115 The meaning of 'sponsored' for the purposes of the guidance is qualified in paragraph 46 as being '*wholly* supported by an award which covers both fees and living costs' (added emphasis). This definition appears to contradict paragraphs 171 and 173 of the Tier 4 policy guidance that go on to explain that 'financial sponsorship is where a student is given money to cover *some or all* his/her course fees and/or living costs' and 'if the student's financial sponsor is only covering *some* of his/her course fees or living costs, he/she must show that he/she has the rest of the money needed' (added emphasis).

3.116 Paragraph 45 explains that within the last 12 months an applicant may have been financially sponsored as a student, a Tier 4 (General) or Tier 4 (Child) student, a student nurse, a student re-sitting an examination, a student writing up a thesis or a postgraduate doctor or dentist. Students currently sponsored by a Government or international scholarship agency or whose financial sponsorship ended within 12 months of their application being made must provide their financial sponsor's unconditional written consent together with their application (paragraph 47). The wording in paragraph 245ZV(f) of the Immigration Rules indicates that the applicant applying for entry clearance who is currently being sponsored or within the last 12 months was sponsored by an official financial sponsor must provide written consent rather than unconditional consent in writing. However, paragraph 245ZX(g) of the Immigration Rules requires the applicant to provide the unconditional written consent from an official financial sponsor when applying for leave to remain.

3.117 Entry Clearance Guidance STY5 helpfully provides a list of the main sponsored programmes for overseas students. The list is quoted directly from the source guidance on the UKBA Visa Services website:

FCO-funded programme	Countries to which applicable
British Marshall Scholarships FCO pays for all tuition fees and provide stipends	USA
Atlantic Fellowships	USA
Commonwealth Scholarship and Fellowship Plan (CSFP) (administered by the British Council and the Association of Commonwealth Universities) (Jointly funded with DFID)	All Commonwealth countries
Chevening Scholars including Jointly Funded Chevening Scholarships (jointly funded by FCO/industry/British universities and other interests)	Some specified or all countries

DFID funded programmes	**Countries to which applicable**
Technical Co-operation Training (TCT)	Developing countries
Commonwealth Scholarship and Fellowship Plan (CSFP) (administered by the British Council and the Association of Commonwealth Universities)	All Commonwealth countries
British Council funded and/or administered programmes	**Countries to which applicable**
United Nations (UN) Awards	All countries
European Commission (EC) Awards	All countries
Department for Department for Business, Enterprise and Regulatory Reform	**Countries to which applicable**
British Overseas Industrial Placement Scheme (BOND)	All countries
Department for Education and Skills funded programmes	**Countries to which applicable**
Overseas Research Students Awards Scheme (ORSAS)	All countries
Fulbright Scholarships	USA
Education and Training Group – British Council Exchange Programmes	All countries

3.118 STY5 goes on to give examples of non-Governmental organisations and institutions sponsor scholarship and award programmes for students wishing to study in the United Kingdom:

- Confederation of British Industries (CBI)
- Commonwealth Secretariat
- Nuffield Foundation
- The Royal Society
- The British Academy
- Welcome Trust
- Rhodes Scholarships Trust
- Goethe Institute
- Hornby Trust (managed by ENTS/GFS)
- European Young Lawyers (GFS/DATS)

- Spanish Banks programmes (GFS/DATS)

3.119 The guidance concludes by stating that 'many UK companies and universities also have similar sponsorship programmes.'[83] Some scholarship programmes are conditional on students fulfilling contractual terms subject to which funding is granted. It is important for students to be aware of the caveats prohibiting further study or switching into other immigration categories on completing studies as they may impede their ability to vary their leave within PBS, for at least 12 months.

3.120 Paragraph 88 of the Tier 4 Policy Guidance contains an additional provision outside the Immigration Rules. The paragraph states that 'if a Tier 4 (General) student has official financial sponsorship which wholly covers their fees and living costs, and the financial sponsor limits the time he/she may study in the UK, the permission to stay will be limited to that length of time plus the usual post-course period allowed.'

Please refer to the documents section for evidential requirements related to official financial sponsorship.

Courses below degree level

3.121 Further restrictions are imposed on students undertaking studies below degree level in paragraphs 245ZV(g) and 245ZX(h) of the Immigration Rules as follows:

> 'If the course is below degree level the grant of leave to remain[84] the applicant is seeking must not lead to the applicant having spent more than 3 years in the UK as a Tier 4 Migrant since the age of 18 studying courses that did not consist of degree level study.'[85]

3.122 Applicants aged 18 years and over cannot spend more than three years in the United Kingdom attending courses which are below degree level (paragraphs 245ZV(g) and 245ZX(h)). Paragraph 86 of the Tier 4 Policy Guidance states that this rule applies regardless of whether the three years are spent studying one course or several while paragraph 87 goes on to provide some reprieve against the rigidity of its application. As stated in **Chapter 7**, this presents an obstacle to continuity of stay in the United Kingdom.

3.123 However, the exemptions in paragraph 87 mean that the limit does not apply retrospectively to students studying under the Immigration Rules in force before 31 March 2009, nor does it apply to Tier 4 (General) students when they were 16 or 17 years old, Tier 4 (Child) students when they were aged 17 years or

83 STY5 List of main sponsored programmes for overseas students, UK Border Agency Visa Services, www.ukvisas.gov.uk/en/ecg/study/listmainsponsoredprogs.

84 In paragraph 245ZV(g) read the words 'leave to remain' as 'entry clearance'.

85 Paragraphs 245ZV(g)(1)–(2) and 245ZX(h)(1)–(2) were deleted by the Statement of Changes in Immigration Rules (HC 1148).

under, or any other non-Tier 4 category allowing study. Provisions related to work and work placements are examined further below.

3.124 From April 2012, the Government intends to set a maximum total period of five years that a Tier 4 (General) migrant can spend studying at degree level and above (NQF Levels 6 and 7/QCF Levels 6 and 7/SCQF Levels 9 to 11). The total time a Tier 4 (General) migrant can then spend in the United Kingdom (counting the period of three years spent studying at below degree level) will be limited to eight years. Some exceptions will be made for advanced courses. Time spent in the United Kingdom studying under the Tier 4 (Child) category will be excluded from these limits. Presumably, these limits will be put into place to prevent students from settling in the United Kingdom under the long residence provision.

Age related requirements

3.125 Pursuant to paragraph 245ZT of the Immigration Rules the Tier 4 (General) route is for migrants aged 16 and over coming to the United Kingdom to study. Paragraphs 245ZV(h) and 245ZX(i) state that a Tier 4 (General) migrant must be at least 16 years old. This is further qualified by paragraph 56 of the Tier 4 Policy Guidance which says students aged 16 or 17 years undertaking a course of study at or above NQF Level 3 have a choice between applying in the Tier 4 (General) or Tier 4 (Child) category. This must be agreed with the sponsor. Those aged 16 or 17 years who are applying under the Tier 4 (Child) category, should refer to the relevant section in this book.

3.126 Under paragraphs 245ZV(i)–(j) and 245ZX(j)–(k) of the Immigration Rules where the applicant is under the age of 18 years, their application must be supported by their parents, just one parent who bears sole responsibility for them, or legal guardian who must confirm that they consent to the arrangements made for the applicant's:

- travel to, reception and care in the United Kingdom (with regard to entry clearance applications); or
- care in the United Kingdom (with regard to applications for leave to remain).

Time restrictions related to extension applications

3.127 Students applying in-country must be conscious of the time gap between the date of expiry of their current leave and the start date of their course of study. Paragraph 245ZX(l) states that:

> 'the applicant must not be applying for leave to remain for the purpose of studies which would commence more than one month after the applicant's current entry clearance or leave to remain granted under these Rules expires.'[86]

86 The words 'granted under these Rules' were inserted by the Statement of Changes in Immigration Rules (HC 908).

3.128 Students whose leave ends more than a calendar month[87] before the start date of the next course of study are expected to leave the United Kingdom and apply for entry clearance at an overseas post (paragraph 89 of the Tier 4 Policy Guidance). Those applying for leave to remain in the United Kingdom will face a mandatory refusal.

3.129 There is nothing in the Tier 4 (General) provisions that requires leave to be refused if it is applied for after previous leave has run out. Therefore, if a Tier 4 (General) migrant fails to submit their extension application in time prior to the expiry of their leave and, as a result, becomes an overstayer, he or she can still submit their application.[88]

Period and conditions of grant

PERIOD OF GRANT

3.130 In accordance with paragraphs 245ZW(a) and 245ZY(a) entry clearance and leave to remain will be granted for the duration of the course subject to the table[89] set out in paragraphs 245ZW(b) and 245ZY(b) and notes accompanying it:

Type of course	**Period of entry clearance/leave to remain to be granted before the course starts**	**Period of entry clearance/leave to remain to be granted after the course ends**
12 months	1 month	4 months
6 months or more but less than 12 months	1 month	2 months
Pre-sessional course of less than 6 months	1 month	1 month
Course of less than 6 months that is not a pre-sessional course	7 days	7 days
Postgraduate doctor or dentist	1 month	1 month

3.131 Paragraph 83 of the Tier 4 Policy Guidance contains its own version of the table. Paragraph 84 states that 'a course will be considered to be 12 months long if

87 See the judgment of QI (para 245ZX(l) considered) Pakistan [2010] UKUT 217 (IAC) (6 July 2010) in which it was held that 'current leave to remain' means substantive leave rather than extended leave under the Immigration Act 1971, s 3C.

88 Entry clearance applications are caught by the general grounds of refusal in paragraph 320(7B) of the Immigration Rules.

89 The contents of tables denoting length of grant of entry clearance and leave to remain are identical and are combined into one table for ease of reference.

it lasts a full calendar year'. The notes following the table in the Immigration Rules state if the grant of entry clearance or leave to remain is made less than one month, or in the case of the course of less than six months that is not a pre-sessional course, less than seven days before the start of the course, entry clearance or leave to remain will be granted with immediate effect. The notes also define a pre-sessional course as 'a course which prepares a student for the student's main course of study in the UK' (paragraph 245ZW(b)(ii) of the Immigration Rules). A pre-sessional course is not otherwise defined in paragraph 6 of the Immigration Rules. Notably, in practice, immigration officials have not been applying the provision related to the period of grant of entry clearance or leave to remain consistently.

CONDITIONS OF GRANT

3.132 Entry clearance or leave to remain will be granted subject to the following conditions (paragraphs 245ZW(c) and 245ZY(c) of the Immigration Rules, respectively):

'(i) no recourse to public funds,
(ii) registration with the police, if this is required by paragraph 326 of these Rules,
(iii) no employment except:
  (1) employment during term time of no more than 20 hours per week and employment (of any duration) during vacations, where the student is following a course of degree level study and is either:
    (a) sponsored by a Sponsor that is a Recognised Body or a body in receipt of public funding as a higher education institution from the Department of Employment and Learning in Northern Ireland, the Higher Education Funding Council for England, the Higher Education Funding Council for Wales or the Scottish Funding Council; or
    (b) sponsored by an overseas higher education institution to undertake a short-term Study Abroad Programme in the United Kingdom.
  (2) employment during term time of no more than 10 hours per week and employment (of any duration) during vacations, where the student is following a course of below degree level study and is sponsored by a Sponsor that is a Recognised Body or a body in receipt of public funding as a higher education institution from the Department of Employment and Learning in Northern Ireland, the Higher Education Funding Council for England, the Higher Education Funding Council for Wales or the Scottish Funding Council,
  (3) employment during term time of no more than 10 hours per week and employment (of any duration) during vacations, where the student is following a course of study at any academic level and is sponsored by a Sponsor that is a publicly funded further education college,[90]

90 Sub-paragraphs (1)–(3) were substituted by the Statement of Changes in Immigration Rules (HC 1148).

(4) employment as part of a course-related work placement which forms an assessed part of the applicant's course and provided that any period that the applicant spends on that placement does not exceed half of the total length of the course undertaken in the UK except where it is a United Kingdom statutory requirement that the placement should exceed half the total length of the course.

(5) Employment as a Student Union Sabbatical Officer, for up to 2 years, provided the post is elective and is at the institution which is the applicant's Sponsor.

(6) Employment as a postgraduate doctor or dentist on a recognised Foundation Programme

provided that the migrant is not self-employed, or employed as a Doctor or Dentist in Training other than a vacancy on a recognised Foundation Programme, professional sportsperson (including a sports coach) or an entertainer, and provided that the migrant's employment would not fill a permanent full time vacancy other than a vacancy on a recognised Foundation Programme or as a sabbatical officer; and

(iv) no study except:

(1) study at the institution that the Confirmation of Acceptance for Studies Checking Service records as the migrant's Sponsor, or where the migrant was awarded points for a visa letter, study at the institution which issued that visa letter unless the migrant is studying at an institution which is a partner institution of the migrant's Sponsor.[91]

(2) until such time as a decision is received from the UK Border Agency on an application which is supported by a Confirmation of Acceptance for Studies assigned by a Highly Trusted Sponsor and which is made while the applicant has extant leave, and any appeal against that decision has been determined, study at the Highly Trusted Sponsor institution which the Confirmation of Acceptance for Studies Checking Service records as having assigned a Confirmation of Acceptance for Studies to the Tier 4 migrant; and

(3) supplementary study.'

In paragraphs 295–328 the Tier 4 Policy Guidance goes on to elaborate on the framework of work and study related conditions set out in the Rules.

WORK RELATED CONDITIONS

3.133 Paragraph 296 of the Tier 4 Policy Guidance states that:

'where a Tier 4 (General) student is following a course at NQF 6/QCF 6/SCQF 9 or above with a sponsor which is a UK Higher Education Institution, or is

91 The words 'unless the migrant is studying at an institution which is a partner institution of the migrant's Sponsor' were inserted into the Immigration Rules by the Statement of Changes in Immigration Rules (HC 908).

undertaking a short-term study abroad degree programme at an overseas Higher Education Institution, the following work is allowed:

- part-time during term-time, which is no more than 20 hours a week;
- full-time during vacations;
- on a work placement as part of the course;
- as a postgraduate doctor or dentist on a recognised Foundation Programme;
- as a student union sabbatical officer for up to two years.'

3.134 Paragraph 297 of the Tier Policy Guidance goes on to state that:

> 'where a Tier 4 (General) student is following a course at NQF 3,4 or 5/QCF 3, 4 or 5/SCQF 6, 7 or 8, with a sponsor which is a UK Higher Education Institution, the following work is allowed:
>
> - part-time during term-time, which is no more than 10 hours a week;
> - full-time during vacations;
> - on a work placement as part of the course;
> - as a student union sabbatical officer for up to two years.'

3.135 In following up the above, paragraph 298 of the Tier 4 Policy Guidance states that:

> 'where a Tier 4 (General) student is following a course at any level with a sponsor which is a publicly funded further education college, the following work is allowed:
>
> - part-time during term-time, which is no more than 10 hours a week;
> - full-time during vacations;
> - on a work placement as part of a course where the Tier 4 (General) student is studying with a Highly Trusted Sponsor or with any sponsor where the course is at NQF 6/QCF 6/SCQF 9 or above.
> - as a student union sabbatical officer for up to two years.'

Therefore, new students who are not sponsored by a higher education institution, a publicly funded further education college or a short-term study abroad degree programme will be prohibited from working while undertaking studies in the United Kingdom (paragraph 299 of the Tier 4 Policy Guidance).[92]

92 85% of respondents (overall number of respondents: 26,382) to the Tier 4 consultation disagreed with the proposal to further limit students' entitlement to work and 56% of respondents (overall number of respondents: 26,279) disagreed with having to simplify the rules governing students' entitlement to work by restricting it to set times. Consultation on the student immigration system: 7th December 2010 to 31st January 2011. Consultation questionnaire results, UK Border Agency, March 2011, p 9 www.ukba.homeoffice.gov.uk/sitecontent/documents/policyandlaw/consultations/students/student-consultation-results.pdf?view=Binary.

3.136 In accordance with paragraph 300, Tier 4 (General) students must not:

- fill a full-time permanent vacancy (except in the case of a recognised Foundation Programme);
- be self-employed;
- employed as a doctor in training (except in the case of a recognised Foundation Programme);
- employed as a professional sportsperson (including coach) or entertainer.

3.137 The UKBA made an announcement about the change in the work related conditions on 3 March 2010.[93] From July 2011, students applying for entry clearance or leave to remain will not be granted permission to work in the United Kingdom unless they are sponsored by a higher education institution or a publicly funded further education institution. Further changes to the work related conditions were announced on 13 June 2011 although these relate to Tier 4 (General) students.[94]

CONDITIONS RELATED TO WORK PLACEMENTS

3.138 A Tier 4 (General) student will be allowed to do a work placement as part of their studies in the United Kingdom provided that the work placement forms an assessed part of the course (paragraph 305 of the Tier 4 Policy Guidance), is not more than 50% of the length of the course in the United Kingdom unless there is a statutory requirement to the contrary (paragraph 306) and the student is (according to paragraphs 305 and 308):

- a Tier 4 (General) student studying a course of degree level study or above; or
- a Tier 4 (General) student studying a foundation degree course; or
- a Tier 4 (General) student studying a course with a Highly Trusted Sponsor; or
- a Tier 4 (General) student enrolled on a higher education course at an overseas higher education institution and is doing part of the course in the UK.

3.139 Tier 4 sponsors will bear responsibility for their students undertaking work placements as part of their course (paragraph 309). For further information about work placements please refer to paragraphs 364–370 of the Sponsor Guidance. Sponsors who are A rated or B rated with an action plan under the Sponsor Guidance in place before 5 September 2011 cannot offer courses to new Tier 4 (General) students that are below QCF or NQF level 6 and include work placements

93 Changes to Tier 4 student visa applications from 3 March 2010, UK Border Agency, 3 March 2010, http://webarchive.nationalarchives.gov.uk/20100303141249/http://www.bia.homeoffice.gov.uk/sitecontent/newsarticles/2010/255022/tier4-visa-applications.

94 Next set of changes to student visa rules is announced, UK Border Agency, 13 June 2011, /www.ukba.homeoffice.gov.uk/sitecontent/newsarticles/2011/june/17-t4-changes.

(with the exception of foundation degrees). From April 2012, only higher education institutions will be able to offer courses including work placements where the minimum ratio of study to work will be 50:50. Students starting new courses including work placements elsewhere can only do so where the minimum ratio of study to work will be 66:33.

CONDITIONS RELATED TO PRE-SESSIONAL COURSES

3.140 Prior to 21 April 2011 most of the conditions attached to pre-sessional courses were set out in the Tier 4 Policy Guidance are outside the Immigration Rules. These have been done away with. Requirements set out in the Tier 4 Policy Guidance as at 21 April 2011 have been brought in line with the amended Immigration Rules.

3.141 The introductory (unnumbered) paragraph preceding paragraph 310 of the Tier 4 Policy Guidance describes a pre-sessional course to prepare a student for the main course of study in the United Kingdom as an intensive English language course or any other course. As per paragraph 310 of the Tier 4 Policy Guidance a Tier 4 (General) student can be given permission to stay to cover both his/her pre-sessional course and the main course of study where the CAS is:

- '• issued by a UK Higher Education Institution to cover both a pre-sessional course of no longer than three months' duration; and
- the applicant has an unconditional offer of a place on a course of degree level study at that UK Higher Education Institution; and
- the course of degree level study commences no later than one month after the end date of the pre-sessional course.'

The above requirements are now in line with paragraph 120A(b) of Appendix A to the Immigration Rules. All other Tier 4 students who do not fall within the above requirements but wish to undertake a pre-sessional course before their main course of study will have to make a separate Tier 4 application to cover each course and both courses must satisfy the full Tier 4 criteria including the course level and the English language testing requirements, where appropriate (paragraph 312 of the Tier 4 Policy Guidance).

STUDY RELATED CONDITIONS

3.142 On 30 September 2009 the UKBA announced that it would be 'tying' Tier 4 students' permission to stay in the United Kingdom to their sponsors provided they made their application on or after 5 October 2009. The relevant part of the announcement reads as follows:

> 'On 5 October 2009, new Tier 4 students' permission to stay in the United Kingdom will be 'tied' to the education provider that is sponsoring them. This will bring Tier 4 in line with other tiers of the points-based system.

From 5 October, every new Tier 4 student will find their sponsor's reference number on the vignette in their passport or on their identity card for foreign nationals.

In future, if a student wants to study with a new Tier 4 sponsor and they made their last application for a Tier 4 visa **on or after 5 October 2009**, they will need to apply for a new Tier 4 visa. They will not be allowed to begin studying with the new education provider until they have received a decision on the outcome of their application – if they do so, they will be committing a criminal offence for which they could be prosecuted or removed from the country.

We have been asked whether students in this situation will be able to begin studying with the new education provider, at their own risk, before they have received a decision on their application. The UK Border Agency cannot condone a criminal offence, and therefore cannot advise students that this is an option for them.'[95]

3.143 This restriction stems from the enactment of the Borders, Citizenship and Immigration Act 2009, s 50. Section 50 inserted sub-paragraph (ia) 'a condition restricting his studies in the United Kingdom' into the Immigration Act 1971, s 3(1)(c). Failure to observe the condition of leave pursuant to the Immigration Act 1971, s 24(1)(b) is an offence punishable on summary conviction with a fine of not more than level 5 on the standard scale or with imprisonment for not more than six months. In accordance with the Tier 4 questions & answers brochure published for students in September 2009 'senior officials within UK Border Agency took the decision that the condition should be applied to new Tier 4 applicants from the earliest opportunity, in parallel with the implementation of phase 3 of Tier 4.'[96] Although s 50(2) allows the Secretary of State to apply the restriction to those granted leave before the Act came into force, it was decided not to use that provision retrospectively at the time.

3.144 On 23 July 2010 the UKBA made an allowance for Highly Trusted Sponsors in the Immigration Rules, thereby relaxing the application of the Borders, Citizenship and Immigration Act 2009, s 50. In his statement the Minister for Immigration stated on 22 July 2010 that:

'In recognition of the high levels of student compliance among Highly Trusted sponsors; I have agreed an additional freedom for their students which is being introduced by the change to the Immigration Rules for Tier 4 (General) and Tier 4 (Child) students today. The change will allow the students of Highly Trusted

95 Two new policy announcements for Tier 4 of the points-based system, UK Border Agency, 30 September 2009, http://webarchive.nationalarchives.gov.uk/20091108000432/http://www.bia.homeoffice.gov.uk/sitecontent/newsarticles/2009/september/pbs-t4-extending-tying.

96 Tier 4 questions & answers, UK Border Agency, September 2009, p 32 www.ukba.homeoffice.gov.uk/sitecontent/documents/employersandsponsors/pointsbasedsystem/t4-qanda-sponsors.

sponsors to commence their studies with them before receipt of UKBA's decision on their application.

In addition, for the avoidance of doubt, I am also making changes today to our general grounds for refusing applicants, (for example on the basis of submitting false documents), to make it absolutely clear that these provisions also apply to applicants who have overstayed their previous permission to be here.'[97]

3.145 Therefore, pursuant to the Tier 4 Policy Guidance (paragraphs 315–318) students who made their last Tier 4 application on or after 5 October 2009 and now want to study with a new Tier 4 sponsor, must apply for new permission to stay (paragraph 315). According to paragraph 316 'a student can start his/her new course before his/her new Tier 4 application has been approved if:

- he/she has applied for permission to stay to study with a Tier 4 sponsor that has a highly trusted sponsor rating; and
- he/she has existing leave to study in the UK; and
- his/her Tier 4 sponsor has assigned a Confirmation of Acceptance for Studies to the student for his/her new course.

A Tier 4 student does this at his/her own risk as it is possible that his/her application will be refused.'

Consequently, students studying with Tier 4 sponsors who have A or B rating[98] cannot commence their new course until their Tier 4 application is approved (paragraph 317).

3.146 In accordance with paragraphs 319–323 of the Tier 4 Policy Guidance, students who made their last Tier 4 application before 5 October 2009 and want to study with a new Tier 4 sponsor from 21 April 2011 must get permission from the UKBA provided they have time left in their existing leave and want to do the same or a different course of study with a new Tier 4 sponsor (paragraph 319). Those who applied for entry clearance or leave to remain between 31 March 2009 and 4 October 2009 must do so by using the Application for Permission to Change Tier 4 Educational Sponsor (T4 (PTS)). The application can only be made by post and costs £160. The application form must be sent to:

UK Border Agency

T4 Permission to Switch
P.O. Box 498
Durham
DH99 1W

97 Written ministerial statement on changes to the immigration points based system, UK Border Agency, 22 July 2010, www.ukba.homeoffice.gov.uk/sitecontent/documents/news/wms-on-the-changes-to-pbs.pdf.
98 A (Trusted) or B (Sponsor).

Prior to 21 April 2011 Tier 4 students could write to the UKBA (migrantreporting@ukba.gsi.gov.uk) and ask for permission by providing the new of the new course, its start and finish dates, and the name of the new Tier 4 sponsor, its address and contact details.

3.147 The UKBA will then consider the switching application and write to the student confirming that he or she is allowed to use his or her existing leave to study with the new Tier 4 sponsor provided that the sponsor is approved by the UKBA and is on the Register of Sponsors, the sponsor wants to act as the student's new Tier 4 sponsor, and the course meets the Tier 4 requirements (paragraph 320).[99] Students can start the new course before getting permission from the UKBA but they will do so at their own risk as permission could be refused (paragraph 321). Under the Immigration Rules, the UKBA can limit a student's permission to stay as a student if he or she changes their Tier 4 sponsor without getting permission (paragraph 322).

3.148 Students must also be aware of policy provisions concerned with taking up a different course of study with the same Tier 4 sponsor (paragraphs 324–326), consequences of finishing the course early (paragraphs 327–328) and supplementary study (paragraph 313).

DOCUMENTS

3.149 In order to make a valid entry clearance or in-country extension application as a Tier 4 (General) student, an applicant must meet the requirements of the Immigration Rules and relevant policy and score 40 points by complying with the points scoring requirements set out in Appendices A and C to the Immigration Rules and providing documents specified in Tier 4 policy guidance. The application must be accompanied by:

- a specified application form;
- photographs;
- specified fee;
- biometric data;
- passports (current and expired);
- BRP or ICFN (if applicable);
- police certificate (if applicable);
- a print-out of an ATAS clearance certificate (if applicable);

99 Students are allowed to continue studying a course at CEFR level A2 or above.

- evidence of English language competence (if applicable);
- letter from parent(s) or legal guardian (applicable to students who are 16 or 17 years old and living independently while studying in the UK);
- specified documents related to CAS and maintenance (funds); and
- documents related to accommodation in the UK (optional, not specified in the Tier 4 policy guidance) (evidence which is not specified in the policy guidance will not go towards scoring points).

3.150 As PBS applications are evidence and content sensitive, applicants must understand which of the documents specified in the Tier 4 policy guidance apply to them and what information they should contain to satisfy the point scoring requirements. Adult students considered to be low risk will have their evidence treated in accordance with the differentiation arrangements. The particulars of each document are outlined in bullet-point, template or narrative form in the Tier 4 policy guidance. Given the changing nature of the Tier 4 policy guidance, the documents and their contents have been modified a number of times since 31 March 2009 and will continue to do so. Therefore, applicants must rely on the Tier 4 policy guidance and other requirements which are in force at the time of the application.

FORMS

3.151

- VAF9 PBS Personal Details form (online or hard copy) must be submitted together with Appendix 8 (in hard copy only) (for use in entry clearance applications).
- Application for a Grant of Leave and Biometric Immigration Document under Tier 4 (General) Student – Main Applicant (Tier 4 (G)[100] (for use in leave to remain applications).
- Application for Permission to Change Tier 4 Educational Sponsor (T4 (PTS)) (for by Tier 4 migrants wishing to change their Tier 4 sponsor).

100 UKBA published a number of versions of the Tier 4 in-country application form from 31 March 2009 including version 03/09 (to be used from 31 March 2009), version 06/09 (to be used from 1 June 2009), version 10/09 (to be used from 5 October 2009), version 02/10 (to be used from 22 February 2010), version 07/10 (to be used from 23 July 2010), version 09/10 (to be used from 6 September 2010), version 11/10 (to be used from 22 November 2010) and version 04/11 (to be used from 6 April 2011). This is not an exhaustive list. In accordance with paragraph 34I of the Immigration Rules 'where an application or claim is made no more than 21 days after the date on which a form is specified under the immigration rules and on a form that was permitted for such application or claim immediately prior to the date of such specification, the application or claim shall be deemed to have been made on the specified form.'

GENERAL SPECIFICATIONS RELATED TO DOCUMENTS

3.152 There are also general specifications that apply to all the documents specified in the Tier 4 policy guidance. According to paragraph 13 of the Tier 4 Policy Guidance, documents must be:

- issued by an authorised official of the issuing organisation;
- be original (unless stated otherwise in the Tier 4 Policy Guidance); and
- be on the official letter-headed paper or stationery of the issuing organisation.

Documents related to maintenance (funds) must be on the official letter-headed paper or stationery of the financial institution, issued by an authorised person and dated no more than one month before the application is submitted.

TRANSLATIONS OF DOCUMENTS IN SUPPORT OF APPLICATIONS MADE IN THE UNITED KINGDOM

3.153 Original documents which are not in English or Welsh must be accompanied by a fully certified translation. The translation must be done by a professional translator or a translation company. In line with paragraph 14 of the Tier 4 Policy Guidance, translations must include:

- the date of translation; and
- details of the translator or the translation company's credentials; and
- confirmation that it is an accurate translation of the original document; and
- the translator or the translation company's contact details; and
- the original signature of the translator or an authorised official at the translation company.

TRANSLATIONS OF DOCUMENTS IN SUPPORT OF APPLICATIONS MADE OUTSIDE THE UNITED KINGDOM

3.154 Original documents which are not in English or Welsh must be accompanied by a full translation that can be independently verified by the UKBA. In line with paragraph 15 of the Tier 4 Policy Guidance, original translations must contain:

- confirmation from the translator or the translation company that it is an accurate translation of the original document; and
- the date of translation; and
- the full name and signature of the translator or an authorised official of the translation company; and
- the translator or the translation company's contact details.

Translations of overseas qualifications or award certificates will not be taken directly as proof of the academic level of the award and will be verified against UK NARIC to assess equivalency (paragraph 16 of the Tier 4 Policy Guidance). These general specifications related to the form in which documents should be presented, are not stipulated in the Immigration Rules. While non-compliance with these specifications is often cited as a reason for refusal, it can be challenged.

DOCUMENTS RELATED TO CAS

3.155 Paragraph 118 of the Tier 4 Policy Guidance states that in order to claim 30 points for a valid CAS, the applicant must send the following documents:

- Paragraphs 119–126 of the Tier 4 Policy Guidance deal with the specified documents related to CAS (excluding students undertaking English language courses at level B2 of the CEFR whose CAS was assigned prior to 21 April 2011 and students undertaking Foundation Programme as Postgraduate Doctors or Dentists);
- Paragraphs 127–132 of the Tier 4 Policy Guidance deal with ATAS related to CAS;
- Paragraphs 133–138 of the Tier 4 Policy Guidance deal with the specified documents related to CAS assigned prior to 21 April 2011 to students undertaking English language courses at level B2 of the CEFR;
- Paragraphs 139–140 of the Tier 4 Policy Guidance deals with the specified documents related to students undertaking Foundation Programme as Postgraduate Doctors or Dentists.

3.156 Applicants should ask their Tier 4 sponsor for a print out of their CAS statement and find out about the evidence that the Tier 4 sponsor used to offer them a place on the course so that they could submit these documents with their application. The specified documents below are named as they are in the policy guidance. Applicants will need to refer to the policy guidance which details the content of each specified document.

- CAS reference number which must be entered on the applicant's Tier 4 (General) application form;
- Documents related to CAS (excluding students undertaking English language courses at level B2 of the CEFR whose CAS was assigned prior to 21 April 2011 and students undertaking Foundation Programme as Postgraduate Doctors or Dentists):
    - — Original certificate of qualification, or
    - — Original transcript of results, or
    - — If assessed by other means (e.g. references, portfolio of artwork, interview or internal test or entrance exam) for a course at NQF level 3 or above, then the applicant does not have to include these documents with the application (although the Tier 4 sponsor must clearly indicate the form of assessment on the CAS), or

- If offered a place on the course because of progress made on the existing course, then the applicant will not have to send any documents with the application (although the Tier 4 sponsor must clearly indicate the form of assessment on the CAS), or
- If the applicant has had their English language competence assessed by way of an English language test, a qualification taught in a majority speaking English country, or a course completed as a Tier 4 (Child) student, the Tier 4 sponsor will need to include this information in the CAS and the applicant will need to add the requisite document to their application. If the Tier 4 sponsor has used an approved English language test to check that the applicant is competent in English language, then the applicant must include the test certificate with the application. However, if the applicant is using Pearson Test of English Academic (PTE Academic), then he/she will not receive a hard copy paper certificate. Instead, they must provide:
  - ♦ A print out of their online score report;

- ATAS Clearance Certificate
  - A print out of the applicant's ATAS clearance certificate;
- Documents related to CAS assigned prior to 21 April 2011 to students undertaking English language courses at level B2 of the CEFR
  - Original certificate of qualification, or
  - Original transcript of results, or
  - Original reference, or
  - If offered a place on the course because of progress made on the existing course, then the applicant will not have to send any documents with the application (although the Tier 4 sponsor must clearly indicate the form of assessment on the CAS);
- Documents related to students undertaking Foundation Programme as Postgraduate Doctors or Dentists
  - Original certificate and/or original transcript of results of a UK recognised degree in medicine or dentistry completed by the applicant whilst in the UK as a student.

DOCUMENTS RELATED TO MAINTENANCE (FUNDS)

3.157 Paragraph 174 of the Tier 4 Policy Guidance states that in order to claim 10 points for maintenance (funds), the applicant must provide evidence that he/she:

- has paid all or part of the course and accommodation fees to the Tier 4 sponsor; and/or
- is receiving official financial sponsorship; and/or
- has sufficient funds to cover the remaining course fees and living costs, if any (either by using his own money, his parents/legal guardian's money or a personal loan).

3.158 Paragraphs 175–191 of the Tier 4 Policy Guidance deal with the specified documents related to maintenance (funds). Difficulties often arise with the evidential requirements in relation to maintenance (funds) and not only because applicants are not able to comply with the substantive requirements. Banks in the UK and overseas have their internal document templates which do not always adhere to the content prerequisites set out in the Tier 4 policy guidance. Applicants are therefore advised to make special requests with reference to the Tier 4 Policy Guidance. With regard to the official financial sponsorship, some Tier 4 sponsors acting as official financial sponsors have made special arrangements with the UKBA and students applying for extension of leave in the UK must be aware of these when answering questions L14 and L17 on the application form. From July 2011 the UKBA will introduce a streamlined application process for low-risk students in respect of documentary evidence of maintenance and qualifications and will also revise its maintenance requirements.

- Documents needed to show money already paid to the Tier 4 sponsor
  - Original paper receipt issued by the UK Tier 4 sponsor confirming that the student has paid all or part of the fees.
- Documents needed to show official financial sponsorship
  - Letter of confirmation from the official financial sponsor on official letter-headed paper or stationery of the organisation of the official financial sponsor and have the official stamp of that organisation on it (advisable to include consent of the official financial sponsor to the applicant making the application in this letter).
- Documents needed to show money available to the student
  - Personal bank or building society statements covering a consecutive 28 day period ending no more than one month before the date of the student's application; or
  - Building society pass book covering a consecutive 28 day period ending no more than one month before the date of the student's application; or
  - Letter from the student's bank confirming funds have been held for a consecutive 28 day period ending no more than one month before the date of the application; or
  - Letter from a financial institution regulated by either the Financial Services Authority or, in the case of overseas accounts, the home regulator (official

regulatory body for the country the institution is in and where the money is held) confirming funds have been held of a consecutive 28 day period ending no more than one month before the date of the application; or

— Letter from a financial institution regulated by either the Financial Services Authority or, in the case of overseas accounts, the home regulator (official regulatory body for the country the institution is in and where the money is held) confirming the loan.

- Using money held by parent(s)/legal guardian
  - — Student's birth certificate showing names of parent(s); or
  - — Student's certificate of adoption showing names of both parent(s) or legal guardian; or
  - — A court document naming the student's legal guardian; and
  - — Letter from parent(s) or legal guardian (which must confirm the relationship between them and consent for use of the funds to study in the UK).

Parental consent for Tier 4 (General) students who are 16 or 17 years old

3.159 In line with paragraphs 192–193 of the Tier 4 Policy Guidance, students who are 16 or 17 year old have a legal right to live independently and make their own accommodation arrangements. Their parent(s) or legal guardian must consent to this and provide the following document:

- A letter from parent(s) or legal guardian confirming the relationship between them and the applicant and giving their consent to the application and to the care, travel and accommodation arrangements. Contents of this letter will vary depending on whether the Tier 4 (General) student is applying for entry clearance or leave to remain.

Tier 4 (General) in-country applications

3.160 Applicants and their dependants will need to submit for biometric data collection at a time specified by the UKBA, depending on whether their application is made by post, courier or at a Public Enquiry Office. If their application is successful, applicants and their dependants will be issued with biometric residence permits. In-country applications for initial grant of leave (switching) or an extension of leave under Tier 4 (General) can be made using the application form noted above either by post, courier or at a Public Enquiry Office at a cost[101] of £386 (for a main applicant applying by post or courier) or £702 (for a main applicant applying at a Public Enquiry Office). The cost of applications to change a Tier 4 sponsor is £160, these can be submitted by post only and sent to the address on the form.

101 Costs were last revised on 6 April 2011.

Applications made by post should be sent to:	Applications made by courier should be sent to:
UK Border Agency Tier 4 PO Box 500 Durham DH99 1WJ	UK Border Agency Tier 4 Millburngate House Millburngate Durham DH97 1PA

Dependants of Tier 4 (General) students

3.161 Entry of family members of Tier 4 (General) students to the UK is regulated by paragraphs 319A–319K of the Immigration Rules, Appendix E to the Immigration Rules and Points Based System (Dependant) Policy Guidance. These provisions are generic and apply to dependants of migrants in such PBS categories as Tier 1, Tier 2, Tier 4 and Tier 5 (Temporary Worker) referred to in the Immigration Rules as Relevant Points Based System Migrants. There is a separate generic application form for dependants of Relevant Points Based System Migrants. Dependants of Tier 4 (General) migrants making a leave to remain application must at the same time apply for a Biometric Immigration Document using the same form (please see above for information about Biometric Immigration Documents). Family members include spouses, civil partners, unmarried or same-sex partners (collectively referred to as 'partners' below) and children under the age of 18 of Tier 4 (General) students. Entry clearance is compulsory for partners and children (paragraphs 319B and 319G of the Immigration Rules).

3.162 Partners must satisfy the requirements set out in paragraph 319C of the Immigration Rules to qualify for entry clearance or leave to remain. These are quoted below:

'(a) The applicant must not fall for refusal under the general grounds for refusal, and if applying for leave to remain, must not be an illegal entrant.

(b) The applicant must be the spouse or civil partner, unmarried or same-sex partner of a person who:

- (i) has valid leave to enter or remain as a Relevant Points Based System Migrant, or
- (ii) is, at the same time, being granted entry clearance or leave to remain as a Relevant Points Based System Migrant.

(c) An applicant who is the unmarried or same-sex partner of a Relevant Points Based System Migrant must also meet the following requirements:

- (i) any previous marriage or civil partnership or similar relationship by the applicant or the Relevant Points Based System Migrant with another person must have permanently broken down,

(ii) the applicant and the Relevant Points Based System Migrant must not be so closely related that they would be prohibited from marrying each other in the UK, and

(iii) the applicant and the Relevant Points Based System Migrant must have been living together in a relationship similar to marriage or civil partnership for a period of at least 2 years.

(d) The marriage or civil partnership, or relationship similar to marriage or civil partnership, must be subsisting at the time the application is made.

(e) The applicant and the Relevant Points Based System Migrant must intend to live with the other as their spouse or civil partner, unmarried or same-sex partner throughout the applicants stay in the UK.

(f) The applicant must not intend to stay in the UK beyond any period of leave granted to the Relevant Points Based System Migrant .

(g) Unless the Relevant Points Based System Migrant is a Tier 1 (Investor) Migrant, there must be a sufficient level of funds available to the applicant, as set out in Appendix E.

(h) An applicant who is applying for leave to remain, must have, or have last been granted, leave:

(i) as the Partner of a Relevant Points Based System Migrant,

(ii) as the spouse or civil partner, unmarried or same-sex partner of a person with leave under another category of these Rules who has since been granted, or is, at the same time, being granted leave to remain as a Relevant Points Based System Migrant, or

(iii) in any other category of these Rules, provided the Relevant Points Based System Migrant has, or is being granted, leave to remain as a Tier 5 (Temporary Worker) Migrant in the creative and sporting subcategory on the basis of having met the requirement at paragraph 245ZQ(b)(ii).

(i) If the Relevant Points Based System Migrant is a Tier 4 (General) Student,[102]

(1) the Relevant Points Based System Migrant must be applying for a course of study of more than six months duration and must have or have last had entry clearance, leave to enter or leave to remain as a Tier 4 (General) Student or Student for a course of more than six months duration within the three months immediately preceding the date of the application; and

(2) the Partner must have or have last had entry clearance, leave to enter or leave to remain as the Partner of a Tier 4 (General) Student or Student with leave for a course of more than six months duration within the three months immediately preceding the date of the application; and

(3) the Relevant Points Based System Migrant and Partner must be applying at the same time; or

102 The word 'Migrant' was supplemented with '(General) Student' by the Statement of Changes in Immigration Rules (HC 908).

(4) the Relevant Points Based System Migrant must be a Government Sponsored student who is applying for or has entry clearance or leave to remain for a course of study that is longer than six months; or

(5) the Relevant Points Based System Migrant must be undertaking a course which is 12 months or longer in duration, and is of postgraduate level study, sponsored by a Sponsor which is a Recognised Body or a body in receipt of funding as a higher education institution from the Department for Employment and Learning in Northern Ireland, the Higher Education Funding Council for England, the Higher Education Funding Council for Wales or the Scottish Funding Council'.[103]

Students applying for their initial grant of leave from 4 July 2011 will be able to sponsor their family members provided their course is at least 12 months in duration and the student is either Government sponsored or undertaking an NQF Level 7/QCF Level 7/SCQF Level 11 or above postgraduate degree course at a higher education institution. Their dependants – spouses/partners and children under the age of 18 – will be able to work.[104] Dependants with existing permission seeking to extend their stay in the United Kingdom will be allowed to do so provided they make their application at the same time as the Tier 4 (General) student applying for extension of leave to undertake a course of study which is six months or longer. See also paragraphs 290–291 of the Tier 4 Policy Guidance.

3.163 Period and conditions of grant of entry clearance and leave to remain are addressed in paragraph 319D of the Immigration Rules. Partners of Tier 4 (General) migrants may be granted entry clearance or leave to remain 'for a period which expires on the same day as the leave granted to the Relevant Points Based System Migrant.' If granted, leave will be subject to partners:

- having no recourse to public funds;
- registering with the police, if required in line with paragraph 326 of the Immigration Rules;
- not being employed as a Doctor or Dentist in Training (subject to further conditions in paragraph 319D(iii));

103 Sub-paragraphs (i)(1)–(5) were inserted by the Statement of Changes in Immigration Rules (HC 1148).

104 51% of respondents (overall number of respondents: 25,988) to the Tier 4 consultation agreed that that only those studying for longer than 12 months should be allowed to bring in their dependants and 73% of respondents (overall number of respondents: 25,958) disagreed that dependants should be banned from working. Consultation on the student immigration system: 7th December 2010 to 31st January 2011. Consultation questionnaire results", UK Border Agency, March 2011, p 10 www.ukba.homeoffice.gov.uk/sitecontent/documents/policyandlaw/consultations/students/student-consultation-results.pdf?view=Binary.

- not being employed if the Tier 4 (General) student is applying for leave for less than 12 months or the Tier 4 (General) student is following a course of study below degree level.

3.164 Children under 18 years wishing to qualify for entry clearance or leave to remain as dependants of Tier 4 (General) migrants must satisfy the following requirements pursuant to paragraph 319H of the Immigration Rules quoted below:

'(a) The applicant must not fall for refusal under the general grounds for refusal, and if applying for leave to remain, must not be an illegal entrant.
(b) The applicant must be the child of a parent who:
 (i) has valid leave to enter or remain as a Relevant Points Based System Migrant, or
 (ii) is, at the same time, being granted entry clearance or leave to remain as a Relevant Points Based System Migrant.
(c) The applicant must be under the age of 18 on the date the application is made, or if over 18 and applying for leave to remain, must have, or have last been granted, leave as the child of a Relevant Points Based System Migrant or as the child of the parent who had leave under another category of these Rules and who has since been granted, or, is at the same time being granted, leave to remain as a Relevant Points Based System Migrant.
(d) The applicant must not be married or in a civil partnership, must not have formed an independent family unit, and must not be leading an independent life.
(e) The applicant must not intend to stay in the UK beyond any period of leave granted to the Relevant Points Based System Migrant parent.
(f) Both of the applicant's parents must either be lawfully present in the UK, or being granted entry clearance or leave to remain at the same time as the applicant, unless:
 (i) The Relevant Points Based System Migrantis [sic] the applicant's sole surviving parent, or
 (ii) The Relevant Points Based System Migrant parent has and has had sole responsibility for the applicant's upbringing, or
 (iii) There are serious or compelling family or other considerations which would make it desirable not to refuse the application and suitable arrangements have been made in the UK for the applicant's care.
(g) Unless the Relevant Points Based System Migrant is a Relevant Points Based System (Investor) Migrant, there must be a sufficient level of funds available to the applicant, as set out in Appendix E.
(h) an applicant who is applying for leave to remain must have, or have last been granted leave as the child of a parent who had leave under any category of these Rules.[105]

105 Prior to 21 April 2011, the wording of paragraph 319H(h) of the Immigration Rules was as follows: 'an applicant who is applying for leave to remain must have, or have last been granted leave'. The wording was amended by the Statement of Changes in Immigration Rules (HC 908).

(i) If the Relevant Points Based System Migrant is a Tier 4 (General) Student,[106]

(1) the Relevant Points Based System Migrant must be applying for a course of study of more than six months duration and must have or have last had entry clearance, leave to enter or leave to remain as a Tier 4 (General) Student or Student for a course of more than six months duration within the three months immediately preceding the date of the application; and

(2) the Child must have or last have had entry clearance, leave to enter or leave to remain as the Child of a Tier 4 (General) Student or Student with leave for a course of more than six months duration within the three months immediately preceding the date of the application; and

(3) the Relevant Points Based System Migrant and Child must be applying at the same time; or

(4) the Relevant Points Based System Migrant must be a Government Sponsored student who is applying for or has entry clearance or leave to remain for a course of study that is longer than six months; or

(5) the Relevant Points Based System Migrant must be undertaking a course which is 12 months or longer in duration, and is of post-graduate level study, sponsored by a Sponsor which is a Recognised Body or a body in receipt of funding as a higher education institution from the Department for Employment and Learning in Northern Ireland, the Higher Education Funding Council for England, the Higher Education Funding Council for Wales or the Scottish Funding Council.[107]

(j) A Child whose parent is a Relevant Points Based System Migrant, who is a Tier 4 (General) Student or Student, and who does not otherwise meet the requirements of paragraph 319H(i):

(1) must have been born during the Relevant Points Based System Migrant's most recent grant of entry clearance, leave to enter or leave to remain as a Tier 4 (General) Student or Student with leave for a course of more than six months duration; or

(2) where the Relevant Points Based System Migrant's most recent grant of entry clearance, leave to enter or leave to remain was to re-sit examinations or repeat a module of a course, must either have been born during a period of leave granted for the purposes of re-sitting examinations or repeating a module of a course or during the Relevant Points Based System Migrant's grant of leave for a course of more than six months, where that course is the same as the one for which the most recent grant of leave was to re-sit examinations or repeat a module; or

106 The word 'Migrant' was supplemented with '(General) Student' by the Statement of Changes in Immigration Rules (HC 908).

107 Sub-paragraphs (i)(1)–(5) were inserted by the Statement of Changes in Immigration Rules (HC 1148).

(3) must have been born no more than three months after the expiry of that most recent grant of leave; and

(4) must be applying for entry clearance."[108]

See paragraphs 290–291 of the Tier 4 Policy Guidance (as in respect of paragraph 319C of the Immigration Rules).

3.165 Period and conditions of grant are set out in paragraph 319I of the Immigration Rules stipulating that entry clearance or leave to remain will be granted to children 'for a period which expires on the same day as the leave granted to the Relevant Points Based System Migrant parent'. If granted, leave will be subject to children:

- having no recourse to public funds;
- registering with the police, if required in line with paragraph 326 of the Immigration Rules;
- not being employed if the Tier 4 (General) student is applying for leave for less than 12 months or the Tier 4 (General) student is following a course of study below degree level.

3.166 Requirements for indefinite leave to remain are set out in paragraphs 319E and 319J of the Immigration Rules. As leave granted to Tier 4 (General) migrants does not lead to settlement outright (unless they switch into another category or qualify under the long residence provisions), partners and children of Tier 4 (General) migrants are unlikely to qualify for indefinite leave to remain under these provisions.

MAINTENANCE (FUNDS)

3.167 Family members must fulfil the maintenance requirement referred to in paragraphs 319C(g) and 319H(g) of the Immigration Rules by satisfying the requirements set out in Appendix E dealing with maintenance (funds) for the family of Relevant Points Based Systems Migrants.

3.168 Moreover, main applicants and their dependants making applications at the same time must be mindful of paragraph 1A(h)[109] of Appendix C to the Immigration Rules which states the following:

> 'Where the application is made at the same time as applications by the partner or child of the applicant (such that the applicant is a Relevant Points Based

108 Sub-paragraphs (j)(1)–(4) were inserted by the Statement of Changes in Immigration Rules (HC 1148).

109 Inserted by the Statement of Changes in Immigration Rules (HC 863) laid before Parliament on 16 March 2011 and in force from 6 April 2011.

System Migrant for the purposes of paragraph 319AA), each applicant must have the total requisite funds specified in the relevant parts of appendices C and E. If each applicant does not individually meet the requirements of appendices C and/or E, as appropriate, all the applications (the application by the Relevant Points Based System Migrant and applications as the partner or child of that relevant Points Based system Migrant) will be refused.'

3.169 This is reflected in paragraph (l) of Appendix E to the Immigration Rules as follows:

> 'Where the application is one of a number of applications made at the same time as a partner or child of a Relevant Points Based System Migrant (as set out in paragraphs 319A and 319F) each applicant, including the Relevant Points Based System Migrant if applying at the same time, must have the total requisite funds specified in the relevant parts of appendices C and E. if each applicant does not individually meet the requirements of appendices C and / or E, as appropriate, all the applications (the application by the Relevant Points Based System Migrant and applications as the partner or child of that Relevant Points Based System Migrant) will be refused.'

3.170 Appendix E stipulates that 'a sufficient level of funds must be available to an applicant applying as the Partner or Child of a Relevant Points Based System Migrant'. In accordance with paragraph 53 of the Points Based System (Dependant) Policy Guidance,[110] for a family member of a Tier 4 (General) migrant this depends on:

'• the length of the course;
• where the main applicant will be studying in the United Kingdom; and
• whether the main applicant already has an established presence studying in the United Kingdom.'

3.171 Paragraph (ba)(i) of Appendix E to the Immigration Rules states that:

'Where the application is connected to a Tier 4 Migrant:
(1) if the Tier 4 (General) Student[111] is studying in inner London (as defined in paragraph 12 of Appendix C), there must be £533 in funds for each month for which the applicant would, if successful, be granted leave under paragraph 319D(a), up to a maximum of £4,797,
(2) if the Tier 4 (General) Student[112] is not studying in inner London, there must be £400 in funds for each month for which the applicant would, if

110 Version 07/11, valid from 4 July 2011.
111 The word 'Migrant' was supplemented with '(General) Student' by the Statement of Changes in Immigration Rules (HC 1148).
112 The word 'Migrant' was supplemented with '(General) Student' by the Statement of Changes in Immigration Rules (HC 1148).

successful, be granted leave under paragraph 319D(a), up to a maximum of £3,600,

and in each case

(3) the applicant must confirm that the funds referred to in (1) or (2) above are:

(i) available in the manner specified in paragraph (f) below for use in living costs in the UK; and

(ii) that the funds will remain available in the manner specified in paragraph (f) below unless used to pay for living costs.'

The UKBA revised its evidential requirements of maintenance by adding a declaration to the dependants' application form asking them to confirm availability of funds to cover living costs. Where concerns arise, checks will be carried out to verify that funds continue to be available.

3.172 Therefore and in accordance with paragraphs 68 and 71 of Points Based System (Dependant) Policy Guidance, the family member must have:

- £533 for living costs for up to a maximum of nine months, if the Tier 4 (General) migrant is studying in inner London; or
- £400 for living costs for up to a maximum of nine months, if the Tier 4 (General) migrant is studying in outer London or elsewhere in the United Kingdom.

3.173 If applying as a partner, the sufficient level of funds must be available to either the applicant or the Tier 4 (General) migrant. If applying as a child, the sufficient level of funds must be available either to the applicant, the Tier 4 (General) migrant or the applicant's other parent who is lawfully present in the United Kingdom or being granted leave at the same time as the child. The funds must be held by the relevant person for 'a consecutive 28-day period of time, ending no earlier than one calendar month before the date of application, if the applicant is applying as the Partner or Child of a Tier 4 (General) Student'[113] (paragraph (g)(ii) of Appendix E).

3.174 In line with paragraph 61 of the Points Based System (Dependant) Policy Guidance, 'a family member of a Tier 4 (General) student must show that he/she has enough money to cover his/her monthly living costs whilst the student is studying in the United Kingdom.' The amount of money will depend on whether the student has an established presence in the United Kingdom and if so, the family member will need to demonstrate availability of a lesser amount of funds. This is not provided for in Appendix E. However, according to paragraphs 74 and 77 of

113 The word 'Migrant' was supplemented with '(General) Student' by the Statement of Changes in Immigration Rules (HC 1148).

the Points Based System (Dependant) Policy Guidance, the family member must have:

- £533 for living costs for up to a maximum of two months, if the Tier 4 (General) migrant is studying in inner London; or
- £400 for living costs for up to a maximum of two months, if the Tier 4 (General) migrant is studying in outer London or elsewhere in the United Kingdom.

3.175 In all cases the dependant must provide specified documents unless he or she is applying at the same time as a Tier 4 (General) student who is considered low risk under the differentiation arrangements (paragraph (j) of Appendix E). Paragraph 319K of the Immigration Rules deals with documentary evidence referred to in Appendix E. Paragraph 319K(a) of the Immigration Rules states that 'where Appendix E of these Rules states that specified documents must be provided, that means documents specified by the Secretary of State in the Points Based system (dependants) Policy Guidance.'[114]

DOCUMENTS

3.176 Family members are required to demonstrate evidence of maintenance (funds) in accordance with Appendix E subject to paragraph (j) of Appendix E. Family members must show that they have held the sufficient level of funds for a consecutive 28-day period[115] by providing the documents listed in paragraphs 96–97 of the Points Based System (Dependant) Policy Guidance:

- Evidence required for applications made under Tier 4
  - — Personal bank or building society statements covering a 28 day period ending no more than one month before the date of the application; or
  - — Building society passbook covering a 28 day period ending no more than one month before the date of the application; or
  - — Letter from the bank confirming funds have been held for a 28 day period ending no more than one month before the date of the application; or
  - — Letter from a financial institution regulated by either the Financial Services Authority or, in the case of overseas accounts, the home regulator (official regulatory body for the country the institution is in and where the money is held) confirming funds covering a 28 day period ending no more than one month before the date of the application.

114 The words 'Tier 1 (General) Points Based System (Dependants) Policy Guidance' were replaced by the words 'Points Based system (dependants) Policy Guidance' on 21 April 2011 by the Statement of Changes in Immigration Rules (HC 908) thus amending an apparent error.

115 In accordance with transitional arrangements in place, family members making in-country applications prior to 1 February 2010 were required to show availability of funds on the day of application.

- Official financial sponsorship or Government sponsor (if the Tier 4 (General) student has official financial sponsorship and it is intended to cover costs of the family member(s))
  — A letter of confirmation from the Tier 4 (General) student's official financial sponsor

In addition, children of Tier 4 (General) migrants who are over the age of 16 must also provide additional evidence in accordance with paragraphs 102–110 of the Points Based System (Dependant) Policy Guidance.

In-country applications by Tier 4 (General) dependants

3.177 Dependants of Tier 4 (General) migrants are subject to biometric requirements. Dependants, applying at the same time as the main applicant, have to pay £193 for postal/courier applications and £351 for applications made at a Public Enquiry Office, unless the dependant is a child aged 18 years or over. Dependants applying separately at a later date and applications made by dependent children aged 18 years or over will attract a charge of £550 for postal and courier applications and £850 for applications made in person at a Public Enquiry Office. Dependants must use a separate PBS (Dependant) application form. This is a generic form that must be used by all PBS dependants including dependants of Tier 4 (General) migrants.

Applications made by post should be sent to:	Applications made by courier should be sent to:
UK Border Agency PBS (Dependants) PO Box 500 Durham DH99 1WJ	UK Border Agency PBS (Dependants) Millburngate House Millburngate Durham DH97 1PA

Tier 4 (Child) migrants

3.178 Tier 4 (Child) migrants must refer to the following provisions before making their entry clearance application:

- Paragraph 245A of the Immigration Rules;
- Paragraphs 245ZZA–245ZZB of the Immigration Rules;
- Paragraphs 121–126 of Appendix A (Attributes) to the Immigration Rules;
- Paragraphs 1A and 15–22 of Appendix C (Maintenance) to the Immigration Rules;

- Paragraphs 320–324 of the Immigration Rules together with Chapter 9, IDI (general grounds of refusal, see modernised guidance);
- Paragraphs 325–326 of the Immigration Rules together with Chapter 10, IDI (police registration, see modernised guidance);
- Tier 4 of the Points Based System – Policy Guidance ('Tier 4 Policy Guidance');
- Photo guidance;
- Study (STY) guidance for use by entry clearance staff (currently being updated);
- Entry Clearance Guidance, STY5, List of main sponsored programmes for overseas students (scholarship and award programmes);
- the Borders, Citizenship and Immigration Act 2009, s 55.

3.179 Applications for entry clearance as a Tier 4 (Child) student must be made either online or on paper using a VAF9 PBS Personal Details form. In addition, applicants must complete a hard copy of a self-assessment point scoring Appendix 9 and submit it together with the VAF9.

3.180 Tier 4 (Child) migrants should be mindful of the following provisions before making their application for leave to remain in the United Kingdom:

- Paragraphs 34–34J of the Immigration Rules (provisions related to forms, procedures and formalities associated with making immigration applications);
- Paragraph 245A of the Immigration Rules;
- Paragraphs 245ZZC–245ZZD of the Immigration Rules;
- Paragraphs 121–126 of Appendix A to the Immigration Rules;
- Paragraphs 1A and 15–22 of Appendix C to the Immigration Rules;
- Tier 4 of the Points Based System – Policy Guidance ('Tier 4 Policy Guidance');
- Photo Guidance;
- Paragraphs 320–324 of the Immigration Rules together with Chapter 9, IDI (general grounds of refusal, see modernised guidance);
- Paragraphs 325–326 of the Immigration Rules together with Chapter 10, IDI (police registration, see modernised guidance);
- Chapter 3, IDI (for information only by those who hold leave granted prior to 31 March 2009);
- Borders, Citizenship and Immigration Act 2009, s 50;
- Borders, Citizenship and Immigration Act 2009, s 55;
- Entry Clearance Guidance, STY5, List of main sponsored programmes for overseas students (scholarship and award programmes).

3.181 Applications for leave to remain in the United Kingdom as a Tier 4 (Child) student must be made using a specified form, Application for a Grant of Leave and Biometric Immigration Document under Tier 4 (Child) Student – Main Applicant (Tier 4 (C)).

Requirements for entry clearance and leave to remain

3.182 This route, which was introduced alongside Tier 4 (General) on 31 March 2009, is for non-EU/EEA children between the ages of four and 18 wishing to come to the United Kingdom to study (paragraph 245ZZ of the Immigration Rules). Paragraph 196 of the Tier 4 Policy Guidance expands on this by stating that 'the Tier 4 (Child) student category is for children coming to the United Kingdom to be educated between four and 17 years old.' The paragraph goes on to say that 'children between four and 15 years old must be educated at independent fee-paying schools' and 'it is not possible for a Tier 4 (Child) student to study at a public funded school' (paragraph 197) while it is possible to study as a publicly funded further education college able to charge for non-EU/EEA students.

3.183 Obtaining entry clearance is mandatory prior to entering the United Kingdom in this category. This applies to visa and non-visa nationals (paragraph 245ZZA of the Immigration Rules).

3.184 As with Tier 4 (General), Tier 4 (Child) requirements for entry clearance and leave to remain are very similar, save for the differences which will be noted as the requirements are examined below.

GENERAL GROUNDS OF REFUSAL

3.185 Under paragraphs 245ZZA(a) and 245ZZC(a) applicants must not fall for refusal under the general grounds of refusal. Also, under paragraph 245ZZC(a) applicants must not have entered the country illegally. These grounds are contained in paragraphs 320 to 324 of the Immigration Rules and are dealt with separately below in this chapter.

POINT SCORING REQUIREMENTS

3.186 There are two core point scoring requirements. Applicants must score:

- a minimum of 30 points under paragraphs 121 to 126 of Appendix A (paragraphs 245ZZA(b) and 245ZZC(c)), and
- a minimum of 10 points under paragraphs 15 to 22[116] of Appendix C (paragraphs 245ZZA(c) and 245ZZC(d)).

116 Covered by paragraphs 15 to 20 of Appendix A prior to 21 April 2011 which were cited as 14 to 18 in the substantive Rules.

3.187 Appendix A deals with attributes. The only attribute a Tier 4 (Child) student is required to have is a valid CAS. In order to claim points for a CAS, there is a range of additional requirements set out in Appendix A that need to be satisfied in order for the CAS to be considered valid. Appendix C relates to maintenance (funds), namely the amount of money students must have and the length of time for which they (or their financial sponsors) must have held it.

CONFIRMATION OF ACCEPTANCE FOR STUDIES

3.188 Tier 4 (Child) students must score 30 points for attributes set out in Appendix A to the Immigration Rules. The available points are shown in the table (Table 17) below:

Criterion	**Points awarded**
Confirmation of Acceptance for Studies	30

The validity of a CAS is defined in the accompanying notes in paragraphs 124–126 of Appendix A.

VALIDITY OF CAS

3.189 In accordance with paragraph 124 a CAS will be considered valid only if:

'(a) where the applicant is under 16, it was issued by an independent, fee paying school,
(b) it was issued no more than six months before the application is made,
(c) the application for entry clearance or leave to remain no more than three months before the start date of the course of study as stated on the Confirmation of Acceptance of Studies,
(d) the Sponsor has not withdrawn the offer since the Confirmation of Acceptance of Studies was issued,
(e) it was issued by an institution with a Tier 4 (Child) Student Sponsor Licence,
(f) the institution must still hold such a licence at the time the application for entry clearance or leave to remain is determined, and
(fa) the migrant must not previously have applied for entry clearance, leave to enter or leave to remain using the same Confirmation of Acceptance for Studies reference number, if that application was either approved or refused (not rejected as an invalid application or withdrawn), and[117]
(g) it contains such information as is specified as mandatory in guidance published by the United Kingdom Border Agency.'

117 This sub-paragraph incorporated into the Immigration Rules on 21 April 2011 the requirement that a CAS reference number can only be used once unless the application in support of which it was provided was rejected as invalid or withdrawn.

3.190 This means that a CAS will only be valid:

- if issued to a child aged four to 15 years old, it was issued by an independent fee-paying school (paragraph 196 of the Tier 4 Policy Guidance);
- for a period of six months (also see paragraph 31 of the Tier 4 Policy Guidance);
- if the application for entry clearance or leave to remain is made no earlier than three months before the start date of the course of study (also see paragraphs 29 of the Tier 4 Policy Guidance);
- if the offer to undertake a course of study with the sponsor has not been withdrawn;
- if it was assigned by a licensed sponsor whose licence is effective at the time the application for entry clearance or leave to remain is determined;
- only once (paragraph 32 of the Tier 4 Policy Guidance);
- if it contains the information specified as mandatory in the UKBA guidance (see also paragraph 26 of the Tier 4 policy guidance).

VALIDITY OF A CAS REFERENCE NUMBER

3.191 In line with paragraph 125 of Appendix A, a CAS reference number will only be considered as valid if:

'(a) the number supplied links to a Confirmation of Acceptance of Studies Checking Service entry that names the applicant as the migrant and confirms that the Sponsor is sponsoring him in the Tier 4 category indicated by the migrant in his application for leave to remain (that is, as a Tier 4 (General) Student or a Tier 4 (Child) Student), and

(b) that reference number must not have been withdrawn or cancelled by the Sponsor or by the United Kingdom Border Agency since it was assigned.'[118]

3.192 This effectively means that the CAS reference number specified by an applicant on the application form must match a related entry on the Confirmation of Acceptance for Studies Checking Service and must not have been withdrawn or cancelled by the sponsor or the UKBA since being issued. Paragraph 34 of the Tier 4 Policy Guidance states that a CAS can be withdrawn or cancelled by the sponsor or the UKBA at any time. It is the sponsor's responsibility to provide the CAS reference number to the applicant (paragraph 27 of the Tier 4 Policy Guidance) and the information contained in the CAS which is relevant to the student's application (paragraph 28 of the Tier 4 Policy Guidance).

118 Paragraph 125(b) of Appendix A to the Immigration Rules was deleted and substituted by virtue of the Statement of Changes in Immigration Rules (HC 908). Wording of paragraph 125(b) prior to substitution: 'that reference number must not have been cancelled by the Sponsor or by the United Kingdom Border Agency since it was assigned.'

Paragraph 125A of Appendix A[119] states that:

> 'Points will only be awarded for a Confirmation of Acceptance for Studies if the applicant:
> (a) Supplies, as evidence of previous qualifications, specified documents that the applicant used to obtain the offer of a place on a course from the Sponsor, or
> (b) Is sponsored by a Highly Trusted Sponsor, is a national of one of the countries listed in Appendix H and is applying for entry clearance in his country of nationality or leave to remain in the UK. The UK Border Agency reserves the right to request the specified documents from these applicants. The application will be refused if the specified documents are not provided in accordance with the requested made.'

As with the Tier 4 (General) category, the UKBA has made different documentary requirements[120] for those Tier 4 students it considers to be 'low risk'.[121] In accordance with paragraph 12 of the Tier 4 Policy Guidance Tier 4 students will qualify under the differentiation arrangements if they are:

- sponsored by a sponsor which has HTS status; and
- applying for entry clearance in the country of their nationality or for leave to remain in the UK;[122] and
- nationals of the following countries listed in Appendix H to the Immigration Rules[123]
  'Argentina
  Australia
  British National Overseas
  Brunei
  Canada
  Chile
  Croatia
  Hong Kong
  Japan
  New Zealand
  Singapore

119 Incorporated by the Statement of Changes in Immigration Rules (HC 1148).
120 These requirements are arguably discriminatory.
121 50% of respondents (overall number of respondents: 25,571) to the Tier 4 consultation agreed that differential requirements should be implemented for high and low risk students and 51% of respondents (overall number of respondents: 25,520) agreed that the UKBA should concentrate on the abuse of evidence as the starting point. Consultation on the student immigration system: 7th December 2010 to 31st January 2011. Consultation questionnaire results, UK Border Agency, March 2011, p 10 www.ukba.homeoffice.gov.uk/sitecontent/documents/policyandlaw/consultations/students/student-consultation-results.pdf?view=Binary.
122 Appendix H to the Immigration Rules adds that 'where an applicant is a dual national, and only one of their nationalities is listed above, he will be able to apply using the different documentary requirements that apply to these nationals, provided he is applying either for entry clearance in his country of nationality listed above or for leave to remain in the UK'.
123 Appendix H was inserted by virtue of the Statement of Changes in Immigration Rules (HC 1148).

South Korea
Taiwan (those who hold a passport issued by Taiwan that includes the number of the identification card issued by the competent authority in Taiwan)
Trinidad and Tobago
United States of America'

This list will normally be reviewed on an annual basis. Under the different documentary requirements, Tier 4 students will normally be required to provide less evidence as indicated in the Tier 4 Policy Guidance. The UKBA reserves the right to request the full set of documents and refuse those applications where such are not provided within a specified time. Aside from the differentiation arrangements, Tier 4 (Child) students under the age of 16 are not required to send any documents with their CAS in any event (paragraph 211 of the Tier 4 Policy Guidance). Students aged 16 or 17 will not be required to send evidence with their CAS only if they qualify under the differentiation arrangements.

ACCEPTABLE COURSE LEVELS

3.193 The course in respect of which the CAS is issued must meet one of the following requirements set out in paragraph 126 of Appendix A:

'(a) be taught in accordance with the National Curriculum,
(b) be taught in accordance with the National Qualification Framework (NQF),
(c) be accepted as being of equivalent academic status to (a) or (b) above by Ofsted (England), the Education and Training Inspectorate (Northern Ireland), Her Majesty's Inspectorate of Education (Scotland) or Estyn (Wales),
(d) be provided as required by prevailing independent school education inspection standards.
(e) is a single course of study, except where the Confirmation of Acceptance for Studies is:
   (i) issued by an independent school to cover both a pre-sessional course and a course at an independent school; and
   (ii) the applicant has an unconditional offer of a place at the independent school; and
   (iii) the duration of the pre-sessional course and period of study at the independent school does not exceed the maximum period of entry clearance or leave to remain that can be granted under paragraphs 245ZZB and 245ZZD of the Immigration Rules.'[124]

3.194 The acceptable levels of courses are elaborated on in paragraph 201 of the Tier 4 Policy Guidance as follows:

'• taught in line with the National Curriculum; or
• taught in line with the National Qualification Framework (NQF); or
• accepted as being the same academic level as the National Curriculum or the National Qualification Framework by Ofsted (England), the Education

124 Paragraph 126(e) of Appendix A added by the Statement of Changes in Immigration Rules (HC 908).

and Training Inspectorate (Northern Ireland), Her Majesty's Inspectorate of Education (Scotland) or Estyn (Wales); or

- taught in line with existing (also known as prevailing) independent school education inspection standards; or
- pre-sessional courses to prepare a Tier 4 (Child) student for the main course of study. The main course of study must meet the conditions above.'

MAINTENANCE (FUNDS)

3.195 Tier 4 (Child) students must score 10 points for maintenance (funds) as per the criteria set out in a table in Appendix C to the Immigration Rules. As noted above, the Immigration Rules erroneously refer to paragraphs 15 to 22 of Appendix C which should be read together with paragraph 1A of Appendix C (see the section on Tier 4 (General) migrants above for reference to paragraph 1A). Points will be awarded subject to the differentiation arrangements (paragraph 16 of Appendix C).

Criterion	**Points awarded**
Where the child is (or will be) studying at a residential independent school: sufficient funds are available to the applicant to pay boarding fees (being course fees plus board/lodging fees) for an academic year.	10
Where the child is (or will be) studying at a non-residential independent school and is in a private foster care arrangement (see notes below) or staying with and cared for by a close relative (see notes below): sufficient funds are available to the applicant to pay school fees for an academic year, the foster carer or relative (who must meet such requirements as are specified in guidance published by the United Kingdom Border Agency) has undertaken to maintain and accommodate the child for the duration of the course, and that foster carer or relative has funds equivalent to at least £500 per month, for up to a maximum of nine months, to support the child while he is in the United Kingdom.	10
Where the child is (or will be) studying at a non-residential independent school, is under the age of 12 and is (or will be) accompanied by a parent, sufficient funds are available to the applicant to pay school fees for an academic year, plus: • if no other children are accompanying the applicant and the parent, £1333 per month of stay up to a maximum of nine months; or • if other children are accompanying the applicant and the parent, £1333 per month, plus £533 per month for each additional child, up to a maximum of nine months.	10

Criterion	**Points awarded**
Where the child is aged 16 or 17 years old and is living independently and studying in inner London: (i) Where the applicant does not have an established presence in the United Kingdom, the applicant must have funds amounting to the full course fees for the first academic year of the course, or for the entire course if it is less than a year long, plus £800 for each month of the course up to a maximum of nine months. (ii) Where the applicant has an established presence in the United Kingdom, the applicant must have funds amounting to the course fees required either for the remaining academic year if the applicant is applying part-way through, or for the next academic year if the applicant will continue or commence a new course at the start of the next academic year, or for the entire course if it is less than a year long, plus £800 for each month of the course up to a maximum of two months.	10
Where the child is aged 16 or 17 years old, is living independently and studying in outer London or elsewhere in the United Kingdom: (iii) Where the applicant does not have an established presence in the United Kingdom, the applicant must have funds amounting to the full course fees for the first academic year of the course, or for the entire course if it is less than a year long, plus £600 for each month of the course up to a maximum of nine months. (iv) Where the applicant has an established presence in the United Kingdom, the applicant must have funds amounting to the course fees required either for the remaining academic year if the applicant is applying part-way through or for the next academic year if the applicant will continue or commence a new course at the start of the next academic year, or for the entire course it is less than a year long, plus £600 for each month of the course up to a maximum of two months.	10

3.196 The accompanying notes at paragraphs 17–22 of Appendix C provide definitions for 'foster care', 'close relative' and 'established presence' emphasising at paragraph 19 that the arrangements made for the child's care in the United Kingdom must comply with the requirements specified in the guidance published by the UKBA. An explanation of what foster care is, according to the Immigration Rules is set out in paragraph 17 as 'children (under 16, or under 18 if disabled) are privately fostered when they are cared for on a full-time basis by a person or persons aged 18 or over, who are not their parents or a close relative, for a period of 28 days or more'. The theme of foster care is developed further in the section dealing with child visitors. A close relative is defined, in line with paragraph 18, as 'a grandparent, brother, sister, step-parent, uncle (brother or half-brother of the child's parent) or aunt (sister or half-sister of the child's parent) who is aged 18 or over.'

3.197 New additional paragraph 20 deals with the calculation of the length of the applicant's course if it includes a part of a month (prior to 21 April 2011 this was dealt with only in the Tier 4 Policy Guidance). Availability of funds is dealt with in paragraph 21. This paragraph incorporates the additional requirements that were previously imputed by the Tier 4 Policy Guidance into the Rules:

> 'Funds will be available to the applicant only where the specified documents show or, where permitted by these rules, the applicant confirms that[125] the funds are held or provided by:
> (i) the applicant (whether as a sole or joint account holder); and/or
> (ii) the applicant's parent(s) or legal guardian(s), and the parent(s) or legal guardian(s) have provided written consent that their funds may be used by the applicant in order to study in the UK; and/or
> (iii) an official financial sponsor which must be Her Majesty's Government, the applicant's home government, the British Council or any international organisation, international company, University or Independent school.'

The newly added Paragraph 21A states that:

> 'No points will be awarded where the specified documents show that the funds are held in a financial institution with which the UK Border Agency is unable to make satisfactory verification checks. A list of financial institutions which do not satisfactorily verify financial statements is published on the UK Border Agency website.'[126]

Reference should be made to paragraph 259 of the Tier 4 Policy Guidance. The list of financial institutions can be found at: www.ukba.homeoffice.gov.uk/sitecontent/documents/studying/financial-institutions.pdf.[127]

3.198 The circumstances in which an applicant, be it a Tier 4 migrant or a student will be considered to have an established presence studying in the United Kingdom are defined in paragraph 22 as follows:

> '(i) has finished a single course that was at least six months long within the applicant's last period of entry clearance, leave to enter or leave to remain, or

125 From the word 'or' to 'that' added by the Statement of Changes in Immigration Rules (HC 1148).
126 Incorporated by the Statement of Changes in Immigration Rules (HC 1148).
127 Not available online at the time of publication.

(ii) is applying for continued study on a single course where the applicant has completed at least six months of that course.'[128]

3.199 Paragraphs 245ZZA(f) and 245ZZC(g) of the Immigration Rules stipulate that:

> 'if a foster carer or a relative (not a parent or guardian) of the applicant will be responsible for the care of the applicant for the care of the applicant:
> (i) the arrangements for the care of the applicant by the foster carer or relative must meet the requirements laid down in guidance published by the United Kingdom Border Agency and the applicant must provide the specified documents to show that this requirement has been met, and
> (ii) the applicant must provide details of the care arrangements as specified in guidance published by the United Kingdom Border Agency.'

3.200 Paragraphs 35–41 of the Tier 4 Policy Guidance provide the breakdown of maintenance requirements:

- The two factors that determine the amount of money an applicant needs to have available in each individual case are the length of the course of study and the place of study (paragraph 35);
- The two components of the maintenance requirement are course fees for the first period of study (if commencing a new course) or the next period of study (if continuing a course) and living costs for up to a maximum of nine months (paragraph 36);
- The amount of course fees will be indicated by the Tier 4 sponsor on a CAS (paragraph 37);
- For those embarking on a new course the Tier 4 sponsor must indicate the course fees for the first year or the entire course, if its duration is less than a year (paragraph 38);
- For those continuing a course and applying for an extension of leave the Tier 4 sponsor must indicate the balance of course fees that remains to be paid (if the student is part way through the academic year) or the course fees payable for the next academic year (if the student is to continue the course at the start of the academic year) (paragraph 39);

128 This paragraph was supplemented by the Statement of Changes in Immigration Rules (HC 908). The wording of this paragraph prior to the changes in force from 21 April 2011 is as follows: 'if the applicant has completed a course that was a least six months long within their last period of leave as a Tier 4 migrant, student or as a Postgraduate Doctor or Dentist, and this course finished within the last four months, or the applicant is applying for continued study on a course where the applicant has completed at least six months of that course and has been studying within the last four months.'

- For those undertaking a Study Abroad Programme the Tier 4 sponsor must indicate the course fees for the first year or the entire course, if its duration is less than a year, or alternatively, indicate that no fees are due (paragraph 40);
- There is no fixed amount of living costs that an applicant must show as this will depend on personal circumstances of each applicant (paragraph 41).

3.201 Paragraphs 217–265 of the Tier 4 Policy Guidance deal with funding issues for boarding and non-boarding child students, course fees, living costs, place of study, established presence, the amount of maintenance (funds) to be shown, money that can be used for the purposes of applying.

BOARDING STUDENTS (PARAGRAPHS 217–223)

3.202 A child student who is being accommodated by their Tier 4 sponsor must have available sufficient funds to pay their school fees for the first year of the course or for the entire course if it is less than a year long. School fees are comprised of:

- course fees; and
- board or lodging fees

3.203 The course fees will be indicated by the child's Tier 4 sponsor on their CAS. If a child student has no fees to pay to the Tier 4 sponsor, it will also be indicated on their CAS. A child student who has already started the course and is applying for a new period of leave to continue the course must show that they have available sufficient funds to pay for the school fees to the end of the current academic year or for the next academic year if the next segment of the course will resume at the start of the next academic year. A child student undertaking a Study Abroad Programme must have available sufficient funds to pay for any school fees payable to the Tier 4 sponsor for the first year of the course or for the entire course if it is less than a year long. If the length of the course exceeds an even number of months, then it will be rounded up to the next month (this is pervasive throughout the Tier 4 policy guidance and has since 21 April 2011 become part of the Immigration Rules).

NON-BOARDING STUDENTS, THEIR COURSE FEES AND LIVING COSTS (PARAGRAPHS 224–237)

3.204 A child student who is not being accommodated by their Tier 4 sponsor must have available sufficient funds to pay course fees and living costs. As far as course fees are concerned, the guidance for boarding students is the same as for non-boarding students. Please refer to 3.202. The amount of living costs depends on the child student's care arrangements in the United Kingdom. In accordance with paragraphs 48–50 of the Tier 4 Policy Guidance, the UKBA must have regard to the need to safeguard children and to promote their welfare in line with the Borders,

Citizenship and Immigration Act 2009, s 55.[129] Therefore, all child students under the age of 18 must have suitable care arrangements for their travel to, reception on arrival and accommodation in the United Kingdom. All arrangements for the children's care and accommodation in the United Kingdom must comply with the relevant legislation and regulations (as described below in the section dealing with child visitors). In paragraph 50 of the Tier 4 Policy Guidance reference is also made to the following additional guidance published by the Department of Health:

'• Accommodation of students under eighteen by further education colleges: national minimum standards and inspection regulations';

'• Boarding schools: national minimum standards, inspection regulations';

'• Residential special schools: national minimum standards, inspection regulations'.

3.205 The provisions set out in Appendix C and the Tier 4 Policy Guidance allow for three care arrangement scenarios which raise concerns due to the limitations they impose. These scenarios are set out in paragraph 225 of the Tier 4 policy guidance as follows:

- '• the Tier 4 (Child) will be staying in the UK with a carer who is a resident British citizen or other UK resident;
- the Tier 4 (Child) will be staying with a parent or a legal guardian who will be accompanying them to the UK (under 12 year olds only);
- the Tier 4 (Child) is 16 or 17 years old and will be living independently in the UK.'

3.206 In accordance with paragraph 232 of the Tier 4 Policy Guidance if the child is staying with a carer who is a resident British citizen or other UK resident, the child must have available funds for the course fees and:

- '• the intended carer has agreed to look after and accommodate the Tier 4 (Child) student in the UK for the length of his/her course;
- the intended carer has at least £500 per month to look after and accommodate the Tier 4 (Child) student in the UK for each month of their course up, to a maximum of nine months; and
- confirmation that the intended carer is a resident British citizen or other UK resident.'

3.207 Child students under the age of 12 years can be accompanied to the United Kingdom by a parent or a legal guardian. Pursuant to paragraph 235 of the Tier 4 Policy Guidance a child student accompanied by a parent or a legal guardian must have available funds to pay for their course fees and:

129 Under the UK Borders Act 2007, s 21, the UKBA issued a code of practice designed to keep children safe from harm: UK Border Agency Code of Practice for Keeping Children Safe from Harm, www.ukba.homeoffice.gov.uk/sitecontent/documents/policyandlaw/consultations/closedconsultations/keepingchildrensafe/codeofpracticechildren?view=Binary.

- '• £533 for living costs for the Tier 4 (Child) student for each month of his/her course up, to a maximum of nine months; and
- £800 for living costs for his/her parent or legal guardian for every month of the Tier 4 (Child) student's course up, to a maximum of nine months.'

3.208 If a parent or a legal guardian is accompanying two or more of their children to the United Kingdom as child students, then under paragraph 236 of the Tier 4 policy guidance each additional child student must have available funds to pay for their course fees and:

- '• £533 for living costs for the Tier 4 (Child) student for each month of his/her course up, to a maximum of nine months.'

3.209 A parent or a legal guardian is expected to come to the United Kingdom as a special visitor (paragraph 234 of the Tier 4 Policy Guidance). While a parent can apply to come to the United Kingdom as a parent of a child at school (see **Chapter 6**), there is no specific immigration category for legal guardians. According to page 8, *Parent of a child at school*, Guidance,[130] a caseworker granting leave to a parent whose child reaches the age of 12 before any leave granted to the parent expires is instructed to advise the parent in writing that 'you will not qualify for further leave to remain in this capacity once your child has reached the age of 12 and that alternative arrangements for their care will thereafter have to be made if it is intended that they should continue their education in the United Kingdom.'

3.210 The alternative care arrangements are limited. Child students over the age of 12 years can stay with a foster carer (paragraphs 51–53 of the Tier 4 Policy Guidance), be looked after by a close relative resident in the United Kingdom or go to a boarding school. Tearing young children away from their parents[131] makes a mockery of the obligations imposed on the Secretary of State by the Borders, Citizenship and Immigration Act 2009, s 55 and should be challenged.

TIER 4 (CHILD) STUDENTS WHO ARE 16 OR 17 YEAR OLD AND LIVING INDEPENDENTLY (PARAGRAPHS 238–253)

3.211 If a child student is 16 or 17 years old and is living independently, the amount of money that must be available to pay for living costs will depend on:

- the location of the site of study (which determines the monthly amount); and
- established presence (which determines whether an applicant can show this amount for a reduced number of months).

130 Modernised Guidance, version 1.0 EXT, valid from 2 August 2011.

131 Who do not qualify in their own right to come to the UK and bring their children over the age of 12 as dependants.

3.212 A 16 or 17 year old child student living independently spending more than 50% of their study time in inner London must show £800 per month for living costs. A 16 or 17 year old child student living independently who is spending more than 50% of their study time in outer London or elsewhere in the United Kingdom must show £600 per month for living costs. If a 16 or 17 year old child student has already paid all or part of accommodation fees before making the application for entry clearance or leave to remain, this amount can be deducted from the total amount that the student must show as being available to him/her for living costs when making the application. This provision does not apply to privately arranged accommodation.

3.213 Inner London encompasses the following boroughs:

- Camden
- City of London
- Hackney
- Hammersmith and Fulham
- Haringey
- Islington
- Kensington and Chelsea
- Lambeth
- Lewisham
- Newham
- Southwark
- Tower Hamlets
- Wandsworth
- Westminster

3.214 A 16 or 17 year old child student living independently who does not have an established presence studying in the United Kingdom must show sufficient funds for living costs for each month of the course up to a maximum of nine months. For such a student the overall amount of funds is made up of the course fees plus:

- £800 for living costs for each month of their course up to a maximum of nine months, if studying in inner London; or
- £600 for living costs for each month of their course up to a maximum of nine months, if studying in outer London or elsewhere in the United Kingdom.

3.215 A 16 or 17 year old child student living independently with an established presence studying in the United Kingdom must show sufficient funds for living costs for each month of the course up to a maximum of two months. For such a student the overall amount of funds is made up of the course fees plus:

- £800 for living costs for each month of their course up to a maximum of two months, if studying in inner London, or
- £600 for living costs for each month of their course up to a maximum of two months, if studying in outer London or elsewhere in the United Kingdom.

3.216 A student can claim points for the reduced levels of living costs regardless of whether they are applying for entry clearance or leave to remain. The definition of 'established presence' is contained in Appendix C (see above) and paragraph 246 of the Tier 4 Policy Guidance. Annex 5 contains a table of maintenance (funds) students with or without an established presence of studying in the United Kingdom will need to demonstrate to claim 10 points.

MONEY THAT CAN BE USED BY A TIER 4 (CHILD) STUDENT AND OFFICIAL FINANCIAL SPONSORSHIP (PARAGRAPHS 254–265)

3.217 A child student can use money held in an account owned by their parents or legal guardians. No additional evidence of the relationship with the child student is required (paragraph 254). This implicitly excludes sponsorship by other family members, friends or relatives. This is a restrictive substantive requirement which, as of 21 April 2011, forms part of the Immigration Rules. Students can also rely on official financial sponsorship to cover all or part of their maintenance (funds) (paragraph 263). The Interpretation Section also contains a general definition of an official financial sponsor for the purposes of Part 6A of the Rules as 'the person or Government that the Certificate of Sponsorship Checking Service or Confirmation of Acceptance for Studies Checking Service records as being the Sponsor for a migrant'. Students can also use a personal loan as evidence of available funds (see documents section) (there is no prohibition against using loans held in the name of a parent(s) or a legal guardian as evidence of funds available to Tier 4 (Child) students). As maintenance (funds) is an evidential requirement, please see the documents section below.

AGE RELATED REQUIREMENTS

3.218 For the purposes of obtaining entry clearance 'the applicant must be at least four years old and under the age of 18' (paragraph 245ZZA(d) of the Immigration Rules) whereas for the purposes of applying for leave to remain 'the applicant must be under the age of 18' (paragraph 245ZZC(e) of the Immigration Rules).

3.219 Under paragraphs 245ZZA(g)–(h) and 245ZZC(h)–(i) of the Immigration Rules a child student must have their application supported by their parents, just one parent who bears sole responsibility for them, or legal guardian who must confirm that they consent to the arrangements made for the applicant's

- travel to, reception and care in the United Kingdom (with regard to entry clearance applications); or
- care in the United Kingdom (with regard to applications for leave to remain).

TIME RESTRICTIONS RELATED TO EXTENSION APPLICATIONS

3.220 Child students applying in-country must be conscious of the time gap between the date of expiry of their current leave and the start date of their course of study. Paragraph 245ZZC(j) of the Immigration Rules states that:

> 'the applicant must not be applying for leave to remain for the purpose of studies which would commence more than one month after the applicant's current entry clearance or leave to remain granted under these Rules expires.'[132]

3.221 Child students whose leave ends more than a calendar month before the start date of the next course of study are expected to leave the United Kingdom and apply for entry clearance at an overseas post (paragraph 208 of the Tier 4 Policy Guidance). Those applying for leave to remain in the United Kingdom will face a mandatory refusal.

OFFICIAL FINANCIAL SPONSORSHIP

3.222 Paragraphs 245ZZA(i) and 245ZZC(k) of the Immigration Rules deal with additional requirements to be satisfied by officially sponsored students:

> 'if the applicant is currently being sponsored by a Government or international scholarship agency, or within the last 12 months has come to an end of such a period of sponsorship, the applicant must provide the written consent of the sponsoring Government or agency to the application and must provide the specified documents to show that this requirement has been met.'

3.223 An explanation of restrictions placed on students with official financial sponsorship is contained in paragraphs 44–47 of the Tier 4 Policy Guidance. Such a restriction is a PBS-wide phenomenon and is not limited to Tier 4. An official financial sponsor is defined in paragraph 44 as 'Her Majesty's Government, the student's home Government, the British Council or any international organisation, international company, university or UK independent school.' The meaning of 'sponsored' for the purposes of the guidance is qualified in paragraph 46 of the

132 The words 'granted under these Rules' were inserted by the Statement of Changes in Immigration Rules (HC 908).

Tier 4 Policy Guidance as being '*wholly* supported by an award which covers both fees and living costs' (added emphasis). This definition appears to contradict paragraphs 263 and 265 of the Tier 4 Policy Guidance that go on to explain that 'financial sponsorship is where a Tier 4 (Child) student is given money to cover *some or all* his/her course fees and/or living costs' and 'if the Tier 4 (Child) student's financial sponsor is only covering *some* of his/her course fees or living costs, he/she must show that he/she has the rest of the money needed' (added emphasis).

3.224 Paragraph 45 of the Tier 4 Policy Guidance explains that within the last 12 months an applicant may have been financially sponsored as a student, a Tier 4 (General) or Tier 4 (Child) student, a student nurse, a student re-sitting an examination, a student writing up a thesis or a postgraduate doctor or dentist. Students currently sponsored by a Government or international scholarship agency or whose financial sponsorship ended within 12 months of their application being made must provide their financial sponsor's unconditional written consent together with their application (paragraph 47). It is evident from the wording of paragraphs 245ZZA(i) and 245ZZC(k) of the Immigration Rules that the official financial sponsor is only required to provide written consent rather than unconditional consent in writing. Therefore, the Immigration Rules take precedence (however, see paragraph 245ZX(g) in respect of leave to remain applications by Tier 4 (General) students).

3.225 Entry Clearance Guidance STY5 lists the main sponsored programmes for overseas students. These are aimed primarily at students undertaking post-16 education in the United Kingdom. Please refer to the section dealing with Tier 4 (General) students above, if relevant.

3.226 Paragraph 207 of the Tier 4 policy guidance contains an additional provision outside the Immigration Rules. The paragraph states that 'if a Tier 4 (Child) student has official financial sponsorship which wholly covers their fees and living costs, and the financial sponsor limits the time he/she may study in the United Kingdom, the permission to stay will be limited to that length of time plus the usual post-course period allowed.'

Please refer to the documents section for evidential requirements related to official financial sponsorship.

Period and conditions of grant

PERIOD OF GRANT

3.227 In accordance with paragraphs 245ZZB(a) and 245ZZD(a) of the Immigration Rules where an applicant is under the age of 16, entry clearance and leave to remain will be granted for a period of no more than one month before the course starts plus a period requested by the applicant equal to the length of the course or a period of six years, whichever is the shorter, plus an additional four months. Where an applicant is 16 years old or over, entry clearance and leave to remain will be granted, in accordance with paragraphs 245ZZB(b) and 245ZZD(b) of the Immigration Rules, for a period of no more than one month before the course starts plus a period requested by the applicant equal to the length of the course or a period of three years, whichever is the shorter, plus an additional four months.

3.228 Paragraphs 205–206 of the Tier 4 Policy Guidance seems to suggest that paragraphs 245ZZB(b) and 245ZZD(b) of the Immigration Rules apply to 16 or 17 year olds and if a child student turns 18 years old, he or she can continue with the course until their permission to stay in the United Kingdom expires. If they want to continue their studies in the United Kingdom, they can do so as Tier 4 (General) students. On 6 April 2010 the UKBA extended the maximum amount of length of leave that a 16 or 17 year old could apply for as a Tier 4 (Child) student from two to three years. As of 21 April 2011, 18 and 19 year old students who were initially given permission to stay prior to 6 April 2010 can apply for additional leave as Tier 4 (Child) students if they are currently studying in the United Kingdom as:

- Tier 4 (Child) students; or
- students under the Immigration Rules in place prior to 31 March 2009 where they were granted leave while they were under 18 years of age.

3.229 Additionally, they must have a valid CAS from their Tier 4 sponsor for the additional period of study. The maximum period of new leave that can be granted to the Tier 4 (Child) student is three years excluding the length of their previous period of leave.[133]

CONDITIONS OF GRANT

3.230 Entry clearance or leave to remain will be granted subject to the conditions set out in paragraphs 245ZZB(c) and 245ZZD(c) of the Immigration Rules:

'(i) no recourse to public funds,
(ii) registration with the police, if this is required by paragraph 326 of these Rules,
(iii) no employment whilst the migrant is aged under 16,
(iv) no employment whilst the migrant is aged 16 or over except:
  (1) employment during term time of no more than 10 hours per week,
  (2) employment (of any duration) during vacations,
  (3) employment as part of a course-related work placement which forms an assessed part of the applicant's course, and provided that any period that the applicant spend on that placement does not exceed half of the total length of the course undertaken in the UK except where it is a United Kingdom statutory requirement that the placement should exceed half the total length of the course,

133 See Appendix A of the Tier 4 Policy Guidance.

(4) employment as a Student Union Sabbatical Officer for up to 2 years provided the post is elective and is at the institution which is the applicant's Sponsor,

provided that the migrant is not self-employed, or employed as a Doctor in Training, a professional sportsperson (including a sports coach) or an entertainer, and provided that the migrant's employment would not fill a permanent full time vacancy other than a vacancy as a sabbatical officer.

(v) no study except:

(1) study at the institution that the Confirmation of Acceptance for Studies Checking Service records as the migrant's Sponsor, or where the migrant was awarded points for a visa letter, study at the institution which issued that visa letter unless the migrant is studying at an institution which is a partner institution of the migrant's Sponsor;[134]

(2) until such time as a decision is received from the UK Border Agency on an application which is supported by a Confirmation of Acceptance for Studies assigned by a Highly Trusted Sponsor and which is made while the applicant has extant leave, and any appeal against that decision has been determined, study at the Highly Trusted Sponsor institution which the Confirmation of Acceptance for Studies Checking Service records as having assigned a Confirmation of Acceptance for Studies to the Tier 4 migrant; and

(3) supplementary study.'

In paragraphs 295–328 the Tier 4 Policy Guidance goes on to elaborate on the framework of work and study related conditions set out in the Rules.

WORK RELATED CONDITIONS

3.231 Paragraph 301 of the Tier 4 Policy Guidance provides that a child student under 16 years old is prohibited from working at all during their time in the United Kingdom. Paragraph 302 goes on to say that a child student who is 16 years old or over is allowed to work subject to the following conditions:

- 'part-time during term-time, which is no more than 10 hours a week;
- full-time during vacations;
- on a work placement as part of the course;
- as a student union sabbatical officer for up to two years.'

3.232 Paragraph 304 adds that child students aged 16 or over can work full-time during vacation periods and during the period between them making an application for extension of stay under the PBS and being granted fresh permission

134 From the words 'unless the migrant' inserted by the Statement of Changes in Immigration Rules (HC 1148).

subject to the limits described in paragraph 302. Paragraph 303 states that a child student must not fill a permanent vacancy, must not be self-employed, employed as a doctor in training or as a professional sportsperson (including coach) or entertainer. It's unlikely that this will apply to most child students.

The UKBA made an announcement about the change in the work related conditions on 3 March 2010.[135] Further changes to the work related conditions were announced on 13 June 2011 although these relate to Tier 4 (General) students.[136]

CONDITIONS RELATED TO WORK PLACEMENTS

3.233 A Tier 4 (Child) student will be allowed to do a work placement as part of their studies in the United Kingdom provided that the work placement forms an assessed part of the course (paragraph 305), is not more than 50% of the length of the course in the United Kingdom unless there is a statutory requirement to the contrary (paragraph 306) and the student is (according to paragraph 305):

'• a Tier 4 (Child) student who is 16 years old or over'

3.234 Paragraph 307 provides that child students who are under 16 years old are prohibited from undertaking work placements as part of their course of study in the United Kingdom. Tier 4 sponsors will bear responsibility for their students undertaking work placements as part of their course (paragraph 309).

CONDITIONS RELATED TO PRE-SESSIONAL COURSES

3.235 Prior to 21 April 2011 most of the conditions attached to pre-sessional courses were set out in the Tier 4 Policy Guidance outside the Immigration Rules. These have been done away with. Requirements set out in the Tier 4 Policy Guidance as at 21 April 2011 have been brought in line with the amended Immigration Rules.

3.236 The introductory (unnumbered) paragraph preceding paragraph 310 of the Tier 4 Policy Guidance describes a pre-sessional course to prepare a student for the main course of study in the United Kingdom as an intensive English language course or any other course. As per paragraph 311 of the Tier 4 Policy Guidance a Tier 4 (Child) student can be given leave covering both the pre-sessional and the main course of study provided that his/her CAS is:

'• issued by an independent school to cover both a pre-sessional course and a course at an independent school; and

135 Changes to Tier 4 student visa applications from 3 March 2010, UK Border Agency, 3 March 2010, http://webarchive.nationalarchives.gov.uk/20100303141249/http://www.bia.homeoffice.gov.uk/sitecontent/newsarticles/2010/255022/tier4-visa-applications.

136 Next set of changes to student visa rules is announced, UK Border Agency, 13 June 2011, www.ukba.homeoffice.gov.uk/sitecontent/newsarticles/2011/june/17-t4-changes.

- the applicant has an unconditional offer of a place on a course at that independent school; and
- the duration of the pre-sessional course and the main course does not exceed maximum length of permission to stay that a Tier 4 (Child) student can be given.'

3.237 The above requirements are now in line with paragraph 126(e)(i)–(iii) of Appendix A to the Immigration Rules. All other Tier 4 students who do not fall within the above requirements but wish to undertake a pre-sessional course before their main course of study will have to make a separate Tier 4 application to cover each course and both courses must satisfy the full Tier 4 criteria including the course level and the English language testing requirements, where appropriate (paragraph 312 of the Tier 4 Policy Guidance).

STUDY RELATED CONDITIONS

3.238 On 30 September 2009 the UKBA announced that it would be 'tying' Tier 4 students' permission to stay in the United Kingdom to their sponsors provided they made their application on or after 5 October 2009. The relevant part of the announcement reads as follows:

> 'On 5 October 2009, new Tier 4 students' permission to stay in the United Kingdom will be 'tied' to the education provider that is sponsoring them. This will bring Tier 4 in line with other tiers of the points-based system.
>
> From 5 October, every new Tier 4 student will find their sponsor's reference number on the vignette in their passport or on their identity card for foreign nationals.
>
> In future, if a student wants to study with a new Tier 4 sponsor and they made their last application for a Tier 4 visa **on or after 5 October 2009**, they will need to apply for a new Tier 4 visa. They will not be allowed to begin studying with the new education provider until they have received a decision on the outcome of their application - if they do so, they will be committing a criminal offence for which they could be prosecuted or removed from the country.
>
> We have been asked whether students in this situation will be able to begin studying with the new education provider, at their own risk, before they have received a decision on their application. The UK Border Agency cannot condone a criminal offence, and therefore cannot advise students that this is an option for them.'[137]

3.239 This restriction stems from the enactment of the Borders, Citizenship and Immigration Act 2009, s 50. Section 50 inserted sub-paragraph (ia) 'a condition

137 Two new policy announcements for Tier 4 of the points-based system, UK Border Agency, 30 September 2009, http://webarchive.nationalarchives.gov.uk/20091108000432/http://www.bia.homeoffice.gov.uk/sitecontent/newsarticles/2009/september/pbs-t4-extending-tying.

restricting his studies in the United Kingdom' into the Immigration Act 1971, s 3(1)(c). Failure to observe the condition of leave pursuant to the Immigration Act 1971, s 24(1)(b) is an offence punishable on summary conviction with a fine of not more than level 5 on the standard scale or with imprisonment for not more than six months. In accordance with the *Tier 4 questions & answers* brochure published for students in September 2009, 'senior officials within UK Border Agency took the decision that the condition should be applied to new Tier 4 applicants from the earliest opportunity, in parallel with the implementation of phase 3 of Tier 4.'[138] Although s 50(2) allows the Secretary of State to apply the restriction to those granted leave before the Act came into force, it was decided not to use that provision retrospectively at the time.

3.240 On 23 July 2010 the UKBA made an allowance for Highly Trusted Sponsors in the Immigration Rules thereby relaxing the application of the Borders, Citizenship and Immigration Act 2009, s 50. In his statement the Minister for Immigration stated on 22 July 2010 that:

> 'In recognition of the high levels of student compliance among Highly Trusted sponsors; I have agreed an additional freedom for their students which is being introduced by the change to the Immigration Rules for Tier 4 (General) and Tier 4 (Child) students today. The change will allow the students of Highly Trusted sponsors to commence their studies with them before receipt of UKBA's decision on their application.
>
> In addition, for the avoidance of doubt, I am also making changes today to our general grounds for refusing applicants, (for example on the basis of submitting false documents), to make it absolutely clear that these provisions also apply to applicants who have overstayed their previous permission to be here.'[139]

3.241 Therefore, pursuant to the Tier 4 Policy Guidance (paragraphs 315–318) students who made their last Tier 4 application on or after 5 October 2009 and now want to study with a new Tier 4 sponsor, must apply for new permission to stay (paragraph 315). According to paragraph 316 'a student can start his/her new course before his/her new Tier 4 application has been approved if:

- he/she has applied for permission to stay to study with a Tier 4 sponsor that has a highly trusted sponsor rating; and
- he/she has existing leave to study in the UK; and
- his/her Tier 4 sponsor has assigned a Confirmation of Acceptance for Studies to the student for his/her new course.

138 Tier 4 questions & answers, UK Border Agency, September 2009, p 32 www.ukba.homeoffice.gov.uk/sitecontent/documents/employersandsponsors/pointsbasedsystem/t4-qanda-sponsors.

139 *Written ministerial statement on changes to the immigration points based system*, UK Border Agency, 22 July 2010, www.ukba.homeoffice.gov.uk/sitecontent/documents/news/wms-on-the-changes-to-pbs.pdf.

A Tier 4 student does this at his/her own risk as it is possible that his/her application will be refused.'

3.242 Consequently, students studying with Tier 4 sponsors who have A or B rating[140] cannot commence their new course until their Tier 4 application is approved (paragraph 317).

3.243 In accordance with paragraphs 319–323 of the Tier 4 Policy Guidance students who made their last Tier 4 application before 5 October 2009 and want to study with a new Tier 4 sponsor from 21 April 2011 must get permission from the UKBA provided they have time left in their existing leave and want to do the same or a different course of study with a new Tier 4 sponsor (paragraph 319). Those who applied for entry clearance or leave to remain between 31 March 2009 and 4 October 2009 must do so by using the Application for Permission to Change Tier 4 Educational Sponsor (T4 (PTS)). The application can only be made by post and costs £160. The application form must be sent to:

UK Border Agency
T4 Permission to Switch
P.O.Box 498
Durham
DH99 1W

Prior to 21 April 2011 Tier 4 students could write to the UKBA (migrantreporting@ukba.gsi.gov.uk) and ask for permission by providing the new of the new course, its start and finish dates, and the name of the new Tier 4 sponsor, its address and contact details.

3.244 The UKBA will then consider the switching application and write to the student confirming that he or she is allowed to use his or her existing leave to study with the new Tier 4 sponsor provided that the sponsor is approved by the UKBA and is on the Register of Sponsors, the sponsor wants to act as the student's new Tier 4 sponsor, and the course meets the Tier 4 requirements (paragraph 320).[141] Students can start the new course before getting permission from the UKBA but they will do so at their own risk as permission could be refused (paragraph 321). Under the Immigration Rules, the UKBA can limit a student's permission to stay as a student if he or she changes their Tier 4 sponsor without getting permission (paragraph 322).

3.245 Students must also be aware of policy provisions concerned with taking up a different course of study with the same Tier 4 sponsor (paragraphs 324–326), consequences of finishing the course early (paragraphs 327–328) and supplementary study (paragraph 313).

140 A (Trusted) or B (Sponsor).
141 Students are allowed to continue studying a course at CEFR level A2 or above.

Documents

3.246 In order to make a valid entry clearance or in-country extension application as a Tier 4 (Child) student, an applicant must meet the requirements of the Immigration Rules and relevant policy and score 40 points by complying with the points scoring requirements set out in Appendices A and C to the Immigration Rules and providing documents specified in Tier 4 Policy Guidance. The application must be accompanied by:

- a specified application form;
- photographs;
- specified fee;
- biometric data;
- passports (current and expired);
- BRP or ICFN (if applicable);
- police certificate (if applicable, to children aged 16 and over);
- letter from parent(s) or legal guardian;
- specified documents related to CAS and maintenance (funds); and
- documents related to accommodation in the United Kingdom (optional, not specified in the Tier 4 Policy Guidance) (evidence which is not specified in the policy guidance will not go towards scoring points).

3.247 As PBS applications are evidence and content sensitive, applicants must understand which of the documents specified in the Tier 4 Policy Guidance apply to them and what information they should contain to satisfy the point scoring requirements. Child students considered to be low risk will have their evidence treated in accordance with the differentiation arrangements. The particulars of each document are outlined in bullet-point, template or narrative form in the Tier 4 Policy Guidance. Given the changing nature of the Tier 4 Policy Guidance, the documents and their contents have been modified a number of times since 31 March 2009 and will continue to do so. Therefore, applicants must rely on the Tier 4 Policy Guidance and other requirements which are in force at the time of the application.

FORMS

3.248

- VAF9 PBS Personal Details form (online or hard copy) must be submitted together with Appendix 9 (in hard copy only) (for use in entry clearance applications).

- Application for a Grant of Leave and Biometric Immigration Document under Tier 4 (Child) Student – Main Applicant (Tier 4 (C)) (for use in leave to remain applications).
- Application for Permission to Change Tier 4 Educational Sponsor (T4 (PTS)) (for Tier 4 migrants wishing to change their Tier 4 sponsor).

GENERAL SPECIFICATIONS RELATED TO DOCUMENTS

3.249 There are also general specifications that apply to all the documents specified in the Tier 4 Policy Guidance. According to paragraph 13 of the Tier 4 Policy Guidance, documents must be:

- issued by an authorised official of the issuing organisation;
- be original (unless stated otherwise in the Tier 4 Policy Guidance); and
- be on the official letter-headed paper or stationery of the issuing organisation.

Documents related to maintenance (funds) must be on the official letter-headed paper or stationery of the financial institution, issued by an authorised person and dated no more than one month before the application is submitted.

TRANSLATIONS OF DOCUMENTS IN SUPPORT OF APPLICATIONS MADE IN THE UNITED KINGDOM

3.250 Original documents which are not in English or Welsh must be accompanied by a fully certified translation. The translation must be done by a professional translator or a translation company. In line with paragraph 14 of the Tier 4 Policy Guidance, translations must include:

- the date of translation; and
- details of the translator or the translation company's credentials; and
- confirmation that it is an accurate translation of the original document; and
- the translator or the translation company's contact details; and
- the original signature of the translator or an authorised official at the translation company.

TRANSLATIONS OF DOCUMENTS IN SUPPORT OF APPLICATIONS MADE OUTSIDE THE UNITED KINGDOM

3.251 Original documents which are not in English or Welsh must be accompanied by a full translation that can be independently verified by the UKBA. In line with paragraph 15 of the Tier 4 Policy Guidance, original translations must contain:

- confirmation from the translator or the translation company that it is an accurate translation of the original document; and

- the date of translation; and
- the full name and signature of the translator or an authorised official of the translation company; and
- the translator or the translation company's contact details.

Translations of overseas qualifications or award certificates will not be taken directly as proof of the academic level of the award and will be verified against UK NARIC to assess equivalency (paragraph 16 of the Tier 4 Policy Guidance). These general specifications related to the form in which documents should be presented are not stipulated in the Immigration Rules. While non-compliance with these specifications is often cited as a reason for refusal, it can be challenged.

DOCUMENTS RELATED TO CAS

3.252 The specified documents below are named as they are in the policy guidance. Applicants will need to refer to the Tier 4 Policy Guidance which details the content of each specified document. Paragraphs 209–216 of the Tier 4 Policy Guidance deal with the specified documents related to CAS.

3.253 Paragraph 209 of the Tier 4 Policy Guidance states that in order to claim 30 points for a valid CAS, the applicant must send the following documents:

- Paragraph 211 of the Tier 4 Policy Guidance deals with the specified documents related to CAS for Tier 4 (Child) students under 16 years old;
- Paragraphs 212–216 of the Tier 4 Policy Guidance deal with the specified documents related to CAS for Tier 4 (Child) students who are 16 or 17 years old.

3.254 Applicants should ask their Tier 4 sponsor for a print out of their CAS statement and find out about the evidence that the Tier 4 sponsor used to offer them a place on the course so that they could submit these documents with their application.

- CAS reference number which must be entered on the applicant's Tier 4 (Child) application form;
- Documents used to get CAS for Tier 4 (Child) students under 16 years old
  - — A child student under the age of 16 years will not need to send any documents apart from citing their CAS reference number;
- Documents used to get CAS for Tier 4 (Child) students aged 16 or 17
  - — Original certificate of qualification, or
  - — Original transcript of results, or

— If assessed by other means (eg references, portfolio of artwork, interview or internal test or entrance exam), then the applicant does not have to include these documents with the application (although the Tier 4 sponsor must clearly indicate the form of assessment on the CAS), or

— If offered a place on the course because of progress made on the existing course, then the applicant will not have to send any documents with the application (although the Tier 4 sponsor must clearly indicate the form of assessment on the CAS).

DOCUMENTS RELATED TO MAINTENANCE (FUNDS)

3.255 Paragraph 266 of the Tier 4 Policy Guidance states that in order to claim 10 points for maintenance (funds), the applicant must provide evidence that he/she:

- has paid all or part of the course and accommodation fees to the Tier 4 sponsor; and/or
- is receiving official financial sponsorship; and/or
- has sufficient funds to cover the remaining course fees and living costs, if any (either by using his own money, his parents/legal guardian's money or a personal loan).

3.256 Paragraphs 267–279 of the Tier 4 Policy Guidance deal with the specified documents related to maintenance (funds). Paragraphs 280–286 of the Tier 4 Policy Guidance deal with additional evidence required depending on the student's care and accommodation arrangements. An applicant must submit evidence to show that all or part of the course and accommodation fees have been paid to the Tier 4 sponsor and/or the applicant is receiving official financial sponsorship and/or has sufficient funds to cover the remaining course fees and living costs (either by using his own money, his parents/legal guardian's money or a personal loan). Applicants are advised to be mindful of the difficulties arising out of the evidential requirements in relation to maintenance (funds).

- Documents needed to show money already paid to the Tier 4 sponsor
  — Original paper receipt issued by the UK Tier 4 sponsor confirming that the student has paid all or part of the fees.
- Documents needed to show official financial sponsorship
  — Letter of confirmation from the official financial sponsor on official letter-headed paper or stationery of the organisation of the official financial sponsor and have the official stamp of that organisation on it (advisable to include consent of the official financial sponsor to the applicant making the application in this letter).

- Documents needed to show money available to the student
  - — Personal bank or building society statements covering a consecutive 28-day period ending no more than one month before the date of the student's application, or
  - — Building society pass book covering a consecutive 28-day period ending no more than one month before the date of the student's application, or
  - — Letter from the student's bank confirming funds have been held for a consecutive 28-day period ending no more than one month before the date of the application, or
  - — Letter from a financial institution regulated by either the Financial Services Authority or, in the case of overseas accounts, the home regulator (official regulatory body for the country the institution is in and where the money is held) confirming funds have been held of a consecutive 28-day period ending no more than one month before the date of the application, or
  - — Letter from a financial institution regulated by either the Financial Services Authority or, in the case of overseas accounts, the home regulator (official regulatory body for the country the institution is in and where the money is held) confirming the loan.
- Additional evidence for a 16 or 17 year old child student living independently
  - — A letter from their parent(s) or legal guardian, confirming their consent (the content of this letter can be incorporated into the parental consent letter).
- Additional evidence for a child student staying with a resident British citizen or other United Kingdom resident who is a close relative or in a private foster care arrangement
  - — A written (undertaking) letter from the intended carer confirming the care arrangement, and
  - — A letter from his/her parent(s) or legal guardian confirming the care arrangement, and
  - — Proof to confirm the intended carer is allowed to be in the United Kingdom, and/or
  - — A copy of the letter of notification from the child's parent(s), legal guardian or intended carer to the United Kingdom local authority (for child students staying in a private foster care arrangement only), and
  - — The United Kingdom local authority's confirmation of receipt (for child students staying in a private foster care arrangement only).

Parental consent for Tier 4 (Child) students

3.257 A Tier 4 (Child) student needs parental consent before they can make an application for entry clearance or leave to remain. Their parent(s) or legal guardian must consent to this and provide the following document:

- A letter from parent(s) or legal guardian confirming the relationship between them and the applicant, giving their consent to the application and to the care, travel and accommodation arrangements. Contents of this letter will vary depending on whether the Tier 4 (Child) student is applying for entry clearance or leave to remain.

Tier 4 (Child) in-country applications

3.258 Applicants will need to submit for biometric data collection at a time specified by the UKBA, depending on whether their application is made by post, courier or at a Public Enquiry Office. If their application is successful, applicants will be issued with biometric residence permits. In-country applications for grant of leave under Tier 4 (Child) category can be made using the application form noted above either by post, courier or at a Public Enquiry Office at a cost[142] of £386 (applying by post or courier) or £702 (applying at a Public Enquiry Office). As explained above, Tier 4 (Child) migrants are not allowed to bring their dependants to the United Kingdom with them. The cost of applications to change a Tier 4 sponsor is £160, these can be submitted by post only and sent to the address on the form.

Applications made by post should be sent to:	Applications made by courier should be sent to:
UK Border Agency Tier 4 PO Box 500 Durham DH99 1WJ	UK Border Agency Tier 4 Millburngate House Millburngate Durham DH97 1PA

Dependants of Tier 4 (Child) students

3.259 Under paragraphs 245ZZA(e) and 245ZZC(f) of the Immigration Rules:

142 Costs were last revised on 6 April 2011.

'the applicant must have no children under the age of 18 who are either living with the applicant or for whom the applicant is financially responsible'.

3.260 Paragraphs 292–293 of the Tier 4 Policy Guidance go on to explain that child students are not allowed to bring their partners with them as their dependants. If they are married or have a partner who wants to come with them, the spouse or partner must make an application in their own right. If child students have children under the age of 18 who live with them and who are financially dependent on them, they are not able to come to the United Kingdom as child students. This creates an obvious obstacle for applicants under the age of 18 who have children of their own unless the applicants are 16 or 17 years old undertaking a course of study for longer than six months and can qualify for leave under another immigration category.

Concessions and transitional arrangements relating to Tier 4 (General) and Tier 4 (Child) students

3.261 The Secretary of State has introduced various temporary concessions and transitional arrangements related to Tier 4 using the Policy Guidance, addenda to it or the UKBA website as vehicles for announcing and implementing temporary changes to the public. The previous list of such arrangements was attached to the Tier 4 Policy Guidance (version 07/10, 23 July 2010) at Appendix 1 and included:

- arrangements for International Baccalaureate Students with awards issued on 5 July 2010;
- arrangements to allow 18 year olds to apply for an additional 12 months permission to stay as a Tier 4 (Child) student;
- transitional arrangements related to changes made on 3 March 2010 and changes made on 6 April 2010; and
- time limited transitional arrangements from 6 April 2010.

3.262 The current list of arrangements is contained at Appendix A to the Tier 4 Policy Guidance (version 06/11, 4 July 2011)[143] and includes:

- arrangements for students using the Pearson Test of English Academic;
- arrangements allowing 18 and 19 year olds to apply for additional permission to stay in the Tier 4 (Child) student category.

Both of these arrangements are explained in more detail elsewhere in this chapter. This version of the Tier 4 Policy Guidance was subsequently updated after 25 August 2011 and Appendix A also includes:

143 Same as in version 04/11, 21 April 2011.

- arrangements for students relying on International Baccalaureate qualifications received on 5 July 2011.

3.263 Below is a selective list of concessions and transitional arrangements introduced over the course of 2009/2010:

- On 20 March 2009 the UKBA inserted into the maintenance section of the Tier 4 policy guidance a transitional arrangement for migrants applying before 1 June 2009 affecting the length of time for which they were required to have held their funds for maintenance prior to application;[144]
- On 1 June 2009 Tier 4 policy guidance was revised to extend the transitional arrangements allowing applicants to show they had the money needed to meet the maintenance requirements on the day that they applied rather than for a period of 28 days prior to the date of their application until 30 September 2009;[145]
- On 5 June 2009 the UKBA agreed that the concession allowing students applying to study for A-levels in the United Kingdom to make entry clearance applications based on a conditional offer would be extended to cover all students waiting for GCSE results who were going on to study A-level equivalent courses on the understanding that the unconditional offer would be submitted by them as soon as it was received;[146]
- On 19 August 2009 the UKBA made urgent provisions for students relying on International Baccalaureate qualifications awarded on 5 July 2009 insofar as their Tier 4 sponsors had to explain in their visa letters or separate letters that they had confirmed the students' results using either the UCAS or International Baccalaureate Office online checking systems;[147]
- On 30 September 2009 the UKBA extended the maintenance concession for Tier 4 applicants who were already in the United Kingdom until February 2010 while those applying outside the UK had to show they had the required funds

144 Changes to Tier 4 migrant guidance, UK Border Agency, 20 March 2009, http://webarchive.nationalarchives.gov.uk/20091003025933/http://www.ukba.homeoffice.gov.uk/sitecontent/newsarticles/changestot4migrantguidance?area=Studying.

145 Points-based system: New application forms for students and for dependants, UK Border Agency, 1 June 2009, http://webarchive.nationalarchives.gov.uk/20100303142009/http://www.ukba.homeoffice.gov.uk/sitecontent/newsarticles/pbs-new-forms-for-students.

146 Concession is extended for potential students awaiting GCSE results, UK Border Agency, 5 June 2009, http://webarchive.nationalarchives.gov.uk/20090804164037/http://www.ukba.homeoffice.gov.uk/sitecontent/newsarticles/extension-for-potential-students?area=Studying.

147 Student visas – provision for students with International Baccalaureate qualifications, UK Border Agency, 19 August 2009, http://webarchive.nationalarchives.gov.uk/20091003025933/http://www.ukba.homeoffice.gov.uk/sitecontent/newsarticles/2009/august/baccalaureate?area=Studying.

for a 28-day period ending no more than a month before the date of their application from 1 October 2009;[148]

- On 12 July 2010 the UKBA published an addendum to the Tier 4 policy guidance making arrangements for students using a loan letter to show that they had sufficient maintenance funds and those relying on International Baccalaureate qualifications awarded on 5 July 2010.[149]

Tier 5 (Youth Mobility Scheme)

3.264 Another temporary category which must be addressed in this chapter is Tier 5 (Youth Mobility Scheme). The scheme is covered by paragraphs 245ZI–245ZL of the Immigration Rules, Appendix A (Attributes), Appendix C (Maintenance) and Appendix G (Countries participating in Tier 5 Youth Mobility Scheme) to the Immigration Rules. The particulars of the scheme are expanded upon in the Tier 5 (Youth Mobility Scheme) of the Points Based System Policy Guidance ('Tier 5 (Youth Mobility Scheme) Policy Guidance').[150] The scheme replaced the youth mobility provisions provided for under the Immigration Rules prior to their abolition on 26 November 2008:

- The Working Holidaymakers Category;
- The Au Pair Category;
- The BUNAC Scheme;
- The Japan Youth Exchange Scheme;
- Gap Year Entrants working in UK schools concession;
- MPs' Research Assistants concession.

3.265 Transitional arrangements for those affected by the abolition of the above categories are rather limited and can be found at paragraphs 36–40 of the Tier 5 (Youth Mobility Scheme) Policy Guidance. The purpose of the scheme is to allow sponsored young people from participating countries to come to the United Kingdom to live and work (subject to restrictions) here temporarily (paragraph 245ZI of the Immigration Rules). Migrants coming to the United Kingdom under

148 Two new policy announcements for Tier 4 of the points-based system, UK Border Agency, 30 September 2009, http://webarchive.nationalarchives.gov.uk/20100303142009/http://www.ukba.homeoffice.gov.uk/sitecontent/newsarticles/2009/september/pbs-t4-extending-tying.

149 Changes to Tier 4 policy guidance, UK Border Agency, 12 July 2010, http://webarchive.nationalarchives.gov.uk/20100823120706/http://www.ukba.homeoffice.gov.uk/sitecontent/newsfragments/29-t4-policy-changes. On 13 July 2010 the new guidance containing a number of policy changes was published but due to errors it was withdrawn and the correct document was published on 14 July 2010.

150 At the time of writing the current version of the guidance (07/10) is for applications made on or after 31 July 2010.

the scheme can also engage in privately funded studies, voluntary work and au pair placements (paragraph 35 of the Tier 5 (Youth Mobility Scheme) Policy Guidance).

3.266 Securing entry clearance prior to coming to the United Kingdom is a mandatory requirement under paragraph 245ZJ of the Immigration Rules. In addition to satisfying entry clearance requirements, an applicant must be a citizen of a country listed in Appendix G and when applying must not exceed the annual allocation of places under this route. Paragraph 57 of the Tier 5 (Youth Mobility Scheme) Policy Guidance explains that each participating country is subject to an annual allocation of places and applications from nationals of these countries will be accepted for consideration only up to the point that the allocation for that year has been filled. Once the annual quota is exceeded, applications will be refused (paragraph 245ZK of the Immigration Rules).

3.267 Migrants applying for entry clearance under the scheme must fulfil the following requirements:

'(a) The applicant must not fall for refusal under the general grounds of refusal.
(b) The applicant must be:
    (i) a citizen of a country listed in Appendix G to these Rules, or
    (ii) a British Overseas Citizen, British Overseas Territories Citizen or British National (Overseas), as defined by the British Nationality Act 1981 and must provide the specified documents to show that this requirement has been met.
(c) The applicant must have a minimum of 40 points under paragraphs 101 to 104 of Appendix A.
(d) The applicant must have a minimum of 10 points under paragraphs 6 to 7 of Appendix C.
(e) The applicant must have no children under the age of 18 who are either living with him or for whom he is financially responsible.
(f) The applicant must not previously have spent time in the UK as a Working Holidaymaker or a Tier 5 (Youth Mobility Scheme) Temporary Migrant.'

3.268 Appendix G to the Immigration Rules lists the following countries participating in the scheme:

- Australia
- Canada
- Japan
- New Zealand
- Monaco

All these countries have Deemed Sponsor status (Annex A of the Tier 5 (Youth Mobility Scheme) Policy Guidance). New countries may join the scheme in time.

3.269 British Overseas Territories Citizens are those who derive their British nationality from their connection with an existing British Overseas Territory set out in Sch 6 to the British Nationality Act 1981. Persons with British National (Overseas) status are those who were British Overseas Territories Citizens by virtue of their connection to Hong Kong and who elected to maintain a British passport as British National (Overseas), a new status created following the return of Hong Kong to China on 30 June 1997. British Overseas Citizens are those who for various reasons remained British after the Overseas Territories with which they were connected became independent (except in relation to Hong Kong in respect of which see above). British Overseas Territories Citizens, British Overseas Citizens and British Nationals (Overseas) are not subject to annual quota.

3.270 An applicant applying for entry clearance under the scheme must score 40 points for attributes under Appendix A and 10 points for maintenance under Appendix C to the Immigration Rules. The points scoring criteria is laid out in paragraphs 101–104 of Appendix A and paragraphs 6–7 of Appendix C. Additionally, applicants must comply with the requirements set out at paragraph 1A of Appendix C and in particular with paragraph 1A(g)[151] which states that 'where the applicant is applying as a … Tier 5 Migrant, the funds must have been under his own control on the date of the application and for the period specified in (b) above.' Applicants must provide documents specified in the policy guidance to score requisite points.

Attributes

3.271

Criterion	**Points awarded**
Citizen of a country in Appendix G or Is a British Overseas Citizen, British Territories Overseas Citizen or British National (Overseas.)	30
Will be 18 or over when his entry clearance becomes valid for use and was under the age of 31 on the date his application was made.	10

151 Inserted by the Statement of Changes in Immigration Rules (HC 863) laid before Parliament on 16 March 2011 and in force from 6 April 2011.

Maintenance (funds)

3.272

Level of funds	*Points awarded*
£1600	10

3.273 Applicants who have children under the age of 18 years old with whom they are living or who are financially dependent on them will not meet the entry clearance requirements. There is no prohibition against applicants having spouses or partners but they are not allowed to bring them to the United Kingdom as their dependants. Those who have spent time in the United Kingdom as working holidaymakers or Tier 5 (Youth Mobility Scheme) temporary migrants in the past will have their applications refused.

Period and conditions of grant

PERIOD OF GRANT

3.274 Paragraph 245ZL of the Immigration Rules lays down the provisions which determine the period and conditions of grant of entry clearance. To successful applicants entry clearance is granted for two years only. Applicants cannot extend their leave beyond the two-year period nor can they switch from this category in-country into any other non-PBS or PBS category.

CONDITIONS OF GRANT

3.275 Pursuant to paragraph 245ZL of the Immigration Rules, entry clearance will be granted subject to the following conditions:

'(a) no recourse to public funds,
(b) registration with the police, if this is required by paragraph 326 of these Rules,
(c) no employment as a professional sportsperson (including as a sports coach), and
(d) no employment as a Doctor or Dentist in Training, unless the applicant has obtained a degree in medicine or dentistry at bachelor's level or above from a UK institution that is a UK recognised or listed body, or which holds a sponsor licence under Tier 4 of the Points Based System, and
(e) no self employment, except where the following conditions are met:
    (i) the migrant has no premises which he owns, other than his home, from which he carries out his business,

(ii) the total value of any equipment used in the business does not exceed £5,000, and

(iii) the migrant has no employees.'

Temporary migrants coming to the United Kingdom under the scheme are prohibited from working as professional sportsmen. However, they are allowed to work as a Doctor or Dentist in Training or be self-employed subject to the above restrictions.

Documents

3.276 In order to make a valid entry clearance application as a Tier 5 (Youth Mobility Scheme) Temporary Migrant, an applicant must meet the requirements of the Immigration Rules and relevant policy and score 50 points by complying with the points scoring requirements set out in Appendices A and C to the Immigration Rules and providing documents specified in the Tier 5 (Youth Mobility Scheme) Policy Guidance. Applicants are not allowed to make leave to remain applications in this category. The application must be accompanied by:

- a specified application form;
- photographs;
- specified fee;
- biometric data;
- BRP or ICFN (if applicable);
- police certificate (if applicable);
- specified documents related to points scoring requirements in Appendices A, C and G;
- specified documents related to securing an exemption from the Doctor or Dentist in Training restriction in Annex D of the Tier 5 (Youth Mobility Scheme) Policy Guidance;
- documents related to accommodation in the UK (optional, not specified in the Tier 5 (Youth Mobility Scheme) Policy Guidance) (evidence which is not specified in the policy guidance will not go towards scoring points).

FORMS

3.277 VAF9 PBS Personal Details form (online or hard copy) must be submitted together with Appendix 7 (in hard copy only).

GENERAL SPECIFICATIONS RELATED TO DOCUMENTS AND THEIR TRANSLATIONS

3.278 There are also general specifications that apply to all the documents specified in the Tier 5 (Youth Mobility Scheme) Policy Guidance. The documents:

- must be original (unless stated otherwise in the Tier 5 (Youth Mobility Scheme) Policy Guidance) (paragraph 13 of the Tier 5 (Youth Mobility Scheme) Policy Guidance);
- related to maintenance (funds) must be on the official letter-headed paper or stationery of the financial institution, issued by an authorised person and dated no more than one month before the application is submitted;
- which are not in English or Welsh must be accompanied by a fully certified translation by a professional translator who must date and sign it (in line with paragraph 14 of the Tier 5 (Youth Mobility Scheme) Policy Guidance).

DOCUMENTS RELATED TO ATTRIBUTES

3.279 Paragraphs 42–46 of the Tier 5 (Youth Mobility Scheme) Policy Guidance deal with the specified documents related to attributes. To score 40 points for attributes, applicants must provide a valid passport confirming that they are a national of a country participating in the scheme or a British Overseas Citizen, British Overseas Territories Citizen or British National (Overseas) and that they are of the required age on the date of the application (between 18 and 31).

DOCUMENTS RELATED TO MAINTENANCE (FUNDS)

3.280 Paragraphs 47–53 of the Tier 5 (Youth Mobility Scheme) Policy Guidance deal with the specified documents related to maintenance (funds). An applicant must submit evidence to show that the requirement of holding £1,600 on the date of the application. Evidence of cash funds or a loan available to the applicant is acceptable. However, a loan letter is not among the specified documents. The specified documents below are named as they are in the policy guidance. Applicants will need to refer to the Tier 5 (Youth Mobility Scheme) Policy Guidance which details the content of each specified document.

- Documents required
  - Building society/Savings account pass book; or
  - Personal bank or Building Society statements; or
  - Letter from bank or Building Society confirming funds; or
  - Letter from a financial institution regulated by the home regulator (official regulatory body for the country in which the institution operates) confirming funds.

DOCUMENTS RELATED TO THE EXEMPTION FROM THE DOCTOR OR DENTIST IN TRAINING RESTRICTION

3.281 Annex D of the Tier 5 (Youth Mobility Scheme) Policy Guidance deals with the evidence which an applicant wishing to be employed as a Doctor or Dentist in Training must provide in order to qualify for the exemption.

- Original certificate of award of the qualification; or
- An original academic reference from the institution that is awarding the degree together with an original academic transcript.

Special visitors

3.282 Persons who wish to undertake short-term, part-time or other types of courses or programmes of study that do not make the grade in accordance with PBS requirements under Tier 4 (General) and Tier 4 (Child) categories, may seek to apply under the special visitor provisions:[152] child visitor (under the age of 18), student visitor (aged 18 and over) and prospective students. Visa nationals wishing to come to the United Kingdom as child or student visitors must apply for entry clearance for that purpose. Non-visa nationals do not require leave as child or student visitors. Entry clearance is mandatory for visa nationals and non-visa nationals seeking to be admitted to the United Kingdom as prospective students.

Child visitors

3.283 Provisions governing child visitor applications are contained in paragraphs 46A–46F of the Immigration Rules,[153] Child Visitors, Guidance,[154] VAT03 Special Visitor: Child Visitors, ECG[155] and VAT04 Special Visitor: Child Visitors Sponsored by Charities, ECG.[156] These should be read in light of the Borders, Citizenship and Immigration Act 2009, s 55 ('BCIA 2009')[157] which commenced on 2 November 2009 and imposes a general duty on the Secretary of State to make arrangements to safeguard and promote the welfare of children in discharging her immigration, asylum, nationality and customs functions. In November 2009 the UKBA published statutory guidance regarding arrangements to be made to its staff and contractors

152 Another category that forms part of the special visitor category, 'Parent of a child at school', is dealt with in Chapter 6.
153 Immigration Rules allow child visitors to undertake sports, entertainer or business visitor activities as long as they satisfy the requirements set out in paragraph 46A.
154 Modernised Guidance, Version 2.0, valid from 22 September 2011.
155 See at http://www.ukvisas.gov.uk/en/ecg/visitandtransit/specialchildv.
156 See at http://www.ukvisas.gov.uk/en/ecg/visitandtransit/childsponsoredcharity.
157 BCIA 2009, s 55 replaced the UK Borders Act 2007, s 21.

in the United Kingdom and overseas entitled Every Child Matters, Change for Children.[158] Under the UK Borders Act 2007,s 21, the UKBA issued a code of practice for keeping children safe from harm.[159]

3.284 This category allows applicants under the age of 18 years to undertake a course of study as well as exchange or educational visits. Children sponsored by charities for short term stays in the United Kingdom should be treated as child visitors. Visit visas are normally granted on a multi-entry basis for six months, 12 months, two years, five years or 10 years.[160] While there is no restriction on the frequency or number of visits that can be made during the period of visa validity, visitors may remain in the United Kingdom for a maximum of six months on any one visit and should only remain for the period of the visit as stated by them, even if, as is normal, they are formally admitted for up to six months.

3.285 A migrant applying for leave to enter as a child visitor needs to satisfy the requirements under paragraph 46A of the Immigration Rules set out below to confirm that the applicant:

> '(i) is genuinely seeking entry as a child visitor for a limited period as stated, not exceeding 6 months or not exceeding 12 months to accompany an academic visitor, provided in the latter case the applicant has entry clearance; and'.

3.286 If a child visitor is admitted for less than six months or 12 months if accompanying an academic visitor, then the child visitor may apply for an extension of stay pursuant to paragraph 46D of the Immigration Rules but should not, as a result of the extension, spend more than six (or 12) months in total in the United Kingdom. There appears to be an irregularity at paragraph 46D(i) which requires applicants to comply with paragraph 41(ii)–(vii) and (x)–(xii). Paragraph 41(v) which was inserted into the Rules on 1 September 2007 requires that the applicant does not intend to undertake a course of study. One can speculate whether this is a deliberate exclusion or a drafting oversight. Reference to paragraph 41(v) is apparently deliberately excluded from paragraph 46A(ii) as a requirement that the child visitor must meet – it is understood that this is precisely to enable child visitors, as opposed to ordinary visitors, to undertake a course of study.

> '(ii) meets the requirements of paragraph 41 (ii)-(iv), (vi)-(vii) and (x)-(xii); and'.

158 Every Child Matters, Change for Children, UK Border Agency, November 2009, www.ukba.homeoffice.gov.uk/sitecontent/documents/policyandlaw/legislation/bci-act1/change-for-children.pdf?view=Binary.

159 UK Border Agency Code of Practice for Keeping Children Safe from Harm, www.ukba.homeoffice.gov.uk/sitecontent/documents/policyandlaw/consultations/closedconsultations/keepingchildrensafe/codeofpracticechildren?view=Binary.

160 Child visitors 'should only be granted a visa which is valid to six months past their 18th birthday', paragraph VAT3.15, Special Visitor: Child Visitors, ECG.

3.287 A child visitor must meet a number of general visitor requirements such as:

- have intention to leave the United Kingdom at the end of the period of stay (paragraph 41 (ii));
- not have intention to take employment in the United Kingdom (paragraph 41(iii));
- not have intention to produce goods or provide services in the United Kingdom and sell goods or services directly to the public (paragraph 41(iv));
- be able to maintain and accommodate himself or herself and any dependants adequately out of own funds without recourse to public funds or be maintained and accommodated adequately together with any dependants by relatives or friends (paragraph 41(vi));
- be able to meet the cost of the return or onward journey (paragraph 41(vii));
- not have intention to marry or form a civil partnership, or give notice of marriage or civil partnership during his or her visit (paragraph 41(x));
- not have intention to receive private medical treatment during his or her visit (paragraph 41(xi));
- not be in transit to a country outside the CTA[161] (paragraph 41(xii)).

'(iii) is under the age of 18; and

(iv) can demonstrate that suitable arrangements have been made for their travel to, and reception and care in the United Kingdom. If a foster carer or relative (not a parent or guardian) will be responsible for the care of the applicant, the arrangements must meet the requirements laid down in guidance published by the UK Border Agency; and'.

3.288 Travel, reception and care arrangements are likely to differ depending on whether the child is accompanied or unaccompanied (**3.291–3.292**). Applicants (parents or guardians making an application on behalf of a child[162]) must provide relevant evidence (depending on the circumstances of an individual case and arrangements made) concerning these arrangements to allay any concerns that immigration officials may have about the child's welfare as these might lead to the application being refused.

161 Common Travel Area.

162 If the application is made by someone other than a parent, a guardian or a social worker with parental rights, additional enquiries may be made as to the identity of the adult accompanying the child in question.

Private foster care[163]

3.289 Information about the intended host family or carer such as their name(s), address and telephone number, as well as the child parents' contact details must be made readily available to an Entry Clearance Officer and/or an Immigration Officer (eg in the form of a letter from the host family). Paragraph VAT3.6, Special Visitor: Child Visitors states that 'children (under 16 years old or under 18 years old if disabled) are privately fostered when they are cared for on a full-time basis by adults, who are not their parents or a close relative, for more than 28 days.' Parents, carers or anyone else involved in making private foster care arrangements (including an approved education provider) must intend to notify the local authority[164] of these arrangements soon after the child's arrival in the United Kingdom. The local authority which has the responsibility for safeguarding and promoting the welfare of children (under the Children Act 2004, s 11) must ensure that private foster carers are suitable. Child Visitors, Guidance confirms a child is not in foster care when

- 'a close relative, parent or legal guardian is looking after them
- the child is part of a group travelling and staying together and accompanied by an adult, for example, a school group'

Parent or guardian in the child's home country or country of habitual residence

3.290

'(v) has a parent or guardian in their home country or country of habitual residence who is responsible for their care and who confirms that they consent to the arrangements for the applicant's travel, reception and care in the United Kingdom; and'.

In light of the provisions in the BCIA 2009, s 55, an Entry Clearance Officer and/or an Immigration Officer must be fully satisfied with the reception and care arrangements for the child in the United Kingdom. In support of their application, applicants should provide a letter of consent from a parent or legal guardian consenting to the arrangements for the child's travel, reception and care in the United Kingdom.[165] If a foster care arrangement is in place, then the letter should also include name and

163 Reference should be made to Part IX of the Children Act 1989 and The Children (Private Arrangements for Fostering) Regulations 2005, SI 2005/1533 (in respect of England and Wales), the Foster Children (Scotland) Act 1984 and The Foster Children (Private Fostering) (Scotland) Regulations 1985 (in respect of Scotland), and The Children (Northern Ireland) Order 1995, SI 1995/755 and The Children (Private Arrangements for Fostering) Regulations (Northern Ireland) 1996, SI 1996/452 (in respect of Northern Ireland).

164 See at www.direct.gov.uk/en/DI1/Directories/Localcouncils/index.htm.

165 Unlike Tier 4 there are no set requirements as to the contents of such a letter of consent.

date of birth of the proposed foster carer, address where the child will be staying, relationship of foster carer to child (if applicable) and authority from the parent or legal guardian for the foster carer to care for the child for the duration of his or her stay in the United Kingdom. If the parents are divorced, then the parent who holds legal custody or sole responsibility must provide the letter of consent.

3.291

'(vi) if a visa national:
  (a) the applicant holds a valid United Kingdom entry clearance for entry as an accompanied child visitor and is travelling in the company of the adult identified on the entry clearance, who is on the same occasion being admitted to the United Kingdom; or
  (b) the applicant holds a valid United Kingdom entry clearance for entry as an unaccompanied child visitor; and'.

In order to be admitted to the United Kingdom as a child visitor, a visa national migrant must hold a valid entry clearance. The child visitor can travel to the United Kingdom in the company of a designated adult or unaccompanied. Entries made on an entry clearance vignette must clearly distinguish between the two. The vignette must state that (a) the child will travel accompanied by and be admitted to the United Kingdom at the same time as an adult, (b) identify the adult (C: CHILD VISITOR ACCOMPANIED: 6 MONTHS, CODE 3). Alternatively, the entry clearance can be endorsed in a way so as to confirm that the child is travelling unaccompanied (C: VISIT CHILD UNACCOMPANIED: 6 MONTHS, CODE 3).

3.292 An accompanied child who seeks to enter the United Kingdom in the company of an adult whose details are not recorded on the vignette should normally be refused. The adult with whom the child intends to enter the United Kingdom can be identified on the child's entry clearance vignette by the adult's passport number, initial and surname. However, if the child seeks to travel with two adults, one after the other, each of the adult's passport numbers will be entered on the child's vignette but not their names (C: CHILD VISITOR ACCOMPANIED: 6 MONTHS CODE 3 Only valid if accompanied by [passport number of first adult] or [passport number of second adult]). As evidence of identity, the accompanying adult who has obtained a replacement passport since the issue of the child's entry clearance must be able to present either:

- the original old expired, cancelled or annulled passport; or
- if the previous passport has been kept back by the issuing authority, the new passport bearing an official stamp referring to the old passport and its number in full.

3.293 Parents or guardians wishing to accompany the child visitor to the United Kingdom, or visit them while there, will need to satisfy relevant visitor requirements under the Immigration Rules in their own right. Parents of children at school under the age of 12 have their own category in the Immigration Rules (see **Chapter 6**).

Course of study

3.294

'(vii) if the applicant has been accepted for a course of study, this is to be provided by an institution which is outside the maintained sector and is:
(a) the holder of a Sponsor Licence for Tier 4 of the Points Based System, or
(b) the holder of valid accreditation from a UK Border Agency approved accreditation body, or
(c) inspected by one of the bodies set out in guidance published by the UK Border Agency, and'.

A child visitor may undertake a course of study during his or her visit offered by an education provider which is outside the maintained sector and holds a Tier 4 sponsor licence,[166] or valid accreditation from a UKBA approved accreditation body such as Accreditation UK, the British Accreditation Council ('BAC'), the Accreditation Service for International Colleges ('ASIC') and the Accreditation Body for Language Services ('ABLS'), or is inspected by one of the following bodies:

- Office for Standards in Education ('Ofsted');
- Her Majesty's Inspectorate of Education (Scotland);
- Estyn (Wales);
- Education and Training Inspectorate (Northern Ireland);
- Independent Schools Inspectorate (ISI) (nationwide).[167]

An independent fee paying school registered with the Department for Children, Schools and Families is a common example.

3.295 As of 21 April 2011 the UKBA revised its policy whereby accreditation by Accreditation UK, BAC, ASIC, ABLS and the Church of England Ministry Division no longer makes education providers eligible for joining the Register of Sponsors. Education providers seeking to become Tier 4 sponsors must meet the educational oversight requirement and be inspected, reviewed or audited by the Quality Assurance Agency ('QAA'), Ofsted (England), Her Majesty's Inspectorate of Education (Scotland), Estyn (Wales), Education and Training Inspectorate (Northern

166 Register of Tier 4 sponsors can be found at www.ukba.homeoffice.gov.uk/sitecontent/documents/employersandsponsors/pointsbasedsystem/registerofsponsorseducation.
167 Paragraph 2.13.7, Chapter 2, IDI. This is not reflected in VAT3.8, ECG.

Ireland), The Bridge Schools Inspectorate (England), Schools Inspectorate Service (England) and ISI (England). Existing sponsors who do not currently meet the educational oversight requirement must do so by the end of 2012 (see **Chapter 4**). It may be deliberate that the special visitor provisions for child visitors have not been revised accordingly allowing those who do not meet the educational oversight requirements to still be recruiting overseas students.

Activity based programme

3.296 A child visitor can also undertake an activity based programme that focuses on skills or interests (e.g. football, painting, dancing, hiking, horse riding, etc) during his or her stay in the United Kingdom. If so, then while it need not be accredited, the organisation delivering the programme must show that it has internal procedures to safeguard children and is regulated by an appropriate regulatory body for the programme it provides (if applicable). The activity programme may include a tuition segment although tuition would have to be an ancillary rather than the main purpose of the programme.

Exchange schemes and educational visits

3.297

> '(viii) if the applicant is undertaking an exchange or educational visit only, this is to be provided by a school in the maintained sector, a non-maintained special school, an independent non fee-paying or an independent fee-paying school, as described in guidance published by the UK Border Agency.'

On 28 August 2009 the UKBA announced a temporary concession for students attending state-maintained schools on exchange or educational visits. This concession was to apply until 31 December 2009. The changes to the Immigration Rules made on 1 January 2010 replaced and superseded the temporary concession.

3.298 Child visitors may undertake an exchange or educational visit during their stay in the United Kingdom. Exchange and educational visits are not classified as a course of study for the purposes of paragraph 46(viii) of the Immigration Rules as their aim and outcome are different. 'Exchange visit programmes are principally about enrichment, broadening horizons and deepening intercultural understanding', states paragraph VAT3.10, Special Visitor: Child Visitors. Please see Child Visitors, Guidance and paragraph VAT3.11, Special Visitor: Child Visitors for definitions of the schools which applicants under this limb must attend and which include maintained schools, independent fee paying schools, independent non-fee paying schools, academies, city technology colleges, non-maintained special schools, various school types in Scotland and Northern Ireland.

Student visitors

3.299 When making an application, applicants must be mindful of paragraphs 56K–56M of the Immigration Rules, Student Visitors, Guidance[168] and VAT09 Special Visitor: Student Visitor, ECG.[169] Student visitors (unlike general visitors) can undertake a short course of study during their stay in the United Kingdom to a maximum of six months. This type of leave may be of particular use to English language students whose level is below B1, distance learners, persons undertaking Executive MBA and other part-time programmes. There is no requirement to study a set number of hours per week or for the course of study to lead to a qualification. Student visitors cannot take any employment, nor undertake work placements as part of their course.

3.300 A person making an application for leave to enter as a student visitor must meet the requirements set out at paragraph 56K of the Immigration Rules in that he or she:

'(i) is genuinely seeking entry as a student visitor for a limited period as stated by him, not exceeding six months; and'

3.301 Persons granted leave to enter as a student visitor cannot switch or extend their leave after entry to the United Kingdom beyond six months. Leave as a student visitor is granted for a maximum of six months and not in line with the duration of the course (C: VISIT: STUDENT: 6 MONTHS CODE 3).

3.302 However, from 10 January 2011, English language students wishing to attend 'exclusively English language courses' (VAT9.10, ECG) can apply for leave for up to 11 months exceptionally outside the Immigration Rules provided they satisfy all the other criteria of the student visitor category (D: STUDENT LTE 11 MONTHS CODE 3; 'VISIT – STUDY ENGLISH LANGUAGE ONLY'). An English language course is defined in VAT9.10, ECG as 'a course where a student is learning English as a Foreign Language'. Mixed courses with only a fraction of time spent learning English will not be eligible. Students seeking to undertake other courses of study for longer than six months must do so pursuant to Tier 4. This extended student visitor route is a ministerial concession available only to applicants outside the United Kingdom. Its operation will be reviewed in the next 12 months. Non-visa nationals wishing to make use of the extended student visitor route must apply for entry clearance in this capacity. Student visitors granted leave under this concession will be required to undergo police registration in line with paragraphs 325–326 and Appendix 2 of the Immigration Rules.

'(ii) has been accepted on a course of study which is to be provided by an institution which is:

168 Modernised Guidance, Version 1.0 EXT, valid from 2 August 2011.
169 See at www.ukvisas.gov.uk/en/ecg/visitandtransit/studentvisitor.

(a) the holder of a Sponsor licence for Tier 4 of the Points Based System, or

(b) the holder of valid accreditation from a UK Border Agency approved accreditation body, or

(c) inspected or audited by one of the bodies set out in guidance published by the UK Border Agency, or

(d) an overseas Higher Education Institution offering only part of their programmes in the United Kingdom, holding its own national accreditation and offering programmes that are an equivalent level to a United Kingdom degree, and'.

3.303 Applicants must provide evidence to confirm that they have been accepted to undertake a course of study by an education provider which

- holds a Tier 4 sponsor licence;[170] or
- is accredited by a UKBA approved accreditation body such as Accreditation UK, the British Accreditation Council (BAC), the Accreditation Service for International Colleges (ASIC) and the Accreditation Body for Language Services (ABLS); or
- is inspected by one of the following bodies:
  - Quality Assurance Agency for Higher Education (nationwide) (QAA);
  - Office for Standards in Education (Ofsted);
  - Independent Schools Inspectorate (ISI) (nationwide);
  - Her Majesty's Inspectorate of Education (Scotland);
  - Estyn (Wales);
  - Education and Training Inspectorate (Northern Ireland) (ETINI).[171]
- is an accredited overseas higher education institution which provides programmes that are of an equivalent level to a UK degree recognised by UK NARIC only part of which are taught in the UK.

3.304 As of 21 April 2011, the UKBA revised its policy whereby accreditation by Accreditation UK, BAC, ASIC, ABLS and the Church of England Ministry Division no longer makes education providers eligible for joining the Register of Sponsors. Education providers seeking to become Tier 4 sponsors must meet the educational oversight requirement and be inspected, reviewed or audited by the Quality Assurance Agency ('QAA'), Ofsted (England), Her Majesty's Inspectorate of Education (Scotland), Estyn (Wales), Education and Training Inspectorate (Northern

170 Register of Tier 4 sponsors can be found at www.ukba.homeoffice.gov.uk/sitecontent/documents/employersandsponsors/pointsbasedsystem/registerofsponsorseducation.

171 Page 9, Student Visitors, Guidance.

Ireland), The Bridge Schools Inspectorate (England), Schools Inspectorate Service (England) and ISI (England). Existing sponsors who do not currently meet the educational oversight requirement must do so by the end of 2012 (see **Chapter 4**). It may be deliberate that the special visitor provisions for student visitors have not been revised accordingly allowing those who do not meet the educational oversight requirements to still be recruiting overseas students.

3.305 Student visitors must meet the following general visitor requirements in paragraph 56K of the Immigration Rules:

'(iii) intends to leave the United Kingdom at the end of his visit as stated by him; and

(iv) does not intend to take employment in the United Kingdom; and

(v) does not intend to engage in business, to produce goods or provide services within the United Kingdom, including the selling of goods or services direct to members of the public; and

(vi) does not intend to study at a maintained school; and

(vii) will maintain and accommodate himself and any dependants adequately out of resources available to him without recourse to public funds or taking employment; or will, with any dependants, be maintained and accommodated adequately by relatives or friends; and

(viii) can meet the cost of the return or onward journey; and

(ix) is not a child under the age of 18; and

(x) meets the requirements set out in paragraph 41 (ix)–(xii).'

3.306 The provisions under paragraphs 41(ix)–(xii) require that an applicant:

- does not intend to do any sports, entertainer or business visitor activities set out in paragraphs 46G(iii), 46M(iii) or 46S(iii) (paragraph 41 (ix));
- does not intend to marry or form a civil partnership, or give notice of marriage or civil partnership during his or her visit (paragraph 41(x));
- does not intend to receive private medical treatment during his or her visit (paragraph 41(xi));
- is not be in transit to a country outside the CTA[172] (paragraph 41(xii)).

Prospective students

3.307 As noted above, from 1 September 2007 entry clearance became mandatory for visa and non-visa nationals seeking to be admitted to the United Kingdom as prospective students. The prospective student category (which includes prospective student nurses and overseas qualified nurses or midwives) regulated by

172 Common Travel Area.

paragraphs 82–87 of the Immigration Rules has been retained after the launch of Tier 4 and is intended for those who need to finalise their study arrangements before commencing a course of study in the United Kingdom. Spouses, civil partners and children of prospective sponsors (or pre-PBS students who applied for leave on or before 30 March 2009) can join them in the United Kingdom pursuant to paragraphs 76–78 (spouses and civil partners) and paragraphs 79–81 (children) of the Immigration Rules.

3.308 Guidance for prospective students and their dependants is contained in VAT10, Special Visitor: Prospective Student, ECG and STY1: Dependants of students and prospective students, ECG. Inclusion of prospective students in the special visitor grouping is an oddity as unlike student visitors, prospective students are not expected to comply with any token visitor requirements. Prospective students have to be able to maintain and accommodate themselves and their dependants without recourse to employment or public funds. There is no age restriction subject to Tier 4 (General) or Tier 4 (Child) requirements.

3.309 Leave is granted for a maximum of six months and is subject to a condition prohibiting employment (D: PROSPECTIVE STUDENT: 6 MONTHS, CODE 3). If leave is granted for less than six months, leave to remain may be granted for a period which takes the total duration of stay up to six months pursuant to paragraph 85 of the Immigration Rules. Under paragraph 82(i)–(ii) prospective students can either switch into leave to remain as a Tier 4 (General) migrant pursuant to paragraph 245ZX or a Tier 4 (Child) migrant pursuant to paragraph 245ZZC or leave the United Kingdom.

3.310 The requirements for leave to enter set out in paragraph 82 of the Immigration Rules that prospective students need to satisfy are listed below:

'(i) can demonstrate a genuine and realistic intention of undertaking, within 6 months of his date of entry:
 (a) a course of study which would meet the requirements for an extension of stay as a student under paragraph 245ZX or paragraph 245ZZC; and
 (b) DELETED
(ii) intends to leave the United Kingdom on completion of his studies or on the expiry of his leave to enter if he is not able to meet the requirements for an extension of stay:
 (a) as a student in accordance with paragraph 245ZX or paragraph 245ZZC; and
 (b) DELETED
(iii) is able without working or recourse to public funds to meet the costs of his intended course and accommodation and the maintenance of himself and any dependants while making arrangements to study and during the course of his studies; and
(iv) holds a valid United Kingdom entry clearance for entry in this capacity.'

Business visitors

3.311 Business Visitors, Guidance[173] defines a business visitor as follows:

> 'The business visitor category is for people who work abroad but intend to visit the UK for a short time to do business on their own or their employer's behalf.'

3.312 VAT11.1, ECG also adds another requirement to this list necessitating that the applicant

'• not be replacing someone in the UK, including for temporary leave periods.'

3.313 The business visitor category includes doctors taking the PLAB test and clinical attachments or dental observer posts.

Doctors taking the PLAB test

3.314 This category pertains to doctors but not dentists. As a starting point, any doctor or international medical graduate wishing to practise medicine in the United Kingdom must register with the General Medical Council ('GMC'). Before a doctor who qualified abroad and whose qualification is not recognised in the United Kingdom can register with the GMC he or she must normally pass the Professional and Linguistic Assessment Board ('PLAB') test to demonstrate their knowledge of medical English and medical competence. The PLAB test consists of two separate stages of assessments, Part 1 and Part 2. Information about the substantive test can be found on the GMC website.[174] Immigration provisions relevant to international medical graduate sitting the PLAB test are set out in paragraphs 75A–75F of the Immigration Rules and VAT15 Business Visitor: Doctors coming for PLAB test, ECG.[175] The current policy guidance appears to be out of step with the most recent developments introduced by the GMC. It may therefore be helpful to read the immigration policy documents alongside GMC requirements for PLAB applicants.

3.315 Before coming to the United Kingdom doctors who are non-EU/EEA/Swiss nationals must provide evidence of knowledge of the English language. Those who are new medical graduates having been awarded a Primary Medical Qualification ('PMQ') from a university where the language of instruction and examination is English may satisfy the language requirement by providing alternative evidence. The same applies to doctors moving to the United Kingdom from an English

173 Modernised Guidance, Version 1.0 ETC, valid from 2 August 2011.

174 See at www.gmc-uk.org/doctors/plab.asp.

175 IDIs relating to this category have been withdrawn and not replaced with modernised guidance at the time of publication.

speaking country where they were required to take an English examination as part of registering with their medical regulatory body and prior to making an application to sit the PLAB test have been practising continuously in a country where the first or native language is English.[176] All others must take the International English Language Testing System ('IELTS') test.

3.316 From 1 February 2011 the GMC introduced the following new alternative evidence requirements by which doctors could demonstrate their knowledge of English:

- 'By holding a primary medical qualification which was taught and examined solely in English and where the final examinations were successfully completed within the 12 months before their application for registration. At least 75% of any clinical interaction, including personal contact with patients, their families and other healthcare professionals, which takes place as part of the course of study, or work, must have been conducted in English.
- By holding a primary medical qualification (taught and examined solely in English) which was awarded to the applicant more than 12 months before they applied for registration (or to sit part 1 of the PLAB test) and where the applicant has been working continuously, for at least two years, in a country where English is the first and native language. At least 75% of any clinical interaction, including personal contact with patients, their families and other healthcare professionals, which takes place as part of the PMQ and as part of the continuous work requirement, must have been conducted in English.
- By requesting that the validity of their IELTS test scores is extended by submitting confirmation that they have undertaken a postgraduate course of study which has been taught and examined solely in English. At least 75% of any clinical interaction, including personal contact with patients, their families and other healthcare professionals, which takes place as part of the course of study, or work, must have been conducted in English.
- By requesting that the validity of their IELTS test scores is extended by submitting confirmation that they have been employed in a country where English is the first and native language.'[177]

3.317 Doctors required to pass the IELTS test must take the academic version. The scoring requirements changed on 1 October 2010. Doctors are now required to achieve an overall score of 7.0 together with a minimum score of 7.0 in each of the four parts of the test including speaking, listening, writing and reading. The scores must be attained in a single sitting. IELTS certificates are valid for two years.

176 English language requirements, GMC, www.gmc-uk.org/doctors/registration_applications/language_proficiency.asp.

177 Changes to the guidance on alternative evidence to demonstrate knowledge of English, GMC, www.gmc-uk.org/doctors/registration_news/8547.asp.

3.318 Visa nationals seeking to enter the United Kingdom to sit the PLAB test must obtain prior entry clearance. There is no mandatory entry clearance requirement for non-visa nationals. Entry clearance would be endorsed as D: PLAB TEST: 6 MONTHS, CODE 4. A person seeking leave in this category may be admitted for a period not exceeding six months (paragraph 75B of the Immigration Rules). The provisions for leave to enter are set out in paragraph 75A of the Immigration Rules requiring that an applicant seeking leave to enter to sit the PLAB test:

'(i) is a graduate from a medical school and intends to take the PLAB Test in the United Kingdom; and
(ii) can provide documentary evidence of a confirmed test date or of his eligibility to take the PLAB Test; and
(iii) meets the requirements of paragraph 41 (iii)–(vii) for entry as a visitor; and
(iv) intends to leave the United Kingdom at the end of the leave granted under this paragraph unless he is successful in the PLAB Test and granted leave to remain to undertake a clinical attachment in accordance with paragraphs 75G to 75M of these Rules.'

3.319 Doctors coming to the United Kingdom to sit the PLAB test must also meet the following general visitor requirements under paragraph 41(iii)–(vii) of the Immigration Rules as stated in paragraph 75A(iii):

'(iii) does not intend to take employment in the United Kingdom, and
(iv) does not intend to produce goods or provide services within the United Kingdom, including the selling of goods or services direct to members of the public, and
(v) does not intend to undertake a course of study; and
(vi) will maintain and accommodate himself and any dependants adequately out of resources available to him without recourse to public funds or taking employment; or will, with any dependants, be maintained and accommodated adequately by relatives or friends; and
(vii) can meet the cost of the return or onward journey; and'.

3.320 Documentary evidence required pursuant to paragraph 75A(ii) of the Immigration Rules may take the form of a letter from the GMC, a test admissions card or email.

3.321 Applicants seeking to extend their leave may do so under paragraph 75D of the Immigration Rules the provisions of which are identical to paragraph 75A of the Immigration Rules save for an additional condition placing a time limit on the period of extension of stay. This is contained in paragraph 75D(v) of the Immigration Rules which stipulates that the applicant:

'(v) would not as a result of an extension of stay spend more than 18 months in the United Kingdom for the purpose of taking the PLAB Test.'

3.322 The maximum period allowed to take both parts of the PLAB test is 18 months. However, if the requirements for leave to remain are met, 'the applicant should normally be granted six months leave to remain at a time.'[178]

3.323 Doctors coming to the United Kingdom to take the PLAB test may undertake periods of clinical attachments while on leave in this category. They do not need to make a discrete application to undertake a clinical attachment unless their leave expires before the period of attachment does. Clinical attachments are addressed separately below. Doctors who have passed their PLAB test are not allowed to switch into any of the remaining skilled employment routes under the PBS.[179]

Clinical attachments or dental observer posts

3.324 This category is aimed at overseas doctors and dentists. Doctors or dentists who seek to enter the profession in the United Kingdom may undertake periods of clinical attachments or dental observation posts in order to gain insight into the local working practices. Clinical attachments or dental observation posts can be undertaken only if they are unpaid and are limited to observation rather than treatment of patients. The provisions governing clinical attachments and dental observation posts are set out in paragraphs 75G–75M of the Immigration Rules and VAT16 Business Visitor: Doctors undertaking clinical attachments; Dentists undertaking clinical observation posts, ECG.[180]

3.325 Foreign doctors or dentists can apply for leave to enter to undertake clinical attachments or dental observation posts. Entry clearance is mandatory for visa nationals. Non-visa nationals can seek admission without having prior entry clearance. The now archived paragraph 2.5.3, Chapter 2, Visitors, IDI states that 'leave to enter should be granted as a person coming up to undertake a clinical attachment or dental observer post on Code 4 for up to six weeks duration'. It went on to say that 'extensions of stay will normally be granted for six week periods up to a maximum stay of 6 months in total.'[181] This reflects paragraph 75H of the Immigration Rules. Entry clearance is endorsed as D: CLINICAL ATTACHMENT: 6 WEEKS, CODE 4 or D: DENTAL OBSERVER: 6 WEEKS, CODE 4.

3.326 Leave to enter requirements are specified in paragraph 75G of the Immigration Rules and stipulate that a person seeking leave to enter to undertake a clinical attachment or dental observer post:

178 Paragraph 2.4.7, Chapter 2, Visitors, IDI (archived).

179 Paragraph 2.4.9, Chapter 2, Visitors, IDI (archived).

180 IDIs relating to this category have been withdrawn and not replaced with modernised guidance at the time of publication.

181 IDIs relating to this category have been withdrawn and not replaced with modernised guidance at the time of publication.

'(i) is a graduate from a medical or dental school and intends to undertake a clinical attachment or dental observer post in the United Kingdom; and
(ii) can provide documentary evidence of the clinical attachment or dental observer post which will:
  (a) be unpaid; and
  (b) only involve observation, not treatment, of patients; and
(iii) meets the requirements of paragraph 41 (iii)–(vii) of these Rules; and
(iv) intends to leave the United Kingdom at the end of the leave granted under this paragraph;
(v) if he has previously been granted leave in this category, is not seeking leave to enter which, when amalgamated with those previous periods of leave, would total more than 6 months.'

3.327 Doctors undertaking clinical attachments and dentists undertaking dental observer posts must also meet the following general visitor requirements under paragraph 41(iii)–(vii) of the Immigration Rules:

'(iii) does not intend to take employment in the United Kingdom, and
(iv) does not intend to produce goods or provide services within the United Kingdom, including the selling of goods or services direct to members of the public, and
(v) does not intend to undertake a course of study; and
(vi) will maintain and accommodate himself and any dependants adequately out of resources available to him without recourse to public funds or taking employment; or will, with any dependants, be maintained and accommodated adequately by relatives or friends; and
(vii) can meet the cost of the return or onward journey; and'.

3.328 Persons seeking further leave to undertake a period of clinical attachment or dental observer post can apply for extension of stay which should normally be granted for a six week period at any one time up to a maximum of six months in total paragraph 75L of the Immigration Rules). Persons with the following leave can undertake clinical attachments or dental observer posts under their existing leave:

- Doctors taking the PLAB test;
- Postgraduate doctors, dentists or trainee general practitioners; and
- Work permit holders who are employed as doctors or dentists.

3.329 Where their period of existing leave is due to expire before the end of their clinical attachment or dental observer post, they can apply for further leave to remain. Applicants with the above leave can switch into this category. However, those with leave to undertake clinical attachments or dental observer posts are not allowed to switch into a skilled employment category under the PBS.

3.330 The extension requirements to be satisfied are set out in paragraph 75K of the Immigration Rules which require that the applicant:

'(i) was given leave to enter or remain in the United Kingdom to undertake a clinical attachment or dental observer post or:
  - (a) for the purposes of taking the PLAB Test in accordance with paragraphs 75A to 75F and has passed both parts of the PLAB Test;
  - (b) as a postgraduate doctor, dentist or trainee general practitioner in accordance with paragraphs 70 to 75; or
  - (c) as a work permit holder for employment in the UK as a doctor or dentist in accordance with paragraphs 128 to 135; and

(ii) is a graduate from a medical or dental school and intends to undertake a clinical attachment or dental observer post in the United Kingdom; and

(iii) can provide documentary evidence of the clinical attachment or dental observer post which will:
  - (a) be unpaid; and
  - (b) only involve observation, not treatment, of patients; and
  - (c) intends to leave the United Kingdom at the end of the leave granted under this paragraph; and
    - (i) meets the requirements of paragraphs 41 (iii)–(vii) of these Rules; and
    - (ii) if he has previously been granted leave in this category, is not seeking an extension of stay which, when amalgamated with those previous periods of leave, would total more than 6 months.'

General grounds of refusal

3.331 Paragraphs 320–323A of the Immigration Rules and attendant IDIs deal with the general grounds for the refusal of entry clearance, leave to enter or variation of leave to enter or remain in the United Kingdom. They also deal with curtailment of leave. Some of the grounds are applied on a mandatory basis, others on a discretionary. It is not the purpose of this section to delve deeply into this expansive subject which has been widely covered in general immigration textbooks such as *Macdonald's Immigration Law & Practice* and *JCWI's Immigration, Nationality and Refugee Law Handbook.* Generally, students must be aware of the mandatory grounds of refusal in respect of entry clearance applications,[182] namely, in particular paragraph 320(7A) (in force since 29 February 2008) and paragraph 320(7B) (in force since 1 April 2008, (see the Statement of Changes in Immigration Rules (HC 321) and last amended on 6 April 2011 as a result of the Statement of Changes in Immigration Rules (HC 863)):

182 Inserted by the Statement of Changes in Immigration Rules (HC 321).

'(7A) where false representations have been made or false documents or information have been submitted (whether or not material to the application, and whether or not to the applicant's knowledge), or material facts have not been disclosed, in relation to the application.

(7B) subject to paragraph 320(7C), where the applicant has previously breached the UK's immigration laws by:

- (a) Overstaying;
- (b) breaching a condition attached to his leave;
- (c) being an Illegal Entrant;
- (d) using Deception in an application for entry clearance, leave to enter or remain (whether successful or not);

unless the applicant:

- (i) Overstayed for 28 days or less and left the UK voluntarily, not at the expense (directly or indirectly) of the Secretary of State;
- (ii) used Deception in an application for entry clearance more than 10 years ago;
- (iii) left the UK voluntarily, not at the expense (directly or indirectly) of the Secretary of State, more than 12 months ago;
- (iv) left the UK voluntarily, at the expense (directly or indirectly) of the Secretary of State, more than 2 years ago; and the date the person left the UK was no more than 6 months after the date on which the person was given notice of the removal decision, or no more than 6 months after the date on which the person no longer had a pending appeal; whichever is the later;[183]
- (v) left the UK voluntarily, at the expense (directly or indirectly) of the Secretary of State, more than 5 years ago; or[184]
- (vi) was removed or deported from the UK more than 10 years ago.[185]

Where more than one breach of the UK's immigration laws has occurred, only the breach which leads to the longest period of absence from the UK will be relevant under this paragraph.'

3.332 A refusal of an entry clearance application pursuant to paragraph 320(7B) of the Immigration Rules means that an applicant will be banned from making further entry clearance applications for up to 10 years. There are three levels of ban ranging from 12 months, five years and 10 years depending on

183 Inserted by the Statement of Changes in Immigration Rules (HC 863) laid before Parliament on 16 March 2011.

184 Inserted by the Statement of Changes in Immigration Rules (HC 863) laid before Parliament on 16 March 2011.

185 Inserted by the Statement of Changes in Immigration Rules (HC 863) laid before Parliament on 16 March 2011.

the severity of breach. There is now extensive case law on what constitutes 'false representations' and 'deception' relating to these provisions. Paragraph 6 of the Immigration Rules defines 'deception' as 'making false representations or submitting false documents (whether or not material to the application), or failing to disclose material facts.'

3.333 The more recent changes inserted into paragraph 320(7B) on 6 April 2011 (HC 863) introduced a new intermediate level of entry ban of two years for those who leave the United Kingdom voluntarily but at the expense of the Secretary of State, whether directly or indirectly, within six months of being served the notice of removal or having exhausted appeal rights, whichever is later. All others who do not leave the United Kingdom by this time will face the five year ban.

3.334 Following intense lobbying in the wake of the introduction of the Statement of Changes in Immigration Rules (HC 321) (which introduced paragraph 320(7B) of the Immigration Rules), the Government was obliged to make some concessions to its severity. Some of those concessions were incorporated into the Immigration Rules, others not. The concessions incorporated into the Immigration Rules were inserted by the Statement of Changes in Immigration Rules (HC 607) from 30 June 2008 and are contained in paragraph 320(7C) which exempts from the operation of paragraph 320(7B) certain family life based applications and circumstances in which the applicant concerned was under 18 at the time of his/her most recent breach of the UK's immigration laws:

> '(7C) Paragraph 320(7B) shall not apply in the following circumstances:
> - (a) where the applicant is applying as:
>   - (i) a spouse, civil partner or unmarried or same-sex partner under paragraphs 281 or 295A,
>   - (ii) a fiancé(e) or proposed civil partner under paragraph 290,
>   - (iii) a parent, grandparent or other dependent relative under paragraph 317,
>   - (iv) a person exercising rights of access to a child under paragraph 246, or
>   - (v) a spouse, civil partner, unmarried or same-sex partner of a refugee or person with Humanitarian Protection under paragraphs 352A, 352AA, 352FA or 352FD; or
> - (b) where the individual was under the age of 18 at the time of his most recent breach of the UK's immigration laws.'

3.335 The Statement of Changes in Immigration Rules (HC 607) also inserted an amendment to ensure that those responsible for very serious previous breaches of the United Kingdom immigration laws, can be excluded, on a discretionary basis, regardless of when the breach took place and even if the application involves family members. The relevant rule is paragraph 320(11) of the Immigration Rules which now reads:

'(11) where the applicant has previously contrived in a significant way to frustrate the intentions of these Rules. Guidance will be published[186] giving examples of circumstances in which an applicant who has previously overstayed, breached a condition attached to his leave, been an Illegal Entrant or used Deception in an application for entry clearance, leave to enter or remain (whether successful or not) is likely to be considered as having contrived in a significant way to frustrate the intentions of these Rules'.

3.336 Students must also refer to **Chapter 4** which deals with the impact of a Tier 4 sponsor having its licence suspended or revoked on students' immigration status and possible curtailment of leave. Specific curtailment powers or power to alter duration of leave were introduced for sponsored migrants under the PBS (initially Tiers 2 and 5) that were inserted into the Immigration Rules by virtue of the Statement of Changes in Immigration Rules (HC 1113) from 27 November 2008. These were amended by the Statement of Changes in Immigration Rules (HC 314) in force from 31 March 2009 to include Tier 4 migrants.[187] The powers to curtail leave under PBS were amended once again by the Statement of Changes in Immigration Rules (HC 908) effective from 21 April 2011. Incorporating all the changes the relevant paragraph 323A of the Immigration Rules now reads as follows:

'In addition to the grounds specified in paragraph 323, the leave to enter or remain of a Tier 2 Migrant, a Tier 4 Migrant or a Tier 5 (Temporary Worker) Migrant may be curtailed, or its duration altered, if:

(a) the migrant's Sponsor ceases to have a sponsor licence (for whatever reason)

(b) the migrant's Sponsor transfers the business for which the migrant works or at which the migrant is studying to another person, that person does not have a sponsor licence and that person:
  (i) fails to apply for a sponsor licence within 28 days of the date of the transfer of the business,
  (ii) applies for a sponsor licence but is refused, or
  (iii) applies for a sponsor licence and is granted one, but not in a category that would allow it to issue a Certificate of Sponsorship to the migrant,

(c) the migrant fails to commence, or ceases, working for the Sponsor, or

(d) in the case of a Tier 4 Migrant:
  (i) the migrant fails to commence studying with the Sponsor, or

186 See paragraphs RFL 7.1–7.4 in RFL07 Frustrating the intentions of the Immigration Rules – paragraph 320(11), ECG (www.ukvisas.gov.uk/en/ecg/refusals/frustratingintentionsofrules) and also that contained in the **'Modernised Guidance' under 'General Reasons for Refusing' (www.ukba.homeoffice.gov.uk/sitecontent/documents/policyandlaw/modernised/general-grounds-refusing/).**

187 Further minor amendments were made by the Statements of Changes in Immigration Rules (HC 7701) on 1 October 2009 and (HC 382) on 23 July 2010.

(ii) the migrant studies at an institution other than that which issued the visa letter on the basis of which the migrant's current entry clearance, leave to enter or leave to remain was granted unless the Sponsor is a Highly Trusted Sponsor, the UK Border Agency has granted written permission for the migrant to change to another Sponsor, or the migrant is studying at an institution which is a partner institution of the migrant's sponsor, or

(iii) the migrant ceases studying with the Sponsor.'

Police registration

3.337 Migrants aged 16 or over who are deemed to be 'relevant foreign nationals' with limited leave to enter or remain for longer than six months must register with the police subject to the conditions set out in paragraphs 325–326 of the Immigration Rules, Appendix 2 to the Immigration Rules and Police Registration guidance. Paragraph 325 defines a 'relevant foreign national' as a person who is aged 16 or over and who is:

'(i) a national or citizen of a country or territory listed in Appendix 2 to these Rules;

(ii) a stateless person; or

(iii) a person holding a non-national travel document.'

3.338 Appendix 2 to the Immigration Rules lists the following 42 countries nationals of which must register with the police:

Afghanistan	Algeria	Argentina	Armenia	Azerbaijan	Bahrain
Belarus	Bolivia	Brazil	China	Colombia	Cuba
Egypt	Georgia	Iran	Iraq	Israel	Jordan
Kazakhstan	Kuwait	Kyrgyzstan	Lebanon	Libya	Moldova
Morocco	North Korea	Oman	Palestine	Peru	Qatar
Russia	Saudi Arabia	Sudan	Syria	Tajikistan	Tunisia
Turkey	Turkmenistan	UAE	Ukraine	Uzbekistan	Yemen

3.339 Paragraph 326(1) of the Immigration Rules states that a condition to register with the police should normally be imposed on a relevant foreign national who has been 'given limited leave to enter the United Kingdom for longer than six months; or limited leave to remain which has the effect of allowing him to remain in the United Kingdom for longer than six months, reckoned from the date of his arrival (whether or not such a condition was imposed when he arrived).' This condition should not normally be imposed on a person who has been granted leave:

- under the SAWS;

- in the Tier 5 (Temporary Worker) category;
- in the Tier 2 (Minister of Religion) category;
- on the basis of marriage or civil partnership with a person present and settled in the United Kingdom;
- as a person exercising access rights to a child resident in the United Kingdom;
- as the parent of a child at school (under 12); or
- following grant of asylum.

3.340 Applicants should refer to the Police Registration guidance (Immigration Directorates Instructions) for details about those who are exempt from the requirement to register with the police, dependants who are required to register and penalties related to applicants who have failed to register (an offence under the Immigration Act 1971,s 26(1)(f)). The guidance contains other related information which applicants should familiarise themselves with.

3.341 In accordance with the guidance:

> 'The applicant must report to the police within:
> - seven days of obtaining the leave (in-UK)
> - seven days of arriving in the country if imposed by an entry clearance officer (ECO) or border force officer
> - seven days of receiving their biometric residence permits.'

3.342 Applicants must report either to their local police or if residing in London, should report to the Overseas Visitors Registration Office ('OVRO'), 180 Borough High Street, London SE1 1LH. They must bring with them to the local police station or to OVRO documents related to their nationality, identity, immigration status (including details of employment or study), marital status and residence in and outside the United Kingdom.

Chapter 4

Manual for Tier 4 Sponsors

How to become a licensed Tier 4 sponsor and recruit international students to study in the United Kingdom

The policy documents informing this chapter

4.01 An education provider wishing to enrol non-EU/EEA nationals for the purpose of studying in the United Kingdom must hold a valid Tier 4 licence. There is no black letter law governing the sponsorship or licensing processes although over time some of the provisions have been imported into the Immigration Rules. The pitfalls of this have been addressed in some detail in **Chapter 2**. At the same time the extraneous materials developed to run the sponsorship and licensing systems have matured with time and have now reached a level of intricacy and volume bordering on confusion. As there is no independent authority overseeing the sponsorship and licensing procedures and no facility for appeals, any confusion in interpreting sophisticated but general provisions set out in the extraneous materials is usually not in the prospective or existing sponsor's favour.

4.02 The purpose of this chapter is to deal with sponsorship procedure and practice. It draws on the author's experience in advising sponsors and such extraneous materials as the Tier 4 of the Points Based System – Policy Guidance ('Sponsor Guidance');[1] relevant Appendices thereto;[2] and the Sponsorship Management

1 Unless otherwise specified, references to the Sponsor Guidance cited throughout this chapter are made in respect of 'Tier 4 of the Points Based System – Policy Guidance', Version 09/11, valid from 5 September 2011. The last few notable guidance notes were released on 5 October 2009, 3 March 2010, 6 April 2010, 1 October 2010, 21 April 2011 and 4 July 2011. A different version of the guidance may be in use at the time of publication of this edition. The content of the present chapter will therefore be varied by the changes made in the guidance. It is simply not practical to compare all the incarnations of the past Sponsor Guidance. Such a comparative exercise would surely produce interesting results and a timeline of changes in policy but is beyond the scope and purpose of this book.

2 Last amended on 6 April 2011 and 21 April 2011.

System Manual ('SMS Manual').[3] Appendix A to the Sponsor Guidance deals with supporting documents, Appendix B with immigration offences, Appendix C with civil penalties and Appendix D with record keeping. The last known version of the Tier 4 of the Points Based System – Highly Trusted Sponsor Guidance ('Highly Trusted Sponsor Guidance') has been withdrawn. The Sponsor Guidance having subsumed key provisions relating to the Highly Trusted Sponsor Scheme now stands as the single policy document to be referred to by prospective sponsors seeking to join the Register of Sponsors and existing sponsors seeking to obtain or maintain Highly Trusted Sponsor status ('HTS status').

4.03 These policy documents are revised by the UK Border Agency ('UKBA') without prior notice from time to time. The general and incongruent fashion in which the provisions contained in them have been written leaves them open to interpretation and uncertainty in application. Due to their fleeting nature it is advisable for sponsors to retain copies of previous versions of the Sponsor Guidance, Appendices and other extraneous documents. In the absence of any black letter law, these materials form the compendium of all that a sponsor is expected to comply with during the lifetime of its licence.

Introduction

4.04 This chapter deals with various aspects of pre-licensing, applying for a licence and post-licensing. It also deals with HTS status and procedures associated with it. It sets out the law in force from 4 July 2011 and policy in force from 5 September 2011 with reference to current and historical extraneous materials and lays down policy proposals for the next year. The two important milestones to bear in mind are April 2012 and end of 2012.

4.05 A prospective sponsor must have in place prior to making an application, systems, procedures and appropriate personnel allowing it to comply with its sponsorship duties. A prospective sponsor must make an application to register as a licensed sponsor and be included on the Register of Sponsors by paying the specified fees and providing required documents. A sponsor licence may be granted or refused depending on the circumstances, adherence to set criteria and outcome of checks. The Register of Sponsors went live on 31 March 2009 supplanting the Register of Education and Training Providers published by DIUS (formerly DfES) the establishment of which is detailed in **Chapter 2**.

4.06 If granted, a licence will be rated on the basis of previous history and conduct. A licensed sponsor will be expected to recruit students by assigning Confirmations of Acceptance for Studies ('CAS') through Sponsorship Management

3 Last updated on 27 September 2011.

System ('SMS') tools while complying with their sponsorship duties. A licensed sponsor must consider the severity of commercial ramifications for its business should its licence be downgraded in rating or revoked[4] as a result of allegations of non-compliance. While these are limited in variety and scope, a prospective or existing licensed sponsor must also be aware of legal remedies available to it should its licence be refused, downgraded or revoked. These are dealt with in **Chapter 5**.

4.07 The immigration law relating to sponsoring students is dealt with in **Chapter 3**. In addition, sponsors should refer to paragraphs 295–451 of the Sponsor Guidance which deal with the practice of sponsoring adult and child students, postgraduate doctors or dentists, sabbatical officers, the level at which courses can be taught,[5] the conditions and length of grant of permission to stay including work related arrangements, allowances made for re-sits of examinations, repeats of study and writing-up, switching courses and sponsors depending on when leave was granted.

Changes and transitional measures

4.08 For the second time implementation of PBS policy relating to international students and their sponsors is being phased in over time as it allows the industry to adjust to changes.[6] From 2 August 2010 onwards the Government has repeatedly signalled its intention to transform the existing student route in line with its five-year policy programme.[7] The purpose of the reform was to make PBS, an objective system by design, more selective.[8] Following an obligatory but short consultation that drew responses from more than 30,000 corporate and individual respondents, the Secretary of State announced the changes to be made to the student visa system on 22 March 2011.[9] This was followed by a written announcement on the UKBA website[10] and publication of a summary of the main changes.[11]

4 The UKBA previously used the term 'withdrawal' of a licence, rather than 'revocation'.

5 Including English language requirements and concessions made for gifted students at universities. The level at which courses can be taught are set out in paragraphs 120 and 120A of Appendix A to the Immigration Rules.

6 See **Chapter 2** for more detail on the implementation of Tier 4 from 31 March 2009 onwards.

7 Tier 4 has been in perpetual flux as it underwent another major review announced by the previous Government on 12 November 2009.

8 Fundamentally, returning immigration law to its pre-PBS days.

9 Column 855 et al, Daily Hansard, House of Commons, Volume 525, www.publications.parliament.uk/pa/cm201011/cmhansrd/cm110322/debtext/110322-0001.htm#11032282000003.

10 *Government outlines overhaul of student visas*, UK Border Agency, 22 March 2011, www.ukba.homeoffice.gov.uk/sitecontent/newsarticles/2011/march/54-student-visas.

11 *Summary of the new student policy*, UK Border Agency, 22 March 2011, www.ukba.homeoffice.gov.uk/sitecontent/documents/news/summary-student-policy.pdf.

4.09 On 31 March 2011 the Government published its statement of intent heralding the changes to unfold over the next 18 months.[12] The statement of intent was accompanied by the Statement of Changes in Immigration Rules (HC 908) and other documents. This occasion marked the second anniversary of Tier 4. This new policy was essentially a product of compromise within the Government. The Statement of Changes in Immigration Rules (HC 908) was criticised by the House of Lords' Merits of Statutory Instruments Committee in its Thirty Ninth Report and "drawn to the special attention of the House on the grounds that it gives rise to issues of public policy likely to be of interest to the House and may imperfectly achieve its policy objectives" for a debate on 16 May 2011.[13]

4.10 The first wave of changes that were introduced on 31 March 2011 commenced on 21 April 2011. These changes as well as transitional arrangements made for sponsors have been incorporated into the fabric of this chapter. Although strongly criticised the actual impact of these changes is yet to be determined.[14] The second set of changes was introduced on 13 June 2011 with the publication of the Statement of Changes in Immigration Rules (HC 1148). These changes came into force on 4 July 2011. This was followed up by the announcements on 13 June 2011 and 28 July 2011 of the additional educational oversight arrangements and on 18 July 2011 of the proposed new HTS criteria.[15] A further set of interim changes regarding HTS status, educational oversight and ratings was implemented on 5 September 2011. Other key changes will be rolled out until the end of 2012. Changes relating to international students, their English language competency, the courses they can take, arrangements regarding work, work placements and dependants are set out in **Chapter 3**.

12 *Student Visas, Statement of Intent and Transitional Measures,* UK Border Agency, March 2011, www.ukba.homeoffice.gov.uk/sitecontent/documents/news/sop4.pdf

13 www.publications.parliament.uk/pa/ld201012/ldselect/ldmerit/137/13703.htm.

14 On 13 June 2011, the UKBA published its impact assessment of the proposed changes. *Reform of the Points Based Student (PBS) Immigration System*, UK Border Agency, 13 June 2011, www.ukba.homeoffice.gov.uk/sitecontent/documents/policyandlaw/ia/reform-students-pbs/ia-students-.pdf?view=Binary. The impact assessment was published '12 weeks after the changes to the policy were announced.' (see *Student Visas: Follow-up*, Home Affairs Committee, House of Commons, Eleventh Report of Session 2010–12, HC 1445, 26 July 2011, para 6 www.publications.parliament.uk/pa/cm201012/cmselect/cmhaff/1445/1445.pdf).

15 Alongside the new HTS criteria, the UKBA also set out the scenarios of how the restrictions imposed by the new requirements will affect sponsors who fail to meet the expectations.

Changes before April 2012

4.11 Consideration will be given to how independent schools[16] can continue to qualify for HTS status. All sponsors must have attained HTS status by April 2012.[17] It was proposed on 18 July 2011 that sponsors must apply for HTS status by a date to be specified by the UKBA otherwise they will be relegated to the status of 'legacy sponsors' (see below) and will result in their licence being revoked in April 2012. Such a date was specified in the Sponsor Guidance as of 5 September 2011.

Changes before the end of 2012

4.12 In order to be able to sponsor new students, all sponsors must meet the new educational oversight requirements by this deadline.[18] It was proposed on 18 July 2011 that existing sponsors who do not have a satisfactory review by one of the approved educational oversight bodies will have to submit their applications by 9 September 2011 to meet this requirement. If they fail to meet the application deadline, they will become 'legacy sponsors' (see below) and their licence will be revoked in April 2012. Further deadlines were announced on 28 July 2011.

Tier 4 Sponsors and sponsor licences

Who can be a licensed sponsor and what is a sponsor licence?

4.13 A sponsor licence is defined in the Immigration Rules for the purposes of Part 6A of the Rules as a 'licence granted by the Secretary of State to a person who, by virtue of such a grant, is licensed as a Sponsor under Tiers 2, 4 or 5 of the Points Based System'. The definition is contained in the Interpretation Section of the Rules and was imported by the Statement of Changes in Immigration Rules (HC 1113) laid before Parliament on 4 November 2008. More specifically, the Sponsor

16 A-rated independent schools acquired HTS status automatically on 21 April 2011. They will hold that status for the initial 12 months. If they wish to retain it, they will need to renew it.

17 65% of respondents (overall number of respondents: 25,132) to the Tier 4 consultation agreed that more should be done to increase accreditation and inspection standards in respect of privately funded further and higher education institutions. *Consultation on the student immigration system: 7th December 2010 to 31st January 2011. Consultation questionnaire results*, UK Border Agency, March 2011, p 11 www.ukba.homeoffice.gov.uk/sitecontent/documents/policyandlaw/consultations/students/student-consultation-results.pdf?view=Binary.

18 See the relevant section in this chapter.

Guidance describes a Tier 4 sponsor in paragraph 18 as an education provider[19] that offers courses of study to full-time students[20] with the exception of state schools (including those with six forms) which cannot hold a Tier 4 licence or admit Tier 4 students (paragraphs 16 and 53 of the Sponsor Guidance). A sponsor licence has been found to be a possession in line with Article 1 of the First Protocol of ECHR.[21]

Types of sponsor licence

4.14 Paragraph 5 of the Sponsor Guidance (version 10/10, 1 October 2010) stated that Tier 4 was divided into two classes of sponsor licence, each bearing their own distinct qualification criteria, application process, benefits and consequences of refusal:

- Standard licence, rated A (Trusted) or B (Sponsor); and
- Highly Trusted licence.

4.15 This division between the two types of licence was intrinsically wrong as a Highly Trusted licence could only be attained by first having a Standard licence in the Tier 4 (General) category. Subsequent policy documents were revised accordingly from 21 April 2011 allowing prospective sponsors to apply for a Tier 4 sponsor licence distinguished by A or B rating, and then upgrade it to a HTS status if deemed suitable.

Highly Trusted Sponsor Scheme and HTS Status

4.16 The Highly Trusted Sponsor Scheme was introduced on 6 April 2010. It is essentially a kite mark of good compliance and good sponsorship and it allows a sponsor to provide courses which are perceived to carry a higher immigration

19 There are three exceptions to this rule whereby a Tier 4 sponsor can also be: (a) the UK Foundation Programme Office which is allowed to sponsor all students undertaking the two year Foundation Programme for postgraduate doctors; (b) the Yorkshire and Humber Strategic Health Authority which is allowed to sponsor all students undertaking the two year Foundation Programme for postgraduate dentists; and (c) a UK based organisation connected by common ownership or control to the overseas university providing part of its degree course programme in the United Kingdom. These exceptions are set out in paragraph 18 of the Sponsor Guidance.

20 This definition requires further clarification as it is only non-EU/EEA students that require a Tier 4 sponsor to study in the United Kingdom.

21 The article provides that 'every natural or legal person is entitled to the peaceful enjoyment of his possessions. No one shall be deprived of his possessions except in the public interest and subject to the conditions provided for by law and by the general principles of international law.' See paragraphs 142–150 and 152 of *New London College Ltd, R (on the application of) v Secretary of State for the Home Department* [2011] EWHC 865 (Admin) (7 April 2011) and *The London Reading College Ltd, R (on the application of) v Secretary of State for the Home Department* [2010] EWHC 2561 (Admin) (18 October 2010) at paras 63–68.

risk such as courses below degree level.[22] As part of its purpose to ensure that all education providers take their immigration responsibilities seriously, HTS status 'recognises sponsors who show a good history of compliance with their sponsor duties and whose students meet the standards of compliance with the terms of their visa or permission to stay in the UK' (paragraph 31 of the Sponsor Guidance).

4.17 Prior to 21 April 2011 when joining the Highly Trusted Sponsor Scheme was optional, sponsors were encouraged to obtain HTS status for its benefits. As obtaining HTS status has become mandatory, the following have become part of the arrangement. Tier 4 sponsors with HTS status are able to exclusively offer courses at National Qualifications Framework ('NQF')/Qualifications and Credit Framework ('QCF') level 3 or equivalent and courses below degree level containing work placement (excluding foundation degrees)[23] while A-rated and B-rated sponsors are allowed to offer courses at NQF/QCF level 4 or above. Sponsors holding HTS status can assign additional CAS to students who have already re-sat their exams twice.

4.18 Students who last applied for Tier 4 leave on or after 5 October 2009 and now wish to move to another institution which is Highly Trusted do not have to wait for a decision to be made in respect of their pending application for leave to remain before commencing their studies. Other benefits offered by the status include the services of an account manager to assist with Points Based System ('PBS') queries and a more lenient attitude to reporting student non-attendance (paragraph 466 of the Sponsor Guidance).

4.19 When prospective sponsors apply for a Tier 4 sponsor licence they are given a unique sponsor licence number (paragraph 221 of the Sponsor Guidance) which stays with them when they obtain HTS status. HTS status is not yet available to Tier 2 or Tier 5 sponsors. All sponsors must obtain HTS status by April 2012 in accordance with the new criteria set out in the Sponsor Guidance as of 5 September 2011.

22 Prior to 21 April 2011, as the majority of independent schools teach students who are under 18 year old, they did not need to use the Tier 4 (General) student route and subsequently register for a discrete Highly Trusted sponsor licence. However, some independent schools who do take on students who are already 18 years old or over would have needed to acquire a Tier 4 (General) licence to apply for a Highly Trusted sponsor licence to continue offering courses at NQF level 3 and equivalent. On 6 April 2010 arrangements were made for students aged 16 or 17 to apply for permission to stay in the UK as Tier 4 (Child) migrants for three years (as opposed to two years for those applying before 6 April 2010). Further arrangements were made on 21 April 2011 for students aged 18 or 19 to apply for an additional 12 months permission to stay in the UK in the Tier 4 (Child) category. Also from 21 April 2011, appropriately accredited independent schools with an A rating automatically acquired Highly Trusted Sponsor status for one year (see further below AQ please be more specific).

23 See paragraph 120A(a)(i) of Appendix A to the Immigration Rules.

How many licences should a prospective sponsor have?

4.20 Whether a sponsor organisation chooses to hold one or more Tier 4 sponsor licences depends on its corporate structure and geographic location (paragraphs 102–111 of the Sponsor Guidance). In any event, the sponsor organisation must be aware how its choice may impact on its ability to recruit Tier 4 students should the sponsor licence be revoked or downgraded. A parent organisation that includes different campuses or locations (denoted 'branches' for the purposes of the Sponsor Guidance) linked by common ownership or control may choose to hold its sponsor licence in the following way:

(a) A single Tier 4 sponsor licence held under the 'head office and all branches' umbrella or as a group of branches segregated by location. If the licence is revoked or downgraded, the decision will apply equally to all the branches covered by the licence affecting students across the board. If a subsequent application is made by any of the branches for an individual licence, evidence of previous misconduct will be taken into consideration. Large education providers with a number of branches will automatically have them included in the licence unless applications are made for individual licences (paragraphs 102, 106, 107 and 109 of the Sponsor Guidance); or

(b) Multiple Tier 4 sponsor licences with each branch holding a separate licence. Conversely, in this instance if the licence is revoked or downgraded, the decision will apply only to the offending branch while others may yet be investigated (paragraphs 102 and 105 of the Sponsor Guidance); or

(c) Grouping a number of branches in a single Tier 4 sponsor licence (paragraph 102 of the Sponsor Guidance).

Instances in which common ownership or control can be demonstrated have been described at paragraph 104 of the current Sponsor Guidance[24] as follows:

- 'one entity controls the composition of the other entity's board; or
- one entity is in a position to cast, or control the casting of, more than half the maximum number of votes that might be cast at a general meeting of the other entity; or
- one entity holds more than half the issued share capital of the other entity (excluding any part of that issued share capital that carries no right to participate in a distribution of either profits or capital beyond a specified amount); or
- both entities have a common parent entity that itself or through other entities meets one of the requirements of the first three bullet points above in relation to both entities that are the subject of the intra-company transfer; or

24 The list has diminished since first being mentioned in the Sponsor Guidance (version 06/11, 4 July 2011)

- one entity is related to the other entity as both entities are party to a joint venture agreement; or
- one entity is related to the other entity in that one entity is party to a joint venture agreement and the other entity is the entity formed by that joint venture agreement.'

4.21 The same options apply to franchises depending on whether each franchise is under the control of the parent organisation or not (paragraphs 110–111 of the Sponsor Guidance). A 'partner institution' that is not connected to the sponsor organisation by common ownership or control may be covered under a single Tier 4 sponsor licence as an exception to (a) above provided that it can demonstrate that it delivers pre-sessional courses to students who will undertake their main course of study with the sponsor organisation. A prospective sponsor must name the pre-sessional provider as a 'branch' on your licence if it is a 'partner institution' regardless of the fact that it may already have a sponsor licence in its own right (paragraph 359 of the Sponsor Guidance).

4.22 Pre-sessional courses are normally English language courses or any other short courses most likely taught at NQF level 3 and equivalent preparing the student to undertake the main course of study. If a 'partner institution' has its sponsor licence revoked, action may also be taken against the sponsor organisation holding the Tier 4 sponsor licence (paragraph 108 of the Sponsor Guidance).

Ratings

4.23 Prior to the introduction of the Highly Trusted Sponsor Scheme, the rating system applicable to licences was limited to A or B rating. In the Command Paper (Cm 6741) of 7 March 2006 it was envisaged that a sponsor's rating would be an expression of their record or policies in sponsoring migrants that 'will determine whether applicants receive more or fewer points for their certificate'[25] depending on whether a sponsor is A or B-rated. This was meant to reward best practice and highlight abuse. However, this commercially disadvantageous vision never materialised instead leading to a more carefully crafted risk assessment system.

4.24 As of 6 April 2010 a Standard licence holder could be awarded A (Trusted) or B (Sponsor) rating. A Highly Trusted licence was not rated as it was considered to be a rating category in itself and it could only be attached to a Tier 4 (General) sponsor. From 21 April 2011 the UKBA reverted to calling A (Trusted) and B (Sponsor) rating simply A and B rating[26] while a Highly Trusted licence was transformed into

25 *A Points-Based System: Making Migration Work for Britain*, 7 March 2006, Cm 6741, Home Office, para 12, www.homeoffice.gov.uk/documents/command-points-based-migration?view=Binary.

26 The Register of Sponsors has not been updated to reflect the change as sponsors are still denoted as A (Trusted) and B (Sponsor).

HTS status. Licence rating is a reflection of a sponsor's performance and the ability for a sponsor to run its operations without detriment to immigration control. Unlike a sponsor licence number, a sponsor's rating or its HTS status are publicly displayed on the Register of Sponsors alongside its name. From 5 September 2011 the sponsor rating system changed.

4.25 Prior 5 September 2011 an A rating was given to sponsors who had all the necessary systems in place to observe their duties and had no evidence of abuse. A B rating was awarded to sponsors who were found wanting in terms of adequacy of their systems or if there was evidence of earlier abuse. This rating was transitional and could be awarded initially, on review following a visit, downgraded to during a licence's lifetime or given on renewal. A B rating also meant more frequent and extensive inspections and compliance with an action plan within a particular timeframe to gain or regain an A rating.

4.26 The Interpretation Section of the Immigration Rules (paragraph 6 of the Rules) describes an A-rated Sponsor as 'a Sponsor which is recorded as being "A-rated" on the register of licensed Sponsors maintained by the United Kingdom Border Agency' and a Highly Trusted Sponsor as 'a sponsor which is recorded as being "Highly Trusted" on the register of licensed sponsors maintained by the United Kingdom Border Agency'. A B-rated Sponsor is defined as 'a sponsor which is recorded as being "B-rated" on the register of licensed sponsors maintained by the United Kingdom Border agency.' This last definition was inserted into the Rules by the Statement of Changes in Immigration Rules (HC 908) laid before Parliament on 31 March 2011.

4.27 Before turning to the practicalities of how to apply for a licence, its cost, period of validity and how to sponsor Tier 4 migrants, it is important to examine the component elements underpinning the system that will prepare your organisation for the rigours of sponsorship in terms of what it needs to have in place before making an application to register.

Pre-licensing

Key personnel

4.28 Before making an application for a sponsor licence, the prospective sponsor must allocate particular roles to 'key personnel' (members of its staff and/or representatives) who must be permanently based in the United Kingdom to fulfil certain responsibilities in the day-to-day management of Tier 4 students. There are four key roles: (1) authorising officer; (2) key contact; (3) level 1 user; and (4) level 2 user, and they can be performed by one person or a group of different people depending on the size and capacity of the organisation. Their duties and assignments have been modified slightly over recent years. If the organisation outsources its human resources function to another organisation, then some of the key roles may be assigned to the employees of that third party organisation. Reference should be made to paragraphs 112–145 of the Sponsor Guidance.

4.29 There can be only one authorising officer and one key contact but more than one level 1 and level 2 user. Only level 1 and level 2 users are given passwords and have varying degrees of instant access to the SMS. Their email addresses must be secure and personal to them. A level 2 user has limited access to the SMS as compared to a level 1 user, and thus fulfils only limited and ancillary functions. If the authorising officer or key contact wants to use the SMS at any level, they must be set up on the system as a user.

4.30 While key personnel have a cascading range of obligations, the sponsor bears the burden of responsibility for the actions of all SMS users including representatives and the authorising officer (paragraph 117 of the Sponsor Guidance). It is arguable that the proposed relationship between the sponsor and key personnel is tantamount to the former assuming vicarious liability under the *respondeat superior*[27] doctrine which may give rise to issues not only in tort but also in contract and employment law. Generally, adverse actions by key personnel rendering the sponsor non-compliant with its duties may result in the sponsor having its licence suspended or revoked, its rating downgraded or the number of CAS it is allowed to assign reduced.

4.31 Given the extent of risk exposure for the sponsor, it is best practice to exercise caution and prudence when appointing key personnel roles to members of staff and representatives (see further **Chapter 5**) including running identity/background checks and checking with professional regulatory bodies[28] and asking for Criminal Records Bureau checks to be done. In turn, the UKBA will run criminal and civil liability checks on the authorising officer, key contact, level 1 user, the director and/or owner and any person involved in the everyday running of the educational establishment (paragraph 121 of the Sponsor Guidance). Checks will be made at the application stage or at any time during the lifespan of the licence, especially if new members of key personnel are brought on board. If any of these individuals have unspent criminal convictions or civil penalties issued against them by the UKBA in the preceding 12 months, the UKBA may refuse the application for a sponsor licence, or, if the licence has already been granted, refuse to accept a person subsequently nominated for a key personnel role and revoke the licence (paragraph 123 of the Sponsor Guidance). Each key personnel role will now be considered in terms of their suitability parameters and responsibilities.

27 A common law doctrine of agency whereby the superior is responsible for the acts of its subordinate.
28 For example, the Law Society of England and Wales (www.lawsociety.org.uk) and the General Council of the Bar (www.barcouncil.org.uk) have member directories accessible online, compartmentalised by names of individual solicitors/barristers and their firms/chambers.

Authorising officer

SUITABILITY PARAMETERS

4.32 Please refer to paragraphs 124–131 of the Sponsor Guidance. The role of an authorising officer is one of a supervisor and a decision maker who projects the will of the sponsor insofar as SMS management and compliance with sponsor duties are concerned. A sponsor must appoint an authorising officer at application stage and this must be reflected on the application form. The person nominated to be an authorising officer should be trustworthy, with an established track record within the organisation and managerial/administrative background. Education providers often assign this role to a director or an owner of a private further education establishment, a principal or head of admissions of a school, or an admissions/ international officer at university although other office holders may also be suitable for this position. If an authorising officer is a non-EU/EEA national, his or her immigration status details may need to be provided during the application process. An authorising officer does not have automatic access to the SMS and must be set up on the system as a level 1 or level 2 user to have access.

4.33 An authorising officer must be:

- a responsible and competent person;
- a paid member of staff or office holder in the sponsor organisation;
- permanently based in the United Kingdom; and
- in place at all times throughout the lifetime of a licence.

In accordance with paragraph 129 of the Sponsor Guidance an authorising officer must not be:

> '• a representative;
> • a contractor or consultant who is contracted for a specific project;[29]
> • a temporary staff member supplied by an agency;[30] or
> • an un-discharged bankrupt.'

4.34 The policy department at the UKBA has provided the following definition of an office holder:

> 'a worker who holds an office is traditionally not considered to be an employee because their office continues in existence independently of the particular office holder who, for the time being, holds the position. However, there are exceptions to this approach, for example, police officers are office holders but, by virtue of specific statutory provision, are treated as employees for the purposes of health

29 For example, IT consultants unless they are full-time members of staff.
30 Such as supply teachers or temporary administrative staff.

and safety legislation. However, a person may be both an office holder and an employee at the same [sic]. The category of workers known as "office holders" includes police constables, prison officers, company directors, trustees, members of the clergy, trade union officials, magistrates and club secretaries. An "office" is a permanent post which exists independently of the person who holds [sic].'[31]

4.35 A further definition of an office holder is provided in paragraph 130 of the Sponsor Guidance:

> 'A person who holds an office under one of the following types of appointment, is likely to be an 'office holder':
>
> - a statutory appointment (such as registered company directors or secretaries, board members of statutory bodies, judges or tribunal members, or crown appointments, fro example, the police);
> - an appointment under the internal constitution of an organisation (such as club treasurers or trade union secretaries);
> - an appointment under a trust deed (such as trustees); or
> - an ecclesiastical appointment (such as members of the clergy).
>
> Paragraph 131 of the Sponsor Guidance goes on to state that 'an office holder is not an employee or a worker. But holding an office does not prevent someone from becoming a worker or an employee. They can be an office holder and an employee if their working arrangements are a contractual relationship and satisfy the test for employee status.'

RESPONSIBILITIES

4.36 An authorising officer will be responsible for:

- the activities of all SMS users (paragraph 128 of the Sponsor Guidance);
- deciding how many members of staff have access to the SMS and at what level (paragraph 126 of the Sponsor Guidance).

Key contact

4.37 Please refer to paragraphs 132–135 of the Sponsor Guidance. It is common practice for one person to combine the roles of the authorising officer and key contact, which may be more advantageous, particularly in smaller organisations. Conversely, the two roles can be fulfilled by two different individuals. The person appointed to this position must be permanently based in the United Kingdom. The key contact does not have automatic access to the SMS and must be set up on the system as a level 1 or level 2 user to have access.

31 Email received from the Customer Contact Centre, North East, Yorkshire and the Humber Region, UK Border Agency, 24 December 2010.

SUITABILITY PARAMETERS

4.38 A key contact must be:

- a paid member of staff or office holder in the sponsor organisation; or
- a representative or an employee of the representative based in the United Kingdom.

4.39 As per paragraph 134 of the Sponsor Guidance a key contact must not be:

- '• a contractor;
- a consultant who is contracted for a specific project;
- an employee of a third party organisation you have engaged to deliver all or part of your HR function; or
- a temporary staff member supplied by an agency.'

RESPONSIBILITIES

4.40 A key contact will be responsible for:

- being the main point of contact between the UKBA and the sponsor should any queries arise about the licence application, submitted documents or payment or at any time during the lifespan of the licence.[32]

Level 1 user

4.41 Please refer to paragraph 136–141 of the Sponsor Guidance. Before a sponsor licence is granted, the prospective sponsor can nominate only one level 1 user. However, once the sponsor licence is granted, it is up to the sponsor to decide how many additional level 1 users to appoint using the SMS. This depends on the sponsor's student capacity, human resources and needs of the organisation. The person appointed to this position must be permanently based in the United Kingdom.

SUITABILITY PARAMETERS

4.42 A level 1 user must be:

- a paid member of staff or office holder in the sponsor organisation; or
- an employee of a third party organisation engaged by the sponsor to deliver all or part of its HR function; or

32 Recent experience has shown that key contacts are called upon only occasionally as most correspondence is addressed to the authorising officer although this may vary from sponsor to sponsor.

- a representative or an employee of the representative based in the United Kingdom.

4.43 As per paragraph 141 of the Sponsor Guidance a level 1 user must not be:

- 'a contractor;
- a consultant who is contracted for a specific project;
- a temporary staff member supplied to you by an employment agency; or
- an undischarged bankrupt.'

RESPONSIBILITIES

4.44 A level 1 user will be responsible for:

- requesting additional level 1 users and adding level 2 users to the SMS or removing them;
- assigning CAS;
- requesting an increase in the number of CAS that can be assigned;
- notifying the UKBA of minor changes;
- completing the change of circumstances section on the SMS to notify the UKBA of more significant changes;
- reporting student activity;
- withdrawing CAS;
- informing the UKBA of changes to study/work placement addresses;
- using the Bulk Data Transfer functionality;
- amending user details.

Level 2 user

4.45 Please refer to paragraphs 142–145 of the Sponsor Guidance. Level 2 users have a more limited range of responsibilities and restricted access to the SMS. The sponsor can appoint as many level 2 users as required while keeping the number to a minimum for effective management and consistency. Level 2 users are appointed after the licence has been issued. The person appointed to this position must be permanently based in the United Kingdom.

SUITABILITY PARAMETERS

4.46 A level 2 user must be:

- a paid member of staff or office holder in the sponsor organisation; or

- an employee of a third party organisation engaged by the sponsor to deliver all or part of its HR function;[33] or
- a temporary member of staff supplied to the sponsor by an employment agency; or
- a representative or an employee of the representative based in the United Kingdom.

4.47 As per paragraph 145 of the Sponsor Guidance a level 2 user must not be:

'• a contractor;
• a consultant who is contracted for a specific project; or
• an undischarged bankrupt.'

RESPONSIBILITIES

4.48 A level 2 user will be responsible for:

- assigning CAS; and
- reporting student activity.

The key personnel are there to ensure that the sponsor adheres to its duties while sponsoring students.

Sponsor Duties

4.49 As explained above, sponsorship is the cornerstone of the PBS and one of the main dogmas underpinning the system is that those who benefit from it most must play a role in safeguarding the system against abuse. When reading this section, reference should be made to paragraphs 452–487 of the Sponsor Guidance and Appendix D to the Sponsor Guidance. As part of this trade-off, sponsors are compelled to observe a number of duties, the variety and austerity of which have gone through a series of transformations, in order to prevent abuse, capture patterns of disconcerting student behaviour and monitor compliance with the Immigration Rules.

4.50 The UKBA put out two papers to punctuate the commencement of its consultation *The Student Immigration System, A Consultation*[34] on 7 December

33 When appointing an employee of a third party organisation to the role of a level 2 user, the address that must be given is the main business address of the third party organisation (paragraph 119 of the Sponsor Guidance).

34 *The Student Immigration System, a Consultation*, UK Border Agency, December 2010, page 5 www.ukba.homeoffice.gov.uk/sitecontent/documents/policyandlaw/consultations/students/student-consultation.pdf?view=Binary. The consultation ran for eight weeks until 31 January 2011.

2010 and the publication of its findings together with the Statement of Changes in Immigration Rules (HC 908) on 31 March 2011 together with policy guidance effective from 21 April 2011. In March 2011 the UKBA published findings of a study into attendance at privately funded colleges analysing compliance of a random sample of 4,000 Tier 4 (General) migrants whose leave was granted between April and September 2010.[35] The three-page précis was supplemented by a four-page statistical summary 'intended to provide an insight into trends only' of breaches of immigration control including detection of forgeries, refusals at ports, enforcement activity.[36]

4.51 Publication of this study at the time of unveiling of the new Government's student policy cannot be coincidental. This piece was preceded by the publication of a research paper in December 2010 whose aim was to 'provide estimates of the proportions of non-EEA students, required to apply for visas under Tier 4 of the Points Based System (PBS)' and to 'provide information on student behaviours, in particular the degree of compliance with their permission to enter the UK between institution types.'[37] One can surmise that the conclusions drawn by these two papers merely serve to justify the current attitudes in immigration policy relating to international students and their sponsors.

4.52 As the system is still in its infancy having had its first full test run since March 2009, the fundamental components such as duties are likely to continue changing to reflect the objectives of the policy makers and pushing the flexibility test further to the point of uncertainty. Although all sponsors have to comply with the same sponsorship duties, those with HTS status are allowed some flexibility in reporting student non-attendance.

4.53 Duties are divided into *generic* (duties that apply to sponsors in all Tiers)[38] and *Tier-specific* (applicable only to a particular Tier).[39] Sponsors are advised to direct their queries about duties to the UKBA by contacting them by email at sponsorshipPBSenquiries@ukba.gsi.gov.uk or by telephone on 0300 1234699 (paragraph 486 of the Sponsor Guidance).

35 *Points Based System Tier 4 Attendance at Privately Funded Colleges*, UK Border Agency, March 2011, www.ukba.homeoffice.gov.uk/sitecontent/documents/aboutus/reports/privately-funded-colleges/report.pdf?view=Binary (last updated on 5 April 2011).

36 *Points Based System Tier 4 Attendance at Privately Funded Colleges, Annex: Background Information*, UK Border Agency, March 2011, www.ukba.homeoffice.gov.uk/sitecontent/documents/aboutus/reports/privately-funded-colleges/annex.pdf?view=Binary (last updated on 5 April 2011).

37 *Overseas Students in the Immigration System, Types of Institution and Levels of Study*, UK Border Agency, December 2010, www.ukba.homeoffice.gov.uk/sitecontent/documents/aboutus/reports/pbs-tier-4/overseas-students-report.pdf?view=Binary (last updated on 17 January 2011).

38 After 5 September 2011, these duties are known as duties that 'apply to all sponsors under the points-based system' (paragraph 454 of the Sponsor Guidance).

39 After 5 September 2011, these duties are known as duties that are 'specific to sponsors who are licensed under certain tiers or categories' (paragraph 454 of the Sponsor Guidance).

4.54 It is left to the sponsor to have in place effective mechanisms used to achieve compliance with the duties. The sponsor duties include: (a) complying with the law; (b) record keeping; (c) reporting; and (d) co-operating with the UKBA. The sponsor also has enhanced additional duties and responsibilities which are varied as the system changes. The practical implications of sponsor duties such as reporting and monitoring student activity have come under considerable criticism, especially in the academic circles.

4.55 Sponsor duties commence from the date of the sponsor licence being granted (paragraph 455 of the Sponsor Guidance). The sponsor is notified of this in writing by a letter approving its licence application (see below). The sponsor will be released from its duties in the following instances:

- if the sponsor surrenders its licence;
- if the sponsor has its licence revoked.[40]

A sponsor becomes responsible for each sponsored student when they issue a CAS to them and their responsibilities end when:

- the sponsor informs the UKBA that they prematurely finished their course of study and plan to leave the UK or apply for new permission to stay in the United Kingdom;
- the sponsored student leaves the country and their leave to stay in the United Kingdom ends; or
- the UKBA gives the sponsored student permission to study with a new sponsor or switch into another immigration category.[41]

Generic duties

RECORD KEEPING AND MONITORING STUDENT IMMIGRATION STATUS

4.56 Paragraph 460 of the Sponsor Guidance directs sponsors to keep all the documents listed in Appendix D to the Sponsor Guidance. Documents must be kept for: (a) the length of time a student is sponsored by the sponsor (if less than a year); (b) one year; (c) until an UKBA official has examined and approved them (whichever is shorter, unless the document must be kept for other reasons). Sponsors must hold on record certain documentation and information related to each of their students and make them available to the UKBA compliance officers when requested. Licensed sponsors must keep documents for each sponsored student as listed in Appendix D to the Sponsor Guidance. If applicable, they must

40 The sponsor will be required to comply with its duties even if its licence is suspended or its rating is downgraded.
41 Paragraph 457 of the Sponsor Guidance.

also familiarise themselves with the provisions of the guidance on preventing illegal working and codes of practice.[42]

4.57 Paragraph 460 of the Sponsor Guidance also states that the UKBA does not "tell you how to store the documents". Prior to 5 September 2011 it was stipulated that documents which were not in English/Welsh had to be accompanied by a certified translation featuring the translator's credentials and a declaration of accuracy. Copies of documents could be kept in electronic or paper format and all the relevant parts of each document had to be clearly visible. While it was not a requirement expressed in the Sponsor Guidance or Appendices, the UKBA had advised a number of sponsors that photocopies of relevant documents should be signed and dated on every page.

4.58 Below is a list of documents in which the author expands on the requirements set out in Appendix D and offers practical solutions:[43]

- a student's passport (while some sponsors may choose to keep a copy of the entire document, the UKBA advises to keep copies of the front cover, bio-page and visa endorsement), an ID card for foreign nationals ('ICFN') or a biometric residence permit ('BRP') issued by the UKBA (bearing details of a student's immigration status and period of validity, name and date of birth, employment restrictions, photograph and fingerprints on front and back of the card) or a United Kingdom immigration status document (a one-sided A4 sheet showing immigration status details and a photograph in the form of a residence permit stamp). As the sponsor is responsible for monitoring student's immigration status, it is also advisable to keep copies of each sponsored student's application for extension of stay allowing them to study in the United Kingdom, a copy of the Royal Mail special or recorded delivery slip and receipt as proof of in-time submission, and copies of certain UKBA correspondence such as an acknowledgment letter, a biometric appointment letter and a letter of approval. As it may take several weeks, depending on the standard of service processing times, from the date of the biometric appointment for postal applications to be considered, this will serve to ensure that any gap in the sponsored student's immigration status between the date of expiry of previous grant of leave and the date of the extension application being approved is accounted for.
- contact details including a residential address in the United Kingdom, a landline and mobile telephone number (the advanced list may be enhanced by details of any email addresses, emergency and next of kin contact numbers). Sponsors have employed various devices to keep these up to date including making this requirement a part of their terms and conditions of business, displaying visible

42 www.ukba.homeoffice.gov.uk/sitecontent/documents/employersandsponsors/preventingillegalworking/.

43 See also *New London College Ltd, R (on the application of) v Secretary of State for the Home Department* [2011] EWHC 865 (Admin) (7 April 2011) at para 108.

notices throughout their premises and sending email reminders to students at regular intervals.

- an ATAS clearance certificate, where applicable and is necessitated by the Immigration Rules. The sponsor must keep either a photocopy of the certificate or the electronic approval received by the sponsor from the Foreign and Commonwealth Office.
- letter of consent from parent(s) or a legal guardian agreeing to the travel, reception and care arrangements being made in respect of students under the age of 18; details of foster care, etc.[44]
  - — documents used by the sponsor to make an offer of a place on the course of study.
  - — attendance record.
- other documents related to students which the UKBA considers relevant.

REPORTING AND TRACKING STUDENT ATTENDANCE

4.59 As of 22 February 2010 with the introduction of CAS it became mandatory for sponsors to use the SMS to report certain information, events and changes in circumstances to the UKBA adversely affecting each sponsored student's enrolment, registration and attendance[45] of their Tier 4 main or pre-sessional[46] course of study and compliance with their immigration status within a specified time limit. Some reports may include mitigating reasons given by the sponsor or student. The reporting duties are set out in paragraphs 461–479 of the Sponsor Guidance. Now sponsors must report on students on the main course of study, a pre-sessional course at a 'partner institution' or on a work placement as part of the course (paragraph 462 of the Sponsor Guidance).

4.60 Sponsor reports are likely to lay the ground for the UKBA to take enforcement action against students such as curtail or cancel their leave and administratively remove them from the United Kingdom. Due to lack of feedback from the UKBA and history of disregard of enforcement policy[47] it is difficult to say in how many instances and with what frequency reports made by sponsors are used to initiate enforcement action against students.[48]

44 While students aged 16 or 17 have the legal right to live independently, they require the consent of their parent(s) or a legal guardian to do this and travel to the United Kingdom without adult supervision (the part relating to travel to and reception in the United Kingdom is particularly relevant in entry clearance applications). The requirement to have consent is set out in the Immigration Rules.

45 See *VB (Student-attendance and progress not equated) Jamaica* [2011] UKUT 119 (IAC) (28 March 2011) in which the Upper Tribunal held that satisfactory progress cannot be assumed from a good attendance record.

46 Undertaken with the main sponsor or at a partner institution named on the sponsor licence.

47 See **Chapter 2** referring to the Daily Mail report regarding the leaked memo of 17 December 2007.

48 Especially those students who are beyond the sponsor's control and have ceased attending their course of study without sponsor authorisation.

4.61 The sponsor's ability to hold on to the status quo of its licence and rating is inextricably linked to the sponsored student's ability to see their course of study through to completion. The reporting duty is not clear cut, as in most circumstances it is left to the sponsor to make a judgment call. It has sparked outrage in the academic circles where the reporting duty has been criticised for breaching the trust between teachers and students.[49] As a matter of good practice, sponsors should ask their sponsored students to keep them informed of any changes that may affect their immigration status and for sponsored students to request written permission from the sponsor for any anticipated absences from the course of study to avoid needless or excessive reports being made that may be detrimental to both the sponsor and the students.

4.62 Student attendance may be tracked electronically through student swipe cards or on paper using class registers. Sponsors who are not involved in assisting students with their Tier 4 applications for extension of stay should ask their sponsored students for a copy of their application (including their application form and proof of submission), and any UKBA correspondence received thereafter to prove that they made an in-time application and have extant leave within the meaning of the Immigration Act 1971, s 3C. It is up to the sponsor to choose the most effective method for tracking attendance and monitoring student immigration status depending on the size and budget of its organisation. Students should be warned of ramifications of non-attendance in writing.

4.63 A number of software development companies offer readymade and customised software products for education providers to administer their HR procedures and sponsorship duties. Depending on the sponsor's requirements and number of students some of the more sophisticated products require hardware support to track student attendance, store scanned records and provide advance warnings of students' leave expiring. A small number of the companies that offer PBS solutions are listed below but are by no means the only outlets on the market that provide such services.

- Infospeed Ltd offering the Class package for English language schools (www.class-systems.com);
- GPSoft offering the EduPro package for English language schools (www.gpsoft.co.uk);
- Perceptive Software offering ImageNow and other platforms for large organisations (www.perceptivesoftware.com/company/about-imagenow.psi);
- Jemmac Software (www.jemmac.com);
- Vizual Management Solutions Ltd (www.time-attendance.co.uk/Home.aspx);
- INSZoom Inc (www1.inszoom.com);

49 See *Fortress Academy,* Manifesto Club Report, Valerie Hartwich, February 2010, www.manifestoclub.com/files/FortressAcademy.pdf.

- Strive Software International (www.strivesoft.co.uk/);
- Tensor plc (www.tensor.co.uk/news/assessment-of-your-hr-systems-for-points-based-migration).

4.64 Information that suggests that a student is engaging in terrorism or any other criminal activity should also be reported to the police. Prior to 22 February 2010 reporting was voluntary and done electronically by sending email reports to MigrantReporting@UKBA.gsi.gov.uk. If the student's leave was granted on the basis of a visa letter (phased out as of 22 February 2010), reporting of information listed in Table 1 below remains voluntary. The sponsor is required to report the following information and events:

TABLE 1 – STUDENTS

Description of event/ information	*Time limit for a report to be made*	*Reasons and details included in a report*
Non-enrolment within the enrolment period stipulated by the sponsor (paragraph 463 of the Sponsor Guidance)	Within 10 working days from the end of the prescribed enrolment period	Any reason given by the student for non-enrolment such as missed flights, decision not to come to the United Kingdom, decision to take up a course with another sponsor, or having their application refused
If the sponsor is A-rated, missing 10 consecutive[50] expected contacts[51] without sponsor authorisation (paragraph 467 of the Sponsor Guidance)	Within 10 working days of the 10th missed contact	Any mitigating reasons given by the student

50 The requirement for *consecutive* expected contacts was added from 21 April 2011.

51 Contracts or interactions include but are not limited to: (a) registration: enrolment, matriculation; (b) attendance of any: lesson, tutorial, lecture, seminar, test, exam, assessment board, meeting with a supervisor or tutor, appointment with a welfare advisor or international student advisor, viva, 'research method' or 'research panel meetings, 'writing up' seminars or 'doctoral workshops'; or (c) submission of: coursework, interim dissertation/ coursework/ reports (paragraph 468 of the Sponsor Guidance).

Description of event/ information	*Time limit for a report to be made*	*Reasons and details included in a report*
If the sponsor has HTS status, missing 10 consecutive expected contacts without sponsor authorisation (paragraph 466 of the Sponsor Guidance)	Within 10 working days of the HTS sponsor completing their checkpoint process[52]	Any mitigating reasons given by the student
Discontinuation of studies including deferrals, student ceasing to attend the course of study or the sponsor withdrawing the student from the course (paragraph 472 of the Sponsor Guidance)	Within 10 working days of the event	Name and address of any new education provider that the student has joined, if known to the sponsor
Student switches to another immigration category or if Tier 4 sponsorship is no longer required for another reason (paragraph 473 of the Sponsor Guidance)	Within 10 working days of the event	Any reasons why Tier 4 sponsorship ceases to be relevant
Significant changes in the student's circumstances related to their course of study such as changes in the course start and end dates, and place of study, or any other changes that differ considerably from the information provided on the CAS (paragraph 476 of the Sponsor Guidance)	Within 10 working days	Affected details such as revised course start and end dates, and change of location/campus

52 HTS sponsors can make two checkpoints (re-registrations) in any 12-month period.

Description of event/ information	*Time limit for a report to be made*	*Reasons and details included in a report*
Any information suggesting that the student is breaching conditions of his/her leave (paragraph 476 of the Sponsor Guidance). Please refer Part 6A of the Immigration Rules, Appendices thereto and current Tier 4 student policy guidance for conditions of entry clearance or leave to remain related to Tier 4 (Child) and Tier 4 (General) students	Within 10 working days	Description of any alleged contravention. For example, working over and above the allowed number of hours during term time

TABLE 2 –SPONSORS

Description of event/ information	*Time limit for a report to be made*	*Reasons and details included in a report*
Any significant changes in the sponsor's circumstances such as becoming insolvent, ceasing trading, directors or owners filing for bankruptcy, being involved in a merger or takeover[53] (which principally affects its ownership structure), expansion of premises to include new locations and campuses (which affect capacity and sponsored students' principal place of study) (paragraph 477 of the Sponsor Guidance)	Within 28 calendar days	Details relevant to the change in circumstances

53 See **4.190**.

Description of event/ information	*Time limit for a report to be made*	*Reasons and details included in a report*
Appointment of a new principal or change of owners at a private further or higher education institution[54] (paragraph 478 of the Sponsor Guidance)	Within 28 calendar days	The name of the new principal or owner must be provided
Details of third parties or intermediaries based in the United Kingdom or abroad such as agents or other education providers working on a referral basis engaged in assisting in the recruitment of Tier 4 students (paragraph 479 of the Sponsor Guidance)	Within reasonable time (unless reported at application stage) as no time is specified by the UKBA	The name and address of the third party

COMPLYING WITH THE IMMIGRATION LAW

4.65 This duty is set out in paragraphs 458–459 of the Sponsor Guidance. It appears to be an overarching duty that lacks definition and has the potential to supersede the functions of officials charged with immigration control. It is controversial insofar as the sponsor must ensure the students' compliance with the immigration law as well as its own with the limited tools and knowledge at its disposal. Failure to comply with this duty adequately will have dire repercussions for the sponsor and the sponsored students. It is no overstatement that immigration law is a complex area of expertise not made simpler by the advent of radical measures to simplify it as it requires comprehensive understanding of the relationship between primary legislation, Immigration Rules, policy guidance and case law.

4.66 It is not clear how erudite sponsors have to be to understand what is involved in complying with this duty. It would be unreasonable to expect the sponsor to have anything more than a basic grasp of the immigration law drawn from the relevant provisions of the Immigration Rules related to students and relevant policy guidance. Nonetheless, in recent years sponsors have developed expert knowledge of this area of immigration law through practical experience. To quote Longmore LJ at paragraph 87 of the judgment in *AA (Nigeria) v Secretary of State for the Home Department* [2010] EWCA Civ 773 (06 July 2010):

54 Failure to report this within the specified time will lead to the sponsor licence being revoked.

> 'I am left perplexed and concerned how any individual whom the Rules affect (especially perhaps a student, like Mr A, who is seeking a variation of his leave to remain in the United Kingdom) can discover what the policy of the Secretary of State actually is at any particular time if it necessitates a trawl through Hansard or formal Home Office correspondence as well as through the comparatively complex Rules themselves. It seems that it is only with expensive legal assistance, funded by the taxpayer, that justice can be done.'

4.67 As part of their commitment to comply with the immigration law, the sponsor must ensure that (in line with paragraph 458 of the Sponsor Guidance) it assigns CAS to students who, to the best of belief, will meet the requirements of the Tier 4 category under which the CAS is assigned and comply with the conditions of their leave. As highlighted above (and in **Chapter 2**), CAS is an expression of good faith by the sponsor insofar as it is issued to the best of the sponsor's knowledge and belief.

4.68 There is also an additional requirement, where such a requirement is imposed by a Local Authority, to hold the appropriate planning permission or Local Planning Authority consent to operate the type or class or business conducted at the trading address (paragraph 459 of the Sponsor Guidance).

4.69 With the meagre means and experience of assessing prospective students for immigration risk the sponsor is required to provide a promise to the best of its knowledge and belief that the student is likely to observe the conditions attached to his or her immigration status. Universities have taken to employing immigration consultants and lawyers to deal with issues related to Tier 4 sponsorship.[55] Sponsors with fewer resources have to rely on in-house expertise. This is of particular concern when assigning CAS for entry clearance purposes where initial contact with potential students is either minimal or conducted entirely via third parties or intermediaries such as agents. Ceding control over recruiting international students to overseas agents with questionable practices has been raised as a concern by the UKBA when citing abuse of sponsorship arrangements.[56]

CO-OPERATING WITH THE UKBA

4.70 Paragraph 485 of the Sponsor Guidance lists three additional duties that the sponsor must comply with to allow UKBA to 'manage the sponsorship system properly':

55 Most universities provide immigration services to their international students through International Offices.

56 British Council provides guidance on engaging third parties or intermediaries for recruiting foreign students.

- allowing UKBA staff access to any of its premises on request as part of announced or unannounced visits;[57]
- observing any action plan and conditions set therein by a B rated sponsor under the Sponsor Guidance in place prior to 5 September 2011;
- seeking to minimise the risk of immigration abuse by complying with any good practice guidance set by the UKBA or any appropriate body within the education sector.

Additional duties specific to Tier 4 sponsors

4.71 Duties specific to Tier 4 sponsors were modified considerably as a result of changes brought in on 3 March 2010, 6 April 2010, 23 July 2010 and 12 August 2010.[58] Further changes were brought in on 21 April 2011 and 4 July 2011 adding to the already heavy burden of compliance. The additional duties are set out in a piecemeal manner in the Sponsor Guidance leaving the sponsor responsible for best practice and internal procedures in adhering to these duties.

ABILITY AND INTENTION TO FOLLOW THE COURSE OF STUDY

4.72 The sponsor may only assign a CAS to a student when it is satisfied that the student intends and is able to follow the course of study in respect of which CAS is being issued (paragraph 382 of the Sponsor Guidance). This requirement is similar to the one enshrined in paragraph 57(ii) of the Immigration Rules prior to 31 March 2009 whereby an immigration official had to subject the student's intention and ability to subjective scrutiny. Instead, the responsibility for assessing both ability and intention of the student to follow the chosen course of study now lies with the education provider and is outside the Immigration Rules. This has attracted criticism from entry clearance officers and immigration officers as it impedes their powers. This concern has been addressed as a result of the changes in the Immigration Rules on 21 April 2011.[59] Paragraph 245ZV(ca) of the Immigration Rules provides that:

> 'Where an applicant has been issued with a Confirmation of acceptance for studies on or after 21 April 2011, the applicant must, if required to do so

57 Visiting officers will usually contact the sponsor they intend to inspect although that is not always the case (paragraph 367 of the Sponsor Guidance). The House of Commons Home Affairs Committee recommended in July 2009 that in order to combat bogus colleges the checks should be 'rigorous and, critically, unannounced' (*Bogus colleges*, House of Commons Home Affairs Committee, HC 595, 21 July 2009, at para 22 www.publications.parliament.uk/pa/cm200809/cmselect/cmhaff/595/595.pdf).

58 Paragraphs 283–286, 291–293 were introduced to the Sponsor Guidance (version 10/10, 1 October 2010) on 3 March 2010 and 6 April 2010. They were modified further when the changes on 23 July 2010 and 12 August 2010 were brought in.

59 This is a far cry from the rhetoric of sharing responsibility with sponsors (see **Chapter 2**).

on examination or interview, be able to demonstrate without the assistance of an interpreter English language proficiency of a standard to be expected from an individual who has reached the standard specified in a Confirmation of acceptance for studies assigned in accordance with appendix a paragraph 118(c) (for the avoidance of doubt, the applicant will not be subject to a test at the standard set out in Appendix a, paragraph 118(c)).'

The same requirement is mirrored in paragraph 324 of the Sponsor Guidance.

4.73 As of 3 March 2010 students embarking on English language courses and courses below NQF Level 6, with the exception of those undertaking Foundation Degrees, must have been competent in English language at a minimum standard of CEFR level B1 (threshold, independent user on the global CEFR scale). The sponsor is responsible for assessing English language competence of students. The suitable form of assessment depends on when the CAS was assigned.[60] Secure English language testing by approved test providers was introduced on 12 August 2010. Further changes related to the English language proficiency came into effect on 21 April 2011 and are described in detail in **Chapter 3**. All sponsors must be familiar with and adhere to the English language testing procedures before issuing CAS. Information about what sponsors should put on a CAS in respect of the English language ability is included in paragraphs 330–334 of the Sponsor Guidance.

4.74 According to *Student Visas, Statement of Intent and Transitional Measures* published on 31 March 2011[61] when assessing whether a migrant can speak English to the required level an UKBA officer would 'test whether the student can hold a simple conversation without an interpreter'. If the student cannot speak English without assistance, his or her entry clearance application or admission to the United Kingdom may be refused subject to confirmation from a senior officer.[62]

4.75 Evidence of the assessment must be clearly stipulated on the CAS and any documents such as degree certificates used in the assessment must be attached to the application by the student. Unlike intention, ability can be tested by tangible means and it is up to the sponsor to decide on the acceptable mode of assessment.

4.76 The sponsor is required to do all that it can to ensure that the sponsored students take up the course of study and see it through to the end. It is difficult to imagine what draconian action the sponsor can take against the students, short of coercion, to guarantee a perfect record of their arrival and completion of the course. As explained above, the sponsor's licence and rating are intertwined

60 Currently, the Immigration Rules distinguish between CAS assigned before or after 21 April 2011. Previously, it depended on whether the CAS was assigned between 3 March 2010 and 11 August 2010, from 23 July 2010 or from 12 August 2010.

61 *Student Visas, Statement of Intent and Transitional Measures*, UK Border Agency, March 2011, www.ukba.homeoffice.gov.uk/sitecontent/documents/news/sop4.pdf.

62 In any event, this must be in line with the Immigration Act 1971.

with this duty and if the UKBA finds unacceptable levels of students not arriving or not completing their courses, it will investigate and take action against the sponsor including revocation of its sponsor licence (paragraph 482 of the Sponsor Guidance).

DUTIES RELATED TO CAS AND WORK PLACEMENTS

4.77 From 4 July 2011 if a sponsored student is changing a course and the new course is not higher up the NQF/QCF/SCQF scale than the previous course, the sponsor will have to vouch for the student's academic progression.[63] This relates to CAS assigned on or after 1 July 2011. Using the CAS 'evidence provided' box on the CAS the sponsor will also be asked to confirm that the new course is complementary to the previous course. The exceptions to this requirement are set out in paragraph 120B of Appendix A to the Immigration Rules. Where a CAS is assigned to a student whose course does not represent progression, action will be taken against the sponsor (paragraph 377 of the Sponsor Guidance).

Sponsors must not issue one CAS covering more than one course unless the student is to undertake a pre-sessional course to prepare for the main course of study (paragraph 386 of the Sponsor Guidance). Where any stage of the course leads to a qualification in its own right, then sponsors must assign a CAS before each stage commences (paragraph 387 of the Sponsor Guidance).

4.78 Only those sponsors who have been endorsed as 'ACCA Approved Learning Partner – student tuition (ALP-st)' at 'Gold' or 'Platinum' levels of quality assurance can issue CAS to students undertaking courses of study leading to an ACCA qualification (paragraph 388 of the Sponsor Guidance). This appears to be an additional accreditation requirement.

4.79 If a student is undertaking a work placement as part of their course, the work placement must be regularly monitored and assessed as part of the course by the sponsor and must:

- be an assessed part of the course; and
- not exceed 50% of the course.

If this duty is not complied with, the UKBA will take action against the sponsor (paragraph 481 of the Sponsor Guidance).

63 53% of respondents (overall number of respondents: 26,764) to the Tier 4 consultation agreed that students wishing to study a new course should be asked to demonstrate evidence of progression to a higher level. *Consultation on the student immigration system: 7th December 2010 to 31st January 2011. Consultation questionnaire results*, UK Border Agency, March 2011, at p 8 www.ukba.homeoffice.gov.uk/sitecontent/documents/policyandlaw/consultations/students/student-consultation-results.pdf?view=Binary. Also see *VB (Student-attendance and progress not equated) Jamaica* [2011] UKUT 119 (IAC) (28 March 2011).

MISCELLANEOUS DUTIES

4.80 The sponsor must also comply with the following duties (paragraph 484 of the Sponsor Guidance):

'• continue to be audited and/or inspected at a satisfactory and existing level;[64]
• offer courses to international students which comply with our conditions;
• notify the local authority of any private foster care arrangements for Tier 4 (Child) students, where appropriate.'

DEFERRAL

4.81 It is the responsibility of the sponsor to judge whether a student's absence is authorised or unauthorised as not every instance is clear cut (paragraph 470 of the Sponsor Guidance). It is also for the sponsor to judge whether following a period of absence the student will be able to resume their studies straight away or will need to repeat a previous period of study to progress further in the course.

4.82 Where a repeat period of study is necessary, the student may be required to defer the course. Any deferral must be reported, as explained above. Once a student has deferred their course of study, their leave will be curtailed and they must leave the United Kingdom with the exception of students sponsored by the Foundation Programme Office (paragraph 475 of the Sponsor Guidance).[65] If the student is in the United Kingdom and defers the course of study following arrival, their leave will cease to be valid. The deferral must be reported by the sponsor and the sponsor must advise the student to leave the United Kingdom. The Sponsor Guidance is silent on whether the UKBA will take any action to curtail the student's leave or whether the sponsor is expected to play the role of an immigration official in asking the student to leave the country.

RESUMPTION OF STUDIES

4.83 In the event where the sponsor informs the UKBA of a student missing 10 consecutive expected contacts (paragraph 469 of the Sponsor Guidance) and the lines of communication between the two are subsequently restored, the sponsor may want to consider taking the student back to continue the course of study. If the sponsor wishes to continue sponsoring the student, the UKBA must be duly notified. However, if the student's leave has already been cancelled, the student will need to make a new application before resuming his or her studies. If the student left the United Kingdom due to a deferral of their studies, they will need to make a fresh entry clearance application. This undoubtedly places an additional financial

64 See also paragraph 483 of the Sponsor Guidance.
65 As their sponsorship will continue until they leave the Foundation Programme for good or change their immigration status.

burden on students in travel and visa fees, and the requirement to demonstrate maintenance funds which may prove to be a barrier to further studies with the sponsor.

WITHDRAWING FROM STUDIES

4.84 As explained above, if the student abandons the course of study or informs the sponsor of leaving the course to go to another institution or the sponsor withdraws the course from the student, the UKBA must be notified within 10 working days of these events being confirmed (paragraph 472 of the Sponsor Guidance).

Criteria for a Tier 4 sponsor licence

4.85 Once the prospective sponsor has assessed its own internal systems and ability to commit resources to managing the SMS, it will need to meet the suitability and eligibility criteria before it can make the online application. In order to be granted a sponsor licence, the prospective sponsor must meet the general requirements, suitability and eligibility criteria all of which are described below. Prospective sponsors must also be mindful of the grounds of refusal (see below) as they feed into the suitability and eligibility criteria for sponsors.

General and Tier specific requirements

4.86 The prospective sponsor must comply with the following general requirements as set out in paragraph 198 of the Sponsor Guidance:

- 'complete the appropriate online sponsor application;
- pay the correct fee;
- provide proof that you are based in the UK;
- be able to provide original or certified copies of the documents listed in Appendix A, unless we say otherwise, to establish that you are genuine and operating or trading lawfully in the UK, and with the appropriate planning permission or local planning authority consent to operate the type or class of business at your trading address;
- meet the suitability requirements;
- show there are no reasons to believe that you are a threat to immigration control; and
- agree to comply with the duties of sponsorship.'

Educational oversight

4.87 In its consultation paper *The Student Immigration System.* the UKBA proposed to introduce stricter accreditation procedures for privately funded education providers in particular, 'from April 2011, as the accreditation of individual education providers within the private further and higher education sectors start to expire, the UK Border Agency will want to ensure the current system of accreditation of these providers is replaced by a system which generates greater confidence in the register of sponsors.'[66] The Home Affairs Committee which published the conclusions of its own inquiry into the student route on 17 March 2011 agreed with the Government's proposal.[67] It also recommended that accreditation should be provided by one body rather than five. The Committee were informed during an evidence session that 'the approval for the five accreditation bodies had lapsed in 2009 and had not yet been renewed.'[68]

4.88 On 31 March 2011 the Government published a number of papers concluding its student review amongst which was *Student Visas, Statement of Intent and Transitional Measures.* In this document the UKBA stated that it had arrangements with the five accreditation bodies 'for a period of two years, which have now lapsed in four cases and in the fifth, due to lapse in May 2011' and that it had no intention of renewing them for the purpose of Tier 4.[69] Instead, private further and higher education providers would have to fulfil different criteria of educational oversight subject to a transitional period starting from 21 April 2011.

PRIOR TO 21 APRIL 2011

4.89 Paragraph 25 of the Sponsor Guidance (version 10/10, 1 October 2010) required prospective sponsors to demonstrate that they:

- 'have been inspected or audited; or
- are subject to review by an appropriate body; or
- hold valid accreditation as outlined below; or
- for overseas providers, directly offer short-term "study abroad" programmes in their own premises in the United Kingdom.'

4.90 Effectively, this meant the following:

- if subject to the system of public reviews, had to show that the education provider had been inspected, audited or reviewed by an appropriate body (see immediately below); or

66 *The Student Immigration System, a Consultation*, UK Border Agency, December 2010, at p 22 www.ukba.homeoffice.gov.uk/sitecontent/documents/policyandlaw/consultations/students/student-consultation.pdf?view=Binary. The consultation ran for eight weeks until 31 January 2011.

67 *Student Visas*, House of Commons Home Affairs Committee, Seventh Report of Session 2010–11, Volume 1, HC 773, 17 March 2011, http://www.parliament.uk/documents/commons-committees/home-affairs/Studentvisas.pdf.

68 *Student Visas*, House of Commons Home Affairs Committee, Seventh Report of Session 2010–11, Volume 1, HC 773, 17 March 2011, at p 31 www.parliament.uk/documents/commons-committees/home-affairs/Studentvisas.pdf.

69 *Student Visas, Statement of Intent and Transitional Measures*, UK Border Agency, March 2011, at p 6 www.ukba.homeoffice.gov.uk/sitecontent/documents/news/sop4.pdf.

- if outside the system of public reviews, had to show that the education provider holds valid accreditation from an appropriate body (see below for a further explanation); or
- if the prospective sponsor is an overseas higher education provider, had to show that the education provider directly offered short-term 'study abroad' programmes in its own premises in the United Kingdom in order to claim exemption from having UK accreditation (see below for a further explanation).

Education providers subject to public reviews[70]

4.91 Education providers ranging from universities to independent schools[71] subject to the system of public reviews by virtue of receiving public funding or having been granted UK degree-awarding powers must demonstrate that they have been inspected, audited or reviewed by one of the following bodies listed in the Sponsor Guidance and the UKBA website:

The Quality Assurance Agency for Higher Education ('QAA') – for education providers anywhere in the United Kingdom. QAA is an independent body carrying out external quality assurance in higher education by visiting universities and colleges to review compliance with their responsibilities, providing guidance on maintaining academic standards and investigating causes for concern. It carries out a number of reviews and audits depending on the country and type of institution. These can be found at www.qaa.ac.uk/reviews/default.asp.

Contact details:

Address: QAA
Head Office
Southgate House
Southgate Street
Gloucester
GL1 1UB

QAA Scotland
183 St Vincent Street
Glasgow
G2 5QD

70 Reference should be made to paragraph 26 of the Sponsor Guidance, version 10/10, 1 October 2010.

71 State schools are not eligible to apply for a sponsor licence (paragraph 28 of the Sponsor Guidance, version 10/10, 1 October 2010).

Tel:	+44 (0)1452 557000 (Head Office) +44 (0)141 572 3420 (Scotland) +44 (0)1452 557 127 (Wales) +44 (0)1452 557044 (International Team)
Fax:	+44 (0)1452 557070 (Head Office and International Team) +44 (0)141 572 3421 (Scotland)
Contact person:	Mr Stephen Jackson (Director of Reviews) Mr Julian Ellis (Institutional Review in Wales) Ms Gillian King (Audit, institutional, collaborative and overseas) Ms Carolyn Campbell (International work)
Email:	comms@qaa.ac.uk (Head Office and Scotland) j.ellis@qaa.ac.uk (Wales) international@qaa.ac.uk (International Team)
Website:	http://www.qaa.ac.uk/

The Independent Schools Inspectorate ('ISI') – for education providers anywhere in the United Kingdom. ISI is a 'not for profit' organisation which is an arm of the Independent Schools Council ('ISC'). ISC represents 1,260 independent schools covering the entire academic range. ISI is responsible for the inspection of these ISC schools pursuant to the Education Act 2002, s 162A, as amended by the Education Act 2005, Sch 8. It reports to Department for Education and is monitored by Ofsted. ISI inspection reports are publicly available at www.isi.net/SearchResults.aspx?s=A&t=a .

Contact details:

Address:	The Independent Schools Inspectorate CAP House 9–12 Long Lane London EC1A 9HA
Tel:	+44 (0)20 7600 0100 (Switchboard) +44 (0)20 7776 8831 (Inspection Queries and Support)
Fax:	+44 (0) 20 7776 8849
Contact person:	Ms Lynn Bappa
Email:	info@isi.net (General) lynn.bappa@isi.net (Ms Lynn Bappa) other contact email addresses are available on the website
Website:	www.isi.net

the Office for Standards in Education ('Ofsted').[72] 'Handbook for the inspection of further education and skills from September 2009' can be downloaded from the Ofsted website.[73]

Contact details:

Address:	Office for Standards in Education Royal Exchange Buildings St Ann's Square Manchester M2 7LA
Tel:	0300 123 4234 (about education or adult skills) 0300 123 1231 (about children's services or any other aspect of its work)
Office hours:	8.00am – 8.00pm, Monday to Friday
Email:	enquiries@ofsted.gov.uk
Website:	www.ofsted.gov.uk/

The Bridge Schools Inspectorate ('BSI') –for education providers in England. BSI was approved by the Secretary of State for Education in 2008 as a body established for the purposes of inspecting selected registered, independent schools under the Education Act 2002,s 162A, as amended by the Education Act 2005, Sch 8. BSI whose work is monitored by Ofsted, inspects schools under the umbrella of the Christian School's Trust ('CST') and the Association of Muslim Schools ('AMSUK') in England. It publishes its inspection reports for each school that it inspects (currently 55 schools) and these can be found categorised by 'school' or 'region' online www.bridgeschoolsinspectorate.co.uk/find_a_school. Its 'Framework for Inspections October 2009' can be found among other useful inspection documents on its website.

Contact details:

Address:	Bridge Schools Inspectorate 72C Woodstock Road Witney Oxfordshire OX28 1DY United Kingdom
Contact person:	Miss Julia Morgan
Office hours:	9.00am – 4.00pm (Monday) 9.00am – 12.30pm (Tuesday–Thursday)

72 The UKBA will accept an Ofsted report from any private, further education provider which offers courses attracting public funding (paragraph 26 of the Sponsor Guidance, version 10/10, 1 October 2010).

73 www.ofsted.gov.uk/Ofsted-home/Forms-and-guidance/Browse-all-by/Other/General/Handbook-for-the-inspection-of-further-education-and-skills-from-September-2009.

Tel:	01993 866060
Email:	bsi@dsl.pipex.com
Website:	www.bridgeschoolsinspectorate.co.uk/home

The Schools Inspection Service ('SIS') – for education providers in England. It is an independent body established and approved by the Secretary of State for Education in 2006 under the Education Act 2002, s 162A, as amended by the Education Act 2005, Sch 8. It inspects registered, independent schools in England and is monitored jointly by Ofsted and Department for Education.[74] It inspects a relatively small number of independent schools and past and recent reports can be found on its website at www.schoolinspectionservice.co.uk/recent_inspections.php.
Contact details:

Address:	The School Inspection Service Tolbury House Bruton Somerset BA10 0DG
Email:	enquiries@schoolinspectionservice.co.uk
Website:	www.schoolinspectionservice.co.uk/index.html

Her Majesty's Inspectorate of Education ('HMIE') – for education providers in Scotland. It inspects and reports on the quality of education in pre-school centres, primary schools, secondary schools, community learning and development services, colleges and residential education provision.
Contact details:

Address:	HM Inspectorate of Education Denholm House Almondvale Business Park Livingston EH54 6GA
Office hours:	8.30am – 5.00pm (Monday–Thursday) 8.30am – 4.30pm (Friday)
Tel:	+44 (0)1506 600 200
Textphone:	+44 (0)1506 600 236
Website:	www.hmie.gov.uk

74 DCSF was renamed Department for Education ('DfE') on 12 May 2010.

Estyn – for education providers in Wales. Estyn is the office of Her Majesty's Inspectorate for Education and Training in Wales. While it is independent, it is funded by the National Assembly for Wales under the Government of Wales Act 1998, s 104. It is responsible for inspecting a wide range of education providers, from nursery schools, primary and secondary schools to adult community-based learning and youth support centres.

Contact details:

Address:	Estyn Anchor Court Keen Road Cardiff CF24 5JW
Tel:	029 2044 6446
Fax:	029 2044 6448
Email:	enquiries@estyn.gov.uk (General Enquiries) Chief-Inspector@estyn.gov.uk (Chief Inspector and for all other communications with Estyn)
Website:	www.estyn.gov.uk

The Education and Training Inspectorate – for education providers in Northern Ireland. It provides inspections services for the Department of Education, Department of Culture, Arts and Leisure and Department for Employment & Learning being responsible for inspecting pre-school and nursery schools, colleges of further and higher education, and youth centres.

Contact details:

Address:	Headquarters of the Education and Training Inspectorate Inspection Services Branch Department of Education Rathgael House 43 Balloo Road Bangor Co Down BT19 7PR
Tel:	028 9127 9726
Fax:	028 9127 9721
Email:	inspectionservices@deni.gov.uk
Website:	www.etini.gov.uk

Education providers not subject to public reviews[75]

4.92 On 24 July 2007 the Government announced that it would be mandatory for private institutions outside the system of private reviews to be accredited before they could recruit international students under the PBS. Under the current system, a private higher education establishment which is outside the system of public reviews will need to have valid accreditation from one of the bodies listed in the Sponsor Guidance and on the UKBA website:

the Office for Standards in Education ('Ofsted').[76] See above for contact details.

Accreditation UK – run by British Council for English language schools, accreditation is awarded for up to four years subject to conditions set out in the Handbook. Check the Accreditation UK Handbook 2010–11 for details of eligibility and application process.[77] A list of providers accredited by Accreditation UK can be accessed at www.britishcouncil.org/accreditation-az-list.htm.
Contact details:

Address:	Accreditation Unit British Council Bridgewater House 58 Whitworth Street Manchester M1 6BB
Tel:	0161 957 7414
Contact person:	Ms Laura Conway, Customer Services Assistant
Email:	accreditation.unit@britishcouncil.org
Website:	www.britishcouncil.org/accreditation-about-us-contact-us.htm

the British Accreditation Council ('BAC') – offers a general accreditation service to a wide range of education providers and courses. Check the BAC Handbook for 2010–11[78] and various addenda on the BAC website which can be accessed at www.the-bac.org/accreditation/handbooks/index.html. Accreditation is awarded for up to four years subject to a successful interim inspection and other requirements set out in the Handbook. A list of providers accredited by BAC

75 Reference should be made to paragraph 29 of the Sponsor Guidance (version 10/10, 1 October 2010).
76 Ofsted has withdrawn its accreditation service but an Ofsted accreditation report produced prior to the service being withdrawn will be accepted provided that it is still valid (paragraph 29 of the Sponsor Guidance, version 10/10, 1 October 2010).
77 www.britishcouncil.org/2010–11_accreditation_handbook-new.pdf.
78 www.the-bac.org/accreditation/handbooks/ahuk0910.pdf.

can be found at www.the-bac.org/colleges/directory/index.html for both UK and international colleges.

Contact details:

Address:	British Accreditation Council 44 Bedford Row London WC1R 4LL
Tel:	+44 (0)20 7447 2584
Fax:	+44 (0)20 7447 2585
Email:	info@the-bac.org (General Enquiries) apply@the-bac.org (Applications for accreditation) finance@the-bac.org (Finance Office) inspections@the-bac.org (Inspection Scheduling)
Website:	http://www.the-bac.org/

Accreditation Service for International Colleges ('ASIC') – offers a general accreditation service to a wide range of education providers and courses. ASIC is an independent body approved by Ofsted to accredit independent further and higher education colleges. The directory of colleges accredited by ASIC are publicly accessible on its website at www.asic.org.uk/collegedirectoryUK.php. Its Accreditation Handbook can be downloaded from www.asic.org.uk/Documents/ASIC%20Handbook.pdf.

Contact details:

Address:	Accreditation Service for International Colleges Laburnum House Drovers Lane Redmarshall Stockton-on-tees TS21 1EL
Tel:	+44 (0)1740 630 956
Fax:	+44 (0)1740 630 956
Email:	info@asic.org.uk
Website:	www.asic.org.uk

the Accreditation Body for Language Services Ltd – a more recent addition to the list of approved accreditation bodies, this is a limited company carrying out initial and repeat inspections of providers of private and independently run English language services – schools, colleges and academies.[79]

79 The company's website lists 33 education providers inspected and accredited by it–www.ablsaccreditation.co.uk/schoolaccinfo.asp.

Its Accreditation Handbook 2011 can be downloaded from its website at www.ablsaccreditation.co.uk/docs/Accreditation_Handbook_2011.pdf.
Contact details:

Address:	The Accreditation Body for Language Services PO Box 316 Great Yarmouth NR30 9EP
Tel:	+44 (0)1493 393471
Email:	info@ablsaccreditation.co.uk
Website:	www.ablsaccreditation.co.uk

the Church of England Ministry Division – offers a quality assurance and accreditation service for education providers offering training for Christian ministry in the participating churches. Further information about quality assurance in ministerial education can be found at www.cofe.anglican.org/lifeevents/ministry/qualityassurance/.
Contact details:

Address:	The Church of England National Offices Church House Great Smith Street London SW1P 3AZ
Tel:	+44 (0)20 7898 1000
Email:	webmaster@c-of-e.org.uk
Website:	www.cofe.anglican.org

4.93 Prior to the new provisions being introduced the UKBA used to accept a provisional Stage 2 accreditation from a new private further education establishment which had been trading for less than 18 months[80] and is in the process of gaining an accreditation from one of the appropriate bodies provided that the education provider obtained full Stage 3 academic accreditation within 12 months. New sponsors with Stage 2 accreditation would be rated B (Sponsor) from the start until they gained full Stage 3 accreditation (paragraph 30 of the Sponsor Guidance, version 10/10, 1 October 2010). Accreditation bodies were required to report to the UKBA[81] when an education provider was stripped of its accreditation and to act promptly to address UKBA concerns. If accreditation is removed during the lifetime of the sponsor licence, the sponsor stands to have its licence revoked forthwith.

80 The trading period of 18 months will start from the point the education provider first commences trading or resumes trading after a period of dormancy.

81 This may give an opportunity for a conflict of interest to arise between the duties owed by accreditation bodies to the UKBA and its members.

FROM 21 APRIL 2011

PROSPECTIVE SPONSORS

4.94 According to paragraph 54 of the Sponsor Guidance when making an application for a Tier 4 sponsor licence, education providers must demonstrate that they:

- 'have been inspected or audited by an appropriate body;
- are subject to review by an appropriate body; or
- for overseas providers, you offer short-term 'study abroad' programmes in your own premises in the UK.'

PUBLICLY FUNDED EDUCATION PROVIDERS

4.95 Education providers who are subject to the system of public reviews by virtue of being publicly funded, having UK degree awarding powers or there being a statutory requirement for inspection must show that they have 'a current and satisfactory full inspection, review or audit by one of the appropriate bodies listed below':[82]

- Quality Assurance Agency for Higher Education (QAA) (UK-wide);
- Office for Standards in Education (Ofsted);
- The Bridge Schools Inspectorate (England);
- Schools Inspection Service (England);
- Education Scotland;[83]
- Estyn (Wales);
- Education and Training Inspectorate (Northern Ireland);
- Independent Schools Inspectorate (ISI) (UK-wide).

PRIVATELY FUNDED EDUCATION PROVIDERS

4.96 Privately funded further, higher and English language education providers wishing to apply for a Tier 4 sponsor licence after 21 April 2011 must also show that they have been inspected, audited or reviewed by one of the above bodies.

82 Paragraph 55 of the Sponsor Guidance.

83 Before the announcement of 28 July 2011, the relevant inspectorate body for Scotland was Her Majesty's Inspectorate of Education. *Confirmation of educational oversight arrangements for Tier 4 sponsors,* UK Border Agency, 28 July 2011, http://www.ukba.homeoffice.gov.uk/sitecontent/newsarticles/2011/july/50-tier-4-sponsors.

Inspectorate	**Providers of privately funded education**
Quality Assurance Agency (QAA) (paragraph 56 of the Sponsor Guidance)	higher education providers and pre-sessional providers throughout the United Kingdom[84]
Independent Schools Inspectorate (ISI), Ofsted, Education Scotland, Estyn, the Bridge Schools Inspectorate (BSI) and the School Inspection Service (SIS) (paragraph 57 of the Sponsor Guidance)	further education providers and English language schools in England, Scotland and Wales
The Bridge Schools Inspectorate (BSI) (paragraph 58 of the Sponsor Guidance)	religious colleges of further education in England and Wales
The School Inspection Service (SIS) (paragraph 58 of the Sponsor Guidance)	Montessori and Steiner providers of further education in England and Wales
Independent Schools Inspectorate (ISI) (paragraph 58 of the Sponsor Guidance)	further education colleges and English language schools in Wales (with the exception of religious, Montessori and Steiner colleges)
Education Scotland (paragraph 58 of the Sponsor Guidance)	further education colleges and English language schools in Scotland
Quality Assurance Agency (QAA) (paragraphs 68–69 of the Sponsor Guidance)	foreign providers offering full recognised overseas degree programmes in the United Kingdom (including accredited US institutions listed on the US Department of Education website and associate members or third party providers of the Association of American Study Abroad Programmes UK (AASAP/UK))

Further education colleges and English language colleges in Northern Ireland are yet to be assigned an appropriate body to inspect, review or audit them.

4.97 Accreditation by one of the bodies listed below will no longer be sufficient for entry of private funded education providers onto the Register of Sponsors:

84 Mixed higher and further education providers should apply to QAA or the appropriate further education inspectorate depending on the ratio of higher education courses to further education courses they offer.

- Accreditation UK;
- The Accreditation Service for British Language Schools (ABLS);
- The Accreditation Service for International Colleges (ASIC);
- The British Accreditation Council (BAC); and
- The Church of England Inspectorate – Ministry Division.

4.98 In *Student Visas, Statement of Intent and Transitional Measures* published on 31 March 2011 it states that those education providers accredited by Accreditation UK, ABLS, ASIC or BAC would be eligible for a Tier 4 sponsor licence provided they meet all the other criteria and make their application before 21 April 2011 or in the case of those accredited by the Church of England Inspectorate – Ministry Division before 10 May 2011.[85]

4.99 By way of an exception, accreditation from the above private accrediting bodies will still be acceptable for education providers who cater for student visitors and child visitors undertaking a course of study and education providers of courses in English for Speakers of Other Languages for the purpose of applying for settlement and citizenship.[86]

EXISTING SPONSORS

4.100 All sponsors must:

- have acquired HTS status by April 2012 (HTS status requirement); and
- have been inspected, audited or reviewed by one of the relevant bodies listed above by the end of 2012 (educational oversight requirement).

Existing sponsors who do not already meet the above requirements will be allowed to stay on the Register of Sponsors provided they continue to comply with their sponsorship duties. They will be subject to an interim limit (see below[87]) until they are able to satisfy both of the requirements (paragraph 76 of the Sponsor Guidance). As soon as the sponsors are able to demonstrate that they satisfy both requirements, the interim limit will be removed. The UKBA has set various deadlines by which existing sponsors who do not meet the educational oversight requirement must apply to the relevant body.[88] The UKBA has also published guidance on how

85 This concession was inserted into the Sponsor Guidance from 4 July 2011 at paragraph 44 (it refers to 21 May 2011 as being the relevant date from which accreditation by the Church of England – Ministry Division is no longer sufficient to meet the criteria for entry onto the Register of Sponsors).

86 *Student Visas, Statement of Intent and Transitional Measures*, UK Border Agency, March 2011, at p 6 www.ukba.homeoffice.gov.uk/sitecontent/documents/news/sop4.pdf.

87 See the section on Interim Limit, **4.179**.

88 See the section on Prospective Sponsors above, **4.94**.

and when sponsors wishing to begin or continue recruiting non-EU/EEA students must apply for HTS status.

Transitional arrangements

4.101 Accreditation by one of the bodies listed below is no longer sufficient for entry of private funded education providers onto the Register of Sponsors (paragraph 70 of the Sponsor Guidance):

- Accreditation UK;
- The Accreditation Service for British Language Schools (ABLS);
- The Accreditation Service for International Colleges (ASIC);
- The British Accreditation Council (BAC); and
- The Church of England Inspectorate – Ministry Division.

4.102 In *Student Visas, Statement of Intent and Transitional Measures* published on 31 March 2011 it stated that those education providers accredited by Accreditation UK, ABLS, ASIC or BAC would be eligible for a Tier 4 sponsor licence provided they met all the other criteria and made their application before 21 April 2011 or in the case of those accredited by the Church of England Inspectorate – Ministry Division before 10 May 2011.[89]

4.103 By way of an exception, accreditation from the above private accrediting bodies will still be acceptable for education providers who cater for student visitors and child visitors undertaking a course of study and education providers of courses in English for Speakers of Other Languages for the purpose of applying for settlement and citizenship.[90]

4.104 Existing sponsors with partial or interim accreditation awarded by one of the above accreditation bodies may wish to pursue full accreditation with them. It does not, however, absolve them of the educational oversight requirement.

4.105 The UKBA made announcements about the appropriate educational oversight arrangements on 13 June 2011 and 28 July 2011. Notably, neither of the approved educational oversight bodies were set up to inspect privately funded education providers at the time of the new requirements coming into force on 21 April 2011. On 13 June 2011 the UKBA announced that QAA and ISI had agreed to extend their remit to reviewing privately funded education providers in England

89 This concession was inserted into the Sponsor Guidance from 4 July 2011 at paragraph 44 (it refers to 21 May 2011 as being the relevant date from which accreditation by the Church of England – Ministry Division is no longer sufficient to meet the criteria for entry onto the Register of Sponsors).

90 *Student Visas, Statement of Intent and Transitional Measures*, UK Border Agency, March 2011, at p 6 www.ukba.homeoffice.gov.uk/sitecontent/documents/news/sop4.pdf.

while negotiations were ongoing with educational oversight bodies operating in Wales, Scotland and Northern Ireland.

Under its agreement with the UKBA, QAA will review:

'• listed bodies;
- other private education providers offering courses normally awarded in accordance with the Frameworks for Higher Education Qualifications; and
- "embedded" colleges offering courses as a pathway into higher education.'[91]

ISI will inspect:

- 'privately funded further education colleges offerings courses on the QCF/NQF, and also English language schools.'[92]

Following a dialogue with the sector, QAA and ISI have published further guidance on their respective websites. Sponsors seeking educational oversight by the end of 2012 must submit their applications to QAA and ISI by 9 September 2011. Private providers of higher education have been able to apply for QAA educational oversight from 18 July 2011. Education providers seeking educational oversight by QAA must be registered at Companies House or be a registered charity, and have the majority of their students undertaking higher education programmes. ISI launched a consultation about the framework and inspection arrangements which ran from 20 June 2011 to 15 July 2011. Further education and English language colleges have been able to register for inspection by ISI online from 1 August 2011. ISI inspections are expected to begin from October 2011. Current sponsors without a satisfactory review by one of the approved review bodies had to meet the deadline of 9 September 2011 to retain their ability to issue new CAS. Deadlines for other types of privately funded education providers were announced on 28 July 2011. Those who do not meet the closing dates for submission of their applications will lose their ability to issue new CAS although they will still have until the end of 2012 to obtain a satisfactory review.

Sponsors who can demonstrate that they have been inspected, audited or reviewed by one of the above bodies applying for a Tier 4 sponsor licence after 21 April 2011 will have twelve months from the date of award of the licence within which to attain HTS status (paragraph 32 of the Sponsor Guidance). They must apply to become HTS at the 'earliest possible opportunity'.[93] Sponsors who join the Register of Sponsors as a result of a successful application made on or after 21 April 2011

91 *Educational oversight of Tier 4 sponsors: enhanced role for QAA and ISI*, UK Border Agency, 13 June 2011, www.ukba.homeoffice.gov.uk/sitecontent/newsfragments/49-oversight-qaa-isi.

92 *Educational oversight of Tier 4 sponsors: enhanced role for QAA and ISI*, UK Border Agency, 13 June 2011, www.ukba.homeoffice.gov.uk/sitecontent/newsfragments/49-oversight-qaa-isi.

93 *Highly Trusted Sponsorship for Tier 4 Sponsors – proposed criteria*, UK Border Agency, 18 July 2011, http://www.ukba.homeoffice.gov.uk/sitecontent/newsarticles/2011/july/28-hts-proposed-criteria.

will not be subject to an interim limit in the sense described below but their CAS allocation will be limited to 50% of their total student body (see below[94]).

Inspectorate	**Providers of privately funded education**	**Deadlines by which an application for inspection, audit or review must be made**
Quality Assurance Agency (QAA)	higher education providers and pre-sessional providers throughout the United Kingdom[95]	9 September 2011
Independent Schools Inspectorate (ISI)	further education providers and English language schools in England and Wales	9 September 2011
The Bridge Schools Inspectorate (BSI)	religious colleges of further education and English language colleges in England and Wales	7 October 2011
The School Inspection Service (SIS)	Montessori and Steiner providers of further education in England and Wales	7 October 2011
Independent Schools Inspectorate (ISI)	further education colleges and English language schools in Wales (with the exception of religious, Montessori and Steiner colleges)	9 September 2011
Education Scotland	further education colleges and English language schools in Scotland	11 November 2011

Further education colleges and English language colleges in Northern Ireland are yet to be assigned an appropriate body to inspect, review or audit them.

94 See the section on Allocation of CAS, **4.173**.

95 Mixed higher and further education providers should apply to QAA or the appropriate further education inspectorate depending on the ratio of higher education courses to further education courses they offer.

The UKBA will publish further guidance on what inspection ratings or grades it expects sponsors to receive in order to meet the educational oversight requirement (paragraph 78 of the Sponsor Guidance). It is remarkable that the UKBA did not qualify this requirement before setting deadlines for application.

LEGACY SPONSORS

4.106 Sponsors who do not meet the set deadlines will become 'legacy sponsors' (paragraph 77 of the Sponsor Guidance). The legacy sponsor status relates only to Tier 4 sponsors (paragraph 83 of the Sponsor Guidance). Legacy sponsors are described in paragraph 79 of the Sponsor Guidance as those who:

- 'do not try to meet the requirements for educational oversight by the deadlines set out in this guidance; or
- do try to meet the new requirements for educational oversight by the deadlines set out in this guidance, but fail; or
- meet the mandatory requirements for highly trusted sponsor but score a 'near miss' on the core measurable requirements and when they re-apply, score a second near miss.'

Those education providers who become legacy sponsors will have their names struck off the Register of Sponsors and have their CAS allocation dialled down to zero. They will not be able to sponsor new students but will be required to comply with their sponsor duties as failure to comply with them will result in their licence being revoked (paragraph 84 of the Sponsor Guidance). However, they will be able to retain existing students until their students' course finishes or the sponsor licence expires (paragraph 80 of the Sponsor Guidance). Where a student needs to apply for extension of leave to complete their course or re-sit an exam, the sponsor will have to apply for a CAS (paragraph 81 of the Sponsor Guidance). Students who have had CAS assigned to them by sponsors who subsequently became legacy sponsors will still be able to apply for leave to enter or remain in the United Kingdom (paragraph 82 of the Sponsor Guidance). Legacy sponsors must apply for HTS status by the set closing dates otherwise their licence will be revoked (paragraph 85 of the Sponsor Guidance).

INDEPENDENT SCHOOLS

4.107 New private independent schools must have undergone formal registration with a Government or other designated body. As they are not expected to have an ISI report, they will need to provide evidence of successful registration with the relevant authority (paragraph 61 of the Sponsor Guidance). This evidence will consist of the following:

- 'England – your school number, issued by the Department for Education (DfE).
- Scotland – your Scottish Executive Education Department (SEED) code.

- Northern Ireland – confirmation of registration letter from the Department of Education Northern Ireland (DENI), School Governance Team.
- Wales – confirmation of registration letter from the Welsh Assembly Government (WAG), School Governance Team, which will include your unique school reference number.'

Independent schools were automatically given HTS status from 21 April 2011 in line with transitional arrangements (see below[96]).Their ability to qualify for HTS status will be reviewed from April 2012 onward.

OVERSEAS HIGHER EDUCATION PROVIDERS

4.108 Overseas higher education providers offering only short-term 'study abroad' programmes in their premises in the United Kingdom are exempt from being subject to educational oversight (see paragraphs 63–69 of the Sponsor Guidance). 'Study abroad' programmes envisage that students who are enrolled in their home country, come to the UK to undertake no more than 50% of their overall course, and will return to their home country to complete their degree course which must be equivalent to a UK degree (paragraph 63 of the Sponsor Guidance).

4.109 The prospective sponsor will need to demonstrate that:

- it holds overseas accreditation which can be confirmed by UK NARIC as a provider of degree level programmes equivalent to UK degree qualifications;
- it teaches only part of its programmes in the United Kingdom;
- it has full legal control of the premises it uses by providing a lease or title deeds to the premises;
- if the teaching facilities are rented from a third party to deliver the programme, the facilities must be within an organisation that holds a Tier 4 sponsor licence and the overseas education provider must provide evidence of having full legal control of the offices used for delivery of the 'study abroad' programme in the United Kingdom (if the third party's Tier 4 sponsor licence is revoked, then the overseas higher education provider must find classroom space with another Tier 4 sponsor within six months of the date of revocation).

4.110 The overseas education provider will not be subject to this concession if:

- it teaches full-time programmes to students enrolled full-time in the United Kingdom (QAA will provide educational oversight); or
- the programme is delivered using a third party such as a UK university.

96 See the section relating to HTS on Automatic qualification and transitional arrangements, **4.144**.

Notably, neither of the approved educational oversight bodies were set up to inspect privately funded education providers at the time of the new requirements coming into force on 21 April 2011. On 13 June 2011 the UKBA announced that QAA and ISI had agreed to extend their remit to reviewing privately funded education providers in England while negotiations were ongoing with educational oversight bodies operating in Wales, Scotland and Northern Ireland.

Under its agreement with the UKBA, QAA will review:

- 'listed bodies;
- other private education providers offering courses normally awarded in accordance with the Frameworks for Higher Education Qualifications; and
- "embedded" colleges offering courses as a pathway into higher education.'[97]

ISI will inspect:

- 'privately funded further education colleges offerings courses on the QCF/NQF, and also English language schools.'[98]

Following a dialogue with the sector, QAA and ISI have published further guidance on their respective websites. Sponsors seeking educational oversight by the end of 2012 must submit their applications to QAA and ISI by 9 September 2011. Private providers of higher education have been able to apply for QAA educational oversight from 18 July 2011. Education providers seeking educational oversight by QAA must be registered at Companies House or be a registered charity, and have the majority of their students undertaking higher education programmes. ISI launched a consultation about the framework and inspection arrangements which ran from 20 June 2011 to 15 July 2011. Further education and English language colleges have been able to register for inspection by ISI online from 1 August 2011. ISI inspections are expected to begin from October 2011. Current sponsors without a satisfactory review by one of the approved review bodies had to meet the deadline of 9 September 2011 to retain their ability to issue new CAS. Deadlines for other types of privately funded education providers were announced on 28 July 2011. Those who do not meet the closing dates for submission of their applications will lose their ability to issue new CAS although they will still have until the end of 2012 to obtain a satisfactory review.

Sponsors who can demonstrate that they have been inspected, audited or reviewed by one of the above bodies applying for a Tier 4 sponsor licence after 21 April 2011 will have twelve months from the date of award of the licence within which to

97 *Educational oversight of Tier 4 sponsors: enhanced role for QAA and ISI*, UK Border Agency, 13 June 2011, www.ukba.homeoffice.gov.uk/sitecontent/newsfragments/49-oversight-qaa-isi.

98 *Educational oversight of Tier 4 sponsors: enhanced role for QAA and ISI*, UK Border Agency, 13 June 2011, www.ukba.homeoffice.gov.uk/sitecontent/newsfragments/49-oversight-qaa-isi.

attain HTS status (paragraph 32 of the Sponsor Guidance). They must apply to become HTS at the 'earliest possible opportunity'.[99] Sponsors who join the Register of Sponsors as a result of a successful application made on or after 21 April 2011 will not be subject to an interim limit in the sense described below but their CAS allocation will be limited to 50% of their total student body (see below[100]).

Eligibility criteria for a Tier 4 sponsor licence and document verification checks

4.111 The UKBA will need to ensure that Tier 4 sponsor licences are awarded to genuine organisations that are likely to comply with their duties. The UKBA considers the following criteria when assessing an application for a sponsor licence (paragraph 215 of the Sponsor Guidance). The organisation must be:

- genuine, operating lawfully in the United Kingdom and complying with all appropriate local planning authority regulations;
- dependable and reliable judging by its background and history;
- capable of carrying out sponsor duties.

With this premise in mind, a sponsor application may go through a variety of investigative checks including on-site visits before it is concluded (paragraph 89 of the Sponsor Guidance). The purpose of on-site visits is to verify that the information provided in the application is accurate (paragraphs 213 and 490 of the Sponsor Guidance). Visiting officers and other third party officials working on behalf of the UKBA will carry identification (paragraph 493 of the Sponsor Guidance). If a check has been carried out before a decision on an application is made, the UKBA will make that decision taking into account the information provided by the prospective sponsor and gathered by its officers during the check (paragraph 496 of the Sponsor Guidance). As a matter of practice, reports written by visiting officers are not disclosed to prospective or existing sponsors but can be made available pursuant to a subject access request under the Data Protection Act 1998.

4.112 In order to satisfy the UKBA that it is a genuine organisation operating lawfully in the United Kingdom, the prospective sponsor must provide relevant supporting documents listed in Appendix A (paragraph 50 of the Sponsor Guidance). Prospective sponsors are asked to provide a number of verifiable documents from Appendix A to enable the UKBA to run paper-based and on-site verification checks (including contacting other Government departments, banks, universities and professional bodies) to be satisfied that the education provider

99 *Highly Trusted Sponsorship for Tier 4 Sponsors – proposed criteria*, UK Border Agency, 18 July 2011, http://www.ukba.homeoffice.gov.uk/sitecontent/newsarticles/2011/july/28-hts-proposed-criteria.
100 See the section on Allocation of CAS, **4.173**.

is: (a) genuine and has an operating or trading presence in the United Kingdom; (b) trustworthy and does not have a history of dishonest conduct or immigration crime; and (c) able to carry out sponsorship duties (paragraph 216 of the Sponsor Guidance). If the prospective sponsor is found to have no operating or trading presence in the United Kingdom, the application will be refused. If such a finding is made after the licence has been granted, the licence will be revoked (paragraph 51 of the Sponsor Guidance).

4.113 Documents provided by prospective sponsors will be checked within 15 working days allowing for enquiries to be made. The results of these enquiries will be recorded using a standard format (paragraph 217 of the Sponsor Guidance).

4.114 In accordance with paragraph 218 of the Sponsor Guidance the checks may result in the following:

- If a document is confirmed as genuine, the application will be considered as normal;
- If a document, whether essential or ancillary, is confirmed as false, the application will be refused;
- If the results of the checks are inconclusive, that document will not be used as evidence in support of the application and further supporting documents may be necessary.

Suitability criteria for a Tier 4 sponsor licence and how it is scored

4.115 The suitability criteria may impact on rating, outcome of a licence application, revocation of an existing licence, CAS limits and review points set for sponsors (paragraphs 86–93 of the Sponsor Guidance). The suitability criteria will be used to decide whether: (a) to grant or refuse an application for a Tier 4 sponsor licence; (b) to grant or refuse an application for HTS status; or (c) to revoke the Tier 4 sponsor licence (paragraph 86 of the Sponsor Guidance).

4.116 A prospective sponsor's suitability is assessed against the criteria set out below which is then scored in the way which will determine the prospective sponsor's rating. With the changes to the sponsor rating system after 5 September 2011, the suitability criteria and the scoring system has been simplified.

The UKBA will assess suitability against the following criteria (set out in paragraphs 87–88 of the Sponsor Guidance):

- HR and compliance systems in place enabling the sponsor to perform its sponsorship duties;
- history of compliance with the Immigration Rules;

- the authorising officer, key contact, level 1 user, director, owner or any person involved in day-to-day running of the educational establishment having a civil penalty for immigration offences;
- the authorising officer, key contact, level 1 user, director, owner or any person involved in day-to-day running of the educational establishment having a criminal conviction for an offence listed in Appendix B or any other convictions save for any convictions which are spent under the Rehabilitation of Offenders Act 1974;
- the authorising officer, key contact, level 1 user, director, owner or any person involved in day-to-day running of the educational establishment having come to the adverse notice of the UKBA.

Each area of suitability will be scored as 'met' (which means that the prospective sponsor has met all of the criteria) or 'not met' (which means that the prospective sponsor has not met one or more of the criteria). An A rating will be awarded to a prospective sponsor who has met all of the above criteria and there are no other countervailing reasons for refusing the application. If the prospective sponsor scores 'not met' in any area of suitability, their application will be refused (paragraph 92 of the Sponsor Guidance). Sponsors who are visited after being granted a licence will be scored again against the suitability criteria (paragraph 93 of the Sponsor Guidance).

Standards of HR systems and compliance

4.117 A prospective sponsor must have in place suitable procedures and a proven track record of compliance against which its ability to abide by sponsorship duties will be assessed. The sponsor must have these procedures in place and must comply with immigration law throughout the lifetime of its sponsor licence. Expanding on the suitability criteria the relevant information about the rating of human resource ('HR') systems and compliance is laid out outside the Sponsor Guidance and can be found on the UKBA website at: http://www.ukba.homeoffice.gov.uk/business-sponsors/points/sponsoringmigrants/HRandcompliance/. The Sponsor Guidance no longer refers to these extraneous provisions (as of 5 September 2011). Nonetheless, these are laid out before for reference only.

4.118 These additional provisions are summarised below. Before awarding a rating or deciding whether to refuse or revoke a licence, specific standards are used to assess:[101]

'• whether you have the correct human resource (HR) systems to make sure that you can meet your sponsorship duties; and

101 These provisions relate to those sponsoring migrant workers.

- whether you are complying with, or have previously complied with, the work permit arrangements and other immigration law.' [102]

HR SYSTEMS

4.119 HR systems are divided into five areas.

Area	Procedures that must be in place	Rating '1'	Rating '2'	Rating '3'
Area 1: Monitoring immigration status and preventing illegal employment	(a) Must keep photocopies or electronic copies of each student's passport, Immigration Status Document or identity card showing their immigration status allowing them to work or study and must be able to make them available to UKBA staff on request, and (b) Must not employ migrants whose permission to stay does not allow them to work or study or has expired.	Procedures are in place to discharge both obligations	Procedures are in place to discharge obligation (a) but not (b)	No procedures in place to keep photocopies or electronic copies of required documents or checks are not sufficient to give adequate protection against illegal working
Area 2: Maintaining migrant contact details	(a) Must keep on file and make available to UKBA staff on request each student's contact details including UK residential address, landline and mobile telephone numbers, and (b) Must update these details as necessary by using an electronic self-service system, carrying out a regular audit or issuing clear instructions to students on when and how to notify the sponsor of any changes.	Procedures are in place to discharge both obligations	Procedures are in place to discharge either obligation only partially	No procedures in place to keep reliable contact details and/or provide them to UKBA staff quickly
Area 3: Recordkeeping	(a) Must keep comprehensive records for each student in line with good practice, and (b) Must store them in such a way as to provide any of the documents that UKBA think relevant quickly.	Procedures are in place to discharge both obligations	Procedures are in place to discharge obligation (a) but not (b) or vice versa	No procedures in place to keep records of migrants

102 *The rating system,* UK Border Agency, www.ukba.homeoffice.gov.uk/employers/points/sponsoringmigrants/HRandcompliance/ratingsystem/.

Area	Procedures that must be in place	Rating '1'	Rating '2'	Rating '3'
Area 4: Migrant tracking and monitoring	In the event that: • a student does not enrol on their course at the expected time, is absent from study for more than 10 working days (misses 10 expected contacts or 2 weeks of a course, depending on the type of education provider) without permission, stops their studies or withdraws from the course, or • if there are any significant changes in the student's circumstances, or • the sponsor stops sponsoring them or suspects that they are breaching conditions of their leave The sponsor must send a report to UKBA within 10 working days from the event. In the event that • there are significant changes in the sponsor's circumstances such as ceasing to trade, becoming insolvent, changing the nature of business, etc The sponsor must send a report to UKBA within 28 working days from the event. The sponsor must also report details of any third parties or intermediaries such as recruitment agents in and outside the UK engaged by it to UKBA. (a) Must ensure that students are monitored sufficiently, and (b) Must have a procedure in place by which a designated person is informed of any circumstances which should be reported to UKBA (as listed above) and then do so within the specified period.	Procedures are in place to discharge both obligations	Procedures are in place to discharge obligation (a) but there are minor problems with the monitoring or reporting which may lead to UKBA not being notified within specified time periods	No procedures in place to discharge either of the obligations

Area	**Procedures that must be in place**	**Rating '1'**	**Rating '2'**	**Rating '3'**
Area 5: Professional accreditations and registrations (relevant to licence applications under Tiers 2 and 5 only)	(a) Must ensure that migrants coming to work for the sponsor are entitled to do so and hold the appropriate professional accreditations or registrations. (b) Must keep copies of the relevant documents and make them available to UKBA staff on request. (c) Must monitor expiry dates and ensure that these are renewed and updated as necessary.	Procedures are in place to discharge all the obligations	Procedures are in place to discharge either obligation only partially	No procedures in place to check and record the details of any legally required professional accreditations and registrations

Compliance

4.120 Depending on the record of past compliance with immigration law and any findings during a pre-licensing visit, a prospective sponsor may be considered to be fully, partially or non-compliant.[103] There is no indication as to the time span over which compliance would be assessed. It is also not explicitly apparent whether a newly established, genuine organisation with trading history of less than 18 months would start off with a clean slate provided that it was compliant with immigration law at the time of applying for a Tier 4 sponsor licence.

Eligibility criteria for HTS status

4.121 In accordance with paragraph 263 of the Sponsor Guidance an existing sponsor must apply for HTS status if:

- it has had its sponsor licence for 12 months in which case it can apply up to one month in advance although the application would not be considered until such time when the full 12 months has passed ;
- it has HTS status but it is about to expire in which case the sponsor can apply to renew up to one month in advance;
- it has had its sponsor licence for more than 12 months but has never previously applied for HTS status;

103 The information set out on the UKBA website relates mainly to work permit arrangements. The standards for assessing compliance of education providers who have not previously engaged in employing migrants are not clearly set out. Presumably, their past compliance may be gauged from any evidence of voluntary monitoring and reporting, and recruiting international students in line with immigration law.

- it has applied for HTS status before but the application was refused.

Prior to 5 September 2011 eligible candidates applying for HTS status were expected to meet nine criteria which were aimed at establishing a higher threshold against immigration abuse and staunch commitment to complying with sponsor duties. The criteria were tenuous and vague as there was no definable benchmark against which a sponsor's performance in respect of student enrolment, attendance, course progression or completion could be measured.[104] In referring to the Highly Trusted Sponsor Scheme in *The Student Immigration System, A Consultation*[105] the Secretary of State said that 'to date less than a third of licensed and active Tier 4 sponsors have met the stringent criteria.'

4.122 The nine criteria first appeared in the standalone Highly Trusted Sponsor Guidance, the last version of which was published on 23 July 2010 and was last set out at paragraph 108 in the unified Sponsor Guidance published on 4 July 2011.

4.123 In the statement of intent published on 31 March 2011 the UKBA committed to reviewing HTS criteria.[106] On 18 July 2011 the UKBA published the proposed new HTS criteria inviting comments to be sent in by 5 August 2011.[107] The new eligibility requirements are now set out in paragraphs 268–274 of the Sponsor Guidance. A sponsor applying for HTS status will be assessed against: (a) mandatory; and (b) core measurable requirements all of which must be met (paragraph 268 of the Sponsor Guidance). The sponsor's eligibility will be assessed on the basis of Tier 4 students whose applications for leave were supported by CAS assigned by it (paragraph 270 of the Sponsor Guidance). Failure to meet on or more of the mandatory requirements will result in the refusal of the HTS application and revocation of the sponsor licence (paragraph 271 of the Sponsor Guidance). If the sponsor meets all of the mandatory requirements, their refusal, enrolment and course completion rates – the core measurable requirements – will be examined more closely and the final score will determine the outcome of the application for HTS status (paragraph 272 of the Sponsor Guidance). Sponsors must score at least 70 points to have their application approved (paragraph 273 of the Sponsor Guidance). Those who score less than 70 points, the sponsor will be in a 'near miss' situation (see below).

104 Despite the stringent criteria, there have been instances of sponsors who have had their sponsor licences revoked and subsequently reinstated being granted HTS status.

105 *The Student Immigration System, a Consultation,* UK Border Agency, December 2010, p 5 www.ukba.homeoffice.gov.uk/sitecontent/documents/policyandlaw/consultations/students/student-consultation.pdf?view=Binary. The consultation ran for eight weeks until 31 January 2011.

106 *Student Visas, Statement of Intent and Transitional Measures*, UK Border Agency, March 2011, p 6 http://www.ukba.homeoffice.gov.uk/sitecontent/documents/news/sop4.pdf.

107 *Highly Trusted Sponsorship for Tier 4 Sponsors – proposed criteria,* UK Border Agency, 18 July 2011, www.ukba.homeoffice.gov.uk/sitecontent/newsarticles/2011/july/28-hts-proposed-criteria.

Stage one: mandatory requirements – all must be passed (reproduced from Table (iv) at paragraph 270 of the Sponsor Guidance)	
Minimum qualifying period	You must have held a Tier 4 sponsor licence for 12 consecutive months. Unless you are applying to renew your HTS status, your licence must have been A-rated for the six months immediately before you apply.
No civil penalties	During the three-year period immediately before you apply, you must not have become liable to pay a civil penalty which still stood once your objection and appeal rights were exhausted.
Refusal rate	Your refusal rate must be less than 20 per cent. This means that of all the CAS you have assigned which students have used to support an application for a visa or permission to stay, the total number of applications we refused must be less than 20 per cent. We will assess this using CAS data from the SMS for the 12-month period immediately before you apply. We will take into account all CASs that students have used and applications we refused during this 12-month period.
Enrolment rate	Your enrolment rate must be at least 90 per cent. This means that of all the CASs you have assigned to students who have been granted a visa or permission to stay, at least 90 per cent must have enrolled on their course within the enrolment period. We will assess this using CAS data from the SMS for the 12-month period immediately before you apply. We will take into account all the CASs students have used in a successful application where the student has enrolled on their course within the past 12 months.
Course completion rate (If none of your students were due to complete their course in the past 12 months then we will not assess you against this requirement.)	Your course completion rate must be at least 85 per cent. This means that at least 85 per cent of students sponsored under Tier 4 who enrol with you, must complete their course We will assess this using all CAS data available from the SMS. To determine your course completion rate we will calculate the number of students whose course was due to end in the past 12 months and who dropped out of their course before the course end date. It does not matter when they started their course. We will then calculate the percentage of drop-outs compared with

	all students who were due to complete their course and subtract this from 100 per cent.
Declaration of academic progression	100 per cent This means that you have, where required, confirmed the student's academic progression on all CASs you have assigned during the past 12 months.

Stage two: core measurable requirements (reproduced from Table (v) at paragraph 272 of the Sponsor Guidance)		
Refusal rate percentage	Less than 5 per cent	0 points deducted
	5.0 – 9.99 per cent	5 points deducted
	10 – 14.99 per cent	10 points deducted
	15 – 19.99 per cent	20 points deducted
Enrolment rate percentage	More than 98 per cent	0 points deducted
	96 – 98 per cent	5 points deducted
	93 –95.99 per cent	10 points deducted
	93 – 92.99 per cent	15 points deducted
Course completion rate percentage	More than 98 per cent	0 points deducted
	95 – 98 per cent	5 points deducted
	90 – 94.99 per cent	10 points deducted
	85 – 89.99 per cent	15 points deducted

Application process

4.124 A prospective sponsor making a licence application for the first time or an existing sponsor making an application to add more Tiers to its licence must make their applications using the online application form. The prospective or existing sponsor must send in their supporting documents listed in Appendix A and correct fee to the UKBA for consideration and checks before a sponsor licence can be awarded and rating assigned. A sponsor wishing to apply for HTS status must have a Tier 4 sponsor licence in place and satisfy the criteria set out above.

Making a Tier 4 sponsor licence application

4.125 Applications for a Tier 4 sponsor licence can only be made using the online application form (paragraph 200 of the Sponsor Guidance). While representatives can help to complete the application form, the application must be submitted by the prospective sponsor (paragraph 204 of the Sponsor Guidance). The same form can be used by an existing sponsor wishing to add more Tiers to its licence.

Register

4.126 To access the application system the prospective sponsor must register online by providing a name and email address. Following this the prospective sponsor will be issued a user ID and a password will be sent separately by email. The prospective sponsor can register at www.points.homeoffice.gov.uk/gui-sponsor-jsf/Register/SponsorRegister.faces.

LOG IN

4.127 Using the user ID and password, the prospective sponsor can then log in and start the application process. The prospective sponsor can log in at www.points.homeoffice.gov.uk/gui-sponsor-jsf/Home/SponsorHome.faces.

COMPLETING THE APPLICATION FORM

4.128 The application must be made using the online application form which can be saved along the way. To assist in preparing the application offline, the prospective sponsor can download a mock hard copy application form at:

www.ukba.homeoffice.gov.uk/sitecontent/documents/employersandsponsors/pointsbasedsystem/mock_sponsor_form.pdf. A copy of this form can be found at Annex A to this chapter. The mock form can only be used as a guide in gathering the necessary information prior to making the application and cannot be submitted in lieu of an online application. To complete the online application form the prospective sponsor will be asked to provide the following information:

- the Tier, category and sub-category or a combination of Tiers, categories and sub-categories in which the application is to be made (paragraphs 201–202 of the Sponsor Guidance);
- details of any previous applications;
- organisation details including address, contact details, trading names, regional exposure, structure, size and sector of work or main economic activity;
- details of registration, exception or exemption for organisations with charitable status;

- PAYE, National Insurance, VAT and Accounts office reference numbers;
- name and registration number of any accrediting or governing body or stock exchange;
- in the section for educational institutions, type of educational oversight body, particulars of inspecting or auditing status;
- names and contact details of authorising officer (including immigration status if he or she is a non-EEA national), key contact and level 1 user;[108]
- details of any convictions or penalties of key personnel;
- supporting documents (prospective sponsors must refer to Appendix A for correct guidance relating to supporting documents);
- payment details.

4.129 Representatives assisting the prospective sponsor with the application will be asked to complete and sign their own section in the application form. The authorising officer will be required to indicate the sponsor's agreement to adhere to the sponsorship duties and to complete and sign the sponsor declaration.

SUBMISSION SHEET

4.130 Once the online application form has been submitted, the prospective sponsor will be guided to the submission sheet page (paragraph 186 of the Sponsor Guidance) which must be printed and completed in black ink. The submission sheet must:

- be an original (not a certified copy);
- list supporting documents for each Tier, category or sub-category (paragraph 184 of the Sponsor Guidance) and all the documents listed as mandatory on the submission sheet can be submitted in original or certified copy form;
- state payment details including the fee payable and payment method; and
- be signed and dated by the authorising officer (each page of the submission sheet must be signed and dated by the authorising officer in the designated space).

4.131 The submission sheet together with supporting documents and payment must be sent to the UKBA within 14 calendar days of the date on which the online application form was completed (paragraph 186 of the Sponsor Guidance). If the

108 The contact address given for each key personnel member must be either the main address of the organisation or the address of its branch or head office being included in the licence. If a representative is allocated the role of key contact or level 1 user, then the representative's main business address must be given (paragraph 119 of the Sponsor Guidance).

prospective or existing sponsor applying to join Tier 4 do not send documents specified in Appendix that are not mandatory or if further documents are required, the UKBA will ask for those documents to be sent within 7 calendar days. If they are not received in time, the application will be refused and the fee will not be refunded.

Applications made by post should be sent to:	Applications made by courier should be sent to:
UK Border Agency PBS Sponsor Licence Applications PO Box 501 Durham DH99 1WH	UK Border Agency Room 326 Millburngate House Durham DH99 1SA

SUPPORTING DOCUMENTS

4.132 The prospective sponsor or an existing sponsor joining Tier 4 must submit documents in support of its licence application. These documents must be either original or certified as a true copy of the original by the issuing authority, a solicitor or a notary public (paragraph 190 of the Sponsor Guidance). Printouts of documents in .pdf must be certified once a certifier has had sight of the original email containing the file (paragraph 191 of the Sponsor Guidance). Documents which are not in English or Welsh must be provided together with a certified translation (paragraph 192 of the Sponsor Guidance).

4.133 Appendix A to the Sponsor Guidance contains a catalogue of supporting documents. The Appendix is compartmentalised by type of organisation and is split into three lists, List A (Mandatory documents), List B (Primary documents with exceptions) and List C (Secondary documents). Most education providers will be required to submit only one item of documentary evidence to confirm that they have complied with the educational oversight requirement. Additional documents may be requested by the UKBA. Supporting evidence must be provided for each branch or partner institution included in the application (paragraph 189 of the Sponsor Guidance). Further guidance for newly established and overseas education providers can be found in Appendix A.

COST OF LICENSING

4.134 The cost of a licence depends on whether the organisation making the application is defined as being a small, medium or large company or a charity by the Companies Act 2006 and the Companies Act 2006 (Amendment) (Accounts and Reports) Regulations 2008, SI 2008/393. The cost also depends on the number of Tiers being applied for and whether the application is made by a prospective or an existing sponsor. Fees payable for a licence will be refunded only if the application is rejected as invalid. They will not be refunded if the application is withdrawn or if it is refused. Organisations wishing to register their head office and branches together must pay a single fee. However, organisations wishing to obtain separate licences for each of its branches must pay individual fees for each branch. There are other costs associated with sponsorship such as fees payable for assigning CAS. B-rated sponsors subject to a sponsorship action plan issued under the Sponsor Guidance prior to 5 September 2011 also had to pay extra fees.

4.135 Application fees must be paid online. From 1 October 2011 payments by cheque are not accepted (paragraph 39 of the Sponsor Guidance).

4.136 Licensing fees relevant to prospective and existing sponsors are set out on the UKBA website (at http://ukba.homeoffice.gov.uk/employers/points/sponsoringmigrats/costs), in the Sponsor Guidance (paragraphs 39–45) and are reproduced selectively below. These are last revised on 6 April 2011.

4.137 Prospective sponsors:

Tier	**Fee for small sponsors or sponsors with charitable status**	**Fee for medium or large sponsors**
Tier 2 and Tier 4	£410	£1,025
Tier 2 and Tier 4 and Tier 5	£410	£1,025
Tier 4 only	£410	£410
Tier 4 and Tier 5	£410	£410

4.138 Existing sponsors wishing to add more Tiers to their licence:

Tier you have already registered under	**Tier you want to add**	**Fee for small sponsors or sponsors with charitable status**	**Fee for medium or large sponsors**
Tier 2 only	Tier 4	£100	£0
	Tier 5	£100	£0
	Tier 4 and Tier 5	£100	£0
Tier 2 and Tier 4	Tier 5	£0	£0
Tier 2 and Tier 5	Tier 4	£0	£0

Tier you have already registered under	**Tier you want to add**	**Fee for small sponsors or sponsors with charitable status**	**Fee for medium or large sponsors**
Tier 4 only	Tier 2	£0	£615
	Tier 5	£0	£0
	Tier 2 and Tier 5	£0	£615
	Highly Trusted Sponsor	£410	£410
Tier 4 and Tier 5	Tier 2	£0	£615
Tier 5 only	Tier 2	£0	£615
	Tier 4	£0	£0
	Tier 2 and Tier 4	£0	£615

Making an application for HTS status

4.139 Sponsors holding a Tier 4 sponsor licence wishing to apply for HTS status can do so by downloading and printing out the appropriate application form, an Application for a Highly Trusted Sponsor Licence Under Tier 4 of the Points Based System ('HTS Application Form').[109] The HTS Application Form can be found at: www.ukba.homeoffice.gov.uk/sitecontent/applicationforms/sponsors/hts-form.pdf (paragraph 265 of the Sponsor Guidance). A copy of it is attached in Annex B.

4.140 Sponsors must complete the relevant sections of the form and provide information about their organisation, how they satisfy the qualifying criteria and about student enrolment, attendance and course levels. The sponsor declaration must be signed and dated by the authorising officer. If the application is not fully completed, it will be returned to the key contact to complete and return within 10 days. If the application form is not returned or returned partially completed, the application will be refused (paragraph 267of the Sponsor Guidance).

4.141 The application can be made by post only and must be sent together with the correct application fee to:

109 The current version is HTS version 09/11 for applications made on or after 5 September 2011. The previous versions of HTS was version 06/10 for applications made on or after 16 June 2010 and version 04/11 for applications made on or after 21 April 2011. Sponsors must download the form valid at the time of application.

UK Border Agency

Highly Trusted Sponsors
PO Box 589
Durham
DH99 1AB

Supporting documents

4.142 During the consideration process, the UKBA may ask the sponsor applying for HTS status to complete and provide a student enrolment and attendance spreadsheet[110] in respect of Tier 4 students to whom the sponsor issued a visa letter or a CAS reflecting the sponsor's performance. Sponsors who are required to complete the spreadsheet will be contacted by the caseworking team and provided a Q&A guidance document. The completed spreadsheet must be provided within 21 days of being requested (paragraphs 494–495 of the Sponsor Guidance). The UKBA may require HTS to provide updated spreadsheets to check compliance throughout the lifetime of their HTS status.

Cost of applying for HTS status

4.143 The cost of applying for HTS status is £410 regardless of whether the organisation is small, medium or large or has charitable status. From 1 October 2011 the UKBA will continue accepting payments by cheque for initial or renewal HTS applications (paragraph 42 of the Sponsor Guidance).

Automatic qualification and transitional arrangements

4.144 With the introduction of Highly Trusted Sponsor Scheme on 6 April 2010, A (Trusted) rated, publicly funded, Tier 4 (General) sponsors subject to public reviews by the QAA, Ofsted, HMIE, Estyn and the Education and Training Inspectorate were automatically deemed to have acquired a Highly Trusted sponsor licence. This is similar to the way publicly funded institutions were dealt with when the DfES Register of Education and Training Providers was introduced in 2004. To be awarded a Highly Trusted sponsor licence these sponsors were required to submit their applications by no later than 30 June 2010. Organisations who submitted their application for a Highly Trusted sponsor licence in time were able to continue offering restricted courses at NQF level 3 and equivalent, and courses below degree

110 The UKBA sent out similar spreadsheets to gauge performance from sponsors under investigation prior to the introduction of the Highly Trusted Sponsor Scheme on 6 April 2010.

level with work placements (excluding foundation degrees) while awaiting the outcome.

4.145 Organisations deemed to have Highly Trusted status who did not apply for a Highly Trusted Sponsor licence by 30 June 2010 or applied but failed to meet the set criteria would have had their status cancelled and reverted back to their Standard licence. Organisations that lost their Highly Trusted status had to cancel any unused CAS issued for restricted courses since 6 April 2010 and notified their potential students accordingly.

4.146 Privately funded organisations that were not automatically deemed to have a Highly Trusted sponsor licence had to submit their application for a Highly Trusted sponsor licence by no later than 30 April 2010 to enable them to continue offering restricted courses while awaiting the outcome of their application. Those privately funded organisations that applied for a Highly Trusted sponsor licence after 30 April 2010 had to wait for an approval of their application before they could offer restricted courses to international students. As of 1 May 2010 privately funded sponsors with a Standard licence were no longer able to offer restricted courses.

4.147 As part of the transitional measures introduced from 21 April 2011, sponsors who are not already Highly Trusted have been given until April 2012 to join the scheme and gain HTS status (as it has become known). From 21 April 2011 all independent schools with A rating and valid accreditation had been automatically awarded HTS status for one year. The full burden of HTS requirements was not imposed on them for the first year. Independent schools with B rating and valid accreditation will be given HTS status only when they are A-rated. New independent schools will be granted HTS status immediately if they have A rating and valid accreditation.

Application outcome

Processing times

4.148 Consideration process starts when the payment has cleared, after five working days for cheques and one working day for credit/debit cards. Having submitted a Tier 4 sponsor licence application a prospective sponsor may have to wait for several weeks for the UKBA to consider the application and carry out any checks including on-site visits, if necessary, before a decision is made (paragraphs 213–214 of the Sponsor Guidance). Applications for HTS status will be subject to a rigorous review. There are currently no service standards for processing licence applications. Content of sponsor licence applications is treated confidentially as are any allegations of abuse of the sponsorship arrangements (paragraphs 197 and 30 of the Sponsor Guidance).

Successful applications

4.149 If the Tier 4 sponsor licence application has been approved, the sponsor will receive a letter notifying it of the decision to grant a licence, specifying the sponsor licence number, rating and CAS allocation (paragraphs 220–221 of the Sponsor Guidance). Any original documents sent with the application will be returned under cover of the letter by recorded delivery sent to the address given for the authorising officer (paragraph 195 of the Sponsor Guidance). If the sponsor has been successful in its HTS status application, it will also receive a letter informing it of the decision, will have its rating on the Register of Sponsors changed to Highly Trusted and will have contact telephone number and email address for the regional team (paragraph 282 of the Sponsor Guidance). From 1 October 2011 the rating will also be updated on the SMS account (paragraph 283 of the Sponsor Guidance).

Validity of a Tier 4 sponsor licence

4.150 A Tier 4 sponsor licence is valid for four years from the date of issue unless it is revoked (paragraph 230 of the Sponsor Guidance). A sponsor wishing to continue sponsoring existing students and recruiting new international students should apply to renew its licence before the date of expiry (paragraphs 230–236 of the Sponsor Guidance). Any Tiers which have been added by a sponsor to a licence during its lifetime will expire at the same time as the original licence (paragraph 231 of the Sponsor Guidance).

Validity of HTS status

4.151 HTS status is valid for 12 months from the date of issue (paragraph 284 of the Sponsor Guidance). The status must be renewed every year.

Unsuccessful applications

4.152 Should the application for a Tier 4 sponsor licence be unsuccessful, the prospective sponsor would receive a notification letter citing reasons for the refusal. Any original documents sent with the application would also be returned by recorded delivery (paragraphs 195 of the Sponsor Guidance). A sponsor applying for HTS status will also be notified of refusal in writing. At the same time refusal of HTS status will lead to the Tier 4 sponsor licence being revoked (paragraph 277 of the Sponsor Guidance).

GROUNDS FOR REFUSING TIER 4 SPONSOR LICENCE APPLICATIONS

4.153 The outcome of an application will depend on whether: (1) the requirements for qualifying for a sponsor licence (set out above) are met; and (2) the existence of any of the specific circumstances in which the UKBA states that it 'will' refuse or 'may' refuse a Tier 4 sponsor licence application. These grounds for mandatory and discretionary refusal are contained in paragraphs 94–100 of the Sponsor Guidance and are partially quoted below. These grounds, which have changed with time, may be cited by the Secretary of State as reasons for refusing a licence application.

MANDATORY GROUNDS OF REFUSAL

4.154 The circumstances in which an application will be refused are set out in paragraph 94 of the Sponsor Guidance as follows:

- 'You, or a relevant person[111] submit any false documents with your application. If this happens, and we believe a criminal offence has been committed, we may prosecute you as well.
- You do not meet the requirements of Tier 4 or the category you are applying for.
- You, or a relevant person are legally prohibited from becoming a company director (unless this is because you are an undischarged bankrupt, although the authorising officer, and any Sponsorship Management System (SMS) User cannot be an undischarged bankrupt).
- You, or a relevant person have previously held a sponsor licence under any tier and we revoked that licence in the six months before your current application.
- We find information that suggests you do not have the processes you need to comply with your sponsorship duties.
- We ask, or have ever asked you or a relevant person to send us evidence so we can decide if you:
  can comply with sponsorship duties; or
  have previously complied with sponsorship duties; or
  complied with previous work permit arrangements; and
  you do not or did not send it to us within the relevant timescales.
- You or a relevant person have ever been dishonest in any previous dealings with us (or the former Immigration and Nationality Directorate or Border and Immigration Agency). Dishonesty includes (but is not restricted to):
  - applying for work permits or certificates of sponsorship when you do not have or are not in the process of establishing, an operating or trading presence in the UK;

111 A relevant person means 'any owner, director, authorising officer, key contact, level 1 user, or anyone involved in your day-to-day running' (paragraph 5 of the Sponsor Guidance).

— making false statements in any application to us, including an application for a work permit; and
— assigning a CAS to a student who you knew did not intend or was not able to follow the course of study for which the CAS was assigned.'

The UKBA will also refuse the application for a Tier 4 sponsor licence if the sponsor or the relevant person associated with it

Offences and civil penalties	**Circumstances**
• have within the last 12 months prior to the date of application, been issued with a civil penalty under Section 15 of the Immigration, Asylum and Nationality Act 2006 for employing one or more illegal workers and remain liable for it upon exhaustion of objections and appeal rights (paragraph 95 of the Sponsor Guidance)	• 'If the fine for at least one of those workers was set at the maximum amount of £10,000, or if the fine was for a repeat offence and set below the maximum amount we will refuse your application if: • you paid the fine within the given time limit and applied within six months of the date the fine became payable; or • You paid the fine after the given time limit and applied within 12 months of the date the fine became payable. • If the fine was for a first offence and set below the maximum amount, we will refuse your application if you paid the fine after the given time limit and applied within six months of the date the fine became payable.'
• have not paid an outstanding illegal working civil penalty since their introduction in February 2008 and remain liable for it upon exhaustion of objections and appeal rights (paragraph 96 of the Sponsor Guidance)	
• have been issued with a civil penalty for one of the other offences in Appendix C to the Sponsor Guidance and have not paid for it (paragraph 97 of the Sponsor Guidance)	• ss 32–37 of the Immigration and Asylum Act 1999 (carrying clandestine entrants) • ss 40–41 of the Immigration and Asylum Act 1999 (carrying

Offences and civil penalties	**Circumstances**
	passengers without proper documents) • s 124 of the Nationality, Immigration and Asylum Act 2002 (bringing passengers to the United Kingdom without authority to carry)
• have been convicted of one of the offences listed on the right unless the conviction is deemed spent under the Rehabilitation of Offenders Act 1974 (paragraph 98 of the Sponsor Guidance)	• 'Any offence under the: • Immigration Act 1971; • Immigration Act 1988; • Asylum and Immigration Appeals Act 1993; • Immigration and Asylum Act 1999; • Nationality, Immigration and Asylum Act 2002; • Immigration, Asylum and Nationality Act 2006; • UK Borders Act 2007 • Trafficking for exploitation. • Any other unspent conviction, especially those which; • in our opinion, indicate that you pose a risk to immigration control, for example, offences involving dishonesty or deception, including any of the offences listed in Appendix B. • in our opinion case doubt upon your suitability, or the suitability of a relevant person to teach or be in contact with students, for example sex offences.'

GROUNDS ON WHICH THE UKBA 'MAY' REFUSE A LICENCE

4.155 The UKBA may refuse a Tier 4 sponsor licence application on the following grounds (paragraph 99 of the Sponsor Guidance):

'• You or a relevant person have a previous record of not complying or poor compliance with the duties of sponsorship, or with the work permit arrangements.
- You or a relevant person have had a sponsor licence revoked by us. You will have to show that you have put right any issues which led to us revoking it before we will consider granting you a new licence
- The Office of the Immigration Services Commissioner (OISC) has removed your authorisation to provide immigration advice, or authorisation of any organisation that you or a relevant person have been involved with in a similar role.'

In the above circumstances the decision to be taken will depend on the seriousness of conduct, the time that has passed since it took place and any mitigating circumstances, and the seriousness of the issues which led to the revocation of the previous licence and what has been done to rectify the situation since the revocation (paragraph 100 of the Sponsor Guidance).

GROUNDS FOR REFUSING HTS APPLICATIONS

4.156 Paragraph 275 of the Sponsor Guidance sets out the grounds for a mandatory refusal of an HTS application. An HTS application may also be refused for any of the reasons for refusing an application for a Tier 4 sponsor licence (paragraph 276 of the Sponsor Guidance).

4.157 In accordance with paragraph 275 of the Sponsor Guidance the application for HTS status will be refused in any of the circumstances cited below:

'• You do not meet one or more of the mandatory requirements.
- You do not send us the evidence we request within the given time limit and/or send incomplete information.
- We revoke your Tier 4 licence before we have been able to decide your application.'

SCORING A 'NEAR MISS' FOR AN HTS APPLICATION

Sponsors who score a near miss on an application for HTS status, namely, less than 70 points, will be allowed to stay on the Register of Sponsors with A rating. The number of CAS they can assign will be limited (paragraph 279 of the Sponsor Guidance). The UKBA will inform the applicant of the outcome of their application in writing including the 'near miss' scores, the number of CAS they can assign, and the time by which they need to reapply for HTS status (paragraph 280 of the Sponsor Guidance). The sponsor will be required to complete a fresh application form and pay the correct fee again when applying again. In accordance with paragraph 281 of the Sponsor Guidance, the outcome of their application will be determined by the following:

- If the sponsor scores 70 points or more, it will be awarded HTS status;
- If the sponsor scores less than 70 points (near miss), it will become a legacy sponsor;
- If the sponsor's application is refused, it will have its Tier 4 sponsor licence revoked.

Applying for a Tier 4 sponsor licence following refusal

4.158 There is no right of appeal against the refusal of an application for a Tier 4 sponsor licence. Prospective sponsors who have been refused a Tier 4 sponsor licence can make a fresh application[112] at any time provided that the reasons for the initial refusal, including being issued with a civil penalty,[113] no longer apply. If the applicant previously held a sponsor licence and it was revoked, the application should only be made once six months have passed since the date of revocation (paragraphs 222–225 of the Sponsor Guidance). **Chapter 5** deals with remedies and, if the prospective sponsor can put things right, this is plainly the simplest and cost-effective means of them rectifying the situation (although the same cannot be said about those who have their sponsor licence revoked as a six month period may spell the end of their business).

Applying for HTS status following refusal

4.159 There is no right of appeal against the refusal of an application for HTS status (paragraph 278 of the Sponsor Guidance). In the event that the refusal of an HTS application leads to revocation of the Tier 4 sponsor licence, see above. If your application for HTS status is scored against mandatory and core measurable criteria and the final score is a 'near miss', please see the section dealing with applications who score less than 70 points.[114]

112 The prospective sponsor will have to complete the online application again, submit supporting evidence together with the correct fee (paragraph 225 of the Sponsor Guidance). The only exception to this if the application as refused in error in which case the prospective sponsor will not have to submit supporting evidence or pay a fee.

113 If the sponsor or another relevant person has been issued with a civil penalty, a fresh application should only reply either 6 or 12 months after after the date of the fine became payable.

114 See 'Scoring a 'near miss' for an HTS application'.

Post-licensing

Ratings

4.160 Prior to 5 September 2011 each application for a Tier 4 sponsor licence was rated either A or B[115] on its merits. Once awarded, the rating would appear alongside the sponsor's name and other particulars on the public Register of Sponsors. If a sponsor held a licence in more than one Tier, in exceptional circumstances a B rating could have been attributed to only one Tier if the sponsor's systems were found lacking.

4.161 Historically, a B rating could be awarded at the outset or as a consequence of the Tier 4 sponsor licence being downgraded. It was a transitional rating as a result of which the sponsor could either achieve an A rating or lose its sponsor licence.

4.162 A B-rated sponsor had to comply with the steps or additional duties set out in an action plan aimed at improving the sponsor's performance to enable it to attain or regain an A rating. Prior to 21 April 2011 the sponsor was not able to issue any or further CAS until it signed up to an action plan. From 21 April 2011 a B-rated sponsor was not be able to assign any CAS to new students, only to existing sponsored students who had Tier 4 leave and were eligible to extend it. If the UKBA discovered that a B-rated sponsor had assigned CAS to new students the sponsor's licence would be revoked immediately. On average, action plans were set for a period of three months although longer or shorter periods could be agreed subject to quarterly reviews pursuant to the terms of the Sponsor Guidance in force prior to 5 September 2011. The maximum period for which a sponsor could be subjected to an action plan was 12 months and if the sponsor was still B-rated after this period, its sponsor licence would be revoked immediately. Failure to comply with an action plan would lead to revocation of the licence. Being B-rated also had implications for eligibility for HTS status.

4.163 Action plans used to be free until 6 April 2010 when a processing fee of £600 was imposed following the Immigration and Nationality Fee Regulations being approved on 10 February 2010. As of 1 October 2010 the fee for an action plan went up to £1,000. B-rated sponsors had to settle their invoice for the action plan fee within 10 working days of the date of the invoice. The action plan would then be issued on receipt of payment. If additional concerns arose while an action

115 Or, between 6 April 2010 and 21 April 2011, A (Trusted) and B (Sponsor).

plan was in force, a new action plan might be needed for which a fee had to be paid. Failure to pay the fee for the initial or new action plan within the set time would have led to an immediate revocation of the sponsor licence.

4.164 From 5 September 2011 sponsors can be rated A or have HTS status, and they are reflected as such on the Register of Sponsors (paragraphs 237 and 240 of the Sponsor Guidance). A is a transitional rating given for 12 months from the time when a new sponsor licence is issued (paragraph 238 of the Sponsor Guidance). By the end of the transitional period the sponsor must be able to apply for HTS status and satisfy its eligibility criteria (paragraph 239 of the Sponsor Guidance). Save for exceptional cases the sponsor's rating will normally be the same across all tiers (paragraph 241 of the Sponsor Guidance). A-rated sponsors cannot offer courses of study at QCF/NQF level 3 and equivalent or courses below degree level with a work placement component. Students undertaking courses with A-rated sponsors cannot re-sit their exams more than twice and cannot commence their studies with an A-rated sponsor until their application for leave has been approved by the UKBA (paragraph 242 of the Sponsor Guidance).

4.165 Existing sponsors whose licence was granted before 5 September 2011 and who are A or B-rated will be subject to transitional arrangements.

Transitional arrangements relating to HTS status		
Circumstances	**Required action**	**Outcome**
sponsors who have had their licence for at least 12 months and have never had HTS status (paragraph 244 of the Sponsor Guidance)	must apply for HTS status by 9 October 2011 (applications are accepted up to one month in advance but decided after that date)	failure to comply will result in the sponsor's licence being revoked
sponsors with HTS status which is due for renewal (paragraph 245 of the Sponsor Guidance)	must apply before expiry of HTS status (applications are accepted up to one month in advance)	failure to comply will result in the sponsor's licence being revoked
sponsors whose applications for HTS status had been previously refused (paragraph 246 of the Sponsor Guidance)	must re-apply by no later than six months after the date of previous refusal or by 9 October 2011 (whichever is the latest)	failure to comply will result in the sponsor's licence being revoked

Circumstances	**Required action**	**Outcome**
sponsors who have not had their sponsor licence for 12 months by 9 October 2011 (paragraph 247 of the Sponsor Guidance)	must apply on completion of the 12 month period (applications are accepted up to one month in advance although not decided until the sponsor has had the licence for 12 months)	failure to comply will result in the sponsor's licence being revoked

Transitional arrangements relating to B-rated sponsor subject to an action plan

There are a number of scenarios for B-rated sponsors and their ability to achieve HTS status is determined by a number of factors:

- B-rated sponsors whose action plan is due for a review will have their action plan reviewed on the basis of the Sponsor Guidance in force at the time when the action plan was issued (paragraph 250 of the Sponsor Guidance). Failure to meet all of the conditions stipulated in the action plan will result in the sponsor's licence being revoked. If, on the other hand, the sponsor meets all the conditions attached to the action plan, its licence will be re-rated to an A rating (paragraph 251 of the Sponsor Guidance).
- If the sponsor has had its licence for 12 months by 9 October 2011, it must apply for HTS status by that date on the proviso that it has been A-rated for the six-month period immediately prior to the date of application. If they have not had their licence for 12 months by 9 October 2011, then they must apply for HTS status as soon as they have completed the 12-month period (paragraphs 252–253 of the Sponsor Guidance). B-rated sponsors who are able to achieve and maintain an A rating for six months prior to the date of application for HTS status will be able to satisfy this requirement (paragraph 254 of the Sponsor Guidance).
- If having partial or interim accreditation with one of the previously approved accreditation bodies is the only reason for the sponsor being B-rated and achieving full accreditation is a condition set in the action plan, then the sponsor may pursue full accreditation although it does not absolve it of having to comply with the educational oversight requirement (paragraphs 255–256 of the Sponsor Guidance). If the sponsor applies for educational oversight by the set deadline and there are no other outstanding concerns about the sponsor, its licence will be re-rated to an A rating and the number of CAS it can assign in the ensuing six-month period will be restricted by the interim limit (paragraph 257 of the Sponsor Guidance).

- If the sponsor is B-rated for a number of reasons including having partial or interim accreditation with one of the previously approved accreditation bodies, then the sponsor must meet all of the conditions set in the action plan by the review date. If the sponsor applies for educational oversight by the set deadline, meets all of the conditions set in the action plan and there are no other outstanding concerns about the sponsor, its licence will be re-rated to an A rating (paragraph 258 of the Sponsor Guidance).
- B-rated sponsors who are not able to achieve and maintain an A rating for six months prior to the date of application for HTS status will be subject to the following arrangements depending on whether they were given a B rating at the outset or as a result of being downgraded from A to B:
  - If the sponsor applied for its licence between 1 March 2011 and 20 April 2011 and it was granted with a B rating, then it must apply for HTS status as soon as it has had its licence for 12 months. Its action plan will be reviewed on the specified date. If, as a result of this, its licence is re-rated to an A rating, it will be given a restricted number of CAS subject to the interim limit. If the sponsor then fails to apply for HTS status by the time it has had its licence for a 12-month period, its licence will be revoked (paragraph 260 of the Sponsor Guidance).
  - If the sponsor applied for its licence before 1 March 2011 and it was granted with a B rating and the sponsor remains B-rated, or if the licence rating was downgraded to B and it remains B-rated, its action plan will be reviewed on the specified date. If, as a result of this, its licence is re-rated to an A rating, it will be given a restricted number of CAS subject to the interim limit. The sponsor must then apply for HTS status after being A-rated for six months. If the sponsor fails to apply for HTS status after six months, its licence will be revoked (paragraph 261 of the Sponsor Guidance).

Transitional arrangements relating to sponsors who have recently had their licence re-rated from A to B rating

The UKBA will allow sponsors who are A-rated at the time when they need to apply for HTS status but have at some point during the preceding six months been B-rated to delay their application for HTS status until they have been A-rated for the six-month period immediately prior to the date of the application. If the sponsor fails to apply for HTS status after six months, its licence will be revoked (paragraph 262 of the Sponsor Guidance).

SMS and CAS

SMS

4.166 SMS is a secure electronic hub linking each sponsor to the licensing authority which allows the licensing authority to have disclosure and control over how the sponsor manages its migrant students. On completion of the licensing formalities a Tier 4 sponsor can start using the SMS for its day-to-day activities such as managing users and their profiles, changing organisation details, complying with sponsorship duties, assigning, viewing, paying for and requesting next year's allocation of CAS. If the sponsor has been successful in obtaining HTS status it will retain the same SMS account as before (paragraph 287 of the Sponsor Guidance). From 1 October 2011 the UKBA has introduced changes to the SMS (paragraph 289 of the Sponsor Guidance).

4.167 Access and operational responsibility for running the SMS is given to level 1 and level 2 users while sponsors are fully accountable for their actions. Their functions and levels of access are described in the 'Key personnel' section above. Level 1 user's username is sent to the authorising officer in the post and password is sent by email. Level 1 or level 2 users must never disclose their password to anyone as disclosure may lead to action being taken against the sponsor (paragraphs 290–292 of the Sponsor Guidance). A sponsor must have at least one SMS user in place throughout the life of its licence (paragraph 294 of the Sponsor Guidance). A user should change their password the first time they log in. If they enter the wrong password three times in a row within 20 minutes, they will be locked out. Sponsors also receive an SMS pack including the SMS user manual on a CD-ROM. An electronic copy of the SMS user manual for Tier 4 ('the SMS Manual') is available at www.ukba.homeoffice.gov.uk/sitecontent/documents/employersandsponsors/sms-user-manual-t4/.

The SMS Manual consists of eight practical e-learning sections complete with screen shots and instructions guiding users through various aspects of the system's functionality:

- Section 1: Introduction
- Section 2: Sponsor profile and user administration
- Section 3: Creating and managing single confirmations of acceptance for studies (CAS)
- Section 4: Creating and managing batches of confirmations of acceptance for studies (CAS)
- Section 5: Transferring ownership and exporting confirmations of acceptance for studies (CAS)
- Section 6: Reporting student (migrant) activity

- Section 7: Payments
- Section 8: Managing your allocations

Bulk data transfer

4.168 Bulk data transfer ('BDT') is an electronic facility allowing Tier 4 sponsors to transfer appropriately formatted student related data in bulk from their internal IT systems to the SMS. BDT Toolkit (version 1.0) was released in October 2009. Following completion of Phase 3 of the Implementation Plan, BDT Toolkit (version 1.1) was put out to enhance BDT functionality from 22 February 2010.[116] Bulk transfer functions use a three-letter country code. Technical data about the BDT Toolkit, XML schema and XSD files can be found at: www.ukba.homeoffice.gov.uk/sitecontent/documents/employersandsponsors/pointsbasedsystem/bulk-data-transfer/.

CAS

4.169 A CAS is a virtual document bearing a unique reference number generated by completing a process through the SMS (paragraph 36 of the Sponsor Guidance). A CAS can only be assigned by a level 1 or level 2 user. It is a confirmation that a sponsor wants to recruit an international student for the purpose of undertaking a course of study in the United Kingdom and that, to the best of the sponsor's knowledge and belief, the student meets the requirements for assigning CAS. The student's entry clearance or leave to remain application will then be assessed against the Immigration Rules by immigration officials who will make the final decision (paragraph 35 of the Sponsor Guidance). With regard to a student migrant, paragraph 392 of the Sponsor Guidance states that the fact that a CAS has been assigned 'does not guarantee that we will grant the student's application.'

4.170 When assigning a CAS to a Tier 4 (General) or Tier 4 (Child) student migrant, the sponsor must follow the SMS instructions and complete all the mandatory and other optional fields that may be relevant to the application including the student's personal details, passport number, nationality, course title, study address, start and end dates of the course, course fees and any accommodation fees due, ATAS details (if applicable) and other information. Further information about how to assign a CAS and what to consider before assigning a CAS is contained in paragraphs 378–399 of the Sponsor Guidance.

116 Covering letter sent by the Stakeholder Management Team to sponsors on 5 February 2010, UK Border Agency, www.homeoffice.gov.uk/sitecontent/documents/employersandsponsors/pointsbasedsystem/bulk-data-transfer/toolkit-from-22-feb/bdt-toolkit-letter.pdf?view=Binary.

4.171 In terms of content, a CAS is similar to a visa letter which became obsolete on 22 February 2010. The SMS can be used to create a single CAS or a batch of CAS, edit and save it for completion at a later time. The sponsor will be logged out of the SMS after 20 minutes of inactivity so a CAS should be saved frequently throughout completion. The sponsor must complete in detail the 'evidence provided'[117] section by stating explicitly how it has assessed the potential student's English language ability and student's ability to follow the course[118] (paragraphs 330–334 of the Sponsor Guidance).

4.172 Once assigned, the sponsor must give the CAS reference number to the student applying for entry clearance or leave to remain.[119] A CAS is valid for six months from the date of issue and can only be used once[120] 'regardless of whether that application is successful or not' (paragraphs 392–393 of the Sponsor Guidance). The sponsor should also provide their sponsor licence number and the information about the course including course title, start and end dates, study address, course and accommodation fees and evidence used to be accepted onto the course of study to enable the student to complete the relevant application form or appendix[121] (paragraph 393 of the Sponsor Guidance).

ALLOCATION OF CAS

4.173 When applying for a Tier 4 sponsor licence a prospective sponsor must provide an estimate of the number of CAS it intends to assign each year to both existing and potential students. The number of CAS must be justified by the prospective sponsor (paragraph 146 of the Sponsor Guidance).

4.174 CAS allocation will depend largely on when the sponsor applied for its licence – before or after 21 April 2011.

117 This has been a bone of contention in some refusals where the sponsor failed to list each item of evidence provided and instead stated the type of documents provided by the student during the admissions process.

118 See *OR (Student: ability to follow course) Bangladesh* [2011] UKUT 166 (IAC) (5 November 2011).

119 Sponsors assigning CAS to migrants in the United Kingdom must understand the rules on switching (see **Chapter 3** and **Chapter 7**). For example, migrants with leave as student visitors or child visitors cannot switch to Tier 4 leave in-country while migrants with leave as prospective students can. Other categories that can switch into Tier 4 leave are listed in the Immigration Rules.

120 See **Chapter 3** for further comment. The UKBA website urges sponsors to 'ensure that the student is likely to apply and pass our points-based assessment, so you do not waste a CAS on an unsuccessful applicant.' (*Cost of a confirmation of acceptance for studies,* UK Border Agency, AQ please insert date www.ukba.homeoffice.gov.uk/employers/points/sponsoringmigrants/costs/confirmationofacceptance/).

121 Sponsors print out and provide a copy of the CAS statement generated by the SMS to the student to be enclosed with their application for entry clearance or leave to remain.

ON OR AFTER 21 APRIL 2011

4.175 Those sponsors who obtain their Tier 4 sponsor licence following an application made on or after 21 April 2011 will be given an allocation of CAS up to a maximum of 50% of their total student body based on the figures provided in the latest inspection report. In this instance the limit may be, as previously:

'• the number of CASs you asked for;
- a lower limit if you are a start-up organisation, have any history of not complying with immigration rules, or you do not justify the number you asked for.'[122]

4.176 In setting the limit, the UKBA will take into account such circumstances as the sponsor's previous record in dealing with the UKBA, the student capacity, type and size of the organisation, length of time it has been operating or trading for and previous compliance when allocating the number of CAS to the sponsor (paragraph 149 of the Sponsor Guidance). The sponsor may ask for increase in the number of CAS using the SMS to make the request (paragraph 150 of the Sponsor Guidance). Once the number of CAS has been agreed, it will be allocated to the SMS and the sponsor will have 12 months during which to assign them. Any unused CAS remaining at the end of the period will expire and will not be rolled over to the following year (paragraph 153 of the Sponsor Guidance). The UKBA may reduce a sponsor's CAS allocation all the way to zero due to change of circumstances or if the sponsor represents a threat to immigration control (paragraph 151 of the Sponsor Guidance). As part of its drive to reduce net migration figures, the Government has introduced an interim limit in CAS allocation for those Tier 4 sponsors who do not meet set conditions from 21 April 2011 (see above[123]). The interim limit will apply only to existing sponsors.

4.177 All education providers applying for a Tier 4 sponsor licence from 21 April 2011 will need to demonstrate that they are subject to the educational oversight requirement (see above). Sponsors who join the Register of Sponsors following an application made on or after 21 April 2011 will have 12 months from the date of grant of the Tier 4 sponsor licence to attain HTS status. They must apply for HTS status as soon as possible on completing the 12 month period. These sponsors will not be subject to an interim limit during the period from 21 April 2011 to 5 April 2012 (paragraph 148 of the Sponsor Guidance) although their CAS allocation will be limited to 50% of the total student body.

4.178 Prospective sponsors must be subject to the system of public reviews at the outset to be eligible to join the Register of Sponsors. Existing sponsors who do not have a satisfactory review by one of the relevant bodies must submit their application by the specified dates in order to meet the educational oversight deadline.

122 Paragraph 148 of the Sponsor Guidance.
123 See the section relating to Educational Oversight after 21 April 2011.

BEFORE 21 APRIL 2011

Sponsors who

- had their licence granted under the Sponsor Guidance in force prior to 21 April 2011; and
- did not have HTS status; and/or
- did not meet the educational oversight requirement; and
- were allowed to stay on the Register of Sponsors subject to the interim limit.

To keep their sponsor licence these sponsors must apply for HTS status and educational oversight by particular dates. See the relevant sections in this Chapter. Annex A (Table A) to the Sponsor Guidance sets out transitional arrangements for those sponsors who have been affected by the changes from 21 April 2011 (reproduced in full below):

Sponsor status	**Impact of new requirements**
• If you are an existing sponsor and you meet the new requirements on both educational oversight and HTS status	• No restriction on your CAS allocation.
• If you are a new sponsor and you meet the new requirements on educational oversight	• You will be granted a licence, but your CAS allocation will be limited to 50 per cent of your total student body. • You must achieve HTS status within 12 months to remain on the sponsor register
• If you are an existing sponsor and you meet the new requirements on educational oversight but not HTS	• If you have been licensed for at least 12 months by 10 October 2011 then you must apply for HTS status by this date. The interim limit will apply to your CAS allocation until you obtain HTS status. • If you have been licensed for less than 12 months on 10 October 2011, then you must apply for HTS status when you have been licensed for 12 months.

Sponsor status	**Impact of new requirements**
	• If you been licensed for at least 12 months but your licence has been B rated for any part of the last 6 months, you must apply for HTS when you have been A rated for 6 months. • If you do not apply for HTS status by the deadlines set out in this guidance, your licence will be revoked.
• If you are an existing sponsor with HTS status but you do not meet the new educational oversight requirements	• You must apply to the appropriate body by the specified deadline and meet the new educational oversight requirements by the end of 2012. The interim limit will continue to apply to your CAS allocation. • If you do not apply for educational oversight with the appropriate body by the specified deadline you will become a legacy sponsor and will not be allowed to sponsor any new students. • If you do apply for educational oversight by the specified deadline then the interim limit will continue to apply to your CAS allocation until you receive a decision on your application for educational oversight.
• If you are an existing sponsor and you do not meet the new requirements on either educational oversight or HTS status	• If you do not apply for educational oversight by the deadlines set out in this guidance you will become a legacy sponsor and will not be allowed to sponsor any new students. Even if you become a legacy sponsor, you must still apply for HTS by the deadlines set out in this guidance if you want to continue sponsoring your existing students.

Sponsor status	Impact of new requirements
	• If you do not apply for HTS by the deadlines set out in this guidance, your licence will be revoked.

INTERIM LIMIT

4.179 The Government's 'immigration cap' which has so far been deployed in an attempt to restrict: (1) the number of Tier 1 (General) migrants who may be admitted with leave to the UK; (2) the number of CoS that may be allocated to individual sponsors and overall under the Tier 2 (General) category, has not been applied to Tier 4 until 21 April 2011. The 'interim' cap applicable to Tier 1 (General) and Tier 2 (General) lasted until 5 April 2011 and further limits of 20,700 CoS applicable to Tier 2 (General) migrants were introduced from 6 April 2011.[124] Tier 1 (General) was abolished altogether on 6 April 2011.[125]

4.180 From 21 April 2011 the UKBA imposed an interim limit on CAS allocation in respect of those existing sponsors who had not attained HTS status and met the educational oversight requirement. The interim limit requirements have been incorporated into the Immigration Rules by virtue of paragraphs 115B–115I of Appendix A to the Immigration Rules.[126] The wording of the rules is quoted in **Chapter 3**. Once both requirements have been satisfied, the limit will be removed on provision of evidence in accordance with paragraph 115I of Appendix A to the Immigration Rules.

4.181 The UKBA has implemented the interim limit by restricting the number of CAS that can be assigned to students. Those sponsors to whom the interim limit applies is known as 'limited sponsors' (paragraph 115F of Appendix A to the Immigration Rules). There is no maximum number of CAS that can be assigned during the interim limit period.[127] Each existing sponsor who is subject to the interim limit will be allocated the number of CAS unique to that sponsor.

4.182 Any CAS allocated[128] to existing sponsors subject to the interim limit which had not been assigned to students would have been automatically withdrawn on 20 April 2011 (paragraph 115G of Appendix A to the Immigration Rules). Conversely, students who have had their CAS assigned to them prior to 21 April 2011 would be able to use them in making entry clearance or leave to remain applications (paragraph 162 of the Sponsor Guidance). CAS allocated to sponsors subject to the interim limit would have to be shared between new and current

124 Statement of Changes in Immigration Rules, HC 863 laid before Parliament on 16 March 2011.
125 Migrants with existing Tier 1 (General) leave are able to make extension and settlement applications under the transitional arrangements.
126 Incorporated by virtue of the Statement of Changes in Immigration Rules (HC 908).
127 Unlike Tier 2 (General).
128 Prior to 21 April 2011.

students for applications to be made in or out of country (paragraph 162 of the Sponsor Guidance). Priority should therefore be accorded to existing students.

4.183 The interim limit will be in force from 21 April 2011 to 5 April 2012 (interim limit period as defined in paragraph 115D of Appendix A to the Immigration Rules) and apply to the following classes of existing sponsors:

- privately funded further and higher education providers or English language providers operating outside the system of public reviews with or without HTS status; and
- publicly funded institutions without HTS status.

4.184 According to paragraph 115E(iii)–(vi) of Appendix A to the Immigration Rules the interim limit will not apply to:

- independent schools; or
- the Foundation Programme Office; or
- the Yorkshire and Humber Strategic Health Authority; or
- sponsors who apply for their Tier 4 sponsor licence on or after 21 April 2011.

Also, in accordance with paragraph 161 of the Sponsor Guidance, the interim limit will not apply to any sponsor who has complied with the HTS status and education oversight requirements.

4.185 As part of Appendix A to the Immigration Rules the UKBA has published a formula on the basis of which CAS will be allocated during the interim limit period. The calculation is contained in paragraph 115H of Appendix A to the Immigration Rules. The calculation relates to the circumstances of sponsors during the period from 1 March 2010 to 28 February 2011 (the comparative period). The formula consists of three key considerations:

- the number of CAS assigned by the sponsor during the comparative period which were
- used in applications for entry clearance or leave to remain during the comparative period, and which
- resulted in a grant of entry clearance or leave to remain during the comparative period.

4.186 The calculation will depend on whether the sponsor was licensed for the entire comparative period, part-way through the comparative period, applied for a Tier 4 sponsor licence before 21 April 2011 but obtained it after the end of the comparative period or became subject to the interim limit from 21 April 2011 onwards. The calculation set out in paragraphs 163–180 of the Sponsor Guidance is summarised in the table below:

Sponsors licensed continuously for the entire comparative period	• The interim limit allocation will equal the total number of CAS assigned during the comparative period which were used in an application which resulted in a grant of entry clearance or leave to remain during the comparative period; • If the total number equals zero, then the sponsor will be given a zero CAS allocation which will render it unable to assign any CAS to new or existing students during the interim limit period.
Sponsors licensed part-way through the comparative period	• The interim limit allocation will equal the total number of CAS assigned during the comparative period which were used in an application which resulted in a grant of entry clearance or leave to remain during the comparative period multiplied by the appropriate factor to take the allocation up to full 12 months; • If the total number equals zero, then the sponsor will be given a zero CAS allocation which will render it unable to assign any CAS to new or existing students during the interim limit period.
Sponsors who applied for a Tier 4 sponsor licence before 21 April 2011 but were not licensed during the comparative period	• If the application for a Tier 4 sponsor licence was submitted after 28 February 2011 and the licence was granted before 21 April 2011, the interim limit allocation will be calculated on the basis of the initial CAS allocation minus 26%; • If the application for a Tier 4 sponsor licence was submitted before 21 April 2011 but the licence was not granted until on or after 21 April 2011, then the interim limit allocation will be calculated on the basis of an indicative CAS figure minus 26%.[129]

129 The indicative CAS figure is based on the estimated number of CAS the sponsor would have requested as part of its application for a Tier 4 sponsor licence. When making an assessment of the request for CAS and setting the appropriate limit, the UKBA will take into account such circumstances as the sponsor's previous record in dealing with the UKBA, the student capacity, type and size of the organisation, length of time it has been operating or trading for.

Sponsors who become subject to the interim limit after 21 April 2011	• If a sponsor becomes subject to the interim period after 21 April 2011[130] because they lose their HTS status and/or cannot satisfy the educational oversight requirement, then the interim limit allocation will depend on whether the sponsor was licensed throughout, part-way or none of the comparative period; • The result of the calculation will then be reduced by the number of CAS the sponsor has assigned which were used in an application which resulted in a grant of entry clearance or leave to remain in the period between 21 April 2011 and the date on which the sponsor became subject to the interim limit.

CANCELLATION, WITHDRAWAL AND REDUCTION OF CAS

4.187 A CAS can be cancelled by the UKBA at any time or withdrawn by the sponsor using the SMS before it has been used to support an application for leave to remain. Applications supported by cancelled CAS will be automatically refused. If the student is in the United Kingdom with entry clearance or leave to remain and their CAS is found to have been assigned improperly (for example, if it was assigned as a result of misrepresentation or fraud), the student's leave will either be curtailed immediately if he/she was actively involved in the CAS being assigned improperly or reduced to 60 calendar days if he/she was not actively involved (paragraphs 426–430 of the Sponsor Guidance). Reducing the number of CAS a sponsor is allowed to assign is one of the actions that can be taken against a non-compliant sponsor who is not already subject to the interim limit. However, grounds for doing so are not explicitly set out in the Sponsor Guidance despite piecemeal references throughout (for example, paragraph 502 of the Sponsor Guidance).

COST OF A CAS

4.188 The fee payable for each CAS is £10. The fee paid for a CAS will not be refunded if it is withdrawn, cancelled or if the migrant does not use it to make an application (paragraph 44 of the Sponsor Guidance).

130 This should not apply to those sponsors who were granted their Tier 4 sponsor licence pursuant to an application made on or after 21 April 2011 as they are: (a) not subject to the interim limit although their CAS allocation is restricted; and (b) have 12 months from the date of grant of their licence to gain HTS status. However, if they can no longer satisfy the educational oversight requirement, they may become subject to the interim limit.

Changes in circumstances

4.189 In line with its duties, a sponsor must report any changes in its circumstances to the UKBA. Most changes can be reported using the SMS or by email. However, some changes including the change of authorising officer, replacing the level 1 user or key contact when there is no other user who can do this using the SMS, appointing or removing a representative, withdrawing an application for a sponsor licence or surrendering a sponsor can only be reported by using the Sponsor Change of Circumstances Form (a copy of which is available in **Annex C** to this chapter) and the SMS from 1 October 2011 (paragraphs 539–549 of the Sponsor Guidance). Sponsors who are subject to the interim limit who meet educational oversight and HTS status requirements during the period of the interim limit must notify their change in circumstances by using the SMS, email (SCOC@ukba.gsi.gov.uk) or by post to:

Sponsor Licensing Unit
UK Border Agency
Vulcan House – 4th Floor Steel
North East, Yorkshire & Humber Region
PO Box 3468
Sheffield
S3 8WA

Changes in ownership

4.190 Paragraphs 550–575 of the Sponsor Guidance give instructions on steps to be taken in the event of a change in ownership of the existing sponsor. As part of its sponsorship duties, changes in ownership during the lifetime of a sponsor licence must be reported to the UKBA. They must also be reported to the relevant educational oversight bodies.

TAKEOVERS AND MERGERS

4.191 If the existing sponsor is taken over or merges with another organisation, then both organisations must take the following steps within prescribed time as summarised in the table below. The report must be made by the sponsor's authorising officer. Any students involved in a merger, de-merger or takeover do not need to make a new application for leave and the new sponsor does not need to assign a new CAS. If the new organisation applies for a Tier 4 sponsor licence and is unsuccessful, any students due to transfer to the new organisation will have their leave curtailed.

If you are being completely taken over or merged with another organisation and your sponsored migrants are transferring to a new organisation[131]	**If you have completely taken over, or merged with another sponsor organisation and their sponsored migrants are transferring to you, you**[132]
• must report the change in ownership and provide details of any students transferring over to the new organisation within 28 days of the change preferably by emailing SCOC@ukba.gsi.gov.uk or using the SMS; and • must report any students not transferring over to the new organisation using the SMS (if their leave was granted on the basis of a CAS) or by emailing MigrantReporting@ukba.gsi.gov.uk (if their leave was granted on the basis of a visa letter); • confirm if the sponsor needs to surrender its licence using the Change of Circumstances form.	• must make a valid application for a Tier 4 sponsor licence, unless it has one, within 28 days of the change; or • if it has a sponsor licence in place, it can use the SMS to request an increase in the number of CAS it can assign if the number of students it expects to sponsor is to go up as a result of the takeover or merger;

PARTIAL TAKEOVERS AND DE-MERGERS

4.192 If a new organisation takes over part of an existing sponsor, or if part of an existing sponsor secedes to establish a new organisation and some of the students transfer to the new organisation, then both organisations must take the steps within prescribed time as summarised in the table below. It may be possible to add the new organisation to the existing sponsor's licence as a branch if the new organisation and the existing sponsor are connected by common ownership or control. Details should be sent to SponsorhipPBSEnquiries@ukba.gsi.gov.uk for assessment.

4.193 If the existing sponsor no longer requires its sponsor licence, then the existing sponsor and the new organisation must take the following steps:

131 Paragraph 558 of the Sponsor Guidance.
132 Paragraphs 559 of the Sponsor Guidance.

If you are the existing sponsor, and the change means that you will no longer have any sponsored students, you[133]	**If you are the new organisation, you**[134]
• must report the change in ownership and provide details of any students transferring over to the new organisation within 28 of the change by emailing MigrantReporting@ukba.gsi.gov.uk; and • may want to surrender the sponsor licence; or • may decide to keep the licence if you wish to sponsor new migrants in the future.	• must make a valid application for a Tier sponsor licence, unless it has one, within 28 days of the change; or • if it has a sponsor licence in place, it can use the SMS to request an increase in the number of CAS it can assign if the number of students it expects to sponsor is to go up as a result of the takeover or merger; and • must report the change, including details of any students the sponsor has accepted full sponsorship responsibility for; and • must report migrant activity for the students who have transferred over by emailing MigrantReporting@ukba.gsi.gov.uk and giving the previous sponsor organisation's name, licence number (if known), the student's details, and details of the change you are reporting.

4.194 If the existing sponsor still requires its sponsor licence, then the existing sponsor and the new organisation must take the following steps:

133 12 Paragraphs 563–565 of the Sponsor Guidance.
134 13 Paragraphs 566–569 of the Sponsor Guidance.

Existing sponsor[135]	**New organisation**[136]
• must report the change in ownership and provide details of any students transferring over to the new organisation within 28 days of the change preferably by emailing SCOC@ukba.gsi.gov.uk; • must notify any changes that need to be made to the CAS allocation in view of the change in ownership;[137] and • must continue reporting on any students who remain under its sponsorship but not the students who have transferred over to the new organisation.	• must make a valid application for a Tier 4 sponsor licence, unless it has one, within 28 days of the change; or • if it has a sponsor licence in place, it can use the SMS to request an increase in the number of CAS it can assign if the number of students it expects to sponsor is to go up as a result of the takeover or merger; and • must report the change, including details of any students the sponsor has accepted full sponsorship responsibility for; and • must report migrant activity for the students who have transferred over by emailing MigrantReporting@ukba.gsi.gov.uk and giving the previous sponsor organisation's name, licence number (if known), the student's details, and details of the change you are reporting.

Non-compliance and its impact on tier 4 sponsors and students

4.195 Licensed sponsors must comply with their sponsorship duties and the rules governing illegal working, if applicable. Failure to comply may lead to the rating being downgraded, sponsor licence being suspended or revoked or CAS allocation being reduced against which there is no right of appeal. It may also, where findings of illegal working are made, lead to a civil penalty being issued. Visiting officers may carry out follow-up checks after the sponsor licence has been granted to ensure that the sponsor continues to meet the required standards and comply with sponsorship duties. These checks may be targeted or carried out at random and may be by telephone, in person or by letter. The UKBA will inform the sponsor of

135 Paragraphs 570–571 of the Sponsor Guidance.
136 Paragraphs 572–575 of the Sponsor Guidance.
137 The existing sponsor's CAS allocation will be reduced to zero if it has no students to sponsor and is unsure as to whether it may need to sponsor any students in the future (paragraph 571 of the Sponsor Guidance).

the outcome of a check in writing. Problems revealed during such checks may lead to a sponsor organisation having its rating downgraded, or its licence suspended or revoked. In the more severe cases, such as where deception has been used to obtain a licence, sponsors or their representatives may be prosecuted (see paragraphs 488–493 of the Sponsor Guidance relating to compliance checks for holders of Tier 4 sponsor licences and paragraphs 494–500 of the Sponsor Guidance relating to compliance checks for holders of HTS status). Failure to comply with its sponsorship duties, being dishonest in dealings with the UKBA and representing a threat to immigration control may cause action to be taken against the sponsor. Particularly, the UKBA may:

- revoke the sponsor's licence;
- suspend the sponsor's licence; or
- reduce the number of CAS it can assign to students.

Suspension[138]

4.196 If the UKBA has reason to believe that the sponsor is breaching its duties and/or poses a threat to immigration control to such an extent that necessitates revocation of its licence, it may suspend the licence while further enquiries are made (paragraph 504 of the Sponsor Guidance[139]). If the licence is suspended, it will be suspended across all Tiers, categories and sub-categories and the sponsor's entry from the public version of the Register of Sponsors will be removed (paragraph 506 of the Sponsor Guidance). If the enquiries conducted by the UKBA do not result in

138 A number of private colleges who were suspended from the Register of Sponsors and/or subsequently had their sponsor licence revoked, sought to challenge the decision(s) made by the Secretary of State by way of a judicial review in the High Court. Some also applied for urgent consideration and sought interim relief. In some of these cases the Secretary of State chose not to contest the claim. In others, the claim proceeded to be heard by a judge or a panel of judges (Divisional Court).These cases serve as examples of a wide range of reasons given by the Secretary of State for suspending and/or revoking a sponsor's licence including non-enrolment and low attendance of students, poor migrant tracking, monitoring and record keeping, student capacity, assessing ability and intention of students to undertake courses of study. Here are some of the cases heard at the High Court: *Bhatti & Ors v Croydon Magistrates Court & Ors* [2009] EWHC 3004 (Admin) (6 November 2009); *Leeds Unique Education Ltd (t/a Leeds Professional College) v Secretary of State for the Home Department* [2010] EWHC 1030 (Admin) (14 May 2010); *The London Reading College Ltd, R (on the application of) v Secretary of State for the Home Department* [2010] EWHC 2561 (Admin) (18 October 2010); *New London College Ltd, R (on the application of) v Secretary of State for the Home Department* [2010] EWHC 2701 (Admin) (19 October 2010); *San Michael College Ltd, R (on the application of) v Secretary of State for the Home Department* [2011] EWHC 642 (Admin) (18 March 2011); *New London College Ltd, R (on the application of) v Secretary of State for the Home Department* [2011] EWHC 865 (Admin) (7 April 2011).

139 This is a stark departure from the wording in the Sponsor Guidance, version 10/09, 5 October 2009 which states at paragraph 328 that 'if we have reason to believe that a sponsor is *seriously* breaching its duties and poses a *major* threat to immigration control (for example, assigning confirmations of acceptance for studies or issuing visa letters to students who do not qualify to come to the United Kingdom), we may suspend its licence while we make further enquiries.' [added emphasis]

revocation of the licence, the suspension will be lifted and the sponsor's entry on the public version of the Register of Sponsors will be reinstated (paragraph 507 of the Sponsor Guidance). The sponsor will not be able to continue assigning CAS during the period of suspension (paragraph 505 of the Sponsor Guidance). Sponsored students will remain unaffected unless the suspension leads to revocation of the licence (paragraph 508 of the Sponsor Guidance). While suspended, the sponsor will have to continue complying with its sponsorship duties (paragraph 505 of the Sponsor Guidance).

Suspension without further investigation

4.197 The UKBA may decide to suspend a sponsor licence where it has sufficient evidence to do so without the need for further investigation. The sponsor will be informed in writing and given detailed reasons for the suspension (paragraphs 514 of the Sponsor Guidance). The sponsor will be given 28 calendar days from the date of the letter to respond in writing and provide evidence. This period may be extended in exceptional circumstances. If the UKBA comes across any new evidence during the 28 calendar day period, it will notify the sponsor giving them a further 28 calendar days to respond to the new findings. The UKBA will then consider the response and may consult any visiting officer familiar with the case for information. The UKBA will notify the sponsor of its decision within 28 calendar days of receiving the response.[140] If no response is received from the sponsor within the set time, the UKBA will proceed either to re-instate the sponsor or revoke its licence. Any action taken as a result of the UKBA's decision will become effective from the date of the notification letter sent to the sponsor by recorded delivery (paragraphs 515 519 of the Sponsor Guidance).

Suspension pending a full investigation

4.198 The UKBA may decide to suspend a sponsor licence where the evidence warrants it pending a full investigation. The sponsor will be given the initial reasons for the suspension and be informed that an investigation will be conducted. Protracted delays in conducting such investigations have been the cause of several judicial challenges. Paragraph 514 of the Sponsor Guidance states that 'it may not be possible at that point to say how long the investigation will take, but we will update the sponsor on our progress at regular intervals.' Any representations or evidence sent to the UKBA during this period will be taken into account as part of the investigation.

4.199 The UKBA will give detailed reasons for the suspension to the sponsor once the investigation has been concluded. The sponsor will be given 28 calendar days

140 Increased from 14 calendar days.

from the date of the letter to respond in writing and provide evidence. This period may be extended in exceptional circumstances. If the UKBA comes across any new evidence during the 28 calendar day period, it will notify the sponsor giving them a further 28 calendar days to respond to the new findings. The UKBA will then consider the response and may consult any visiting officer familiar with the case, other law enforcement agencies, Government departments, agencies, local authorities, the police, foreign Governments and/or other body for information. The UKBA will notify the sponsor of its decision within 28 calendar days of receiving the response.[141] If no response is received from the sponsor within the set time, the UKBA will proceed to either re-instate the sponsor or revoke its licence. Any action taken as a result of the UKBA's decision will become effective from the date of the notification letter sent to the sponsor by recorded delivery (paragraphs 515–519 of the Sponsor Guidance). Even if the UKBA does not revoke the sponsor's licence following a period of suspension it may still reduce the number of CAS and draw attention to the areas to be assessed during the next visit (paragraph 520 of the Sponsor Guidance).

Impact of suspension on students

4.200 During the period of suspension the sponsor will not be able to assign any CAS. Students applying for entry clearance or leave to remain with a valid CAS during the period of suspension will not have their applications considered until the suspension has been resolved. Where a student intends to undertake a pre-sessional course with a partner institution whose licence has been suspended, their application for leave will not be considered. If a student has been granted entry clearance on the basis of a CAS issued by the sponsor but has not yet travelled to the United Kingdom, the student will be allowed to enter and commence studies (paragraphs 508–513 of the Sponsor Guidance). This allowance comes with the following warning:

> 'We do advise all students to check the status of their sponsor's licence before they travel and we recommend that students do not travel to the UK if their sponsor's licence has been suspended.'[142]

4.201 While the sponsor's representations are being prepared by the sponsor or considered by the UKBA, sponsored students already in the United Kingdom on the basis of a CAS will not be told about the suspension[143] (paragraph 513 of the Sponsor Guidance).

141 Increased from 14 calendar days.
142 Paragraph 512 of the Sponsor Guidance.
143 Given that the suspended sponsor's entry will be taken off the public version of the Register of Sponsors, such a measure may seem fatuous.

Revocation[144]

MANDATORY GROUNDS FOR REVOCATION

4.202 Paragraphs 521–522 of the Sponsor Guidance set out the circumstances in which the UKBA 'will' or 'may' revoke the sponsor licence. The circumstances in which revocation is mandatory are if:

'• We find, after your licence has been granted, that you gave false information on your sponsor licence application.
- You stop trading or operating for any reason including insolvency.
- You stop being accredited with, or inspected or audited by, any body that you were accredited, inspected or audited by to meet the requirements set out in this guidance on educational oversight. We will not immediately revoke your licence if your accreditation is with any of the accreditation bodies previously approved by us and your accreditation expires. In these circumstances the future status of your licence will depend on whether or not you can meet the full requirements for educational oversight and highly trusted sponsor status as set out in this guidance.
- You are an existing sponsor and (where required) do not apply for educational oversight by the relevant agency by the dates specified as deadlines elsewhere in this guidance and do not obtain this by the end of 2012.
- You do not apply for highly trusted sponsor status by the dates specified as deadlines elsewhere in this guidance.
- Your highly trusted sponsor status expires and you do not apply in time to renew it.
- Your application for highly trusted sponsor status is refused.
- You also have a Tier 2 and/or Tier 5 licence and you have certified that a migrant under Tier 2 and/or Tier 5 will not claim state benefits, and that migrant then did claim benefits, with your knowledge.
- The courses you offer to sponsored students under Tier 4 (General) are below the level allowed according to whether you are an A-rated sponsor or have highly trusted sponsor status, unless the student is exempt because they applied before 5 October 2009. This does not apply to supplementary studies which can be at any level.
- Any work placement associated with a course for Tier 4 (General) students, or for child students age 16 and over, accounts for more than 50 per cent of the total length of the course (except where there is a UK statutory requirement for the work placement to take up more than 50 per cent of the course).
- The study element of any course you offer to sponsored students is not taken on your premises.

144 Referred to as 'withdrawal' prior to 21 April 2011.

- You have offered places and assigned CASs for students who are not from the countries we define as 'majority English-speaking countries', without first properly assessing their English language ability. This also applies to CASs you issued before 21 April 2011 when you were required to assess English language ability for students studying English language courses or courses below degree level (excluding foundation degrees).
- You are an A rated sponsor and you have offered places to Tier 4 (General) students on courses at QCF or NQF level 3 (or equivalent).
- You are an A rated sponsor and you have offered places to Tier 4 (General) students for courses below degree level (excluding foundation degrees) which include a work placement.
- You have offered places to Tier 4 (General) students and the main course of study does not lead to an approved qualification for our purposes.
- You have assigned a CAS to a Tier 4 (General) student to take a distance learning course or a course designed only to support students taking distance learning courses.
- You or a relevant person are issued with a civil penalty for employing one or more illegal workers, and the fine for at least one of those workers stood at the maximum £10,000 once your objection and appeal rights have been exhausted.
- You or a relevant person are issued with a civil penalty as above for a first offence, where the fine is below the maximum amount, and you have failed to pay the fine in full or set up a payment instalment plan with us, by the 29th day after you are notified of liability which may be after an initial objection or appeal determination.
- You or a relevant person, are issued with a civil penalty as above for another offence within the period that your sponsor licence is valid and you are still liable once your objection and appeal rights have been exhausted.
- You or a relevant person are paying a civil penalty fine by an agreed payment instalment plan and you breach the conditions of that plan.
- You do not hold, or you stop holding, appropriate planning permission or local planning authority consent to operate your type or class of business at your trading address (where this is a local authority requirement).
- You or a relevant person are convicted of one of the following offences (unless the conviction is spent under the Rehabilitation of Offenders Act 1974):
  - any offence under the Immigration Act 1971;
  - any offence under the Immigration Act 1988;
  - any offence under the Asylum and Immigration Appeals Act 1993;
  - any offence under the Immigration and Asylum Act 1999;
  - any offence under the Nationality, Immigration and Asylum Act 2002;
  - any offence under the Immigration, Asylum and Nationality Act 2006;
  - any offence under the UK Borders Act 2007;

- any offence under the National Minimum Wage Act or related to benefit fraud;
- trafficking for exploitation; or
- any other offence which, in our opinion, indicates that you or a relevant person are a risk to immigration control, for example, offences involving dishonesty or deception, including any of the offences listed in Appendix B

- you or a relevant person are dishonest in any dealings with us. This includes, among other things:
- making false statements, or failing to disclose any essential information, when applying for a sponsor licence; or
- making false statements, or failing to disclose any essential information, when assigning a CAS.'

B-rated sponsors subject to an action plan under the Sponsor Guidance in force before 5 September 2011 will have their sponsor licence revoked in the following circumstances:

- 'You have been B-rated and you have not complied with your current action plan within the specified target date for completing it.
- You have been B-rated and you have not complied with an action plan for 12 months or more.
- You are a private further or higher education institution and you have not reported a change in your ownership or the appointment of a new principal within 28 days of the change.
- You have been given or downgraded to a B rating under the guidance in place before 5 September 2011 and you have failed to pay the action plan fee within 14 calendar days.
- You have used a CAS to sponsor a new student when we gave it to you specifically to extend an existing student's permission to stay.
- You continue to sponsor a student after they have failed a re-sit twice, or repeated a period of study twice.'

In any of the above circumstances, the sponsor licence will be revoked with immediate effect of which the UKBA will inform the sponsor in writing. The sponsor has no right to appeal this decision nor will the sponsor be eligible to make a fresh licence application for a period of six months following the revocation. Unless the decision can be successfully challenged by way of a judicial review claim, the latter is most likely to have a devastating impact on any education provider, its ability to continue trading and its students (paragraph 523 of the Sponsor Guidance).

DISCRETIONARY GROUNDS FOR REVOCATION

4.203 The circumstances in which the UKBA may revoke the sponsor licence are set out in paragraph 524 of the Sponsor Guidance and arise if:

- '• You or a relevant person are convicted of an offence that we consider to be serious, unless the conviction is spent under the Rehabilitation of Offenders Act 1974.
- You or a relevant person becomes legally prohibited from acting as a company director.
- You or a relevant person becomes an undischarged bankrupt.
- You fail to comply with any of your duties.
- You fail to keep any of the documents specified in Appendix D of this guidance.
- We find that students that you have sponsored have not complied with the conditions of their permission to stay in the UK.
- You, or any organisation that you or a relevant person have been involved with in a similar role, have their authorisation removed by the Office of the Immigration Services Commissioner (OISC). (This applies to people or organisations that provide immigration advice or services.)
- You assign a stating that the course represents progression but you cannot show how you assessed the progression, or we are concerned about how you assessed it; or
- We find, after you have assigned a CAS stating that there is academic profession, that there is no academic progression.
- Any of your users of the (SMS) disclose their SMS password to another person.
- You have no authorising officer.
- You have no SMS users.
- You do not supply, when requested and within the specified time limit, any document we request to support any changes that you have reported to us using the SMS or the sponsor change of circumstances form.
- You are an A-rated sponsor and you continue to sponsor a student after they have failed a re-sit twice, or repeated a period of study twice.
- You issue a CAS to a student who obtains a visa using it, but fails to enrol when they enter the UK.
- You do not have enough control over any overseas agent acting on your behalf. For example we may find evidence:
- of a significant increase in the volume of applications from a particular part of the world with no explanation; and/or
- that we are refusing significant volumes of student applications from a particular part of the world.'

4.204 The Sponsor Guidance does not define precisely the exceptional circumstances in which the UKBA may *not* revoke the sponsor licence should one of the circumstances listed above arise. However, the Sponsor Guidance indicates that the UKBA will consider mitigating evidence (paragraph 525 of the Sponsor Guidance).While the sponsor licence may not always be revoked, the UKBA may immediately suspend it and withdraw any CAS which have not yet been used in an application.

Impact of revocation[145] *on students*

4.205 If the sponsor licence has been withdrawn, the UKBA will take the following action against sponsored students (paragraphs 526–530 of the Sponsor Guidance):

- cancel with immediate effect leave of any students who are believed to have been actively involved in any act of dishonesty by the sponsor whose licence has been revked and the students will have to leave the United Kingdom voluntarily or face enforcement action; and
- reduce the length of leave of any students who were not actively involved in any wrongdoing to 60 calendar days[146] to give them an opportunity to find and transfer to a new sponsor[147] and if any of these students have less than six months of their leave remaining, then their leave will not be curtailed.[148]

4.206 The UKBA will take action including detention and removal against any students who remain in the United Kingdom after their leave has expired. Thus any future entry clearance applications that they may make may be refused under paragraph 320(7B) of the Immigration Rules leading to a ban of up to 10 years. Any CAS assigned by a sponsor whose licence has been withdrawn will be automatically invalidated and any applications for entry clearance or leave to remain made based on these CAS will be refused. Students who have already been granted entry clearance at the time of withdrawal but not yet travelled to the United Kingdom will have their entry clearance cancelled under paragraph 30A(ii) of the Immigration Rules.[149] If they have travelled to the United Kingdom,

145 Referred to as 'withdrawal' prior to 21 April 2011.

146 See *Patel (Tier 4 – no '60-day extension') India* [2011] UKUT 187 (IAC) (13 April 2011) in which the Upper Tribunal held that the 60 day restriction runs from the time when the Secretary of State notifies the student of the imposition of restriction following revocation of the sponsor licence.

147 Students will need to make a fresh application to join their new sponsor. Their ability to start their course straight away will depend on whether they made their last application for Tier 4 leave pre or post 5 October 2009 and whether their new sponsor has a Highly Trusted sponsor licence. It may be difficult or impossible for many of the students to satisfy their maintenance obligations in respect of course fees unless they receive a substantial refund from their former sponsor to pay for the course with the new sponsor. See the decision in *Thakur (PBS decision – common law fairness) Bangladesh* [2011] UKUT 151 (IAC) (23 March 2011) where a Tier 4 (General) student did not have an adequate opportunity to enrol with another sponsor following revocation of his sponsor's licence.

148 Those students who have not found a new sponsor within 60 calendar days will have to leave the United Kingdom or face enforcement action.

149 Paragraph 30A(ii) of the Immigration Rules states that an entry clearance may be revoked if the Entry Clearance Officer is satisfied that 'a change of circumstances since the entry clearance was issued has removed the basis of the holder's claim to be admitted to the United Kingdom, except where the change of circumstances amounts solely to his exceeding the age for entry in one of the categories contained in paragraphs 296–316 of these Rules since the issue of the entry clearance'.

their entry to the United Kingdom will be refused under paragraph 321(ii) of the Immigration Rules[150] (paragraphs 528–530 of the Sponsor Guidance).

Application for a new sponsor licence following revocation[151] or HTS status following removal

4.207 Prior to 21 April 2011 sponsors who had their sponsor licence withdrawn could make a fresh application at any time provided that the reasons for the withdrawal (revocation), including being issued with a civil penalty,[152] no longer applied (paragraphs 408–409 of the Sponsor Guidance, version 10/10, 1 October 2010). From 21 April 2011 the UKBA introduced a major hurdle on the way to rejoining the Register of Sponsors (see below).

4.208 After 21 April 2011, sponsors who have had their Tier 4 sponsor licence revoked cannot apply to rejoin the Register of Sponsors for a period of six months from the date of revocation unless the licence has been revoked in error. The licence cannot be reinstated once revoked. An application to rejoin the Register of Sponsors will be treated as a fresh application subject to the procedures described earlier in this chapter. If the licence has been revoked in error, the sponsor will be exempt from having to pay the fee or submit supporting documents (paragraphs 531–532 of the Sponsor Guidance).

Surrendering a licence

4.209 A sponsor wishing to surrender its sponsor licence can do so by completing the Sponsor Change of Circumstances Form (a copy of the form can be found at Annex C) although from 1 October 2011 sponsors can use the SMS for this purpose. The sponsor can surrender the licence in one or all the Tiers, categories and sub-categories it is registered for. The organisation will then be removed from the Register of Sponsors in the relevant Tiers, categories and sub-categories and will

150 Paragraph 321(ii) of the Immigration Rules states that a person seeking leave to enter the United Kingdom who holds an entry clearance which was duly issued to him and is still current may be refused leave to enter only where the Immigration Officer is satisfied that 'a change of circumstances since it was issued has removed the basis of the holder's claim to admission, except where the change of circumstances amounts solely to the person becoming over age for entry in one of the categories contained in paragraphs 296–316 of these Rules since the issue of the entry clearance.'

151 Referred to as 'withdrawal' prior to 21 April 2011.

152 If the sponsor or another relevant person has been issued with a civil penalty for the maximum amount under the Immigration, Asylum and Nationality Act 2006, s 15 for employing illegal workers, a fresh application should not be made until six months after the date of the penalty has passed.

no longer be able to sponsor international students, having surrendered its licence in Tier 4. The sponsor will have to demonstrate by providing evidence that it no longer has any migrants that require sponsorship. If the sponsor has students that it is responsible for at the time of surrendering the licence, the sponsor's licence will be revoked, the students' permission to stay in the United Kingdom will be 'removed'[153] and they may be removed from the United Kingdom. The sponsor can apply for a new sponsor licence at any time[154] (paragraphs 576–582 of the Sponsor Guidance).

Renewing a sponsor licence and HTS status

4.210 A sponsor wishing to continue sponsoring international students must apply to renew its Tier 4 sponsor licence before its expiry every four years. If an application for renewal is made before the expiry of the sponsor licence, the sponsor will be able to continue sponsoring existing international students and issue CAS to potential students until a decision is made in respect of the application. The renewal application will be processed in the same manner as an application for a new licence. The sponsor will not normally be required to provide the same supporting documents it sent with the original application although it will normally be required to provide the most recent inspection report. Any other documents may be asked for if required. If the sponsor lets its licence expire and it does not renew it, then it will not be able to assign any CAS, act as a sponsor, and its existing sponsored students' leave will be cancelled (paragraphs 230–236 of the Sponsor Guidance).

4.211 Paragraphs 284–286 of the Sponsor Guidance state that HTS status is valid for 12 months from the date of award. To renew HTS status, the sponsor must apply every 12 months before it expires. Renewal applications will be assessed against the full HTS criteria in place at the time the application is made. Sponsors renewing their HTS status are advised to do so up to a month before expiry of their current HTS status.[155] Sponsors who have successfully renewed their HTS status will be subject to an interim CAS limit until they are able to comply with the educational oversight requirement. If the status expires before being renewed, the sponsor will have its licence revoked.

153 Possibly, cancelled or curtailed but not certain from the wording.

154 This is not the case in the event of the licence being revoked given the six month limitation.

155 *Highly Trusted Sponsorship for Tier 4 Sponsors – proposed criteria,* UK Border Agency, 18 July 2011, www.ukba.homeoffice.gov.uk/sitecontent/newsarticles/2011/july/28-hts-proposed-criteria.

Key dates

4.212

Deadlines for applying for educational oversight	9 September 2011, 7 October 2011 and 11 November 2011
Deadline for applying for HTS status	9 October 2011 (unless other factors intervene)
Deadline by which education oversight must be obtained	End of 2012
Deadline by which HTS status must be obtained	April 2012
Interim limit period	21 April 2011 – 5 April 2012
Comparative period	1 March 2010 – 28 February 2011

Useful contacts

4.213

Contact details	Purpose
SponsorshipPBSenquiries@ukba.gsi.gov.uk	General sponsorship enquiries including allegations of abuse of the sponsorship arrangements
sponsor.visits@ukba.gsi.gov.uk	Enquiries related to on-site visits
SponsorLicensingEnquiries@ukba.gsi.gov.uk or 0300 123 4699	General licensing enquiries including identity checks in respect of any visiting officers
MigrantReporting@ukba.gsi.gov.uk	Reporting any changes related to sponsored students whose leave was granted on the basis of a visa letter
SCOC@ukba.gsi.gov.uk	Reporting changes in ownership and other changes
HTSLicenceEvidence@ukba.gsi.gov.uk	To be used by sponsors who do not wish to apply for a Highly Trusted Sponsor licence
UKBApublicenquiries@ukba.gsi.gov.uk	General or specific enquiries about the licence application process
ccfeedback&sugge@ukba.gsi.gov.uk	General comments on the service provided by the contact centre
T4GiftedStudents@UKBA.gsi.gov.uk	Notification of CAS assigned to a gifted student
Tier4HTSReview@UKBA.gsi.gov.uk	Responses to HTS review

Annex A:

4.214

APPLICATION FOR A SPONSOR LICENCE

This printable version of the sponsor application form is designed to be used for reference when completing the online form. This copy of the form should not be completed – it is for reference only. To apply online go to:

https://www.points.homeoffice.gov.uk/gui-sponsor-jsf/SponsorHome.faces

Application for a Sponsor Licence

Category

We are not taking registration applications for Tier 3 at the moment.

You must fill in all fields as you go through the application unless we say otherwise.

1. Under what category is your organisation applying to become a sponsor?

Choose the categories you want to register under (you can choose more than one).

Tier 2 (skilled workers with a job offer)

General ☐
Intra company transfers (ICT) ☐
Sports people ☐
Ministers of religion ☐

Tier 4 (Students)

Students ☐

Tier 5 (Temporary Workers)

Creative and sporting ☐
Government authorised exchange ☐
International agreement ☐
Religious worker ☐
Charity worker ☐

Previous application(s)

2. Are you already on the register of sponsors? *Tick box

- Yes ☐
- No ☐

If yes, give your sponsor licence number (SLN): ☐

Previous application(s)

3. Have you applied to join the register of sponsors before but been unsuccessful? *Tick box*

2

- Yes ☐
- No ☐

If yes, give the application number we gave you.

☐

4. Give your organisation's details: (Please see guidance)

- Name of your organisation ☐
- Address ☐
- Address 2 (optional) ☐
- Address 3 (optional) ☐
- City or town ☐
- County or Area or District ☐
- Postcode ☐
- Country ☐
- Telephone number ☐
- Organisation Website (optional) ☐

5. Give your Head Office details, if different from your organisation's details (optional):

- Name of your organisation ☐
- Address ☐
- Address 2 (optional) ☐
- Address 3 (optional) ☐
- City or town ☐
- County or area or district ☐
- Postcode ☐
- Country ☐
- Telephone number ☐

- Organisation Website (optional)

6. If your organisation has traded under any other name in the last four years, give previous names starting with the most recent (same details required as listed in Q5 above)

You can add your previous trading names to the table by choosing Add
Once you have details in the table, you can edit them by choosing Edit
You can delete details by choosing Select and then Delete

Trading name	From	To	Select

(Radio buttons to be inserted entitled: ADD, EDIT and DELETE)

7. If your organisation has traded under any other name in the last four years, give previous names starting with the most recent.

You can save your details by choosing Save.

You can add more trading names by choosing 'Save' and then 'Add' to add another name.

(Radio buttons to be inserted entitled RESET, BACK, SAVE and SAVE & ADD)

8. Select the regions your organisation works in now. You can choose more than one.*Drop down list*

Regions:
- Wales
- Scotland
- Northern Ireland
- United Kingdom
- England – East of England
- England – East Midlands
- England – London
- England – North East
- England – North West
- England – South East
- England – South West
- England – West Midlands
- England – Yorkshire and the humber
- England – all regions

Your organisation

9. Select the size of your organisation. *Drop down list*

- Micro organisation (0 – 9 employees)
- Small organisation (10 – 50 employees)
- Medium organisation (51 – 250 employees)
- Large organisation (251 + employees)

10. Select the sector your organisation works in? Choose the one that explains your organisation's **main** economic activity. (Drop down list)

Accommodation
Activities auxiliary to financial services and insurance activities
Activities of extraterritorial organisations and bodies
Activities of head offices; management consultancy activities
Activities of households as employers of domestic personnel
Activities of membership organisations
Advertising and market research
Air transport
Architectural and engineering activities; technical testing and analysis
Civil engineering
Computer programming, consultancy and related activities
Construction of buildings
Creative, arts and entertainment activities
Crop and animal production, hunting and related service activities
Education
Electricity, gas, steam and air conditioning supply
Employment activities
Extraction of crude petroleum and natural gas
Financial service activities, except insurance and pension funding
Fishing and aquaculture
Food and beverage service activities
Forestry and logging
Gambling and betting activities
Human health activities
Information service activities
Insurance, reinsurance and pension funding, except compulsory social security
Land transport and transport via pipelines
Legal and accounting activities
Libraries, archives, museums and other cultural activities
Manufacture of basic metals
Manufacture of basic pharmaceutical products and pharmaceutical preparations

Manufacture of beverages
Manufacture of chemicals and chemical products
Manufacture of coke and refined petroleum products
Manufacture of computer, electronic and optical products
Manufacture of electrical equipment
Manufacture of fabricated metal products, except machinery
Manufacture of food products
Manufacture of furniture
Manufacture of leather and related products
Manufacture of machinery and equipment n.e.c.
Manufacture of motor vehicles, trailers and semi-trailers
Manufacture of other non-metallic mineral products
Manufacture of other transport equipment
Manufacture of paper and paper products
Manufacture of rubber and plastic products
Manufacture of textiles
Manufacture of tobacco products
Manufacture of wearing apparel
Manufacture of wood and of products of wood and cork, except furniture; manufacture of articles of straw and plaiting materials
Mining of coal and lignite
Mining support service activities
Motion picture, video and television programme production, sound recording and music publishing activities
Office administrative, office support and other business support activities
Other manufacturing
Other mining and quarrying
Other personal service activities
Other professional, scientific and technical activities
Postal and courier activities
Printing and reproduction of recorded media
Programming and broadcasting activities
Public administration and defence; compulsory social security
Publishing activities
Real estate activities
Remediation activities and other waste management services
Rental and leasing activities
Repair and installation of machinery and equipment
Repair of computers and personal and household goods
Residential care activities
Retail trade, except of motor vehicles and

motorcycles
Scientific research and development
Security and investigation activities
Services to buildings and landscape activities
Sewerage
Social work activities without accommodation
Specialised construction activities
Sports activities and amusement and recreation activities
Telecommunications
Travel agency, tour operator and other reservation service and related activities
Undifferentiated goods-and services-producing activities of private households for own use
Veterinary activities
Warehousing and support activities for transportation
Waste collection, treatment and disposal activities; materials recovery
Water collection, treatment and supply
Water transport
Wholesale and retail trade and repair of motor vehicles and motorcycles
Wholesale trade, except of motor vehicles and motorcycles

11. Is your organisation registering as a head office, a United Kingdom branch, a single body or another type of body? *Drop down list* (Please see guidance)

- Franchise
- Group of Branches
- Head Office
- Head Office and all United Kingdom Branches
- Parent Company with Subsidiaries
- Single Body
- Subsidiary of a Parent Company
- United Kingdom Branch
- Other

If you have answered other or group of branches, give details:

12. Select your type of organisation. Choose one that best explains your type of organisation. (Drop down list)

- Branch Office of an Overseas Company
- Central and Local Government Department; Body; Quango or Agency Public Body.
- Charity
- Company Limited by Guarantee

- Company Incorporated under the Industrial and Provident Societies Act 1968
- Franchise
- Hotel and / or Catering Establishment
- Limited Liability Partnership
- Nursing Homes / Care Homes
- Overseas Government or International Organisation or Diplomatic Mission
- Partnership
- Private Limited Company / Limited Liability Company
- Public Limited Company
- Religious and / or Faith Body
- Representative Office of an Overseas Company
- Sole Trader
- Sporting Organisation
- University or Educational Institution
- Unlimited Company

13. Select how long your organisation has been trading for? *Drop down list

- 0 to 6 months
- Over 6 to 12 months
- Over 12 to 18 months
- Over 18 to 36 months
- Over 36 months +

14. Is your organisation registered with Her Majesty's Revenue & Customs (HMRC) to pay PAYE, national insurance or VAT? *Tick box*

- Yes
- No

If yes, give details of at least one:

- PAYE reference number *Text Field*
- Accounts office reference number *Text Field*
- VAT registration number *Text Field*

15. Are you registered on the London Stock Exchange or a Financial Service Authority approved stock exchange(s)? *Tick box* (Link to FSA website) ****

- Yes
- No

If yes, give the name of the stock exchange(s) and the registration number(s). (Please see guidance) (Link to FSA website)

16. Does your organisation NEED to be registered or accredited to a governing body to operate legally in the United Kingdom? *Tick box*

- Yes
- No

If yes, you must add your accreditation or registration details to the table by choosing Add.

Once you have details in the table, you can edit them by choosing Edit.
You can delete details by choosing Select and then Delete

Name	Number	Expiry date	Select

17. Does your organisation NEED to be registered or accredited to a governing body to operate legally in the United Kingdom?
Name **Free text box **
Number (optional) ** Free text box**
Expiry date (optional) ** Free text box **

(Radio buttons to be inserted entitled: ADD, EDIT and DELETE)

18. Is your organisation registered or accredited with a governing body even if you do NOT NEED to do so to operate legally in the United Kingdom? *Tick box*

- Yes
- No

If yes, you must add your accreditation or registration details to the table by choosing Add.
Once you have details in the table, you can edit them by choosing Edit.
You can delete details by choosing Select and then Delete

Name	Number	Expiry date	Select

19. Is your organisation registered or accredited with a governing body even if you do NOT NEED to do so to operate legally in the United Kingdom
Name **Free text box **
Number (optional) ** Free text box**
Expiry date (optional)** Free text box **

(Radio buttons to be inserted entitled: ADD, EDIT and DELETE)

Your organisation
20. Is your organisation employing migrant workers or sponsoring overseas students (non-EEA nationals) NOW? *Tick box* (Please see guidance)

- Yes
- No

If yes, give the number: [ ]

21. Has an external representative helped you to fill in your application?

- Yes
- No

(For testing usage Q22 to 27 are tier specific questions as mentioned in the navigation doc)

Registering as a charity
22. If your organisation is a charity in England, Scotland or Wales, select whether you are registered, excepted or exempt according to the legislation in your country. Select the Northern Ireland option if you are based in Northern Ireland. *Drop down list*

Registration status:
- Registered
- Excepted
- Exempt
- Based in Northern Ireland
- None of the above (Please see guidance)

23. Give your charity registration number (optional):(Please see guidance) *Text Field*

[ ]

Your educational institution
24. Select the type that best describes your institution. *Drop down list*

Type of institution:
- Academy Schools – England
- Catholic Maintained School - Northern Ireland
- City Technology Colleges
- Controlled School - Northern Ireland
- English Language School
- Grant Aided School – Scotland
- Grant Maintained Integrated School - Northern Ireland
- Independent school
- Independent School - Scotland
- LA (Local Authority) – England
- LA (Local Authority) – Scotland
- LEA (Local Education Authority) - Wales
- Non Maintained Special Schools - England
- Private Institution of Further or Higher Education
- Specialist School or College

- State Maintained School - England
- University or Tertiary college
- Voluntary Grammar School - Northern Ireland
- Other

If other, give details

Publicly funded
25. Are you a University, Educational Institution or other organisation that is publicly funded? *Tick box*

- Yes
- No

Inspecting or auditing body
26. If your organisation is under the system of reviews, you must show that you have been inspected or audited by an appropriate body. Select from the list of bodies.*Drop down list*

List of bodies:
- Education and Training Inspectorate (Northern Ireland)
- Estyn (Wales)
- Her Majesty's Inspectorate of Education (Scotland)
- Independent Schools Inspectorate (ISI)
- Office for Standards in Education (OfSTED)
- Quality Assurance Agency for Higher Education (UK-wide)
- None of these

Accreditation
27. If your organisation is not under the system of reviews, you must show that you hold valid accreditation from a body approved by us. Or that you are an overseas higher education institution that offers part-term study abroad programmes in your locations in the United Kingdom. Select your accreditation body or overseas university with a United Kingdom campus. *Drop down list*

Accreditation or status:
- Accreditation Service for International Colleges (ASIC)
- Accreditation UK
- British Accreditation Council (BAC)
- Office for Standards in Education (OfSTED)
- Overseas Universities with a UK Campus
- None of these (Please see guidance)

28. Tier 2 General

Number of certificates of sponsorship

Enter the estimated number of certificates of sponsorship needed in your first year for this category on the register of sponsors, giving reasons why you need this number.

Number of certificates of sponsorship:

Reasons:

29. Tier 2 Intra company transfers (ICT)

Number of certificates of sponsorship

Enter the estimated number of certificates of sponsorship needed in your first year for this category on the register of sponsors, giving reasons why you need this number.

Number of certificates of sponsorship:

Reasons:

30. Tier 2 Sports people

Number of certificates of sponsorship

Enter the estimated number of certificates of sponsorship needed in your first year for this category on the register of sponsors, giving reasons why you need this number.

Number of certificates of sponsorship:

Reasons:

Sporting body

For Tier 2 sports people, select your sport and then the appropriate sporting body that you are endorsed by. For Tier 5, select other if not applicable.

Sport:
- Association football
- Basketball
- Boxing
- Cricket
- Horse racing
- Ice hockey
- Kabaddi
- Lacrosse
- Polo
- Rugby League
- Rugby Union
- Snooker
- Speedway
- Tier 5: other (Insert button entitled: Find body)

Sporting body:

• The Football Association • The Football Association of Wales • The Irish Football Association • The Scottish Football Association • England Basketball • British Boxing Board of Control • England and Wales Cricket Board • Cricket Scotland • Irish Cricket Union • British Horse Racing Board • The Jockey Club • Ice Hockey UK • England Kabaddi Federation • English Lacrosse Association • Hurlingham Polo Association • Rugby Football League	• TIER5 Aikido • TIER5 American football • TIER5 Angling • TIER5 Aquathlon • TIER5 Archery • TIER5 Arm wrestling • TIER5 Artistic skating (roller) • TIER5 Association football • TIER5 Athletics • TIER5 Australian rules football • TIER5 Badminton • TIER5 Ballooning • TIER5 Ballroom dancing • TIER5 Basketball • TIER5 Baseball/Softball • TIER5 Baton twirling • TIER5 Biathlon • TIER5 Bicycle polo • TIER5 Billiards • TIER5 BMX • TIER5 Bobsleigh • TIER5 Boccia • TIER5 Bowls • TIER5 Boxing

• Wales Rugby League • Scotland Rugby League • Rugby Football Union • Welsh Rugby Union • Scottish Rugby Union • Irish Rugby Football Union • World Professional Billiards & Snooker Assoc • British Speedway Promoters Association • Speedway Control Bureau	• TIER5 Camogie • TIER5 Canoeing • TIER5 Caving • TIER5 Chinese martial arts • TIER5 Clay pigeon shooting • TIER5 Cricket • TIER5 Croquet • TIER5 Curling • TIER5 Cycling • TIER5 Dance sport • TIER5 Darts • TIER5 Disability sport • TIER5 Diving • TIER5 Dragon boat racing • TIER5 Duathlon • TIER5 Equestrian • TIER5 Exercise and fitness • TIER5 Fencing • TIER5 Folk dancing • TIER5 Flying • TIER5 Fives • TIER5 Futsal • TIER5 Gaelic football • TIER5 Gliding • TIER5 Golf • TIER5 Gymnastics • TIER5 Handball • TIER5 Hang gliding and paragliding • TIER5 Harness racing • TIER5 Health and beauty exercise • TIER5 Highland games • TIER5 Hockey • TIER5 Horse racing • TIER5 Horse riding • TIER5 Hovering • TIER5 Hurling • TIER5 Ice hockey • TIER5 Ice skating • TIER5 Jet skiing • TIER5 Judo • TIER5 Ju jitsu • TIER5 Kabaddi • TIER5 Karate • TIER5 Keep fit • TIER5 Kendo • TIER5 Knee boarding

	• TIER5 Korfball • TIER5 Lacrosse • TIER5 Land-sailing/Yachting • TIER5 Luge • TIER5 Model aircraft flying • TIER5 Modern pentathlon • TIER5 Motor cycling • TIER5 Motor cruising • TIER5 Motor sports • TIER5 Mountain biking • TIER5 Mountaineering • TIER5 Movement and dance • TIER5 Netball • TIER5 Octupush • TIER5 Orienteering • TIER5 Parachuting • TIER5 Petanque • TIER5 Polo • TIER5 Polocrosse • TIER5 Pool • TIER5 Powerboating • TIER5 Power lifting • TIER5 Puck hockey (roller) • TIER5 Quoits • TIER5 Rafting (white / wild water) • TIER5 Rackets • TIER5 Racquetball • TIER5 Rambling • TIER5 Real tennis • TIER5 Roller sports • TIER5 Rounders • TIER5 Rowing • TIER5 Rugby league • TIER5 Rugby union • TIER5 Sailing / yachting • TIER5 Shinty • TIER5 Shooting • TIER5 Show jumping • TIER5 Skateboarding • TIER5 Skater hockey (roller) • TIER5 Skeleton • TIER5 Skiing • TIER5 Skipping • TIER5 Snooker • TIER5 Snowboarding • TIER5 Softball • TIER5 Sombo

	• TIER5 Speedway • TIER5 Speed skating (roller) • TIER5 Squash • TIER5 Sub aqua • TIER5 Surf life saving • TIER5 Surfing • TIER5 Swimming and diving • TIER5 Table tennis • TIER5 Tae kwon do • TIER5 Tang soo do • TIER5 Tennis • TIER5 Tenpin bowling • TIER5 Trampolining • TIER5 Triathlon • TIER5 Tug of war • TIER5 Unihoc • TIER5 Volleyball • TIER5 Wakeboarding • TIER5 Water polo • TIER5 Water skiing • TIER5 Weightlifting • TIER5 Windsurfing • TIER5 Wrestling • TIER5 Yoga

31. Tier 2 Ministers of religion

Number of certificates of sponsorship

Enter the estimated number of certificates of sponsorship needed in your first year for this category on the register of sponsors, giving reasons why you need this number.

Number of certificates of sponsorship:

Reasons:

Faith body

Select the faith that you are a member of **Drop down list**
Faith:

- Christian

- Muslim
- Hindu
- Sikh
- Jewish
- Buddhist
- Other

32. Tier 4 (students)

Number of confirmation of acceptance of studies

Enter the estimated number of confirmation of acceptance of studies needed in your first year on the register of sponsors, giving reasons why you need this number.

Number of confirmation of acceptance of studies:

Reasons:

33. Tier 5 Creative and sporting

Number of certificates of sponsorship

Enter the estimated number of certificates of sponsorship needed in your first year for this category on the register of sponsors, giving reasons why you need this number.

Number of certificates of sponsorship:

Reasons:

Sporting body endorsement

For Tier 2 sports people, select your sport and then the appropriate sporting body that are endorsed by. For Tier 5, select other if not applicable.

Sport:**Same drop down list as shown in Q30**

Sporting body: **Same drop down list as shown in Q30**

Creative organisation

If you are a creative organisation, select your type

Type of organisation: ** Drop down list**
- Creative – Dance
- Creative – Film & television
- Creative – Theatre
- Creative – Music
- Sporting
- Other creative category

If other, give details [ ]

34. Tier 5 Government authorised exchange

Number of certificates of sponsorship

Enter the estimated number of certificates of sponsorship needed in your first year for this category on the register of sponsors, giving reasons why you need this number.

Number of certificates of sponsorship: [ ]

Reasons: [ ]

Overarching body

Have you got permission from the appropriate United Kingdom government department to act as an overarching body?

Yes [ ]
No [ ]

35. Tier 5 International Agreement

Number of certificates of sponsorship

Enter the estimated number of certificates of sponsorship needed in your first year for this category on the register of sponsors, giving reasons why you need this number.

Number of certificates of sponsorship:

Reasons:

Your organisation

Select the type of organisation that best describes you.**Drop down list**

Type of organisation:

- A private sector company in the UK
- An international non-commercial body with a base in the UK (e.g. NATO)
- An international commercial company with a base in the UK and overseas
- A diplomatic household (as defined in the Vienna Convention on Diplomatic Relations 1961) with a base in the UK
- A diplomatic mission in the UK
- Other

If other, give details

36. Tier 5 Religious worker

Number of certificates of sponsorship

Enter the estimated number of certificates of sponsorship needed in your first year for this category on the register of sponsors, giving reasons why you need this number.

Number of certificates of sponsorship:

Reasons:

Faith body

Select the faith that you are a member of **Drop down list**

Faith:
- Christian
- Muslim
- Hindu
- Sikh
- Jewish
- Buddhist
- Other

37. Tier 5 Charity worker

Number of certificates of sponsorship

Enter the estimated number of certificates of sponsorship needed in your first year for this category on the register of sponsors, giving reasons why you need this number.

Number of certificates of sponsorship: [ ]

Reasons: [ ]

38. Supporting documents

To prove your organisation is genuine and has an established trading presence in the United Kingdom, you must send your supporting documents with your submission sheet, within 10 working days of submitting your application.

The type of documents you send depends on the type of your organisation and category that you are applying for. You must select a total of four documents.

You must check the guidance for the most up-to-date list of documents you must send.

You can choose Reset to clear this screen and re-enter your supporting documents.

Mandatory documents

The following documents are mandatory and you must send them with your application.

Documents	To be sent	Sent with a previous sponsor application

Primary documents

The following documents are primary and you must send them with your application.

Documents	To be sent	Sent with a previous sponsor application

Secondary documents (optional)

The following documents are secondary and you may send them with your application.

Documents	To be sent	Sent with a previous sponsor application

Authorising officer

You must appoint an authorising officer who is responsible for registering your organisation on the register of sponsors. The authorising officer must be based in the United Kingdom.

39. Fill in all fields for your authorising officer.

- Title: (If other, give the title):
- First name(s):
- Last name:
- Previously known as if applicable (optional):
- Address where employed:
- Postcode:
- Country:
- Telephone number:
- Email address:
- Date of birth:
- Country of nationality:
- National Insurance number:
- Position within the organisation:

40. If the AO is a non-EEA national, and is under immigration control, give their details (Please see guidance)

- Immigration status (optional):
- Home Office reference number if known (optional):
- Expiry date of current leave to enter or leave to remain (optional):
- Passport number (optional):

Key Contact

You must appoint a key contact who is the main point of contact within your organisation. If your organisation has overseas branches you can only appoint a key contact who is based in the United Kingdom branch of the organisation. The key contact must be based in the United Kingdom.

41. Will the authorising officer be the key contact?

Yes ☐
No ☐

42. Fill in all fields for your key contact.

- Title: (If other, give the title): ☐
- First name(s): ☐
- Last name: ☐
- Previously known as if applicable (optional): ☐
- Address where employed: ☐
- Postcode: ☐
- Country: ☐
- Telephone number: ☐
- Email address: ☐
- Date of birth: ☐
- Country of nationality: ☐
- National Insurance number: ☐
- Position within the organisation: ☐

43. If the AO is a non-EEA national, and is under immigration control, give their details (Please see guidance)

- Immigration status (optional): ☐
- Home Office reference number if known (optional): ☐

- Expiry date of current leave to enter or leave to remain (optional):
- Passport number (optional):

Level 1 user

You must appoint one level 1 user only who is based in the United Kingdom. Your level 1 user is the member of staff you want to access the sponsor management system.

44. Select who will be the level 1 user:

Authorising officer ☐
Key contact ☐
Other ☐

45. Fill in all fields for your level 1 user.

- Title: (If other, give the title): ☐
- First name(s): ☐
- Last name: ☐
- Previously known as if applicable (optional): ☐
- Address where employed: ☐
- Postcode: ☐
- Country: ☐
- Telephone number: ☐
- Email address: ☐
- Date of birth: ☐
- Country of nationality: ☐
- National Insurance number: ☐
- Position within the organisation: ☐

46. If the AO is a non-EEA national, and is under immigration control, give their details (Please see guidance)

- Immigration status (optional): ☐
- Home Office reference number if known (optional): ☐

25

- Expiry date of current leave to enter or leave to remain (optional):
- Passport number (optional):

47. Convictions or penalties

You must tell us if any of the staff in your application have any convictions or penalties.

Has the authorising officer, key contact or level 1 user been:

- convicted of an offence in the list of immigration offences which undermine immigration control (Appendix B of the guidance). (Convictions that are 'spent' under the Rehabilitation of Offenders Act 1974 will not be taken into account); or
- convicted of any other offence which is still 'unspent'; or
- issued with a fixed or civil penalty (a fine) five years before the date of this application in the list of civil penalties (Appendix C of the guidance), unless that penalty was withdrawn by us or cancelled on appeal; or
- an un-discharged bankrupt, or is legally prevented from becoming or acting as a company director.

Yes
No

If yes, give details of the conviction or penalty and the date it was given.

Conviction or penalty details:

Representatives

Only fill this in if you are a third party, for example a legal representative, helping a sponsor with their application.

Previous application

48. Have you helped a sponsor with an application to join the register of sponsors or a migrant to apply under the points-based system before?

Yes ☐
No ☐

If yes, give your representative's PBS reference number (if known):

☐

Representative details

49. Fill in all details

- Name of representative organisation: ☐
- Contact name in your organisation: ☐
- Address: ☐
- Postcode: ☐
- Country: ☐
- Is it a United Kingdom based organisation: (Please see guidance)

  Yes ☐
  No ☐
- Telephone number ☐
- Email address ☐

50. Select how you are qualified to operate under Section 84 of the Immigration and Asylum Act 1999.

Regulation status:

- Regulated by the OISC ☐
- Exempt from OISC regulation ☐
- Not regulated by the OISC ☐

51. Give your Office of the Immigration Service Commissioner (OISC) number

52. If you are not regulated by the OISC select the designated professional body that authorises you to practice. *Tick box*

The Faculty of Advocates	
The General Council of the Bar	
The General Council of the Bar of Northern Ireland	
The Institute of Legal Executives	
The Law Society	
The Law Society of Northern Ireland	
The Law Society of Scotland	

53. Give your professional body membership number (if applicable).

54. Are you the registration or authorisation holder?

Yes

No

If no, give the name of your supervisor

55. If you are not regulated by OISC or a designated professional body and do not have to be, are you:

- authorised by an EE body responsible for the regulation of the provision of legal advice in that EEA state; or
- employed or supervised by the person regulated as defined in section 84(2)(d), (e) and (f) of the IAA 1999?

Yes

No

If yes, give the name of the registered or accredited EEA body or enter not applicable.

Give your supervisor's name (if applicable)

56. Are you under a category of person specified in an Order made by The Secretary of State under subsection 84(4)(d) of the Immigration Asylum Act 1999?

Yes

No (please see guidance)

If yes, give details

Representative's declaration

57. You must agree with all the statements for the application to be successful.

Read the declaration and tick the box if you agree with all the following statements if you are a representative helping a sponsor with their application.

- I have been appointed by the organisation to assist with this application
- I confirm that the organisation has completed and verified the application, and the application is, to the best of my knowledge and belief, true and correct.
- I am aware that it is an offence under the Immigration Act 1971, as amended by the Immigration and Asylum Act 1999 and the Nationality, Immigration and Asylum Act 2002, to do an act which facilitates the commission of a breach of immigration law by an individual who is not a citizen of the European Union, knowing or having reasonable cause to believe that the act has this effect.

Tick the box if you agree with all the statements	☐
Date (dd/mm/yyyy)	
Name	
Name of representative organisation	
Position within organisation	

Sponsor duties

58. As a sponsor, you must fulfil certain duties to make sure immigration controls stay effective. The objectives of these duties are to:

- prevent abuse of assessment procedures;
- capture early any patterns of migrant behaviour which cause concern;
- address possible weaknesses in your processes which cause those patterns; and
- monitor compliance with immigration rules.

You must agree to comply with your sponsor duties for the application to be successful. Find a list of all sponsor duties (link to http://www.ukba.homeoffice.gov.uk/employers/points/sponsorduties/), which you must read before ticking the box to agree.

Tick the box if you agree with all the statements. ☐

Date (dd/mm/yyyy)	
Name of Authorising Officer	
Position within organisation	

Sponsor declaration

59. Fill in this section if you are the authorising officer.

You must agree with all the statements for the application to be successful.

Read the declaration, and tick the box to say you have understood and agree with all the statements.

- I agree to comply with my sponsor duties.
- I understand that if I do not comply with the rules of the sponsor licensing system I may lose my licence and be removed from the register of sponsors, which would mean that I could no longer sponsor overseas nationals (other than nationals of European Economic Area (EEA) member states) wanting to come to the United Kingdom, to work for or study with me. The leave of any existing non-EEA migrant workers or students under Tiers 2 to 5 of the points based system may also be curtailed.
- The information I have given in this online application is complete, accurate and true to the best of my knowledge.
- I will inform you without delay if there is a material change in my circumstances or new information relevant to this application becomes available before this application is decided.
- I agree to co-operate with your officials, when they are carrying out checks on our compliance with our sponsor duties.
- I understand that if I knowingly make any false representations or submit any false documents, the application will be refused and I may be prosecuted.
- I understand that it is an offence under section 25 of the Immigration Act 1971 to do an act which facilitates a breach of immigration law by an individual who is not a citizen of the European Union, or if I know or have reasonable cause to believe that it may so facilitate.
- The information provided by me to you will be treated in confidence but it may be disclosed to other law enforcement agencies, United Kingdom government departments, agencies, local authorities, foreign governments and other bodies for immigration or research purposes and to help them to carry out their functions.
- I understand you may ask for or check information from other law enforcement agencies, government departments, agencies, local authorities, the police, foreign governments and other bodies for immigration, research or security purposes or to help you carry out your work.
- I understand you can use the information given in this application for training and research purposes.

Tick the box if you agree with all the statements ☐

Date (dd/mm/yyyy) ____________

Name of Authorised Officer	
Position within organisation	

32

PBS Sponsor's Licence Application submission sheet

Your application has been submitted successfully. You must **print** this submission sheet and complete **(using black ink)** the relevant sections including your fee. Call the Customer Contact Centre on 0114 207 4074 if you have any queries. We advise you take a copy for your records.

Part 1: Your Application:
PBS SPONSOR'S LICENCE APPLICATION REFERENCE NUMBER:]
Date submitted:
Organisation name:
Key Contact details
Name:
Address:
[Address line 1]
[Address line 2]
[Address line 3]
[Address line 4]
[Address line 5]
[Postcode]

Telephone number:
Email:
Preferred method of contact:

Your supporting evidence: Tick each box to confirm you have included the document with this submission sheet.

Document Type 1 ☐
Document Type 2 ☐ (box will need to expand as necessary)
Document Type 3 ☐
Document Type 4 ☐

I have read and understood the sponsor declaration and agree to comply with my sponsor declaration and duties.

Authorising officer's name:
Position in organisation:
Authorising officer's signature:
Date submitted:

[The signature **must** be the authorising officer's.]

For Office Use Only
Date received ______________
Received by ______________

33

Part 2: PAYMENT DETAILS

Application Details:
PBS SPONSOR'S LICENCE APPLICATION REFERENCE NUMBER:
Date submitted
Organisation name:
Key Contact details
Name:
Address:
[Address line 1]
[Address line 2]
[Address line 3]
[Address line 4]
[Address line 5]
[Postcode]

Telephone number:
Email address:
Preferred method of contact:

Payment Details:
Chosen Method of Payment: **[Card]**.

Please debit my: Visa ☐ Mastercard ☐ Delta ☐ Maestro (UK) ☐
Amount: **[£nnn]**
Name on Card
Card Number
Card Details Valid from / Expiry date / Issue No (Maestro) CVV No
Signature Date

OR

Payment Details:
Chosen Method of Payment: **[Cheque].** Enclose a cheque for **[£nnn]** making the cheque payable to Home Office PBS Sponsorship. Please fill in the following:
Account No Sortcode Cheque No

OR

Payment Details:
Amount: **[£nnn]**
Chosen Method of Payment: **[No payment required – fee already paid].**

34

Send both pages of the submission sheet with your documents and fee (if paying by cheque) to:

Border and Immigration Agency
PBS Sponsor's Licence Application
PO Box 501
Durham
DH99 1WH

We must receive your signed submission sheet and fee at the above address by [submitted date + 14] for your application to be considered.

Annex B:

4.215

Home Office
UK Border Agency

HTS
version 09/11

APPLICATION FOR HIGHLY TRUSTED SPONSOR STATUS UNDER TIER 4 OF THE POINTS BASED SYSTEM

This form is for use by organisations that already hold a Tier 4 Sponsor Licence

Please check on the website at www.ukba.homeoffice.gov.uk that this is the current form for use on the date that you apply.

You are advised to read the help text at the front of this form and separate guidance notes that are available on our website. Please read them before making your application.

Applications on this form can be made by post only. The postal address is:

UK Border Agency
Highly Trusted Sponsors
PO Box 589
Durham
DH99 1AB

This form is for applications made on or after 5 September 2011

HTS - APPLICATION FORM

HIGHLY TRUSTED SPONSOR STATUS APPLICATION FORM - HELP TEXT

This leaflet contains essential information to help you to complete the HTS application form, including guidance on paying for an application and help for specific questions.

Who should apply using this form?

Highly Trusted Sponsor status is only available to organisations that already hold a Tier 4 Sponsor licence and this application form should only be completed by such an organisation.

If you do not currently hold a Sponsor licence that includes Tier 4, but you want to be able to sponsor students under Tier 4, you should apply using the online application on our website. You should also read the associated guidance which is also available on our website at www.ukba.homeoffice.gov.uk/employers/.

Submitting a valid application

You will only be considered to have submitted a valid application if the following has been complied with:

The application form has been completed and submitted by prepaid post

The correct application fee has been paid

All sections of the form are complete

The declaration is signed by the Authorising Officer

Any necessary supporting documents have been submitted

The applicable fee

Please refer to our website for the latest applicable fee http://www.ukba.homeoffice.gov.uk/employers/points/sponsoringmigrants/costs/

How can you pay?

You can pay by any of the following methods:

- Cheque/Bankers Draft
- Postal Order
- Credit card – MasterCard or Visa (including Electron)
- Debit Card – Delta, Maestro* (including Solo)

* Maestro – we can only accept Maestro cards issued in the UK.

We will reject and return all applications where the payment cannot be banked, including any of the following reasons:

- no payment is included with your application;
- the amount provided or authorised does not cover the fee required;
- the cheque has not been signed or dated correctly;
- the debit or credit card details have not been completed correctly.

Cheques and postal orders

You must make the cheque or postal order payable to "Home Office PBS Sponsorship" and cross the cheque A/C Payee only.

Please write the organisation name on the back of the cheque or postal order and keep the postal order receipt(s). Please make sure that the date and the amount (words and figures) are correct and that the cheque is signed properly.

Attach your cheque or postal order(s) to the front of the application form.

Completing Section A

To ensure that your payment is processed without any delay, please follow this guidance when completing Section A of this form (Payment Details).

A2 The organisation's name, as stated on your Sponsor licence.

A3 The contact name for this application. This person must be the Authorising Officer named on your current standard Tier 4 Sponsor

HTS Application Form (version 09/11) - page 2

HTS - APPLICATION FORM

licence.

A4 The address for correspondence which should be the same as that on your Sponsor licence.

Methods of payment

A5 Tick one of the boxes to show which method of payment you are using.

A6 – A8 If paying by cheque, enter the bank account number, sort code and cheque number.

Paying by credit/debit card

A9 The name as displayed on the credit/debit card.

A10 Card number – this is the long number across the centre of the card.

A11-A13 Enter the details where available on the card.

A14 The Card Verification Value (CVV) is a three-digit security code, found on the back of the card on the signature strip – it consists of the last 3 digits.

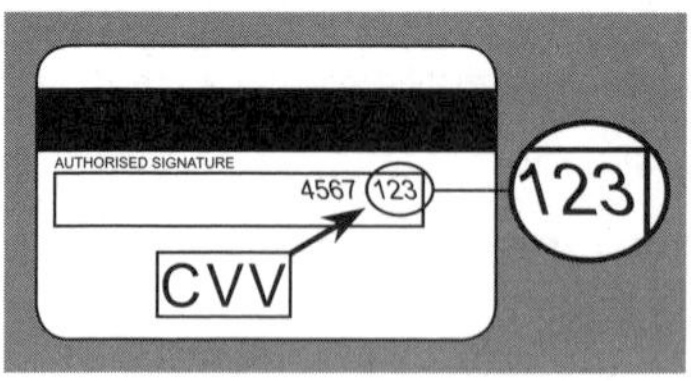

<u>If you do not provide the CVV number, we cannot take your payment and your application will be rejected as invalid.</u>

A15 For card payments, tick to confirm the payment to be taken.

A16 – A17 Card holder's signature – the person named on the credit/debit card must sign and date these sections.

Completing Section B

B1 – B3 You should supply full details of your organisation's name, sponsor licence number and correspondence address and these should match the details on your existing Sponsor licence.

B4 – B7 You should give a named contact for this application. This must be the Authorising Officer on your existing Tier 4 Sponsor licence. The Authorising Officer must give his/her details in Section F and sign the declaration.

Completing Section C

C1 - C2 Give details of your inspection or accreditation body.

Completing Section D

There are two stages in considering your application. The first stage is where we assess you against the "mandatory requirements" – these requirements are covered in this section.

If you meet all of these mandatory requirements we will then look more closely at your "core measurable requirements" which are refusal rate, enrolment rate and course completion rate.

You will be scored on these requirements and the final score will determine the outcome of your HTS application.

Please note, we have not included questions relating to refusal rate, enrolment rate or course completion rate as we will assess these aspects of your application based on CAS data from the Sponsor Management System for the 12 month period immediately before you make your HTS application.

D1 - 2 Provide details of your current licence status.

D3 Organisations cannot be granted HTS status if they have become liable for the payment of a civil penalty which still stands

HTS Application Form (version 09/11) - page 3

HTS - APPLICATION FORM

once any objection and appeal rights have been exhausted, within the 3 year period immediately prior to making this application.

D4 This is a declaration from yourself that, where required, each CAS you have issued in the 12 months prior to you making this application includes a confirmation of the student's academic progression.

Completing Section E

This section should be completed by the current Authorising Officer named on your current standard Tier 4 Sponsor licence.

Consideration process

The fee charged is for the processing and consideration of the application. This fee will be payable once the application form is received by the UK Border Agency or its payment processing agent, regardless of the outcome of the application.

We cannot begin the consideration process until payment has cleared. We allow 5 working days for payments made by cheque to clear; credit/debit cards and postal orders will clear immediately.

Should the application be withdrawn at any time during the consideration process the fee will not be refunded.

HTS Application Form (version 09/11) - page 4

HTS - APPLICATION FORM

A. Payment Details

There is help text available at the front of this form.
Please complete this form in block capitals and black ink.

A1. The applicable fee:
The fee for consideration of this application is £410

A2. Organisation name:

A3. Contact name:

A4. Address for correspondence in the UK:

Postcode

A5. Please select the method of payment from the list below

UK postal order (payable to 'Home Office PBS Sponsorship') - go to question A17 ☐

Cheque (payable to 'Home Office PBS Sponsorship') - go to question A6 ☐

Visa / Mastercard - go to question A9 ☐

Delta / Maestro - go to question A9 ☐

A6. Account number

A7. Sort code

A8. Cheque number

A9. Name on card

A10. Card number (the long number across the centre of the card)

A11. Valid from /

A12. Expiry /

A13. Issue number (where available)

A14. CVV security number (3 digit number on back of card)

A15. Amount - please tick to confirm the fee of £410 ☐

A16. Cardholder's signature

A17. Date (DD/MM/YYY)

HTS Application Form (version 09/11) - page 5

HTS - APPLICATION FORM

This page is intentionally blank

HTS Application Form (version 09/11) - page 6

HTS - APPLICATION FORM

Help with filling in this form is available in the notes at the front. Please read these notes prior to filling in the application as errors may result in your application being rejected.

You must complete all questions applicable to your organisation. Please note that this application will not be valid if it is not completed fully.

B. Organisation details

B1. Organisation name:

Highly Trusted Sponsor status is only available to existing Tier 4 Sponsor licence holders. For more information, please refer to the policy guidance "Tier 4 of the Points Based System" which is available on our website at http://www.ukba.homeoffice.gov.uk/sitecontent/documents/employersandsponsors/pbsguidance/

B2. Please enter your Sponsor Licence Number (SLN):

B3. Address for correspondence in the UK:

Postcode

B4. Contact name:

B5. Position within organisation:

B6. Contact telephone number:

B7. Contact email address:

Now continue to Section C.

HTS - APPLICATION FORM

C. Accreditation / Educational Oversight Requirements

The questions in this section ask about your Tier 4 Sponsor licence. You should answer all questions that apply to your organisation.

C1. Which organisation is your institution subject to an inspection from?

C2. What is the date of the last inspection by the organisation named at C1?

Now continue to Section D

HTS - APPLICATION FORM

D. MANDATORY REQUIREMENTS

D1. Has your organisation held a Tier 4 sponsor licence for the last 12 consecutive months?

Yes ☐ Proceed to question D2 **No** ☐ Your application will be refused

D2. Has your organisation held an A-rated Tier 4 sponsor licence for the 6 months immediately prior to you making this application?

Yes ☐ Proceed to question D3 **No** ☐ Your application will be refused

D3. Has your organisation become liable for a civil penalty, which still stands once your objection and appeal rights have been exhausted, during the 3-year period immediately prior to you making this application?

Yes ☐ Your application will be refused **No** ☐ Proceed to question D4

D4. Have you confirmed, where applicable, student progression on 100% of CAS assigned during the last 12 months?

Yes ☐ Proceed to section E **No** ☐ Your application will be refused

HTS Application Form (version 09/11) - page 9

HTS - APPLICATION FORM

E. Sponsor Declaration

The Authorising Officer named on your existing Tier 4 licence must sign and agree with all statements for the application to be successful.

This is my organisation's application for Highly Trusted Sponsor status.

I can confim that I am compliant with my sponsor duties and will continue to adhere to these duties for the duration of my organisation's licence.

I understand that if I do not comply with the rules of the sponsor licensing system I may lose my Tier 4 Sponsor licence and be removed from the register of sponsors, which would mean that I could no longer sponsor overseas nationals (other than nationals of European Economic Area (EEA) member states) wanting to come to the United Kingdom, to work for or study with me. The leave of any existing non-EEA migrant workers or students under Tiers 2 to 5 of the points based system may also be curtailed.

The information I have given in this application is complete, accurate and true to the best of my knowledge.

I will inform you without delay if there is a material change in my circumstances or new information relevant to this application becomes available before this application is decided.

I agree to co-operate with your officials, when they are carrying out checks on our compliance with our sponsor duties.

I understand that if I knowingly make any false representations or submit any false documents, the application will be refused and I may be prosecuted.

I understand that it is an offence under section 25 of the Immigration Act 1971 to do an act which facilitates a breach of immigration law by an individual who is not a citizen of the European Union, or if I know or have reasonable cause to believe that it may so facilitate.

The information provided by me to you will be treated in confidence but it may be disclosed to other law enforcement agencies, United Kingdom government departments, agencies, local authorities, foreign governments and other bodies for immigration or research purposes and to help them to carry out their functions.

I understand you may ask for or check information from other law enforcement agencies, government departments, agencies, local authorities, the police, foreign governments and other bodies for immigration, research or security purposes or to help you carry out your work.

I understand you can use the information given in this application for training and research purposes.

Authorising Officer's name:

Position within Organisation:

Authorising Officer's Signature:

Date (DD/MM/YYY):

Home Office
UK Border Agency

HTS
version 09/11

APPLICATION FOR HIGHLY TRUSTED SPONSOR STATUS UNDER TIER 4 OF THE POINTS BASED SYSTEM

This form is for use by organisations that already hold a Tier 4 Sponsor Licence

Please check on the website at www.ukba.homeoffice.gov.uk that this is the current form for use on the date that you apply.

You are advised to read the help text at the front of this form and separate guidance notes that are available on our website. Please read them before making your application.

Applications on this form can be made by post only. The postal address is:

UK Border Agency
Highly Trusted Sponsors
PO Box 589
Durham
DH99 1AB

This form is for applications made on or after 5 September 2011

Annex C:

4.216

Home Office
UK Border Agency

Sponsor
Change of
Circumstances
VERSION 04/2011

SPONSOR CHANGE OF CIRCUMSTANCES FORM

You can get more information from our website at www.ukba.homeoffice.gov.uk or by emailing SponsorshipPBSEnquiries@ukba.gsi.gov.uk

The address to which you must post your Sponsor Change of Circumstances Form is:

Sponsor Casework Operations
UK Border Agency
PO Box 3468
Sheffield
S3 8WA

This form is to be used for applications made on or after 6 April 2011

SPONSOR CHANGE OF CIRCUMSTANCES FORM

This form should only be used to report the following changes:

Requested Change	**Who has authority to sign the form**
Replacing the Authorising Officer	New Authorising Officer
Appointing a new Level 1 User where there are no other Level 1 Users who can make the request via SMS	Any existing Key Personnel
De-activating a Level 1 User where there are no other Level 1 Users who can make the request via SMS	Any existing Key Personnel
Replacing the Key Contact	Any existing Key Personnel
Appointing a new representative, removing a representative or appointing an additional representative	Existing Authorising Officer or new Authorising Officer if the change is being reported on the same form
Surrender a tier/category/licence	Existing Authorising Officer

If the request is not authorised as above it will be rejected and the form will be returned to you.

1. Indicate the changes you wish to make below:

Replacing an Authorising Officer (complete Q2, 3, 4, 5, 6, 7 & 14) ☐

Appointing a new Level 1 User (complete Q2, 3, 4, 5, 6, 7, 9 & 14) ☐

De-activating a Level 1 User (complete Q2, 3, 4, 5, 6, 7, 8 & 14) ☐

Replacing the Key Contact (complete Q2, 3, 4, 5, 6, 7, 9 & 14) ☐

Appointing a new or additional representative, or removing an existing representative, (complete Q2, 3, 4, 10, 14 & Annex A) ☐

Request to surrender an existing sponsor licence or a tier and/or category of an existing sponsor licence (complete Q2, 3, 4, 11,12,13, & 14) ☐

Sponsor Change of Circumstances Form (Version 04/11) - page 2 of 9

SPONSOR CHANGE OF CIRCUMSTANCES FORM

2. Who are you? (tick box for each option)

Existing Authorising Officer ☐
New Authorising Officer ☐
Key Contact ☐
Level 1 User ☐

3. What is your Sponsor Licence Number?

4. What is the name of your Sponsor organisation?

5. If you are replacing the Authorising Officer, Level 1 User or Key Contact, give details of the new appointment. *(If you wish to appoint more than one individual you should complete a separate sheet for each).*

Which role are you replacing? (tick box for each option)

Authorising Officer ☐ Level 1 User ☐ Key Contact ☐

Give new details:

Title (Mr Mrs Miss Ms Dr Other – enter title):

First Name(s):

Last Name(s):

Previously known as (if applicable):

Address where employed:

Postcode:

Sponsor Change of Circumstances Form (Version 04/11) - page 3 of 9

SPONSOR CHANGE OF CIRCUMSTANCES FORM

Telephone number:

Email address:

Date of birth: D D M M Y Y Y Y

Nationality:

National Insurance Number:

Position within the organisation:

6. If he/she is a non-EEA national, and under immigration control, you must provide details here. You must include a copy of the individual's bio data page from their passport along with a copy of the Leave to Remain/Enter or their Biometric Residence Permit if applicable.

Immigration status:

Home office reference number (if known):

Expiry date of their current leave to enter or leave to remain:

D D M M Y Y Y Y

Passport number:

Sponsor Change of Circumstances Form (Version 04/11) - page 4 of 9

SPONSOR CHANGE OF CIRCUMSTANCES FORM

It is mandatory to complete question 7.

7. Has he/she been:

- convicted of an offence in the list of immigration offences which undermine immigration control (Appendix B of the guidance). (Convictions that are 'spent' under the Rehabilitation of Offenders Act 1974 will not be taken into account); or
- convicted of any other offence which is still 'unspent', please include driving related convictions; or
- issued with a fixed or civil penalty five years before the date of this request in the list of civil penalties (Appendix C of the guidance), unless that penalty was withdrawn by us or cancelled on appeal; or
- an un-discharged bankrupt, or is legally prevented from becoming or acting as a company director.

Yes ☐ (give details of the conviction or penalty and the date it was given in the box below)

No ☐

8. If you wish to de-activate any existing Level 1 Users you must list the name(s) here.

SPONSOR CHANGE OF CIRCUMSTANCES FORM

9. If you are replacing the existing Level 1 User or Key Contact, indicate whether they are an employee of your organisation or a representative. (Tick box for each option)

☐ Employee

☐ Representative

You should ensure the representative firm is listed as the representative on your Sponsor Licence. If they are not, you must complete Question 10 – Appointing a new representative.

10. Indicate if you are removing an existing legal representative and/or appointing a new legal representative.

Removing a representative? ☐

Confirm their details:

Name of the representative's organisation

Name of contact

Address

Postcode

Email address

Telephone number

Representative's OISC registration number or details of exemption:

Appointing a new representative? ☐

Appointing an additional representative? ☐

Sponsor Change of Circumstances Form (Version 04/11) - page 6 of 9

SPONSOR CHANGE OF CIRCUMSTANCES FORM

Give new details:

Name of the representative's organisation:

Name of contact:

Address:

Postcode:

Email address:

Telephone number:

Representative's OISC registration number or details of exemption:

If you are appointing a new or additional legal representative you must ensure Annex A is completed and enclosed with this form.

11. If you are surrendering your sponsor licence, you must provide the reasons for this request. If you are currently licensed for more than one tier or category, you must indicate which tiers, categories or subcategories you wish to surrender.

SPONSOR CHANGE OF CIRCUMSTANCES FORM

12. If you are surrendering your licence as part of a merger or takeover you must give full details in the box below.

13. If you are surrendering your sponsor licence you must confirm the following:

1) Do you currently sponsor any migrants (or have you transferred any migrants to a new organisation as part of a merger/takeover or TUPE transfer) or;

2) Do you have any outstanding certificates of sponsorship/confirmation of acceptance for study assigned to a migrant application?

If yes, give full details (name, DOB, nationality, passport number and Certificate of Sponsorship number) of the migrants below.

Please note, if you have more than three migrants you should complete an appropriate table or spreadsheet with all the relevant details (as above) and submit it with this form.

It is mandatory to complete question 14.

14. Declaration

I hereby declare the above information is, to the best of my knowledge and belief, true and correct.

You must refer to the 'What are Key Personnel?' section of the sponsor guidance to ensure you are fully aware of the roles and responsibilities for each Key Personnel role.

Name:

Name of organisation:

Position within organisation:

Signature:

Date:

ALL SIGNATURES MUST BE ORIGINAL, the form will be returned if it is not signed or the signatures are photocopies or scanned copies.

Sponsor Change of Circumstances Form (Version 04/11) - page 8 of 9

Chapter 5

Legal remedies and legal representation for Tier 4 sponsors and migrants

Legal and other remedies

5.01 This section deals with a number of legal and other remedies available to migrants and sponsors under the Points Based System ('PBS'). The Secretary of State has imposed various limitations on the remedies available. This section provides a broad summary of the options. PBS migrants and sponsors should seek professional legal advice before proceeding to take any action.[1]

Administrative Review

5.02 Under the PBS, entry clearance applicants have been divested of a full right of appeal and have instead been given an entitlement to a non-statutory reconsideration procedure, Administrative Review, by an immigration official. One of the main criticisms levelled at this substitution of a judicial review for a bureaucratic one is that it lacks impartiality.[2] At the same time, PBS applicants have retained a limited right of appeal under the Nationality, Immigration and Asylum Act 2002, s 84(1)(b) and (c).[3] Administrative Review is a policy driven scheme[4] allowing applicants to have refusal decisions which they believe to have been made in error, reviewed free of charge. For students making entry clearance applications Administrative Review was introduced alongside Tier 4 on 31 March 2009.

1 In some cases, where circumstances permit, it may be advisable to make a fresh application.

2 Paragraph 144, House of Commons Home Affairs Committee Thirteenth Report of Session 2008–09, 'Managing Migration: The Points Based System', HC 217-I, 1 August 2009. http://www.publications.parliament.uk/pa/cm200809/cmselect/cmhaff/217/21711.htm

3 On the grounds that the decision is unlawful under the Race Relations Act 1976, s 19B or the Human Rights Act 1998, s 6.

4 Administrative Review under the Points Based System, 1 April 2008, http://www.parliament.uk/deposits/depositedpapers/2008/DEP2008-0829.pdf

5.03 A request for Administrative Review must be made on the Administrative Review Request Notice[5] within 28 days from the date of the refusal notice. Applicants are limited to making a single request per refusal decision unless the refusal has been upheld on review but for different reasons. Late requests may be accepted exceptionally. Reviews are conducted by an Entry Clearance Manager at the post that was responsible for making the refusal decision or another post (and who was not previously involved with the case).

5.04 No additional documents or new evidence must be submitted with the request unless required by the reviewer. New evidence will otherwise be disregarded and returned to the applicant with the outcome of the review unless the refusal decision was made on the general grounds pursuant to paragraphs 320(7A) or 320(7B) of the Immigration Rules. These provisions provide for mandatory refusals where, for example, a false document or false representation has been employed. For a refusal to be based on such a ground, the Entry Clearance Officer would have to prove not only that the document or representation was false in the sense of wrong or inaccurate, but also that the appellant acted dishonestly.[6]

5.05 The reviewer will review the refusal decision in its entirety to check that:

- 'points have been correctly awarded;
- documents have been corrected assessed; and
- verification checks have been properly carried out.'[7]

The reviewer may recommend for the refusal decision to be overturned should they find that the Entry Clearance Officer:

- 'failed to properly consider evidence submitted with the original application;
- failed to apply the Immigration Rules correctly;
- made a mistake in processing the application;
- failed to give adequate reasons for refusing entry clearance. In this case, the administrative reviewer will recommend the Entry Clearance Officer revoke the original refusal and serve a new refusal notice giving a full explanation for the refusal.'[8]

5.06 The official carrying out the review will notify the applicant of his or her decision within 28 days from the date of receipt of the request notice. If the reviewer is unable to complete the review within 28 days, the applicant will be informed in

5 A copy of the Administrative Review Request Notice can be downloaded at http://www.ukvisas.gov.uk/resources/en/docs/1903073/pbsadminreviewrequest (archived)

6 See *AA (Nigeria) v Secretary of State for the Home Department* [2010] EWCA Civ 773 (6 July 2010).

7 Paragraph 21, Annex 4, Tier 4 of the points based system Policy Guidance (version 07/11, 4 July 2011).

8 Paragraph 22, Annex 4, Tier 4 of the points based system Policy Guidance (version 07/11, 4 July 2011).

writing of when to expect a decision. The review may result in the refusal decision being upheld for the same or revised reasons or being overturned. If the decision has been upheld for the same reasons, the applicant will be notified of this by letter and will not be entitled to a further review. If the decision has been upheld but the reasons for the refusal have been modified, the applicant will be served with a GV51 refusal notice and may be entitled to have the fresh reasons administratively reviewed. Where a decision has been overturned, the applicant will be informed by letter and requested to submit their passport for endorsement with entry clearance.

Appeals

5.07 The Tribunals, Courts and Enforcement Act 2007 established the First-tier Tribunal and the Upper Tribunal, each divided into a number of chambers.[9] On 15 February 2010 Immigration and Asylum Chambers were established in both tiers[10] superseding the Asylum and Immigration Tribunal. Both chambers are independent judicial bodies which form part of the HM Courts & Tribunals Service,[11] an agency run under the auspices of the Ministry of Justice.

5.08 The purpose of the First-tier Tribunal (Immigration and Asylum Chamber ('IAC')) is to consider appeals against decisions made by the Secretary of State and other immigration authorities (namely Entry Clearance Officers, in respect of decisions officially made at posts abroad, and Immigration Officers, in respect of decisions officially made at UK ports of entry) in matters concerning asylum, immigration and nationality. From the First-tier Tribunal (IAC), appeals lie to the Upper Tribunal (IAC). The Upper Tribunal is a superior court of record with a status equivalent to the High Court.

5.09 A person who has received a notice of decision to refuse leave to remain in the United Kingdom as a PBS migrant will be entitled to a full right of appeal pursuant to the Nationality, Immigration and Asylum Act 2002, s 82(1) ('2002 Act'). The appeal may be brought on one or more of the grounds listed in s 84 of the 2002 Act. In order to exercise the right of appeal the person named in the notice of decision must file a notice of appeal against the decision made by the Secretary of State with the First-tier Tribunal within a set time.[12]

5.10 In respect of all PBS and some non-PBS applications made at a post abroad, the right of appeal against a refusal is restricted. A decision to refuse an application

9 The Tribunals, Courts and Enforcement Act 2007, ss 3 and 7. The First-tier Tribunal and the Upper Tribunal may be organised into a number of chambers by order made by the Lord Chancellor together with the Senior President of Tribunals.

10 Established by the First-tier Tribunal and Upper Tribunal (Chambers) Order 2008.

11 Created on 1 April 2011 by bringing together Her Majesty's Courts Service and the Tribunals Service.

12 Rule 6 of the Asylum and Immigration Tribunal (Procedure) Rules 2005, SI 2005/230, version in force from 29 November 2010.

for entry clearance by general visitors, business visitors, academic visitors, doctors on clinical attachments and dental observers, student visitors, prospective students, all PBS categories, and dependants applying at the same time as the main applicant who has been refused, may appeal only on human rights and race discrimination grounds pursuant to s 84(1)(b) and (c) of the 2002 Act (ie on the basis that the decision is unlawful by virtue of the Race Relations Act 1976, s 9B and/or the Human Rights Act 1998, s 6).

5.11 Persons entitled to a full right of appeal ('appellants') must file their notice of appeal with the First-tier Tribunal not later than five working days from the date of service of the notice of decision if the appellant is in detention under the Immigration Acts or ten working days[13] from the date of service of the notice of decision in any other case.[14] If sent by post, the notice of decision is considered to have been received two days after the date stated on the notice. Where an appellant may exercise a right of appeal against a decision made in the United Kingdom from outside the United Kingdom,[15] notice of appeal must be given not later than 28 days after departure from the country or the date of receipt of the notice of decision.[16] If sent by post, the notice of decision is considered to have been received 28 days after the date stated on the notice.

5.12 The appeal form must be completed in English and any supporting documents lodged with the First-tier Tribunal must be in English or accompanied by a translation into English signed by the translator certifying its accuracy.[17] The appeal form must state the name and address of the appellant and a representative (if one has been nominated to act on behalf of the appellant), list any documents on which the appellant seeks to rely as evidence, include the notice of decision or provide reasons for not including it, be signed and dated by the appellant or representative on the appellant's instructions.[18] The form invites appellants to set out their grounds of appeal and reasons therefor.

5.13 The appellant may also provide details of any witness who will give evidence in support of the appeal and indicate whether the appellant,[19] the representative or any witness will require an interpreter. Appellants must state their preference

13 Calculation of time for service must be done in line with rule 57 of the Asylum and Immigration Tribunal (Procedure) Rules 2005, SI 2005/230version in force from 29 November 2010.

14 Rule 7(1) of the Asylum and Immigration Tribunal (Procedure) Rules 2005, SI 2005/230 version in force from 29 November 2010.

15 For example they do not have a right of appeal exercisable from inside the United Kingdom.

16 Rule 7(2) of the Asylum and Immigration Tribunal (Procedure) Rules 2005 , SI 2005/230 version in force from 29 November 2010.

17 Rule 52 of the Asylum and Immigration Tribunal (Procedure) Rules 2005, SI 2005/230 version in force from 29 November 2010.

18 Rule 8 of the Asylum and Immigration Tribunal (Procedure) Rules 2005, SI 2005/230 version in force from 29 November 2010.

19 The appellant is entitled to the services of an interpreter (Rule 49A of the Asylum and Immigration Tribunal (Procedure) Rules 2005, SI 2005/230 version in force from 29 November 2010).

as to how they wish for the appeal to be disposed of. This can be done either on the papers (meaning the appeal will be dealt with on the basis of the information contained in the appeal form and documentary evidence submitted in support of the appeal without a hearing) or at an oral hearing (meaning the appeal will be dealt with at a hearing – whether or not the appellant attends).[20] In accordance with rule 55 of the Asylum and Immigration Tribunal (Procedure) Rules 2005 supporting documents may be submitted to the First-tier Tribunal or served on any party by post, fax, via a document exchange, by email or in person (if served on an individual).[21]

5.14 Paragraph 8.2 of the Practice Directions[22] gives the best practice for the preparation of trial bundles for hearings as follows:

'(a) all documents must be relevant, be presented in logical order and be legible;

(b) where the document is not in the English language, a typed translation of the document signed by the translator, and certifying that the translation is accurate, must be inserted in the bundle next to the copy of the original document, together with details of the identity and qualifications of the translator;

(c) if it is necessary to include a lengthy document, that part of the document on which reliance is placed should, unless the passages are outlined in any skeleton argument, be highlighted or clearly identified by reference to page and/or paragraph number;

(d) bundles submitted must have an index showing the page numbers of each document in the bundle;

(e) the skeleton argument or written submission should define and confine the areas at issue in a numbered list of brief points and each point should refer to any documentation in the bundle on which the appellant proposes to rely (together with its page number);

(f) where reliance is placed on a particular case or text, photocopies of the case or text must be provided in full for the Tribunal and the other party; and

(g) large bundles should be contained in a ring binder or lever arch file, capable of lying flat when opened.'

5.15 There have been recent developments relating to evidence that can be relied on at the appeal. The Commencement Order for the UK Borders Act 2007,

20 Rule 19 of the Asylum and Immigration Tribunal (Procedure) Rules 2005, SI 2005/230 version in force from 29 November 2010.

21 The First-tier Tribunal website currently indicates that it does not accept service of documents by email.

22 Practice Directions, Immigration and Asylum Chambers of the First-tier Tribunal and the Upper Tribunal, in force from 15 February 2010. Preparation of trial bundles in the form prescribed in paragraph 8.2 is not mandatory in every case although it is of the highest importance in particularly complex cases.

s 19 came into force on 23 May 2011.[23] PBS migrants are required to submit specified documents with their applications and this evidence is checked, verified and considered by the UK Border Agency ('UKBA'). The purpose of s 19 is to confine the type of new evidence that can be adduced for consideration at appeal to the documents that the appellant submitted with the PBS application.

5.16 Section 85(4) of the 2002 Act allows the tribunal to consider evidence 'about any matter which it thinks relevant to the substance of the decision including evidence which concerns a matter arising after the date of the decision'. However, the scope of s 85(4) is restricted by the exceptions cited in s 85A inserted into the 2002 Act by the UK Borders Act 2007, s 19. Section 85A(3) of the 2002 Act states that if the appeal is against an immigration decision made under the PBS to refuse leave to enter the United Kingdom or vary leave to enter or remain in the United Kingdom resulting in a person having no leave and the appeal relies wholly or partly on the grounds that:

- the decision is not in accordance with the Immigration Rules (s 84(1)(a) of the 2002 Act);
- the decision is otherwise not in accordance with the law (s 84(1)(e) of the 2002 Act); and
- the person who made the decision should have exercised the discretion conferred by the Immigration Rules differently (s 84(1)(f) of the 2002 Act)

then in accordance with s 85A(4) of the 2002 Act the Tribunal may consider evidence adduced by the appellant only if it –

> '(a) was submitted in support of, and at the time of making, the application to which the immigration decision related,
> (b) relates to the appeal in so far as it relies on grounds other than those specified in subsection (3)(c),
> (c) is adduced to prove that a document is genuine or valid, or
> (d) is adduced in connection with the Secretary of State's reliance on a discretion under immigration rules, or compliance with a requirement of immigration rules, to refuse an application on grounds not related to the acquisition of "points" under the "Points Based System".'

5.17 If lodging the appeal from inside the United Kingdom, appellants must send IAFT-1 form together with copy supporting documents to the following address or fax number:[24]

23 'Commencement of Section 19 of the United Kingdom Borders Act 2007', Ministerial Statement, Home Office, 19 May 2011.

24 These details will also be indicated on the relevant appeal form.

First-tier Tribunal (Immigration and Asylum Chamber)

Administrative Support Centre Birmingham
P.O. Box 14619
Birmingham
B16 6FQ
Fax: 0121 450 6391

If lodging the appeal from outside the United Kingdom against a decision made in the United Kingdom, appellants must send IAFT-3 form together with copy supporting documents to the following address or fax number:

First-tier Tribunal (Immigration and Asylum Chamber)
P.O. Box 6987
Leicester
United Kingdom
LE1 6ZX
Fax: 0044 (0)116 249 4214

The Tribunal Customer Enquiry Unit is open from 8.30am to 5.30pm from Monday to Friday and can be contacted by telephone on 0845 6000 877 or fax on 01509 221403.

5.18 The notice of appeal will then be served on the respondent, the Secretary of State and her officials, by the First-tier Tribunal. The respondent must file with the First-tier Tribunal and serve on the appellant the notice of decision and other documents related to the decision being appealed.[25] Once the appeal is listed,[26] the First-tier Tribunal will inform every party to the appeal of the date, time and place of the appeal hearing in writing and may give directions relating to the conduct of the appeal.[27] The appeal may be withdrawn or abandoned.[28] A hearing may be adjourned in line with the Asylum and Immigration Tribunal (Procedure) Rules 2005.[29] Applications for adjournment of appeals listed for hearing must be made not later than 5pm one clear working day prior to the date of hearing and supported by full reasons.[30]

25 Rule 13 of the Asylum and Immigration Tribunal (Procedure) Rules 2005, SI 2005/230 version in force from 29 November 2010.

26 Depending on the complexity of a case and directions given by the First-tier Tribunal, there may be hearings to decide on a preliminary issue, a Case Management Review hearing, a For Mention Only/ Pre-hearing Review hearing or a substantive hearing.

27 Rules 45 and 46 of the Asylum and Immigration Tribunal (Procedure) Rules 2005, SI 2005/230 version in force from 29 November 2010.

28 Rules 17 and 18 of the Asylum and Immigration Tribunal (Procedure) Rules 2005, SI 2005/230 version in force from 29 November 2010.

29 See the Asylum and Immigration Tribunal (Procedure) Rules 2005, SI 2005/230, rr 21 and 47.

30 Paragraph 9 of the Practice Directions, Immigration and Asylum Chambers of the First-tier Tribunal and the Upper Tribunal, in force from 15 February 2010.

5.19 Appeals are heard by one or more Immigration Judges and non-legal members of the First-tier Tribunal who are appointed by the Lord Chancellor in line with the Tribunals, Courts and Enforcement Act 2007. The Immigration Judge or a panel of judges will decide whether the appeal should be allowed or dismissed.[31] There are a number of hearing centres across the country. The decision will then be promulgated by way of a written determination and served on the parties to the appeal.

5.20 Either party may apply for permission to appeal to the Upper Tribunal on any point of law arising from a decision made by the First-tier Tribunal.[32] Such an application must first be made in writing to the First-tier Tribunal on form IAFT-4. If the application is unsuccessful, the appellant can apply directly to the Upper Tribunal using form IAUT-1. The time limits for making an application to the First-tier Tribunal for permission to appeal to the Upper Tribunal are set out in the Asylum and Immigration Tribunal (Procedure) Rules 2005, r 24. Procedures involved in making an application to the Upper Tribunal for permission to appeal are laid out in the Tribunal Procedure (Upper Tribunal) Rules 2008, r 21.[33] The appellant or the respondent may also apply for permission to appeal to the Court of Appeal on any point of law arising from a decision made by the Upper Tribunal.[34]

5.21 At the moment, filing a notice of appeal is free of charge. However, from October 2011 the Ministry of Justice will introduce fees for appeals to the Immigration and Asylum Chamber of the First-tier Tribunal in order to move some of the costs of administering justice from taxpayers to direct users.[35] Fees of £80 and £140 will be payable for paper and oral appeals respectively. The fee system will be reviewed regularly and will operate subject to a number of exemptions. Although no refunds will be given for out of time, invalid or withdrawn appeals, judges will be given discretionary power to award costs to recover appeal fee charges against the UKBA in certain circumstances, such as in cases where the decision should have clearly been made in favour of the appellant on the strength of the evidence provided to the UKBA at the time of the initial decision. No fee will be charged for onward appeals to the Upper Tribunal for the time being.

31 Under the Tribunals, Courts and Enforcement Act 2007, s 29 the First-tier Tribunal does not have the power to make any order to award costs.

32 The Tribunals, Courts and Enforcement Act 2007, s 11. In addition, both chambers have the power to review their decisions either on their own initiative or on application (Tribunals, Courts and Enforcement Act 2007, ss 9 and 10).

33 Version in force from 1 April 2011.

34 The Tribunals, Courts and Enforcement Act 2007, s 13.

35 'Introducing fee charges for appeals in the Immigration and Asylum Chambers of the First-tier Tribunal and the Upper Tribunal', Response to Consultation CP(R) 10/10, 9 May 2011 HM Courts & Tribunals Service, part of the Ministry of Justice.

Judicial Review

5.22 Decisions that are outside the scope of the statutory appeal system may be susceptible to a challenge in public law by a Judicial Review (often referred to simply as 'JR') in the Administrative Court, a division of the High Court.[36] Judicial Review is an administrative law procedure by which a claim can be brought against any enactment, decision, action or failure to act by inferior courts and tribunals, public bodies and persons exercising a public function including the immigration authorities.[37] The Administrative Court on a Judicial Review has wide powers, including the power to quash a decision and the power to order an action to be taken. Where an individual or an entity (eg a college) is aggrieved by something done (or not done) by a public authority, (eg an immigration official), legal advice should be sought to establish whether Judicial Review may be an appropriate remedy in the circumstances[38] and if so, what steps must be undertaken.

5.23 In particular, persons outside the United Kingdom, including PBS migrants, who have a limited right of appeal, or those who have no right of appeal, may be able to challenge an action, a failure to act or a decision made by the Secretary of State or her officials using the Judicial Review mechanism. Furthermore, sponsors who do not have a right of appeal against actions taken by the Secretary of State or her officials[39] relating to sponsor licences may be able to contest the following by way of a Judicial Review:

- refusal of an initial or renewal application for a sponsor licence;
- delay in making a decision in respect of an initial or renewal application for a sponsor licence;
- refusal of an initial or renewal application for Highly Trusted Sponsor ('HTS') status;
- delay in making a decision in respect of an initial or renewal application for HTS status;
- imposition of a B rating and having to comply with the terms of an action plan as a result of an application for a sponsor licence or a downgrading;
- rating review prompted by a visit from a visiting officer, any information received from the sponsor or an unsuccessful application for HTS status;
- reduction of allocation of Certificates of Acceptance for Studies;

36 The Administrative Court sites are the Royal Courts of Justice in London, Birmingham Civil Justice Centre, Cardiff Civil Justice Centre, Leeds Combined Centre and Manchester Civil Justice Centre.

37 Rule 52.1 of Part 54 Judicial Review and Statutory Review, Civil Procedure Rules 1998 (55th update to the Civil Procedure Rules in force from 6 April 2011; updates 56 and 57 are expected in Octover 2011).

38 A form of alternative dispute resolution such as the Parliamentary Ombudsman may be more appropriate than litigation.

39 For example, officials from the Sponsor Licensing Unit.

- downgrading of a sponsor licence rating from A to B;
- suspension of a sponsor licence;
- delay in making a decision relating to suspension of a sponsor licence;
- revocation of a sponsor licence.[40]

5.24 Before making a Judicial Review claim, claimants must comply with the Pre-Action Protocol for Judicial Review[41] by sending a letter to the proposed defendant. The letter should 'contain the date and details of the decision, act or omission being challenged and a clear summary of the facts on which the claim is based'.[42] It should also include other details as set out in Annex A to the Pre-Action Protocol for Judicial Review. The defendant, the Secretary of State, should normally be allowed 14 days to respond.

5.25 The Judicial Review procedure can only be used by a party who has locus standi,[43] and a claim will seek one or more of the following: a mandatory order,[44] a prohibiting order,[45] a quashing order,[46] a declaration, an injunction or damages.[47] A remedy can also be sought under the Human Rights Act 1998.[48] After complying with the Pre-Action Protocol by sending a 'letter before claim' (and allowing at least 14 days for a response), the next step is to make the claim itself, which is a two-stage process: firstly the permission of the court is required to bring the claim, and then the claim is brought. A claim for permission to apply for Judicial Review must be filed promptly and in any event not later than three months after the grounds for it first arose.[49] This is done using form N461 and paying the court fee of £60.

40 This is not an exhaustive list and there may be other causes for action. Some private colleges have taken action against decisions made by the Secretary of State to suspend and/or revoke their sponsor licences. See *Bhatti & Ors v Croydon Magistrates Court & Ors* [2009] EWHC 3004 (Admin) (6 November 2009); *Leeds Unique Education Ltd (t/a Leeds Professional College) v Secretary of State for the Home Department* [2010] EWHC 1030 (Admin) (14 May 2010); *The London Reading College Ltd, R (on the application of) v Secretary of State for the Home Department* [2010] EWHC 2561 (Admin) (18 October 2010); *New London College Ltd, R (on the application of) v Secretary of State for the Home Department* [2010] EWHC 2701 (Admin) (19 October 2010); *San Michael College Ltd, R (on the application of) v Secretary of State for the Home Department* [2011] EWHC 642 (Admin) (18 March 2011); *New London College Ltd, R (on the application of) v Secretary of State for the Home Department* [2011] EWHC 865 (Admin) (7 April 2011).

41 http://www.justice.gov.uk/guidance/courts-and-tribunals/courts/procedure-rules/civil/contents/protocols/prot_jrv.htm.

42 Paragraph 10 of the Pre-Action Protocol for Judicial Review, Civil Procedure Rules 1998, SI 1998/3132.

43 Requirement to show sufficient connection to the issue at the heart of the claim.

44 Previously known as an order of mandamus.

45 Previously known as an order of prohibition.

46 Previously known as an order of certiorari.

47 Rules 54.2 and 54.3 of Part 54 Judicial Review and Statutory Review, Civil Procedure Rules 1998.

48 Rule 54.6 of Practice Direction 54A and paragraph 15 of Practice Direction 16, Civil Procedure Rules 1998.

49 Part 54.5(1) of Part 54 Judicial Review and Statutory Review, Civil Procedure Rules 1998. The time limit cannot be extended by agreement between the parties. Part 54.5

5.26 The claimant must complete the claim form and enclose with it documents in accordance with the requirements set out at Civil Procedure Rules, Rule 54.6 of Part 54 and Practice Direction 54A. The claimant may at the same time make an application for urgent consideration asking the court to grant interim relief. This application can be made using form N463 and may be granted, should a judge consider that the claimant has arguable grounds for Judicial Review and the balance of convenience is in the claimant's favour. The claimant must file with the Administrative Court two copies of a paginated and indexed bundle containing the claim[50] and serve the claim on the defendant within seven days of the date of issue of the claim. In this instance, the claim must be served on the Treasury Solicitor's Department acting on behalf of the Secretary of State, The Treasury Solicitor's Department, One Kemble Street, London, WC2B 4TS, email: thetreasurysolicitor@tsol.gsi.gov.uk.

5.27 There are two substantive grounds for a Judicial Review: illegality and irrationality, and one procedural: procedural impropriety. In the case of *Council of Civil Service Unions v Minister for the Civil Service* [1983] UKHL 6 Lord Diplock stated that:

> 'By "illegality" as a ground for judicial review I mean that the decision-maker must understand correctly the law that regulates his decision-making power and must give effect to it. Whether he has or not is par excellence a justiciable question to be decided, in the event of dispute, by those persons, the judges, by whom the judicial power of the state is exercisable.
>
> By "irrationality" I mean what can by now be succinctly referred to as "*Wednesbury* unreasonableness" (*Associated Provincial Picture Houses Ltd, v. Wednesbury Corporation* [1948] 1 KB 223). It applies to a decision which is so outrageous in its defiance of logic or of accepted moral standards that no sensible person who had applied his mind to the question to be decided could have arrived at it. Whether a decision falls within this category is a question that judges by their training and experience should be well equipped to answer, or else there would be something badly wrong with our judicial system. To justify the court's exercise of this role, resort I think is today no longer needed to Viscount Radcliffe's ingenious explanation in *Edwards v. Bairstow* [1956] A.C. 14 of irrationality as a ground for a court's reversal of a decision by ascribing it to an inferred though unidentifiable mistake of law by the decision-maker. "Irrationality" by now can stand upon its own feet as an accepted ground on which a decision may be attacked by judicial review.
>
> I have described the third head as "procedural impropriety" rather than failure to observe basic rules of natural justice or failure to act with procedural fairness towards the person who will be affected by the decision. This is because susceptibility to judicial review under this head covers also failure by an

50 Civil Procedure Rules 1998, Paragraph 5.9 of Practice Direction 54A.

administrative tribunal to observe procedural rules that are expressly laid down in the legislative instrument by which its jurisdiction is conferred, even where such failure does not involve any denial of natural justice.'

The party served with the claim and wishing to participate in the Judicial Review must file an acknowledgement of service with the Administrative Court and serve it on the claimant within 21 days of service of the claim. The acknowledgement of service must stipulate the defendant's intention to dispute the claim and set out grounds of defence.[51] If, in light of the claim made and the grounds of defence submitted in response, the court grants the claimant permission to apply for Judicial Review, the claimant will need to pay a further £215 to the court and the final stage (consideration of the claim) will occur (usually in the form of an inter partes[52] substantive hearing in open court).

Complaints

5.28 In the event of a complaint arising out of any action taken by the UKBA leading to injustice or hardship as a consequence of maladministration, applicants and sponsors should first bring the matter to the attention of the office or team responsible. It is arguable, however, that the internal complaint-handling procedure is not appropriate for sponsors who have had their licences suspended or revoked. If the complainant is an applicant who is outside the United Kingdom, they should first approach the Visa Application Centre where the application was made.[53] The complaint can be made using a paper based 'Complaint registration form'.[54] The turnaround time for dealing with initial complaints is 20 working days unless they involve an allegation of serious professional misconduct in which case an investigation may take up to 12 weeks.

5.29 The way in which a complaint has been handled can then be reviewed by a local customer service unit, if made in the United Kingdom, which will report its findings within 20 working days of the date of the review request. A request for a further investigation of complaints made outside the United Kingdom can be made to the Head of UK Customer Services up to three months after the date of the initial complaint. The complainant can make a claim for reimbursement of

51 Rule 54.8 of Part 54 Judicial Review and Statutory Review, Civil Procedure Rules 1998.

52 Ie with all parties present or represented.

53 Alternatively, their sponsor in the United Kingdom can send the complaint to the Visa Customer Services Unit of International Group in Croydon.

54 A form to be lodged outside the United Kingdom can be found on the International Group's website at http://www.ukvisas.gov.uk/en/aboutus/enquiries/complaints and a form for complaints made in the United Kingdom can be found at the UKBA's website at http://www.ukba.homeoffice.gov.uk/contact/makingacomplaint/dealingwithyourcomplaint/.

costs incurred as a direct result of maladministration which must be supported by documentary evidence. The UKBA will consider reimbursing costs 'if they were reasonable, unavoidable and a direct consequence of our actions'.[55] In the absence of financial loss, the UKBA may consider making a consolatory payment.

5.30 Complaints relating to PBS applications made in the United Kingdom and issues dealt with by the sponsorship and employers' helpline are considered by the North East, Yorkshire and the Humber customer service unit. A complaint can be sent to the unit by post at the address listed in the table below. Alternatively, the unit can be contacted by telephone on 0114 207 2966, fax on 0114 207 2906 or email: NEYHCustomers@ukba.gsi.gov.uk. For a further independent investigation of their complaints, complainants who are resident in the United Kingdom and have completed the internal complaints handling process can approach the Member of Parliament ('MP' – member of the House of Commons) for the constituency in which they live and, via that MP, submit a complaint to the Parliamentary Ombudsman: see the next section, below.

5.31

Scotland and Northern Ireland customer service unit	Scotland and Northern Ireland Region CSU, Festival Court 1, 200 Brand Street, Glasgow G51 1DH
North West customer service unit	North West Region CSU, PO Box 99, Manchester M90 3WW
North East, Yorkshire and the Humber customer service unit	North East, Yorkshire and the Humber Region CSU, PO Box 3468, Sheffield S3 8WA
Midlands and East of England customer service unit	Midlands and East of England CSU, PO Box 1004, Peterborough PE1 9GH
Wales and South West customer service unit	Wales and South West CSU, 3rd Floor, General Building, 31–33 Newport Road, Cardiff CF24 0AB
London and South East customer service unit	London and South East Region CSU, PO Box 1863, Croydon CR9 3UF

55 'How we will deal with your complaint', UK Border Agency, http://www.ukba.homeoffice.gov.uk/contact/makingacomplaint/dealingwithyourcomplaint/.

5.32 Further investigation of complaints made outside the United Kingdom:

Head of UK Visa Customer Services	Visa Services Directorate, International Group UKBA, c/o Lunar House, 40 Wellesley Road, Croydon, CR9 2BY, fax: 0870 336 9240, email: visacomplaints@homeoffice.gsi.gov.uk

Parliamentary Ombudsman

5.33 The office of the Parliamentary Commissioner for Administration, otherwise known as the Parliamentary Ombudsman, stems from the Parliamentary Commissioner Act 1967.[56] Over the years the Act has been amended by other primary legislation and statutory instruments informing the scope of the Ombudsman's powers. The Ombudsman is accountable to Parliament by way of the Public Administration Select Committee. The Ombudsman is appointed by Her Majesty for a term of seven years to investigate actions of Government departments, corporations and unincorporated bodies listed in Sch 2 to the Act.[57] The Home Office is among the Government departments that the Ombudsman is mandated to investigate. The UKBA, an executive agency of the Home Office, falls under that remit.

5.34 The Ombudsman may investigate any action 'taken in the exercise of administrative functions of that department or authority, in any case where –

(a) a written complaint is duly made to a member of the House of Commons by a member of the public who claims to have sustained injustice in consequence of maladministration in connection with the action so taken; and

(b) the complaint is referred to the Commissioner, with the consent of the person who made it, by a member of that House with a request to conduct an investigation thereon.'[58]

5.35 The Ombudsman is precluded from conducting investigations relating to any action in respect of which other legal remedies exist such as an appeal, reference or review to or before a tribunal or proceedings in a court of law 'provided that the Commissioner may conduct an investigation notwithstanding that the person aggrieved has or had such a right or remedy if satisfied that in the particular circumstances it is not reasonable to expect him to resort or have resorted to it.'[59]

56 The current serving Ombudsman is Ann Abraham.

57 The Ombudsman does not investigate actions taken by local councils. They are within the remit of the Local Government Ombudsman.

58 The Parliamentary Commissioner Act 1967, s 5(1).

59 The Parliamentary Commissioner Act 1967, s 5(2).

5.36 There is no definitive explanation or exhaustive list of what constitutes 'maladministration'. Maladministration may include:

- 'failure to provide a service
- delay that could have been avoided
- faulty procedures, or failing to follow correct procedures
- not telling you about any rights of appeal open to you
- unfairness, bias or prejudice
- giving advice which is misleading or inadequate
- refusing to answer reasonable questions
- rudeness and not apologising for mistakes
- mistakes in handling your claims
- not putting things right when something has gone wrong'[60]

5.37 A complaint can be made by any individual or body of persons resident in the United Kingdom, or their personal representatives, to an MP not later than 12 months from the date on which the complainant first had notice of the matter being complained of save for situations where special circumstances exist and the Ombudsman agrees to conduct an investigation into a complaint made outside that period.[61] There is no fee for making a complaint.

5.38 The principal officer of the department or authority against which the complaint is made will be given an opportunity to comment on the allegations made in the complaint.[62] An investigation into the complaint will be conducted in private and the procedure for conducting the investigation will be determined by the Ombudsman.[63] Each complaint is dealt with on its merits as there is no automatic right to an investigation by the Ombudsman. Once a complaint is received, the Ombudsman will acknowledge its receipt within two working days, undertake steps to establish its eligibility for investigation and if accepted, will move to a detailed assessment to determine whether there is evidence of administrative fault or service failure which has caused injustice or hardship, and a reasonable prospect of achieving a satisfactory outcome. This may lead to an in-depth investigation and take several months to resolve.

5.39 As part of its investigation the Ombudsman may require a Government Minister, an officer or member of the department or authority named in the complaint to provide information or documents relevant to the investigation.[64] The results of the investigation will be reported to the MP who made the request for the investigation to be conducted and the principal officer of the

60 'What is maladministration?', ADRnow (administered by the Advice Services Alliance), http://www.adrnow.org.uk/go/SubPage_85.html#ser.
61 The Parliamentary Commissioner Act 1967, s 6(1), (3) and (4).
62 The Parliamentary Commissioner Act 1967, s 7(1).
63 The Parliamentary Commissioner Act 1967, s 7(2).
64 The Parliamentary Commissioner Act 1967, s 8(1).

department or authority against which the complaint lies.[65] While findings of the Parliamentary Ombudsman are binding on the public body, its recommendations are not. In a case where the injustice that has been caused to the complainant as a result of maladministration has not and will not be remedied, the Ombudsman may, if appropriate, lay before each House of Parliament a special report on that case.[66]

5.40 However, before involving an MP the complainant should first complain directly to the organisation against which maladministration is alleged allowing it a chance to respond to allegations and put matters right. The UKBA offers a two-step complaints handling process. The Ombudsman expects each complainant to have completed the internal complaints procedure at first instance (see the section 'Complaints', immediately above) before approaching an MP unless there are exceptional reasons for not having done so. If the complainant is not satisfied with the way the complaint has been handled internally, they can approach an MP. This can be done using the complaint form 'Making a complaint to the Parliamentary Ombudsman' which must be completed by the complainant, signed by an MP and sent to the Ombudsman together with documentary evidence of maladministration.

5.41 In its document 'Principles for Remedy' the Ombudsman has set out guiding principles for public bodies to follow in providing remedies for injustice or hardship arising from maladministration or service failure using the broad tenets of public law. This document should be read together with the Ombudsman's 'Principles of Good Administration' and 'Principles of Good Complaint Handling'. Where maladministration or service failure has caused injustice or hardship, the Ombudsman would expect the responsible Government department or authority to restore the complainant to the situation they were in prior to maladministration or service failure taking place, or, if this is not possible, to compensate them appropriately. Remedies may be pecuniary (ie financial) or non-pecuniary. Criteria for deciding what remedy to offer should be clear and remedies should be fair, reasonable and proportionate to the injustice or hardship suffered. Public bodies must be mindful to protect public funds and must not exceed their legal powers when deciding what remedies are appropriate.

5.42 In 'Principles for Remedy' the Ombudsman outlines a range of remedies:

- 'an apology, explanation, and acknowledgement of responsibility
- remedial action, which may include reviewing or changing a decision on the service given to an individual complainant; revising published material; revising procedures to prevent the same thing happening again; training or supervising staff; or any combination of these

65 The Parliamentary Commissioner Act 1967, s 10(1) and (2).
66 The Parliamentary Commissioner Act 1967, s 10(3).

- financial compensation for direct or indirect financial loss, loss of opportunity, inconvenience, distress, or any combination of these.'[67]

5.43 The complainant must show a direct causal link between maladministration and financial loss suffered. The document provides a formula for calculating pecuniary compensation. A public body should:

- 'calculate payments for financial loss by looking at how much the complainant has demonstrably lost or what extra costs they have incurred
- apply an appropriate interest rate to payments for financial loss, aimed at restoring complainants to the position they would have been in if the maladministration or poor service had not occurred
- consider what interest rate to pay and explain the reasons for the chosen rate.'

5.44 A public body should also take the following factors into account when deciding on the level of financial compensation for inconvenience or distress:

- 'the impact on the individual – for example whether the events contributed to ill health, or led to prolonged or aggravated injustice or hardship
- the length of time taken to resolve a dispute or complaint
- the trouble the individual was put on in pursuing the dispute or complaint.'

5.45 PBS migrants and sponsors can resort to using the service provided by the Parliamentary Ombudsman in seeking a remedy from the UKBA by way of consolatory payments for inconvenience or other forms of restitution including those for financial loss. The Ombudsman has discretion in deciding whether to accept their complaint depending on whether they have or are planning to take legal action.[68] Sponsors may suffer injustice or hardship resulting from the way in which the UKBA has dealt with suspension or revocation of their licences leading to financial loss or, worse, insolvency.[69]

5.46 The Ombudsman can be contacted at:

The Parliamentary and Health Service Ombudsman
Millbank Tower
Millbank
London
SW1P 4QP
Helpline: 0345 015 4033

67 This may include compensation for costs incurred in pursuing the complaint and any inconvenience, distress or both caused by poor complaint handling.

68 See the Parliamentary Commissioner Act 1967, s 5(2).

69 Including other actions taken by the UKBA associated with administration and regulation of the sponsorship and licensing scheme.

Fax: 0300 061 4000
Email: phso.enquiries@ombudsman.org.uk
Website: www.ombudsman.org.uk

A local member of the House of Commons can be found at findyourmp.parliament.uk or by contacting the House of Commons Information Office on 020 7219 4272.

Legal representation

Introduction

5.47 With the introduction of the PBS and the sponsorship system alongside it, the role of immigration practitioners has been redefined and adjusted in line with the needs of migrants and sponsors, and the restrictions imposed by the fledgling scheme, namely, objectification of substantive immigration law, simplification of its application and limitation of out of country appeal rights.

5.48 PBS has affected employers and education providers, their HR departments, admission offices and administrative staff assigned to carry the immigration burden in accordance with the new system's requirements. Equally, the scheme has also impacted on migrants and their ability to satisfy new entry clearance or in-country initial application and switching provisions. There is scope for legal representatives to provide legal assistance to migrants as well as sponsors. PBS allows sponsors and migrants to appoint legal representatives and yet, in the opinion of a number of practitioners, their capacity to act for their clients impartially has been ostensibly fettered.[70]

Legal representatives

5.49 Persons who can provide immigration advice or immigration services[71] are defined by statute. Section 84 of the Immigration and Asylum Act 1999[72] deals with the provision of immigration services:

> '(1) No person may provide immigration advice or immigration services unless he is a qualified person.

70 See 'Are immigration solicitors an endangered species?', The Law Gazette, 15 April 2010, www.lawgazette.co.uk/in-practice/are-immigration-solicitors-endangered-species

71 'Immigration advice' and 'immigration services' are defined by the Immigration and Asylum Act 1999, s 82.

72 http://www.opsi.gov.uk/acts/acts1999/ukpga_19990033_en_8.

(2) A person is a qualified person if—
  (a) he is registered with the Commissioner or is employed by, or works under the supervision of, such a person;
  (b) he is a member or employee of a body which is a registered person, or works under the supervision of such a member or employee;
  (c) he is authorised by a designated professional body to practise as a member of the profession whose members are regulated by that body, or works under the supervision of such a person;
  (d) he is registered with, or authorised by, a person in another EEA State responsible for regulating the provision in that EEA State of advice or services corresponding to immigration advice or immigration services or would be required to be so registered or authorised were he not exempt from such a requirement;
  (e) he is authorised by a body regulating the legal profession, or any branch of it, in another EEA State to practise as a member of that profession or branch; or
  (f) he is employed by a person who falls within paragraph (d) or (e) or works under the supervision of such a person or of an employee of such a person.

(3) If a registered person's registration has limited effect (by virtue of paragraph 2(2) of Schedule 6), neither paragraph (a) nor (b) of subsection (2) authorises the provision of advice or services falling outside the scope of that registration.

(4) Subsection (1) does not apply to a person who—
  (a) is certified by the Commissioner as exempt ("an exempt person");
  (b) is employed by an exempt person;
  (c) works under the supervision of an exempt person or an employee of an exempt person; or
  (d) who falls within a category of person specified in an order made by the Secretary of State for the purposes of this subsection.

(5) A certificate under subsection (4)(a) may relate only to a specified description of immigration advice or immigration services.

(6) Subsection (1) does not apply to a person—
  (a) holding an office under the Crown, when acting in that capacity;
  (b) employed by, or for the purposes of, a government department, when acting in that capacity;
  (c) acting under the control of a government department; or
  (d) otherwise exercising functions on behalf of the Crown.

(7) An exemption given under subsection (4) may be withdrawn by the Commissioner.'

5.50 In exercising the powers conferred by the Immigration and Asylum Act 1999, ss 84(4)(d) and 166[73] the Secretary of State enacted the Immigration and Asylum

73 Dealing with regulations and orders exercisable by statutory instrument.

Act 1999 (Part V Exemption: Relevant Employers) Order 2003, SI 2003/3214 on 8 December 2003[74] thus extending the Immigration and Asylum Act 1999, s 84 to persons providing immigration advice or immigration services to employees or prospective employees or members of their immediate family.[75] Furthermore, the Immigration and Asylum Act 1999, s 84 was extended to include licensed sponsors under Tiers 2 and 4 by the Immigration and Asylum Act 1999 (Part V Exemption: Licensed Tiers 2 and 4) Order 2009 which came into force on 31 March 2009. The Order states:

> '3.(1) Subject to paragraphs (2) and (3) for the purposes of section 84(4)(d) of the Act the following persons shall be specified, namely persons who are licensed sponsors of Tier 2 and Tier 4 migrants and who provide immigration advice or immigration services free of charge to those migrants or their immediate family.
>
> (2) The immigration advice or services given must be restricted to matters relating to the migrant's application under Tier 2 or Tier 4 of the Points-based system or to an application for entry clearance, leave to enter or leave to remain made by that person's immediate family and which is dependent on the migrant's application under Tier 2 or Tier 4 of the Points-based system.
>
> (3) For the purposes of paragraph (1), the person providing the immigration advice or immigration services must be the licensed sponsor.'[76]

5.51 According to paragraph 205 of the current Tier 4 of the Points Based System – Policy Guidance ('Sponsor Guidance')[77] a representative is a person who is qualified to provide immigration advice or services in accordance with the Immigration and Asylum Act 1999, s 84, by:

- being regulated by the Office of the Immigration Services Commissioner (OISC); or
- exempt from the requirement to be regulated by Ministerial Order; or
- being otherwise compliant with s 84; or
- being a regulated member of a designated professional body, or are working under the supervision of such a person.

The list of qualified persons under the Immigration and Asylum Act 1999, s 84 includes persons registered with or authorised by a person in another EEA State responsible for regulating immigration advice or immigration services in that country or authorised by a body regulating the legal profession in that EEA State.

74 In force from 1 January 2004.

75 www.legislation.gov.uk/uksi/2003/3214/article/3/made.

76 www.legislation.gov.uk/uksi/2009/506/article/3/made.

77 In force from 5 September 2011.

The Immigration and Asylum Act 1999, s 84(4) discharges a person or a category of persons who are certified as exempt by the OISC or classified as exempt by Ministerial Order from the requirement to be a qualified person under the Immigration and Asylum Act 1999, s 84(1).

5.52 Therefore, by virtue of the Immigration and Asylum Act 1999 (Part V Exemption: Licensed Tiers 2 and 4) Order 2009, Tier 4 (and Tier 2) licensed sponsors can offer immigration advice or immigration services as long as provision of the same is done free of charge, is limited to matters concerning the migrant's Tier 4 (and Tier 2) application and that of their dependants, and for as long as sponsors remain licensed. This Ministerial Order exempting Tier 4 (and Tier 2) licensed sponsors from any form of regulation[78] raises questions of suitability, skills, expertise and quality of immigration advice or immigration services provided by them. The current Sponsor Guidance does not deal with this issue. Presumably, the Ministerial Order was necessary to prevent Tier 4 (and Tier 2) sponsors falling foul of the Immigration and Asylum Act 1999, s 91 when having to advise students on various immigration matters pertaining to the PBS. Prior to the commencement of the Ministerial Order only publicly funded institutions of further and higher education and their student unions (including some institutions providing approved courses for degrees awarded by universities) were authorised to provide immigration advice by a block exemption.

5.53 Section 86 of the Immigration and Asylum Act 1999[79] lists the designated professional bodies:[80]

- The Law Society;
- The Law Society of Scotland;
- The Law Society of Northern Ireland;
- The Institute of Legal Executives;
- The General Council of the Bar;
- The Faculty of Advocates;
- The General Council of the Bar of Northern Ireland;

78 Save for the Secretary of State withdrawing their sponsor licence.

79 Sections 86(1)(a), (d) and (e) of the Act were repealed by the Legal Services Act 2007 (Commencement No 6, Transitory, Transitional and Saving Provisions) Order 2009, SI 2009/3250 which came into force on 1 January 2010 effectively excluding the Law Society, the Institute of Legal Executives and the General Council of the Bar from the list of designated bodies. This appears to be a transitional oversight which will be repaired when Part 3 of Schedule 18 (Immigration Advice and Immigration Services) of the Legal Services Act 2007 is activated. In the meantime, the Legal Services Act 2007 (Commencement No. 10) Order 2011 SI 2011/720 in force from 1 April 2011 activates Parts 1 and 2 of Sch 18 of the Legal Services Act 2007.

80 See Appendix B for a list of contact details of the relevant professional regulatory bodies.

5.54 *Legal remedies and legal representation for Tier 4 sponsors and migrants*

If a designated professional body 'has consistently failed to provide effective regulation of its members in their provision of immigration advice or immigration services'[81] the Secretary of State may by order remove its name from the list. Acting in contravention of the Immigration and Asylum Act 1999, s 84 is an offence under s 91 of the same Act. Despite being a highly regulated area, immigration practice is open to abuse in and outside the United Kingdom. It should be noted that commercial partners[82] and administrative staff at visa application centres cannot give immigration advice and cannot interfere with an application other than accept it from an applicant in order to forward it to the relevant British post. Students often rely on word of mouth, education and tourist agents, and the Internet for immigration advice.[83]

5.54 By virtue of the above, a representative can be:

- a person who is either regulated or certified as exempt by the OISC (eg a human resources consultant, an admissions/international officer, an immigration adviser;
- a person regulated by a designated professional body (eg a solicitor, barrister, legal executive or advocate);
- a person registered with or authorised by a person in another EEA State responsible for the provision of immigration advice or immigration services, or authorised by a body regulating the legal profession in that country;
- a category of persons classified as exempt by Ministerial Order (eg a Tier 4 licensed sponsor).

5.55 A representative cannot act on behalf of sponsors if it does not fall within one of these categories or is not based in the United Kingdom. However, the same does not apply to a representative acting on behalf of migrants as advisers based in other jurisdictions outside the United Kingdom are not subject to regulation, and in particular, to the Immigration and Asylum Act 1999, s 84. Territoriality is an issue of concern.

5.56 Immigration advisers are regulated by OISC (the office is currently held by Suzanne McCarthy) under the powers given to the Commissioner by the Immigration And Asylum Act 1999 while solicitors and barristers are regulated by the Law Society (or one of its constituent parts now known as the Solicitors Regulation Authority) and the Bar Standards Board (or its emanations in Northern Ireland and Scotland).

81 Section 86(2), http://www.legislation.gov.uk/ukpga/1999/33/section/86.

82 Such as VFS Global and WorldBridge.

83 'Tier 4: students' experiences (applying from outside the UK)', UK Council for International Student Affairs, December 2009, http://www.ukcisa.org.uk/files/pdf/about/tier4_student_survey.pdf.

5.57 OISC regulates immigration advisers in accordance with the Commissioner's Code of Standards and Rules, processes applications for registration or exemption[84] from immigration advisers, maintains and publishes the register of advisers[85] and promotes good practice by immigration advisers pursuant to the Immigration and Asylum Act 1999, ss 82 and 85. From 2 November 2009 to 29 January 2010 (extended to 25 February 2010) OISC ran a consultation on revising its 'Guidance on Competence' the report on which was published on 27 May 2010.[86]

5.58 Prior to that the UKBA conducted a consultation from 14 May 2009 to 6 August 2009, 'Oversight of the Immigration Advice Sector', concerned with 'the shape of future regulation of the Immigration advice and services sector.' The proposal was to address oversight of the immigration advice sector within the Immigration Simplification Bill. The consultation paper offered three options for consideration:

- Option 1: leave OISC and the regulation of immigration advice and service broadly as it is;
- Option 2: consolidate OISC legislation, amend its functions and revenue raising ability;
- Option 3: bring regulation of immigration advice under the Legal Services Act.

It was indicated that Option 2 was the preferred option. According to partial impact assessment published on 4 March 2009, the objective of Government intervention 'is to provide an improved regulatory framework for the immigration advice and services sector that ensures the provision of high quality immigration advice and discourages and punishes those who operate outside the regulatory framework or seek to abuse individuals seeking advice.'[87] The UKBA published its response to the consultation on 12 November 2009[88] which set out the steps to be taken by the UKBA 'to achieve our goals of providing more effective oversight of the sector and better value for the taxpayer … by consolidating and improving the OISC's legislative powers and introducing new measures that will allow for greater

84 'Should I apply for registration or exemption?', OISC, http://www.oisc.gov.uk/how_to_become_an_immigration_adviser/should_i_apply_for_registration_or_exemption/.

85 OISC, Register of Immigration Advisers, http://www.oisc.gov.uk/people_seeking_immigration_advice/register_of_immigration_advisers/.

86 OISC, http://www.oisc.gov.uk/latest_information/consultations/.

87 'Impact Assessment of proposals to address oversight of the immigration advice sector within the Immigration Simplification Bill', UK Border Agency, 4 March 2009, http://webarchive.nationalarchives.gov.uk/20091123090744/http://www.ukba.homeoffice.gov.uk/sitecontent/documents/aboutus/consultations/closedconsultations/oversight_of_the_immigration_adv/oversight_immigration_advice/impact_assessment?view=Binary.

88 'Oversight of the immigration advice sector, Consultation Response, November 2009', UK Border Agency, http://webarchive.nationalarchives.gov.uk/20091123090744/http://www.ukba.homeoffice.gov.uk/sitecontent/documents/aboutus/consultations/closedconsultations/oversight_of_the_immigration_adv/oversight_immigration_advice/oversight-of-immigration-advice?view=Binary.

levels of intervention against those who are incompetent or unfit, looking to abuse individuals seeking immigration advice/services or abuse the system'.

5.59 Regulation over immigration practice has been tightened gradually. From 30 April 2001 a person other than a barrister, solicitor or legal executive who provided immigration advice or immigration services without being registered or exempted from registration under the Immigration and Asylum Act 1999 was committing an offence. As of 1 April 2004 giving advice in connection with an application for an immigration employment document became tantamount to giving immigration advice on relevant matters under the Nationality, Immigration and Asylum Act 2002, s 123 (amending the Immigration and Asylum Act 1999, s 82).

5.60 Effective from 1 April 2005 the Legal Services Commission compelled all advisers (including solicitors) who conducted publicly funded immigration and asylum work to be accredited under its Immigration and Asylum Accreditation Scheme (IAAS).[89] Accreditation became compulsory. The scheme now provides five levels of accreditation: (a) Level 1 Probationer; (b) Level 1 Accredited Caseworker; (c) Level 2 Probationer; (d) Level 2 Senior Caseworker; and (e) Level 3 Advanced Caseworker. As of 1 July 2009[90] the scheme has been administered by the Law Society and assessment carried out by Central Law Training.

5.61 Solicitors, registered foreign lawyers, registered European lawyers, recognised bodies and recognised sole practitioners regulated by the Solicitors Regulation Authority who conduct privately funded immigration work can do so by virtue of Rule 20.01 (Rights and Obligations of Practice) of the Solicitors' Code of Conduct[91] and are not subject to mandatory accreditation under the IAAS.

Sponsors

5.62 As noted above, for PBS purposes, representatives acting on behalf of sponsors[92] must be based in the United Kingdom. Representatives based overseas cannot act on behalf of sponsors and cannot be added to the Sponsorship Management System ('SMS').[93] Depending on the size and structure of the organisation, having an external legal representative can provide the sponsor with a degree of protection. Representatives will be given their own PBS reference

89 Reference should be made to the Legal Services Commission website dealing with the IAAS at http://www.legalservices.gov.uk/civil/immigration/accreditation.asp.

90 Reference should be made to the Law Society website for current information concerning its administration of the IAAS at http://www.lawsociety.org.uk/productsandservices/accreditation/accreditationimmigrationasylum.page.

91 Solicitors' Code of Conduct 2007,rule 20 http://www.sra.org.uk/rule20/.

92 Licensed sponsors in Tiers 2, 4 and 5.

93 Otherwise known as the Sponsor Management System.

number which they can quote for a migrant or a sponsor in the relevant part of a PBS application form.

5.63 Representatives acting on behalf of sponsors cannot:

- act as an authorising officer;
- apply for a licence on the sponsor's behalf;
- issue visa letters[94] on behalf of Tier 4 sponsors.

They (or their employees) can:

- assist in preparing an application for a licence;[95]
- be Level 1 or 2 users and be set up on the SMS as such;
- be a key contact appointed by an authorising officer.

5.64 A representative helping a sponsor with their licence application must agree to the following declaratory statements by ticking the appropriate box.[96]

- 'I have been appointed by the organisation to assist with this application.
- I confirm that the organisation has completed and verified the application, and the application is, to the best of my knowledge and belief, true and correct.
- I am aware that it is an offence under the Immigration Act 1971, as amended by the Immigration and Asylum Act 1999 and the Nationality, Immigration and Asylum Act 2002, to do an act which facilitates the commission of a breach of immigration law by an individual who is not a citizen of the European Union, knowing or having reasonable cause to believe that the act has this effect.'

5.65 In order to appoint a representative and retain its services under the PBS after obtaining a licence, a sponsor must:

- notify the UKBA using the Change of Circumstances form or, from 1 October 2011 via the SMS account;[97]

94 Prior to 22 February 2010.

95 If it is found that an application for a sponsor licence was submitted by a representative on behalf of a prospective sponsor, the application will be refused and the UK Border Agency will retain the application fee.

96 A copy of a sample Application for a Sponsor Licence form which is to be used as reference only when completing the online form can be found at http://www.ukba.homeoffice.gov.uk/sitecontent/documents/employersandsponsors/pointsbasedsystem/mock_sponsor_form.pdf. 'Representative's declaration' is cited on page 29 of the sample application form.

97 The UKBA will not deal with a representative directly unless the representative has been formally appointed by a sponsor.

- add each of the representative individual employees to the SMS as Level 1 or 2 users and set the level of access required.

5.66 Only Level 1[98] and 2 users have access to the SMS. A representative can be appointed to be a Level 1 or 2 user to operate the system remotely. In both cases the authorising officer will bear responsibility for the representative acting as an SMS user. As Level 1 or 2 users, representatives are expected to perform the key personnel functions outlined in **Chapter 4**. Any acts performed by a representative on behalf of a sponsor as an SMS user will be treated as acts of the sponsor. If a representative is appointed as key contract or a Level 1 user, the sponsor must provide the representative's main business address. As discussed below, there may be instances that may put immigration practitioners at odds with their responsibilities as representatives to sponsors. Any non-compliance with or contravention of the sponsorship duties by a representative acting on behalf of a sponsor as an SMS user may ultimately lead to a raft of penalties including but not limited to suspension or withdrawal of a sponsor licence.

5.67 As accountability is key to operating the system effectively, it seems only reasonable for lawyers and legal advisers to be able to assist employers or education providers in their role as sponsors with administrative and legal issues arising out of the PBS.

5.68 In order to become a sponsor, an organisation has to undergo rigorous compliance checks to establish its suitability and eligibility and legal representatives are often tasked to assist along the way on a wide range of issues. It has now become established practice. However, in the months preceding the introduction of the SMS in November 2008,[99] questions concerning the ability of immigration practitioners to act even-handedly on behalf of their clients started surfacing in the face of stringent prevention of illegal working measures laden with civil and criminal penalties. One of the core concerns magnified by the new provisions was that according to the UKBA published codes, the UKBA was prepared to accept 'audits' of prospective sponsors carried out by immigration practitioners 'approved' by the UKBA in lieu of visits and checks by UKBA compliance officers provided that these audits specified the prospective sponsors' immigration failings to date.

5.69 Legal representatives acting for prospective sponsors may have found themselves in a role where they were primarily serving the interests of the UKBA leading to ethical questions concerning conflict of interest, confidentiality, duty not to mislead, independence and general client care. This arrangement brought duties owed by immigration practitioners regulated by the Commissioner or designated professional bodies to clients and to the UKBA into stark contrast. This concerns the following classes of professionals:

98 In December 2009, the UKBA announced in its 'All Points' news bulletin (Issue 5) that 'currently 854 (around 40%) of Tier 4 Sponsors have more than one Level 1 User registered on SMS'.
99 In respect of Tiers 2 and 5.

- Solicitors who are regulated by the Solicitors Regulation Authority and governed by the Solicitors' Code of Conduct 2007 (a new Code of Conduct will come into force on 6 October 2011);[100]
- Solicitors who are regulated by the Law Society of Scotland and governed by the Code of Conduct for Scottish Solicitors 2002 replaced by the Standards of Conduct on 1 January 2009;[101]
- Solicitors who are regulated by the Law Society of Northern Ireland and governed by the Solicitors' Practice Regulations 1987;[102]
- Barristers who are regulated by the Bar Standards Board and governed by the Code of Conduct;[103]
- Barristers who are regulated by the Bar Library and governed by the Code of Conduct for the Bar of Northern Ireland;[104]
- Advocates who are regulated by the Faculty of Advocates and guided by the Guide to the Professional Conduct of Advocates;[105]
- Legal executives who are regulated by the ILEX Professional Standards and governed by the Code of Conduct and Guides to Good Practice;[106]
- Advisers who are regulated by the OISC and governed by the Code of Standards.[107]

5.70 The announcement that legal advisers would be able to produce audit reports in support of licence applications called their position into question as such reports would effectively replace the work done by UKBA visiting officers and turn lawyers into auditors whose responsibility went far beyond their mere advisory capacity. In September 2008 the UKBA published a list on its website consisting of two City law firms who were called the UKBA's 'trusted partners'. This implied exclusivity granted to these two firms by the UKBA to provide certain immigration services to prospective sponsors. The stakeholders and legal community, in general, met the position taken by the UKBA with dismay.

100 Solicitors Regulation Authority, Solicitors' Code of Conduct 2007, www.sra.org.uk (this version of the Code of Conduct may be superseded by the new Code of Conduct coming into force on 6 October 2011).
101 The Law Society of Scotland, Standards for Scottish Solicitors, www.lawscot.org.uk.
102 The Law Society of Northern Ireland, Solicitors' Practice Regulations 1987, www.lawsoc-ni.org.
103 The Bar Standards Board, Code of Conduct (8th edition, came into effect on 31 October 2004), www.barstandardsboard.org.uk.
104 The Bar Library, Code of Conduct for the Bar of Northern Ireland (adopted on 6 March 2003), www.barlibrary.com.
105 The Faculty of Advocates, Guide to the Professional Conduct of Advocates (5th edition, October 2008), www.advocates.org.uk.
106 ILEX Professional Standards, Code of Conduct, www.ilex.org.uk.
107 OISC, The Code of Standards (Second Edition), www.oisc.gov.uk.

5.71 ILPA wrote to the Chief Executive of the UKBA, Lin Homer, on 18 September 2008 raising concerns. The list in question was taken down from the UKBA website on 23 September 2008[108] and 32 firms were invited to meet with the UKBA on 25 September 2008 to assess their suitability to be included on an extended list of accredited organisations. UKBA published accreditation criteria on its website under *'Providing Advice and support to prospective sponsors'*[109] on 23 September 2008. The Law Society reacted quickly and wrote to the Head of Immigration Group at the UKBA, Matthew Coats, on 24 September 2008 underlining the primary areas of concern:

> 'The Law Society has serious concerns about the UKBA accrediting solicitors in relation to the Points Based System. As you know, solicitors practising in England and Wales are obliged to comply with the Solicitors' Code of Conduct 2007, which provides, amongst other duties, that solicitors must not allow their independence to be compromised and must act in the best interests of each client. The Society is interested in ensuring that solicitors will not be placed in a position where duties owed to their clients may potentially conflict with solicitors' interests in acquiring and maintaining accreditation.'[110]

5.72 There is no publicly available evidence to suggest what assurances have been provided to the Law Society by the UKBA since then to alleviate practitioners' concerns. In the meantime, on 25 September 2008 ILPA was sent a response to its letter of 18 September 2008 by Lin Homer who attempted to placate ILPA and defend the UKBA's own position in embarking 'on the process of listing sources of additional support for sponsors':[111]

> '... we wanted to do more to support business by working with a range of companies who came to us with ideas on how they could provide "audit" services which would give applicants confidence that their systems and processes were suitable to enable them to act as sponsors. We made it absolutely clear to the organisations involved that we could not countenance any "exclusive" arrangement and that we wanted to encourage a range of firms to provide similar services in due course.'[112]

108 This was confirmed in writing by Lin Homer, then Chief Executive of the UK Border Agency, in a response to ILPA dated 25 September 2008.

109 No longer available.

110 Letter from the Law Society signed by Mark Stobbs, Director of Legal Policy, addressed to Matthew Coats, Head of Immigration, Immigration Group, UK Border Agency dated 24 September 2008, pp 98–99, CLT Conferences, 'Migrant Workers and the New Points Based System', 19 May 2009.

111 See enclosed in the pack.

112 Letter from the UK Border Agency signed by Lin Homer, Chief Executive, addressed to Sophie Barrett-Brown, Chair of ILPA dated 25 September 2008, pp 96–97, CLT Conferences, 'Migrant Workers and the New Points Based System', 19 May 2009.

5.73 From October 2008 more organisations were invited to 'express an interest' if they could show that:

- 'the advice they provided was in line with the guidance and support tools provided by the UK Border Agency;
- they had appropriately trained staff undertaking sponsor support activity; and
- they had in place a reporting framework which provides the UK Border Agency with evidence that all required checks have been completed for each client application.'[113]

5.74 Following the initial assessment on 25 September 2008 a small number of organisations[114] were included on the extended list entitled 'Organisations assessed as advisers to prospective sponsors under the Points-based System'. At the time, the website page offering additional support for employers[115] stated that the list included organisations:

> "'... who have demonstrated to us a good understanding of the sponsorship arrangements and have provided us with evidence about the type of checks and services they will make when working with clients. They are able to provide prospective sponsors with a document which assesses their readiness to make a sponsorship application. Prospective sponsors can then ***choose*** whether to submit this document to us in support of their sponsorship application. Where such documents are submitted to us, we will not ***normally*** duplicate the checks we expect these organisations to have already made.' [added emphasis]

5.75 The list itself was prefaced by the following disclaimer:[116]

> 'The list covers only those organisations that we have assessed satisfactorily to date. The fact that a particular adviser is not listed does not indicate that the firm is not eligible for inclusion in the future. ***Prospective sponsors are free to appoint any adviser they choose.***
>
> We have no formal relationship or contract with the listed organisations nor do we accredit them. There is no relationship with us which should have any impact on the normal operation of the client-adviser relationship. They are listed here to provide those prospective sponsors who need reassurance about their application with a range of possible providers who have demonstrated sponsorship services to our satisfaction.' [added emphasis]

113 At the time of writing this information is no longer available on the UKBA website.

114 Which as at 19 May 2009 stood at 66 law firms and consultancies in accordance with the list available at pp.100–101, CLT Conferences, 'Migrant Workers and the New Points Based System', 19 May 2009.

115 At the time of writing this information is no longer available on the UKBA website.

116 At the time of writing this information is no longer available on the UKBA website. However, it can be found at pp100–101, CLT Conferences, 'Migrant Workers and the New Points Based System', 19 May 2009.

It can be argued that while the wording of the foreword does not explicitly state so, the fact that prospective sponsors could choose to rely on an audit report produced by one of the accredited firms, which would then be accepted in place of an on-site visit by UKBA officials, appears to imply that the responsibility for pre-requisite checks has been shared out between prospective sponsors and legal advisers with the UKBA shouldering a negligible burden. On the face of readily available evidence, the concerns that came to the surface in the autumn of 2008 endure and, as a consequence, it is left to immigration practitioners to ensure good practice.

Migrants

5.76 Acting on behalf of Tier 4 migrants, as well as students and academics who fall outside the ambit of the PBS, does not present legal representatives with as many obstacles as acting for sponsors under the PBS and it remains the migrants' prerogative to appoint a representative of their choice be it in or outside the United Kingdom.

5.77 When acting on behalf of migrant students or their dependants in respect of their initial or switching in-country Tier 4 application, representatives have to sign a declaration:

- 'I have been appointed by the student to make this application.
- I confirm that the student has completed and verified the application and the application is, to the best of my knowledge and belief, true and correct.
- Once the UK Border Agency has decided the application, I will give the student[117] all correspondence from the UK Border Agency relating to the decision.
- I am permitted to give immigration advice and immigration services by Section 84 of the Immigration and Asylum Act 1999.
- I am aware that it is an offence under the Immigration Act 1971, as amended by the Immigration and Asylum Act 1999 and the Nationality, Immigration and Asylum Act 2002, to do an act which facilitates the commission of a breach of immigration law by an individual who is not a citizen of the European Union, knowing or having reasonable cause to believe that the act has this effect.'

5.78 The evolution of Tier 4, its gradual, protracted roll-out from 31 March 2009 to 22 February 2010, two extensive reforms (one of which will be ongoing until at least the end of 2012) and frequent changes to substantive immigration law and policy, have turned student immigration into an area of complexity, making more

117 Or 'the applicant' when acting on behalf of a dependant.

migrants seek specialist advice. With the effective removal of discretion as part of the PBS scheme, restrictions imposed by the Borders, Citizenship and Immigration Act 2009 on studies as of October 2009 and loss of out of country appeal rights, immigration practitioners are relied on to challenge unreasonable decisions with an ever decreasing array of legal remedies at their disposal.

Annex

Contact details of relevant regulatory bodies

5.79 The Office of the Immigration Services Commissioner
5th Floor
Counting House
53 Tooley Street
London
SE1 2QN
Tel: 0845 000 0046
Fax: +44 (0) 207 211 1553
Website: www.oisc.gov.uk

The Law Society
113 Chancery Lane
London
WC2A 1PL
Tel: +44 (0) 207 242 1222
Fax: +44 (0) 207 831 0344
Website: www.lawsociety.org.uk

The Law Society Office in Wales
Capital Tower
Greyfriars Road
Cardiff
CF10 3AG
Tel: +44 (0) 29 2064 5254
Fax: +44 (0) 29 2022 5944
Email: wales@lawsociety.org.uk

The Law Society of Scotland
26 Drumsheugh Gardens
Edinburgh
EH3 7YR
Tel: +44 (0) 131 226 7411
Fax: +44 (0) 131 225 2934
Email: lawscot@lawscot.org.uk
Website: www.lawscot.org.uk

The Law Society of Northern Ireland
96 Victoria Street
Belfast
BT1 3GN
Tel: +44 (0) 28 9023 1614
Fax: +44 (0) 28 9023 2606
Website: www.lawsoc-ni.org

The Institute of Legal Executives
Kempston Manor
Kempston
Bedford
MK42 7AB
Tel: +44 (0) 1234 841000
Email: info@ilex.org.uk
Website: www.ilex.org.uk

The General Council of the Bar
289–293 High Holborn
London
WC1V 7HZ
Tel: +44 (0) 207 242 0082
Fax: +44 (0) 207 831 9217
Website: www.barcouncil.org.uk

The General Council of the Bar of Northern Ireland
The Bar Library
91 Chichester Street
Belfast
BT1 3JQ
Tel: +44 (0) 2890 562349
Fax: +44 (0) 2890 562350
Email: chief.executive@barcouncil_ni.org.uk
Website: www.barlibrary.com

The Faculty of Advocates
Parliament House
Edinburgh
EH1 1RF
Tel: +44 (0) 131 226 5071
Email: clerkoffaculty@advocates.org.uk
Website: www.advocates.org.uk

Chapter 6

Manual for academics, researchers and parents

Miscellaneous temporary categories for academic staff, parents of children at school and sponsored researchers

Introduction

6.01 There are provisions in the Immigration Rules allowing academic and teaching staff,[1] lecturers, trainers, researchers and other professional academicians and practitioners to visit and work in the United Kingdom in visitor and Points Based System ('PBS') categories, depending on the terms of their stay. Ordinarily, individuals wishing to work in the United Kingdom would apply under Tier 2 (General)[2] unless they qualify on points under Tier 1 (General).[3] However, due to the Government's intention to reduce net migration numbers, these categories are mired by interim limits and a higher points threshold. Tier 1 (General) and Tier 2 (General) are dealt with separately in **Chapter 7**.

6.02 This chapter is devoted to temporary and short-term migration routes related to education not covered in **Chapter 3**: academic visitors, visiting professors, parents of children under 12 at school in the United Kingdom and sponsored researchers. Academic visitors and visiting professors belong to the business visitor category, parents of children at school is a sub-type of the special visitor category and sponsored researchers form part of the Government authorised exchange sub-category of Tier 5 (Temporary Worker) route.

1 One such category related to teachers or language assistants coming to the United Kingdom under approved exchange schemes allowed for permit free employment outside the Work Permit Scheme pursuant to paragraphs 110–115 of the Immigration Rules. This category was deleted by the Statement of Changes in Immigration Rules (HC 1113) on 27 November 2008.
2 More appropriately, under Sections P and M of the Codes of Practice.
3 This is no longer the case for entry clearance applications from 23 December 2010 and for in-country applications from 6 April 2011.

Academic visitors and visiting professors

6.03 Prior to 27 November 2008 when it was brought into the Immigration Rules[4] under the umbrella of the business visitor category, academic visitors were granted concessionary leave outside the Immigration Rules. A category for visiting professors was also introduced into the Immigration Rules on 27 November 2008. Immigration requirements for academic visitors and visiting professors are set out in paragraphs 46G–46L of the Immigration Rules which weaves them into the business visitor category. Policy guidances related to these categories are contained on page 13, Guidance, Business Visitors[5] (academic visitors), page 15, Guidance, Business Visitors[6] (visiting professors), VAT12 Business Visitor: Academic Visitor, ECG and VAT13 Business Visitor: Visiting Professors, ECG.

6.04 The requirements for leave to enter as an academic visitor are contained in paragraph 46G of the Immigration Rules. The provisions related to academic visitors in paragraph 46G of the Immigration Rules will be met provided that the migrant:

> '(i) is genuinely seeking entry as a Business Visitor for a limited period as stated by him:
>
> ...
>
> (b) not exceeding 12 months if seeking entry as an Academic Visitor'[7]

6.05 Entry clearance is mandatory for those seeking more than six months leave to enter. Non-visa nationals seeking leave for six months or less do not require prior entry clearance. Entry clearance is normally issued for 12 months in this category (D: ACADEMIC VISITOR: UP TO 12 MONTHS, CODE 3). Extensions will not be granted beyond this maximum period (paragraph 46J of the Immigration Rules).

> '(ii) meets the requirements of paragraphs 41(ii)-(viii) and (x)-(xii)'[8]

6.06 An academic visitor must meet a number of general visitor requirements such as:

- have intention to leave the United Kingdom at the end of the period of stay (paragraph 41(ii));
- not have intention to take employment in the United Kingdom (paragraph 41(iii));
- not have intention to produce goods or provide services in the United Kingdom and sell goods or services directly to the public (paragraph 41(iv));

4 Inserted by the Statement of Changes in Immigration Rules (HC 1113).
5 Modernised Guidance, Version 1.0EXT, valid from 2 August 2011.
6 Modernised Guidance, Version 1.0EXT, valid from 2 August 2011.
7 Paragraph 46G(i)(b) of the Immigration Rules.
8 Paragraph 46G(ii) of the Immigration Rules.

- not have intention to undertake a course of study (paragraph 41(v));
- be able to maintain and accommodate himself or herself and any dependants adequately out of own funds without recourse to public funds or be maintained and accommodated adequately together with any dependants by relatives or friends (paragraph 41(vi));
- be able to meet the cost of the return or onward journey (paragraph 41(vii));
- not be a child under the age of 18 (paragraph 41(viii));
- not have intention to marry or form a civil partnership, or give notice of marriage or civil partnership during his or her visit (paragraph 41(x));
- not have intention to receive private medical treatment during his or her visit (paragraph 41(xi));
- not be in transit to a country outside the CTA[9] (paragraph 41(xii)).

'(iii) intends to do one or more of the following during his visit:

...

(d) to act as an Academic Visitor but only if he has been working as an academic in an institution of higher education overseas, or in the field of their academic expertise immediately prior to seeking entry.'[10]

6.07 An academic visitor is described as 'a person who is from an overseas academic institution or who is highly qualified within his own field of expertise seeking leave to enter the UK to carry out research and associated activities for his own purposes' in paragraph 6 of the Immigration Rules. According to provisions on page 13, Guidance, Business Visitors and paragraph VAT12.1, VAT12 Business Visitor: Academic Visitor, ECG academic visitors must be either:

- an academic who is either
  - (a) on sabbatical leave from an overseas academic institution wishing to come to the United Kingdom to carry out private research;
  - (b) taking part in arranged formal exchange arrangements with their United Kingdom colleagues with any salary being paid by the academic's own overseas institution (including doctors);
  - (c) coming to share knowledge or experience or to have informal discussions with their colleagues in the United Kingdom; or
  - (d) taking part in a single conference or seminar but not for profit; or
- eminent senior doctors and dentists coming to take part in research, teaching or clinical practice.

9 Common Travel Area.

10 Paragraph 46G(iii)(d) of the Immigration Rules.

6.08 Academic visitors cannot receive funding for their work from any United Kingdom source, save for payments of expenses, reasonable honoraria or payments on an exchange basis (paragraph VAT12.1). Individuals with leave as academic visitors cannot switch into a PBS employment category (paragraph VAT12.7), nor can they switch into a PBS study category (see **Chapter 7**).

6.09 There are also those who are unlikely to qualify as academic visitors:

Type of individuals	Suggested alternative routes
Recent graduates who are unlikely to have reached the level of expertise within their field	Tier 1 (Post-Study Work), if graduated in the United Kingdom in the last 12 months with an eligible qualification (before the category's abolition in April 2012); otherwise, Tier 2 (General) to work or Tier 4 (General) to undertake further studies
Postgraduate researchers entering the United Kingdom for the purpose of studying for an accredited UK academic qualification rather than to undertake academic research work	Tier 4 (General) to study or Tier 2 (General) to work
Lecturers	Tier 2 (General) to undertake paid work or business visitor provided they are coming to the United Kingdom for a conference or seminar which is a single or occasional event, which is not a commercial venture and from which organisers are not making a profit
Individuals on sabbatical leave from private research companies	Depending on circumstances, may be eligible under a number of visitor and PBS categories
Sponsored researchers[11]	Tier 5 (Temporary Worker), Government authorised exchange sub-category or business visitor if coming to the United Kingdom to share knowledge or experience or to hold informal discussions with colleagues in the United Kingdom

11 From 9 May 2005 the academic visitors concession no longer included provisions for entry to the United Kingdom of sponsored researchers. Individuals seeking entry to undertake sponsored research in the United Kingdom were expected to do so as work permit holders.

6.10 Academic visitors may be accompanied or joined by their spouses or civil partners and dependant children. Those who are visa nationals must apply for entry clearance. Any extensions of stay must be granted in line with the leave granted to the academic visitor. Dependants may apply for entry clearance as general visitors (pursuant to paragraph 41 of the Immigration Rules) and child visitors (pursuant to paragraph 46A of the Immigration Rules). Dependants who are non-visa nationals may be admitted to the United Kingdom as general or child visitors without having prior entry clearance for a period of up to six months. Visa and non-visa nationals wishing to come to the United Kingdom for longer than six months can be granted entry clearance for a period not exceeding 12 months. The requirement for a child visitor not to study at a school in the maintained sector may be waived in respect of a child who is a dependent of an academic visitor. However, admission decisions rest with the school.

6.11 Paragraphs 46G-46L of the Immigration Rules also make provision for visiting professors who are classified as business visitors. Paragraph VAT13.1, VAT13, Business Visitor: Visiting Professors, ECG and page 15, Guidance, Business Visitors stipulate that students from overseas academic institutions who come to the United Kingdom on Study Abroad programmes can be accompanied by professors and teachers to oversee their studies provided they are employed and paid by an overseas institution and do not intend to base themselves or seek employment in the United Kingdom. Visiting professors and teachers may undertake some teaching at the United Kingdom institution hosting the students whose studies they are supervising.

> '(i) is genuinely seeking entry as a Business Visitor for a limited period as stated by him:
>
> ...
>
> (a) not exceeding 6 months'[12]

6.12 Entry clearance is not mandatory for persons seeking to be admitted to the United Kingdom as visiting professors save for visa nationals (C: VISIT – VISITING PROFESSOR: 6 MONTHS. CODE 3). Six months is the maximum period for which entry clearance can be granted and extensions beyond that will not be granted (paragraph 46J of the Immigration Rules).

> '(ii) meets the requirements of paragraphs 41(ii)-(viii) and (x)-(xii)'[13]

Same as academic visitors (see above).

> '(iii) intends to do one or more of the following during his visit:
>
> ...
>
> (e) to act as a Visiting Professor.'[14]

12 Paragraph 46G(i)(a) of the Immigration Rules.
13 Paragraph 46G(ii) of the Immigration Rules.
14 Paragraph 46G(iii)(e) of the Immigration Rules.

A visiting professor is a term defined in paragraph 6 of the Immigration Rules as 'a person who is seeking leave to enter the United Kingdom as an academic professor to accompany students who are studying here on Study Abroad Programmes.'

6.13 Persons applying for entry clearance as academic visitors or visiting professors may do so online or, in countries where online forms are not accepted, academic visitors may make their entry clearance applications using VAF1E forms at a cost of £76.00 (for up to 12 months).[15] Academic visitors wishing to extend their leave in country can do so by using FLR(BID) application form. Visiting professors do not have a specific hard copy application form assigned to them but may apply using the business visitor form VAF1C.

6.14 The business visitor category offers other limited options to be considered by visiting academics and teachers in the alternative:

- Advisers, consultants, trainers and troubleshooters to the branch based in the United Kingdom of the same group of companies as the visitor's overseas company who must remain employed and paid by the overseas company (paragraph 46G(iii)(h) of the Immigration Rules; page 20, Guidance, Business Visitors; paragraph VAT11.2.2, VAT11 Business Visitor, ECG);
- Visitors providing one-off training on techniques and work practices used in the United Kingdom (paragraph 46G(iii)(i)(a)–(b) of the Immigration Rules; page 21, Guidance, Business Visitors; paragraph VAT11.2.3, VAT11 Business Visitor, ECG);
- Speakers coming to the United Kingdom for a one-off conference organised on a non-profit basis (one of the 'permissible activities' covered by paragraph 46G(iii)(a) of the Immigration Rules; page 10, Guidance, Business Visitors; paragraph VAT11.2.4, VAT11 Business Visitor, ECG).

Parents of children at school

6.15 This category is for parents who wish to accompany or join their children who are under the age of 12 and studying in the United Kingdom at an independent fee-paying day school pursuant to leave as Tier 4 (Child) students. They can come to the United Kingdom for a maximum of 12 months as long as they comply with several general visitor requirements. In addition to having adequate funds for maintenance and accommodation, they must demonstrate adequate and reliable funds for maintaining a second home in the United Kingdom. Parents of children at school are classified as special visitors and are governed by paragraphs 56A–56C of the Immigration Rules. Relevant policy guidance can be found in Guidance, Visitor

15 Cost in effect from 6 April 2011.

Parent of a child at school[16] and paragraph VAT05, Special Visitor: Parents with children under 12 at school in UK, ECG. Visa nationals and persons seeking entry for up to the maximum of 12 months must obtain entry clearance before travelling to the United Kingdom (C: VISIT: CHILD AT SCHOOL: 6 MONTHS: CODE 3 and C: VISIT: CHILD AT SCHOOL: 12 MONTHS: CODE 3). Once the child reaches the age of 12, parents will not qualify for further leave to remain.

6.16 Requirements for leave to enter or remain are set out in paragraph 56A of the Immigration Rules and they are as follows:

'(i) the parent meets the requirements set out in paragraph 41 (ii)–(xii); and'[17]

Namely, the parent must fully comply with the general visitor requirements:

- have intention to leave the United Kingdom at the end of the period of stay (paragraph 41(ii));
- not have intention to take employment in the United Kingdom (paragraph 41(iii));
- not have intention to produce goods or provide services in the United Kingdom and sell goods or services directly to the public (paragraph 41(iv));
- not have intention to undertake a course of study (paragraph 41(v));
- be able to maintain and accommodate himself or herself and any dependants adequately out of own funds without recourse to public funds or be maintained and accommodated adequately together with any dependants by relatives or friends (paragraph 41(vi));
- be able to meet the cost of the return or onward journey (paragraph 41(vii));
- not be a child under the age of 18 (paragraph 41(viii));
- not to have intention to do any sports, entertainer or business visitor activities set out in paragraphs 46G(iii), 46M(iii) or 46S(iii) (paragraph 41(ix));
- not have intention to marry or form a civil partnership, or give notice of marriage or civil partnership during his or her visit (paragraph 41(x));
- not have intention to receive private medical treatment during his or her visit (paragraph 41(xi));
- not be in transit to a country outside the CTA[18] (paragraph 41(xii)).

'(ii) (1) if the child has leave under paragraphs 57 to 62 of these Rules, the child is attending an independent fee paying day school and meets the requirements set out in paragraph 57(i) to (ix), or

16 Modernised Guidance, version 1.0 EXT, valid from 2 August 2011.
17 Paragraph 56A(i) of the Immigration Rules.
18 Common Travel Area.

(2) if the child is a Tier 4 (Child) Student, the child is attending an independent fee paying day school and meets the requirements set out in paragraph 245ZZA (if seeking leave to enter) or 245ZZC (if seeking leave to remain); and'[19]

Please refer to **Chapter 3** for information about Tier 4 (Child) students and their care arrangements. Notably, there are no similar provisions made for child visitors.

6.17 Paragraph 56A of the Immigration Rules goes on to impose further requirements:

'(iii) the child is under 12 years of age; and
(iv) the parent can provide satisfactory evidence of adequate and reliable funds for maintaining a second home in the United Kingdom; and
(v) the parent is not seeking to make the United Kingdom his main home; and
(vi) the parent was not last admitted to the United Kingdom under the Approved Destination Status Agreement with China.'[20]

6.18 Parents applying for entry clearance may do so online. There is no specific hard copy application form designed for this sub-type of the special visitor category. Applicants may use the general visitor application form VAF1A. The cost of making an entry clearance application is £265.[21]

Sponsored researchers

6.19 The sponsored researchers category used to form part of the Business and Commercial category of the work permit scheme.[22] Prior to 9 May 2005, there was a provision for sponsored researchers in the academic visitor concession (see above). Under the deleted work permit scheme researchers would undertake funded research at a host institution. From 27 November 2008[23] the sponsored researchers scheme was incorporated into the Tier 5 (Temporary Worker) route. The route is divided into five sub-categories: creative and sporting, charity worker, religious worker, Government authorised exchange and international agreement. Sponsored researchers come within the Government authorised exchange category.

19 Paragraph 56A(ii)(1)–2) of the Immigration Rules.
20 Paragraph 56A(iii)–(vi) of the Immigration Rules.
21 Cost in effect from 6 April 2011.
22 The Business and Commercial internal guidance, Working in the UK casework instructions, can be found at http://www.ukba.homeoffice.gov.uk/sitecontent/documents/policyandlaw/businessandcommercialcaseworker/wpukguidancesponsoredresear1.pdf?view=Binary.
23 Inserted by the Statement of Changes in Immigration Rules (HC1113).

6.20 Paragraphs 245ZM–245ZS of the Immigration Rules deal with the Tier 5 (Temporary Worker) route. Provisions governing dependants of Tier 5 migrants are generic for all PBS dependants (paragraphs 319A–319E of the Immigration Rules and Appendix E (for spouses, civil partners, unmarried or same sex partners) and paragraphs 319F–319K of the Immigration Rules and Appendix E (for children)). Applicants must comply with the requirements set out at paragraph 1A of Appendix C and in particular with paragraph 1A(g) of Appendix C to the Immigration Rules[24] which states that 'where the applicant is applying as a … Tier 5 Migrant, the funds must have been under his own control on the date of the application and for the period specified in (b) above'. Moreover, main applicants and their dependants making applications at the same time must be mindful of another new addition to the Immigration Rules made on 6 April 2011 in paragraph 1A(h) of Appendix C to the Immigration Rules which states the following:

> 'Where the application is made at the same time as applications by the partner or child of the applicant (such that the applicant is a Relevant Points Based System Migrant for the purposes of paragraph 319AA), each applicant must have the total requisite funds specified in the relevant parts of appendices C and E. If each applicant does not individually meet the requirements of appendices C and/or E, as appropriate, all the applications (the application by the Relevant Points Based System Migrant and applications as the partner or child of that relevant Points Based system Migrant) will be refused.'

6.21 Applicants and their dependants must refer to Tier 5 (Temporary Worker) of the Points Based System Policy Guidance ('Tier 5 (Temporary Worker) Policy Guidance'),[25] Points Based System (Dependant) Policy Guidance (for applications in the United Kingdom) and Points-based System Tier 5 (Temporary Worker) visa application guide (for applications outside the United Kingdom). These must be up to date and relevant at the time of application.

6.22 Paragraph 245ZM of the Immigration Rules explains that the aim of Tier 5 (Temporary Worker) migrant route is to encourage those 'whose entry helps to satisfy cultural, charitable, religious or international objectives.' More particularly, the aim of the Government authorised exchange sub-category is explained in paragraph 397 of the Tiers 2 and 5 Sponsor Guidance:[26]

> 'This category is for migrants coming to the United Kingdom through approved schemes that aim to share knowledge, experience and best practice. This category cannot be used to fill job vacancies or provide a way to bring unskilled labour to the United Kingdom'.

24 Inserted by the Statement of Changes in Immigration Rules (HC 863) laid before Parliament on 16 March 2011 and in force from 6 April 2011.

25 Version referred to in this chapter is for applications made on or after 14 December 2010.

26 Version 04/11, for applications made on or after 6 April 2011. Previous version of the Tiers 2 and 5 Sponsor Guidance was for applications made on or after 21 December 2010.

6.23 Paragraph 245ZM of the Immigration Rules contains definitions of 'consecutive engagements' and 'period of engagement' for the purposes of paragraphs 245ZM–245ZS. All migrants arriving in the United Kingdom and wishing to enter as Tier 5 (Temporary Worker) migrants must have prior entry clearance with the exception of non-visa nationals in the creative and sporting sub-category seeking entry for three months or less (paragraph 245ZN(b)).

6.24 Migrants wishing to qualify for entry clearance, leave to enter or remain and indefinite leave to remain must not fall for refusal under the general grounds of refusal and not be illegal entrants (see **Chapter 3**). Leave is granted subject to migrants registering with the police, having no recourse to public funds and not being employed by anyone other than their sponsor or, if being sponsored in the Government authorised exchange sub-category, any person for whom the sponsor directs the migrant to work. Tier 5 (Temporary Worker) migrants are allowed to engage in supplementary employment.

6.25 Migrants wishing to qualify for entry clearance or leave to enter must satisfy the requirements set out in paragraph 245ZO of the Immigration Rules which require applicants to score a minimum of 30 points under paragraphs 105 to 112 of Appendix A (Attributes) to the Immigration Rules and a minimum of ten points under paragraphs 8 to 9 of Appendix C (Maintenance) to the Immigration Rules. This means scoring a total of 40 points. There is no English language requirement for Tier 5 (Temporary Worker) migrants.

6.26 Applicants under the age of 18 must have their application supported either by parents, a parent who has sole legal responsibility or a legal guardian who must consent to the arrangements made for the child's travel to, reception and care in the United Kingdom. Further special care arrangements to be made pursuant to the Borders, Citizenship and Immigration Act 2009, s 55 are outlined in Points-based System Tier 5 (Temporary Worker) –visa application guide. Requirements for leave to remain are similar subject to the applicant having or having last been granted entry clearance, leave to enter or remain in one of the categories listed in paragraph 245ZQ(b) of the Immigration Rules (which lists switching categories) and subject to paragraph 245ZQ(e) of the Immigration Rules which states that:

> 'The Certificate of Sponsorship Checking Service entry to which the Certificate of Sponsorship reference number for which points under Appendix A were awarded relates must record that the applicant is being sponsored in the same subcategory of the Tier 5 (Temporary Worker) Migrant route as the one in which he was being sponsored when he was last granted entry clearance or leave to remain as a Tier 5 (Temporary Worker) Migrant.'

6.27 Paragraph 133 of the Tier 5 (Temporary Worker) Policy Guidance states that the applicant:

'will need to pass the test that is in force at the time he/she applies and this could be different to the test that was in place when the applicant first came to the United Kingdom. The exception is non visa nationals entering the United Kingdom under the Creative and Sporting sub-category for a period of less than three months, who have not obtained entry clearance. An applicant, in this situation, will not be able to extend his/her leave.'

6.28 According to paragraph 245ZP(d) of the Immigration Rules leave will be granted to Tier 5 (Temporary Worker) migrants in the Government authorised exchange sub-category for a period commencing 14 days before the beginning of the period of engagement and ending 14 days after the end of that period of engagement or for two years, whichever is shorter. Migrants in the Government authorised exchange sub-category are able to extend their stay up to the maximum time in that sub-category depending on the outcome of a calculation of period of leave in paragraph 245ZR(b) of the Immigration Rules:

'(i) the length of the period of engagement, as recorded in the Certificate of Sponsorship Checking Service entry, plus 14 days (or, where the applicant has consecutive engagements, a period beginning on the first day of the first period of engagement and ending 14 days after the last day of the last period of engagement) or

(ii) the difference between the period that the applicant has already spent in the UK since his last grant of entry clearance or leave to enter as a Tier 5 (Temporary Worker) Migrant and:

...

(2) 2 years, If he Is being sponsored in the religious workers, government authorised exchange or international agreement subcategories,

whichever of (i) or (ii) is the shorter.'

Tier 5 (Temporary Worker) migrants in the Government authorised exchange sub-category do not qualify to apply for indefinite leave to remain under paragraph 245ZS of the Immigration Rules.

6.29 Migrants applying under the Government authorised exchange sub-category must be sponsored by an overarching body operating a scheme. In turn, the scheme must be supported by a Government department. According to paragraph 405 of the Tiers 2 and 5 Sponsor Guidance, the overarching body assigning a Certificate of Sponsorship ('CoS') to the migrant guarantees that the migrant:

- 'is seeking entry to the United Kingdom to work or train temporarily here through an approved exchange scheme;
- does not intend to establish a business in the United Kingdom; and
- meets the requirements of the individual exchange scheme.'

6.30 According to paragraph 401 of the Tiers 2 and 5 Sponsor Guidance schemes supported by Government departments must adhere to the following requirements:

- 'The exchange scheme must not harm the resident labour market. Migrants coming to the UK to take part in work experience schemes must not fill vacancies in the workforce and must do work that is additional to your normal staffing requirements.
- Any work the migrant undertakes must be at a skill level of S/NVQ 3 or above. The only exception to this is where the migrant is coming to the UK through a scheme set up as part of the EU Lifelong Learning Programme, where the migrant may undertake vocational education and training at a lower skill level.
- The employment must conform with all relevant UK and European legislation, such as the National Minimum Wage Act and the EC working hours directives.
- The exchange scheme must include measures that protect it from being abused.'

Individual employers and organisations cannot sponsor migrants in this sub-category (see paragraph 399 of Tiers 2 and 5 Sponsor Guidance). The sponsored researchers scheme, which is supported by the Department of Business, Innovation and Skills ('DBIS'), is one of two exceptions to this rule as it allows individual higher education institutions to sponsor researchers qualifying under the Government authorised exchange sub-category (paragraph 125 of Tier 5 (Temporary Worker) Policy Guidance). The other exception is where the employer is a Government department or an Executive agency of a Government department. Higher education institutions wishing to recruit sponsored researchers 'must already be licensed as a Tier 4 sponsor.'[27]

6.31 A sponsored researcher is not a defined term under paragraph 6 of the Immigration Rules, although a description of it is given at paragraph VAT12.2, VAT12 Business Visitor: Academic Visitor, ECG, nor is it mentioned anywhere else in the Immigration Rules save for paragraph 245ZQ(v). At paragraph VAT12.2 a sponsored researcher is described as 'a person who wishes to come to the United Kingdom to lead or to take part in any formal research project' and these are in turn classified as being 'those hosted but not necessarily funded by a United Kingdom research institution including universities, non-commercial research organisations, charitable organisations and national research council.' The paragraph goes on to say that 'the sponsored researcher fills a research post and works under the full or partial control of the institution, which will itself benefit from the research.'

27 See 'Tier 5 (Temporary workers – government authorised exchange'", Sponsoring Migrants, UK Border Agency, http://www.ukba.homeoffice.gov.uk/...points/sponsoringmigrants/eligibility/tier5govauthorisedexchange/.

6.32 The general requirements for entry clearance, leave to enter or remain are set out in the Immigration Rules, as above. The requirements specific to the Government authorised exchange sub-category to which the sponsored researcher scheme belongs are dealt with primarily in policy guidance, as was the case under the work permit scheme. Whatever little and broadly worded guidance there is for individual higher education institutions and sponsored researchers contained in paragraphs 397–406 of the Tiers 2 and 5 Sponsor Guidance and paragraphs 124–128 of the Tier 5 (Temporary Worker) Policy Guidance, it is very limited in content. The generic Tier 5 (Temporary Worker) application form[28] (for in-country applications) and Appendix 6 (for entry clearance applications made overseas) appear to be ill-suited to finding out whether an applicant satisfies the requirements specifically related to the Government authorised exchange sub-category given that applicants are not asked questions about the scheme under which they are seeking leave[29] or whether that scheme meets Government approval.

Attributes (Appendix A)

6.33 Tier 5 (Temporary Worker) migrants applying for entry clearance, leave to enter or remain must score 30 points for attributes with reference to Table 15 in paragraph 107 of Appendix A to the Immigration Rules.

Criterion	**Points Awarded**
Holds a Tier 5 (Temporary Worker) Certificate of Sponsorship	30

In order to meet this requirement, applicants must provide a valid CoS reference number for sponsorship in this category. The same reference number can only be used once when applying entry clearance or leave to remain. The number will be considered valid if:

- the entry in the Certificate Sponsorship Checking Service confirms that the applicant is the migrant being sponsored as a Tier 5 (Temporary Worker) migrant in the sub-category as indicated by the applicant in the application (paragraph 109 of Appendix A);
- it was assigned to the migrant no more than three months before the application for entry clearance, leave to remain is made unless the migrant is applying for leave to enter and has previously been granted leave to enter using the same number (paragraph 109A(a));

28 Version 04/11, for applications made on or after 6 April 2011. Previous version 12/10 – for applications made on or after 14 December 2010.

29 Oddly, at G4, applicants are asked whether they hold shares in the United Kingdom company or connected business. This seems to be copied over from a Tier 2 application form.

- the application for entry clearance or leave to remain is made no more than three months before the start date of the employment (paragraph 109A(b));
- it has not been cancelled by the sponsor or the UK Border Agency since being assigned (paragraph 109A(c));
- it was issued by an A-rated sponsor unless the application is for leave to remain and the application has or was last granted leave as a Tier 5 migrant, an overseas Government employee or a work permit holder (paragraph 109A(d)).[30]

Additional requirements are contained in paragraphs 110–112 of Appendix A to the Immigration Rules.

Maintenance (funds) (Appendix C)

6.34 Maintenance provisions for Tier 5 (Temporary Worker) migrants are contained in paragraphs 8 and 9 of Appendix C to the Immigration Rules. These should be read together with paragraph 1A of Appendix C to the Immigration Rules[31] which post *Pankina*[32] specifies the length of time for which funds need to have been held by the applicant to score points. Tier 5 (Temporary Worker) migrants must score 10 points for funds by satisfying the requirements set out in the table in paragraph 9 of Appendix C (copied verbatim below) and providing specified documents. The list of documents accepted as evidence to satisfy the maintenance (funds) criteria is given in the Tier 5 (Temporary Worker) Policy Guidance.

Criterion	**Points Awarded**
has £800; or The Sponsor is an A rated Sponsor and the Certificate of Sponsorship Checking Service confirms that the Sponsor has certified that the applicant will not claim public funds during his period of leave as a Tier 5 (Temporary Worker) Migrant. Points will only be awarded if the applicant provides a valid Certificate of Sponsorship reference number with his application.	10

30 This provision was inserted into the Immigration Rules on 6 April 2011 (HC 863).
31 Most recently amended by the Statement of Changes in Immigration Rules (HC 863).
32 *Secretary of State for the Home Department v Pankina* [2010] EWCA Civ 719.

Government authorised exchange schemes

6.35 The sponsored researcher scheme is just one of a number of Tier 5 Government authorised exchange schemes approved by the UKBA for the purposes of this subcategory. The UKBA has published two lists of such schemes[33] and their particulars. A selective composite list of approved schemes, combining the essential details from both lists, related to education is produced below for ease of reference. For further information, please refer to the UKBA prepared lists, *Approved Tier 5 Government Authorised Exchange Schemes* and *Approved Tier 5 Government Authorised Exchange Schemes – Details/Contacts*:

Scheme and date of approval	Scheme purpose	Name of overarching body (sponsor) and supporting department	Contact details and UK coverage
Name: American Institute for Foreign Study (AIFS) **Date of approval:** 27 January 2010	A programme for US undergraduate education majors and postgraduate students.	**Overarching body:** AIFS (UK) Ltd **Supporting department:** Department for Business, Innovation and Skills (DBIS)	**Contact:** Ailsa Brookes AIFS (UK) Ltd Tel: 020 7636 0761 Email: abrookes@aifs.co.uk **UK coverage:** England
Name: AIESEC Internships **Date of approval:** 9 September 2009	The scheme is part of AIESEC's global exchange programme in which 4000 graduates participate every year.	**Overarching body:** AISEC **Supporting department:** Department for Business, Innovation and Skills (DBIS)	**Contact:** Helen McAvoy Vice President, Business Development AIESEC UK Ltd 29–31 Cowper Street London EC2A 4AT Tel: 020 7549 1800 Email: Helen@aiesec.co.uk Website: www.aiesec.co.uk **UK coverage:** All UK

33 'Approved Tier 5 Government Authorised Exchange Schemes', September 2011, http://www.ukba.homeoffice.gov.uk/sitecontent/documents/workingintheuk/gae-list.pdf and 'Approved Tier 5 Government Authorised Exchange Schemes – Details/Contacts', August 2010, http://www.ukba.homeoffice.gov.uk/sitecontent/documents/workingintheuk/gae-details.pdf/.

Scheme and date of approval	Scheme purpose	Name of overarching body (sponsor) and supporting department	Contact details and UK coverage
Name: Broadening Horizons **Date of approval:** 17 July 2009	Brings to the UK Taiwanese teachers who are professionally qualified to teach Mandarin as a second language.	**Overarching body:** The Sir Bernard Lovell Language School **Supporting department:** Department for Children, Schools and Families (DCSF)	**Contact:** The Sir Bernard Lovell Language School North Street Oldland Common BS30 8TS Tel: 01454 868 020 Email: contact@broadeninghorizons-uk-taiwan.com Website: www.broadeninghorizons-uk-taiwan.com **UK coverage:** England
Name: British Universities North America Club (BUNAC) Blue Card Internships – 'Intern in Britain' **Date of approval:** 22 May 2009	The scheme provides a well-controlled pathway for a wide range of organisations in the UK to offer and to benefit from work experience opportunities (internships) for eligible students and recent graduates.	**Overarching body:** BUNAC **Supporting department:** Department for Business, Innovation and Skills (DBIS)	**Contact:** BUNAC Tel: 020 7251 3472 Email: iib@bunac.org.uk Website: www.bunac.org/usa/interninbritain **UK coverage:** All UK
Name: Chevening Programme **Date of approval:** 2 November 2009	The programme includes scholars and researchers attending the UK Environment Programme's World Conservation Monitoring Centre in Cambridge, the Oxford Centre for Islamic Studies and the Clore Leadership programme.	**Overarching body:** British Council **Supporting department:** Foreign and Commonwealth Department (FCO)	**Contact:** Email: chevening.online@britishcouncil.org Website: www.chevening.com **UK coverage:** All UK

Scheme and date of approval	**Scheme purpose**	**Name of overarching body (sponsor) and supporting department**	**Contact details and UK coverage**
Name: Commonwealth Exchange Programme **Date of approval:** 9 March 2009	The programme offers teachers the opportunity to work in different education systems in another country.	**Overarching body:** League for the Exchange of Commonwealth Teachers (LECT)/ CfBT Education Trust **Supporting department:** Department for Children, Schools and Families (DCSF)	**Contact:** LECT CfBT Education Trust 60 Queens Road Reading RG1 4BS Tel: 0118 902 1000 Fax: 0118 902 1739 Email: info@lect.org.uk Website: www.lect.org.uk **UK coverage:** All UK
Name: Commonwealth Scholarships and Fellowships Plan (CSFP) **Date of approval:** 24 July 2009	Annual scheme made available to developing Commonwealth countries. Participants undertake academic, medical or professional research fellowships.	**Overarching body:** British Council **Supporting department:** Department for International Development (DFID)	**Contact:** Commonwealth Scholarships Commission Tel: 020 7380 6700 Website: www.cscuk.org.uk **UK coverage:** All UK
Name: Erasmus **Date of approval:** 20 February 2009 (Scotland) 26 February 2009 (England) 6 April 2009 (Wales)	It is a European Commission educational exchange programme for HE students and teachers.	**Overarching body:** British Council British Council Wales British Council Scotland British Council Northern Ireland	**Contact:** Tel: 02920 924311 Email: Erasmus@britishcouncil.org **UK coverage:** Wales, Scotland, England, Northern Ireland
		Supporting department: Scottish Government (Scotland) Department for Business, Innovation and Skills (DBIS) (England) Welsh Assembly Government (Wales)	

Scheme and date of approval	Scheme purpose	Name of overarching body (sponsor) and supporting department	Contact details and UK coverage
Name: Foreign Language Assistants Programme **Date of approval:** 4 December 2008 (Scotland) 5 December 2008 (England) 19 December 2008 (Northern Ireland) 6 April 2009 (Wales)	Working with partner organisations overseas to provide opportunities for young people to work as language assistants in the UK.	**Overarching body:** British Council British Council Wales British Council Scotland British Council Northern Ireland **Supporting department:** Scottish Government (Scotland) Department for Children, Schools and Families (DCSF) (England) Welsh Assembly Government (Wales) Department of Education (Northern Ireland)	**Contact:** Website: www.britishcouncil.org **UK coverage:** Wales, Scotland, England, Northern Ireland
Name: Fulbright UK/US Teacher Exchange Programme **Date of approval:** 5 December 2008 (England) 5 December 2008 (Scotland) 19 December 2008 (Northern Ireland)	Run by British Council in collaboration with the US State Department for outstanding UK/US teachers to trade places.	**Overarching body:** British Council British Council Wales British Council Scotland British Council Northern Ireland	**Contact:** Tel: 02890 24 8220 ext 226 Email: Fulbright@britishcouncil.org UK coverage: Wales, Scotland, England, Northern Ireland
		Supporting department: Scottish Government (Scotland) Department for Children, Schools and Families (DCSF) (England) Welsh Assembly Government (Wales) Department of Education (Northern Ireland)	

Scheme and date of approval	Scheme purpose	Name of overarching body (sponsor) and supporting department	Contact details and UK coverage
Name: Glasgow Caledonian University International exchange programme **Date of approval:** 22 May 2009	Offers students work experience, cultural diversity and personal development through the exchange programme.	**Overarching body:** Glasgow Caledonian University **Supporting department:** Scottish Government	**Contact:** Gerald Shaw Industrial Placement Officer Tel: 0141 331 3206 Email: Gerald@gcal.ac.uk Website: www.gcal.ac.uk **UK coverage:** Scotland
Name: Grundtvig **Date of approval:** 6 April 2009	The programme which aims to strengthen the European dimension in adult education and lifelong learning funds a range of activities: assistantships, in-service training, learner workshops, visits and exchanges.	**Overarching body:** ECOTEC Research and Consulting Ltd **Supporting department:** Department for Business, Innovation and Skills (DBIS)	**Contact:** Tier 5 ECOTEC Tel: 0845 199 1919 Email: tier5@ecotec.com Website: www.grundtvig.org.uk **UK coverage:** All UK
Name: IAESTE Date of approval: 15 December 2008 (Scotland) 19 December 2008 (Northern Ireland) 26 February 2009 (England) 6 April 2009 (Wales)	IAESTE UK provides science, engineering and applied arts graduates with training experience relevant to their studies through work placements	**Overarching body:** British Council British Council Wales British Council Scotland British Council Northern Ireland	**Contact:** Tel: 020 7389 4771 Email: iaeste@britishcouncil.org **UK coverage:** Wales, Scotland, England, Northern Ireland
		Supporting department: Scottish Government (Scotland) Department for Business, Innovation and Skills (DBIS) (England) Welsh Assembly Government (Wales) Department of Education (Northern Ireland)	

Scheme and date of approval	Scheme purpose	Name of overarching body (sponsor) and supporting department	Contact details and UK coverage
Name: Law Society Tier 5 scheme for migrant lawyers **Date of approval:** 26 February 2009	It is open to law firms based in England and Wales and covers placements, internships and secondments offered to lawyers and law students from other countries coming to the UK for primarily non-economic purposes.	**Overarching body:** The Law Society of England and Wales **Supporting department:** Ministry of Justice	**Contact:** Email: tier5@lawsociety.org.uk Website: www.lawsociety.org.uk **UK coverage:** England and Wales
Name: Leonardo da Vinci **Date of approval:** 6 April 2009	It is part of the European Commission's Lifelong Learning Programme and is open to any organisation involved in vocational training in the countries participating in the programme.	**Overarching body:** ECOTEC Research and Consulting Ltd **Supporting department:** Department for Business, Innovation and Skills (DBIS)	**Contact:** Tier 5 ECOTEC Tel: 0845 199 2929 Email: tier5@ecotec.com Website: www.leonardo.org.uk **UK coverage:** All UK
Name: Lord Chancellor's Training Scheme for Young Chinese Lawyers **Date of approval:** 4 March 2010	The programme is organised to enable Chinese lawyers to obtain practical experience in commercial law, litigation and court procedure.	**Overarching body:** British Council **Supporting department:** Ministry of Justice	**Contact:** Tel: 020 7389 4253 Website: www.britishcouncil.org.uk **UK coverage:** All UK

Scheme and date of approval	Scheme purpose	Name of overarching body (sponsor) and supporting department	Contact details and UK coverage
Name: Mandarin Teachers Programme **Date of approval:** 10 August 2009	The programme is run by the Confucius Institute at the Specialist School and Academies Trust in collaboration with the Office of Chinese Language Council International (Hanban) and Peking University through which a number of Chinese teachers come to the UK for one academic year to supporting the teaching and learning of Mandarin Chinese.	**Overarching body:** Specialist Schools and Academies Trust **Supporting department:** Joint International Unit (on behalf of DCSF)	**Contact:** Tel: 020 7802 2300 Email: chiensenetworks@ssatrust.org.uk **UK coverage:** England and Wales
Name: Mountbatten Programme **Date of approval:** 9 March 2009	The programme offers participants a one-year experience in London combining full-time work with seminars, self-assessment, and projects leading to a professional qualification, a postgraduate certificate or an MBA in International Business Practice.	**Overarching body:** St Mary's University College Twickenham **Supporting department:** Department for Business, Innovation and Skills (DBIS)	**Contact:** St Mary's University College Twickenham Waldegrave Road Strawberry Hill Twickenham TW1 4SX Tel: 020 8240 4000 Email: international@smuc.ac.uk Website: www.smuc.ac.uk **UK coverage:** England
Name: US-UK Education Commission (aka The US-UK Fulbright Commission) **Date of approval:** 4 June 2009	The aim is to foster mutual understanding between the US and the UK through academic exchange by the awarding of merit based scholarships.	**Overarching body:** The US-UK Education Commission (aka The US-UK Fulbright Commission) **Supporting department:** Joint International Unit (on behalf of DBIS)	**Contact:** www.fulbright.co.uk **UK coverage:** All UK

Scheme and date of approval	Scheme purpose	Name of overarching body (sponsor) and supporting department	Contact details and UK coverage
Name: UK-China Graduate Work Experience Programme **Date of approval:** 7 January 2009	This is programme for employers to access the UK and China's most promising talent and for graduates to take part in work placements.	**Overarching body:** GTI Recruiting Solutions **Supporting department:** Department for Business, Innovation and Skills (DBIS)	**Contact:** Richard Barrett Project Manager GTI Recruiting Solutions Tel: 020 7061 1913 Email: ukchinagrad@gtisolutions.co.uk Website: www.ukchinagrad.com **UK coverage:** England
Name: UK-India Graduate Work Experience Programme **Date of approval:** 3 July 2009	The programme gives Indian graduates the opportunity to take part in salaried internships with companies in the UK.	**Overarching body:** GTI Recruiting Solutions **Supporting department:** Department for Business, Innovation and Skills (DBIS)	**Contact:** Emma Waltham Project Manager GTI Recruiting Solutions Tel: 020 7061 1912 Email: ukindiagrad@groupgti.com Website: www.ukindiagrad.com **UK coverage:** England
Name: UK-India Education and Research Initiative **Date of approval:** 26 February 2009 (England) 6 April 2009 (Wales)	This is a five year initiative designed to facilitate education and research co-operation between the two countries.	**Overarching body:** British Council British Council Wales British Council Scotland British Council Northern Ireland **Supporting department:** Department for Business, Innovation and Skills (DBIS) (England) Welsh Assembly Government (Wales)	Contact: Website: www.ukieri.org **UK coverage:** Wales, England, Scotland and Northern Ireland

Scheme and date of approval	Scheme purpose	Name of overarching body (sponsor) and supporting department	Contact details and UK coverage
Name: Welsh Language Teaching Programme in Patagonia **Date of approval:** 22 May 2009	The programme aims to strengthen the use of the Welsh language in Patagonia by bringing Patagonians to Wales to improve their language fluency and bilingual environments. The project is managed by the British Council in collaboration with the Wales-Argentina Society and Cardiff University's Welsh Language Teaching Centre for Adults.	**Overarching body:** British Council Wales **Supporting department:** Welsh Assembly Government	**Contact:** Website: http://www.britishcouncil.org/wales-education-welsh-language-project.htm **UK coverage:** Wales

6.36 It is a requirement for applicants and their dependants to submit to biometric data collection at a time specified by the UKBA, depending on whether their application is made by post, courier or at a Public Enquiry Office. If their application is successful, applicants and their dependants will be issued with biometric residence permits. Entry clearance applications can be made using online forms or hard copy forms, VAF9 (for main applicants) and VAF10 (dependants). The cost to the main applicant of making an entry clearance application is £190.[34] In-country applications for a grant of leave under Tier 5 (Temporary Worker) category can be made using a Tier 5 (Temporary Worker) application form either by post, courier or at a Public Enquiry Office at a cost of £190[35] (for a main applicant applying by post or courier) or £648[36] (for a main applicant applying at a Public Enquiry Office). Dependants, applying at the same time as the main applicant, have to pay £95[37] for postal applications and £324[38] for applications made at a Public Enquiry Office, unless the dependant is a child aged 18 years or over. There are reduced fees for certain nationalities and their dependants. Dependants applying at a later date and applications made by dependent children aged 18 years or over will attract

34 Cost in effect from 6 April 2011.
35 Cost in effect from 6 April 2011.
36 Cost in effect from 6 April 2011.
37 Cost in effect from 6 April 2011.
38 Cost in effect from 6 April 2011.

a charge of £550[39] for postal and courier applications and £850[40] for applications made in person at a Public Enquiry Office. Dependants must use a separate PBS (Dependant) application form.

Applications made by post should be sent to:	Applications made by courier should be sent to:
UK Border Agency Tier 5 (Temporary Worker) PO Box 506 Durham DH99 1WB	UK Border Agency Tier 5 (Temporary Worker) Millburngate House Millburngate Durham DH97 1PA

39 Cost in effect from 6 April 2011.
40 Cost in effect from 6 April 2011.

Chapter 7

Looking ahead: Where do I go from here?

Introduction

7.01 This chapter contemplates, in view of the recent or proposed future changes to the law, the road ahead for migrants in the student or related categories, who, as their current period of leave draws to an end, sit down to consider their switching or extension options with a view to staying in the country permanently or taking steps to become British citizens. As the Government seeks to break the links between temporary and permanent migration, migrants are left with fewer choices.

Intention to leave

Historical note

7.02 Prior to 31 March 2009 paragraph 57(vi) of the Immigration Rules required a student to demonstrate his or her intention 'to leave the United Kingdom at the end of his studies'.[1] With the introduction of provisions allowing degree students to switch into employment related categories, this requirement began losing its potency and became more difficult to apply in practice. Paragraph 131A[2] of the Immigration Rules in effect from 18 September 2002 allowed students who successfully completed UK degree level courses to switch to work permit employment in-country upon qualification provided that they:

- entered the United Kingdom or were given leave to remain as students in line with paragraphs 57 to 62 of the Immigration Rules;[3] and;

1 Immigration Rules (HC 395), Margaret Phelan and James Gillespie *Immigration Law Handbook*, (6th edn, OUP, 2009).
2 Inserted by the Statement of Changes in Immigration Rules (Cmnd 5597) on 18 September 2002.
3 Paragraph 131A(i) of the Immigration Rules (HC 395).

- had completed a recognised UK degree course at either a UK publicly funded further or higher education institution, or a *bona fide* private education institution which maintains satisfactory records of enrolment and attendance;[4] and;
- held a valid Home Office immigration employment document;[5] and;
- if sponsored by their Government or international scholarship agency, had the written consent of their official sponsor;[6] and;
- met general work permit requirements set out in paragraph 128(ii) to (vi).[7]

7.03 Similar provisions were made for student nurses, postgraduate doctors and dentists under paragraph 131B of the Immigration Rules.[8] Participants of the Science and Engineering Graduate Scheme ('SEGS'), subsequently succeeded by the International Graduates Scheme ('IGS'), were allowed to extend their stay to take employment pursuant to paragraph 131C of the Immigration Rules.[9]

7.04 If an immigration official was satisfied that an applicant intended, and was able, to follow a chosen degree level course of study,[10] he was to assume that the applicant had a reasonable prospect of success in his studies making him eligible for employment. Chapter 3, Section 3, IDIs, recommended that 'in such cases the intention to leave requirements should be disregarded, and considerations should concentrate on the other aspects of the rules, with particular emphasis on the applicant's ability and intention to follow the course of study.'[11] The policy was introduced on 17 October 2001 by the Secretary of State in a concession outside the Immigration Rules.[12] Intentions of students whose courses did not lead to a UK degree were under more scrutiny. In respect of them, immigration officials were instructed to make enquiries into their intentions only 'where there is reason to believe the applicant does not intend to go home'.[13]

4 Paragraph 131A(ii) of the Immigration Rules (HC 395).
5 Paragraph 131A(iii) of the Immigration Rules (HC 395).
6 Paragraph 131A(iv) of the Immigration Rules (HC 395).
7 Paragraph 131A(v) of the Immigration Rules (HC 395).
8 Inserted by the Statement of Changes in Immigration Rules (Cmnd 5597) on 18 September 2002 and amended by HC 645 on 30 November 2005.
9 Inserted by the Statement of Changes in Immigration Rules (Cmnd 6339) on 1 October 2004 and amended by HC 7075 on 1 May 2007.
10 Policy provided for the same considerations to apply to applicants applying for degree courses conditional on successful completion of a foundation programme or English language course, IDI June 2009, Chapter 3, Section 3.
11 Paragraph 20.2, IDI June 2009, Chapter 3, Section 3, http://www.ukba.homeoffice.gov.uk/sitecontent/documents/policyandlaw/IDIs/idischapter3/section3/section3.pdf?view=Binary.
12 Duran Seddon, *Immigration, nationality and refugee law handbook* (2006 edition, JCWI p 259)
13 Paragraph 20.2, IDI June 2009, Chapter 3, Section 3, http://www.ukba.homeoffice.gov.uk/sitecontent/documents/policyandlaw/IDIs/idischapter3/section3/section3.pdf?view=Binary.

7.05 On 25 October 2004 the Government introduced SEGS,[14] participants in which were able to apply for leave to enter or remain in the United Kingdom for a period not exceeding 12 months provided they had successfully completed and obtained a bachelor degree (with second class honours or above), master's degree or PhD in a subject approved by the Department for Education and Skills ('DfES') in the 12 months prior to application, intended to seek or take work during the period of leave and were able to maintain and accommodate themselves.

7.06 SEGS was launched to encourage non-EU/EEA graduates in physical sciences, mathematics and engineering to pursue a career in the United Kingdom. SEGS participants were able to switch into employment (paragraphs 128–135H of the Immigration Rules) or business category (paragraphs 200–210H of the Immigration Rules). From 3 April 2006 SEGS was revised to reflect a provision made in the Chancellor's Pre-Budget Report published on 5 December 2005 allowing 'all international students on completion of a post-graduate degree, or an undergraduate degree in a shortage sector, to work in the UK for up to 12 months'.[15] The scheme was expanded allowing graduates with a postgraduate degree in any subject commenced on or after 1 May 2006 to participate in SEGS. Fresh Talent: Working in Scotland scheme ('FT: WISS'), comparable to SEGS, was launched on 22 June 2005.[16]

7.07 SEGS was replaced by IGS on 1 May 2007[17] broadening the eligibility criteria of the scheme. On the same day DfES lists of eligible undergraduate courses which were drawn up 'based on trends in numbers of UK students graduating'[18] were removed. While retaining the basic features similar to SEGS,[19] IGS widened the eligibility criteria and presented new possibilities to graduates who obtained their UK recognised bachelor, master's degrees and PhDs, or postgraduate certificates and postgraduate diplomas in any subject on or after 1 May 2007.[20] FT: WISS was brought in line with IGS from 1 May 2007.[21] Concessionary arrangements

14 Paragraphs 135O–135T were inserted by the Statement of Changes in Immigration Rules (Cmnd 6339) on 25 October 2004. Paragraph 135O(i) was substituted by HC 1016 from 3 April 2006 expanding SEGS so that those who commenced a master's degree or PhD after 1 May 2006 were eligible to apply regardless of the subject. Paragraphs 135O–135T were deleted on 30 June 2008.

15 Paragraph 7, Policy Background, Explanatory Memorandum to the Statement of Changes in Immigration Rules laid on 30 March 2006 (HC 1016).

16 Inserted by the Statement of Changes in Immigration Rules (HC 104) on 22 June 2005 by paragraphs 143A–143F. Paragraph 143A(i), (ii) and (v) was substituted by Cmnd 7075 on 1 May 2007.

17 Inserted by the Statement of Changes in Immigration Rules (Cmnd 7075) on 1 May 2007 substituting paragraphs 135O–135T.

18 Paragraph 7, Policy Background, Explanatory Memorandum to the Statement of Changes in Immigration Rules laid on 4 April 2007 (Cm 7075).

19 At paragraph 135O(i)(a) of the Immigration Rules for graduates who obtained their bachelor degrees in a subject approved by DfES completed before 1 May 2007.

20 Paragraph 135O(i)(b) and (c) of the Immigration Rules.

21 Paragraph 143A(i) substituted by by the Statement of Changes in Immigration Rules (Cmnd 7075) on 1 May 2007.

were put in place for those who completed their master's degree or PhD before 1 May 2007. Other qualifications such as Higher National Diplomas, Higher National Certificates, honorary or Foundation degrees were not eligible under IGS. The new scheme presented 'no identifiable impact on the public sector.'[22]

7.08 While leave granted under IGS did not lead to settlement, it allowed participants to switch into work permit employment (paragraphs 128–135 of the Immigration Rules), the Highly Skilled Migrant Programme (paragraphs 135A–135H of the Immigration Rules), categories for persons intending to establish themselves in business (paragraphs 200–210 of the Immigration Rules) or innovator category (paragraphs 210A–210H of the Immigration Rules). Chapter 5, Section 3, IDIs, conceded that 'this is not a permanent migration route, and the applicant would then need to switch into one of the four categories listed above if they wanted to pursue their career in the United Kingdom in the long term.'[23] Switching into IGS was limited to those with valid leave as students, student nurses, for the purpose of re-sitting examinations or writing up a thesis.

7.09 From 1 October 2004 under paragraph 135DB[24] of the Immigration Rules students were given permission to switch into the Highly Skilled Migrant Programme provided they:

- entered the United Kingdom or were given leave to remain as a student;[25]
- obtained a degree qualification on a recognised degree course at a UK publicly funded further or higher education institution or a bona fide UK private education institution;[26]
- if sponsored by their Government or international scholarship agency, had written consent of their official sponsor to remain in the United Kingdom as a highly skilled migrant;[27] and
- met the requirements set out in paragraph 135A(i)–(iii).[28]

Provisions were also made for postgraduate doctors and dentists[29] and in time for participants of SEGS and FT: WISS.

22 Explanatory Memorandum to the Statement of Changes in Immigration Rules laid on 4 April 2007 (Cm 7075).
23 IDI (undated), Chapter 5, Section 13, http://www.ukba.homeoffice.gov.uk/sitecontent/documents/policyandlaw/IDIs/idischapter5/section13/section13.pdf?view=Binary.
24 Inserted by the Statement of Changes in Immigration Rules (Cmnd 6339) on 1 October 2004.
25 Paragraph 135DB(i) of the Immigration Rules (HC 395).
26 Paragraph 135DB(ii) of the Immigration Rules (HC 395).
27 Paragraph 135DB(iii) of the Immigration Rules (HC 395).
28 Paragraph 135DB(iv) of the Immigration Rules (HC 395).
29 Paragraphs 135DB, 135DC, 135DE and 135DH were last inserted into the Immigration Rules on 5 December 2006 (HC 1702) but deleted on 29 February 2008 (HC 321) and moved to Appendix D to the Rules.

7.10 With the noticeable disappearance of the 'intention to leave' requirement from 17 October 2001, Government policy gradually enabled a wider class of overseas graduates to stay on in the United Kingdom after completing their studies and advance their careers, while, at the same time, further retrenching switching arrangements into the student route. On 1 October 2004 the Immigration Rules introduced a restriction on in-country switching into the student category.[30] At the time non-visa nationals entering the United Kingdom as visitors could be granted permission to stay as students provided they had been accepted on a course of study at degree level or above. Other visitors, visa nationals and non-visa nationals alike, accepted on courses below degree level, were prohibited from switching into the student route in-country without having prior entry clearance. On 3 April 2006 paragraph 60(i) of the Immigration Rules was changed further to require non-visa national visitors accepted onto courses at degree level or above to have entry clearance as a student or prospective student before being allowed to switch into the student route.[31] Mandatory entry clearance became a requirement for students and prospective students from 1 September 2007 'to ensure that we only allow those people who can be said to have a legitimate expectation to progress into the student route to do so.'[32] This included those with leave as students re-sitting an examination, work permit holders, sabbatical officers, and participants in SEGS, IGS or FT: WISS. This was a seminal shift towards the mentality accepted under the Points Based System ('PBS').

7.11 From 1 October 2004 paragraph 60(vi) of the Immigration Rules was amended to reduce the maximum total period of leave granted to students undertaking consecutive short courses below degree level from four to two years[33] 'to limit the scope for students to take successive short courses'.[34] The definition of 'degree level study' was imported into paragraph 6 of the Rules on the same date. There was no analogous provision related to short courses for students seeking entry clearance under paragraph 57 of the Immigration Rules although the IDIs stated that where 'a similar situation is encountered in relation to a student seeking entry to continue his previous stay after a short absence abroad, it is likely that refusal in accordance with paragraph 57(v) will be justified'.[35] This disparity was rectified under the PBS.

30 Paragraph 60(i) was substituted by the Statement of Changes in Immigration Rules (Cmnd 6339) on 1 October 2004.

31 Paragraph 60(i) was substituted by the Statement of Changes in Immigration Rules (HC 1016) on 3 April 2006. Non-visa nationals who were granted leave to enter as a visitor prior to 1 July 2006 were not subject to these changes (paragraph 60(i)(b)).

32 Explanatory Memorandum to the Statement of Changes in Immigration Rules laid on 3 April 2007 (Cm 7074).

33 Paragraph 60(vi) was amended by the Statement of Changes (Cm 6339) as of 1 October 2004 to say 'would not, as a result of an extension of stay, spend more than 2 years on short courses below degree level (ie courses of less than 1 years duration, or longer courses broken off before completion).'

34 Paragraph 19, IDI June 2009, Chapter 3, Section 3, http://www.ukba.homeoffice.gov.uk/sitecontent/documents/policyandlaw/IDIs/idischapter3/section3/section3.pdf?view=Binary.

35 Paragraph 19, IDI June 2009, Chapter 3, Section 3. Paragraph 57(v) requires the applicant to leave the United Kingdom at the end of his studies.

7.12 *Looking ahead: Where do I go from here?*

Current considerations

7.12 Opening the student route to so many switching exceptions eventually rendered the 'intention to leave' requirement ineffective, barely enforceable and open to challenge in view of the ample discretion to discount it from the scale of consideration. This kind of discretionary and subjective treatment of the Rules could not be allowed under the PBS which required rigidity and objectivity in approaching the Rules. Despite this, prompted by the number of students who have stayed on in the United Kingdom since2004[36] the 'intention to leave' requirement has been revisited by the Government as part of its extended review of the student route.[37]

7.13 In 'The Student Immigration System' consultation paper published on 7 December 2010 the Government made the following proposal

> 'We also wish to consider whether students wishing to extend their studies should be required to return home to apply overseas for a new visa, in order to mark the fact that their initial stay has expired and that they leave the UK in line with their original intention, prior to a new permission to enter. In general we wish to challenge the perception that once a student visa has been obtained, an extended stay in the UK will be permitted.'

Studies have shown that 92% of 26,912 respondents disagreed with this.[38] Instead, the Government will introduce an overall limit on the time spent in the United Kingdom studying in the Tier 4 (General) category from April 2012.[39]

Switching

Switching into Tier 4 (General) and Tier 4 (Child) categories

7.14 Mandatory entry clearance for students was introduced with effect from 31 March 2009. The requirement for students to leave at the end of their studies was plainly absent and remains so from the Immigration Rules. However, from

36 'The Migrant Journey', Home Office, Lorrah Achato, Mike Eaton and Chris Jones, September 2010, http://rds.homeoffice.gov.uk/rds/pdfs10/horr43c.pdf.

37 *The Student Immigration System, a Consultation,* UK Border Agency, December 2010, http://www.ukba.homeoffice.gov.uk/sitecontent/documents/policyandlaw/consultations/students/student-consultation.pdf?view=Binary. The consultation closed on 31 January 2011.

38 Page 8, *Consultation on the student immigration system: 7th December 2010 to 31st January 2011. Consultation questionnaire results*, UK Border Agency, March 2011, http://www.ukba.homeoffice.gov.uk/sitecontent/documents/policyandlaw/consultations/students/student-consultation-results.pdf?view=Binary.

39 *Student Visas, Statement of Intent and Transitional Measures*, UK Border Agency, March 2011, http://www.ukba.homeoffice.gov.uk/sitecontent/documents/news/sop4.pdf.

April 2012 Tier 4 (General) students will be able to spend a maximum of five years undertaking degree level courses.

7.15 Switching arrangements under the PBS are stated to be inflexible and the Secretary of State has sought to remove policies allowing switching outside the Immigration Rules. Nonetheless, the Secretary of State has the power either under the Prerogative or under the Immigration Act 1971, s 4 to exercise discretion to cover situations not governed by the Immigration Rules and nothing in the Immigration Rules or related policies can fetter the Secretary of State from exercising that discretion. Paragraphs 245ZX(b) and 245ZZC(b) of the Immigration Rules[40] and policy guidance provide exhaustive lists of mostly deleted immigration categories allowing migrants, vast numbers of pre-PBS remnants, to switch or be absorbed into the general and child student routes, respectively.

7.16 An adult applicant who has or was last granted entry clearance, leave to enter or remain as:

- a Tier 4 (General) student;
- a Tier 4 (Child) student;
- a Tier 1 (Post-Study Work) migrant;
- a Tier 2 migrant;
- a participant in IGS or SEGS;
- a participant in the FT: WISS;
- a postgraduate doctor or dentist;
- a prospective student;
- a student;
- a student nurse;
- a student re-sitting an examination;
- a student writing-up a thesis;
- a Student Union Sabbatical Officer; or
- a work permit holder

can extend their permission to stay or switch into Tier 4 (General) migrant route in-country.

7.17 The child category is naturally more restrictive and thus only those who have or were last granted entry clearance, leave to enter or remain as:

40 Immigration Rules HC 395, as at 4 July 2011.

- Tier 4 migrants;
- students; or
- prospective students

are allowed to apply for leave to remain as Tier 4 (Child) migrants or to switch into this category.

7.18 There are provisions in the Immigration Rules and policy to frustrate perpetual students. These apply to Tier 4 (General) students of 18 years old or over. Paragraph 245ZV(g) of the Immigration Rules sets out requirements for applicants seeking entry clearance:

> '(g) If the course is below degree level the grant of entry clearance the applicant is seeking must not lead to the applicant having spent more than 3 years in the UK as a Tier 4 Migrant since the age of 18 studying courses that did not consist of degree level study'.

7.19 The same requirement is reflected in the extension of stay provisions at paragraph 245ZX(h) of the Immigration Rules. Paragraphs 85–87 of the Tier 4 of the Points Based System – Policy Guidance ('Tier 4 Policy Guidance')[41] go on to explain that adult students are not allowed to spend more than three years studying in the United Kingdom below bachelor's degree level 'in his/her lifetime' implying cumulative aggregation of time. As opposed to the Rules in effect prior to 31 March 2009, these provisions no longer refer to 'short courses'. Students can undertake one or several courses during the three year period which excludes the time a student has spent on courses below degree level under:

- 'the student rules that were in place before 31 March 2009; or
- Tier 4 (General) when they were 16 or 17 years old; or
- Tier 4 (Child) when they were aged 17 years or under; or
- any other non Tier 4 category which permits study'.[42]

A further hindrance to continuity of stay is the prohibition at paragraph 245ZX(l) of the Immigration Rules against applying for leave to remain for the purpose of studies commencing more than one month after the expiry of a student's current permission to stay. Paragraph 89 of the Tier 4 Policy Guidance stipulates that students whose leave runs out more than one calendar month before the start date of their intended course 'will be expected to return overseas and apply from outside the UK'. If they submit their application in the United Kingdom, it will be refused.

41 Version 07/11, 4 July 2011.
42 Paragraph 84, Tier 4 Policy Guidance (version 04/11, 21 April 2011).

Switching from Tier 4 and other student related categories into other PBS routes

7.20 PBS switching provisions for student related categories of applicants are shown in the following table which is indicative but not exhaustive:

Applicants with permission to stay as	can switch into the following PBS categories
• Tier 4 migrants	• Tier 1 (General) • Tier 1 (Post-Study Work) • Tier 1 (Investor) • Tier 1 (Entrepreneur) • Tier 2 (General) • Tier 2 (Sportsperson) • Tier 2 (Minister of Religion)
• students	• Tier 1 (General) • Tier 1 (Post-Study Work) • Tier 1 (Investor) • Tier 1 (Entrepreneur) • Tier 2 (General) • Tier 2 (Sportsperson) • Tier 2 (Minister of Religion)
• student nurses	• Tier 1 (General) • Tier 1 (Post-Study Work) • Tier 1 (Investor) • Tier 1 (Entrepreneur) • Tier 2 (General) • Tier 2 (Sportsperson) • Tier 2 (Minister of Religion)
• students re-sitting an examination	• Tier 1 (General) • Tier 1 (Post-Study Work) • Tier 1 (Investor) • Tier 1 (Entrepreneur) • Tier 2 (General) • Tier 2 (Sportsperson) • Tier 2 (Minister of Religion)
• students writing-up a thesis	• Tier 1 (General) • Tier 1 (Post-Study Work) • Tier 1 (Investor) • Tier 1 (Entrepreneur) • Tier 2 (General) • Tier 2 (Sportsperson) • Tier 2 (Minister of Religion)

7.21 *Looking ahead: Where do I go from here?*

Applicants with permission to stay as	can switch into the following PBS categories
• postgraduate doctors or dentists	• Tier 1 (General) • Tier 1 (Entrepreneur) • Tier 2 (General) • Tier 2 (Sportsperson) • Tier 2 (Minister of Religion)
• participants in IGS, SEGS or FT: WISS	• Tier 1 (General) • Tier 1 (Post-Study Work) transitional arrangements • Tier 1 (Entrepreneur) • Tier 2 (General) • Tier 2 (Sportsperson) • Tier 2 (Minister of Religion)
• Student Union Sabbatical Officers	• Tier 2 (General) • Tier 2 (Sportsperson) • Tier 2 (Minister of Religion)

General overview of PBS routes

7.21 It is important to know how to navigate your way around these different routes when considering making an application. Although these PBS routes exhibit signs of homogeny in that they share some common traits, they are far from uniform. Applicants are advised to consider the source materials mentioned below before making an application. The overview below summarises the relevant points.

7.22 While undertaking a course of study is not expressly prohibited, Tier 1 and 2 migrants must be mindful of the purpose and conditions of their leave before taking up studies. Paragraph 459 of the Tiers 2 and 5 Sponsor Guidance[43] states that migrants who are employed under Tier 2 (as well as Tier 5, see **Chapter 3** and **Chapter 6**) may undertake courses of study and there is no limit either on the number of hours they can study, type of study or level of course as long as 'any study done does not interfere with their ability to carry out the job they have been employed to do.' Courses do not have to be undertaken with a Tier 4 sponsor.

7.23 Prior to 6 April 2011, Tier 1 was divided into four sub-categories: Tier 1 (General), Tier 1 (Investor), Tier 1 (Entrepreneur) and Tier 1 (Post-Study Work). Changes that occurred on 6 April 2011 saw the addition of a new sub-category, Tier

43 References made to Tiers 2 and 5 Sponsor Guidance hereinafter refer to version 04/11, valid from 6 April 2011.

1 (Exceptional Talent), which came fully into force on 9 August 2011. At the same time Tier 1 (General) became a residual category closed to new applicants. Tier 2 is also divided into four sub-categories: Tier 2 (General), Tier 2 (Sportsperson), Tier 2 (Minister of Religion) and Tier 2 (Intra-Company Transfer). Tier 2 (Intra-Company Transfer) is further divided into three sub-categories, namely, Established Staff, Graduate Trainee and Skills Transfer. Tiers 1 and 2 (as well as Tiers 4 and 5) were introduced in the Isle of Man by the Statement of Changes in Immigration Rules from 26 July 2010.[44] Although the Channel Islands have not adopted the PBS, they recognise Tier 2 (Minister of Religion) and Tier 5 (Youth Mobility Scheme).

7.24 In the United Kingdom the provisions informing applicants of requirements are contained in the Immigration Rules, the Appendices to the Immigration Rules (which are part of the Rules themselves as laid before Parliament) and Policy Guidance and Entry Clearance Guidance.[45] The Immigration Rules deal with the purpose, requirements for entry clearance, leave to remain and indefinite leave to remain, period, conditions and curtailment of grant and transitional arrangements, if any. Appendices A (Attributes), B (English language) and C (Maintenance (Funds)) to the Immigration Rules outline point-scoring criteria for each category within a Tier. With the exception of Tier 1 (Investor) and Tier 1 (Exceptional Talent) migrants, applicants must score points under all three Appendices in order to satisfy the requirements (these vary depending on whether they are applying for entry clearance or leave to remain). Tier 1 (Investor) migrants must score points under Appendix A only. When applying for entry clearance Tier 1 (Exceptional Talent) migrants must score points under Appendix A only, however, when applying for leave to remain, points must be scored under Appendices A and B.

7.25 The constitutional standing of Policy Guidance has been subject to judicial scrutiny (see **Chapter 2**). From a practical point of view, its function is to provide guidance in respect of each PBS route, to unpack each point scoring component and to specify required evidence. Under the Immigration Rules themselves, it is suggested that the Policy Guidance is there in order to state what forms of *evidence* will be required in order to satisfy various requirements under the Immigration Rules. However, as highlighted in *Pankina*,[46] the difficulty has been that, in many cases, Policy Guidance amounts to imposing substantive requirements of its own. Policy Guidance also contains general information about self-assessment, verification and other checks conducted in respect of documents, appeal rights, and any other instructions relevant to each category. Particular attention should be paid to the wording of specified documentation and details contained therein. Evidence and its format are the backbone of a successful PBS application.

44 Statement of Changes in Immigration Rules, SD No: 62/05, http://www.gov.im/lib/docs/cso/immigrationrulesjuly262010.pdf (no longer available).

45 Entry clearance guidance contains 'copies of instructions used by visa staff on the handling of entry clearance and visa applications made outside the United Kingdom' as per the introductory note at http://www.ukvisas.gov.uk/en/ecg/.

46 *Secretary of State for the Home Department v Pankina* [2010] EWCA Civ 719.

Applications

7.26 Applicants can find relevant application forms on the International Group (http://www.ukvisas.gov.uk/)[47] and the UK Border Agency ('UKBA') (http://www.ukba.homeoffice.gov.uk/) websites. These were merged into a unified website on 4 September 2011 (http://www.ukba.homeoffice.gov.uk) combining information about in and out of country applications.

Entry clearance applications are made using electronic application forms available at http://www.visa4uk.fco.gov.uk/ although some posts still accept paper-based forms. Applicants are then required to submit their signed application forms, self-assessment Appendices, supporting documents, photographs, biometrics and consular fees, normally by prior appointment, at British posts overseas (the UKBA acting through British Embassy, British Consulate or British High Commission) mostly through their commercial partners, Worldbridge and VFS Global. British diplomatic missions do not interface directly with applicants. Submission procedures, as well as processing times, vary depending on the post and should be ascertained in advance by contacting the relevant Visa Application Centre.

7.27 To be valid, leave to remain applications must be made on relevant forms and submitted together with specified documents as defined in paragraphs 34A–34J of the Immigration Rules[48] (see also **Chapter 3**). In-country applications can be made by post, by courier or using the premium service at Public Enquiry Offices[49] (with the exception of Tier 1 (Investor) and Tier 1 (Entrepreneur) categories) at an uplifted fee. In some cases, super premium service launched on 6 April 2010 is also available.[50] Applications can also be submitted online using the 'Apply online' facility using interactive or paper based forms.[51] Service standards and processing times vary accordingly. Information about processing times can be found on the unified UKBA website. It became necessary for Tier 1 migrants and their dependants to apply for a biometric residence permit from 14 December 2010.

7.28 Tier 1 is outside the sponsorship scheme. Tier 2 requires an applicant to have a Certificate of Sponsorship ('CoS') issued by a Tier 2 licensed sponsor and a job offer before they can make an immigration application. Entry clearance is mandatory for Tier 1 and Tier 2 migrants subject to switching arrangements and applicants must not fall for refusal under the general grounds for refusal contained in paragraphs 320 to 323A of the Immigration Rules or be illegal entrants. PBS

47 New look website was launched on 20 September 2010.

48 These were made under the Immigration, Asylum and Nationality Act 2006, s 50(1). Application forms and related procedures were previously specified in The Immigration (Leave to Remain) (Prescribed Forms and Procedures) Regulations 2007, SI 2007/882, which were withdrawn on 29 February 2008 (refer to Chapter 1A, Section 1, IDI, Mar/10 (archived)).

49 Public Enquiry Offices operate in Croydon, Solihull, Sheffield, Liverpool, Glasgow, Belfast and Cardiff.

50 http://www.ukba.homeoffice.gov.uk/contact/super-premium/. The fee for using this service was reduced from £15,000 to £6,000 on 6 April 2011. Tier 1, Tier 2 and Tier 5 migrants can use this service.

51 http://apply.ukba.homeoffice.gov.uk.

migrants must register with the police in line with paragraph 326 of the Immigration Rules and must not have recourse to public funds.

7.29 In respect of applications made for leave in the Tier 1 and Tier 2 categories there is an additional requirement for students, postgraduate doctors or dentists, student nurses, students writing-up a thesis, students re-sitting an examination and Tier 4 migrants sponsored by a Government or international scholarship agency to provide an unconditional written consent of the sponsor (Government or agency) to the application and specified documents. Those wishing to qualify for indefinite leave to remain[52] must have sufficient knowledge of English language and life in the United Kingdom in line with paragraphs 33BA of the Immigration Rules unless they are under the age of 18 years or aged 65 and over at the time of making the application. They must also not have any unspent convictions within the meaning of the Rehabilitation of Offenders Act 1974.

7.30 Spouses, civil partners, unmarried or same-sex partners of PBS migrants are catered for by paragraphs 319A–319E of the Immigration Rules and Appendix E to the Immigration Rules. There are also provisions for children of PBS migrants at paragraphs 319F–319K of the Immigration Rules and Appendix E to the Immigration Rules. Specified documents are listed in the PBS (Dependant) Policy Guidance.

Cap on economic migration

7.31 On 28 June 2010 the Immigration Rules were amended with effect from 19 July 2010[53] so as to place interim limits on entry clearance applications and to increase the points threshold for attributes from 75 to 80 (with some exceptions) for Tier 1 (General) applicants. The new Rules introduced on 6 April 2010[54] and amended on 19 July 2010 favoured high-earners as opposed to those with higher education, as applicants with previous earnings of £150,000 or over would be awarded 80 points without having to demonstrate any qualifications. Given the reduction in points awarded for PhDs[55] and growing demand for higher income, switching into Tier 1 (General) would have been an uphill struggle for most recent graduates, teaching assistants or academics.

7.32 In line with the Government's effort 'to reduce net migration, to reduce any adverse social impacts of immigration, and to continue to attract the brightest and the best people to the UK',[56] the Rules were modified further on 15 July 2010

52 Save for Tier 1 (Post-Study Work) migrants.
53 Inserted by the Statement of Changes in Immigration Rules (HC 59).
54 Inserted by the Statement of Changes in Immigration Rules (HC 439).
55 From 6 April 2010.
56 *Migration Interim Limits (PBS Tier 1 and Tier 2)*, Impact Assessment, UK Border Agency, 28 June 2010, http://www.ukba.homeoffice.gov.uk/sitecontent/documents/aboutus/consultations/limits-on-non-eu-migration/ia-migration-interim-limit.pdf?view=Binary.

with effect from 19 July 2010[57] so as to empower the Secretary of State to limit the number of CoS available under the Tier 2 (General) migrant category, to be assigned to sponsors generally and to any specific sponsor in any one period with limits to be 'specified in the Points Based System guidance.'[58] This nod to Policy Guidance in the wording of paragraph 63A of Appendix A to the Immigration Rules was contrary to Sedley LJ's finding in *Pankina* that:

> '… the statutory recognition of rules which are to have the character, and, on appeal, the force of law requires such rules to be certain. That does not shut out extraneous forms of evidence of compliance, so long as these are themselves specified, but it does in my judgment shut out criteria affecting individuals' status and entitlements which … (a) have not themselves been tendered for parliamentary scrutiny, and (c) even if ascertainable at that point of time, may be changed without fresh scrutiny. As to (b), while the fact that the criterion absorbed into the rules comes from a policy document makes nonsense of the notion of policy.'

7.33 The intention behind the Rules laid on 15 July 2010 was to limit approvals 'at a level 1,300 (or around 6%) below 2009 levels for the equivalent period for this category'.[59] No public consultation was undertaken in relation to interim limits for Tier 1 and Tier 2 categories. They were implemented stealthily to prevent a surge or 'a spike in intake of applications'.[60] One of the risks identified in the impact assessment paper associated with interim limits is that 'some applicants, who will view Tiers 1 and 2 as "too difficult" to get into, will then displace into other routes.' One such possibility was, of course, the student route.

57 Paragraph 63A, Appendix A inserted by the Statement of Changes in Immigration Rules (HC 96).

58 Paragraph 63A, Appendix A inserted by the Statement of Changes in Immigration Rules (HC 96).

59 *Migration Interim Limits (PBS Tier 1 and Tier 2)*, Impact Assessment, UK Border Agency, 28 June 2010, http://www.ukba.homeoffice.gov.uk/sitecontent/documents/aboutus/consultations/limits-on-non-eu-migration/ia-migration-interim-limit.pdf?view=Binary. Some publications refer to 1,300 as being approximately 5%, one of these being *Coalition commits to impose migration limit*, UK Border Agency, 28 June 2010, http://www.ukba.homeoffice.gov.uk/sitecontent/newsarticles/2010/268071/43-impose-migration-limit1. The interim limit was further discussed in the Government's statement made on 28 June 2010 and noted in *'Immigration limit for Tier 2 (General) of the points-based system'*, UK Border Agency, 28 June 2010, http://www.ukba.homeoffice.gov.uk/sitecontent/newsfragments/28-intro-limit-for-t2-pbs and *'Immigration limit for Tier 1 (General) of the points-based system'*, UK Border Agency, 19 July 2010, http://www.ukba.homeoffice.gov.uk/sitecontent/newsfragments/27-intro-limit-for-t1-pbs.

60 *Migration Interim Limits (PBS Tier 1 and Tier 2)*, Impact Assessment, UK Border Agency, 28 June 2010, http://www.ukba.homeoffice.gov.uk/sitecontent/documents/aboutus/consultations/limits-on-non-eu-migration/ia-migration-interim-limit.pdf?view=Binary. Some publications refer to 1,300 as being approximately 5%, one of these being *Coalition commits to impose migration limit*, UK Border Agency, 28 June 2010, http://www.ukba.homeoffice.gov.uk/sitecontent/newsarticles/2010/268071/43-impose-migration-limit1. The interim limit was further discussed in the Government's statement made on 28 June 2010 and noted in *'Immigration limit for Tier 2 (General) of the points-based system'*, UK Border Agency, 28 June 2010, http://www.ukba.homeoffice.gov.uk/sitecontent/newsfragments/28-intro-limit-for-t2-pbs and *'Immigration limit for Tier 1 (General) of the points-based system'*, UK Border Agency, 19 July 2010, http://www.ukba.homeoffice.gov.uk/sitecontent/newsfragments/27-intro-limit-for-t1-pbs.

7.34 On 28 June 2010 the Government began a period of consultation with regard to annual limits. Following the consultation[61] which ended on 17 September 2010, and advice provided by the Migration Advisory Committee, the Secretary of State intended to impose annual limits on economic migration and other changes to drive down the number of non-EU/EEA migrants coming to the United Kingdom from April 2011.[62] The consultation paper, *'Limits on non-EU economic migration,* proposed parameters of the intended quotas. In the meantime, the Migration Advisory Committee conducted its own consultation on the levels of limits entitled *Consultation by the Migration Advisory Committee on the level of an annual limit on economic migration to the UK.*[63]

7.35 The interim cap on immigration was the focus of a judicial review to which the Joint Council for Welfare of Immigrants ('JCWI') was a party. The Government vowed to 'rigorously defend'[64] the action. On 21 October 2010 it was announced that the monthly limit for Tier 1 (General) applications made at overseas posts had been reached. Such an announcement was to be published monthly. As a result of its consultation, the Migration Advisory Committee released its report on 'Limits on Tier 1 and Tier 2 for 2011/12 and supporting policies'[65] in November 2010. The Committee reiterated that the evidence received by it weighed heavily in favour of protecting Tier 2. At the same time at paragraphs 10.13–10.14 of the report it made the following suggestions for Tier 1 (General) in order to meet the Government policy objectives:

- 'a **reduction** in the number of entry clearance visas issued, compared to 2009, in the range of **3,150 to 6,300**; and
- a **limit** on the number of Tier 1 entry clearance visas in the range of **8,000 to 11,100** in 2011/12.

...

- periodically recalibrating the Tier 1 General points table in order to ensure that it appropriately selects the most skilled migrants; and
- introducing the requirement of being employed in skilled graduate-level occupations at the extension stage.
- revising the methodology for updating the multipliers and putting in place new salary multipliers as quickly as possible.'

61 ILPA provided a notable response to the Migration Advisory Committee's consultation on 7 September 2010, http://www.ilpa.org.uk/.

62 *Coalition commits to impose migration limit*, UK Border Agency, 28 June 2010, http://www.ukba.homeoffice.gov.uk/sitecontent/newsarticles/2010/268071/43-impose-migration-limit1.

63 See http://www.ukba.homeoffice.gov.uk/sitecontent/documents/aboutus/workingwithus/mac/mac-consultation-annual-limit/0610/mac-consultation-annual-limit?view=Binary.

64 *Minister defends immigration limit,* UK Border Agency, 24 September 2010, http://www.ukba.homeoffice.gov.uk/sitecontent/newsarticles/2010/sept/66-immigration-limit.

65 *Limits on Tier 1 and Tier 2 for 2011/12 and supporting policies*, Migration Advisory Committee, November 2010, http://www.ukba.homeoffice.gov.uk/sitecontent/documents/aboutus/workingwithus/mac/mac-limits-t1-t2/report.pdf?view=Binary

7.36 *Looking ahead: Where do I go from here?*

7.36 On 1 November 2010 the UKBA published refined criteria to be applied to requests for initial or additional allocation of Certificates of Sponsorship (using application form COS(AR)).[66] This apparent concession by the Government had undermined the going judicial review. JCWI carried on with the challenge which resulted in the interim cap (the manner in which it was implemented) being declared invalid on 17 December 2010.[67] The Secretary of State changed the Immigration Rules on 21 December 2010 (HC 698) to quantify the size of the cap (10,832) to run until 5 April 2011 inclusive (by inserting paragraphs 63B–63K into Appendix A to the Immigration Rules). On 23 December 2010 the Secretary of State closed down the entry clearance route for Tier 1 (General) migrants. From 6 April 2011 Tier 1 (General) became a residual category. An Annual limit was introduced from 6 April 2011 by paragraph 80A of the Immigration Rules.[68] In the period between 6 April 2011 and 5 April 2012 the Secretary of State will be entitled to limit the allocation of CoS to sponsors under Tier 4 (General) to 20,700.

Tier 1 (General)

7.37 On 23 November 2010 the Government expressed an intention to delete this category in 2011 stating that

> 'The old tier one – supposedly the route for the best and the brightest – has not attracted highly-skilled workers. At least 30% of Tier One migrants work in low-skilled occupations such as stacking shelves, driving taxis or working as security guards and some don't have a job at all. So we will close the Tier One general route.
>
> Instead, I want to use tier one to attract more investors, entrepreneurs and people of exceptional talent.'[69]

7.38 As stated above, on 23 December 2010 this route was closed to overseas applicants by virtue of the Statement of Changes in Immigration Rules (HC 698). In its Statement of Intent published on 16 February 2011 the UKBA indicated that those migrants who are not already in Tier 1 (General) will not be able to switch into it from 6 April 2011. Those with leave under Tier 1 (Post Study Work), its predecessor categories or Tier 4 will be able to switch into Tier 2 (General) instead. Tier 1 (General) will remain open for those who have existing leave to enter or remain under Tier 1 (General), the Highly Skilled Migrant Programme or the

66 *Requests for additional certificates of sponsorship: refined criteria*, UK Border Agency, 1 November 2010, http://www.ukba.homeoffice.gov.uk/sitecontent/newsarticles/2010/nov/01-additional-cos.

67 *Joint Council for the Welfare of Immigrants, R (on the application of) v Secretary of State for the Home Department* [2010] EWHC 3524 (Admin).

68 Statement of Changes in Immigration Rules (HC 863).

69 *Immigration limits oral statement*, Home Office, 23 November 2010, http://www.homeoffice.gov.uk/publications/parliamentary-business/oral-statements/limits-statement/.

deleted categories for writers, composers and artists, and self-employed lawyers (former concession outside the Rules) allowing them to extend their stay in the United Kingdom.[70] Nonetheless, it is necessary to deal with Tier 1 (General) as part of this chapter while it is still in force even in a residual capacity.

After 23 December 2010 but prior to 6 April 2011

7.39 In this section, reference is made to the Immigration Rules as they were when amended by the Statement of Changes in Immigration Rules (HC 698) in force from 23 December 2010 and to the Tier 1 (General) Policy Guidance (for applications made on or after 23 December 2010).

7.40 Tier 1 (General), a natural successor of the Highly Skilled Migrant Programme, was introduced in three stages: on 29 February 2008 for highly skilled migrants applying in the UK, in India from 1 April 2008, and from 30 June 2008 throughout the world.[71] Its purpose was to encourage highly skilled migrants who wish to work, or become self-employed in the United Kingdom.[72] Paragraph 6 of the Immigration Rules described a Tier 1 (General) migrant as 'a migrant who is granted leave under paragraphs 245A to 245D of these Rules.'[73]

7.41 Requirements for entry clearance or leave to remain were set out in paragraph 245C of the Immigration Rules, paragraphs 1 to 31 of Appendix A (applicants must score 75 or 80 points), paragraphs 1 to 2 of Appendix B (applicants must score 10 points) and paragraphs 1 to 3 of Appendix C (applicants must score 10 points). Prior to 23 December 2010, pursuant to paragraph 245D of the Immigration Rules entry clearance was granted for a period of 2 years. Leave to remain was granted for a period of 3 years (to those who were last granted leave as Tier 1 (General) migrants under the Rules in place on or after 6 April 2010, as HSMP migrants, innovators, investors, self-employed lawyers, writers, composers or artists).[74] A Tier 1 (General) migrant, according to paragraph 245D(d)(iii) of the Immigration Rules, could not be employed as a doctor or dentist in training 'unless the applicant:

1) has obtained a degree in medicine or dentistry at bachelor's level or above from a UK institution that is a UK recognised or listed body, or which holds a sponsor licence under Tier 4 of the Points Based System; or

70 *Tier 2 of the Points Based System, Statement of Intent, Transitional Measures and Indefinite Leave to Remain*, UK Border Agency, February 2011, http://www.ukba.homeoffice.gov.uk/sitecontent/documents/aboutus/reports/soi-tier2/.

71 Inserted by the Statements of Changes in Immigration Rules (HC 321) and (HC 607).

72 Prior to 6 April 2011, paragraph 245A, Immigration Rules (HC 395) and paragraph 44 of Tier 1 (General) Policy Guidance (for applications made on or after 23 December 2010).

73 This definition does not reflect the changes inserted by the Statement of Changes in Immigration Rules (HC 698), (HC 863) and (HC 908).

74 To all others leave to remain will be granted for a period of 2 years.

2) is applying for leave to remain and has, or has last been granted, entry clearance, leave to enter or leave to remain that was not subject to any condition restricting their employment, and has been employed during that leave as a Doctor or Dentist in Training.'

7.42 In order to be exempt, applicants must satisfy the evidential requirements set out at Annex D of the Policy Guidance. Tier 1 (General) migrants also could not be employed as professional sportspersons (paragraph 245D(d)(iv) of the Immigration Rules).

7.43 Tier 1 (General) leads to settlement and indefinite leave to remain is granted to those who have spent a continuous period of 5 years (unless the application is made under the terms of the HSMP ILR Judicial Review Policy Document) lawfully in the United Kingdom with the most recent period of leave being Tier 1 (General) in a combination with a number of other categories (paragraph 245E of the Immigration Rules). Paragraph 245E(c) stated that:

> 'The applicant must be economically active in the UK, in employment or self-employment or both.'

7.44 Transitional arrangements were in place for those who on 29 February 2008 were in the United Kingdom, on 1 April 2008 in India, or on 30 June 2008 elsewhere and were in the process of applying to become highly skilled migrants (paragraph 245F of the Immigration Rules). Paragraph 1A of Appendix A to the Immigration Rules offered transitional arrangements for applicants who enrolled on eligible Master of Business Administration programmes listed in paragraph 58A of the same Appendix on or before 29 June 2008 and submit their application within 12 months of completing their qualifying degree.

7.45 The points scoring requirements were as follows:

Attributes (Appendix A)

Applicants must score:

- at least 75 points provided they were last granted leave as a Tier 1 (General) migrant, a writer, composer or artist, or as a self-employer lawyer; or
- at least 80 points if the applicant does not fall under the above exception.

Qualifying MBA graduates applying under the transitional arrangements would be awarded 80 points for attributes (paragraph 1A of Appendix A).

7.46 Attributes for Tier 1 (General) migrants are broken down into four criteria, namely, age, qualifications, previous earnings and UK experience with variable points available in each one. Points value differed depending on whether the applicant is making an initial or extension application. Due to the historical aspect of conditions attributable to extension applications, the requirements related to attributes are drawn from the Immigration Rules and Policy Guidance (for applications made on or after 23 December 2010).

5–20 points	**Age**			
	Initial Applications		Extension Applications by applicants who have or were last granted leave as Tier 1 (General) migrants, writers, composers or artists, or self-employed lawyers under the Rules in place before 6 April 2010	
	below 30	20 points	Below 31	20 points
	30–34	10 points	31–32	10 points
	35–39	5 points	33–34	5 points
			Extension Applications by Highly Skilled Migrants	
			below 30	20 points
			30–31	10 points
			32–33	5 points
			Extension Applications by applicants who were granted initial leave under Tier 1 (General) under the Rules in place after 5 April 2010	
			below 32	20 points
			32–36	10 points
			37–41	5 points
30–45 points[75] **30–50 points**[76]	**Qualifications**[77]			
	Initial Applications		Extension Applications by applicants who have or were last granted leave as a Highly Skilled Migrant, Tier 1 (General) migrants, writers, composers or artists, or self-employed lawyers under the Rules in place before 31 March 2009	

5–20 points	**Age**			
	PhD	45 points	PhD	50 points
	Master's degree	35 points	Master's degree	35 points
	Bachelor's degree	30 points	Bachelor's degree	30 points
			Extension Applications by applicants who have or were last granted leave as a Tier 1 (General) migrant under the Rules in place between 31 March 2009 and 5 April 2010	
			PhD	50 points
			Master's degree	35 points
			Extension Applications by applicants who have or were last granted leave as a Tier 1 (General) migrant under the Rules in place after 5 April 2010 and including the Rules in place after 19 July 2010	
			PhD	45 points
			Master's degree	35 points
			Bachelor's degree	30 points
5–80 points	**Previous earnings**[78]			
	Initial Applications		**Extension Applications** **Extension Applications by applicants who have or were last granted leave as a Highly Skilled Migrant, Tier 1 (General) migrants, writers, composers or artists, or self-employed lawyers under the Rules in place before 31 March 2009**	
	£25,000–£29,999	5 points	£16,000–£17,999	5 points
	£30,000–£34,999	15 points	£18,000–£19,999	10 points
	£35,000–£39,999	20 points	£20,000–£22,999	15 points
	£40,000–£49,999	25 points	£23,000–£25,999	20 points
	£50,000–£54,999	30 points	£26,000–£28,999	25 points
	£55,000–£64,999	35 points	£29,000–£31,999	30 points
	£65,000–£74,999	40 points	£32,000–£34,999	35 points
	£75,000–£149,999	45 points	£35,000–£39,999	40 points
	£150,000 or more	80 points	£40,000 or more	45 points

5–20 points	**Age**		
		Extension Applications by applicants who have or were last granted leave as a Tier 1 (General) migrant under the Rules in place between 31 March 2009 and 5 April 2010	
		£20,000–£22,999	15 points
		£23,000–£25,999	20 points
		£26,000–£28,999	25 points
		£29,000–£31,999	30 points
		£32,000–£34,999	35 points
		£35,000–£39,999	40 points
		£40,000 or more	45 points
		Extension Applications by applicants who have or were last granted leave as a Tier 1 (General) migrant under the Rules in place after 5 April 2010 and including the Rules in place after 19 July 2010	
		£25,000–£29,999	5 points
		£30,000–£34,999	15 points
		£35,000–£39,999	20 points
		£40,000–£49,999	25 points
		£50,000–£54,999	30 points
		£55,000–£64,999	35 points
		£65,000–£74,999	40 points
		£75,000–£149,999	45 points
		£150,000 or more	**75/80[79] points**
5 points	**UK experience**		
	Initial Applications	Extension Applications by applicants who have or were last granted leave as Tier 1 (General) migrants, writers, composers or artists, or self-employed lawyers under the Rules in place before 6 April 2010	
	To claim points applicants must have: • successfully scored points for previous earning at least £25,000 of which must have been made in the UK; or • undertaken a full-time course of study in the UK of at least one full academic year and been awarded a qualification at bachelor's degree level or above which should have been awarded no more than five years before making the application.	Applicants may claim for previous earnings if: • they scored points in the section for pervious earnings; and • the relevant earnings were made in the UK.	

5–20 points	**Age**	
		Extension Applications by applicants who have or were last granted leave as a Tier 1 (General) migrant under the Rules in place after 5 April 2010 and including the Rules in place after 19 July 2010
		Applicants may claim for previous earnings if: • they scored points in the section for pervious earnings; and • the relevant earnings were made in the UK.

English language (Appendix B)

7.47 Applicants must score 10 points for English language. They could demonstrate their competence in one of the ways described below with reference to the Immigration Rules and by providing evidence specified in the Policy Guidance. According to paragraph 2 of Appendix B, '10 points will only be awarded to an applicant in Tier 1 (General) or Tier 1 (Entrepreneur) if the applicant:

(a) has the level of English language shown in the table below and:

(i) provides an original English language test certificate[80] from an English language test provider[81] approved by the Secretary of State for these purposes, which clearly shows the applicant's name; the qualification obtained (which must meet or exceed the level shown in the table below); and the date of the award, or

(ii) has obtained an academic qualification (not a professional or vocational qualification) which is deemed by UK NARIC[82] to meet or exceed the recognised standard of a Bachelor's or Master's degree or a PhD in the UK, and which UK NARIC has confirmed was taught or researched in English to the level indicated in the table below, and provides the specified documents, or

75 For initial applications.

76 For extension applications.

77 Qualifications below include equivalent vocational or professional qualifications.

78 From salaried employment and self-employment. Overseas earnings can be converted using OANDA at http://www.oanda.com/currency/classic-converter/.

79 75 points in line with the Rules in place after 6 April 2010 and 80 points in line with the Rules in place after 19 July 2010.

80 Those waiting to sit their test must give the UKBA the date of their test within 10 working days of submitting the application and once the results are received these should be provided within 5 working days.

81 The current list of test providers can be found at: http://www.ukba.homeoffice.gov.uk/sitecontent/applicationforms/pbs/approvedenglishtests.pdf.

82 National Academic Recognition Information Centre for the United Kingdom, http://www.naric.org.uk/.

Level of English language	**Points**
A knowledge of English equivalent to level C1 of the Council of Europe's Common European Framework for Language Learning[83] or above	10

(a) is a national of one of the following countries:
Antigua and Barbuda
Australia
The Bahamas
Barbados
Belize
Canada
Dominica
Grenada
Guyana
Jamaica
New Zealand
St Kitts and Nevis
St Lucia
St Vincent and the Grenadines
Trinidad and Tobago
USA,
and provides the specified documents, or

(b) has obtained an academic qualification (not professional or vocational qualification), which is deemed by UK NARIC to meet or exceed the recognised standard of a Bachelor's or Master's degree or a PhD in the UK, from an educational establishment in one of the following countries:
Antigua and Barbuda
Australia
The Bahamas
Barbados
Belize
Dominica
Grenada
Guyana
Ireland
Jamaica
New Zealand
St Kitts and Nevis

83 Council of Europe, CEFR, http://www.coe.int/t/dg4/linguistic/CADRE_EN.asp.

St Lucia
St Vincent and The Grenadines
Trinidad and Tobago
the UK
the USA,
and provides specified documents, or

(c) has ever been granted leave as a Tier 1 (General) Migrant or a Tier 1 (Entrepreneur) Migrant or Business person, or

(d) has ever been granted leave as a Highly Skilled Migrant, if that leave was granted under these Rules at a time when they included the changes which came into force on 5 December 2006.'

Maintenance (funds) (Appendix C)

7.48 An applicant applying for entry clearance or leave to remain as a Tier 1 (General) migrant must score 10 points for funds. If the funds were obtained by the applicant when he/she was in the United Kingdom, the funds must have been obtained while the applicant had valid permission to stay and was not in breach of any conditions attached to the leave. Therefore, students whose employment is restricted should be mindful of this stipulation. Dependants of Tier 1 (General) migrants would also have to demonstrate sufficient funds in their own right. Pursuant to the judgement in Secretary of State for the Home Department v Pankina [2010] EWCA Civ 719, the Secretary of State conceded that historical applications for entry clearance or leave to remain made by migrants and their dependants up to and including 22 July 2010 would be eligible for reconsideration in line with the resulting policy document.[84]

7.49 With effect from 23 July 2010 Appendix C to the Immigration Rules was amended to lay down a requirement at paragraph 1A, previously specified in Policy Guidance only, to have the maintenance funds 'for a consecutive 90-day period of time, ending no earlier than one calendar month before the date of application.'[85] This requirement relates to those applying for entry clearance, leave to enter or remain in the United Kingdom as Tier 1 (other than Tier 1 (Investor)), Tiers 2 and Tier 5 migrants from 23 July 2010.

84 *Points-Based System Maintenance (Funds): Policy Document*, 23 July 2010, UK Border Agency, http://www.ukba.homeoffice.gov.uk/sitecontent/documents/news/pbs-pol-guid-maintenance.pdf.

85 Paragraph 1A(b) inserted by the Statement of Changes in Immigration Rules, HC 382, with effect from 23 July 2010.

10 points	**Maintenance (funds)** **10 points will only be awarded if an applicant:**			
	Application for entry clearance		**Application for leave to remain**	
	(a) applying for entry clearance, has the level of funds shown in the table below and provides the specified documents, or		(b) applying for leave to remain, has the level of funds shown in the table below and provides the specified documents.[86]	
	£2,800	**10 points**	**£800**	**10 points**

AFTER 6 APRIL 2011

7.50 The Statement of Changes in Immigration Rules (HC 863) was laid before Parliament on 16 March 2011 making Tier 1 (General) a residual sub-category closed for newcomers. The new Rules came into force on 6 April 2011 and were further amended by the Statement of Changes in Immigration Rules (HC 908) from 21 April 2011. Due to the general reshuffle and renumbering of paragraphs within Part 6A of the Immigration Rules, Tier 1 (General) provisions are dealt with by paragraphs 245C to 245CE of the Immigration Rules. The point scoring requirements are set out in paragraphs 7 to 34 of Appendix A to the Immigration Rules, paragraphs 1 to 2 of Appendix B to the Immigration Rules and 1 to 3 of Appendix C to the Immigration Rules. The Rules are supported by Tier 1 (General) Policy Guidance (for applications made on or after 6 April 2011, version 04/11).

7.51 Pursuant to paragraph 245CA of the Immigration Rules applicants who have or have last been granted entry clearance, leave to enter or remain as Tier 1 (General) migrants, highly skilled migrants, writers, composers or artists or self-employed lawyers can apply for extension of stay under this sub-category. No other type of migrant can switch into this category.

7.52 In order to qualify for leave to remain, applicants must score:

- 75 points under paragraphs 7 to 34 of Appendix A if they have or have had leave as Tier 1 (General) migrants, highly skilled migrants, writers, composers or artists or self-employed lawyers under the Immigration Rules in place before 19 July 2010 and have not been granted leave in any other categories since then; or
- 80 points under paragraphs 7 to 34 of Appendix A in all other cases; and
- 10 points under paragraphs 1 to 2 of Appendix B; and
- 10 points under paragraphs 1 to 3 of Appendix C.

86 Paragraph 2, Appendix C (Maintenance (Funds)), Immigration Rules (HC 395).

7.53 *Looking ahead: Where do I go from here?*

7.53 Leave to remain will be granted subject to applicants having no recourse to public funds, registering with the police, not working as doctors or dentists in training unless they can meet stipulated requirements, and not working as professional sportspersons:

- for a period of 2 years to applicants who have or was last granted leave as a Tier 1 (General) migrant under the Immigration Rules in place before 6 April 2010; or
- for a period of 3 years in all other cases.

7.54 In order to qualify for indefinite leave to remain pursuant to paragraph 245CD of the Immigration Rules, Tier 1 (General) migrants must meet the following requirements:

- must have a continuous period of 5 years lawful leave of which the most recent must have been spent with leave as a Tier 1 (General) migrant in any combination with categories such as Tier 1 (General) migrant, highly skilled migrant, worker permit holder, innovator, self-employer lawyer, writer composer or artist, Tier 2 (General) migrant, Tier 2 (Minister of Religion) migrant, Tier 2 (Sportsperson) migrant, or Tier 2 (Intra-Company Transfer) migrant;[87]
- must not fall for refusal under the general grounds of refusal and must not be illegal entrants;
- must score 75 points under paragraphs 7 to 34 of Appendix A if they have or have had leave as Tier 1 (General) migrants, highly skilled migrants, writers, composers or artists or self-employed lawyers under the Immigration Rules in place before 19 July 2010 and have not been granted leave in any other categories since then; or
- 80 points under paragraphs 7 to 34 of Appendix A in all other cases; and
- must not have any unspent convictions within the meaning of the Rehabilitation of Offenders Act 1974;
- must have sufficient knowledge of the English language and life in the United Kingdom pursuant to paragraph 33BA of the Immigration Rules unless they are under the age of 18 years or aged 65 and over at the time of making the application.

7.55 If the application is being made under the terms of the HSMP ILR Judicial Review Policy document, applicants:

87 Provided that the continuous period of 5 years lawful leave includes a period of leave granted to the applicant as a Tier 2 (Intra-Company Transfer) migrant under the Immigration Rules in force prior to 6 April 2010.

- must have a continuous period of 4 years lawful leave[88] of which the most recent must have been spent with leave as a Tier 1 (General) migrant in any combination with categories such as Tier 1 (General) migrant, highly skilled migrant, worker permit holder, or innovator;
- must not fall for refusal under the general grounds of refusal and must not be illegal entrants;
- must be economically active in the United Kingdom, in employment or self-employment, or both;
- are exempt from the requirement to have no unspent convictions within the meaning of the Rehabilitation of Offenders Act 1974;
- are exempt from having to demonstrate sufficient knowledge of the English language and life in the United Kingdom pursuant to paragraph 33BA of the Immigration Rules.

Paragraph 245CE of the Immigration Rules deals with transitional arrangements for highly skilled migrants. Further policy governing applications for settlement is contained in Chapter 6A, IDIs.[89]

Attributes (Appendix A)

7.56 Paragraphs 7–9 of Appendix A to the Immigration Rules deal with the general point scoring requirements in the following way:

- applicants applying for leave to remain or indefinite leave to remain must score 75 points if they have or have had leave as Tier 1 (General) migrants, highly skilled migrants, writers, composers or artists or self-employed lawyers under the Immigration Rules in place before 19 July 2010 and have not been granted leave in any other categories since then;
- applicants applying for leave to remain or indefinite leave to remain must score 80 points if they do not fall within the above criteria;
- applicants applying for leave to remain or indefinite leave to remain under the terms of the HSMP ILR Judicial Review Policy document are not required to score points for attributes.

The notes in Appendix A deal with the substance of each point scoring requirement: qualifications (paragraphs 13–17), previous earnings (paragraphs 18–30), UK experience (paragraphs 31–32) and age (paragraphs 33–34).[90]

88 If the applicant applied to join the Highly Skilled Migrant Programme between 3 April 2006 and 7 November 2006, then they must have a continuous period of 5 years lawful leave in the United Kingdom.

89 Section 1, Chapter 6A, http://www.ukba.homeoffice.gov.uk/sitecontent/documents/policyandlaw/IDIs/idichapter6a/section1/section1.pdf?view=Binary.

90 Provisions that were previously contained solely in the Tier 1 (General) Policy Guidance have been brought into Appendix A making them more resistant to a *Pankina* type challenge.

7.57 Table 2 (the contents of which are reproduced below exactly) makes provisions for those applying for leave to remain or indefinite leave to remain where the applicants have or have had leave as Tier 1 (General) migrants, highly skilled migrants, writers, composers or artists or self-employed lawyers under the Immigration Rules in place before 6 April 2010 and have not been granted leave in any other categories since then.

Qualification	**Points**	**Previous earnings**	**Points**	**UK Experience**	**Points**	**Age (at date of application for first grant)**	**Points**
Bachelor's degree (see paragraph 13 below)[91]	30	£16,000–£17,999.99 (see paragraph 18 below)[92]	5	If £16,000 or more of the previous earnings for which points are claimed were earned in the UK	5	Under 28 years of age	20

91 Paragraph 13 of Appendix A states that an applicant will be awarded no points for a Bachelor's degree if:
'(a) his last grant of entry clearance was as a Tier 1 (General) Migrant under the rules in place between 31 March 2009 and 5 April 2010, or
(b)(i) he has had leave to remain as a Tier 1 (General) Migrant under the rules in place between 31 March 2009 and 5 April 2010, and
(ii) his previous entry clearance, leave to enter or leave to remain before that leave was not as a Highly Skilled Migrant, as a Writer, Composer or artist, as a self-employed lawyer, or as a Tier 1 (General) Migrant.'

92 Paragraph 18 of Appendix A states that an applicant will be awarded no points for previous earnings of less than £20,000 if:
'(a) his last grant of entry clearance was as a Tier 1 (General) Migrant under the rules in place between 31 March 2009 and 5 April 2010, or
(b)(i) he has had leave to remain as a Tier 1 (General) Migrant under the rules in place between 31 March 2009 and 5 April 2010, and
(ii) his previous entry clearance, leave to enter or remain before that leave was not as a Highly Skilled Migrant, as a Writer, Composer or artist, as a self-employed lawyer, or as a Tier 1 (General) Migrant.'

93 Paragraph 18 of Appendix A states that an applicant will be awarded no points for previous earnings of less than £20,000 if:
'(a) his last grant of entry clearance was as a Tier 1 (General) Migrant under the rules in place between 31 March 2009 and 5 April 2010, or
(b)(i) he has had leave to remain as a Tier 1 (General) Migrant under the rules in place between 31 March 2009 and 5 April 2010, and
(ii) his previous entry clearance, leave to enter or remain before that leave was not as a Highly Skilled Migrant, as a Writer, Composer or artist, as a self-employed lawyer, or as a Tier 1 (General) Migrant.

Qualification	Points	Previous earnings	Points	UK Experience	Points	Age (at date of application for first grant)	Points
Master's degree	35	£18,000–£19,999.99 (see paragraph 18 below)[93]	10	If £16,000 or more of the previous earnings for which points are claimed were earned in the UK		28 or 29 years of age	10
PhD	50	£20,000–£22,999.99	15			30 or 31 years of age	5
		£23,000–£25,999.99	20				
		£26,000–£28,999.99	25				
		£29,000–£31,999.99	30				
		£32,000–£34,999.99	35				
		£35,000–£39,999.99	40				
		£40,000 or more	45				

7.58 Table 3 (the contents of which are reproduced below exactly) goes on to make provisions for all other applications.

Qualification	Points	Previous earnings	Points	UK Experience	Points	Age (at date of application for first grant)	Points
Bachelor's degree	30	£25,000–£29,999.99	5	If £25,000 or more of the previous earnings for which points are claimed were earned in the UK	5	Under 30 years of age	20
Master's degree	35	£30,000–£34,999.99	15			30 to 34 years of age	10

Qualification	**Points**	**Previous earnings**	**Points**	**UK Experience**	**Points**	**Age (at date of application for first grant)**	**Points**
PhD	45	£35,000–£39,999.99	20			35 to 39 years of age	5
		£40,000–£49,999.99	25				
		£50,000–£54,999.99	30				
		£55,000–£64,999.99	35				
		£65,000–£74,999.99	40				
		£75,000–£149,999.99	45				
		£150,000 or more	80[94]				

English language (Appendix B)

7.59 Applicants applying for leave to remain must score 10 points under paragraphs 1 to 2 of Appendix B. Please see the section referring to the provisions prior to 6 April 2011. Paragraph 2(a) of Appendix B has been amended. No amendments have been made to paragraphs 2(b)–(e) of Appendix B as cited above. Paragraph 2(a) of Appendix B states the following:

'(a) has the level of English language shown in the table below and:
  (i) provides an original English language test certificate from an English language test provider approved by the Secretary of State for these purposes, which is within its validity date and clearly shows:
    (1) the applicant's name;
    (2) the qualification obtained, which must meet or exceed the level shown in the table below in all four components (reading, writing, speaking and listening), unless the applicant

94 In line with the Rules in place after 6 April 2010 (amended by the Statement of Changes in Immigration Rules (HC 439) laid before Parliament on 18 March 2010) 75 points would be awarded for previous earnings of £150,000 or more. In line with the Rules in place after 19 July 2010 (Table 2 of Appendix A was further amended by the Statement of Changes in Immigration Rules (HC 59) laid before Parliament on 28 June 2010) 80 points would be awarded for previous earnings of £150,000 or more.

was exempted from sitting a component on the basis of his disability,[95] and

(3) the date of the award, or

(ii) has obtained an academic qualification (not a professional or vocational qualification) which is deemed by UK NARIC to meet the recognised standard of a Bachelor's degree in the UK, and:

(1) provides the specified evidence as set out in the appropriate Tier 1 guidance, published on the UK Border Agency website, to show he has the qualification, and

(2) UK NARIC has confirmed that the degree was taught or researched in English to level C1 of the Council of Europe's Common European Framework for Language learning or above, or'

7.60 Paragraphs 128–155 of the Tier 1 (General) Policy Guidance deal with English language assessment and specified documents which must be provided to claim points. As far as English language tests are concerned, applicants will need to use the list of approved English language tests published at: http://www.ukba.homeoffice.gov.uk/sitecontent/applicationforms/new-approved-english-tests.pdf.

Maintenance (funds) (Appendix C)

7.61 Applicants applying for leave to remain must score 10 points under paragraphs 1 to 3 of Appendix C. Please see the section referring to the provisions prior to 6 April 2011 as these remain unchanged. However, paragraph 1A of Appendix C has been amended to include new provisions related to

- the funds being in one or more foreign currencies;
- the funds being under the applicant's own control on the date of application and during specified period (as consecutive 90-day period of time for Tier 1 (General) migrants);
- each applicant meeting the requirements set out in Appendices C and E where the main applicant is applying together with dependants failing which all the applications will be refused.

7.62 Applicants and their dependants need to submit for biometric data collection at a time specified by the UKBA, depending on whether their application is made by post, courier or at a Public Enquiry Office. If their application is successful,

95 Paragraph 138 of the Tier 1 (General) Policy Guidance states that 'applicants with disabilities (for example, hearing difficulties) are not exempt from the English language requirement. They should contact a test provider for details of support that can be provided while taking the test.'

applicants and their dependants will be issued with biometric residence permits. Applications for extension of leave under Tier 1 (General) can be made using a Tier 1 (General) application form either by post, courier or at a Public Enquiry Office at a cost[96] of £1,000 (for a main applicant applying by post or courier) or £1,300 (for a main applicant applying at a Public Enquiry Office). Applications can also be made using the UKBA 'Apply Online' facility.[97] Dependants, applying at the same time as the main applicant, have to pay £500 for postal applications and £650 for applications made at a Public Enquiry Office, unless the dependant is a child aged 18 years or over. There are reduced fees for certain nationalities and their dependants. Dependants applying at a later date and applications made by dependent children aged 18 years or over will attract a charge of £550 for postal and courier applications and £850 for applications made in person at a Public Enquiry Office. Dependants must use a separate PBS (Dependant) application form.

Applications made by post should be sent to:	Applications made by courier should be sent to:
UK Border Agency Tier 1 PO Box 496 Durham DH99 1WQ	UK Border Agency Tier 1 Millburngate House Millburngate Durham DH97 1PA

Tier 1 (Entrepreneur)

7.63 Tier 1 (Entrepreneur) sub-category was inserted into the Immigration Rules by the Statement of Changes (HC 607) from 30 June 2008 phasing out businessperson and innovator categories. It was last revamped on 6 April 2011.[98] The purpose of Tier 1 (Entrepreneur) is to provide a route for migrants 'who wish to establish, join or take over one or more businesses in the UK' (paragraph 245D of the Immigration Rules). Paragraph 46 of the Tier 1 (Entrepreneur) Policy Guidance (for applications made on or after 6 April 2011, version 04/11) describes this sub-category as being 'for those investing in the United Kingdom by setting up or taking over, and being actively involved in the running of one or more businesses in the United Kingdom.'

96 Costs as at 6 April 2011.

97 http://apply.ukba.homeoffice.gov.uk/iapply.portal.

98 See the Statement of Changes in Immigration Rules (HC 863). Despite an indication given in the *Tier 2 of the Points Based System, Statement of Intent, Transitional Measures and Indefinite Leave to Remain*, UK Border Agency, February 2011, http://www.ukba.homeoffice.gov.uk/sitecontent/documents/aboutus/reports/soi-tier2/ that changes relating to Tier 1 (Investor) and Tier 1 (Entrepreneur) routes would be set out 'separately as soon as possible', no further announcement was made until the publication of the Statement of Changes in Immigration Rules (HC 863) on 16 March 2011.

7.64 A Tier 1 (Entrepreneur) migrant is defined in paragraph 6 of the Immigration Rules as 'a migrant who is granted leave under paragraphs 245H to 245N of these Rules.' This definition is out of date as since 6 April 2011 the Tier 1 (Entrepreneur) route is dealt with by paragraphs 245D to 245DF of the Immigration Rules. Under paragraph 245D(b) of the Immigration Rules 'business' is defined as 'an enterprise for (i) a sole trader, (ii) a partnership, or (iii) a company registered in the UK.' Paragraph 48 of Appendix A to the Immigration Rules clarifies this further by stating that a 'business will be considered to be in the UK if: (i) it is trading within the UK economy; (ii) it has a registered office in the UK, except where the applicant is registered with HM Revenue & Customs as self-employed and does not have a business office; (iii) it has a UK bank account; and (iv) it is subject to UK taxation.'

7.65 Requirements for entry clearance are set out in paragraph 245DB of the Immigration Rules and requirements for leave to remain are detailed in paragraph 245DD of the Immigration Rules. Applicants submitting initial or extension applications must score 75 points for attributes as set out in paragraphs 35 to 53 of Appendix A, 10 points for English language as per paragraphs 1 to 3 of Appendix B and have sufficient maintenance (funds) as set out in paragraphs 1 to 2 of Appendix C. In accordance with paragraph 245DC of the Immigration Rules entry clearance is granted for a period of 3 years and 4 months while leave to remain will be granted for a period of 2 years to applicants who have or were last granted leave as Tier 1 (Entrepreneur) migrants and for 3 years to everyone else (paragraph 245DE of the Immigration Rules). One of the key conditions of grant is 'no employment other than working for the business or businesses which he has established, joined or taken over.'[99]

7.66 As far as curtailment is concerned, paragraph 245DE(c) provides that:

> 'Without prejudice to the grounds for curtailment in paragraph 323 of these Rules, leave to enter or remain granted to a Tier 1 (Entrepreneur) Migrant may be curtailed if, within 6 months of the date specified in paragraph (d), the applicant has not done one or more of the following things:
> (i) registered with HM Revenue and Customs as self-employed,
> (ii) registered a new business in which he is a director, or
> (iii) registered as a director of an existing business.'

7.67 According to paragraph 245DE(d), the date referred to above is:

> '(i) the date of the applicant's entry to the UK, in the case of an applicant granted entry clearance as a Tier 1 (Entrepreneur) Migrant where there is evidence to establish the applicant's date of entry to the UK,

99 Paragraphs 245DC(iii) and 245DE(b)(iii) of the Immigration Rules.

(ii) the date of the grant of entry clearance to the applicant, in the case of an applicant granted entry clearance as a Tier 1 (Entrepreneur) Migrant where there is no evidence to establish the applicant's date of entry to the UK, or
(iii) the date of the grant of leave to remain to the applicant, in any other case.'

7.68 Paragraph 245DE(e) goes on to state that:

'Paragraph 245DE(c) does not apply where the applicant's last grant of leave prior to the grant of the leave that he currently has was as a Tier 1 (Entrepreneur) Migrant, a Businessperson or an Innovator.'

7.69 Applicants wishing to make the grade for indefinite leave to remain must meet the criteria set out in paragraph 245DF of the Immigration Rules:

- must not fall for refusal under the general grounds of refusal and must not be illegal entrants;
- must score 75 points under paragraphs 35 to 53 of Appendix A;
- must not have any unspent convictions within the meaning of the Rehabilitation of Offenders Act 1974;
- must have sufficient knowledge of the English language and life in the United Kingdom pursuant to paragraph 33BA of the Immigration Rules unless they are under the age of 18 years or aged 65 and over at the time of making the application.

Further policy governing applications for settlement is contained in Chapter 6A, IDIs.[100]

Attributes (Appendix A)

7.70 Applicants applying for entry clearance must score 75 points in line with Table 4 accompanied by notes in paragraphs 40 to 45 in Appendix A to the Immigration Rules whereas those making extension and indefinite leave to remain applications must comply with requirements set out in Tables 5 and 6 respectively concerned with investment and business activity. These tables are complemented by explanatory notes at paragraphs 46 to 53 in Appendix A of the Immigration Rules. The point scoring requirements are split into sections.

7.71 Applicants who wish to apply for entry clearance will need to demonstrate that:

- they have access to not less than £200,000;
- or have access to not less than £50,000 which has been funded by one or more:
  - registered venture capitalist firms regulated by the Financial Services Authority; or

100 Section 1, Chapter 6A, http://www.ukba.homeoffice.gov.uk/sitecontent/documents/policyandlaw/IDIs/idichapter6a/section1/section1.pdf?view=Binary.

- UK Entrepreneurial seed funding competition endorsed on the UK Trade and Investment website, or
- UK Government Departments and made available by the relevant Department for the specific purpose of establishing or expanding a business based in the United Kingdom;

- the money is held in one or more regulated financial institutions;
- the money is disposable in the United Kingdom.

7.72 This route is also available to pairs of entrepreneurs or entrepreneurial teams without the requirement for increased levels of funding, provided they both have equal control over the funds.

The entrepreneur is required:

- to invest or have invested on his behalf £200,000 or £50,000 (whichever applies) directly into one or more businesses in the United Kingdom; and
- to register within six months of entry with HM Revenue & Customs as self employed; or to register a new business in which they are a director; or to register as a director of an existing company;
- to remain engaged in business activity;
- to establish a new business or businesses that create the equivalent of at least two full time jobs for settled UK workers for at least 12 months; or to take over or join an established business and with their services or investment to create the equivalent of at least two full time jobs for settled UK workers for at least 12 months.

After five years of continuous lawful residence, applicants can qualify for indefinite leave to remain in the United Kingdom if they can show that they are still engaged in active business and meet the requirements as above.

7.73 Alternatively, a Tier 1 (Entrepreneur) migrant can fast-track their way to settlement without the need to make an intermediate extension application at any point after three years of leave provided that:

- the applicant has created 10 full time jobs for resident workers for at least 12 months; or
- the company has generated a total turnover of £5 million over the three-year period (for start-up companies), or an additional £5 million in turnover compared with the preceding three-year period (for existing businesses).

Migrants pursuing settlement after five years under the accelerated scheme or five years will be able to be absent from the United Kingdom for up to 180 days in any 12 calendar months. This is not currently reflected in nationality law or policy.

The wording below is taken from Tables 4, 5 and 6 in Appendix A to the Immigration Rules (reproduced below exactly).

7.74 *Looking ahead: Where do I go from here?*

TABLE 4 – FOR ENTRY CLEARANCE APPLICATIONS

7.74

Investment	**Points**
(a) The applicant has access to not less than £200,000, or (b) The applicant has access to not less than £50,000 from: (i) one or more registered venture capitalist firms regulated by the Financial Services Authority, (ii) one or more UK Entrepreneurial seed funding competitions which is listed as endorsed on the UK Trade & Investment website, or (iii) one or more UK Government Departments, and made available by the Department(s) for the specific purpose of establishing or expanding a UK business.	**25**
The money is held in one or more regulated financial institutions	**25**
The money is disposable in the UK	**25**

TABLE 5 – FOR LEAVE TO REMAIN APPLICATIONS

7.75

Investment and business activity	**Points**
The applicant has invested, or had invested on his behalf, not less than £200,000 (or £50,000 if, in his last grant of leave, he was awarded points for funds of £50,000 from one of the sources listed in Table 4 paragraph (b) above) in cash directly into one or more businesses in the UK.	**20**
The applicant has: (a) registered with HM revenue and Customs as self-employed, or (b) registered a new business in which he is a director, or (c) registered as a director of an existing business. Where the applicant's last grant of entry clearance, leave to enter or leave to remain was as a Tier 1 (Entrepreneur) Migrant, the above condition must have been met within 6 months of his entry to the UK (if he was granted entry clearance as a Tier 1 (Entrepreneur) Migrant and there is evidence to establish his date of arrival to the UK), or, in any other case, the date of the grant of leave to remain.	**20**
On a date no earlier than three months prior to the date of application, the applicant was: (a) registered with HM revenue and Customs as self-employed, or (b) registered a new business in which he is a director, or (c) registered as a director of an existing business.	**15**

Investment and business activity	**Points**
The applicant has: (a) established a new business or businesses that has or have created the equivalent of at least two new full time jobs for persons settled in the UK, or (b) taken over or invested in an existing business or businesses and his services or investment have resulted in a net increase in the employment provided by the business or businesses for persons settled in the UK by creating the equivalent of at least two new full time jobs. Where the applicant's last grant of entry clearance or leave to enter or remain was as a Tier 1 (Entrepreneur) Migrant, the jobs must have existed for at least 12 months of the period for which the previous leave was granted.	**20**

TABLE 6 – FOR INDEFINITE LEAVE TO REMAIN APPLICATIONS

7.76

Row	**Investment and business activity**	**Points**
1.	On a date no earlier than three months prior to the date of application, the applicant was: (a) registered with HM Revenue and Customs as self-employed, or (b) registered a new business in which he is a director, or (c) registered as a director of an existing business.	**20**
2.	The applicant has: (a) established a new UK business or businesses that has or have created the equivalent of X new full time jobs for persons settled in the UK, or (b) taken over or invested in an existing UK business or businesses and his services or investment have resulted in a net increase in the employment provided by the business or businesses for persons settled in the UK by creating the equivalent of X new full time jobs where X is at least 2. Where the applicant's last grant of entry clearance or leave to enter or remain was as a Tier 1 (Entrepreneur) Migrant, the jobs must have existed for at least 12 months of the period for which the previous leave was granted.	**20**

Row	Investment and business activity	Points
3.	The applicant has spent the specified continuous period lawfully in the UK, with absences from the UK of no more than 180 days in any 12 calendar months during that period. The specified period must have been spent with leave as a Tier 1 (Entrepreneur) Migrant, as a Businessperson and/or as an Innovator, of which the most recent period must have been spent with leave as a Tier (1) (Entrepreneur) Migrant. The specified continuous period is: (a) 3 years if the number of new full time jobs, X, referred to in row 2 above is at least 10, (b) 3 years if the applicant has: (i) established a new UK business that has had an income from business activity of at least £5 million during a 3 year period in which the applicant has had leave as a Tier 1 (Entrepreneur) Migrant, or (ii) taken over or invested in an existing UK business and his services or investment have resulted in a net increase in income from business activity to that business of £5 million during a 3 year period in which the applicant has had leave as a Tier 1 (Entrepreneur) Migrant, when compared to the immediately preceding 3 year period, or (c) 5 years in all other cases.	**35**

English language (Appendix B) and Maintenance (funds) (Appendix C)

7.77 Tier 1 (Entrepreneur) migrants must score 10 points in each of these point scoring categories by satisfying the same requirements as Tier 1 (General) migrants.

7.78 From 6 April 2011 entrepreneurs wishing to secure funding in the United Kingdom can use Prospective Entrepreneur visitor category dealt with under paragraphs 56N to 56Q of the Immigration Rules.[101] Prospective entrepreneurs can spend up to 6 months in the United Kingdom in order to secure backing for their business from one or more of registered venture capitalist firms regulated by the Financial Services Authority; or UK Entrepreneurial seed funding competition endorsed on the UK Trade and Investment website, or UK Government Departments

101 Inserted by the Statement of Changes in Immigration Rules (HC 863) laid before Parliament on 16 Mach 2011.

and made available by the relevant Department for the specific purpose of establishing or expanding a business based in the United Kingdom. Applicants are then able to switch into the Tier 1 (Entrepreneur) sub-category in-country provided the necessary requirements are met. The Government is also seeking to encourage other wealth creators such as innovative student entrepreneurs to stay in the United Kingdom.

7.79 Applicants and their dependants need to submit for biometric data collection at a time specified by the UKBA. If their application is successful, applicants and their dependants will be issued with biometric residence permits. In-country applications for initial grant of leave (switching) or an extension of leave under Tier 1 (Entrepreneur) can be made using a Tier 1 (Entrepreneur) application form either by post or courier only at a cost[102] of £1,000 (for a main applicant applying). Applications for leave as a Tier 1 (Entrepreneur) cannot be made using the premium service. Applications can also be made using the UKBA 'Apply Online' facility.[103] Dependants, applying at the same time as the main applicant, have to pay £500. There are reduced fees for certain nationalities and their dependants. Dependants applying at a later date and applications made by dependent children aged 18 years or over will attract a charge of £550 for postal and courier applications.

Applications made by post should be sent to:	Applications made by courier should be sent to:
UK Border Agency Tier 1 PO Box 496 Durham DH99 1WQ	UK Border Agency Tier 1 Millburngate House Millburngate Durham DH97 1PA

Tier 1 (Investor)

7.80 Tier 1 (Investor) sub-category replaced the investor route on 30 June 2008.[104] This route was most recently modified on 6 April 2011 by the Statement of Changes in Immigration Rules (HC 863).[105] As with entrepreneurs, the aim is to attract more investors to the United Kingdom by offering variable levels of

102 Costs as at 6 April 2011.

103 http://apply.ukba.homeoffice.gov.uk/iapply.portal.

104 Inserted by the Statement of Changes in Immigration Rules (HC 607).

105 Despite an indication given in the *Tier 2 of the Points Based System, Statement of Intent, Transitional Measures and Indefinite Leave to Remain*, UK Border Agency, February 2011, http://www.ukba.homeoffice.gov.uk/sitecontent/documents/aboutus/reports/soi-tier2/ that changes relating to Tier 1 (Investor) and Tier 1 (Entrepreneur) routes would be set out 'separately as soon as possible', no further announcement was made until the publication of the Statement of Changes in Immigration Rules (HC 863) on 16 March 2011.

investment ranging from £1 million to £10 million in exchange for accelerated qualification periods for settlement depending on the amount of investment.

7.81 The meaning of a Tier 1 (Investor) migrant as contained in paragraph 6 of the Immigration Rules is that of 'a migrant who is granted leave under paragraphs 245O to 245U of these Rules.' This definition is out of date as since 6 April 2011 the Tier 1 (Investor) route is dealt with by paragraphs 245E to 245EF of the Immigration Rules. This route is for high net worth individuals making a substantial financial investment to the UK (paragraph 245E of the Immigration Rules). Applicants are able to enter into employment, self-employment or start their own business. Requirements for entry clearance and leave to remain are set out in paragraphs 245EB and 245ED of the Immigration Rules, respectively, which include an applicant having to score 75 points under paragraphs 54 to 65 of Appendix A to the Immigration Rules. Applicants do not have to score any points under Appendix B or C to the Immigration Rules.

7.82 Entry clearance will be granted for three years and four months subject to conditions of grant such as the restriction on employment as a doctor or dentist in training (unless the requirements at paragraph 245EC(iii) of the Immigration Rules and Annex D of Policy Guidance (for applications made on or after 6 April 2011, version 04/11) are satisfied). The same restriction applies to extension applications (paragraph 245EE(iii) of the Immigration Rules). Leave to remain is granted either for two years to an applicant who has or was last granted leave as a Tier 1 (Investor) migrant or for three years to anyone else. Leave to enter or remain may be curtailed subject to paragraph 245EE(c) as follows:

> 'Without prejudice to the grounds of curtailment in paragraph 323 of these Rules, leave to enter or remain as a Tier 1 (Investor) Migrant may be curtailed if within 3 months of the date specified in paragraph (d), the applicant has not invested, or had invested on his behalf, at least £750,000 of his capital in the UK by way of UK Government bonds, share capital or loan capital in active and trading UK registered companies other than those principally engaged in property investment.'

7.83 According to paragraph 245EE(d), the date referred to above is:

> '(i) the date of the applicant's entry to the UK, in the case of an applicant granted entry clearance as a Tier 1 (Investor) Migrant where there is evidence to establish the applicant's date of entry to the UK,
>
> (ii) the date of the grant of entry clearance to the applicant, in the case of an applicant granted entry clearance as a Tier 1 (Investor) Migrant where there is no evidence to establish the applicant's date of entry to the UK, or
>
> (iii) the date of the grant of leave to remain to the applicant, in any other case.'

7.84 Paragraph 245EE(e) states that:

'Paragraph 245EE(c) does not apply where the applicant's last grant of leave prior to the grant of the leave that he currently has was as a Tier 1 (Investor) Migrant or as an investor.'

7.85 Applicants wishing to make the grade for indefinite leave to remain must meet the criteria set out in paragraph 245EF of the Immigration Rules:

- must not fall for refusal under the general grounds of refusal and must not be illegal entrants;
- must score 75 points under paragraphs 54 to 65 of Appendix A;
- must not have any unspent convictions within the meaning of the Rehabilitation of Offenders Act 1974;
- must have sufficient knowledge of the English language and life in the United Kingdom pursuant to paragraph 33BA of the Immigration Rules unless they are under the age of 18 years or aged 65 and over at the time of making the application.

Further policy governing applications for settlement is contained in Chapter 6A, IDIs.[106]

Attributes (Appendix A)

7.86 A Tier 1 (Investor) applicant must score 75 points for attributes. Point scoring requirements for applications for entry clearance or leave to remain are set out in Table 7 of Appendix A to the Immigration Rules. Points contained in Table 8 of Appendix A to the Immigration Rules are for those applicants who are applying for leave to remain and have or were last granted entry clearance, leave to enter or remain as a Tier 1 (Investor) migrant or as an investor. Applicants wishing to apply for indefinite leave to remain must refer to Table 9. Notably, requirements for accelerated settlement are not reflected in the entry clearance provisions. Explanatory notes to Tables 7, 8 and 9 are contained in paragraphs 59 to 65 in Appendix A to the Immigration Rules.

7.87 At entry clearance stage, applicants must evidence that they have held the requisite funds of at least £1 million in a regulated financial institution and disposable in the United Kingdom for at least three months prior to making the application. If they have not held the full amount of funds for that length of time or are unable to evidence it for the entire three-month period, then they must also provide evidence of the source of the money.

106 Section 1, Chapter 6A, http://www.ukba.homeoffice.gov.uk/sitecontent/documents/policyandlaw/IDIs/idichapter6a/section1/section1.pdf?view=Binary.

7.88 *Looking ahead: Where do I go from here?*

7.88 The source of funds, if evidenced sufficiently, can include the following:

- a gift;
- deeds of sale;
- funds held in a business;
- a will;
- divorce settlements; or
- award of winnings.

7.89 To qualify for extension of leave, applicants will be required to invest funds three months after the initial entry to the United Kingdom as a Tier 1 (Investor) migrant in accordance with the requirements set out in Table 8 below. The level of investment must have been maintained throughout the period of leave, but it does not necessarily need to be the same investment that was made in the first three months.

7.90 After five years of continuous lawful residence, applicants can qualify for indefinite leave to remain in the United Kingdom if they can show that the level of investment has been maintained throughout the entire period save for first three-month grace period and that they have been out of the United Kingdom for more than 180 days in any 12 calendar months. This is not currently reflected in nationality law or policy.

7.91 If a greater level of investment is made then it is possible to acquire settlement sooner without being required to make the intermediate application for extension of leave, as follows:

- If the level of investment is at least £5 million[107] then settlement can be applied for after three years of leave as a Tier 1 (Investor).
- If the level of investment is at least £10 million[108] then settlement can be applied for after two years of leave as a Tier 1 (Investor).

7.92 In either case the respective level of investment must have been maintained throughout the corresponding period of time (other than the first three months of your leave to remain). Migrants pursuing settlement at an accelerated pace can be out of the United Kingdom for no more than 180 days in any 12 calendar months.

The point scoring requirements for entry clearance and leave to remain are as follows (reproduced exactly below):

107 Or £10 million in personal assets and money under their control and disposable in the UK amounting to not less than £5 million which has been loaned by a UK regulated financial institution

108 Or £20 million in personal assets and money under their control and disposable in the UK amounting to not less than £10 million which has been loaned by a UK regulated financial institution.

TABLE 7

7.93

Assets	**Points**
The applicant: has money of his own under his control held in a regulated financial institution and disposable in the UK amounting to not less than £1 million; or (i) owns personal assets which, taking into account any liabilities to which they are subject, have a value exceeding £2 million, and (ii) has money under his control held in a regulated financial institution and disposable in the UK amounting to not less than £1 million which has been loaned to him by a UK regulated financial institution.	**75**

The point scoring requirements for leave to remain are as follows (reproduced below exactly):

TABLE 8

7.94

Assets and investment	**Points**
The applicant: has money of his own under his control in the UK amounting to not less than £1 million, or (i) owns personal assets which, taking into account any liabilities to which they are subject, have a value of not less than £2 million, and (ii) has money under his control and disposable in the UK amounting to not less than £1 million which has been loaned to him by a UK regulated financial institution.	**30**
The applicant has invested not less than £750,000 of his capital in the UK by way of UK Government bonds, share capital or loan capital in active and trading UK registered companies, subject to the restrictions set out in paragraph 65 and has invested the remaining balance of £1,000,000 in the UK by the purchase of assets or by maintaining the money on deposit in a UK regulated financial institution.	**30**

Assets and investment	**Points**
The investment referred to above was made within three months of his entry to the UK (if he was granted entry clearance as a [sic] as a Tier 1 (Investor) Migrant and there is evidence to establish his date of arrival in the UK), or the date of the grant of entry clearance as a Tier 1 (Investor) Migrant (if there is no evidence to establish his date of arrival to the UK), or, in any other case, the date of the grant of leave to remain as a Tier 1 (Investor) Migrant and in each case the investment has been maintained for the whole of the remaining period of that leave; or The migrant has, or was last granted, entry clearance, leave to enter or leave to remain as an Investor.	**15**

The point scoring requirements for indefinite leave to remain are as follows (reproduced below exactly):

7.95

Row	**Assets and investment**	**Points**
1.	The applicant: (a) (i) has money of his own under his control in the UK amounting to not less than £10 million, or (ii) (1) owns personal assets which, taking into account any liabilities to which they are subject, have a value of not less than £20 million, and (2) has money under his control and disposable in the UK amounting to not less than £10 million which has been loaned to him by a UK regulated financial institution, or (b) (i) has money of his own under his control in the UK amounting to not less than £5 million, or (ii) (1) owns personal assets which, taking into account any liabilities to which they are subject, have a value of not less than £10 million, and (2) has money under his control and disposable in the UK amounting to not less than £5 million which has been loaned to him by a UK regulated financial institution, or	**20**

Row	Assets and investment	Points
	(c) (i) has money of his own under his control in the UK amounting to not less than £1 million, or (ii) (1) owns personal assets which, taking into account any liabilities to which they are subject, have a value of not less than £2 million, and (2) has money under his control and disposable in the UK amounting to not less than £1 million which has been loaned to him by a UK regulated financial institution,	
2.	The applicant has invested not less than 75% of the specified invested amount of his capital in the UK by way of UK Government bonds, share capital or loan capital in active and trading UK registered companies, subject to the restrictions set out in paragraph 65 below, and has invested the remaining balance of the specified invested amount in the UK by the purchase of assets or by maintaining the money on deposit in a UK regulated financial institution. The specified invested amount is: (a) £10,000,000 if the applicant scores points from row 1(a) above, (b) £5,000,000 if the applicant scores points from row 1(b) above, or (c) £1,000,000 if the applicant scores points from row 1(c) above.	**20**
3.	The applicant has spent the specified continuous period lawfully in the UK, with absences from the UK of no more than 180 days in any 12 calendar months during that period. The specified continuous period must have been spent with leave as a Tier 1 (Investor) Migrant and/or as an Investor, of which the most recent period must have been spent with leave as a Tier 1 (Investor) Migrant. The specified continuous period is: (a) 2 years if the applicant scores points from row 1(a) above, (b) 3 years if the applicant scores points from row 1(b) above, or (c) 5 years if the applicant scores points from row 1(c) above.	**20**

Row	Assets and investment	Points
4.	The applicant has maintained the full specified invested amount referred to in the relevant part of row 2 throughout the relevant specified continuous period referred to in row 3, other than in the first 3 months of that period and, in relation to time spent with leave as a Tier 1 (Investor) Migrant, has provided specified documents to show that this requirement has been met. When calculating the specified continuous period, the first day of that period will be taken to be the day 3 months before the full specified amount is invested.	**15**

7.96 Paragraph 65 of Appendix A excludes the following types of investment:

'(a) an offshore company or trust,
(b) Open-ended investment companies, investment trust companies or pooled investment vehicles,
(c) Companies mainly engaged in property investment, property management or property development,
(d) Deposits with a bank, building society or other enterprise whose normal course of business includes the acceptance of deposits,
(e) ISAs, premium bonds and saving certificates issued by the National Savings and Investment Agency (NS&I), for an applicant who has, or last had leave as a Tier 1 (Investor) Migrant, or
(f) Leveraged investment funds.'

7.97 Applicants and their dependants need to submit for biometric data collection at a time specified by the UKBA. If their application is successful, applicants and their dependants will be issued with biometric residence permits. In-country applications for initial grant of leave (switching) or an extension of leave under Tier 1 (Investor) can be made using a Tier 1 (Investor) application form either by post or courier only at a cost[109] of £1,000 (for a main applicant applying). Applications for leave as a Tier 1 (Investor) cannot be made using the premium service. Applications can also be made using the UKBA 'Apply Online' facility.[110] Dependants, applying at the same time as the main applicant, have to pay £500. There are reduced fees for certain nationalities and their dependants. Dependants applying at a later date and applications made by dependent children aged 18 years or over will attract a charge of £550 for postal and courier applications. Dependants must use a separate PBS (Dependant) application form.

109 Costs as at 6 April 2011.
110 http://apply.ukba.homeoffice.gov.uk/iapply.portal.

Applications made by post should be sent to:	Applications made by courier should be sent to:
UK Border Agency Tier 1 PO Box 496 Durham DH99 1WQ	UK Border Agency Tier 1 Millburngate House Millburngate Durham DH97 1PA

Tier 1 (Post-Study Work)

7.98 On 23 November 2010, in addressing the House of Commons the Secretary of State announced the Government's plan to 'consult on closing the Post Study route, which last year allowed some 38 thousand foreign graduates to enter the UK labour market at a time when one in ten UK graduates were unemployed.'[111] This is intended to break the link between temporary and permanent migration and dissuade graduate students from staying on in the United Kingdom to look for work. On 7 December 2010 the Government published a consultation paper in which its proposal is stated as follows:

> 'We therefore propose to close the Tier 1 Post Study Work route. We also invite views on any necessary transitional arrangements.
>
> We recognise there are other options short of closing the route entirely. These could include, for example, restricting it to those with a higher degree such as a PhD. However any option short of closure must ensure that access is tightly restricted to the very brightest and best. We believe that a student's primary motivation for coming to the UK should be the prospect of obtaining a world class education here, not of being able to work afterwards; especially when entry to work is in any case possible through direct entry to Tier 2, which in turn ensures that the student finds a skilled job rather than potentially filling unskilled jobs for up to two years.'[112]

7.99 In its November 2010 report *Limits on Tier 1 and Tier 2 for 2011/12 and supporting policies*[113] the Migration Advisory Committee noted at paragraph 9.140 that the previous Government had commissioned research to be

111 *Immigration limits oral statement*, Home Office, 23 November 2010, http://www.homeoffice.gov.uk/publications/parliamentary-business/oral-statements/limits-statement/.

112 *The Student Immigration System, a Consultation*, UK Border Agency, December 2010, http://www.ukba.homeoffice.gov.uk/sitecontent/documents/policyandlaw/consultations/students/student-consultation.pdf?view=Binary. The consultation ran for eight weeks until 31 January 2011.

113 *Limits on Tier 1 and Tier 2 for 2011/12 and supporting policies*, Migration Advisory Committee, November 2010, http://www.ukba.homeoffice.gov.uk/sitecontent/documents/aboutus/workingwithus/mac/mac-limits-t1-t2/report.pdf?view=Binary

conducted by the Department for Business, Innovation and Skills into the foreign students' experience of the Tier 1 (Post Study Work) route and whether it was determinative in them choosing to study in the United Kingdom. Part of the research had been completed but not published by the time the Committee's report was released and the second and final part of the research will be finished by the end of 2011. On 31 March 2011 the Government published a statement of intent hailing closure of the Tier 1 (Post Study Work) category by April 2012.[114] The Tier 2 (General) route will remain a possibility for recent graduates applying for graduate level jobs.[115]

7.100 Tier 1 (Post-Study Work) category was launched on 30 June 2008[116] replacing IGS and associated categories (see the historical note above). On 16 March 2011 the Statement of Changes in Immigration Rules (HC 863) was laid before Parliament proposing changes to the Tier 1 (Post-Study Work) route. These changes were minimal. The new Rules have been in force since 6 April 2011.

7.101 The aim of Tier 1 (Post-Study Work) is 'to retain the most able international graduates who have studied in the United Kingdom', says Tier 1 (Post-Study Work) Policy Guidance (for applications made on or after 19 July 2011, version 04/11). It adds that 'it will also enhance the United Kingdom's overall offer to international students.' Its intention is to provide a passage to highly skilled or skilled work under Tier 1 or Tier 2 categories now limited by the revised switching restrictions. In fact, paragraph 245F of the Immigration Rules states that the purpose of this route 'is to encourage international graduates who have studied in the UK to stay on and do skilled or highly skilled work.' As a bridging category, Tier 1 (Post-Study Work) is a means to an end. It does not lead directly to settlement.

7.102 Paragraph 6 of the Immigration Rules defines a Tier 1 (Post-Study Work) Migrant as a 'migrant who is granted leave under paragraphs 245V to 245ZA of these Rules.' However, due to the renumbering that occurred as a result of the new Rules coming into force on 6 April 2011, this route is covered by paragraphs 245F to 245FE of the Immigration Rules. Applicants applying for entry clearance must score

114 *Student Visas, Statement of Intent and Transitional Measures*, UK Border Agency, March 2011, http://www.ukba.homeoffice.gov.uk/sitecontent/documents/news/sop4.pdf

115 On 7 June 2011 the Law Society began canvassing opinion from law firms regarding difficulties faced by students undertaking the accelerated Legal Practice Course which is of less than 12 months duration. Students who have leave as Tier 4 (General) migrants are unable to switch in-country to Tier 2 (General) and are having to submit their entry clearance applications in their home countries. The Law Society stated that "it is likely that the UKBA will review the rules for switching from Tier 4 to Tier 2 in time for April 2012" ("Immigration status of accelerated LPBC students", The Law Society, 7 June 2011, http://www.lawsociety.org.uk/newsandevents/news/view=newsarticle.law?NEWSID=436401.

116 Inserted by the Statement of Changes in Immigration Rules (HC 607).

75 points under paragraphs 66 to 72 of Appendix A, 10 points under paragraphs 1 to 3 of Appendix B and 10 points under paragraphs 1 to 2 of Appendix C. Applicants who have previously been granted entry clearance or leave to remain as a Tier 1 (Post-Study Work) migrant or participant of IGS, SEGS or FT: WISS will not meet the entry clearance requirements.

7.103 Entry clearance is granted for two years with a restriction on employment as a doctor or dentist in training (unless an applicant can satisfy the requirements set out at paragraph 245FC(c) of the Immigration Rules and Annex B of Tier 1 (Post-Study Work) Policy Guidance). To meet requirements for leave to remain under paragraph 245FD of the Immigration Rules an applicant must not previously have been granted entry clearance or leave to remain as a Tier 1 (Post-Study Work) migrant, must score points in Appendices A to C, and must have or have last been granted entry clearance, leave to enter or remain as a participant in IGS, SEGS or FT: WISS, or as a student, student nurse, student re-sitting an examination, student writing-up a thesis, a Tier 4 migrant or as a postgraduate doctor or dentist. An applicant who has or was last granted leave as a participant in FT: WISS must be a British National (Overseas), British Overseas Territories Citizen, British Overseas Citizen, British Protected Person or a British subject as per the British Nationality Act 1981. Period of grant of leave to remain is set out in paragraph 245FE(a) as follows:

> 'Leave to remain will be granted:
> (i) for a period of the difference between 2 years and the period of the last grant of entry clearance, leave to enter or remain, to an applicant who has or was last granted leave as a Participant in the Fresh Talent: Working in Scotland Scheme, as a Participant in the International Graduates Scheme (or its predecessor the Science and Engineering Graduates Scheme). If this calculation results in no grant of leave then leave to remain is to be refused;
> (ii) for a period of 2 years, to any other applicant.'

This provision should be read together with paragraphs 84 to 89 of Tier 1 (Post-Study Work) Policy Guidance.

Attributes (Appendix A)

7.104 An applicant must score 75 points for attributes as set out in Table 10 (the contents of which are reproduced below exactly save for footnotes). Explanatory notes are provided at paragraphs 69 to 72 of Appendix A to the Immigration Rules. Applicants should refer to Tier 1 (Post-Study Work) Policy Guidance which separates this table into point scoring requirements for initial applications and those made under transitional arrangements.

TABLE 9

7.105

Qualifications	**Points**
The applicant has been awarded: (a) a UK recognised bachelor or postgraduate degree,[117] or (b) a UK postgraduate certificate in education or Professional Graduate Diploma or Education,[118] or (c) a Higher National Diploma ('HND') from a Scottish institution.[119]	**20**
(a) The applicant studied for his award at a UK institution that is a UK recognised or listed body,[120] or which holds a sponsor licence under Tier 4 of the Points Based System, or (b) If the applicant is claiming points for having been awarded a Higher National Diploma from a Scottish Institution, he studied for that diploma at a Scottish publicly funded institution of further or higher education, or a Scottish bona fide private education institution which maintains satisfactory records of enrolment and attendance. The Scottish institution must: (i) be on the list of Education and Training Providers list on the Department of Business, Innovation and Skills website, or (ii) hold a Sponsor licence under Tier 4 of the Points Based System.[121]	**20**

117 For a UK degree to be recognised, it must have been awarded by a UK recognised body which is an institution conferred with degree awarding powers by a Royal Charter, an Act of Parliament or the Privy Council. This includes all UK universities and some HE colleges. See http://www.bis.gov.uk/policies/higher-education/recognised-uk-degrees for a list of UK recognised bodies. See all the relevant statutory instruments, the Education (Recognised Bodies) (England) Order 2007, SI 2007/2688 which list all the recognised bodies pursuant to s 214(2)(a) or (b) of the Education Reform Act 1988 and the Education (Recognised Bodies) (England) (Amendment) Order 2008, SI 2008/2889.

118 It is not necessary for bodies awarding PGCEs and PGDEs to be recognised. Foundation degrees, honorary degrees, qualifications awarded in the UK by overseas awarding bodies, qualifications undertaken solely at an overseas campus of UK institutions, professional and vocational qualifications, and postgraduate certificates and diplomas (apart from PGCE and PGDE) are expressly ineligible (paragraph 59 of the Tier 1 (Post-Study Work) Guidance).

119 For an HND to be acceptable, it must be at level 8 on the Scottish Credit and Qualifications Framework. See the interactive SCQF at http://www.scqf.org.uk/features/Framework.htm.

120 A UK recognised body is as described above while a UK listed body is an institution that is not a UK recognised body but which provides full courses that lead to the award of a degree by a UK recognised body. All the degrees awarded by UK recognised bodies at their own institution or through listed bodies are recognised degrees. See. http://www.bis.gov.uk/policies/higher-education/recognised-uk-degrees.

121 The provision for Scottish institutions was inserted by the Statement of Changes in Immigration Rules (HC 863).

Qualifications	**Points**
The applicant's periods of UK study and/or research towards his eligible award were undertaken whilst he had entry clearance, leave to enter or leave to remain in the UK that was not subject to a restriction preventing him from undertaking a course of study and/or research.	**20**
The applicant made the application for entry clearance or leave to remain as a Tier 1 (Post-Study Work) Migrant within 12 months of obtaining the relevant qualification or within 12 months of completing a United Kingdom Foundation Programme Office affiliated Foundation Programme as a postgraduate doctor or dentist.	**15**
The applicant is applying for leave to remain and has, or was last granted, leave as a Participant in the International Graduates Scheme (or its predecessor, the Science and Engineering Graduates Scheme) or as a Participant in the Fresh Talent: Working in Scotland Scheme.	**75**

English language (Appendix B)

7.106 Applicants will score 10 points if they have achieved 75 points under Appendix A (paragraph 3 of Appendix B to the Immigration Rules).

Maintenance (funds) (Appendix C)

7.107 Applicants must score 10 points for maintenance (funds). The requirements are the same as for Tier 1 (General) and Tier 1 (Entrepreneur) migrants outlined above.

Applicants and their dependants will need to submit for biometric data collection at a time specified by the UKBA, depending on whether their application is made by post, courier or at a Public Enquiry Office. If their application is successful, applicants and their dependants will be issued with biometric residence permits. In-country applications for grant of leave under Tier 1 (Post-Study Work) can be made using a Tier 1 (Post-Study Work) application form either by post, courier or at a Public Enquiry Office at a cost[122] of £594 (for a main applicant applying by post or courier) or £918 (for a main applicant applying at a Public Enquiry Office). Applications can also be made using the UKBA 'Apply Online' facility.[123] Dependants, applying at the same time as the main applicant, have to pay £297 for postal applications and £459 for applications made at a Public Enquiry Office, unless the dependant is a child aged 18 years or over. There are reduced fees for

122 Costs as at 6 April 2011.
123 http://apply.ukba.homeoffice.gov.uk/iapply.portal.

certain nationalities and their dependants. Dependants applying at a later date and applications made by dependent children aged 18 years or over will attract a charge of £550 for postal and courier applications and £850 for applications made in person at a Public Enquiry Office. Dependants must use a separate PBS (Dependant) application form.

Applications made by post should be sent to:	Applications made by courier should be sent to:
UK Border Agency Tier 1 PO Box 496 Durham DH99 1WQ	UK Border Agency Tier 1 Millburngate House Millburngate Durham DH97 1PA

Tier 1 (Exceptional Talent)

7.108 The Statement of Changes in Immigration Rules (HC 863) laid before Parliament on 16 March 2011 added a fifth sub-category to Tier 1 – Tier 1 (Exceptional Talent). The Rules governing this sub-category came into force on 6 April 2011. Even with the Rules in place, the sub-category did not immediately become operational as its structure was still in development. On 19 July 2011 the Government presented to Parliament a further Statement of Changes in Immigration Rules (HC 1436) dedicated solely to expanding and clarifying the provisions relating to Tier 1 (Exceptional Talent) with the view to opening the new scheme to applicants from 9 August 2011.

7.109 Prior to 9 August 2011 the purpose of this sub-category was defined in paragraph 245B of the Immigration Rules as being 'for those who are internationally recognised as world leaders or potential world-leading talent in the fields of science and the arts and who wish to work in the UK'. On 9 August 2011 paragraph 245B of the Rules was substituted for a tighter definition encompassing a more specific group of 'internationally talented individuals in the fields of science, humanities, engineering and the arts, who wish to work in the UK'. The sub-category's purpose is extended to 'those who are already internationally recognised at the highest level as world leaders in their particular field, or who have already demonstrated exceptional promise and are likely to become world leaders in their particular area.'

7.110 The requirements to be met by applicants from 9 August 2011 are set out at paragraphs 245B–245BF of the Immigration Rules. The point scoring requirements are contained in paragraphs 1 to 6 of Appendix A to the Immigration Rules pursuant to which applicants applying for entry clearance, leave to remain or indefinite leave to remain must score 75 points and paragraphs 1 to 9 of Appendix B to the Immigration Rules pursuant to which applicants applying for leave to remain must score 10 points. Eligibility criteria are set out two extraneous documents on the UKBA website.[124]

7.111 Applicants must obtain entry clearance in this sub-category before coming to the United Kingdom (paragraph 245BB of the Immigration Rules). Applicants must also have a Tier 1 (Exceptional Talent) Unique Reference Number ('URN') assigned by the UKBA. The URN is defined in paragraph 6 of the Immigration Rules as a "unique reference number issued for the purposes of managing Tier 1 (Exceptional Talent) Limit and provided by the UK Border Agency to an applicant prior to making his application as a Tier 1 (Exceptional Talent) Migrant." The number is valid for 10 working days from the date of issue. It can only be used once (not unlike a CoS or a CAS) and cannot be granted to the same applicant more than three times in the period from 9 August 2011 to 5 April 2012. The URN must relate to the designated competent body (see below) the applicant seeks endorsement from in support of the application (paragraph 245BB(b) of the Immigration Rules). A request for a URN can be made by email sent to Tier1ExTalentEoI@UKBA.gsi.gov.uk. Once a URN is assigned, applicants can submit their application to the relevant British diplomatic post abroad together with supporting documents which will be assessed against the eligibility criteria set by the designated competent bodies in the relevant field. There are no provisions made for switching in paragraph 245BD of the Immigration Rules. There is no access into this route from any other category. Entry clearance is granted for three years and four months subject to the applicant having no recourse to public funds, registering with the police, not working as a doctor or dentist in training or as a professional sportsperson. Leave to remain is granted for two years subject to the same conditions (paragraph 245BE of the Immigration Rules). Applicants will qualify for indefinite leave to remain if they have spent a continuous period of five years lawfully in the United Kingdom only in this capacity, do not have any unspent convictions within the meaning of the Rehabilitation of Offenders Act 1974 and have sufficient knowledge of the English language and life in the United Kingdom in accordance with paragraph 33BA of the Immigration Rules unless they are under the age of 18 years or aged 65 and over at the time of making the application. Further policy governing applications for settlement is contained in Chapter 6A, IDIs.[125] Under paragraph 323B of the Immigration Rules a Tier 1 (Exceptional Talent) migrant may have their leave to enter or remain curtailed if the designated competent body withdraws its endorsement of the migrant which led to the grant of leave (see also paragraph 6 of Appendix A to the Immigration Rules).

124 *Eligibility Criteria: Arts Council England,* UK Border Agency, http://www.ukba.homeoffice.gov.uk/sitecontent/documents/workingintheuk/t1-et/arts-criteria.pdf and *Eligibility Criteria: British Academy, Royal Academy of Engineering, Royal Society*, UK Border Agency, http://www.ukba.homeoffice.gov.uk/sitecontent/documents/workingintheuk/t1-et/science-criteria.pdf.

125 Section 1, Chapter 6A, http://www.ukba.homeoffice.gov.uk/sitecontent/documents/policyandlaw/IDIs/idichapter6a/section1/section1.pdf?view=Binary.

Attributes (Appendix A)

7.112 An applicant must score 75 points for attributes as set out in Table 1 (the contents of which are reproduced below exactly). Table 1 is split into two parts. Explanatory notes are provided at paragraphs 4 to 6 of Appendix A to the Immigration Rules. Applicants should refer to Tier 1 (Exceptional Talent) Policy Guidance for information related to specified documents.

Applications for entry clearance

7.113

Criterion	**Points**
Endorsed by Designated Competent Body	**75**

Applications for leave to remain and indefinite leave to remain

7.114

Criterion	**Points**
The applicant is economically active in his expert field as previously endorsed by a Designated Competent Body, in employment or self-employment or both; and that Designated Competent Body has not withdrawn its endorsement of the applicant	**75**

A designated competent body is defined in paragraph 6 of the Immigration Rules as 'an organisation which has been approved by the UK Border Agency to endorse applicants as a Tier 1 (Exceptional Talent) Migrant.' There are four designated competent bodies each responsible for a particular discipline:

- The Arts Council – applications in the fields of arts and culture;
- The Royal Society – applications in the fields of natural sciences and medical science research;
- The Royal Academy of Engineering – applications in the field of engineering;
- The British Academy – applications in the fields of humanities and social sciences.

7.115 When the Rules relating to this sub-category initially came into force on 6 April 2011 it was envisaged that a limit of 1,000 endorsements would apply to applications for entry clearance made in the period between 6 April 2011 and 5 April 2012 with the limit being divided into 700 endorsements in the field of science and 300 endorsements in the field of the arts. The limit of 1,000 endorsements will now be divided between the four designated competent bodies: the Arts Council

(300 endorsements), the Royal Society (300 endorsements), the Royal Academy of Engineering (200 endorsements) and the British Academy (200 endorsements). The relevant period during which the limit will apply is between 9 August 2011 and 5 April 2012 (paragraph 4(b) of Appendix A). From 9 August 2011 to 30 November 2011 the UKBA will make available 500 endorsements to be allocated. The other 500 endorsements can be allocated in the period from 1 December 2011 to 5 April 2012 (paragraph 5(b) of Appendix A). Endorsements will be made in line with the criteria agreed between the designated competent bodies and the UKBA The endorsement must not have been withdrawn when the application for entry clearance is made (paragraph 6 of Appendix A).

English language (Appendix B)

7.116 Initially, paragraph 245BD(c) of the Immigration Rules (in force from 6 April 2011) required applicants to score 10 points for maintenance under paragraphs 1 to 2 of Appendix C. From 9 August 2011, however, applicants applying for leave to remain must score a minimum of 10 points under paragraphs 1 to 9 of Appendix B pursuant to paragraph 245BD(c) of the Immigration Rules.[126] For the purposes of satisfying the English language requirement, Tier 1 (Exceptional Talent) migrants are grouped together with Tier 2 migrants.

Tier 2 migrants

7.117 Although Tier 2 consists of four sub-categories, this section is principally concerned with the Tier 2 (General) migrant route in keeping with the subject matter of this book and its relevance to students, academics and sponsors. The requirements inserted by the Statement of Changes in Immigration Rules (HC 863) on 16 March 2011 in force from 6 April 2011 have changed the way in which sponsors can assign CoS to migrants, the minimum skill and salary levels, the English language and other requirements bringing about an extensive reform of the Tier 2 route. These changes were preceded by an announcement by the Secretary of State on 23 November 2010[127] and a detailed statement of changes on 16 February 2011.[128]

7.118 Provisions for Tier 2 migrants came into effect on 27 November 2008[129] replacing, among other deleted categories, the work permit scheme. Tier 2

126 Inserted by the Statement of Changes in Immigration Rules (HC 1436).

127 *Immigration limits oral statement*, Home Office, 23 November 2010, http://www.homeoffice.gov.uk/publications/parliamentary-business/oral-statements/limits-statement/.

128 *Tier 2 of the Points Based System, Statement of Intent, Transitional Measures and Indefinite Leave to Remain*, UK Border Agency, February 2011, http://www.ukba.homeoffice.gov.uk/sitecontent/documents/aboutus/reports/soi-tier2/.

129 Inserted by the Statement of Changes in Immigration Rules, HC 1113.

(General) is the route which allows UK employers to employ non-EU/EEA workers to fill a particular vacancy that cannot be filled by a British or EU/EEA worker (paragraph 245H of the Immigration Rules). Any job in the Tier 2 (General) sub-category must correspond to a graduate level occupation offering a salary of no less than £20,000, which ensures that the resident labour market is not undercut.

7.119 Before a Tier 2 sponsor can issue a CoS, the sponsor must ensure that the proposed job meets all the conditions of the relevant code of practice with reference to the Standard Occupational Classification. The number of CoS that can be allocated to sponsors for the purpose of assigning them to applicants applying for entry clearance as Tier 2 (General) migrants has been capped at 20,700 in the period from 6 April 2011 to 5 April 2012. These CoS are classified as 'restricted'. Other Tier 2 sub-categories are not affected by the limit and CoS associated with these are known as 'unrestricted' (see **7.135** *et seq*).

7.120 An occupation can be on the Shortage Occupation List which means that there are not enough resident workers to take up the available jobs.[130] The list has been updated in line with the Graduate Occupations List recommended by the Migration Advisory Committee. In respect of all other jobs corresponding to graduate level occupations the sponsor is required to undertake a Resident Labour Market Test ('RLMT') and to demonstrate that no appropriately skilled settled worker can fill the vacancy. After 14 December 2009, all job vacancies have to be advertised for 28 calendar days using the services of Jobcentre Plus, national newspapers or professional journals, milk rounds (if the code of practice allows it), rolling recruitment programmes, recruitment agencies, Internet and headhunters.

7.121 There are certain exemptions to the RLMT.[131] One such exemption is when a migrant is already employed in the job and has leave as a Tier 1 (Post-Study Work) migrant, a participant of IGS, SEGS or FT: WISS. A person switching from these categories must have worked in the job for at least six months before the date of application.

7.122 Paragraphs 245H to 245HF of the Immigration Rules cover three of the four Tier 2 sub-categories (with the exception of Tier 2 (Intra-Company Transfer) which is dealt with in paragraphs 245G to 245GF of the Immigration Rules). Some provisions dealing with curtailment of leave and particulars of certain changing requirements are only dealt with, arguably contrary to *Pankina*,[132] in the Policy Guidance. Tier 2 relies heavily on extraneous documents although this has become less so with the incorporation of the Statement of Changes in Immigration Rules (HC 863).

130 *Government-approved shortage occupation list for Tier 2 of the Points-Based System*, UK Border Agency, 29 April 2010, http://www.ukba.homeoffice.gov.uk/sitecontent/documents/workingintheuk/shortageoccupationlist.pdf.

131 The limited waiver of the RLMT for jobs paying a salary of £130,000 or more has been abolished.

132 *Secretary of State for the Home Department v Pankina* [2010] EWCA Civ 719

7.123 For the purpose of these provisions 'length of the period of engagement' and 'working for the same employer' are defined at paragraph 6 of the Rules:

> '"length of the period of engagement" is the period beginning with the employment start date as recorded on the Certificate of Sponsorship Checking Service entry which relates to the Certificate of Sponsorship reference number for which the migrant was awarded points under Appendix A and ending on the employment end date as recorded in the same entry', and
>
> '"working for the same employer" includes working for the same business or concern as at the time of the earlier grant of leave if that business or concern has, since that date, merged or been taken over by another entity.'

7.124 Requirements for entry clearance and leave to remain for Tier 2 (General) migrants are set out in paragraphs 245HB and 245HD of the Immigration Rules, respectively. Common requirements related to Tier 2 (General) are set out below:

Minimum points to be scored:

a) 50 points under paragraphs 76 to 84A of Appendix A to the Immigration Rules (paragraphs 245HB(b) and 245HD(j)). More specifically, Tier 2 (General) migrants must score points under paragraphs 76 to 79D of Appendix A (paragraphs 245HC(f)(i) and 245HE(h)(i)),

b) 10 points under paragraphs 5 to 10 of Appendix B to the Immigration Rules (paragraphs 245HB(e) and 245HD(l)), and

c) 10 points under paragraphs 4 to 5 of Appendix C to the Immigration Rules (paragraphs 245HB(f) and 245HD(m)).

Minimum age of applicants:

a) at least 16 years old (paragraphs 245HB(h) and 245HD(n)),

b) if under the age of 18, parents or one parent, provided that parent has sole responsibility, or legal guardian of an applicant must:
   - support the application (paragraphs 245HB(i) and 245HD(o)); and
   - give their consent to the applicant's travel, reception and care arrangements in the UK (paragraph 245HB(j)) as applications for leave to remain are only concerned with care arrangements at paragraph 245HD(p)).

Shareholding:

a) applicants whose sponsor is a limited company must not own more than 10% of the company's shares (paragraphs 245HB(k) and 245HD(q)).

7.125 As for all the other PBS categories, entry clearance is a mandatory requirement (paragraph 245HA of the Immigration Rules). Pursuant to paragraph

245HD(b) of the Rules, if an applicant is applying for leave to remain as a Tier 2 (General) migrant, then he or she must have or have last been granted entry clearance, leave to enter or remain in the United Kingdom in one of the 24 categories listed in that paragraph.

7.126 The key provisions dealing with the period of grant of entry clearance to Tier 2 (General) migrants are set down in paragraph 245HC of the Rules. Entry clearance is granted for a period equal to the length of the period of engagement plus one month, or a period of three years and one month, whichever is shorter, with effect from 14 days before the start of employment in the United Kingdom or with immediate effect if entry clearance is granted less than 14 days before that date. Calculation of the period of leave to remain for Tier 2 (General) migrants is a more complex algorithm requiring reference to paragraph 245HE of the Rules.

7.127 Tier 2 (General) migrants who have been granted entry clearance, leave to enter or remain can only work for their sponsor subject to any notification of a permissible change in their employment (paragraphs 245HC(e)(iii)(1) and 245HE(g)(iii)(1)), be engaged in supplementary employment (paragraphs 245HC(e)(iii)(2) and 245HE(g)(iii)(2)) or do voluntary work (paragraphs 245HC(e)(iii)(3) and 245HE(g)(iii)(3)).

7.128 Requirements for indefinite leave to remain are contained in paragraph 245HF of the Rules. To qualify for indefinite leave to remain an applicant must have spent a continuous period of five years lawfully in the United Kingdom with the most recent period being as a Tier 2 migrant in a combination with any of the ten categories listed at paragraph 245HF(c). Their sponsors must certify in writing that they still require them for employment and that the applicants are paid at or above the appropriate rate for the job as stated in the codes of practice. Qualification of foreign workers for indefinite leave to remain is under review pending the results of *Employment-Related Settlement, Tier 5 and Overseas Domestic Workers, A Consultation,* pursuant to which the Secretary of State is seeking to break the link between temporary and permanent leave. The intention of the review is to deprive the majority of foreign workers of an automatic right to settlement in the United Kingdom.[133]

7.129 The applicants must also not fall for refusal under the general grounds of refusal and must not be illegal entrants, must not have any unspent convictions within the meaning of the Rehabilitation of Offenders Act 1974 and must have sufficient knowledge of the English language and life in the United Kingdom

133 *Employment-Related Settlement, Tier 5 and Overseas Domestic Workers, A Consultation,* UK Border Agency, June 2011, http://www.ukba.homeoffice.gov.uk/sitecontent/documents/policyandlaw/consultations/employment-related-settlement/employment-related-consultation?view=Binary. The consultation ran from 9 June 2011 to 9 September 2011.

pursuant to paragraph 33BA of the Immigration Rules unless they are under the age of 18 years or aged 65 and over at the time of making the application.

Attributes (Appendix A)

7.130 Migrants must score a minimum of 50 points for sponsorship and appropriate salary. Applicants are not longer scored on the basis of their qualifications. Applicants applying for entry clearance or leave to remain must refer to the point scoring requirements which are set out in Table 11A (the contents of which are reproduced exactly) and accompanying notes at paragraphs 77 to 79D which establish the validity of a CoS (paragraphs 77 to 77F), deal with shortage occupations (paragraph 78), job offers with a salary of £150,000 or more (paragraph 78A) and those jobs that pass the RLMT test (paragraph 78B), post-study workers applying to switch (paragraph 78C), continuing to work in the same job for the same sponsor (paragraph 78D) and define the parameters of appropriate salary (paragraph 79 to 79D).

TABLE 11A

7.131

Certificate of Sponsorship	**Points**	**Appropriate salary**	**Points**
Shortage occupation	**30**	Appropriate salary	**20**
Job offer with a salary of £150,000 or more	**30**		
Job offer passes resident labour Market Test	**30**		
Post-Study Work	**30**		
Continuing to work in the same job for the same Sponsor	**30**		

CERTIFICATE OF SPONSORSHIP

7.132 In order to score points for the sponsorship criteria, migrants must have a valid CoS reference number (paragraph 77A). The only CoS to be allocated to sponsors in the period from 6 April 2011 to 5 April 2012 are CoS to be assigned to applicants for entry clearance as allocated to sponsors under the annual limit, CoS to be assigned to applicants for leave to remain, and CoS to be assigned to applicants whose job pays the gross annual salary of £150,000 or more (paragraph 77B). The CoS reference number must correspond to a Certificate of Sponsorship

Checking Service entry made in respect of the migrant and the sponsor (paragraph 77C). To be valid the CoS reference number must have been assigned to the migrant no more than three months after the sponsor was allocated the CoS (if subject to the annual limit) (paragraph 77C(b), no more than three months before the application for entry clearance of leave to remain is made (paragraph 77C(c)) and the application is made no more than three months before the start of the employment (paragraph 77C(d)).

7.133 The number must not have been withdrawn or cancelled by either the sponsor or the UKBA after being assigned to the migrant (paragraph 77C(f)) and the sponsor is A-rated (paragraph 77C(g)). The number can only be used in respect of one application (paragraph 77C(e)). Points will only be scored by the migrant in the sponsorship criteria in line with the requirements set out in paragraphs 77D to 77F are satisfied.

APPROPRIATE SALARY

7.134 Points will be awarded on the basis of the applicant's gross annual salary as recorded in the Certificate of Sponsorship Checking Service entry (paragraph 79). No points will be awarded unless the salary is £20,000 per annum unless the applicant is applying for leave to remain (paragraph 79A). No points will be awarded if the salary is less than the appropriate salary indicated in the codes of practice (paragraph 79B). If the applicant is paid on an hourly basis then consideration for what constitutes appropriate salary will be based on earnings up to a maximum of 48 hours per week (paragraph 79C).

ANNUAL LIMIT

7.135 In the period from 6 April 2011 to 5 April 2012 the annual limit for CoS to be allocated to sponsors has been set at 20,700 (paragraph 80A). CoS have been divided into 'restricted' and 'unrestricted'. If the role a sponsor wishes to fill is subject to the limit, the sponsor needs to apply to the Secretary of State for a restricted CoS before being able to assign it to a migrant (paragraph 80C). The point scoring requirements for making applications for CoS under the annual limit are set out in Table 11B (the contents of which are reproduced exactly). The sponsor must score at least 32 points for a 'Type of Job' and 'Salary on Offer' for the application to be granted (paragraph 80D). The provisions set out in Table 11B are accompanied by notes in paragraphs 81 to 81G.

7.136 The following categories are not affected by the limit and CoS for these types of applications are classified as 'unrestricted':

- Tier 2 (Intra-Company Transfer) migrants;
- Tier 2 (Sportsperson) migrants;
- Tier 2 (Minister of Religion) migrants;

- Tier 2 migrants extending their period of leave with their original employer or those with valid leave extending their stay by switching to a new employer;
- Migrants applying for entry clearance to fill a role paying a salary of £150,000 or more;
- Migrants with leave in other categories applying to switch in-country into Tier 2 (General);
- Tier 2 migrants or work permit holders subject to transitional arrangements.

TABLE 11B

7.137

Type of job	**Points**	**Salary on offer**	**Points**
Shortage Occupation	**75**	£20,000 – £20,999.99	**2**
PhD-level occupation code and job passes resident labour Market Test	**50**	£21,000 – £21,999.99	**3**
Job passes resident labour Market Test	**30**	£22,000 – £22,999.99	**4**
		£23,000 – £23,999.99	**5**
		£24,000 – £24,999.99	**6**
		£25,000 – £25,999.99	**7**
		£26,000 – £26,999.99	**8**
		£27,000 – £27,999.99	**9**
		£28,000 – £31,999.99	**10**
		£32,000 – £45,999.99	**15**
		£46,000 – £74,999.99	**20**
		£75,000 – £99,999.99	**25**
		£100,000 – £149,999.99	**30**

MONTHLY ALLOCATIONS

7.138 The annual limit has been divided into monthly allocations (paragraph 82) which may be adjusted (paragraph 82D). Each monthly allocation set out in Table 11C specifies the number of available CoS (paragraph 82A). Applications submitted by sponsors for CoS will be considered against each monthly allocation (paragraph 82B) and may be deferred if received in the following application period (paragraph 82C). The UKBA began accepting applications for restricted CoS from 16 March 2011. Table 11C is accompanied by notes at paragraphs 83 to 84A informing the reader of how applications made by sponsors are to be considered against monthly allocations.

TABLE 11C

7.139

Application Period	**Provisional monthly allocation**
Up to 6 April 2011	4,200
7 April – 5 May 2011	1,500
6 May 2011 – 5 June 2011	1,500
6 June 2011 – 5 July 2011	1,500
6 July 2011 – 5 August 2011	1,500
6 August 2011 – 5 September 2011	1,500
6 September 2011 – 5 October 2011	1,500
6 October 2011 – 5 November 2011	1,500
6 November 2011 – 5 December 2012	1,500
6 December 2012 – 5 January 2012	1,500
6 January 2012 – 5 February 2012	1,500
6 February 2012 – 5 March 2012	1,500

English language (Appendix B)

7.140 A Tier 2 (General) migrant must score 10 points for English language. In accordance with paragraph 6 of Appendix B an applicant will only score 10 points if:

'(a) The applicant has the level of English shown in the table below and:

(i) provides an original English language test certificate from an English language test provider approved by the Secretary of State for these purposes, which is within its validity period and clearly shows:

(1) the applicant's name,

(2) the qualification obtained, which must meet or exceed the level that the Secretary of State specifies in the guidance as being required to meet the standard laid down in the table below in all four components (reading, writing, speaking and listening), and:

(3) the date of the award, or

(ii) has obtained an academic qualification (not a professional or vocational qualification) which is deemed by UK NARIC to meet the recognised standard of a Bachelor's degree in the UK, and
  (1) provides the specified evidence to show he has the qualification, and
  (2) UK NARIC has confirmed that the degree was taught or researched in English to level C1 of the Council of Europe's Common European Framework for Language learning or above, or
(iii) in the cases referred to in row 1 of the table below, the applicant has obtained an academic qualification (not a professional or vocational qualification) which is deemed by UK NARIC to meet or exceed the recognised standard of a Bachelor's or Master's degree in the UK, and provides the specified evidence to show that:
  (1) he has the qualification, and
  (2) the qualification was taught or researched in English,
  and

(b) one or more of paragraph 2(b)-2(e), 7 or 8 applies to the applicant.'

7.141 Paragraphs 2(b)–2(e) of Appendix B relate to nationals of majority English-speaking countries, academic qualifications deemed by UK NARIC to meet or exceed the recognised standard of a Bachelor's or Master's degree or a PhD in the UK from an educational institution in one of the majority English-speaking countries, those who have been granted leave as Tier 1 (General), Tier 1 (Entrepreneur) migrants, business persons or highly skilled migrants (if leave was granted under the Rules which included the changes in place from 5 December 2006).

7.142 Rows 1 and 2 relate to applications for leave to remain and entry clearance in the Tier 2 (General) sub-category. Where an applicant is applying for leave to remain as a Tier 2 (General) migrant and they have or were last granted entry clearance, leave to enter or remain:

- as a Tier 2 (General) migrant under the Rules in force prior to 6 April 2011;
- a qualifying work permit holder, a representative of an overseas newspaper, news agency or broadcasting organisation;
- a member of the operational ground staff of an overseas-owned airline; or
- a Jewish Agency employee;

their English language ability must that of a basic user.

7.143 Where an applicant is making an application for entry clearance or leave to remain (in all other instances save for those set out above) as a Tier 2 (General) migrant, he or she must demonstrate a level of English equivalent to level B1 of the Council of Europe's Common European Framework for Language Learning or above. In cases referred to in rows 1 and 2 points will be awarded in line with paragraphs 7 to 9 of Appendix B.

Maintenance (funds) (Appendix C)

7.144 A Tier 2 (General) migrant must score 10 points for funds. The applicant must demonstrate the funds by providing specified documents. This requirement will also be met if the applicant:

- has an immigration status in one of the categories listed below, or
- is applying for leave to remain as a Tier 2 (General) migrant on the basis of the post-study work provisions, or
- is provided with a written undertaking by his or her sponsor, provided the sponsor is A-rated, to maintain and accommodate the migrant up to the amount of at least £800 up to the end of the first month of his employment, should it become necessary.

7.145 More precisely, the requirements are set out in paragraph 5 of Appendix C to the Immigration Rules:

'(a) the applicant has the level of funds shown in the table below and provides the specified documents, or

Level of funds	**Points awarded**
£800	**10**

(b) the applicant has entry clearance, leave to enter or leave to remain as:
(i) a Tier 2 Migrant,
(ii) a Jewish Agency Employee,
(iii) a member of the Operational Ground Staff of an Overseas-owned Airline,
(iv) a Minister of Religion, Missionary or Member of a Religious Order,
(v) a Representative of an Overseas Newspaper, News Agency or Broadcasting Organisation, or
(vi) a Work Permit Holder, or

(c) he is applying for leave to remain as a Tier 2 (General) Migrant and obtains points under the post-study work provisions in Table 11A of Appendix A, or

(d) the Sponsor is an a rated Sponsor and has certified on the Certificate of Sponsorship that, should it become necessary, it will maintain and accommodate the migrant up to the end of the first month of his employment. The Sponsor may limit the amount of the undertaking but any limit must be at least £800. Points will only be awarded if the applicant provides a valid Certificate of Sponsorship reference number with his application.'

7.146 Applicants and their dependants will need to submit for biometric data collection at a time specified by the UKBA, depending on whether their application is made by post, courier or at a Public Enquiry Office. If their application is successful, applicants and their dependants will be issued with biometric residence permits. In-country applications for a grant of leave and biometric immigration under Tier 2 can be made using a Tier 2 application form either by post, courier or at a Public Enquiry Office at a cost[134] of £550 (for a main applicant applying by post or courier) or £850 (for a main applicant applying at a Public Enquiry Office). Applications can also be made using the UKBA 'Apply Online' facility.[135] Dependants, applying at the same time as the main applicant, have to pay £275 for postal applications and £425 for applications made at a Public Enquiry Office, unless the dependant is a child aged 18 years or over. There are reduced fees for certain nationalities and their dependants. Dependants applying at a later date and applications made by dependent children aged 18 years or over will attract a charge of £550 for postal and courier applications and £850 for applications made in person at a Public Enquiry Office. Dependants must use a separate PBS (Dependant) application form.

Applications made by post should be sent to:	Applications made by courier should be sent to:
UK Border Agency Tier 2 PO Box 506 Durham DH99 1WB	UK Border Agency Tier 2 Millburngate House Millburngate Durham DH97 1PA

Extending Stay In The United Kingdom Through Marriage Or Partnership

7.147 Migrants may wish to extend their stay in the United Kingdom on the basis of their relationships with persons who have settled status in the United Kingdom or are EU/EEA nationals. By way of preserving family unity, the Immigration Rules make provisions *inter alia* for leave to enter or remain for:

- spouses and civil partners of persons present and settled in the United Kingdom or entering at the same time for settlement (paragraphs 281–289 subject to paragraphs 277–280);
- fiancé(e)s and proposed civil partners of persons present and settled in the United Kingdom (paragraphs 290–295 subject to paragraph 289AA); and

134 Cost as at 6 April 2011.
135 http://apply.ukba.homeoffice.gov.uk/iapply.portal.

- unmarried and same-sex partners of persons present and settled in the United Kingdom (paragraphs 295A–295O subject to paragraph 295AA).

These provisions are subject to a requirement that both parties, the migrant and the sponsor in the United Kingdom, are aged 21 or over unless serving as a member of HM Forces.[136] Family migration route is currently under review with changes coming in April 2012.[137]

7.148 Paragraphs 56D–56F of the Immigration Rules introduced a special visitor category for those wishing to apply for leave to enter as a visitor for marriage or to enter a civil partnership on the basis of:

- their intention to give notice of marriage or civil partnership or marry or form a civil partnership, and
- satisfactory evidence of arrangements made to give notice or marry (subject to satisfying the requirements set out in paragraphs 41(i)–(ix) and 41(xi)–(xii) of the Immigration Rules).

7.149 As of 29 November 2010 any migrant who wishes to apply to enter or remain in the United Kingdom as a spouse, civil partner, fiancé(e), proposed civil partner, unmarried partner or same-sex partner must demonstrate their ability to speak and understand English at level A1 of the Council of Europe's Common European Framework of Reference. The requirement to demonstrate English language ability was integrated into the Immigration Rules by the Statement of Changes in Immigration Rules (Cm 7944).[138] This requirement applies to nationals of a country outside of EU/EEA and Switzerland who are in a relationship with a person present and settled in the United Kingdom.

7.150 The following classes of applicants will be deemed to have met this requirement on presentation of required evidence:

- nationals of a majority English-speaking country such as Antigua and Barbuda, Australia, the Bahamas, Barbados, Belize, Canada, Dominica, Grenada, Guyana, Jamaica, New Zealand, St Kitts and Nevis, St Lucia, St Vincent and the Grenadines, Trinidad and Tobago and the USA;

136 Provision inserted by the Statement of Changes in Immigration Rules (HC 1113) on 27 November 2008. However, in the judgement handed down on 21 December 2010, *Quila & Ors v Secretary of State for the Home Department & Ors* [2010] EWCA Civ 1482, the Court of Appeal was asked to decide 'whether the ban contained in paragraph 277 of the immigration rules on the entry for settlement of foreign spouses between the ages of 18 and 21 is a lawful way of dealing with the problem of forced marriages'. The court declared that the application of paragraph 277 to the appellants was invalid. However, it did not go as far as striking down the Rule.

137 *Family Migration, A Consultation,* UK Border Agency, July 2011, http://www.ukba.homeoffice.gov.uk/sitecontent/documents/policyandlaw/consultations/family-migration/consultation.pdf?view=Binary. The consultation ran from 13 July to 6 October 2011.

138 Paragraphs 281(i)(a)(ii)–(vi) and 284(ix)(a)–(ix)(e) of the Immigration Rules.

- applicants who have obtained an academic qualification (save for a professional or vocational qualification) considered by UK NARIC to meet the recognised standard of a Bachelor's degree in the United Kingdom taught at an education institution in a majority English-speaking country listed above;
- applicants who have obtained an academic qualification (save for a professional or vocational qualification) considered by UK NARIC to meet the recognised standard of a Bachelor's degree in the United Kingdom (taught or researched in English or assessed and verified by UK NARIC as being taught or researched in English).

7.151 By way of a concession the UKBA will accept any Master's or PhD qualification obtained in the same way as Bachelor's degrees described above. This concession will be brought into the Immigration Rules in June 2011.[139]

7.152 Nationals of other countries who do not fall into the above categories will need to demonstrate their English language ability by passing an acceptable English language test with one of the test providers approved by the UKBA unless:

- they are aged 65 or over at the time of making the application; or
- they are considered by the Secretary of State to have a physical or mental condition preventing them from meeting this requirement; or
- there are considered by the Secretary of State exceptional compassionate circumstances preventing them from meeting this requirement.

On 6 April 2011 the UKBA published a new list of approved English language test providers for applications made under Tiers 1, 2 and 4 of the PBS and spouse and partner applications. On 8 July 2011 the UKBA updated this list to include

'• new acceptable test certificates for business language testing service (BULATS);
- clarification that we accept the test of English as a foreign language (TOEFL) ibt test (internet based test); and
- new test scores for tests conducted by Pearson'.[140]

The new updated list of approved English language tests can be found at http://www.ukba.homeoffice.gov.uk/sitecontent/applicationforms/new-approved-english-tests.pdf. This new list is broken down by awarding body, level, minimum grade required, test certificate validity and documents which are required with the application.

139 *Information for applicants on the new English language requirement for partners*, UK Border Agency, http://www.ukba.homeoffice.gov.uk/sitecontent/documents/partners-other-family/guidance-for-applicants.pdf.

140 *"Changes to the new list of English language test and providers"*, UK Border Agency, 8 July 2011, http://www.ukba.homeoffice.gov.uk/sitecontent/newsarticles/2011/july/13-list-of-english-language.

Long-term residents of a country where there is no test centre are exempt from the requirement.[141]

7.153 Non-EU/EEA family members of EU/EEA nationals exercising Treaty rights of residence in the United Kingdom can join their relatives in the United Kingdom.[142] Direct family members include spouses or civil partners, children under 21 or dependent children over 21 and dependent direct relatives in the ascending line such as parents and grandparents.[143] Extended family members may include dependent family members such as brothers, sisters and cousins and durable partners such as unmarried partners.[144] Non-EU/EEA family members who are visa nationals must obtain prior entry clearance in the form of an EU/EEA family permit[145] which is granted free of charge before they can travel to the United Kingdom in this capacity.

7.154 Migrants who are not yet married or have not yet formed a civil partnership with a person who is present and settled in the United Kingdom or an EU/EEA national but wish to do so in the United Kingdom can either:

- apply from overseas in the visitor for marriage or civil partnership category (for those who plan to leave the United Kingdom after the ceremony) or fiancé(e) and proposed civil partner category (for those who want to stay in the country following the marriage or registration of the civil partnership), or
- give a registrar notice to marry or register a civil partnership and apply for leave to remain in the United Kingdom in the spouse and civil partner category (from 9 May 2011 migrants subject to immigration control are no longer required to hold a Certificate of Approval).

7.155 Notice to marry or register a civil partnership must be given at a designated office. There are 76 designated offices in England and Wales while all registration offices in Scotland and Northern Ireland are designated. Registration in England and Wales is in person with both partners in attendance. In Scotland and Northern Ireland registration can be done by post. Once a notice is given there is a waiting period of 15 days (in England and Wales) and 14 days (in Scotland and Ireland) before a marriage or registration ceremony can take place. Notice is valid for one year in England, Wales and Northern Ireland and three months in Scotland and

141 At the time of publication there are no test centres in Angola, Burkina Faso, Cambodia, Cape Verde, Central African republic, Chad, Comoros, Congo, Democratic Republic of Congo, Dominican Republic, Equatorial Guinea, Eritrea, Gabon, Guinea, Guinea-Bissau, Ivory Coast, Kiribati, Lesotho, Liberia, Madagascar, Maldives, Rwanda, Samoa, Sao Tome Principe, Seychelles, Sierra Leone, Somalia, Swaziland, Togo, Wallis and Futuna Islands.

142 Chapter 3, Issue of an EEA family permit, European Casework Instructions, http://www.ukba.homeoffice.gov.uk/sitecontent/documents/policyandlaw/ecis/chapter3.pdf?view=Binary.

143 Article 2 of the Free Movement Directive (2004/38/EC) which came into force on 30 April 2006.

144 Article 3(2) of the Free Movement Directive (2004/38/EC) which came into force on 30 April 2006.

145 Using VAF5 application form.

marriage or registration of a civil partnership must ensue within that time. Once married or in a civil partnership, migrants such as students may apply to switch into the spouse or civil partner category using the FLR(M) form in the United Kingdom pursuant to paragraph 284 of the Immigration Rules provided that:

'(i) the applicant has limited leave to enter or remain in the United Kingdom which was given in accordance with any of the provisions of these Rules, other than where as a result of that leave he would not have been in the United Kingdom beyond 6 months from the date on which he was admitted to the United Kingdom on this occasion in accordance with these Rules, unless the leave in question is limited leave to enter as a fiance or proposed civil partner; and

(ii) is married to or the civil partner of a person present and settled in the United Kingdom; and

(iii) the parties to the marriage or civil partnership have met; and

(iv) the applicant has not remained in breach of the immigration laws; and

(v) the marriage or civil partnership has not taken place after a decision has been made to deport the applicant or he has been recommended for deportation or been given notice under Section 6(2) of the Immigration Act 1971 or been given directions for his removal under section 10 of the Immigration and Asylum Act 1999; and

(vi) each of the parties intends to live permanently with the other as his or her spouse or civil partner and the marriage or civil partnership is subsisting; and

(vii) there will be adequate accommodation for the parties and any dependants without recourse to public funds in accommodation which they own or occupy exclusively; and

(viii) the parties will be able to maintain themselves and any dependants adequately without recourse to public funds; and

(ix)(a) the applicant provides an original English language test certificate in speaking and listening from an English language test provider approved by the Secretary of State for these purposes, which clearly shows the applicant's name and the qualification obtained (which must meet or exceed level A1 of the Common European Framework of Reference) unless:

- (i) the applicant is aged 65 or over at the time he makes his application; or
- (ii) the Secretary of State considers that the applicant has a physical or mental condition that would prevent him from meeting the requirement; or;
- (iii) the Secretary of State considers there are exceptional compassionate circumstances that would prevent the applicant from meeting the requirement; or

(ix)(b) the applicant is a national of one of the following countries: Antigua and Barbuda; Australia; the Bahamas; Barbados; Belize; Canada; Dominica; Grenada; Guyana; Jamaica; New Zealand; St Kitts and Nevis; St Lucia; St Vincent and the Grenadines; Trinidad and Tobago; United States of America; or (ix)(c) the applicant has obtained an academic qualification (not a professional or vocational qualification), which is deemed by UK NARIC to meet the recognised standard of a Bachelor's degree in the UK, from an educational establishment in one of the following countries: Antigua and Barbuda; Australia; The Bahamas; Barbados; Belize; Dominica; Grenada; Guyana; Ireland; Jamaica; New Zealand; St Kitts and Nevis; St Lucia; St Vincent and The Grenadines; Trinidad and Tobago; the UK; the USA; and provides the specified documents; or

(ix)(d) the applicant has obtained an academic qualification (not a professional or vocational qualification) which is deemed by UK NARIC to meet the recognised standard of a Bachelor's degree in the UK, and
- (1) provides the specified evidence to show he has the qualification, and
- (2) UK NARIC has confirmed that the degree was taught or researched in English, or

(ix)(e) has obtained an academic qualification (not a professional or vocational qualification) which is deemed by UK NARIC to meet the recognised standard of a Bachelor's degree in the UK, and provides the specified evidence to show:
- (1) he has the qualification, and
- (2) that the qualification was taught or researched in English.'

Certificate of Approval Scheme

7.156 Prior to 9 May 2011 migrants who were subject to immigration control had to obtain a Certificate of Approval ('CoA') before being able to marry in the United Kingdom. British citizens, EU/EEA or Swiss nationals, family members of an EU/EEA national exercising Treaty rights of residence in the United Kingdom, those with a certificate of entitlement and all others not subject to immigration control did not have to obtain prior permission in the form of a CoA.

7.157 Provisions governing the Certificate of Approval Scheme are contained in the Asylum and Immigration (Treatment of Claimants, etc) Act 2004, ss 19–25 ('2004 Act') and Civil Partnership Act 2004, Sch 23. Correspondingly, they came into force on 1 February 2005 by way of the Immigration (Procedure for Marriage) Regulations 2005, SI 2005/15[146] and on 5 December 2005 by way of the Immigration (Procedure for Formation of Civil Partnerships) Regulations 2005, SI 2005/2917. The Scheme was launched in response to the Government's concerns of a growing number of sham marriages but has since undergone a series of amendments following judgments in the *Baiai* case (see below) in which the

146 The Scheme was extended to the Isle of Man by the Immigration (Isle of Man) Order 2008, SI 2008/680.

Joint Council for Welfare of Immigrants and the AIRE Centre acted as interveners. The Scheme was abolished with effect from 9 May 2011.

Historical note on the Certificate of Approval Scheme

7.158 Changes to the Scheme, a summary of which can be found in an UKBA policy document entitled 'Important Information Regarding Certificate of Approval for Marriage or Civil Partnership Applications',[147] were made following:

- the High Court judgment of 10 April 2006 that declared the 2004 Act, s 19(3) to be incompatible with Articles 12 and 14 of the ECHR. Section 19(3) was found to amount to an unlawful interference with Article 12 (right to marry) and was discriminatory on the grounds of nationality and religion given the Church of England exemption contrary to Article 14 (prohibition on discrimination) (*Baiai & Ors v Secretary of State for the Home Department & Anor* [2006] EWHC 823 (Admin));[148]

- the Court of Appeal judgment of 23 May 2007 in *Secretary of State for the Home Department v Baiai & Ors* [2007] EWCA Civ 478 which upheld the ruling of the High Court;

- the House of Lords judgment of 30 July 2008 in *Baiai & Ors, R (On The Application of) v Secretary of State For The Home Department* [2008] UKHL 53 which held the 2004 Act,s 19(1) to be incompatible with Article 14 as read together with Article 12. The declaration of incompatibility made by the lower courts was set aside save as to the discrimination between civil and Anglican marriages in respect of the 2004 Act, s 19(1) (instead of s 19(3)). Section 19(3) sets out the requirement to obtain the permission of the Secretary of State before entering into marriage whereas s 19(1) grants exemption for marriages conducted in the Church of England.

7.159 The Government failed to remedy the declaration of incompatibility within a reasonable time. On several occasions the Joint Committee on Human Rights wrote to the Government prompting it to provide information regarding progress in dealing with this matter.[149] The delay in dealing with the declaration of incompatibility following the House of Lords ruling in *Baiai* was reported by

147 See at http://www.ukba.homeoffice.gov.uk/sitecontent/documents/visitingtheuk/coaguidance.pdf.

148 This was followed by a claim for damages heard on 10 May 2006 in *Baiai & Ors, R (on the application of) v Secretary of State for the Home Department & Anor* [2006] EWHC 1035 (Admin) which also considered an additional issue of the impact of section 19 on applicants who are present in the UK unlawfully.

149 Paragraphs 145–155, *'Joint Committee on Human Rights, Enhancing Parliament's role in relation to human rights judgments'*, Fifteenth Report of Session 2009–10, HL Paper 85/HC 455, published on 26 March 2010, House of Lords and House of Commons, http://www.publications.parliament.uk/pa/jt200910/jtselect/jtrights/85/85.pdf.

the Joint Committee on 26 March 2010. In suspending the requirement to pay a specified fee for a CoA application[150] the Government felt it had adequately addressed the House of Lords' criticism that 'the fees associated with the Certificate of Approval scheme could interfere with the right of needy applicants to marry.'[151]

7.160 In a communiqué to the Joint Committee dated 12 November 2009 the Government said that 'the UK Border Agency has sought for some time to bring marriages after Anglican preliminaries in England and Wales within the CoA scheme but has been unable to find a workable solution.'[152] Instead, it was proposed to do away with the whole Certificate of Approval Scheme by way of 'a Remedial Order under Section 10 of the Human Rights Act.'[153] The Joint Committee welcomed the decision to bring forward a Remedial Order but expressed a concern that the Scheme would continue to operate and called on the Government to publish a draft Order as soon as possible 'in the light of the earlier prolonged delay in this case.'[154]

7.161 The coalition Government issued a response to the Joint Committee's report on 27 July 2010 in which it stressed its commitment to removing the incompatibility found in respect of the Certificate of Approval Scheme by laying a non-urgent Remedial Order (under the Human Rights Act 1998, s 10) before Parliament before the summer recess with a view to it coming into force by the end of 2010 or early in 2011, subject to Parliamentary scrutiny. The response went on to say that:

> 'The proposed Remedial Order will abolish the Certificate of Approval scheme so that those subject to immigration control who wish to marry in the UK and the Isle of Man will have the freedom to give notice of marriage without

150 The suspension commenced on 9 April 2009. Since 31 July 2009 migrants who applied between 2005 and 2009 have been able to apply for a refund of the fees paid for their CoA application. The repayment scheme came to an end on 31 July 2010.

151 Paragraph 149, *Joint Committee on Human Rights, Enhancing Parliament's role in relation to human rights judgments,* Fifteenth Report of Session 2009–10, HL Paper 85/HC 455, published on 26 March 2010, House of Lords and House of Commons, http://www.publications.parliament.uk/pa/jt200910/jtselect/jtrights/85/85.pdf.

152 Paragraph 149, *Joint Committee on Human Rights, Enhancing Parliament's role in relation to human rights judgments,* Fifteenth Report of Session 2009–10, HL Paper 85/HC 455, published on 26 March 2010, House of Lords and House of Commons, http://www.publications.parliament.uk/pa/jt200910/jtselect/jtrights/85/85.pdf.

153 Paragraph 149, *Joint Committee on Human Rights, Enhancing Parliament's role in relation to human rights judgments,* Fifteenth Report of Session 2009–10, HL Paper 85/HC 455, published on 26 March 2010, House of Lords and House of Commons, http://www.publications.parliament.uk/pa/jt200910/jtselect/jtrights/85/85.pdf.

154 Paragraph 152, *Joint Committee on Human Rights, Enhancing Parliament's role in relation to human rights judgments,* Fifteenth Report of Session 2009–10, HL Paper 85/HC 455, published on 26 March 2010, House of Lords and House of Commons, http://www.publications.parliament.uk/pa/jt200910/jtselect/jtrights/85/85.pdf.

having first to seek permission of the Secretary of State. This will ensure that the incompatibility with the Convention will be removed. Though the current exemption for the Anglican Church only relates to marriages, not to civil partnerships, and thus there was no discrimination in the application of the scheme to civil partnerships, the Remedial Order will also repeal the Certificate of Approval scheme in relation to civil partnerships. This will ensure consistency between the treatment of civil partnerships and marriages.'[155]

The rationale for abolishing the CoA by way of a statutory instrument and not primary legislation and foregoing public consultation is given in the Explanatory Memorandum to the draft Order.[156]

7.162 On 26 July 2010 the Government announced its intention to abolish the Certificate of Approval Scheme and laid the draft Asylum and Immigration (Treatment of Claimants, etc) Act 2004 (Remedial) Order 2010. Two years after the House of Lords judgment, the Government was finally forced to concede defeat and pronounce that the Scheme was 'no longer an effective method of preventing sham marriage.'[157] The Explanatory Note to the Remedial Order[158] stated that:

> 'In order to remove the incompatibility, Article 2 makes changes to sections 19 and 20 of the 2004 Act, to remove the Certificate of Approval Scheme, as it applies in England and Wales.[159] Article 2 also makes consequential amendments to sections 21 to 23 of the 2004 Act in respect of Scotland and Northern Ireland, and to section 25. Article 4 makes consequential amendments to Schedule 23 to the Civil Partnership Act 2004 in order to remove the Certificate of Approval Scheme as it applies to civil partnerships in England and Wales, Scotland and Northern Ireland.'

7.163 On 4 April 2011 the Remedial Order was approved by Parliament. The Asylum and Immigration (Treatment of Claimants, etc) Act 2004 (Remedial) Order 2011, SI 2011/1158 came into force on 9 May 2011 marking the end of the Scheme. Those wishing to give notice to marry or register a civil partnership from 9 May 2011 will have to do so at a designated register office but will no longer need to have a CoA, entry clearance for the purpose of entering into marriage or registering a civil partnership, or settled status in the United Kingdom.

155 *Responding to human rights judgments, Government Response to the Joint Committee on Human Rights' Fifteenth Report of Session 2009–10,* July 2010, Cm 7892, http://www.justice.gov.uk/responding-human-rights-judgements-2009-2010.pdf.

156 See at http://www.opsi.gov.uk/si/si2010/draft/em/ukdsiem_9780111500644_en.pdf.

157 *Changes to the certificate of approval scheme,* UK Border Agency, 26 July 2010, http://www.ukba.homeoffice.gov.uk/sitecontent/newsfragments/32-coa-changes.

158 See at http://www.opsi.gov.uk/si/si2010/draft/ukdsi_9780111500644_en_2.

159 The Order also applies to the Isle of Man.

Settlement on the basis of long residence

7.164 As a starting point, temporary leave granted to students, student nurses, students re-sitting an examination, students writing-up a thesis, postgraduate doctors or dentists, sabbatical officers, participants in IGS, SEGS or FT: WISS, Tier 4 or Tier 1 (Post-Study Work) migrants does not lead to settlement. Those on temporary leave can either switch into a category that leads to settlement (see **7.21–7.146**, although the Government has put up various barriers to settlement throughout 2010/11), enter into marriage or partnership with a person present and settled in the United Kingdom, EEA or Swiss national (see **7.147–7.163**, although this route is also under review) or, after a lengthy period spent in the United Kingdom apply for indefinite leave to remain on the basis of long residence, which we come to address in this section. As noted throughout this book the Government has indicated its intention to sever the connection between temporary migration for work, study and settlement. Settlement provisions have been revised from 6 April 2011 with the introduction of a new income requirement for some categories, tightening up of the English language requirement and criminality test.

7.165 Aside from the provisions relating to settlement under the specific categories of admission, there is also a route to settlement through long residence. In accordance with requirements prescribed in paragraph 276B of the Immigration Rules, a person, to be granted indefinite leave to remain, subject to public interest considerations and countervailing factors, must have resided in the United Kingdom[160] continuously and lawfully for 10 years or more, or accumulated 14 years of continuous residence of any legality, have no unspent convictions within the meaning of the Rehabilitation of Offenders Act 1974[161] and have sufficient knowledge of the English language and life in the United Kingdom. Students often fall foul of the 'lawful' and 'continuous' requirements under the long residence category. Most commonly, continuity of leave is broken by absences from the United Kingdom for a period of six months or more at any one time and a total of more than 18 months of absences in the 10/14 year period.

7.166 The other end of the scale is balanced by the totality of applicants' personal and family circumstances and their ties to the United Kingdom. Caseworkers must consider any reasons why it would be undesirable for an applicant to be granted indefinite leave to remain on the basis of long residence. The factors that caseworkers should take into consideration in all cases pursuant to paragraph 276B(ii) of the Immigration Rules[162] are age, strength of connections in the

160 Time spent in the Republic of Ireland, Channel Islands or the Isle of Man does not count as residence in the UK for the purpose of long residence rules.

161 Paragraph 276B(iii) of the Immigration Rules. Introduced on 6 April 2011 by the Statement of Changes in Immigration Rules (HC 863).

162 Previous criminal record and nature of any offence was excluded from this list by virtue of the changes to the Immigration Rules on 6 April 2011. The new criminality test was introduced by the Statement of Changes in Immigration Rules (HC 863).

United Kingdom, personal history, including character, conduct, associations and employment record, domestic circumstances, compassionate circumstances and any representations made on the applicants' behalf. Conversely, these same reasons, provided they are favourable, may serve to demonstrate the depth of a person's commitment to the United Kingdom.

7.167 Paragraph 276A(a) of the Immigration Rules defines 'continuous residence' as:

> 'residence in the United Kingdom for an unbroken period, and for these purposes a period shall not be considered to have been broken where an applicant is absent from the United Kingdom for a period of 6 months or less at any one time, provided that the applicant in question has existing limited leave to enter or remain upon their departure and return, but shall be considered to have been broken if the applicant:
> (i) has been removed under Schedule 2 of the 1971 Act, section 10 of the 1999 Act, has been deported or has left the United Kingdom having been refused leave to enter or remain here; or
> (ii) has left the United Kingdom and, on doing so, evidenced a clear intention not to return; or
> (iii) left the United Kingdom in circumstances in which he could have had no reasonable expectation at the time of leaving that he would lawfully be able to return; or
> (iv) has been convicted of an offence and was sentenced to a period of imprisonment or was directed to be detained in an institution other than a prison (including, in particular, a hospital or an institution for young offenders), provided that the sentence in question was not a suspended sentence; or
> (v) has spent a total of more than 18 months absent from the United Kingdom during the period in question.'

7.168 Paragraph 276A(b) defines 'lawful residence' as:

> 'residence which is continuous residence pursuant to:
> (i) existing leave to enter or remain; or
> (ii) temporary admission within section 11 of the 1971 Act where leave to enter or remain is subsequently granted; or
> (iii) an exemption from immigration control, including where an exemption ceases to apply if it is immediately followed by a grant of leave to enter or remain.'

Historical note on the long residence provisions

7.169 The history of long residence provisions hails back to Article 3(3) of the European Convention on Establishment which states that 'nationals of any

Contracting Party who have been lawfully residing for more than ten years in the territory of any other Party may only be expelled for reasons of national security or if the other reasons mentioned in paragraph 1 of this article are of a particularly serious nature.'[163] For a number of years before finding their way into the Immigration Rules on 1 April 2003 (paragraphs 276A–276D, HC 538), long residence provisions were applied on a discretionary basis by way of a concession. The inclusion of the provisions in the Rules meant that decisions under the concession were made yet more amenable to appeal under the Nationality, Immigration and Asylum Act 2002.

7.170 As far as the eligibility under the concession is concerned, Timothy Kirkhope, Parliamentary Under-Secretary of State for the Home Department, stated on 8 February 1996 in the House of Commons that 'we do not distinguish between nationals of the contracting parties and other overseas nationals.'[164] In fact, under the concession the provision in Article 3(3) was extended 'to include all foreign nationals, to grant indefinite leave rather than simply refrain from removing such a person; and to allow those who have been here illegally to benefit.'[165]

7.171 Even after the incorporation of the long residence provisions into the Rules, the old concession continued to co-exist alongside the Rules for a few years regardless of its apparently outdated wording:

> '1. Introduction
> There is no provision within the Immigration Rules for a person to be granted indefinite leave to remain solely on the basis of the length of his or her residence.
> The grant of indefinite leave to remain on the basis of lengthy continuous residence is discretionary, each case should be considered on its merits.
> ...
>
> 10. Refusal of Indefinite Leave to Remain
> Applications that do not meet the criteria set out in the above paragraphs should normally be refused unless the circumstances are particularly exceptional and it would, in view of those exceptional circumstances be unreasonable to consider removal. Any case where it is proposed to refuse the application despite the lengthy residence should be referred to a senior officer.

163 *European Convention on Establishment (ETS No. 19)*, entered into force on 23 February 1965 and ratified by the UK on 14 October 1969, University of Minnesota Human Rights Library, http://www1.umn.edu/humanrts/euro/ets19.html.

164 House of Commons Hansard Written Answers, 8 February 1996, http://www.publications.parliament.uk/pa/cm199596/cmhansrd/vo960208/text/60208w08.htm (accessed 21 September 2010).

165 Long Residence Concession, Chapter 18, IDI, September 2004.

Applications for indefinite leave to remain on the basis of long residence which fall for refusal should be refused under Paragraph 322(1) of HC 395 (no provision in the Rules).'[166]

7.172 This irregularity was examined in *OS (10 years' lawful residence Hong Kong* [2006] UKAIT 00031, promulgated on 20 March 2006. In its determination the Asylum and Immigration Tribunal, remarked that:

'5. At a hearing before the Immigration Judge, the Home Office Presenting Officer stated that the concession had been withdrawn when the rules relating to long residence were introduced. That was not true. Not only had the concession not been withdrawn then, but we were told by both parties before us that on 28 February 2006 the concession still appeared on the Home Office website, within the Immigration Directorate's instructions. The chapter in question is Chapter 18, headed "The Long Residence Concession" and the version we have seen is dated September 2004.'

7.173 The Tribunal found that the concession is not to be used as an aid to the interpretation of the Rule (paragraph 16), but at the same time:

'19. Despite the errors to which we have drawn attention in the wording of Chapter 18 of the Immigration Directorate's instructions, it seems to us that the co-existence of the Rules and the concession is entirely understandable. The Rules give, in essence, a right to indefinite leave to remain after ten years' lawful residence, but that right is contingent on there having been no illegality. The concession survives the introduction of the Rule to lay out the terms of an exercise of discretion to grant indefinite leave to remain after ten years residence which has not been entirely lawful. It is better to have a right than to have the possibility of benefit under a discretion.

...

22. Thus, although we have held that the <u>terms</u> of the concession cannot be used as an aid to interpreting the Rule, the <u>existence</u> of the concession helps to make it clear that the Rule means exactly what it says. Cases that fall outside the Rule are amply dealt with by the concession.'

7.174 The concession was removed after the decision in *OS* [2006] UKAIT 00031 (paragraph 9)[167] although its co-existence with the Rules was not found to be reprehensible, and replaced subsequently by Chapter 18, Long Residence, IDI, May/07 (issued on 4 May 2007). The wording in paragraph 2.1.3, Chapter 18, IDI, "Time Spent Out of the United Kingdom", dealing with continuity of residence,

166 Long Residence Concession, Chapter 18, IDI, September 2004.

167 *TT (Long residence – "continuous residence" – interpretation) British Overseas Citizen* [2008] UKAIT 00038.

came under scrutiny in *TT (Long residence – 'continuous residence' – interpretation) British Overseas Citizen* [2008] UKAIT 00038.

7.175 In TT, the Tribunal held that in stating that 'a person who leaves the UK when one period of leave expires, and comes back with a fresh grant of leave, will not be resuming his continuous residence, but will instead be starting a new period of residence in the UK' paragraph 2.1.3 purported to interpret 'existing limited leave' at paragraph 276A(a) of the Immigration Rules as 'same leave' and this was found to be inconsistent with the purpose of the provision in the Rules (paragraph 23 of the determination).

7.176 Following the decision that 'a period of continuous residence, as defined in paragraph 276A(a), is not broken in circumstances where a person with leave to remain in the United Kingdom obtains further leave from an Entry Clearance Officer while temporarily outside the United Kingdom prior to the expiry of the leave to remain',[168] caseworkers were advised on 22 August 2008 to put the following cases on hold until further notice:

> 'when the applicant has; [sic]
>
> - left the UK with valid leave on the date of their departure and;
> - subsequently re-entered the UK with a <u>different</u> grant of leave than the one they had when they departed.
> - this includes applications where the applicant has had a gap of leave <u>whilst outside the UK</u> between their old leave expiring and obtaining new Entry Clearance or Leave to Enter. Please note this applies to 10 year lawful residence cases, as long as the applicant is <u>outside the UK</u> during the gap in their leave. 10 year cases where the applicant has a gap of leave while they are <u>in the UK</u> should be refused as normal.'[169]

7.177 On 9 September 2008 caseworkers were given a further instruction that:

> 'C**ontinuous residence** should not be considered to have been broken if an applicant had valid leave on the date that they departed the UK and valid leave on the date that they re-entered. **We will no longer treat *'existing'* leave to mean the *same* leave.**
>
> Continuity of residence is not broken if an applicant re-enters the UK with a different grant of valid leave than the one they had when they departed.
>
> ...

168 *TT (Long residence – "continuous residence" – interpretation) British Overseas Citizen* [2008] UKAIT 00038.

169 Long Residence, Continuous Residence, Interim Operational Instruction from Performance Directorate, Immigration Group, 103/589, 22 August 2008.

> **Continuous *lawful* residence** in 10 year long residence cases should not be considered to have been broken if the applicant has a gap in leave whilst they were outside the UK … Any gaps in valid leave while the applicant was in the UK should be considered to have broken continuous lawful residence.'[170]

7.178 The IDIs were amended. In its judgment handed down on 19 January 2009 in *ZH (Bangladesh) v Secretary of State for the Home Department* [2009] EWCA Civ 8, a case concerned with the 14 year provision, the Court of Appeal defined the role of the IDI as follows:

> 'Two things seem reasonably clear. One is that the IDI does not have, and cannot be treated as if it possessed, the force of law. The other is that, at least in a case such the present one, the IDI must have a legitimate bearing in the sense that it would be wrong for the immigration judge to adjudicate in ignorance of it. Between these poles one can locate two further propositions. First, albeit its author is in law the author of the immigration rules, the IDI is not an aid to the construction of those rules. Secondly, and assuming always that it sits, as it must, within the four corners of the rule to which it relates, the IDI's significance cannot depend on whether it steers caseworkers towards a restrictive or a generous application of the rule.'[171]

7.179 The IDIs currently in use were last updated on 22 April 2009.[172] They are positively brimming with discretion.[173] Unlike the PBS, the system is flexible and generous as applications are considered on a case-by-case basis depending on individual circumstances of applicants. Paragraph 2.2.4 of Chapter 18, IDI, which was modified in line with casework instructions, states that:

> 'Continuous residence should be considered to have been broken if the applicant has spent a total of more than 18 months absent from the United Kingdom during the period in question.
>
> Subject to that, continuous residence shall not be considered to have been broken where an applicant is absent from the United Kingdom for a period of 6 months or less at any one time, *provided that the applicant has existing limited leave to enter or remain upon his departure and return* (see Example 1).
>
> To benefit from this, an applicant must have valid leave on the date that they departed the UK and valid leave on the date that they returned. Please note that this does not have to be the same grant of leave on departure and return (see

170 Casework Instruction, Long Residence – Continuous Residence, 103/596, 9 September 2008, http://www.whatdotheyknow.com/request/4429/response/10727/attach/html/4/Casework%20Instruction%20103%20596.doc.html.

171 *ZH (Bangladesh) v Secretary of State for the Home Department* [2009] EWCA Civ 8 at para 32.

172 This page of the IDI was last updated on 5 October 2010.

173 Chapter 18, IDI, April 2009, can be accessed at http://www.ukba.homeoffice.gov.uk/sitecontent/documents/policyandlaw/IDIs/idischapter18/longresidence/Long_Residence_IDI-_final_d1.pdf?view=Binary.

> Example 2). Nor is it necessary for the leave to be in the same category (i.e. an applicant can depart the UK with leave as a student and return with leave as a work permit holder). As long as the applicant has valid leave on both the date of departure and the date they return, they will not have broken continuous residence.'

7.180 Contrary to instructions given to caseworkers in September 2008 to consider 'any gaps in valid leave while the applicant was in the UK' (as above) to have broken continuous lawful residence, paragraph 2.3.3 of Chapter 18, IDI says that:

> 'If an applicant has a **single** short gap in lawful residence through making one **single** previous application out of time by a few days (not usually more than 10 calendar days out of time), caseworkers should use discretion granting ILR, **so long as the application meets all the other requirements.**
>
> It would **not usually** be appropriate to exercise discretion when an applicant has **more than one** gap in their lawful residence due to submitting more than one of their previous applications out of time, as they would not have shown the necessary commitment to ensuring they have maintained lawful leave throughout their time in the UK.
>
> It may be appropriate to use your judgement in cases where an applicant has submitted a single application more than 10 days out of time if there are extenuating reasons for this (e.g. postal strike, hospitalisation, administrative error on our part etc). This must be discussed with a Senior Caseworker.'

7.181 Applicants are advised to read the IDIs and the Rules before making an application. While there is no provision in the Immigration Rules to grant indefinite leave to enter, IDIs allow for discretion to be exercised outside the Rules where an applicant meets all the other criteria set out in paragraph 276B of the Rules. Applications for indefinite leave to remain on the basis of long residence must be made using SET(O) application forms. These applications can no longer be made at a Public Enquiry Office. Applications can also be made using the UKBA 'Apply Online' facility.[174] Postal applications cost £972[175] and must be sent to:

UK Border Agency

SET(O)

Indefinite Leave to Remain
PO Box 591
Durham
DH1 9FS

174 http://apply.ukba.homeoffice.gov.uk/iapply.portal.
175 Cost from 6 April 2011.

7.182 There is no provision for dependants in the long residence category and, as the IDIs provide, 'any dependants specified in paragraph 34D (spouse, civil partner, unmarried or same-sex partner and/or child under the age of 18) included on the application form should normally be refused on the basis that there is no provision in the immigration rules.' The IDIs go on to say that 'should the main applicant be granted ILR, family members will need to apply under the relevant categories of the rules relating to spouses, civil partners and dependant [sic] children of persons present and settled in the UK.' These provisions can be found in Part 8 of the Immigration Rules (family members). This route, for all its flexibility, does not sit comfortably with the Government's efforts to discourage irregular migration, to cut net migration figures, and if so, we may see it disappear entirely or in part in not too distant future.

British citizenship

7.183 British nationality law is complex and multifarious. Its legacy stems from the depths of British colonial history. The last[176] Government's enthralment to the concept of civic unity prompted a systematic revision of what British citizenship should be all about and led to the Borders, Citizenship and Immigration Act 2009 ('BCIA 2009'). The new legislation made some liberal amendments to existing naturalisation and registration provisions set out in the British Nationality Act 1981 ('BNA 1981')[177] but mainly amended naturalisation law in line with a substantial restructuring of immigration control. The naturalisation provisions were at the last instance amended by the Nationality, Immigration and Asylum Act 2002 and by the Civil Partnership Act 2004.

7.184 Students and individuals in related categories who have become settled (ordinarily resident without time restrictions)[178] through switching, marriage or long-term residence may consider becoming British citizens unless there are constraints which prevent them from having dual nationality. Broadly speaking, the BNA 1981 sets out the rules for acquisition of British citizenship by birth, adoption, abandonment, descent, naturalisation and registration. Adults with foreign or Commonwealth nationality, who fulfil set prerequisites, may naturalise as British citizens, but minors (under the age of 18 years old) can only register as British citizens. Registration is subject to a variety of precursory factors determining eligibility. This section is concerned primarily with the current state of naturalisation law and its future. Sections related to naturalisation in Part 2 of BCIA 2009 are not in force at the time of writing, nor are there any current plans to implement them.

176 In power before May 2010.

177 Although the rigidity of the provision on absences during the qualifying period are of warranted concern.

178 See Laurie Fransman QC, *Fransman's British Nationality Law* (3rd edn, Bloomsbury Professional, 2011), sections 13.2.2 and 13.2.3.

7.185 Naturalisation provisions are currently detailed in BNA 1981, s 6 and Sch 1. The Secretary of State has the discretion to disregard some of the requirements contained there although the core requirements cannot be waived. Legislative provisions are further supported by nationality policy contained in Volume 1, Chapter 18 of Nationality Instructions and Annexes A to F.[179] Section 6 states the following:

> '(1) If, on an application for naturalisation as a British citizen made by a person of full age and capacity, the Secretary of State is satisfied that the applicant fulfils the requirements of Schedule 1 for naturalisation as such a citizen under this subsection, he may, if he thinks fit, grant to him a certificate of naturalisation as such a citizen.
>
> (2) If, on an application for naturalisation as a British citizen made by a person of full age and capacity who on the date of the application is married to a British citizen, or is the civil partner of a British citizen the Secretary of State is satisfied that the applicant fulfils the requirements of Schedule 1 for naturalisation as such a citizen under this subsection, he may, if he thinks fit, grant to him a certificate of naturalisation as such a citizen.'

7.186 Section 6(2) applies to spouses and civil partners of British citizens. Migrants applying for naturalisation as British citizens will need to fulfil the following requirements in accordance with BNA 1981, s 6 and Sch 1:

- be aged 18 or over; and
- be of sound mind; and
- intend to have their home or main home in the United Kingdom (or continue in Crown Service, the service of an international organisation of which the United Kingdom is a member, or the service of a company or association established in the United Kingdom) (Sch 1, para 1(1)(d); this provision does not apply to those applying under s 6(2)); and
- can communicate in English, Welsh or Scottish Gaelic to an acceptable level (Sch 1. paras 1(1)(c) and 3(e)); and
- must have sufficient knowledge of life in the United Kingdom (which means having passed a Life in the UK test) (Sch 1, paras 1(1)(ca) and 3(e)); and
- be of good character (Sch 1, paras 1(1)(b) and 3(e)); and
- meet the residential requirements.

7.187 To satisfy the residential requirements, migrants must:

179 Chapter 18 and Annexes thereto can be found at: http://www.ukba.homeoffice.gov.uk/sitecontent/documents/policyandlaw/nationalityinstructions/nichapter18/.

- be resident in the United Kingdom for at least five years (for those applying under s 6(1)) or at least three years (for those applying under s 6(2)); and
- have been lawfully present in the United Kingdom at the start of the residential qualifying period, be it five or three years; and
- have not spent more than 450 days outside the United Kingdom during the five year period (Sch 1, para 1(2)(a)) or 270 days outside the United Kingdom during the three year period (Sch 1, para 3(a)); and
- have not spent more than 90 days outside the United Kingdom in the last 12 months of the residential qualifying period (Sch 1, paras 1(2)(b) and 3(b)); and
- not have been in breach of the immigration rules at any stage during the residential qualifying period (Sch 1, paras 1(2)(d) and 3(d)).

Also, migrants applying under s 6(1) must be free from immigration time restrictions for the last 12 months of the residential qualifying period prior to making their naturalisation application (Sch 1, para 1(2)(c)) while those applying under s 6(2) must be free from immigration time restrictions on the date of application (Sch 1, para 3(d)). Applications for naturalisation are made using Form AN. Applications can also be made using the UKBA 'Apply Online' facility.[180] Migrants and their dependants must qualify in their own right before making an application. The costs of applying for citizenship are normally revised annually. From 6 April 2011 the costs of applying are £836 for a single applicant and £1,294 for a married couple.

7.188 On 3 July 2007 the Government published a Green Paper entitled 'The Governance of Britain' the purpose of which was to address the questions of accountability of the executive and expansion of the rights and responsibilities of citizens. The Government charged Lord Goldsmith QC 'to carry out a review of citizenship, looking both at legal aspects and other issues including civic participation and social responsibility.'[181] Lord Goldsmith commenced his review on 5 October 2007 and on 11 March 2008 delivered his recommendations in the body of his report, 'Citizenship: Our Common Bond', in which he proposed that:

> '... government should give consideration to moving towards a system of rules whereby people who have come to the UK either have limited leave to be here or they have to apply to become citizens. Our system for allowing people to access citizenship should be rigorous but it should also make a clear distinction between people who are temporary residents and people who are

180 http://apply.ukba.homeoffice.gov.uk/iapply.portal.

181 Paragraph 193, Part 4, *The Governance of Britain*, CM 7170, 3 July 2007, http://www.official-documents.gov.uk/document/cm71/7170/7170.pdf.

here permanently – and hence people who ought to share in a common sense of belonging, with the rights and responsibilities that go along with that.'[182]

7.189 Preceding the publication of Lord Goldsmith's report, on 20 February 2008 the Secretary of State announced that 'the rights and benefits of citizenship will be available to those who can demonstrate a commitment to our shared values and a willingness to contribute to the community'.[183] The Secretary of State put forward a new 'citizenship deal' encapsulated in a Green Paper, 'The Path to Citizenship: Next Steps in Reforming the Immigration System',[184] running in tandem with far-reaching plans to simplify immigration law and strengthen UK borders already underfoot. The Green Paper which launched a nationwide consultation was summarised as follows:

- 'a three stage route to citizenship, including a new probationary period of citizenship, requiring new migrants to demonstrate their contribution to the UK at every stage or leave the country;
- full access to benefits being delayed until migrants have completed the probationary period;
- migrants having to improve their command of English to pass probation;
- anyone committing an offence resulting in prison being barred from becoming a citizen;
- those committing minor offences being required to spend longer in the new probationary period of citizenship;
- migrants contributing to a new fund for managing the transitional impacts of migration, providing extra financial help to communities experiencing change from migration; and
- migrants getting involved in their communities through volunteering being able to graduate to British citizenship more quickly."[185]

7.190 The three routes to citizenship were through work, family and protection and the three steps that migrants would have needed to take on the path to citizenship were temporary residence, probationary citizenship and British

182 *Citizenship: Our Common Bond*, 11 March 2008, http://www.justice.gov.uk/docs/citizenship-report-full.pdf. The White Paper: *The Governance of Britain – Constitutional Renewal* and Draft Constitutional Renewal Bill published on 25 March 2008 did not make any mention of Lord Goldsmith's recommendations.

183 *Prime Minister launches contract for foreign national seeking British citizenship,* UK Border Agency, 20 February 2008, http://webarchive.nationalarchives.gov.uk/20080609134125/http://www.bia.homeoffice.gov.uk/sitecontent/newsarticles/primeministerlaunchescontract.

184 *The Path to Citizenship: Next Steps in Reforming the Immigration System*, Border and Immigration Agency, February 2008, http://webarchive.nationalarchives.gov.uk/20080609134125/http://www.ukba.homeoffice.gov.uk/sitecontent/documents/aboutus/consultations/closedconsultations/pathtocitizenship/pathtocitizenship?view=Binary.

185 *Prime Minister launches contract for foreign national seeking British citizenship,* UK Border Agency, 20 February 2008, http://webarchive.nationalarchives.gov.uk/20080609134125/http://www.bia.homeoffice.gov.uk/sitecontent/newsarticles/primeministerlaunchescontract.

citizenship or permanent residence. Therefore, a migrant following the current somewhat linear route to citizenship would be faced with a fork in the road. The option to switch from permanent residence to citizenship at a later date would be retained. To encourage integration, the Government offered to promote active citizenship. Tier 4 and 5 migrants, their dependants and visitors would be ineligible for citizenship or permanent residence.

7.191 The consultation was wrapped up by 14 May 2008 and its results were published on 14 July 2008 concluding that foreign nationals wishing to become British citizens would 'have to earn the right to stay'.[186] On the face of it, earned citizenship had little new to offer as the requirements to speak English and obey the law had been inherent in the law for many years before. On closer inspection, however, by enhancing the burden of responsibilities for those wishing to tread the path to citizenship, the Government also restricted full access to some of the benefits enjoyed by migrants along the way. One such restriction would have been imposed on access to 'home rate' fees for higher education students. Only British citizens and permanent residents could benefit from fees at 'home rates'.[187]

7.192 On 14 January 2009 the Borders, Citizenship and Immigration Bill was introduced to Parliament and published the following day requiring 'all migrants to speak English and obey the law if they want to gain citizenship and stay permanently in Britain – while speeding up the path to citizenship for those who contribute to the community by being active citizens'.[188] On 14 July 2009 came the announcement that the Borders, Citizenship and Immigration Bill was undergoing consideration in Parliament with a view to amending certain sections in the BNA 1981. Passage of the Bill was accompanied by spirited debate in both Houses of Parliament[189] and the Bill received Royal Assent on 21 July 2009.

7.193 New registration provisions commenced on 13 January 2010 and the new 'earned citizenship' provisions contained in BCIA 2009, Part 2, ss 39–41 and 47–49

186 *The Path to Citizenship: Next Steps in Reforming the Immigration System, Government Response to Consultation*, UK Border Agency, July 2008, http://webarchive.nationalarchives.gov.uk/20080609134125/http://www.ukba.homeoffice.gov.uk/sitecontent/documents/aboutus/consultations/closedconsultations/pathtocitizenship/governmentreponsetoconsultation?view=Binary.

187 Currently, apart from refugees, EU, EEA and Swiss nationals and family members, students settled and ordinarily resident in the UK can benefit from home rates, depending on the educational establishment. The definition of 'settled' is contained in BNA 1981, s 50. Please also refer to the information provided by the UK Council for International Student Affairs to see which category you fit into as far as fees are concerned – http://www.ukcisa.org.uk/student/info_sheets/tuition_fees_ewni.php#categories_home.

188 *Government's new bill shakes up the route to citizenship*, UK Border Agency, 15 January 2009, http://webarchive.nationalarchives.gov.uk/20090120164230/http://www.bia.homeoffice.gov.uk/sitecontent/newsarticles/new-bill-route-to-citizenship.

189 *Borders, Citizenship and Immigration Act 2009, Ministerial Statements*, Elinor Harper and Steve Symonds, ILPA, http://www.ilpa.org.uk/publications/Ministerial%20Statements%20BCI%20Act%202009.pdf.

amending sections of BNA 1981[190] dealing with naturalisation were reserved until July 2011. BCIA 2009 includes a two year grace period for migrants who have already been given indefinite leave to remain on the date when earned citizenship is introduced or migrants who have applied for indefinite leave to remain before the date when earned citizenship is introduced. If the naturalisation provisions contained in Part 2 of BCIA 2009 were to be implemented, they would need to be accompanied by changes in the Immigration Rules to introduce new immigration criteria for 'temporary residence leave', 'probationary citizenship leave', 'permanent residence leave' etc.

7.194 Sections 39–41 and 47–49 of Part 2, BCIA 2009 omit, substitute and insert amendments into ss 6(1), (2), 41 and 50, and naturalisation requirements set out in the corresponding paragraphs of BNA 1981, Sch 1. Notable amendments include:

Section 39(2) of BCIA 2009 substitutes BNA 1981, Sch 1, para 1(2)introducing the following requirements:

(a) 'that the applicant ("A") was in the United Kingdom at the beginning of the qualifying period;
(b) that the number of days on which A was absent from the United Kingdom in each year of the qualifying period does not exceed 90;
(c) that A had a qualifying immigration status for the whole of the qualifying period;
(d) that on the date of the application A has probationary citizenship leave, permanent residence leave, a qualifying CTA entitlement, a Commonwealth right of abode or a permanent EEA entitlement;
(e) that, where on the date of the application A has probationary citizenship leave granted for the purpose of taking employment in the United Kingdom, A has been in continuous employment since the date of the grant of that leave;
(f) that A was not at any time in the qualifying period in the United Kingdom in breach of the immigration laws.'

7.195 After Sch 1, para 2, s 39(11) inserts paragraph 2A which reads:

(1) 'A person has a qualifying immigration status for the purposes of paragraph 1(2) if the person has
  (a) qualifying temporary residence leave;
  (b) probationary citizenship leave;
  (c) permanent residence leave;
  (d) a qualifying CTA entitlement;
  (e) a Commonwealth right of abode; or
  (f) a temporary or permanent EEA entitlement.

190 As well as certain sections in Hong Kong (War Wives and Widows) Act 1996, British Nationality (Hong Kong) Act 1997, Nationality, Immigration and Asylum Act 2002, UK Borders Act 2007 and others.

(2) A person who is required for those purposes to have a qualifying immigration status for the whole of the qualifying period need not have the same qualifying immigration status for the whole of that period.'

7.196 Section 40 of BCIA 2009 goes on to substitute or otherwise amend the requirements for naturalisation under s 6(2). Section 41 of the Act deals with the qualifying period under s 6. The qualifying period for those making applications under BNA 1981, s 6(1), (2) are eight and five years, respectively, unless an applicant meets an 'activity condition', reducing the qualifying period to six and three years, respectively. The activity condition is a reference to what the Government called active citizenship at consultation stages. In the 'Government Response to Consultation' published on 14 July 2008 the Government agreed that 'active citizenship will be a means to speed up progress and not a mandatory requirement for citizenship.'[191] Section 41(1) of BCIA 2009 inserting paragraph 4B into Sch 1 of BNA 1981 provides at para 4B(5) that:

'The applicant meets the activity condition if the Secretary of State is satisfied that the applicant
(a) has participated otherwise than for payment in prescribed activities; or
(b) is to be treated as having so participated.'

7.197 The activity condition would have been prescribed by regulations. Section 41(5) of the BCIA 2009 inserts sub-section (8) into BNA 1981, s 41:

'Any regulations (whether alone or with other provision)
(a) under subsection (1)(a) for prescribing activities for the purposes of paragraph 4B(5)(a) of Schedule 1; ...
...
may not be made unless a draft has been laid before and approved by a resolution of each House of Parliament.'

7.198 Since commencement, BCIA 2009 has been generally examined by practitioners in *Blackstone's Guide to The Borders, Citizenship and Immigration Act 2009*[192] and *Fransman's British Nationality Law (Third Edition)*. After a six month hiatus the Secretary of State announced on 5 November 2010 that the Government would not be introducing the earned citizenship provisions as it found them to

191 Page 18, *The Path to Citizenship: Next Steps in Reforming the Immigration System, Government Response to Consultation,* UK Border Agency, July 2008, http://webarchive.nationalarchives.gov.uk/20080609134125/http://www.ukba.homeoffice.gov.uk/sitecontent/documents/aboutus/consultations/closedconsultations/pathtocitizenship/governmentreponsetoconsultation?view=Binary.
192 *Blackstone's Guide to The Borders, Citizenship and Immigration Act 2009,* (Oxford University Press, 2010).

be 'too complicated, bureaucratic and, in the end, ineffective.'[193] Instead, on 23 November 2010 the Secretary of State revealed the Government's intention to 'end the link between temporary and permanent migration.'[194] In light of changes to the number of allowed absences,[195] the Government will now need to consider corresponding amendments to nationality policy for Tier 1 (Investors) and Tier 1 (Entrepreneurs).

193 *The Home Secretary's Immigration Speech*, Home Office, 5 November 2010, http://www.homeoffice.gov.uk/media-centre/speeches/immigration-speech. This announcement was in keeping with the contents of a Daily Mail article published on 6 September 2010, *Student visa crackdown as immigration minister vows to cut number of arrivals by tens of thousands*, http://www.dailymail.co.uk/news/article-1309369/Student-visa-crackdown-immigration-minister-vows-cut-number-arrivals.html.

194 *Immigration limits oral statement*, Home Office, 23 November 2010, http://www.homeoffice.gov.uk/publications/parliamentary-business/oral-statements/limits-statement/.

195 180 days in any 12 calendar months.

Chapter 8

The view of Tier 4 through the eyes of end users

Introduction

8.01 As this book is intended for practical use by laymen as well as practitioners, its critique of the current system should be broader than the scope of substantive immigration law and the sobriety of legal argument allow it to be. In general terms, immigration law and policy are shaped by fundamental principles of public good and national security, domestic socio-political considerations and international obligations, and once enacted, are enforced by the serpentine machinery of Governmental and quasi-Governmental bodies whose role it is to control and manage them.

8.02 By utilising stakeholders[1] and impact analysts, drawing on feedback from public consultations and research by migration think tanks,[2] the Government has signalled what seems to be a more inclusive approach to policy development. In view of this, policy makers would be remiss in dismissing some of the constructive (and reactive) criticisms expressed by the end users of the Points Based System ('PBS'): academics, sponsors and students, which form the substance of this chapter.

8.03 While the evidence is more anecdotal than systematic, and piecemeal research conducted so far is less than conclusive, it is apparent that a proportion of the end users have voiced their opposition to the PBS through active campaigns, publications, lobbying and judicial challenges. News of the PBS and its implementation throughout 2009/2010 and continued reforms in 2010/2011 have been met with varying degrees of acceptance across the disparate quarters of the education sector. The Government has proposed to overhaul the system even further to make it more selective and it is these proposals that will colour

1 As part of the Joint Education Taskforce, the Stakeholder Management Team, Forms & Guidance Subgroup (set up following requests from the education sector) and IT Working Group.

2 Such as the Migration Advisory Committee, http://www.ukba.homeoffice.gov.uk/aboutus/workingwithus/indbodies/mac/.

the discussion on student migration for most of 2011/2012. The purpose of this chapter is to raise awareness of these views and the source materials rather than to provide a definitive summary of them.

Academics

8.04 Opposition to the new regulations has taken on different forms. These range from court proceedings to ongoing events and campaigns organised by student and/or staff groups, associations and unions within (and outside) of universities supported by politicians, lobbyists, peers and human rights lawyers. Campaigns encourage principled non-compliance and are ultimately geared towards scrapping the system whereas court actions target specific and most severely prejudicial aspects of the scheme on the basis of detailed grounds.[3]

8.05 On the eve of Tiers 2 and 5 being introduced alongside the Sponsorship Management System ('SMS') in November 2008, a wave of protest rippled across university academia. On 10 November 2008 the Guardian published an open letter signed by Ian Grigg-Spall (academic chair, National Critical Lawyers Group[4]), Sally Hunt (University and College Union), Tony Benn, Professor Bill Bowring (Birkbeck School of Law, University of London), and Liz Davies (chair, Haldane Society of Socialist Lawyers). The letter read:

> 'The new immigration rules for overseas students to be introduced in March 2009 by the Border Agency are very worrying (New points system, November 5). These rules would require universities to report any absences by overseas students from lectures, seminars or tutorials, or any failure to submit any assessment on time. In other words, the university is being asked to act as an immigration officer and set up a surveillance unit over these students. This goes far beyond the present monitoring of student progress systems in universities, which has as its basic purpose assisting students to reach their full potential.
>
> In our view it is hard to justify such detailed monitoring of overseas students, even for immigration control purposes. Surely the Border Agency just needs to know students have registered and are at the university? It does not need to have this constant monitoring. This police-like surveillance is not the function of universities, and alters the educational relationship between students and their teachers in a very harmful manner. University staff are there to help the students develop intellectually and not to be a means of sanctioning these students. The proposals are discriminatory as they apply only to overseas students and non EU students. They represent a possible breach of article 8 (right to a private life) and

3 An account of various court proceedings is given in **Chapter 5**.

4 NCLG spearheaded its own 'Campaign against the New Immigration Rules' by publishing a petition on its website at http://www.nclg.org.uk/Conference%202009/ImmigrationRules.htm.

article 3 (degrading treatment) of the European convention on human rights and the Human Rights Act 1998. We would urge universities, MPs and others to join us in opposing these rules and calling for the government to withdraw them.'[5]

8.06 Academics baulked at the requirement to monitor student attendance and report on student activity to the UK Border Agency ('UKBA') which, they argued, went against their professional ethos and would lead to damaging the trust in the relationships between students and teaching staff. The University and College Union ('UCU')[6] which represents more than 120,000 academics, lecturers, researchers and others in the higher and further education strata picked up the mantle at a seminar on 28 April 2009 resolving to raise the profile of the campaigns against the PBS at the annual congress held on 27–29 May 2009.

8.07 The UCU carried a number of motions during the congress, strongly condemning the PBS for being against principal values of academic freedom and equality which also impact on the contractual terms of academic and related staff, working conditions and race relations matters. On 29 May 2009 the UCU resolved to launch 'a campaign of non-compliance with all such policing and surveillance duties (including recording details from foreign national students, supplying personal details to other institutions in our capacity as external examiners, assessors and lecturers, and refusal to request such details on behalf of our own institutions from external examiners, assessors and lecturers)'.[7] The congress agreed:

'1. to reaffirm its opposition to the new Home Office regulations
2. to ask members not to commence implementation of these regulations until the human rights and workload issues that arise from the new regulations are appropriately dealt with.'[8]

In October 2009 the UCU published its guidance on the PBS informing its members of the new duties they might be asked to perform by their college or university and providing them with model letters they can use to request information concerning the impact of the PBS on their employment contracts, health and safety and equality.[9]

5 'Academics are not immigration officials', Guardian, http://www.guardian.co.uk/politics/2008/nov/10/immigration-policy-immigration-and-public-services.

6 The UCU was formed on 1 June 2006 as a result of AUT and NATFHE joining forces.

7 *Socio-Legal Newsletter*, No 59, SLSA, autumn/winter 2009, http://www.kent.ac.uk/nslsa/content/view/58/255.

8 The UCU guidance on points based immigration, October 2009, http://www.ucu.org.uk/media/pdf/4/7/ucu_pbiguidance_oct09.pdf.

9 The UCU guidance on points based immigration, October 2009, http://www.ucu.org.uk/media/pdf/4/7/ucu_pbiguidance_oct09.pdf.

8.08 The spirit of revolt spread like wildfire. 'Universities Without Borders',[10] a faction of students and academics from the University of Kent, and a fusion of Goldsmiths UCU[11] and Goldsmiths Students Union, 'Students Not Suspects'[12] set up blogs to run their campaigns in opposition to the PBS. 'Students Not Suspects' held a number of campaign events and meetings, including an open meeting under the banner of 'Freedom of Thought = Freedom of Movement // Students ≠ Suspects // Universities ≠ Border Agents //' on 2 December 2009. Goldsmiths, fast becoming the hub of insurrection against the PBS, published a series of 'Departmental Statements of Opposition' dating from December 2009 to March 2010. In the statements the academics invite their colleagues at Goldsmiths and across the University of London to resist implementation of some of the sponsorship duties, and in particular, the attendance monitoring duty.[13]

> 'The new regulations make us do a policing job in our classrooms, turning both academic and administrative staff into agents of the UK Border Agency. We object to this for reasons both political and professional. We are concerned that the regulations represent possible breaches of European human rights conventions and seriously threaten our students' rights to mobility, privacy and education. Although recent changes to implementation of the law have expanded the scope of student monitoring and reporting--with the result that policies explicitly targeting the monitoring and reporting of information about non-EU students have been expanded to include the monitoring and reporting of information about all students--this does not disguise the fact that these policies are discriminatory in intent and will very likely be discriminatory in practice.'[14]

8.09 Public statements against the PBS have also been made by Goldsmiths UCU, UCU Black Members' Standing Committee, UCU Black Members, University of Kent, Manchester Metropolitan University, the Institute of Race Relations and the National Critical Lawyers Group[15] with many universities such as the University of St Andrews, SOAS and UCL, and civil rights campaign organisations such as the Manifesto Club and campaigners such as Helena Kennedy QC and Frances Webber joining the sprawling campaign. On 16 October 2010 the author attended the morning session of a conference on 'the consequences of the new immigration system in universities and colleges' organised by the University of London Union,

10 http://universitieswithoutborders.blogspot.com/.

11 http://homepages.gold.ac.uk/ucu/pbsicampaign.html.

12 In one of its briefing packs, 'Students not Suspects' explain that they 'are a broad and growing coalition of students, staff and campaigners who are opposed to the new Home Office rules. While we are based at Goldsmiths (University of London), we see ourselves as acting [sic] solidarity with anyone affected by the Points-Based System for Immigration, as well are anyone opposed to the rules.'

13 Which, of course, became mandatory as at 22 February 2010.

14 http://studentsnotsuspects.blogspot.com/p/goldsmiths-departmental-statements-of.html.

15 NCLG is an umbrella organisation that was fostered at the Kent Law School which provides a forum for discussion of law by academics, students, practitioners and politicians.

entitled 'Points-Based Immigration System in Context: Research and Campaign Strategies'. The speakers talked about immigration and education issues in very broad terms. Lobbying and campaigning continue as the Government has unveiled its new plans for the student route to be rolled out over the next 18 months.

Sponsors

8.10 The author conducted a sample survey of sponsors, stakeholders,[16] associations[17] and accreditation bodies[18] by way of a questionnaire sent out in June 2010. Instead of collecting statistical data, the aim of the survey was to draw out general views on the impact of Tier 4. Questionnaires were sent out to 190 sponsors by email and consisted of 22, mainly open, questions, listed below. Questionnaires were also dispatched to 21 stakeholders, associations and accreditation bodies by post and email, and consisted of 21, mainly open, questions, listed below.

	Questions posed to sponsors	**Questions posed to stakeholders**
1.	Please state the full name of your organisation and is your organisation on the Tier 4 Register of Sponsors?	Please state the full name of your organisation.
2.	How many students does your organisation have?	How many members does your organisation have?
3.	When was your organisation established?	What kind of education providers are they? Please list the type of organisation and their number within your membership (eg private colleges 35, independent schools – 50, etc).
4.	What is your overall assessment of Tier 4 and its efficacy?	What is your overall assessment of Tier 4 and its efficacy?

16 For example, BUILA, AIHEP, Independent Schools Council, British Council, Study UK, QISAN/ASIC, English UK, Universities UK, etc. from the Joint Education Taskforce which consists of 31 members and 'is composed of representatives from across the education sector and government. The aim of the JET is to support partnership working across government and with all the key stakeholder groups on immigration issues affecting international students', *All Points*, Issue No 2, September 2009, the UK Border Agency, at the time of writing this information is no longer available on the UKBA website.

17 For example, The Independent Association of Prep Schools, the Association of Governing Bodies of Independent Schools, the Boarding Schools' Association, Council of British International Schools, Society of Headmasters and Headmistresses of Independent Schools and others.

18 For example, BAC, AoC, Accreditation UK and others. Following the changes to the Immigration Rules and policy on 21 April 2011, these accreditation bodies no longer play a point in Tier 4.

8.10 *The view of Tier 4 through the eyes of end users*

	Questions posed to sponsors	Questions posed to stakeholders
5.	In what way, if any, has Tier 4 affected your organisation?	In what way, if any, has Tier 4 affected your organisation?
6.	Has the feedback received by you from your students been generally positive or negative?	Has the feedback received by you from your members been positive or negative?
7.	What do you see as key concerns related to Tier 4?	What are seen as your members' key concerns related to Tier 4?
8.	Do you agree that sponsors should share responsibility with the immigration authorities and play an active role in safeguarding the system from immigration abuse? Please state your reasons.	Do you agree that sponsors should share responsibility with the immigration authorities and play an active role in safeguarding the system from immigration abuse? Please state your reasons.
9.	If so, what is your opinion on the way this proposition has translated into sponsors having to adhere to duties which see them policing students and reporting on their behaviour?	If so, what is your opinion on the way this proposition has translated into sponsors having to adhere to duties which see them policing students and reporting on their behaviour?
10.	Do you think the relationship between education providers and their students has been undermined as a result of the sponsor duties? If so, please describe how. In which part of the education sector is this felt particularly acutely?	Do you think the relationship between education providers and their students has been undermined as a result of the sponsor duties? If so, please describe how. In which part of the education sector is this felt particularly acutely?
11.	There are no provisions in the immigration legislation which give statutory authority to the sponsorship and licensing scheme. It is policy driven and thrives on flexibility outside the realm of parliamentary scrutiny to implement revisions.	There are no provisions in the immigration legislation which give statutory authority to the sponsorship and licensing scheme. It is policy driven and thrives on flexibility outside the realm of parliamentary scrutiny to implement revisions.

	Questions posed to sponsors	**Questions posed to stakeholders**
	Tier 4 sponsor guidance has been modified several times since 31 March 2010 introducing changes in such a manner and of such nature as to incite parliamentary censure and judicial challenges. How has the legal uncertainty affected your organisation and your students?	Tier 4 sponsor guidance has been modified several times since 31 March 2010 introducing changes in such a manner and of such nature as to incite parliamentary censure and judicial challenges. How has the legal uncertainty affected your members?
12.	The UK Border Agency makes unilateral decisions when it comes to licensing. While sponsors are able to make representations against a decision to suspend their licence, they do not have a right of appeal against: 1) refusal of an application for a licence; 2) a decision to withdraw a licence. Sponsors are able to reapply or have the decisions judicially reviewed. Given the wide-ranging consequences for sponsors, should you, as a sponsor, be deprived of a right of appeal? If no, what alternatives would you propose?	The UK Border Agency makes unilateral decisions when it comes to licensing. While sponsors are able to make representations against a decision to suspend their licence, they do not have a right of appeal against: 1) refusal of an application for a licence; 2) a decision to withdraw a licence. Sponsors are able to reapply or have the decisions judicially reviewed. Given the wide-ranging consequences for sponsors, should they be deprived of a right of appeal? If no, what alternatives would you propose?
13.	Have you been: 1) B-rated and asked to comply with an action plan; 2) had the number of their CAS reduced; 3) suspended; 4) had their Tier 4 licence withdrawn; 5) other.	Have any of your members been: 1) B-rated and asked to comply with an action plan; 2) had the number of their CAS reduced; 3) suspended; 4) had their Tier 4 licence withdrawn; 5) other.

	Questions posed to sponsors	Questions posed to stakeholders
		Please state: a) how many of your members have had action taken against them by the UK Border Agency since 31 March 2009; b) what kind of action was taken against them ((1) – (5)); c) what were the reasons given by the UK Border Agency, if known; d) what effect did the action have on the members and their students; e) what steps did the members take to mitigate the effects of the action.
14.	If you have had any form of action taken against you by the UK Border Agency as described above: what effect did the action have on your organisation and your students? what steps did you take to mitigate the effects of the action (eg make a fresh application to the UK Border Agency, ask your accreditation/inspection body to mediate, apply to have the decision judicially reviewed?)	What impact has Tier 4 had on your members' business?
15.	What impact, if any, has Tier 4 had on the commercial and administrative aspects of your business?	How many of your members become insolvent or ceased trading as a direct result of UK Border Agency actions?
16	Has your organisation been able to maintain the same level of business in recruiting non-EEA students as before 31 March 2009?	Has your organisation been called upon by the members to mediate between them and the UK Border Agency in any dispute related to the above at 13? Did you agree to participate in such disputes and been able to resolve them? If so, what was the outcome?

	Questions posed to sponsors	**Questions posed to stakeholders**
17.	In the period from 31 March 2009 to 22 February 2010, how many of the students out of the overall number to whom you issued visa letters have been able to obtain entry clearance or in-country extension of stay as a Tier 4 student on the first attempt?	If your organisation is an inspection or accreditation body, do you feel there is potential for a conflict of interest arising between your professional obligations towards the UK Border Agency and the responsibility to your members?
18.	In the period from 22 February 2010 to date, how many of the students out of the overall number to whom you issued CAS have been able to obtain entry clearance or in-country extension of stay as a Tier 4 student on the first attempt?	If your organisation is a stakeholder on the Joint Education Taskforce, how do you think your participation has shaped Tier 4 policy?
19.	Can you list top three reasons given by the UK Border Agency for refusing entry clearance or in-country extension of stay to your sponsored students?	Do you think that Tier 4 presents an effective model for averting abuse of immigration control as opposed to previous attempts? If yes, to what degree? If no, what would you propose to improve the current system?
20.	Do you think that Tier 4 presents an effective model for averting abuse of immigration control as opposed to previous attempts? If yes, to what degree? If no, what would you propose to improve the current system?	In the document published in May 2010, *'The Coalition: our programme for government'*, the coalition government pledged to introduce new measures to minimise abuse of the immigration system, citing the student route as an example. What measures do you think the current government will seek to bring in to reinforce the existing Tier 4?

8.11 *The view of Tier 4 through the eyes of end users*

	Questions posed to sponsors	Questions posed to stakeholders
21.	In the document published in May 2010, *'The Coalition: our programme for government'*, the coalition government pledged to introduce new measures to minimise abuse of the immigration system, citing the student route as an example. What measures do you think the current government will seek to bring in to reinforce the existing Tier 4?	In your opinion, what does the future hold for Tier 4?
22.	In your opinion, what does the future hold for Tier 4?	

8.11 As at 30 June 2010, the author had received 10 responses from sponsors and 3 responses from stakeholders, associations and accreditation bodies. The taciturn reaction of stakeholders and accreditation bodies is telling and their responses are too inadequate to form a part of this study. The sponsor respondents consisted of independent schools, English Language Teaching ('ELT') schools, an academy and a community school established from 1968 through to 2008[19] with the number of students taught at each institution ranging from 40 to approximately 1,000. At the time, six respondents[20] were on the Register of Sponsors, two respondents[21] had their sponsor licences irrevocably withdrawn with one becoming insolvent, two respondents[22] had their licences withdrawn but these were reinstated following a judicial challenge, and one respondent[23] had its licence suspended but reinstated following an inspection by compliance officers. Questions were grouped together to gain comprehensive insight into their experiences and some of the respondents' notable comments are quoted below.

Key concerns and general assessment of Tier 4[24]

8.12 The respondents cited a variety of concerns associated with the Tier 4 category. While some have accepted that the concept is generally good, they feel

19 Six of the educational establishments opened between 1968 and 1997, and four were founded in the years from 2003 to 2008.
20 Respondents C, D, F, G, H and I.
21 Respondents A and B.
22 Respondents C and G.
23 Respondent D.
24 Questions 4, 5 and 7.

that its execution has been less than effective. The respondents have highlighted the following as the key concerns affecting their institutions:

- loss of business including prospective students through increased restrictions on students, confusion at the British diplomatic posts abroad;[25]
- financial losses, loss of reputation and damage to staff;[26]
- inefficient operation due to extra administrative work[27] with one respondent commenting that 'generally T4 seems over-bureaucratic and victimising';
- unclear and ambiguous guidance including information on the UKBA website;[28]
- continual, arbitrary and frequent changes to the regulations and guidance which make it difficult to be up to speed with the requirements;[29]
- inability of students to switch institutions without having to make a fresh application;[30]
- raising the English language bar[31] which has led one respondent to conclude that 'UKBA has absolutely no understanding of the role that English language tuition performs in benefiting the UK economy';
- imposing responsibility of immigration officers on sponsors;[32]
- application process being time consuming and costly to students;[33]

Shared responsibility for immigration control[34]

8.13 In its response to the author's request under the Freedom of Information Act 2000 on 3 August 2010, the UKBA provided an altered perspective on the concept of 'shared responsibility' now deeply entrenched in the PBS. This view presents a perceptible departure from the propositions made in Government literature prior to May 2010:[35]

> **'2. What gives the Secretary of State for the Home Department power to 'share responsibility' for immigration control with sponsors?**
>
> The power to set down rules and statements of practice to be followed in the administration of the 1971 Act is set out in Section 3(2) of the Act, as outlined in

25 Respondents C, D, F and H.
26 Respondents C and G.
27 Respondents D, I and J.
28 Respondents A, D and H.
29 Respondents D, F
30 Respondents D and F.
31 Respondents C, D, F, H and I.
32 Respondents B, G and F.
33 Respondent E.
34 Question 8.
35 See **Chapter 4**.

the previous answer. Sponsorship allows employers and education providers to make decisions about migrants from outside the UK who wish to work or study with them, in line with ordinary practice in recruitment of employees or students. However, the final decision on whether or not to grant entry clearance or leave to remain is firmly the responsibility of the SSHD. A decision by a Sponsor [sic] to accept an individual as an employee or student is not determinative of an application for Entry Clearance or Leave to Remain.'[36]

8.14 Understandably, academics do not see themselves being complicit with the Big Brother establishment in policing their students or becoming immigration officers. Frances Webber argued on the pages of 'Red Pepper' magazine that 'the Government is sacrificing the futures of thousands of would-be students and educational institutions – and the relationship between students and their educators, who should not be required to act as an unpaid arm of the immigration police".[37] Sponsors, on the other hand, who have a keen interest in recruiting genuine students see sharing responsibility with the immigration authorities and playing an active role in safeguarding the system from immigration abuse as an opportunity to exercise their rights as stakeholders. 80% of the respondents who took part in the author's survey agreed with this as can be seen from their comments:

Respondent A stated:

> 'It needs to be a joint effort between the sponsors and the authorities'.

Respondent C stated:

> 'I am convinced by the stakeholder principle and sharing some of the responsibility as we would expect to gain from an efficient and safe system. However we are not gaining today.'

Respondent E stated:

> 'Every organisation has a duty of care and as such we should ensure that any accreditation or legal systems [sic] is supported.'

Respondent F stated:

> 'We are more than ready to play a role in assessing the validity of each application. However we are not treated as stakeholders.'

Respondent I stated:

> 'If schools are given the authority to recruit international students, they should also have the responsibility to make sure this isn't being abused.'

36 Letter from Freedom of Information Team, North East, Yorkshire and the Humber Region, UK Border Agency sent to Ms Elena Tsirlina, Blokh Solicitors, by email on 3 August 2010.

37 *Informers in the classroom*, Red Pepper, Frances Webber, 2 February 2010, http://www.redpepper.org.uk/Informers-in-the-classroom.

However, Respondent G disagreed, saying:

> 'It is right that all citizens/institutions should have a duty to report breaches of the law to the UK authorities but not that they should adopt responsibility for enforcing the law itself – this is the role of the state, answerable to the judiciary, the legislature and, ultimately, via democratic processes, the electorate as a whole.'

Sponsorship duties and their impact on relationships with students[38]

8.15 The authors of *'Academics as Borders Guards?'* encapsulate the position held by protesting academics insofar as:

> '... it is inimical to the functions and core values of higher education, and those who teach there, to be spying and reporting on their students. These measures fundamentally betray the trust and destroy the openness upon which academic processes and the ethics of the university depend. They are immoral. Nor should university staff be performing mini-Stasi roles for the immigration authorities in filing and submitting personal information about their colleagues from abroad: the data collection functions of immigration authorities are not the rightful province of universities, nor are observing and reporting their attendance patterns and compliance with immigration requirements. We have a duty to cling to whatever remains of the ethic of the university.'[39]

8.16 The author's survey established that the respondents have a range of opinions on having to adhere to sponsor studies and their impact on the relationship between education providers and students.

- Respondents A and E felt that it was right for sponsors to report any misconduct by students in contravention to their immigration conditions;
- Respondents B, C and D thought that while it may be a natural consequence of sharing responsibility, the administrative burden of compliance is excessive and difficult to police;
- Respondents H and I could not discern any ostensible changes between new and previous requirements to monitor students' attendance;
- Whereas Respondent G was opposed to the state imposing such duties on sponsors considering it 'a denigration of accountability on the part of the state and a perversion of natural justice'.

38 Questions 9 and 10.
39 *Socio-Legal Newsletter*, No 59, SLSA, autumn/winter 2009, http://www.kent.ac.uk/nslsa/content/view/58/255.

8.17 *The view of Tier 4 through the eyes of end users*

As far as the relationship between educators and students is concerned, Respondents A, C, E and H thought that it was not undermined as a result of sponsors exercising their duties. However, Respondents B, D, G and I felt that the relationship would suffer as a result as 'education providers cannot force students to follow strict guidelines without almost bullying them to comply' and 'students feel they are being unfairly targeted and that UKBA treats them as "suspects".' Respondent F believed that 'the relationship remains strong, but students are frequently at a loss to understand the reasons for what we have to do.'

Impact of legal uncertainty[40]

8.17 There is no apparent statutory basis behind sponsorship and licensing schemes and these are driven entirely by policy. Broad and often ambiguous policies[41] offer a wide scope for interpretation to sponsors who have to implement them. Generality of policy provisions is dictated by the disparity and diversity within the education sector. In effect, it means that sponsors are left to read between the lines and use their own ingenuity when applying the rigid requirements to their own distinctive environments. They know that getting it wrong leads to deplorable consequences but this is hardly an objective exercise across the board. Predictably, changing policies give rise to misinterpretation and confusion.

8.18 In its newsletter the Socio-Legal Studies Association ('SLSA') expressed concern over higher education ('HE') institutions interpreting their sponsorship duties very differently:

> 'confusing the monitoring of academic progress with the requirement to report "bogus students". Amongst a generally confused response are an increasing number of instances of over-zealous interpretations of these new rules, resulting in practices which are inhumane and discriminatory, while the atmosphere for non-EU students and colleagues is becoming increasingly hostile and surrounded with doubt and suspicion'.[42]

8.19 In the recent High Court and Court of Appeal decisions judges ruled on the use of policy guidance and the UKBA stipulated its position on what statutory provisions give grounding to the sponsorship scheme in its response under the Freedom of Information Act 2000 on 3 August 2010.[43] While the Secretary of State and the courts have been wrangling over issues of illegality and irrationality, the

40 Question 11.

41 Tier 4 Sponsor Guidance was issued on 31 March 2009 and updated on 1 August 2009, 5 October 2009, 26 November 2009, 22 February 2010, 3 March 2010, 6 April 2010, 23 July 2010, 1 October 2010 and 21 April 2011 either as a standalone policy document or, in the earlier versions, in combination with Tier 2 and Tier 5 provisions.

42 *Academics as Border Guards?*, Socio-Legal Newsletter, No 59, SLSA, autumn/winter 2009, http://www.kent.ac.uk/nslsa/content/view/58/255.

43 See **Chapter 2** and **Chapter 5**.

respondents who took part in the author's survey have felt the wide-ranging effects of legal uncertainty.

Respondent C stated:

> 'The uncertainty of where rules will lie in the future and frequency with which changes have been made has meant that we have had to spend a huge number of manhours [sic] in keeping abreast with the latest regulations. Students have become exasperated and frustrated. Many have voted with their feet and either left the UK or chosen other destinations. Our revenue has been significantly impacted.'

Respondent D stated:

> 'It seems that UKBA has been given Carte Blanche to produce whatever changes they wish to stop foreigners coming into Britain.'

Respondent E stated:

> 'The uncertainty has impacted on our organisation in many ways. All staff are acutely aware of this threat of effective closure hanging over our heads. They are also aware that there are many centres which have been allowed to continue to trade while flaunting [sic] the new regulations, simply because certain accreditation bodies were admitted to the scheme which had no basis or foundation of professional conduct. The lack of legal due process is astonishing to all in this organisation, let alone in the sector as a whole. The situation, lurching from one change to another, is also highly distracting, in that senior staff are spending hugely disproportionate amounts of time on administering illogical and unlawful regulations.'

Right of appeal for sponsors[44]

8.20 This is a subject matter that has been lightly touched upon in **Chapter 2**. The current[45] Tier 4 of the Points Based – Police Guidance ('Sponsor Guidance') states at paragraph 222 that 'you have no right of appeal if we refuse your application. You may reapply at any time but you must ensure that the reasons we refused you no longer apply.' Equally, there is no right of appeal against a decision to refuse an HTS application (paragraph 278 of the Sponsor Guidance) or revoke the sponsor licence (paragraph 523 of the Sponsor Guidance). In addition, as of 21 April 2011, sponsors who have been stripped of their licence cannot make an application to get back on the Register of Sponsors for six months from the date of decision to revoke the licence. Sponsors have a prospect of defending themselves by making representations against a decision to suspend their licence but with the

44 Question 12.
45 Version 09/11, 5 September 2011.

Secretary of State playing the dual role of prosecutor and the appellate authority a just outcome is moot. Sponsors are therefore left with a limited array of options. They can either make a fresh application to the same body that revoked it in the first place six months following the revocation or apply to have the original decision judicially reviewed. At least 70% of those responding to the author's questionnaire recognised the need for a right of appeal for sponsors with one respondent adding that there should also be a right to sue for damages for losses caused by the UKBA.

8.21 Respondent G suggested that, 'the power to remove/suspend schools should be removed from UKBA itself, the inspectorate, and given to an independent authority which is not prey to political pressure from above. The reports of UKBA officers should be provided to a committee composed to education professionals, representatives of UKBA itself and representatives from accrediting bodies.'

Actions taken against sponsors and their impact[46]

8.22 Sponsors can be castigated for their conduct in a variety of ways, each more severe than the one preceding it, ranging from downgrading of ratings[47] and having their Confirmation of Acceptance for Studies ('CAS') numbers reduced, to suspension and revocation of licences. An additional hurdle for existing sponsors who do not meet the new requirements introduced on 21 April 2011 is having an interim limit imposed on the number of CAS that can be allocated to them between 21 April 2011 and 5 April 2012. Any of these actions can be taken against sponsors by themselves or in a combination. Two of the respondents[48] had their sponsor licences revoked with one becoming insolvent. It had a devastating impact on the institutions, and led to loss of income, jobs and ability of students to complete their courses. Respondents C and G had their licences revoked but these were reinstated having initiated judicial review proceedings. Action taken against them resulted in financial loss and lasting reputational damage and for one of them the outcome was 'near fatal'. Respondent D, an umbrella organisation consisting of five schools not licensed together, had one of its licences suspended but reinstated following an inspection by compliance officers. It said that 'the inspection which reinstated the school was the third inspection by UKBA within a six month period – which destabilised the students, seeing Immigration Officers continually visiting the school.'[49]

46 Questions 13, 14, 15 and 16.

47 For Standard sponsors.

48 Respondents A and B.

49 It is worth noting that the reputational damage that may be caused to the business of a sponsor by the UKBA intervention could be devastating. Most privately funded sponsors rely on goodwill and positive 'word of mouth' to draw in students. Reputation is a fragile concept that takes time to build up. This heightens the duty of procedural fairness incumbent on the UKBA in investigating performance of a licensed sponsor and in deciding what action to take.

8.23 The remainder of the respondents[50] who had no action taken against them felt the additional administrative burden of having to align their systems with the SMS. 100% of the respondents said that they were not able to recruit as many non-EEA students as they were able to before 31 March 2009 with one conceding that it was not due to the introduction of Tier 4.

8.24 In issue 5 of the monthly bulletin for Tier 4 sponsors, *'All Points'*, the UKBA stated that on 18 January 2010 it 'suspended a number of colleges from the Tier 4 register of sponsors.' It further warned that 'where the UK Border Agency has intelligence or evidence to suggest that as a sponsor you have not been meeting your obligations and are therefore posing a risk to effective immigration control, we will suspend your licence and investigate these concerns. If found to be complicit your licence will be revoked.'[51]

8.25 On 25 January 2010 Lord Naseby asked the Government in the House of Lords Main Chamber debate what action had been taken in the previous six months to prevent illegal immigration through the use of 'bogus' colleges. The Parliamentary Under-Secretary of State, Home Office, Lord West of Spithead[52] took to the floor to reveal that 'in the last six months we have carried out around 600 inspections, suspending 140 and revoking 15 tier licences.'[53]

8.26 In his interview with Manifesto Club on 26 January 2010, Dominic Scott, Chief Executive of the UK Council for International Student Affairs alluded to 56 colleges recently being suspended without 'being told of the evidence or allegations against them'.[54] On 4 February 2010, it was reported that out of '142 suspended colleges' more than a quarter were state schools.[55] The same publication announced that a

50 Respondents E, F, H, I and J.

51 *All Points*, Issue No 5, the UK Border Agency, at the time of writing this information is no longer available on the UKBA website.

52 Lord West, who was appointed to the post on 29 June 2007 and had the responsibility for security, resigned on 11 May 2010.

53 House of Lords, Main Chamber Debates, 25 January 2010, http://services.parliament.uk/hansard/Lords/bydate/20100125/mainchamberdebates/part004.html and *"140 colleges suspended over immigration"*, The Independent, 25 January 2010, http://www.independent.co.uk/news/education/education-news/140-colleges-suspended-over-immigration-1878648.html .

54 *Fortress Academy*, Manifesto Club Report, Valerie Hartwich, February 2010, http://www.manifestoclub.com/files/FortressAcademy.pdf .

55 Which should not have been granted a Tier 4 licence pursuant to paragraphs 16 and 53 of the Sponsor Guidance (version 09/11, 5 September 2011). The provision concerning state schools has been in place from the inception of Tier 4 and has not changed much in substance.

number of suspended colleges were taking the UKBA to court.[56] It was clear that the information available in the public domain was neither consistent nor reliable. The author resolved to ask the UKBA for clarification of some of the information pertaining to suspension and/or withdrawal of sponsor licences and their impact on the sponsors and sent a request under the Freedom of Information Act 2000 on 27 April 2010. The author received a response from the Freedom of Information Team, UKBA on 3 August 2010 (reference 14899/1173), the relevant part of which is quoted below:

'6. Please provide a list of colleges suspended from the Register of Sponsors in the period from August 2009 to February 2010.
I can confirm that we do hold the information you are interested in. However, I am unable to communicate this information to you pursuant to the exemption under section 31 (1) (e) and 43 (2) of the Freedom of Information Act 2000. Please see Annex A for an explanation of the reasons for this decision.

7. Please provide a list of colleges who had their licences revoked in the same period.
I can confirm that this information is held by the UK Border Agency . We intend to publish the information you have requested in September 2010 on the UK Border Agency website.
Section 22 (1) allows us to exempt information if it is intended for future publication. Please see Annex B for an explanation of the reasons for this decision.

8. How many of these education providers were (a) a threat to immigration control, (b)) not a bona fide private education institution as defined by paragraph 6 of the Immigration Rules HC395 (as amended).
The vast majority of Tier 4 Sponsors who have been revoked would have been considered to pose a threat to Immigration control in some way. For example 328 of the guidance notes state: *If we have reason to believe that a sponsor is*
seriously breaching its duties and poses a major threat to immigration control (for example, assigning confirmations of acceptance for studies or issuing visa letters to students who do not qualify to come to the United Kingdom), we may suspend its licence while we make further enquiries. A sponsor will not be able to assign any confirmations of acceptance for studies and should

56 *Blacklisted UK colleges take Border Agency to court,* The Register, 4 February 2010, http://www.theregister.co.uk/2010/02/04/ukba_student_visa/. See also *Bhatti & Ors v Croydon Magistrates Court & Ors* [2009] EWHC 3004 (Admin) (6 November 2009); *Leeds Unique Education Ltd (t/a Leeds Professional College) v Secretary of State for the Home Department* [2010] EWHC 1030 (Admin) (14 May 2010); *The London Reading College Ltd, R (on the application of) v Secretary of State for the Home Department* [2010] EWHC 2561 (Admin) (18 October 2010;, *New London College Ltd, R (on the application of) v Secretary of State for the Home Department* [2010] EWHC 2701 (Admin) (19 October 2010); *San Michael College Ltd, R (on the application of) v Secretary of State for the Home Department* [2011] EWHC 642 (Admin) (18 March 2011); *New London College Ltd, R (on the application of) v Secretary of State for the Home Department* [2011] EWHC 865 (Admin) (7 April 2011).

not issue any visa letters while it is suspended. All sponsors must continue to comply with all of their sponsor duties throughout the period of suspension.

In addition the following would also be considered as a threat to immigration control (the list is not endless):

- ☐ Not reporting or monitoring migrant activity
- ☐ Migrant leave to remain/visa expiry dates not consistently updated on internal systems
- ☐ Students not undertaking the requisite amount of study time – missing lectures on a regular basis.

9. Please provide a list of colleges who had the suspension and revocation decisions judicially challenged.

   Information held by a public authority is exempt information if it is held **only by virtue of being contained in**-

   - ☐ **(a)** any document filed with, or otherwise placed in the custody of, a court for the purposes of proceedings in a particular cause or matter,
   - ☐ **(b)** any document served upon, or by, a public authority for the purposes of proceedings in a particular cause or matter, or
   - ☐ **(c)** any document created by-
     - ☐ **(i)** a court, or
     - ☐ **(ii)** a member of the administrative staff of a court, for the purposes of proceedings in a particular cause or matter.

10. How many of those who challenged these decisions through the courts were subsequently re-instated on the Register of Sponsors and why?

    Information held by a public authority is exempt information if it is held only by virtue of being contained In-

    - ☐ **(a)** any document filed with, or otherwise placed in the custody of, a court for the purposes of proceedings in a particular cause or matter,
    - ☐ **(b)** any document served upon, or by, a public authority for the purposes of proceedings in a particular cause or matter, or
    - ☐ **(c)** any document created by-
      - ☐ **(i)** a court, or
      - ☐ **(ii)** a member of the administrative staff of a court, for the purposes of proceedings in a particular [sic]

11. What was the annual fee income to the budget from foreign students in 2007/2008, 2008/2009 and 2009/2010 respectively?

    The annual fee budget for 2007/8, 2008/9 and 2009/10 was £43,250,695, £37,126,515 and £50,028,108 respectively.

12. What has been the estimated cost to small business and in particular, to private colleges) brought about by the suspension and revocation decisions made in the period specified above.

    We do not hold this information.

13. How many sponsors in the education sector became insolvent and ceased trading as a result of the Secretary of State for the Home Department's actions under the sponsorship scheme.

8.26 *The view of Tier 4 through the eyes of end users*

We do not hold this Information. Revocation does not automatically result in closure of the educational establishment...

Annex A

Section 31 (1) (e) allows us to exempt information if its disclosure would, or would be likely to, prejudice the operation of immigration controls. We cannot disclose details of suspended Institutions [sic] directly as this would have a detrimental effect on those affected, who, if they are able to fully overcome the issues that have been identified, may make another application. Any disclosure of this detail would invariably damage the institution and also affect any legal proceedings that are ongoing.

Suspension of the sponsorship licence is a stage in an investigative process and may not lead to revocation. The UK Border Agency must be able to regulate the sponsorship mechanism freely and without restriction from external influence.

The use of this exemption also requires us to consider whether the public interest in maintaining the exemption stated above outweighs the public interest in disclosing the information.

We have considered the public interest there may be in disclosing the information to you. There is a public interest in disclosure to ensure that there is public confidence in the points-based licensing system and how the UK Border Agency is policing it.

We have also considered the public interest in maintaining the exemption to the duty to communicate. There is strong public interest in ensuring that the relationship between educational institutions and the UK Border Agency is preserved.

Furthermore, the UK Border Agency must be allowed the necessary space and confidentially in which to carry out the compliance process. If we have reason to believe that an educational establishment is in serious breach of its duties and poses a threat to immigration control we may suspend its licence. This period of suspension allows us to consider all the facts of the case. Sponsors have 28 days in which to respond to their suspension and the UK Border Agency will then respond within 14 days of receiving this response. All educational establishments are removed from the register of sponsors following suspension.

We have considered whether in all the circumstances of the case the public interest in maintaining the exemption outweighs the public interest in disclosing the information. We have concluded that the balance of the public interests identified lies in favour of maintaining the exemption because the greater public interest lies in ensuring that UK Border Agency officials are allowed to administer the compliance process and interact with educational establishments without undue outside influence.

Section 43 (2) allows us to exempt information if its disclosure under this Act would, or would be likely to, prejudice the commercial interest of any persons.

If we were to disclose the information you have requested, it may prejudice the commercial interests of the educational establishment concerned. As you will aware suspension of a licence does not always lead to eventual revocation.

The use of this exemption also requires us to consider whether in all the circumstances of the case the public interest in maintaining the exemption stated as above outweighs the public interest in disclosing the information.

We have considered the public interest there may be in the circumstances of this case in disclosing the information to you. There is a public interest in the disclosure of this information as it will provide the public with additional information relating to educational establishments and their current status.

We have considered whether in all the circumstances of the case the public interest in maintaining the exemption outweighs the public interest in disclosing the information. We have concluded that the balance of public interest lies in ensuring the UK Border Agency can continue to maintain its business relationship with its Tier 4 sponsors during periods of suspension and that they in turn are allowed to continue their normal business activities whilst cooperating with the UK Border Agency during suspension. Please note that suspension of an educational establishment's licence allows the UK Border Agency to further investigate any issues of non-compliance and that there are a variety of reasons why an educational establishment may be suspended including administrative reasons.

Annex B

The use of exemption 22(1) requires consideration of whether it is:

- ☐ Reasonable In all the circumstances to withhold the information until the intended publication date of September 2010, and
- ☐ Whether in all circumstances of the case the public interest in maintaining the exemption stated above outweighs the public interest in disclosing the information.

This is a two stage test but the central issue is whether in all the circumstances it is reasonable and in accordance with the public interest to require you to wait until September 2010 for publication.

We recognise that there may be a public interest in disclosing this information to you now and that this may also weigh in favour of it being unreasonable to make you wait until the intended publication date. We have considered the following:

- ☐ It is important that the public have access to information regarding educational establishments that have had their licenses revoked as without this information it is difficult to ascertain if an education establishment's licence has been suspended or revoked.

- ☐ Immediate disclosure would allow those that have made Freedom of Information requests to obtain this information sooner rather than later.

But there are also public interest reasons for maintaining the exemption to the duty to communicate which weigh in favour of it being reasonable to require you to wait for publication until September 2010. We have considered the following:

- ☐ There is a strong public interest in permitting the UK Border Agency to publish revocation information in a manner and form of its own choosing which could be undermined by immediate disclosure.
- ☐ Publication would undermine UK Border Agency's established pre-publication procedures, which includes internal consultation about the content and format of the final information being established on the UK Border Agency website.
- ☐ Unnecessary concern could be caused to both sponsors and students by piecemeal disclosure.

After balancing these conflicting arguments around the date of publication, we have concluded not only that it is reasonable to require you to wait for publication in September 2010 but also that the balance of the public interests identified favours maintaining the exemption. This is not least because we believe that in this case the overall public interest lies in favour of ensuring that the UK Border Agency is able to plan publication of information in a managed and coherent way, and this would not be possible if immediate disclosures were made.'[57]

8.27 In disclosing information pertaining to the author's request dated 27 April 2010 the UKBA used public interest exemptions pursuant to sub-paragraphs 22(1) (information intended for future publication), 31(1)(e) (law enforcement), 32(2) (court records) and 43(2) (commercial interests) of the Freedom of Information Act 2000[58] thus revealing very little of any intrinsic value save for the fact that the UKBA intended to publish a list of colleges whose licences were revoked in September 2010. The logic used by the UKBA in refusing to divulge particulars of suspended colleges is noteworthy and ironic for the following reasons:

- The UKBA argues that disclosure would be detrimental for suspended colleges 'who, if they are able to fully overcome the issues that have been identified, may make another application'. However, in order to make a fresh application the sponsor licence has to be revoked first. Paragraph 408 of the Tier 4 Sponsor

57 Letter from Freedom of Information Team, North East, Yorkshire and the Humber Region, UK Border Agency sent to Ms Elena Tsirlina, Blokh Solicitors, by email on 3 August 2010.

58 http://www.legislation.gov.uk/ukpga/2000/36/contents.

Guidance (version 10/10, 1 October 2010) stated that 'the sponsor can apply to rejoin the register if its licence was withdrawn because of an error or failure to do something that the sponsor can show it has corrected.'

- Now the UKBA's argument is even more unreasonable given that after 21 April 2011, 'if we revoke your licence, we will not reinstate it. You will have to wait a minimum of six months from the date we revoked the licence before you can apply to rejoin the sponsor register, unless we revoked your licence by mistake' (paragraph 531 of the Tier 4 Sponsor Guidance, version 09/11, 5 September 2011).
- 'Any disclosure of this detail would invariably damage the institution' as suspension may not lead to revocation, the UKBA reiterates, but at the same time 'all educational establishments are removed from the register of sponsors following suspension.' Likewise, a sponsor will continue to be off the Register of Sponsors following revocation of its licence. An absence of a sponsor from the Register of Sponsors, whether temporary or permanent, invariably damages a sponsor's reputation and good standing as ordinary students and agents simply cannot tell the difference between the reasons for their removal.
- The UKBA is keen to preserve public confidence in the PBS and its relationship with educational institutions while having 'the necessary space and confidentiality in which to carry out the compliance process' and to 'interact with educational establishments *without undue outside influence*' (added emphasis). Notably, sponsors are given 28 calendar days to make representations to the UKBA following suspension and the UKBA has 28 calendar days[59] in which to inform the sponsor of its final decision. If any new evidence comes to light during the 28-day period, the sponsor will be given another 28 days to respond to the new evidence (paragraphs 515–517 of the Sponsor Guidance). As there is no right of appeal, redressing the balance is a drawn out and partial process shielded from public scrutiny which is unlikely to benefit the weaker party *without undue outside influence* of lawyers and courts.
- Further, the UKBA insists that disclosure may 'prejudice the commercial interests' of sponsors. Contrary to this concern, the UKBA has previously acknowledged that every institution removed from the Register of Sponsors faces financial loss. This is in no small measure attributable to the fact that a sponsor's income is reduced by the number of new overseas students it is unable to recruit[60] during the often protracted suspension period. Suspended sponsors cannot assign any CAS (paragraphs 505 and 509 of the Sponsor Guidance) nor will the UKBA consider any applications for leave for any student with valid CAS issued by a sponsor whose licence has been suspended (paragraph 441 of the Tier 4 Sponsor Guidance). Should the suspension develop into revocation of

59 Fourteen calendar days prior to 21 April 2011.

60 And any existing students who are concerned about the sponsor's precarious status and may wish to transfer to another education provider.

the sponsor's licence, it is likely to lead to a large proportion of the sponsor's students leaving the institution altogether. Moreover, from 21 April 2011, B-rated sponsors cannot assign any CAS either (from 5 September 2011, the status of B-rated sponsors became even more precarious). Existing sponsors who do not meet the new requirements of having to be subject to the system of public reviews (educational oversight) and having HTS status are restricted in their ability to recruit new international students due an interim limit imposed on 21 April 2011.

8.28 On 3 November 2010 the House of Commons Home Affairs Committee published its First Report of Session 2010–11 on the Immigration Cap. When giving evidence before the Committee on 20 July 2010 the Minister for Immigration was asked whether it was the Government's intention to cap student migration. He responded by saying that 'we are looking at the whole student area partly in terms of numbers but also in terms of the problems experienced by legitimate businesses, languages colleges and so on.'[61] In a letter addressed to the Chair of the Committee dated 20 September 2010 which forms part of the evidence presented by the Committee the Minister for Immigration wrote:

> 'You have asked for the number of colleges that have closed down since the Home Affairs Committee's last report in July 2009. We have suspended 214 Tier 4 sponsors since 21 July 2009 and revoked 48 licences. Since the launch of Tier 4 we have revoked a total of 53 sponsor licenses. The number of non-EEA students affected by closures or restrictions on the operation of colleges is 43,300. *The UK Border Agency does not have the power to close down colleges as the Agency's licence relates only to non-EEA students coming under T4 of the Points Based System'*[62] (added emphasis)

The concluding sentence in the Minister's letter makes the propositions made in the last section of **Chapter 2** all the more potent and feasible.

8.29 On 6 December 2010 the Minister announced in the House of Commons that 'I hope he will be encouraged to learn that since the Government came to office in May, we have revoked 24 tier 4 sponsor licences for bogus colleges, 40% more than the number revoked by the last Government. We have also discovered by researching the figures that in some sectors of the education world – especially private sector further education colleges – 26% of students are not complying with the visas with which they entered the country. That means that tens of thousands of

61 *Immigration Cap*, House of Commons Home Affairs Committee, First Report of Session 2010–11, HC 361, 3 November 2010, p 66 http://www.publications.parliament.uk/pa/cm201011/cmselect/cmhaff/361/361.pdf.

62 *Immigration Cap*, House of Commons Home Affairs Committee, First Report of Session 2010–11, HC 361, 3 November 2010, p 130, Ev 73 http://www.publications.parliament.uk/pa/cm201011/cmselect/cmhaff/361/361.pdf.

students are breaking the rules in some way each year. That is simply unacceptable, and we will deal with it."[63]

8.30 In his speech on reforming the immigration system on 1 February 2011, the Minister elaborated further on the number of sponsor licences that have been suspended or withdrawn:

> 'Since tier 4 started the UK Border Agency has revoked the sponsorship licence of 58 colleges. They were all privately funded colleges of further education. The UK Border Agency has also suspended (since the launch of tier 4) a total of 247 sponsors, of which 208 are privately funded.
>
> There are 248 B rated sponsors on the register, who are having to take remedial action to satisfy the UK Border Agency they are fit to remain on the register. 220 of these are privately funded.
>
> Understandably this concerns me deeply, so I have been turning over the stones in this area. I have to report that some unpleasant things have crawled out. Let me share some of the facts I have discovered.
>
> On the UK Border Agency sponsor register of 2298 licensed colleges, 744 are private colleges, excluding independent schools registered with the Department for Education. Only 34 of the 744 have identified themselves as being subject to OFSTED inspection. And of those 744, 131 – or 18 per cent - have so far attained highly trusted sponsor status. To compare with the public education bodies, 76 per cent of them are highly trusted.
>
> As of mid-January of this year, the 613 private colleges who are not highly trusted have had the ability to sponsor a total of 280,000 international students between them. Looking in detail at these figures, 120,000 of the 280,000 have been assigned to individuals, and 91,000 of these were used in visa applications in the past 12 months. That's up to 91,000 people coming here to "study" at institutions which are not verified as highly trusted. The potential for abuse is clearly enormous.
>
> I have also looked more closely at the 58 colleges whose licences have been revoked. 14,000 visas were issued for these colleges, of which at least 12,000 were issued since 2009. IT and business courses were popular among their international students and they charged fees averaging £3700 a year.'[64]

Another update was made to Parliament during the Home Office Questions on 9 May 2011:

63 Column 16, House of Commons Debates, 6 December 2010, volume 520, part 85, http://www.publications.parliament.uk/pa/cm201011/cmhansrd/cm101206/debtext/101206-0001.htm#1012067000018

64 *Reforming the immigration system*, Home Office, 1 February 2011, http://www.homeoffice.gov.uk/media-centre/speeches/immigration-reform. The Minister referred to these figures in giving evidence to the House of Commons Home Affairs Committee on 8 February 2011.

8.31 *The view of Tier 4 through the eyes of end users*

> 'In the past 12 months we have revoked 21 tier 4-sponsored licences and suspended more than 70. We are also increasing our enforcement activities to drive out the widespread abuses we have found.'[65]

The same was confirmed by the Minister for Immigration in his response to the independent report on the use of intelligence by the UKBA: '70 bogus colleges have had their licenses suspended following information being received from the public.'[66] As part of that latest statistic, Glasgow Caledonian University became the first university to have its licence suspended on 20 April 2011.

Efficacy of Tier 4 in the battle against immigration abuse and its future[67]

8.31 Respondents A, C, D and E felt that to a degree, Tier 4 presents an effective model for prevention of immigration abuse. One said that 'Tier 4 if properly managed will work very well, however the issue of abuse and one would expect that the Government would try to work along private colleges and support them towards better policing the system rather than bully.' Respondent F thought that reverting back to the old system would be better and Respondents H and I adopted a 'wait and see' approach. Respondents offered an assortment of ideas on how to improve the system including making it more robust with safeguards against mistakes, counting students in and out of the country, stricter immigration controls overseas, ensuring that only those schools that meet good educational standards can provide academic services and greater scrutiny of agents. Respondent B suggested that the coalition Government would introduce a cap on sponsors while Respondent G thought that there could be a cap on student numbers. A selection of opinions voiced by the respondents on the future of the scheme is quoted below:

Respondent A:

> '... unless there is trust between the sponsors and UKBA seen as partnership for the good of the Nation, Tier 4 will not achieve ultimate goals.'

Respondent B:

> 'The way things are going, hundreds of thousands of students will go 'underground' rather than return home and there will be an enormous gap in availability of staff for instance in nursing/residential homes. Tier 4 could therefore achieve exactly the opposite to what it is set up to do.'

65 Column 891, Daily Hansard, House of Commons, 9 May 2011, http://www.publications.parliament.uk/pa/cm201011/cmhansrd/cm110509/debtext/110509-0001.htm#11050912000022.

66 *'System "getting better" says immigration minister'*, Home Office, 13 May 2011, http://www.homeoffice.gov.uk/media-centre/news/system-getting-better.

67 Questions 20, 21 and 22.

Respondent D:

> 'It is not true that foreign students are depriving English students of places at University – they are funding them. It is not true that students are depriving English men of work – they are studying so do not have the time to spare. It is time for common sense – and joined-up thinking.'

Respondent F:

> 'I doubt the present government is listening, despite the massive opportunity for expanding this huge but largely invisible export industry'.

Respondent G:

> 'In the event of an improvement in the UK's economy, recognition of the contribution that immigration has made to our country's prosperity in the past will ensue amongst the populace as a whole followed by a change of policy from the Government *vis a vis* Tier 4. In the event of worsening in the economy, I would hope the wider realisation that students are not 'immigrants' in the first place, but rather a source of much needed income to the economy, would lead to a similar change of policy.'

Respondent I:

> 'Going in the right direction with accreditation of institutions, but still needs to be less bureaucratic and remember that students are firstly paying customers, not potential criminals.'

8.32 In fact, as a result of the consultation that ran from 7 December 2010 to 31 January 2011 and in line with its intended policy, the Government introduced an interim cap on the number of CAS that can be allocated to existing sponsors who do not meet both of the following requirements from 21 April 2011:[68]

- be inspected/audited/reviewed by one of the following bodies (educational oversight):
  - — Quality Assurance Agency (QAA) for Higher Education (UK-wide);
  - — Ofsted;
  - — The Bridge Schools Inspectorate (England);
  - — Schools Inspection Service (England);
  - — Her Majesty's Inspectorate of Education (Scotland);
  - — Estyn (Wales);
  - — Education and Training Inspectorate (Northern Ireland);

68 See **Chapter 4**.

— Independent Schools Inspectorate (ISI) (UK-wide)

- have Highly Trusted Sponsor (HTS) status.

Existing sponsors who do not meet the educational oversight requirement have until the end of 2012 to comply with it (see **Chapter 4** for application deadlines to comply with the educational oversight requirement). Those who do not yet have HTS status will have until April 2012 to meet this requirement (see **Chapter 4** for application deadlines to comply with the HTS status requirement).

Students[69]

8.33 In May 2009 the University of St Andrews Students' Association conducted an opinion poll in which 920 of its students expressed their thoughts on the new regulations and its results accompanied by a litany of critical comments showed that:

- 66% of the institution's current overseas students felt that they would either be unwilling or financially unable to accept an offer to study in the UK had they applied under the new regulations;
- 75% of British and EU students felt the new regulations were either negative or very negative.[70]

Nonetheless, in the survey conducted on 7 September 2009, when the UCU asked its members to gauge if they had witnessed a downturn in student numbers, 81.4% of respondents answered in the negative.[71]

8.34 On 16 September 2009 the UKBA stopped accepting new Tier 4 applications for long-term English and NVQ/equivalent level 3 and below courses at the Fuzhou, Guangzhou[72] and Shenzhen (South China) visa application centres.[73] This was said to be a temporary measure 'whilst we carry out an investigation to ensure applications are genuine and that students coming through these centres

69 Tier 4 (Child) migrants, a category not without its share of problems, are noticeably left without a voice.

70 *Response to Tier 4 immigration regulations*, June 2009, the University of St Andrews Students' Association, http://www.st-andrews.ac.uk/~ucu/pdf/pbi/pbi_booklet.pdf.

71 *Points Based Immigration*, Appendix 2, page 17, UCU PBI Survey, snapshot at 7 September 2009, http://www.ucu.org.uk/media/pdf/4/7/ucu_pbiguidance_oct09.pdf.

72 As a result of the suspension of Tier 4 in this province, 2,500 Tier 4 applications had been put on hold. See *An inspection of the visa section in Guangzhou*, Independent Chief Inspector of the UK Border Agency, May–August 2010, http://icinspector.independent.gov.uk/wp-content/uploads/2010/12/An-inspection-of-the-visa-section-in-Guangzhou.pdf.

73 VFS Global China, http://www.vfs-uk-cn.com/news.aspx. Previous visa fraud related to student visas was identified and investigated in Guangzhou in September 2008 (page 34, UKBA Business Plan, April 2009).

are compliant'.[74] On 20 November 2009 the UKBA announced that the restriction would remain in place until further notice.[75] On 12 August 2010 lifted the suspension at the three visa application centres for all courses with the exception of English language courses:[76]

> 'In South China there is a continuing suspension on students applying for Tier 4 visas to study English language courses, this includes any pre sessional course that includes English language. However, there are three exceptions. Students applying for a pre-sessional English Language course will be able to apply if they have:
>
> 1) an offer for a Foundation Degree at NQF5, for any course at NQF6 or above or for a Scottish HND, where the CAS is being issued by the same institution, or a partner institution named on the licence of the institution offering the main course. If the main course is unconditional it should be referred to on the CAS. If the main course is conditional, the applicant will need to submit a copy of their conditional offer letter with their application.
>
> Or
>
> 2) a conditional offer for any of those courses listed at point 1 above, where the pre sessional is being taken at a separate institution. In this case the applicant will need to submit a copy of their conditional offer letter for the main course with their application, the pre sessional must be at a minimum of B2 level of the Common European Framework of Reference, and the applicant must be at B1 level. A SELT is not required.
> 3) an unconditional offer for a NQF level 3, 4 or 5 course and the CAS has been issued for both the pre sessional and main course – in this case a SELT will be required to prove the applicant is at B1 level and the pre sessional must be at a minimum B2 level.
>
> Students in Southern China cannot apply for Tier 4 visas to study pre-sessional English language courses and other pre-sessional courses which include English as part of the course and which progress conditionally to courses **below** NQF level 6 (excluding Foundation Degrees and Scottish HNDs). This suspension will be kept under review.'

8.35 From 1 February 2010 the UKBA stopped accepting new Tier 4 applications at New Delhi, Jalandhar and Chandigarh (North India), Dhaka, Sylhet and Chittagong (Bangladesh) and Kathmandu (Nepal). The UKBA stated that it had been receiving 'unusually high volumes' of Tier 4 applications in these locations 'during a time which is normally the low season for student applications' and it had

74 *All Points*, Issue No 2, September 2009, the UK Border Agency, at the time of writing this information is no longer available on the UKBA website.

75 VFS Global China, http://www.vfs-uk-cn.com/news.aspx.

76 VFS Global China, http://www.vfs-uk-cn.com/news.aspx.

taken the action to ensure 'proper scrutiny of these applications.'[77] It was reported by the BBC on 30 January 2010 that 'in the last three months of last year, there were 13,500 applications from northern India alone, compared with 1,800 in the same period of 2008'[78] and this was the precursor to the action taken by the UKBA. On 12 August 2010 the UKBA lifted the continuing suspensions in North India, Nepal and Bangladesh with the same restrictions on English language courses as in South China.

8.36 In the February 2010 report *Fortress Academy* the Manifesto Club[79] focused on the increase in late arrivals and no shows of international students for the academic year 2009–2010 due to processing delays at overseas posts and suspension of visa routes in some parts of Asia and the increase in visa refusals for international students[80] including refusals for a number of trivial reasons.[81] In the August 2009 issue of the news bulletin for Tier 4 sponsors, *All Points*, published by the UKBA, it was noted that the vast majority of Tier 4 refusals was caused by the visa letter not containing all the required information.[82] In the next issue of the bulletin, the publishers stated that 'analysis of refused cases has shown that 60–65% of refusals are caused by mandatory information not being included on visa letters or the maintenance requirement not being satisfied'.[83]

8.37 The UK Council for International Student Affairs ('UKCISA') conducted two surveys focusing on students making entry clearance and in-country extension of stay applications the results of which were published in December 2009 and March 2010 respectively. Both surveys asked students to rate their experience of application process, its length, problems with documentation and ability to satisfy requirements, costs, biometrics, dependants and quality of service. Neither of the surveys has touched on the subject of suspensions and withdrawals of sponsor licences and their impact on students.

The key findings of the December 2009 survey are quoted below:

- '33% found the **cost** of a student visa was reasonable: 65% disagreed

77 *All Points*, Issue No 5, the UK Border Agency, at the time of writing this information is no longer available on the UKBA website.

78 'UK suspends Indian student applications', BBC News, http://news.bbc.co.uk/1/hi/uk/8489349.stm.

79 *Fortress Academy*, Manifesto Club Report, Valerie Hartwich, February 2010, http://www.manifestoclub.com/files/FortressAcademy.pdf.

80 'Tough visa rules deterring overseas students coming to the UK, Guardian, 21 July 2009, http://www.guardian.co.uk/education/2009/jul/21/visa-rules-deterring-overseas-students-to-uk.

81 *UCU report, Points Based Immigration Seminar*, UCU, 28 April 2009, http://www.ucu.org.uk/media/pdf/k/g/pbs_seminarreport_apr09.pdf.

82 *All Points*, Issue No 1, August 2009, the UK Border Agency, at the time of writing this information is no longer available on the UKBA website. In a 15 May 2009 press release sponsors were reminded to ensure that any visa letters issued to prospective students were completed correctly as a significant number of visa letters received by UKBA contained errors.

83 *All Points*, Issue No 2, September 2009, the UK Border Agency, at the time of writing this information is no longer available on the UKBA website.

- 59% were satisfied with the **speed and efficiency** of the application process
- 41% found the **application form and guidance** straightforward to complete
- One in four of those who needed to provide **translation of documents**, had difficulty doing so
- 49% had difficulty in providing **proof of funds**
- 38% encountered difficulties in the cost and/or time of travel for **biometrics**
- 63% found the **UKBA website** helpful: 12% said it was unhelpful and another 25% either did not know or had not used it
- 43% had to pay up to £50 in **additional costs** such as attending biometrics appointments or arranging translation of documents, etc; 20% up to an additional £99, 15% up to additional £200 and 16% £200 or more

One in three students requiring an **ATAS** certificate found this a problematic part of the process'[84]

The key findings from the March 2010 survey are also quoted below:

- 'only 36% found the **process** quick and efficient in the UK compared to 59% overseas.
- only 50% of those applying to extend in the UK found the **application form** easy to complete, compared to 68% applying overseas.
- only 15% applying in the UK thought the **cost** was reasonable compared to 33% applying overseas. 48% strongly disagreed that the cost was reasonable in the UK compared to 24% of those who applied overseas.'[85]

The author's own survey[86] demonstrates that:

- 80% of respondents stated that the feedback received from their students and/or agents has been negative with some students reacting to the new regulations with 'anger, frustration and disbelief';[87]

- In the period from 31 March 2009 to 22 February 2010, 35%–99% of students have been able to obtain entry clearance or in-country extension of stay on first attempt;

84 *Tier 4: students' experiences (applying from outside the UK)*, UK Council for International Student Affairs, December 2009, http://www.ukcisa.org.uk/files/pdf/about/tier4_student_survey.pdf.

85 *Students' experiences of extending their visas in the UK under Tier 4*, UK Council for International Student Affairs, March 2010, http://www.ukcisa.org.uk/files/pdf/about/tier4_student_survey_uk.pdf.

86 In response to questions 6, 17, 18 and 19 of the author's questionnaire, above.

87 Respondent F.

8.38 *The view of Tier 4 through the eyes of end users*

- In the period from 22 February 2010 to the date of the survey between 70% and 95% have been able to obtain entry clearance or in-country extension of stay on first attempt.

Respondents listed the following top three reasons given by the UKBA for refusing applications:

- Lack of maintenance (funds) evidence or insufficient funds – 70%
- Lack of evidence of English language level or insufficient level – 30%
- Errors or omissions on the application form, visa letter or CAS – 20%

The conclusions drawn by the surveys are hardly a glowing testament to the accomplishments achieved by the new regulations. To the contrary, the torrent of commentary complementing each survey's findings is rather damning. And yet, despite fears of dwindling numbers and students turning away from the United Kingdom to undertake their studies elsewhere, the Home Office figures published in the media on 2 August 2010 exposed a paradox in that 313,011 non-EEA students were granted visas in the 12 months up to March 2010 together with 31,385 dependants, as compared to 235,295 students and 24,780 dependants in the previous year.[88]

8.38 However, on closer examination, the quarterly statistics for April–June 2010[89] while conceding that there was an increase of 35% in the combined number of Tier 4 students and student visitor visas issued in the year to 30 June 2010, showed that the actual breakdown of Tier 4 students granted entry clearance in the year from July 2009 to June 2010 was 278,940 together with 28,210 dependants and the number of grants of an extension of leave to remain was 103,460 students together with 18,915 dependants. The summary noted that 'the number of entry clearance visas issued ("out of country") under PBS is an indicator of the level of immigration for employment or study of non-EEA nationals, although it shows intention to travel, rather than entry to the UK. The number of grants of an extension ("in country") under PBS is an indicator of changes in the length of stay in the UK for these migrants.'[90]

88 'Student visas policy reviewed to minimise abuse', BBC News, 2 August 2010, http://www.bbc.co.uk/news/uk-10834526 .

89 *Control of Immigration, Quarterly Statistical Summary*, Home Office, April–June 2010, 26 August 2010, http://rds.homeoffice.gov.uk/rds/pdfs10/immiq210.pdf.

90 *Control of Immigration, Quarterly Statistical Summary*, Home Office, April–June 2010, 26 August 2010, http://rds.homeoffice.gov.uk/rds/pdfs10/immiq210.pdf .

Tier 4 review 2010/2011

8.39 True to its five-year policy programme published on 20 May 2010, *The Coalition: our programme for government,*[91] the Minister of State for Borders and Immigration[92] announced on 2 August 2010 that he would be conducting 'an urgent review of the whole student visa system' to make sure that 'we can continue to attract the brightest and best to this country but also to stop that route being used as a scam.'[93] With reference to suspensions of the Tier 4 migrant route in North India, Bangladesh and Nepal, the Minister said that 'there was clearly a large-scale scam going on.'[94] On returning from a three-day trip to India and discussing immigration policy with government ministers, the Minister made the following observations in a British-Indian publication on 2 September 2010:

> 'It is important to make sure that genuine students are protected from exploitation by bogus colleges in the UK. The UK Border Agency are shutting down bogus colleges and targeting the criminals who exploit those desperate to come to the UK.
>
> It is not only bogus colleges who exploit those who genuinely want to come to the UK to study. A key topic during my meetings in India was our joint efforts to tackle the activities of unscrupulous agents. Dodgy agents play a significant role in orchestrating much of the abuse of the visa rules, in particular for student visas.'[95]

8.40 On 6 September 2010 the Minister of State for Borders and Immigration gave a speech at the Royal Commonwealth Society defining the Government

91 The aims of this document are reflected in Home Office's *Business Plan 2011–2015* updated on 13 May 2011 which aims to 'deliver an improved migration system that commands public confidence and serves our economic interests. Limit non-EU economic migrants, and *introduce new measures to reduce inflow and minimise abuse of all migration routes, for example the student route.* Process asylum applications more quickly, and end the detention of children for immigration purposes.' (added emphasis) http://www.number10.gov.uk/wp-content/uploads/HO-Business-Plan1.pdf.

92 Damian Green, appointed 13 May 2010.

93 'UK immigration system barely "fit for purpose" Damian Green has suggested', Telegraph, 2 August 2010, http://www.telegraph.co.uk/news/7923094/UK-immigration-system-barely-fit-for-purpose-Damian-Green-has-suggested.html.

94 'UK immigration system barely "fit for purpose" Damian Green has suggested', Telegraph, 2 August 2010, http://www.telegraph.co.uk/news/7923094/UK-immigration-system-barely-fit-for-purpose-Damian-Green-has-suggested.html.

95 *We welcome the brightest and best,* Home Office, 2 September 2010, http://www.homeoffice.gov.uk/media-centre/news/brightest-and-best.

immigration policy.[96] His speech reflected on the results of the Home Office research report, The Migrant Journey,[97] which concluded that:

> 'The findings relating to the study route appear to be consistent with the pattern expected for students coming to the UK. A small proportion of students on one-year courses leave the system fairly early, while those on mid-length courses (e.g. graduate and postgraduate degrees) are likely to remain in the UK for three years or more. The small proportion of migrants still in the system as a student in 2009 may represent either those on longer-term career education (e.g. medical students) or those individuals who have undertaken more than one course of study. *Less than five per cent of the 2004 cohort had been granted settlement at the end of 2009.'* (added emphasis)

8.41 The Minister drew the following conclusions which indicated the direction in which policies related to the student route would head in the not too distant future:

> 'I want a student visa system which encourages the entry of legitimate students coming to study legitimate courses. For me that certainly means students coming to study at universities, students who are equipped to study the courses to which they have subscribed and who fulfil their academic obligations, students who at the end of their period of leave return to their country of origin. That is good for the students concerned, it is good for the institutions they study in, and it is good for Britain.'

8.42 This response appeared to be blind to the immigration provisions allowing students to *legitimately* continue their studies or switch into work or marriage related categories leading to settlement. Given that there is no requirement under the Tier 4 route for students to have intention to leave the United Kingdom at the end of their studies, the Minister's comments came across as ignorant of the current state of immigration law related to students. He went on to draw a question mark over the future of private institutions:

> 'Of course we are the ideal country for others to come to learn English. But I want to ensure those who come here to study at language schools or any other institutions play by the rules and leave when their visas expire. We estimate we are bringing more than ninety thousand people into Britain every year to do courses below degree level at private institutions. We need to decide whether

96 *Damian Green's speech: The Real Immigration Question*', Home Office, 7 September 2010, http://www.homeoffice.gov.uk/media-centre/speeches/Damian-Green-real-immigration.

97 *The Migrant Journey*, Home Office, Lorrah Achato, Mike Eaton and Chris Jones, September 2010, http://rds.homeoffice.gov.uk/rds/pdfs10/horr43c.pdf. Read *The Migrant Journey,* Home Office, Lorrah Achato, Mike Eaton and Chris Jones, August 2011, http://www.homeoffice.gov.uk/publications/science-research-statistics/research-statistics/immigration-asylum-research/horr57/horr57-report?view=Binary for up to date findings.

this is right and also whether it is the best thing in each case for the students themselves, given the high financial commitments required of them.'

This line of reasoning takes its cue from the former Prime Minister's speech on immigration on 12 November 2009 which prompted a rapid review of the Tier 4 categories and resulted in changes to Tier 4 policy announced on 3 March 2010.[98] Concerns expressed by the English language sector during the *EnglishUK* judicial review proceedings[99] could only be exacerbated in view of what was to come.

8.43 The aim of the Government for the next five years is to upgrade the PBS from a simple tool to a smarter, more discerning system that is able to select 'the brightest and the best' amongst applicants to suit the needs of the country. In his speech of 6 September 2010, the Minister suggested that 'steady downward pressure on many routes to long-term immigration' should be applied from now on in order to meet the Government's net migration commitment.[100] This commitment is reinforced in the Home Office's *Business Plan 2011–2015*:

> 'We will deliver an improved migration system that commands public confidence and serves our economic interests. It will be more efficient and less open to abuse and will reduce the number of non-EU migrants. We are developing policies to meet this objective. As a result of these policies we anticipate net migration will be in the tens of thousands in future.'[101]

8.44 The ministerial speech of 6 September 2010 determined the current course of the Government aiming to sever links between the temporary and permanent migration by doing away with routes which encourage students to stay on in the United Kingdom to enter the job market here. Although the Government had not yet set about reforming the student route, this intention was clearly stated in speeches given by the Secretary of State on 5 November 2010:

> 'We will follow exactly the same principle as in the skilled work route – a more selective approach, which attracts the highly skilled, the talented and the genuinely needed, but reduces numbers overall by weeding out those who do not deserve to be allowed in. The sheer number of students coming in, and the large proportion of total inward migration this represents, means we cannot delay in taking this necessary and decisive action …

98 *Changes to Tier 4 student visa applications from 3 March 2010*, UK Border Agency, 3 March 2010, http://webarchive.nationalarchives.gov.uk/20100303141249/http://www.bia.homeoffice.gov.uk/sitecontent/newsarticles/2010/255022/tier4-visa-applications

99 *English UK Ltd, R (on the application of) v Secretary of State for the Home Department* [2010] EWHC 1726 (Admin).

100 It is difficult to distinguish it from the commitment made by the previous Government in the UKBA's April 2009 Business Plan to deliver 'increased selectivity together with increased enforcement activity against illegal immigration and illegal working' expected to lead to a fall in numbers as a result.

101 *Business Plan 2011–2015*, Home Office, 13 May 2011, http://www.number10.gov.uk/wp-content/uploads/HO-Business-Plan1.pdf.

8.45 *The view of Tier 4 through the eyes of end users*

> Studying a course in Britain should not give someone the right to settle in Britain. Settling in Britain should be a cherished right, not an automatic add on to a temporary way in. That does not mean bolting our borders shut. It means welcoming the brightest and the best ... and people who can help our economy.'[102]

23 November 2010:

> 'By introducing a system that is more selective and more robust, the Government is aiming to stamp out abuse while continuing to attract the top students to our top universities ...
>
> We estimate that nearly half of all students coming here from abroad are coming to study a course below degree level where levels of compliance with immigration requirements are not high enough ...
>
> We must also have a more robust system to ensure that students leave the country at the end of their legitimate stay.'[103]

8.45 On 23 November 2010 the Secretary of State also announced that an eight week consultation would be launched seeking views on the measures to reduce the number of international students coming to the United Kingdom:

- 'for adult students, focussing Tier 4 on higher level courses and those offered by Highly Trusted Sponsors
- introducing tougher entry criteria such as English language competence
- ensuring students wishing to extend their studies show evidence of academic progression
- improving the accreditation process for education providers, alongside more rigorous inspections'[104]

In the Home Affairs Committee report on the immigration cap the Government was urged to direct its efforts towards 'tackling bogus colleges and those who overstay their visas in order to seek employment, than penalising legitimate students.'[105]

8.46 The consultation, *The Student Immigration System, a Consultation*, proposed key areas of restrictions to be imposed on international students and their sponsors in the United Kingdom aimed primarily at reducing net migration numbers.

102 *The Home Secretary's immigration speech*, Home Office, 5 November 2010, http://www.homeoffice.gov.uk/media-centre/speeches/immigration-speech.

103 *Government sets the first annual limit for non-European workers*, Home Office, 23 November 2010, http://www.homeoffice.gov.uk/media-centre/press-releases/non-european-workers

104 *Government sets the first annual limit for non-European workers*, Home Office, 23 November 2010, http://www.homeoffice.gov.uk/media-centre/press-releases/non-european-workers

105 *Immigration Cap*, Home Affairs Committee, House of Commons, First Report of Session 2010–11, HC 361, 3 November 2010, p 35 http://www.publications.parliament.uk/pa/cm201011/cmselect/cmhaff/361/361.pdf.

To coincide with the consultation the Government published a research paper, *Overseas Students in the Immigration System, Types of Institution and Levels of Study*, highlighting flaws in compliance among students studying below degree levels courses at privately funded institutions.[106] The consultation was open to the public from 7 December 2010 to 31 January 2011[107] despite the Government's *Code of Practice on Consultation* which states that:

> '2.1 Under normal circumstances, consultations should last for a minimum of 12 weeks. This should be factored into project plans for policy development work. Allowing at least 12 weeks will help enhance the quality of the responses. This is because many organisations will want to consult the people they represent or work with before drafting a response to Government and to do so takes time.
>
> 2.2 If a consultation exercise is to take place over a period when consultees are less able to respond, e.g. over the summer or Christmas break, or if the policy under consideration is particularly complex, consideration should be given to the feasibility of allowing a longer period for the consultation.'[108]

8.47 The consultation attracted 30,851 online responses and over 300 responses sent by email and post.[109] More substantive reports were published by think tanks and organisations concerned with student migration and education policy:

- 'Pathway to prosperity: making student immigration work for universities and the economy';[110]
- 'The Student Immigration System: a consultation, Response from the Bell Educational Trust';[111]
- 'Universities UK response to the student immigration system – a consultation';[112]

106 *Overseas Students in the Immigration System, Types of Institution and Levels of Study*, UK Border Agency, December 2010, http://www.ukba.homeoffice.gov.uk/sitecontent/documents/aboutus/reports/pbs-tier-4/overseas-students-report.pdf?view=Binary

107 *The Student Immigration System, a Consultation*, UK Border Agency, December 2010, http://www.ukba.homeoffice.gov.uk/sitecontent/documents/policyandlaw/consultations/students/student-consultation.pdf?view=Binary.

108 http://www.berr.gov.uk/files/file47158.pdf.

109 *Consultation on the student immigration system: 7th December 2010 to 31st January 2011. Consultation questionnaire results*, UK Border Agency, March 2011, http://www.ukba.homeoffice.gov.uk/sitecontent/documents/policyandlaw/consultations/students/student-consultation-results.pdf?view=Binary.

110 CentreForum, Thomas Brooks with Chris Nicholson, February 2011, http://www.centreforum.org/assets/pubs/pathways-to-success.pdf.

111 Bell Educational Trust, 11 February 2011, http://www.bell-worldwide.com/media-centre/downloads/The%20Student%20Immigration%20System%20Consultation%20-%20Response%20from%20Bell%20Educational%20Trust%20January%202011.pdf.

112 Universities UK, 11 February 2011, http://www.universitiesuk.ac.uk/Publications/Documents/UUKresponseToTheStudentImmigrationSystem.pdf.

8.48 *The view of Tier 4 through the eyes of end users*

- 'The UKBA's Proposed Restrictions on Tier 4 visas: implications for University recruitment of overseas students';[113]
- 'Student Migration in the UK';[114]
- 'Points Based System Tier 4 Attendance at Privately Funded Colleges';[115]
- 'Student immigration reforms and their anticipated economic impacts'.[116]

8.48 In a speech made on 1 February 2011 the Minister for Immigration announced the closure of the consultation and mapped out the road ahead:

> 'My task is to reduce the numbers coming, increase the numbers leaving when their visas are up and to eliminate abuse of the system. So I am taking action to tighten our migration system across all entry routes for non EEA-migrants – work, students and family – and to break the link between temporary routes and permanent settlement. Some of these measures will take effect in the short term. Others will set us on a long-term road to sustainable immigration, where Britain benefits economically and culturally from new skills and backgrounds, but in a context where people are at ease with the changes they see around them.'

8.49 Following an extensive inquiry into the student route and analysis of the Government's consultation, the Home Affairs Committee published its report on *Student Visas* on 17 March 2011[117] making recommendations and offering alternatives to the proposals made by the Government in its consultation document. One of the issues over which the Committee disagreed with the Government was whether students should be classified as migrants. The message that was sent by the Committee to the Government was encapsulated in the statement made by its chairman, Rt Hon Keith Vaz that accompanied the publication of the report:

> 'Students are not migrants. They come from all over the world to study here, contributing to the economy both through payment of fees and wider spending.

113 Higher Education Policy Institute, Edward Acton, 18 February 2011, http://www.hepi.ac.uk/files/The%20UKBAs%20Proposed%20Restrictions%20on%20Tier%204%20visas%20-%20implications%20for%20University%20recruitment%20of%20overseas%20students.pdf

114 Institute for Public Policy Research, Sarah Mulley and Alice Sachrajda, 22 February 2011, http://www.ippr.org.uk/members/download.asp?f=%2Fecomm%2Ffiles%2Fstudent+migration+Feb2011%2Epdf.

115 UK Border Agency, March 2011, http://www.ukba.homeoffice.gov.uk/sitecontent/documents/aboutus/reports/privately-funded-colleges/report.pdf?view=Binary

116 All-Party Parliamentary Group on Migration, 2 March 2011, http://www.appgmigration.org.uk/sites/default/files/APPG_migration-international%20students-briefing_paper.pdf.

117 *Student Visas*, Home Affairs Committee, House of Commons, Seventh Report of Session 2010–11, Volume I, HC 773, 17 March 2011, http://www.parliament.uk/documents/commons-committees/home-affairs/Studentvisas.pdf.

Whilst we are right to seek to eliminate bogus colleges and bogus students, we need to ensure that we continue to attract the brightest and the best.

The Government's policy ought to be evidence-based. Generating policy based on flawed evidence could cripple the UK education sector. In the case of international students this could mean a significant revenue and reputational loss to the UK. We strongly urge the Government to examine the data which it currently uses to extrapolate migration figures and recognise that for any genuine student the doors to Britain's fine education institutions are always open. If the door is shut they will simply study elsewhere.'[118]

8.50 On 22 March 2011 the Secretary of State announced the changes to the student visa system[119] also publishing its research paper on attendance at privately funded colleges.[120] On 31 March 2011 the Government published the Statement of Changes in Immigration Rules (HC 908) incorporating the first wave of changes coming into force from 21 April 2011. *Student Visas, Statement of Intent and Transitional Measures* published on the same date as a written ministerial statement,[121] revised Tier 4 sponsor and student policy guidance set out the changes to be phased in stages by the end of 2012.

8.51 Home Office's *Business Plan 2011–2015* updated on 13 May 2011 set out its aims as corresponding with those described in the statement of intent and they are to 'implement first proposals arising from the review of the student visa system to prevent abuse with the likely consequence of reducing net migration' through to December 2012 and to 'implement final set of proposals through rule changes to student visas' by April 2012.[122]

118 *Home Affairs Committee publishes report on student visas,* House of Commons, 17 March 2011, http://www.parliament.uk/business/committees/committees-a-z/commons-select/home-affairs-committee/news/110317-student-visas-release/. The Home Affairs Committee went on to reiterate its concerns about immigration statistics and ill timed impact assessment of forthcoming reforms in its follow-up report, *Student Visas: Follow-up,* Home Affairs Committee, House of Commons, Eleventh Report of Session 2010-12, HC 1445, 26 July 2011, http://www.publications.parliament.uk/pa/cm201012/cmselect/cmhaff/1445/144502.htm.

119 *Government outlines overhaul of student visas,* UK Border Agency, 22 March 2011, http://www.ukba.homeoffice.gov.uk/sitecontent/newsarticles/2011/march/54-student-visas.

120 *Points Based System Tier 4 Attendance at Privately Funded Colleges,* UK Border Agency, March 2011, http://www.ukba.homeoffice.gov.uk/sitecontent/documents/aboutus/reports/privately-funded-colleges/report.pdf?view=Binary (last updated on 5 April 2011) and *Points Based System Tier 4 Attendance at Privately Funded Colleges, Annex: Background Information,* UK Border Agency, March 2011, http://www.ukba.homeoffice.gov.uk/sitecontent/documents/aboutus/reports/privately-funded-colleges/annex.pdf?view=Binary (last updated on 5 April 2011)

121 *Written ministerial statement: Statement of Changes in Immigration Rules*, UK Border Agency, 31 March 2011, http://www.ukba.homeoffice.gov.uk/sitecontent/documents/news/wms-tier4.pdf.

122 *'Business Plan 2011–2015',* Home Office, 13 May 2011, http://www.number10.gov.uk/wp-content/uploads/HO-Business-Plan1.pdf.

8.52 *The view of Tier 4 through the eyes of end users*

Conclusion

8.52 The threat represented by the idea of 'bogus colleges' has somewhat waned, its credibility lost to the Government's historical failure to keep ongoing abuse in check. Over the years it has been reduced to a familiar media soundbite wheeled out by speech writers to convince the more conservatively minded among us to accept the necessity of tougher immigration controls on overseas students and the education industry catering to them.

8.53 It is doubtless that since its commencement on 31 March 2009 the PBS has incalculably affected the education sector although to a different extent across the board. Despite their best efforts academic campaigners, at least on the higher education front, do not speak with one voice. Their emerging discontent which has impinged on their relationships with the institutions to which they belong is yet to find cohesion and, for that matter, coherence. It is noticeable that private further education institutions, who are themselves sponsors, hold views which are similar to the concerns expressed by the academic campaigners. The private further education sector has been hit the hardest with some being permanently stripped of their sponsor licences. But this is just the beginning and if this piecemeal revolt grows beyond its current proportions, then it is likely to envelop both the further and higher education academia[123] and hold considerable weight in any public interest argument.

8.54 In the course of the next 18 months the Government will be bearing down the pressure on foreign students to reduce their numbers. The same pressure will be felt in the private education sector. A good understanding of the immigration law and procedures will be essential to all those wishing to come to this country to study as well as those wishing to recruit foreign students.

123 Who have been embroiled in tuition fees debates since the publication of the report dubbed 'The Browne Review', *Securing a Sustainable Future For Higher Education*, published on 12 October 2010. The report recommended reducing reliance on Government funding and regulation affecting not only the tuition fee limits but also teaching grants, maintenance fees and loans and bursary payments and left universities fighting for survival alongside private institutions. The proposals spurned on mass student protests around the United Kingdom. The Government won the vote on tuition fees in Parliament on 9 December 2010. *Securing a Sustainable Future for Higher Education, An Independent Review of Higher Education Funding and Student Finance*, 12 October 2010, prepared by a panel chaired by Lord Browne of Magindley, http://www.bis.gov.uk/assets/biscore/corporate/docs/s/10-1208-securing-sustainable-higher-education-browne-report.pdf.

Index